The Urban Politics Dictionary

THE
URBAN
POLITICS
DICTIONARY

John W. Smith
Planning Board
Village of Beverly Hills, Michigan

John S. Klemanski
Oakland University

ABC-CLIO

Santa Barbara, California
Oxford, England

Library of Congress Cataloging-in-Publication Data

Smith, John William, 1938–
 The urban politics dictionary / John W. Smith, John S. Klemanski.
  p. cm.—(Clio dictionaries in political science)
 Includes bibliographical references and index.
  1. Municipal government—Dictionaries. 2. Municipal government—
United States—Dictionaries. 3. Municipal government—Canada—
Dictionaries. I. Klemanski, John S. II. Title. III. Series.
 JS48.S65 1990   320.8'5'03—dc20   90-37221

ISBN 0-87436-533-3 (alk. paper)
ISBN 0-87436-534-1 (pbk: alk. paper)

97 96 95 94 93 92 91 90   10 9 8 7 6 5 4 3 2 1 (hc)
97 96 95 94 93 92 91 90   10 9 8 7 6 5 4 3 2 1 (pbk)

ABC-CLIO, Inc.
130 Cremona Drive, P.O. Box 1911
Santa Barbara, California 93116-1911

Clio Press Ltd.
55 St. Thomas' Street
Oxford, OX1 1JG, England

This book is printed on acid-free paper ∞.
Manufactured in the United States of America

To Lena and Galen Smith
and
Mary Marshall, James Klemanski,
and Lorna Klemanski

Clio Dictionaries in Political Science

The African Political Dictionary
Claude S. Phillips

The Arms Control, Disarmament, and Military Security Dictionary
Jeffrey M. Elliot and Robert Reginald

The Asian Political Dictionary
Lawrence Ziring and C. I. Eugene Kim

The Constitutional Law Dictionary, Volume 1: Individual Rights
Ralph C. Chandler, Richard A. Enslen, and Peter G. Renstrom

The Constitutional Law Dictionary, Volume 1: Individual Rights, Supplement 1
Ralph C. Chandler, Richard A. Enslen, and Peter G. Renstrom

The Constitutional Law Dictionary, Volume 2: Governmental Powers
Ralph C. Chandler, Richard A. Enslen, and Peter G. Renstrom

The Dictionary of Political Analysis, Second Edition
Jack C. Plano, Robert E. Riggs, and Helenan S. Robin

The Electoral Politics Dictionary
Peter G. Renstrom and Chester B. Rogers

The European Political Dictionary
Ernest E. Rossi and Barbara P. McCrea

The International Law Dictionary
Robert L. Bledsoe and Boleslaw A. Boczek

The International Relations Dictionary, Fourth Edition
Jack C. Plano and Roy Olton

The Latin American Political Dictionary
Ernest E. Rossi and Jack C. Plano

The Middle East Political Dictionary
Lawrence Ziring

The Peace and Nuclear War Dictionary
Sheikh R. Ali

The Presidential-Congressional Political Dictionary
Jeffrey M. Elliot and Sheikh R. Ali

The Public Administration Dictionary, Second Edition
Ralph C. Chandler and Jack C. Plano

The Public Policy Dictionary
Earl R. Kruschke and Byron M. Jackson

The Soviet and East European Political Dictionary
Barbara P. McCrea, Jack C. Plano, and George Klein

The State and Local Government Political Dictionary
Jeffrey M. Elliot and Sheikh R. Ali

The Urban Politics Dictionary
John W. Smith and John S. Klemanski

Forthcoming

The American Law Dictionary, 1991
Peter G. Renstrom

The International Development Dictionary, 1991
Gerald W. Fry and Galen R. Martin

The International Organizations and World Order Dictionary, 1991
Sheikh R. Ali

SERIES STATEMENT

Language precision is the primary tool of every scientific discipline. That aphorism serves as the guideline for this series of political dictionaries. Although each book in the series relates to a specific topical or regional area in the discipline of political science, entries in the dictionaries also emphasize history, geography, economics, sociology, philosophy, and religion.

This dictionary series incorporates special features designed to help the reader overcome any language barriers that may impede a full understanding of the subject matter. For example, the concepts included in each volume were selected to complement the subject matter found in existing texts and other books. Most volumes utilize a subject-matter chapter arrangement that is useful for classroom and study purposes.

Entries in all volumes include an up-to-date definition plus a paragraph of *Significance* in which the authors discuss and analyze the term's historical and current relevance. Most entries are also cross-referenced, providing the reader an opportunity to seek additional information related to the subject of inquiry. A comprehensive index, found in both hardcover and paperback editions, allows the reader to locate major entries and other concepts, events, and institutions discussed within these entries.

The political and social sciences suffer more than most disciplines from semantic confusion. This is attributable, *inter alia,* to the popularization of the language, and to the focus on many diverse foreign political and social systems. This dictionary series is dedicated to overcoming some of this confusion through careful writing of thorough, accurate definitions for the central concepts, institutions, and events that comprise the basic knowledge of each of the subject fields. New titles in the series will be issued periodically, including some in related social science disciplines.

—Jack C. Plano
Series Editor

CONTENTS

A Note on How To Use This Book, **xii**

Preface, **xiii**

The Urban Politics Dictionary, **3**

Index, **589**

A NOTE ON HOW TO USE THIS BOOK

The Urban Politics Dictionary organizes all entries alphabetically for easy access by the student or researcher. In addition, a comprehensive general index lists all of the defined terms and many related subsidiary terms, as well as laws, court cases, institutions, and particular cities and urban areas.

Three components of this book add to its usefulness as a reference text. First, a *See also* section immediately follows each definition. This lists related terms that are also defined in the dictionary. Put together, these terms can provide a richness and texture to a particular urban issue for novice and expert alike. Second, each term includes a *Significance* section. After providing a basic definition for every term, we have "spread our wings" a bit. The *Significance* sections contain the historical and contemporary political and economic import of the term. They often include perspectives of authors who represent an approach or school of thought.

Finally, a *Suggested Reading* list follows the *Significance* section. For about one-third of the terms, there are no suggested readings. This is because the term seems self-evident without bibliographic support, there is little or no helpful material for the term, or no recent literature seems relevant. For some terms, we have included many suggested readings. In this category are some of the more controversial or complicated terms, as well as those considered "theoretical" or "fundamental" to urban politics. For example, *camouflaged case studies* and the community power terms—*pluralism* and *reputational analysis*—have had a long and controversial history and have been central to urban investigation since the early 1900s. *Urban political economy* and *Marxist urban analysis* are terms with strong theoretical underpinnings. *Neighborhood, community, participation,* and *urban political machine* represent examples of fundamental urban politics terms. In compiling bibliographies, we have tried to include recent literature. Many of the works listed themselves contain comprehensive bibliographies.

PREFACE

The major purpose of a dictionary is to record word usage. This *Urban Politics Dictionary* provides definitions and discussions of significance for approximately 600 main entries. For words with more than one meaning, we have attempted to sort and catalog these different meanings. Where appropriate, we have included etymologies if they clarify a definition.

Geographically, this dictionary emphasizes the United States and Canada. However, the scope of the subject matter parallels the great variety, breadth, and depth of urban politics itself. We have covered the social and political tumult of the 1960s, the fiscal crisis of the 1970s, the retrenchment and attempts at revitalization of the 1980s, and we have attempted to anticipate some of the new interests of the 1990s. The total of 600 terms is approximately double the average number of entries for the other dictionaries in this series.

In addition, there are several peripheral research areas, conventionally called subdisciplines within the social sciences, which we added to our urban politics core. The academic apple always will be sliced artificially, and urban politics never will be an academically neat field of inquiry. The cognate fields that most frequently relate (not in any ordinal ranking) are

> Physical planning
> Municipal law
> Urban geography
> Urban sociology
> Urban economics
> Urban demography
> Public administration
> Public policy analysis

We feel this dictionary fills a substantial void that has existed for many years. A number of reference works specifically relating to urban politics have been published in the past, but virtually all are out of print. ABC-CLIO's *State and Local Government Political Dictionary,* by Jeffrey M. Elliot and Sheikh R. Ali, is the only related work currently in print of which we are aware. The 1984 publication of the *Encyclopedia of Community Planning and Environmental Management,* by Marilyn Spigel Schultz and Vivian Loeb Kasen, also touches on some of the terms we treat in the pages that follow.

Modern dictionaries have a burden not shared by earlier works. Ours is an era of data banks, information storage, and retrieval (for example, LOCAL EXCHANGE™, DIALOG™, and LOGIN™) and of "descriptor items," by which we store our literature. With the growth of computer-assisted research, our library systems have been forced into producing specialized thesauruses, or lists of descriptors used to key input. As the social sciences have responded to this change, they have become more rigorous in their terminology. After a list of terms is collected, it is necessary to record definitions that reflect agreed-upon usage.

As a result, we have systematically relied upon several types of sources to build our initial glossary. These include government documents, trade books and textbooks in all of the disciplines noted above, popular and professional journals, and reference works. The sources we consulted were published in the past 50 years, with emphasis on the past three decades.

This dictionary is written for those who need clarification of the myriad of terms relating to city politics and urban life. These would include students of the social sciences; researchers on urban affairs; journalists; state, county, and local officials or employees; and other practitioners such as planners who deal with urban issues.

This project has taken approximately three years. We hope the reader can see the love for urban politics that the authors share, after teaching a combined 37 years. We have many colleagues and friends to thank for their advice and support during the book's completion. Literally scores of academics and practitioners volunteered their valuable time to comment on various drafts of a term or two in their area of expertise. Some who reviewed a number of terms deserve special mention. Professors Alan DiGaetano, Robert K. Whelan, Jr., Richard P. Wang, Ellis Perlman, Laura Reese, Carl Dibble, Barbara Suhay, and Robert Sinclair all provided thoughtful advice, suggested reading material, and offered friendly criticism.

City planner Phil McKenna and county planner Ed E. Bayer, Village Manager George Majoros, and Judge Joseph Burtell added their practitioners' sensibilities to many of the terms. The following libraries provided substantial service: The Eshelman Library; the Purdy Library; the Kresege libraries at Oakland University, University of Detroit, and Wayne State University; the Edward and Helen Mardigian Library; and the City of Detroit Municipal Reference Library, a branch of the Detroit Public Library.

Two research assistants eased the burden of Professor Klemanski immeasurably. Annette Graziani located facts to help with the important detail work of a reference book this size. Chris Reynolds performed beyond our wildest expectations, taking responsibility for many of the social terms and tackling all of the housing terms. Without their efforts, this book could not have been completed on time. We hope Annette and Chris received as much from the dictionary as they gave, and we wish them well in graduate school. The authors would also like to thank the Department of Political Science at Oakland University and its chair, William A. Macauley, for the generous support given to this project.

The ABC-CLIO staff always was available and helpful. Heather Cameron, Vice President; Richard Bass, Managing Editor, Books; and Judyl Mudfoot, Project Editor, Books, made our task much easier. Series Editor Jack C. Plano read every entry and offered sage advice in keeping our writing simple, brief, and direct.

David L. Good of the *Detroit News* edited the typescript and greatly improved the final product. Joyce Fisher and Kathleen Prantner also edited selected entries. Barbara Levantrosser typed and retyped our drafts. To all of these people, we owe a great debt.

—John W. Smith
Beverly Hills, MI
—John S., Klemanski
Rochester, MI, and London, England

The Urban Politics Dictionary

A

A-95 Review   A procedure required by an Office of Management and Budget (OMB) directive that mandated regional coordination and planning in metropolitan areas as a condition of federal funding. Circular A-95 was officially entitled *Evaluation, Review, and Coordination of Federal and Federally Assisted Programs and Projects*. Originally released in 1966 by the Bureau of the Budget and substantially revised in 1971, it was revoked by President Ronald Reagan on April 30, 1983. During the 1960s, the federal government sought to reduce central city–suburban tensions by imposing greater metropolitan and regional planning. Circular A-95 was written to force some cooperation through automatic regional review of local activities, especially grant applications, as they would affect the regional planning being promoted by the federal government. These reviews usually were conducted by regional planning agencies or Councils of Governments (COGs). *See also* BALKANIZATION; COUNCIL OF GOVERNMENTS; EXECUTIVE ORDER 12372; INTERGOVERNMENTAL COOPERATION ACT OF 1968.

Significance   The federal government recognized by the 1960s that regional cooperation was a natural response to the demographic and economic changes occurring in U.S. metropolitan areas and should be encouraged. At the same time, competition and tension among cities over federal grants began to isolate cities from one another. Cooperation and regional planning were encouraged through several federal statutes and policies, including the Intergovernmental Cooperation Act of 1968 and the A-95 Review mandate. Federal Regional Councils and metropolitanwide Councils of Governments (COGs) also were encouraged because they could further reduce tensions, help coordinate planning, and facilitate implementation of regional service delivery. The A-95 Review process was replaced by President Reagan's Executive Order 12372, which became effective on September 30, 1983.

This order directed executive departments and agencies to develop regulations for intergovernmental programs that received federal funding. This new process gave expanded discretion to state governments regarding the review process and continued President Reagan's general thrust of reducing federal involvement in social programs.

Suggested Reading

Mogulof, Melvin B. *Governing Metropolitan Areas: A Critical Review of Council of Governments and the Federal Role.* Washington, DC: Urban Institute, 1971.

U.S. Bureau of the Budget. *Evaluation, Review, and Coordination of Federal and Federally Assisted Programs and Projects.* Washington, DC: Government Printing Office, 1966.

Abandonment   The withdrawal of an individual, firm, or household from an undesirable or uninhabitable building. Abandoned buildings are considered removed from the housing stock and of no further use. Generally, buildings that are unoccupied and targeted for demolition are not considered abandoned, assuming the property will be put to another use. To reduce fire hazards and for safety reasons, city fire officials regularly survey their jurisdictions to determine which structures are believed to be abandoned and to take measures to remove these structures or secure them in such a manner that they will not become safety hazards. *See also* BLIGHT; DISINVESTMENT, URBAN; FILTERING THEORY, HOUSING; *IN REM* PROPERTY; REDLINING; TAX DELINQUENCY; VACANCY CHAIN.

Significance   Abandonment is the last in a series of urban disinvestment decisions. A building may go through many stages before abandonment occurs. The neighborhood in which the building is located may be declining economically. A landlord withdraws services from a building that is becoming a poor investment as a result of redlining, low rents, disinvestment, or deterioration. The mortgage and property taxes are permitted to become delinquent. Lack of maintenance and larger tax delinquencies reduce the possibility of reinvestment in the building. Vandalism and criminal activities may intrude into a building left vacant. Abandonment became a critical problem in some U.S. cities during the early 1970s. For example, in two months during 1970, the North Lawndale neighborhood in Chicago lost 2.6 percent of its housing units to abandonment. By 1971, the city of St. Louis had lost 4 percent of its housing stock. Several attempts have been made to cope with the abandonment crisis in U.S. cities, including altering the federal rental and mortgage subsidy programs. However, in some cities the mortgage subsidy program created tremendous scandals. Substandard houses were built, building inspectors were bribed to approve the structures, and families were moved in under federal subsidies. Banks approved loans for families whose incomes were not necessarily adequate to meet the monthly payments, because the federal government insured all loans. Families often abandoned these houses because the structures were unlivable, they could not make their mortgage payment, and they had no real stake in the property, having made very low down payments, often as little as $100. Such scandals as occurred in Detroit forced the reorganization of the mortgage subsidy program, although rent subsidies still exist.

Suggested Reading

National Urban League. *National Survey of Housing Abandonment.* New York: National Urban League, 1971.
Solomon, Arthur P., and Kerry D. Vandell. "Alternative Perspectives on Neighborhood Decline." *Journal of the American Planning Association,* vol. 48, no. 1 (1982), pp. 81–98.
Sternlieb, George, and Robert W. Burchell. *Residential Abandonment: The Tenement Landlord Revisited.* New Brunswick, NJ: Center for Urban Policy Research, 1973.
Sternlieb, George, et al. "Housing Abandonment in the Urban Core." *Journal of the American Institute of Planners,* vol. 40, no. 5 (1974), pp. 321–332.

Abrogation   Repeal of a civil or criminal statute or ordinance by a legislative body. The antonym of *abrogation* is *rogation,* the base term, which in Roman antiquity meant the submission of a proposed law to the people for their acceptance. Rogation is a formal *creation* or passage of a law. When the legislature adds a clause to a law or ordinance already on the books, it is called *subrogation. Implied abrogation* takes place when the legislature changes an old law or ordinance by passing a new one directly contrary to it without formally taking the former law off the books. If the legislature takes away only some portion of the law but leaves the balance, the action is called *derogation.* A rarely used but useful term combines subrogation and derogation: *Obrogation* takes place when a legislature modifies or annuls a law or ordinance in whole or in part by passing a new and contrary one. To continue or extend a law is *prorogation.* The formal common-law concept that describes a court invalidating a statute or ordinance that has slipped into disuse for want of enforcement over time or because of a change in circumstances is called *desuetude.* In turn, long-established practice, or *consuetude,* may pass into formal statutory law from mere custom. Abrogation works prospectively, whereas court invalidation works retroactively.

Significance   These are technical terms for civil law and ordinance making and changing, the most frequently used among them being abrogation. All are valuable but seldom-utilized concepts that force solons to distinguish properly among making, modifying, extending, overturning in part or in totality, overtly or inadvertently, by themselves or by others, the formal and informal rules of society. Few new topics come before local legislative bodies; modification of existing ordinances occupies the bulk of their deliberations. Lawmakers spend much time innovating; they chronically forget to cull older ordinances and clean up codes after courts exercise negative judicial review. A related legal term using the rogation suffix does not apply to this series: *subrogation,* as used in creditor-debtor relations to describe substituting an individual in place of an original creditor.

***Ad Hoc* Body**   A group established on a temporary basis or to perform a special or particular function. *Ad hoc* bodies include committees, commissions, study groups, and task forces that are usually appointed and less often elected for a specific and limited-time mission. When used by a legislature, they are usually composed of blue ribbon personnel to search or research a topic and report back by a date certain. Less than three months to report back is considered insufficient for part-time personnel to address a complex issue; more than a year suggests that the sponsoring body's intent was to deflect attention away from a hot issue. Legislative-sponsored temporary bodies usually are selected by the rule of odd numbers and commissioned to report back in writing. Executive-sponsored temporary bodies usually consist of personnel from several departments, and possibly outsiders, to implement a complex solution or investigate and report back on a cross-department problem. Often identified by the name of the chair, these groups have the options of writing a unanimous report, splitting into majority and minority reports, or even writing concurring opinions. At the urban level, few temporary bodies appoint professional staff, as is commonly done at the state and national levels. Also, as permanent corporations at the local level, *ad hoc* bodies are charged with a special purpose, such as disposing of solid waste or coordinating public transportation. *See also* CITIZEN ADVISORY BOARD; SPECIAL DISTRICT.

Significance   *Ad hoc* or temporary bodies are selected both to solve issues and to postpone solving them. Final reports sometimes are published but often just internally circulated; occasionally they are "received" and kept as study reports, to deflect criticism from the sponsor. Some reports are converted into policy by ordinance or executive order, some were never intended to be more than artifacts, and some are not even properly filed for later retrieval. Examples of topics studied include charter revision, charges of corruption or conflict of interest, change of status from village to city, privatization of a city service, annexation, selection of a manager, site selection for a new facility, departmental restructuring, and optimum funding for capital projects. *Ad hoc* special-purpose authorities fragment metropolitan areas even more by another layer of authority. They frequently are not popularly elected, have low visibility, and perform technical functions.

Suggested Reading
Smith, Robert G. *Ad Hoc Governments: Special Purpose Transportation Authorities in Britain and the United States.* Beverly Hills: Sage, 1974.

Ad Valorem   According to value, or in proportion to wealth, from the Latin. In international trade, an *ad valorem* duty is a customs tax levied on the value of imported goods. On real and personal property, it is a tax based on a proportion of value, which in turn is determined by an assessor's evaluation. This evaluation is subject to one or two reviews. Gross yield from such a tax is a function of assessed millage times value. A sales tax is also *ad valorem*. *See also* ASSESSMENT; MILLAGE; TAX, PERSONAL PROPERTY; TAX, REAL PROPERTY.

Significance   An *ad valorem* tax system is effective if it is based on a fair and consistent assessment system. As inflation increases, so does tax yield. Assessing is both an art and a science, although not an exact science. Most local governments rely heavily on this type of system. Taxpayers must believe their property is being equitably valued and taxed, or there will be widespread dissatisfaction and, perhaps, active opposition.

Adult-Only Community   The 1988 Fair Housing Amendments Act became effective in 1989 and prohibits most adult-only communities. It is part of Title VIII of the Civil Rights Act of 1968. The act bars discrimination against those in a *familial* status, namely those who have one or more children or are pregnant. Exemptions are made on health and safety grounds. The act permits retirement communities based exclusively on residency of those 62 and older, as well as communities with at least 80 percent of the units housing persons 55 or older who are provided with such facilities as communal dining rooms. State and nationally sponsored facilities for the elderly also are expressly exempt. *See also* FAMILY; LEVITTOWN; NEW TOWN.

Significance   Under the Fair Housing Amendments of 1988, 42 U.S.C. 3601 et seq., age-segregated communities and complexes are limited or prohibited in order to protect the rights of families and children. Some 15 states already had passed such antidiscrimination statutes. Substantial litigation designed to implement the federal statute followed the law's passage. Administrative rules of the Department of Housing and Urban Development are found at 24 CFR. Studies in the mid-1980s found that most apartments banned children, and young families were having a difficult time locating suitable accommodations. Communities within Zephyrhills, Florida, and Youngtown, Arizona, for example, discriminated against permanent residents under the ages of 15, 18, or 19 to meet the goal of establishing a haven for older people. The Del E. Webb communities were directly affected. They had developed four Sun Cities, three in Arizona and one in Nevada, housing more than 64,000 people who were required to meet a minimum age of 45. The issue is particularly important because the median age of the U.S. population is greater than 31 and is increasing.

Suggested Reading
Wals, Gretchen. "The Necessity for Shelter: States Must Prohibit Discrimination against Children in Housing." *Fordham Law Journal*, vol. 15, no. 2 (1987), pp. 481–532.

Advisory Commission on Intergovernmental Relations (ACIR)
A permanent, bipartisan, independent body created by Congress in 1959 (30 U.S.C. 42) to study, monitor, and help improve the interaction of federal, state, and local governments. The ACIR has published studies of governmental finances, taxation issues, reapportionment of state legislatures, public employee strikes, the grants-in-aid system, annexation, and federal aid for urban development. The ACIR Board consists of 26 members who serve two-year terms. The board membership formally represents all branches and levels of government, in addition to the public at large. To that end, three U.S. senators and three U.S. representatives are selected by the president of the Senate and the House Speaker, respectively; three members each from the federal executive branch and the general public are chosen by the president; four governors and four mayors are selected by their respective governing bodies; three county representatives are selected by the National Association of Counties; and three representatives are nominated by the Council of State Governments, who are then chosen by the president. Over the years, the ACIR has employed a relatively small staff of analysts and professionals, never exceeding 50 persons.
See also FISCAL FEDERALISM; INTERGOVERNMENTAL RELATIONS.

Significance   The creation of the Advisory Commission on Intergovernmental Relations was prompted by the changing federal grants-in-aid system, particularly as more federal funding became available and greater federal restrictions were placed on grant program operations. The ACIR was preceded (1953–1955) by the Kestnbaum Commission, a temporary body that conducted the first formal evaluations of intergovernmental relationships. Over the years, the ACIR has developed a reputation for accurate, high-quality research produced for an audience that includes academics and practitioners as well as members of Congress. Its reports and recommendations have helped the cause of fiscal reforms such as block grants and revenue sharing. However, the ACIR has experienced criticism of interpretations of its research findings. The ACIR's conclusions regarding a perceived "overload, hypercomplexity, and dysfunctionality" of the intergovernmental grant system have been questioned by scholars conducting similar research. In addition, its paradigm of a too complicated intergovernmental system suggests a political perspective that supports increased privatization of public services and greater recipient discretion on spending federal funds. Such a perspective promotes certain values concerning important issues of civil rights, accountability, and standards of operation that are central to current political and partisan debates. Should the ACIR associate too closely with one party or perspective, its credibility will suffer considerably.

Suggested Reading

Advisory Commission on Intergovernmental Relations. *The Federal Role in the Federal System, An Agenda for American Federalism: Restoring Confidence and Competence,* A-86. Washington, DC: Government Printing Office, June 1981.

———. *The Intergovernmental Grant System: An Assessment and Proposed Policies,* A-62. Washington, DC: Government Printing Office, June 1978.

Schechter, Stephen L., ed. "Symposium: The Advisory Commission on Intergovernmental Relations." *Publius: The Journal of Federalism,* vol. 14, no. 3 (1984).

U.S. Senate, Committee on Government Operations, 93rd Congress, 2nd Session. *Advisory Commission on Intergovernmental Relations: 15-Year Report.* Washington, DC: Committee Print, October 1974.

Affirmative-Action Programs   Governmental or private business actions designed to remedy past discrimination against racial minorities, women, and other designated "protected groups." Affirmative-action programs usually involve hiring and other employment practices and admission to educational institutions. An affirmative-action plan must include hiring or admission goals, methods that will be used to increase minority representation, and other positive measures for correcting past practices. Unlike a commitment to future nondiscrimination, affirmative-action plans require active steps to utilize underrepresented group members. Federal policy regarding affirmative action began with Executive Orders of the Franklin Roosevelt, John Kennedy, and Lyndon Johnson administrations. At the local level of government, the 1972 Equal Employment Opportunity Act (42 U.S.C. 2000 et seq.) made local governments subject to Title VII of the 1964 Civil Rights Act, which barred employment discrimination. *See also* LOCAL MERIT SYSTEM; SET-ASIDE.

Significance   Affirmative-action programs to correct past discrimination have affected all levels of government as well as substantial portions of the private sector. All institutions receiving federal money must formulate and implement affirmative-action employment or admissions plans and report on them regularly. The role of local governments in enforcing affirmative-action policy has been particularly important, because many of the jobs are at this level. Intense controversy over affirmative-action plans emerged after the late 1960s, when many of these plans began. Questions of numeric goals, the ideal scope of an affirmative-action plan, proper testing procedures, and the role of labor unions and seniority systems all have created much disagreement. The U.S. Supreme Court left standing both affirmative-action programs and the possibility of reverse discrimination in *Board of Regents, University of California, Davis v. Bakke,* 438 U.S. 265 (1978). They ruled that affirmative-action plans are valid if factors in addition to race are included in school admissions decisions. In other cases, federal district courts have ordered local governments to hire only minority applicants until racial and/or gender imbalances have been corrected. Historically, the imbalances appeared most egregiously in local police and fire departments. The issue of reverse discrimination alleged by whites passed over for hiring, promotion, or admission to professional schools has framed much of the legal and political battle. In 1989, the U.S. Supreme Court rendered decisions in three cases that will affect affirmative-action plans in hiring, minority contract set-asides, and reverse discrimination cases. The Rehnquist Court chipped away at some of the earlier decisions supporting affirmative-action plans. *Martin v. Wilks,* 104 L Ed 2d 835 (1989), undercut Court-approved affirmative-action plans by giving increased authority to white males claiming reverse discrimination in employment and promotion decisions. Also on the basis of reverse discrimination, in *City of Richmond v. J. A. Croson Co.,* 102 L Ed 2d 854 (1989), the Court voided use of set-aside programs for minority contractors in cases where cities did not have clear proof of past discrimination against minority-owned contractors. In *Ward's Cove Packing Co. v. Antonio,* 104 L Ed 2d 733

(1989), plaintiffs were severely restricted in their ability to prove discrimination by use of statistical data showing the effect, if not the intent, of bias.

Suggested Reading

Bussell, Horace G. "Result-Oriented Affirmative Action." *ICMA Municipal Year Book, 1975.* Washington, DC: International City Management Association (1976), pp. 163–170.
Cayer, N. Joseph, and Roger C. Schaefer. "Affirmative Action and Municipal Employees." *Social Science Quarterly,* vol. 62, no. 3 (1981), pp. 487–494.
Dometrius, Nelson C., and Lee Sigelman. "Assessing Progress toward Affirmative Action Goals in State and Local Government: A New Benchmark." *Public Administration Review,* vol. 44, no. 3 (1984), pp. 241–246.
Ricucci, Norma M. "Female and Minority Employment in City Government: The Role of Unions." *Policy Studies Journal,* vol. 15, no. 1 (1986), pp. 3–15.
Stein, Lana. "Representative Local Government: Minorities in the Municipal Work Force." *Journal of Politics,* vol. 48, no. 3 (1986), pp. 694–713.
Warner, Rebecca L., and Brent S. Steel. "Affirmative Action in Times of Fiscal Stress and Changing Value Priorities: The Case of Women in Policing." *Public Personnel Management,* vol. 18, no. 3 (1989), pp. 291–309.

Agenda Setting   The early stage of public-policy formation in which a problem is placed before government for attention. Agenda setting answers the question, "Where do public-policy issues originate?" Not all issues placed on the agenda are solved by government. Some are shelved when public interest wanes; some are simply downgraded as more pressing topics emerge. All agendas are limited to a few issues because of the finite number of topics decision makers can study and the restricted resources available for solving them. Truncated discussions of major issues never fully brought to public attention for robust debate are called *nondecisions.* Each of the three branches uses special nomenclature to describe its current set of issues formally under deliberation: Legislatures work with calendars, executives with agendas, and courts with dockets. *See also* CASE STUDY; STATE OF THE CITY ADDRESS; TRIAGE POLITICS.

Significance   It is as important to set the public agenda as to solve it. Calling the political tune limits the subjects open to legitimate debate. Keeping issues off the agenda and creating a hidden agenda are major techniques for manipulating power. Agendas are set in place like the many pieces of a puzzle. (1) One source of agenda items is indeed a mayor either reacting to daily problems or, less commonly, creating long-term policy. Few officials look beyond the next election. (2) A large portion of the formal institutional agenda is set by routine, by the budget cycle and fiscal year, or by renewal of agencies under sunset provisions. (3) Natural disasters also set agendas, for example the 1906 San Francisco earthquake, the lower Mississippi River flood of 1927, and Hurricane Frederic, which struck Mobile, Alabama, in 1979. The Chicago blizzard of January–February 1979 toppled Mayor Michael A. Bilandic and brought Jane Byrne into office with a promise, which she fulfilled, of spending millions on snow-removal equipment and plans. (4) Innovators using technological change set agendas, such as entrepreneurs hoping to install cable television, or public health officials wishing to place fluorides in water in order to prevent dental caries. (5) Leaders of ideological and social movements force agenda changes, as in the case of conservatives pressing for privatization of service delivery, efficiency-conscious groups wanting city-manager government, or, earlier, progressives bent on reforming urban machines. (6) Higher levels of government set local agendas by imposing new state mandates or withholding federal transfer payments. (7) Judges are a major force in setting local political agendas. Examples include forced reapportionment of all local legislative bodies, court-imposed school busing, and court-ordered scatter-site housing. (8) The mass media rightly claim the ability to set part of the public agenda through prominent coverage of investigative reporting. This was previously known as muckraking. (9) A large part of urban political-science literature focuses on the unique role of interest groups, especially elites, in formulating a city's agenda. (10) Nonelite groups also affect agendas, but less often and only with the aid of confrontational tactics. This is the message of such outside agitators as the Association of Community Organizations for Reform Now (ACORN) and, earlier, Saul Alinsky. (11) Finally, direct democracy tactics, such as the initiative and recall, enlarge the civic agenda, by-passing conventional institutional processes and going over the elected leaders' heads to the people. In general, most predictable public-policy agenda items favor the *status quo*. Unpredictable events such as a riot may expand public dialogue, often to the advantage of the citizens. After the urban riots of the 1960s, influence over the community agenda partially shifted to urban coalitions such as New Detroit. This brought about more open dialogue on priorities between corporate and elected leaders and heretofore disfranchised inner-city black groups.

Suggested Reading

Bachrach, Peter, and Morton S. Baratz. *Power and Poverty: Theory and Practice.* New York: Oxford University Press, 1970. (Coiners of the term *nondecisions.*)

Banfield, Edward C. *Political Influence.* Glencoe, IL: Free Press, 1961. (Case study of six citywide Chicago policies between 1957 and 1958.)

Cobb, Roger W., and Charles Elder. *Participation in American Politics: The Dynamics of Agenda-building,* 2nd ed. Baltimore: Johns Hopkins University Press, 1972, 1983.

Crenson, Matthew A. *The Un-politics of Air Pollution: A Study of Non-decision-making in the Cities.* Baltimore: Johns Hopkins University Press, 1971. (Based on case studies of Gary and East Chicago, Indiana.)

Daniel, Pete. *Deep'n as It Come: The 1927 Mississippi River Flood.* New York: Oxford University Press, 1977.

Jones, Charles O. *An Introduction to the Study of Public Policy,* 3rd ed. Monterey, CA: Brooks/Cole, 1984.

Kotter, John, and Paul Lawrence. *Mayors in Action.* New York: John Wiley, 1974. Chap. 4, "Agenda Setting."

Aid to Families with Dependent Children (AFDC)   A federally funded program that provides support for children with only one parent or relative. In 1986, eligible families needed an annual income of less than $3,200 to qualify and could not have more than $1,000 in assets. AFDC is one of four federal programs that originally were mandated with the passage of the Social Security Act of 1935. In the case of AFDC, the federal government provides grants to state governments, which implement the program. Within general guidelines imposed by the federal government, each state has discretion over benefits, eligibility, and amount (if any) of additional benefits provided by the state. About 26 states also offer an AFDC-UP (Unemployed Parent) program for two-parent families with children in which the principal wage earner is unemployed. In 1986, the average AFDC payment per family was about $347, with substantial variation across the states. For example, average payments at the extremes totaled $516 in Alaska and $89 in Mississippi. Cost of this program in 1986 exceeded $14 billion.

Significance   The period of the Great Depression became an important turning point in the amount of governmental involvement in macroeconomic policymaking and in public support through various social programs. Yet Aid to Families with Dependent Children and its companion programs represented a middle ground in public assistance during periods of economic distress. The programs of Social Security and unemployment compensation, for example, are paid for by separate taxation systems. AFDC and Supplemental Security Income (SSI) programs were intended to provide support for those eligible while avoiding institutionalizing those in need. In the case of children eligible under AFDC, a more traditional home and family life could potentially be realized under this program, rather than placing these children in foster homes or sending them to other public institutions.

Suggested Reading
Albert, Vicky N. *Welfare Dependence and Welfare Policy: A Statistical Study.* Westport, CT: Greenwood Press, 1988.
Chernick, Howard. "Block Grants for the Needy: The Case of AFDC." *Journal of Policy Analysis and Management,* vol. 1, no. 2 (1982), pp. 209–222.
Hanson, Russell L. "The 'Content' of Welfare Policy: The States and Aid to Families with Dependent Children." *Journal of Politics,* vol. 45, no. 3 (1983), pp. 771–785.

Air Rights   Ownership of the space above the surface of land. Initially such rights were attached to property but now may be sold separately or even leased for purposes of building. In property law, air rights also include the free access to air and light that belongs to an owner of land or a building by custom or statute. This was the initial well-established rationale for setbacks and height limits on buildings. The law protects adjacent properties by securing access to the direct penetration of the sun's rays and any view of a lake or ocean. Because of high demand for space, especially in Manhattan, zoning regulations have changed airspace rights. They can be consolidated into one package from adjacent parcels and conveyed to third parties for purposes of building above long-secured surface structures such as railroad beds and low-level brownstone structures.

Significance   Air rights were an unambiguous and long-standing portion of property law until the crunch for room and the technology of modern architecture made them an important source of available, buildable space in the 1970s. The two major buildings built on air rights are Madison Square Garden and Two Penn Plaza in New York City. "Lollipop" units are built on these air rights, so called because they architecturally resemble the candy, with the vertical elevator shaft "stick" topped by the "candylike" condominium. Development of air rights is a political issue only in cities such as San Francisco, New York, and Chicago, where central business district (CBD) land costs reach the greatest magnitude.

Suggested Reading
Kennedy, Terrence. "New York City Zoning Resolution Section 12-10: A Third Phase in the Evolution of Airspace Law." *Fordham Urban Law Journal,* vol. 11, no. 4 (1983), pp. 1039–1056.
Wright, Robert R. *The Law of Airspace.* Indianapolis: Bobbs-Merrill, 1968.

Alderman   A member of a city council that is divided into single-member districts or wards. "Alderman" is derived from the Old English "aldor man," an elder or patriarch, and has been used since the thirteenth century to designate the chief officer of a ward in England. Whereas a borough or ward has an alderman, a city council elected at large has councilmen or, in gender-free English, council members or councilpersons. *See also* AT-LARGE ELECTION; UNICAMERAL.

Significance   In nineteenth-century American cities using a bicameral city legislature, the upper chamber often was referred to as a Board of Aldermen, with a member designated as an alderman. Where the term is still in use, as in Chicago, it is associated with mayor-council governments using ward elections. From the outset, the term has been one of honor.

Alternative School   A learning environment, with student enrollment on a voluntary basis, that provides choices and options for students, teachers, and parents. Alternative schools—public or private— are characterized by curricula and teaching methods outside the mainstream of standardized education. Emphasis is placed on a diversity of student learning environments. The philosophy underlying the alternative school approach posits that different students learn best in different ways. Parkway, the first known alternative school, opened in Philadelphia in 1968. Parkway resulted from an idea by Clifford Brenner, then an assistant to Philadelphia's mayor, who suggested that city facilities such as art museums be used as alternative classrooms because Philadelphia had no funding for school buildings. The use of citywide environments became known as "classrooms without walls." In 1970, there were fewer than 24 alternative schools, but by 1980, 90 percent of the larger urban school districts were providing some form of nonstandardized learning within their school systems.

Significance   The concept of some kind of alternative education became popular during the 1960s as black militants and members of the New Left attacked standardized education as oppressive and racist. Standardized public education had become an important part of the assimilation process during the nineteenth century as waves of immigration brought many diverse ethnic groups and cultures to the large cities of the United States. By the 1960s, this assimilation was viewed negatively by groups that considered it an effective means of separating minorities from knowledge about their cultural background. They felt that standardized education contributed to this separation by often ignoring or demeaning the contributions of ethnic or racial minorities. Because large urban centers have diverse populations, alternative schools have received greater acceptance in larger cities than in smaller, more homogeneous communities.

Suggested Reading
Glatthorn, Allan A. *Alternatives in Education: Schools and Programs.* New York: Dodd, Mead, 1975.
Smith, Vernon H., Robert Barr, and Daniel Burke. *Alternatives in Education: Freedom to Choose.* Bloomington, IN: Phi Delta Kappa Educational Foundation, 1976.

Amenities   Pleasant and aesthetically agreeable qualities of a project or place. As applied to contemporary architecture and urban planning, amenities encompass those features that go beyond utilitarian standards to the creation of a pleasurable ambience. Landscape architectural amenities include natural vegetation; conveniently located parks, plazas, recreation facilities, and arboretums; and commons, greenbelts, and fountains. Interior architectural amenities range from barrier-free access for the handicapped, clean-air circulation, sunlight, and indoor recreation facilities to aesthetic decoration. The urban planning concept of amenities includes conveniently located schools, soundproof and billboard-free expressways, multiuse community houses, ample parking lots, interbuilding covered walkways, intermodal public transit, public access beaches, concert halls, and public artwork. When amenities are added by private developers, municipalities may add incentives such as permitting more stories to a building or easing setback requirements. *See also* NEW TOWN; POLICE POWER; QUALITY OF LIFE; ZONING.

Significance   Well-laid-out cities inherently provide amenities that rural life cannot. However, gigantic buildings placed on a treeless landscape surrounded by "air you can see" represent the underside of cities. Urban conveniences that do not degrade the environment are the promise of urban design. Amenities were fundamental to the vision of Pierre Charles L'Enfant in his plan for Washington, D.C., Frederick Law Olmsted in his public parks for New York City and Chicago, and Frank Lloyd Wright in his model Broadacre City. The planned community of Reston, Virginia, included such amenities as optimum population scale and the juxtaposition of living and work space. The amenity of a temperate climate in the sunbelt cities of Atlanta and San Diego competes against the stimulating intellectual climate of the snowbelt's Princeton and Madison.

Suggested Reading
Miller, Brown, et al. *Innovation in New Communities.* Cambridge, MA: MIT Press, 1972.
Spreiregen, Paul D., ed. *On the Art of Designing Cities: Selected Essays of Elbert Peets.* Cambridge, MA: MIT Press, 1968.

American Council To Improve Our Neighborhoods (ACTION)
A national education and reform organization focusing on urban
living and encouraging citizen participation in urban policymaking.
ACTION's subtitle, the National Council for Good Cities, illustrates its
reformist and educational intentions. The organization's board of
directors was composed of leaders in the business and academic communities. Several policy-related committees of ACTION were staffed
by volunteer researchers, including the issue areas of housing and
community development. ACTION also sponsored conferences, academic research, and lobbying activity to promote the livability of cities.
ACTION became absorbed into the National Urban Coalition (NUC),
which has headquarters in Washington, D.C. The NUC supports a
staff of 30 and has more than 40 local affiliate groups across the
nation. *See also* URBAN COALITION.

Significance   ACTION is one example of the variety of good-government educational and reform groups that are also known as goo-
goos. They seek to improve the quality of life in American cities.
ACTION and NUC bring together academic researchers and progressive leaders in business. ACTION also supported research that
sought to improve the physical attractiveness of cities. It promoted
conferences that combined the talents of urban planners, policy analysts, and architects. Though the ACTION acronym has been defunct
since its 1967 merger with the National Urban Coalition, this good-
government reform group should not be confused with ACTION the
independent federal agency that uses the same name, which is not an
acronym, and administers several volunteer programs, such as VISTA
and Foster Grandparents.

**American Federation of State, County and Municipal Employees
(AFSCME)**   A public employee union founded in 1936 with headquarters in Washington, D.C. AFSCME organizes police officers, clerical workers, sanitation employees, and most other classifications of
employees who work in state and local government, except for fire
fighters and teachers. The union is a member of the American Federation of Labor–Congress of Industrial Organizations (AFL-CIO). *See
also* AFFIRMATIVE-ACTION PROGRAMS; LOCAL MERIT SYSTEM; PUBLIC EM-
PLOYEE STRIKE.

Significance   AFSCME became an increasingly influential labor and
political power during the 1960s as it began to advocate the right to
bargain collectively and the right of public employees to strike. Until
that time, public policy toward public employee unions and their right

to strike was restrictive or, at best, unclear. With legal recognition as collective bargaining representatives, public employee unions such as AFSCME witnessed tremendous membership growth. While membership in most private-sector unions declined after 1960, AFSCME grew from 235,000 to more than 1 million members during the 1960s and 1970s. However, unionism among public employees varies across cities and states. Although more than half of all state and local government employees were organized by 1980, approximately one-third of the state governments do not recognize or bargain with such unions. Among those states not recognizing public employee unions are Alaska, Georgia, Kansas, Texas, Utah, and Virginia. AFSCME has been at the center of many of the legal and political battles regarding the right of public employees to unionize, the use of merit versus seniority systems in public employment practices, the proper use and scope of affirmative-action plans, and the limits of privatization.

Annexation   The absorption of adjacent unincorporated territory into a political jurisdiction. Annexation is physical expansion by a government aiming to achieve political and administrative integration. In the urban context, such expansions usually are motivated by the desire to expand the population base, capture revenue, acquire land, or a combination of these. There is no single legal annexation procedure in the United States because annexation is controlled by state law. In all states, basic rules are governed by state constitutions or statutes. The takeover target can resist through its own timely incorporation or by defending the *status quo*. In some states it is possible for land that has been annexed to be detached later in a detachment procedure if, within a specified period, the subject area receives no benefits or is dedicated to agriculture. Incorporated municipalities or school districts that have equal legal status are said to *merge*. Such a merger is properly called *consolidation*. This has been a major trend in school districts since the 1940s. *See also* BOUNDED CITIES, TYPES OF; CONSOLIDATION; DETACHMENT; ENCLAVE; METROPOLITANIZATION.

Significance   Annexation is a major political tool in the United States outside the northeastern quadrant. Between 1960 and 1970, annexation accounted for about 90 percent of central-city population increases. Between 1950 and 1960, annexation increased central-city populations by 6 million. In 1962 alone, more than 950 square miles were annexed. Between 1980 and 1985, annexation added 1 million people and more than 3,000 square miles to cities. Between 1950 and 1960, 78 percent of Tucson's population increase was a result of annexation; for Phoenix in the same period the same percentage was 76. The annexed land must be contiguous to the central city; some states allow for expansion into submerged lands. Some states prohibit contiguous annexation by the "long lasso," in which the unincorporated area is to be attached only by means of a rope of narrow highway. Chicago, Houston, and Denver have annexed international airports. Chicago's is the busiest in the nation; Denver's is the country's largest in acreage. Cities do not always annex all the land within their boundaries; such internal undigested parcels are known as *enclaves*. Some states allow for unilateral expansion, some mandate mutual consent, some designate judicial overview, and some create state boundary commissions to serve as outside referees. In some states, such as Mississippi, an outside authority may require the sponsoring city to issue an impact statement to prove that the attached area will benefit from uniform service delivery. In states such as Michigan where cities can merge with one another, petitions have to be signed by at least 5 percent of the registered voters within the affected area. Central cities in the Northeast and elsewhere often cannot annex territory because the surrounding area is all incorporated. Detroit, for example, is entirely surrounded by 19 suburbs and the Detroit River, which is an international boundary. If an annexation is designed to dilute minority voting rights, it is subject to court challenge under the Voting Rights Act of 1965 (42 U.S.C. 1973C). This happened in the Alabama case of *City of Pleasant Grove v. United States,* 479 U.S. 462 (1987). The successor municipality is liable for all preexisting debt. Annexation may be a viable political option to capture suburban development. In the sunbelt, recently incorporated urbanized areas with council-manager governments are most likely to use annexation with surrounding communities of similar social standing. Tabular data on annexation activity reported by state and city are published by population and land scale in the International City Management Association (ICMA) *Municipal Year Book.*

Suggested Reading

Advisory Commission on Intergovernmental Relations. *The Challenge of Local Government Reorganization.* Washington, DC: Government Printing Office, 1974. Chap. 5.

Murphy, Thomas P. "Race-Base Accounting: Assigning the Costs and Benefits of a Racially Motivated Annexation." *Urban Affairs Quarterly*, vol. 14, no. 2 (1978), pp. 169–193.

Ozog, James W. "Judicial Review of Municipal Annexations under Section 5 of the Voting Rights Act." *Urban Law Annual*, vol. 12, no. 6 (1976), pp. 311–320.

Zimmerman, J. F. "The Federal Voting Rights Act: Its Impact on Annexation." *National Civic Review*, vol. 66 (1977), pp. 278–283.

Antirecession Fiscal Assistance   Funding provided by the federal government to states and cities to combat downturns in the local economy. This program was created by Title II of the 1976 Public Works Employment Act (42 U.S.C. 6701). Congress initially appropriated $1.25 billion for the program, which was to last from July 1976 to September 1977. Under a recommendation from President Jimmy Carter, this measure was extended until September 1978 and provided for an additional $2.25 billion in funding. These funding programs were formula grants, in which cities and states received funding based on various indicators of fiscal and urban distress, primarily a high unemployment rate. Cities receiving the most aid during the first four years of the program were Baltimore, Newark, and Buffalo. Qualifying localities received two-thirds of the available money, with qualifying states receiving the remainder. *See also* FISCAL CRISIS; NATIONAL URBAN POLICY.

Significance   Antirecession fiscal assistance to cities became an important part of the federal urban-aid programs after the energy crisis of the early 1970s. Countercyclical aid was deemed a necessary part of federal support for many cities caught in fiscal crises that were not of their own creation or within their control to solve. Cities were caught in the bind of high unemployment rates coupled with the increased demand and need for social services. Antirecession fiscal assistance was viewed as a temporary measure. During President Carter's administration, such fiscal distress was viewed as more permanent, and federal funding was increased. With President Ronald Reagan's election in 1980, much of the antirecession fiscal assistance funding was reduced, then eliminated in 1983.

Apartheid   In South Africa, legally sanctioned separation of the races, especially for residential purposes, as controlled by the minority group to ensure racial purity, cultural superiority, and political hegemony. *Apartheid* comes from the Dutch and means "to set apart." Apartheid has been the official policy of South Africa since 1948 to ensure white dominance over the other three government-defined races and to allow whites to exploit blacks as a source of inexpensive labor. Apartheidlike processes were used by French colonists in urban areas of northwestern Africa to segregate the "superior" Europeans from the "inferior" native Arabs, Berbers, and Jews. Likewise, apartheidlike practices have been used in the United States, where numerically outnumbered whites manipulated public housing and urban renewal to set apart blacks into crowded segregated residences and hence to segregate public school districts. In the 1960s, the U.S.

Supreme Court invalidated a tortuous, 28-sided, racially gerrymandered city boundary that was designed to discriminate against the majority black population of Tuskegee, Alabama, in Macon County, the highest-percentage black county in the United States. *See also* DIVESTMENT; RESTRICTIVE COVENANT.

Significance   Apartheid is a particularly offensive system of legally imposed racial separation established by minorities against majorities. Racism, officially imposed inequality, and exploitation are inherent in such a system. Explicit in apartheid is an ideology of racial superiority and a fear of tolerating even casual residential contact, although workplace contact may be encouraged.

Suggested Reading
Abu-Lughod, Janet L. *Rabat: Urban Apartheid in Morocco.* Princeton: Princeton University Press, 1980.
Lowi, Theodore J. *The End of Liberalism: The Second Republic of the United States,* 2nd ed. New York: W. W. Norton, 1979. (Chap. 9 deals with apartheid in Iron City, a camouflaged southern metro area of 100,000.)
Smith, David M. *Living under Apartheid: Aspects of Urbanism and Social Change in South Africa.* New York: Allen & Unwin, 1982.
Taper, Bernard. *Gomillion versus Lightfoot: Apartheid in Alabama.* New York: McGraw-Hill, 1962. (Case study of the 1960 Tuskegee, Alabama, and Macon County racial gerrymandering court case.)

Appraisal   Systematic third-party estimate of the value or usefulness of real estate. Although appraisal and assessment occasionally are used interchangeably, appraisal generally designates a nongovernmental estimate of the worth of property. Reasons for obtaining an appraisal include determining sale, loan, and eminent domain *valuation*. The most common type of appraisal is a valuation to determine market, insurable, liquidation, or improvement value. A second and less common type is an *evaluation* appraisal to determine a parcel's uses or potential. *See also* ASSESSMENT; EMINENT DOMAIN.

Significance   Appraisal is a general term for estimate of worth, one subtype of which is an assessment. Public bodies occasionally use appraisals to aid courts in calculating compensation in land condemnation cases, whereas assessments are regularly used by governments to determine the official value of land, against which a millage is levied. Both appraisers and assessors work in the private sector, although usually assessors are full-time public officials. Some assessors are elected, but most are appointed. An appraisal does not always equal an assessment on the same property. They are estimates of worth calculated for different purposes. Appraisals are commissioned by buyers, sellers, lenders, and the government and are usually private information. Assessments can be commissioned only by governments with tax assessment powers, review boards, or the courts and are usually a matter of public record. There are several professional associations for appraisers, such as the American Society of Appraisers (ASA), the Society of Real Estate Appraisers (SRA), and the American Society of Real Estate Counselors of the National Association of Realtors, designated as Counselors of Real Estate (CRE). Calculations of worth are computed by four approaches: original cost, replacement cost, market comparisons, and income generation. Two professional associations in the field, the American Institute of Real Estate Appraisers and the Society of Real Estate Appraisers, Inc., both subscribe to statements of professional ethics.

Suggested Reading

American Institute of Real Estate Appraisers. *The Appraisal of Real Estate,* 9th ed. Chicago: AIREA, 1987.

Friedman, Edith Judith, ed. *Encyclopedia of Real Estate Appraising,* 3rd ed. Englewood Cliffs, NJ: Prentice-Hall, 1978.

International Association of Assessing Officers. *Property Assessment Valuation.* Chicago: IAAO, 1977.

Society of Real Estate Appraisers. *Real Estate Appraisal Principles and Terminology,* 2nd ed. Chicago: SREA, 1973.

Arbitration   Private, nonprofit, and voluntary quasi-judicial conflict resolution using less formal standards of due process than those employed in public courts of law. Arbitration is an alternative to formal litigation. Arbitration is limited to disputes, the boundaries of which are determined beforehand by the competing parties or by the "four corners of the contract." The arbitrator is limited in his or her findings to disputes and remedies found in the contract or in some cases where the arbitration system is relatively unstructured, by pre-agreement between the parties. There may be any odd number of arbitrators. Technically only the submitted dispute and hearing are called arbitration. The decision is called an *award.* In government employee disputes, awards are always made a matter of public record. Advisory arbitration, which recommends settlements, sometimes is employed in local government contracts when collective bargaining collapses. Grievance arbitration is employed as the last stage in management-labor disputes over interpretation of an in-place contract. Interest arbitration at the local government level adjudicates disputes, even after a strike, to settle the meaning of clauses in collective bargaining contracts. Arbitration is distinguished from *conciliation,* in which there is no submission beforehand regarding the boundaries of a dispute. Arbitration also is distinguished from *mediation,* which is conflict resolution by a disinterested third party whose advice can be freely accepted or rejected. Awards can be appealed to public courts, in which the arbitration award's finality and enforcement over public bargaining units is usually but not invariably upheld, frequently by refusal of the courts to consider the award. *See also* MEDIATION.

Significance   Arbitration is an alternative system of dispute resolution in the private and not-for-profit sectors. It is almost always conducted by the American Arbitration Association (AAA), with offices in all principal cities. The arbitration procedure in state and local government varies in each state. Some states have created employment relations commissions, with varying forms of arbitration for local government employees, including binding arbitration. Some states also have formed arrangements for collective bargaining and resultant arbitration by state employees. Since World War II, arbitration has been the preferred method for settling industrial disputes over contract provisions. Since 1969, federal employees have had binding arbitration over their contract provisions. Arguments in favor of arbitration litigation include time savings, cost savings, and, in the private sector, the ability to conduct disputes in private. Because the AAA charges fees for providing services in proportion to the amount in dispute, all but the most complicated cases do indeed save money and are settled with dispatch. When public utility disputes or public employee groups such as police and fire fighters are involved, there is a major argument against arbitration. It means private decision makers not accountable to the electorate are making policy outside the public forum. The awards may force mayors and city councils to shrink other portions of the municipal budget. Where state statute mandates attendance at arbitration, called *compulsory arbitration,* and where the arbitrator's decisions are final, called *binding arbitration,* the results allegedly diminish public scrutiny and electoral accountability and debase democratic accountability.

Suggested Reading

Delaney, John, Peter Feuille, and Wallace Hendricks. "The Regulation of Bargaining Disputes: A Cost-Benefit Analysis of Interest Arbitration in the Public Sector." In David B. Lipsky and David Lewis, eds., *Advances in Industrial and Labor Relations: A Research Annual.* Vol. 3. Greenwich, CT: JAI Press, 1986, pp. 83–118.

El Kouri, Frank, and Edna Asper El Kouri. *How Arbitration Works,* 4th ed. Washington, DC: Bureau of National Affairs, 1985.

Lester, Richard A. *Labor Arbitration in State and Local Government: An Examination of Experience in Eight States and New York City.* Princeton, NJ:

Industrial Relations Section, Firestone Library, 1984. Research Report Series No. 124. (The eight states are Pennsylvania, Michigan, Minnesota, Wisconsin, Massachusetts, New York, Iowa, and New Jersey.)

Architectural Review Board   A multimember body of residents created by ordinance and usually appointed by an elected council or commission to preserve and protect the existing built-up environment by regulating the design of new buildings. Architectural review boards control the content of the owner's and designer's expression and possess power in some instances to prohibit building permits because of excessive conformity or dissimilarity with the balance of the community. Some of the standards involve taste, harmony, and proportion. Boards often are charged with ruling on beauty for its own sake, but more commonly aesthetic concerns are combined with protecting the market value of nearby structures. Some boards work with all types of plans, some primarily with residences or businesses. Often neighbors in a subdivision invoke bylaws against offending and nonconforming houses, as in the case of a proposed Georgian-style home along a street of contemporary designs. *See also* BUILDING PERMIT; HISTORIC PRESERVATION; ZONING, AESTHETIC.

Significance   There is usually little controversy about an architectural review board that reviews safety and health standards of new buildings. This is a widely accepted exercise of the general welfare proviso as, for example, in the mandating of sprinklers in buildings designed for general public occupancy. Communities also have established *historic preservation review boards* to ensure that buildings are restored with a certain degree of fidelity to the original. It is the review of new buildings that causes so much litigation because the community is imposing standards of beauty that are arguably subjective. Designers cry that the city crimps self-expression and that vague and indefinite review standards are unconstitutionally impermissible. To stand up to judicial scrutiny, review boards should have enabling ordinances that are tightly written to allow for agreed-upon standards. Most boards provide for some due process appeals to a zoning board or the city council. Even if the boards are staffed in part by architects, poorly drafted guidelines may fall under judicial scrutiny. In practice, review boards often bargain with developers and designers, agreeing to compromises in such areas as facade, exterior building materials, setbacks, open spaces, and roof lines. Many such boards have been created as a result of a city's having to tolerate a particularly displeasing or disproportionately large building that it was unable to prevent for want of any public review standards. State law is divided on the effectiveness of these review boards, and many challenges undoubtedly will continue to be made by disgruntled owners and architects.

Suggested Reading
Crumpler, Thomas. "Architectural Controls: Aesthetic Regulations of the Urban Environment." *Urban Lawyer,* vol. 6, no. 3 (1973), pp. 622–644.
Kalis, Annette B. "Architectural Expression: Police Power and the First Amendment." *Urban Law Annual,* vol. 16 (1979), pp. 273–304.
Poole, Samuel E. III. "Architectural Appearance Review Regulations and the First Amendment: The Good, the Bad, and the Consensus Ugly." *Urban Lawyer,* vol. 19, no. 2 (1987), pp. 287 ff.

Army Corps of Engineers   A unit of the U.S. Army that administers and implements major construction and development projects. The Corps coordinates the Civil Works Program, which focuses on flood and erosion control, the development of hydroelectric power, navigation channels, and other water resource projects. The Corps has operated since 1824 and is responsible for such large undertakings as the Tennessee Valley Authority (TVA) project and reversing the direction of the Chicago River.

Significance   The Army Corps of Engineers has gained considerable authority over water resource management since its inception. In many cases of erosion control and recreational projects, the cost usually is shared equally by the federal and relevant local governments. Recently, the Corps has become more involved in political struggles as water pollution issues have become the center of attention for many environmental and conservation groups. Federal law gives the Corps extensive regulatory powers over wetland protection, coastal waters, all navigable waters and their tributaries, recreational areas, and wildlife protection. In addition, the Corps administers a permit program that determines the extent of dredging, filling, and discharging of material into navigable water, and it oversees the construction of boat ramps, piers, dams, and wharves. It often surveys navigable rivers to determine 25- and 100-year floodplains, in which buildings generally are not allowed. Though the Corps is part of the Department of Defense, it has enjoyed considerable independence through substantial support from Congress.

Assessment   An official government estimate of the value of real and tangible personal property for the purpose of levying an *ad valorem* property tax. The tax is measured in mills, one mill yielding one dollar of revenue per $1,000 of assessed valuation. Real property consists of land and improvements attached thereto; tangible personal property consists of movable physical assets such as machinery. Assessments are assigned for preparing a tax base for supporting ongoing, general, local governmental service. The assessment ratio can be anywhere from 100 cents on the dollar to 60 percent of value in West Virginia, to not more than 50 percent of market value in Michigan. Frequency of assessments is as important as accurate on-site inspection. State agencies may do some assessment; more commonly counties, townships, cities, and villages do the task. Actual assessors may work in-house or on contract. They may be elected or appointed or promoted under a Civil Service system. Special training is required in most jurisdictions; certification programs may be required. Some states differentiate levels of expertise. Special assessments are allowed in most jurisdictions for *ad hoc* public improvements deemed to yield special benefit for an identifiable area or class. Examples include sewer improvements, localized flood control, and street improvements. *See also* APPRAISAL; MILLAGE; TAX BASE; TAX ROLL.

Significance   Revenue generated from *ad valorem* property taxes is the major resource for local government budgets. All *ad valorem* taxes must be based on competent assessments. But assessing is an art, not an exact science. As long as property is used as the basis of spreading taxes, there will be high levels of controversy over assessments. In theory, assessed value divided into the local budget should equal the millage rate. Rather than fighting tax rates, property owners tend to focus on their particular assessments. Anticipating this, most jurisdictions set up a two-tier administrative review, one local and one at a higher level, often called a board of equalization. The appeal process may be lengthy, lasting more than a year. Further appeals on the assignment of value may be made to the courts, but usually only on limited grounds. A major landowner who wins a lowered assessment forces the municipality to suffer a quick and substantial shortfall. The community may also be liable for payment with interest on overpayment of back taxes. Large segments of land are exempt from assessment, such as churches that are owned and occupied as nonprofit institutions. Parcels of land owned by other jurisdictions, such as colleges, parks, public roads, and post offices, are exempt from taxes under the doctrine of intergovernmental tax immunity, established in *McCulloch v. Maryland*, 4 Wheaton 316 (1819). Assessments should not be confused with *appraisals*, which are estimates of value made by private evaluators; the two figures on the same property are often different. It is assumed that councils, commissions, and boards will not apportion the millage before they know the aggregate assessment.

Because urban renewal is based on the taking of private property for public purpose for a just compensation with due process, conventional and specially appointed appraisers play a critical role in assigning the amount paid for taking all or part of a property for the general public benefit. Courts are routinely asked to review these estimates. Common issues in litigation include questions of equal and uniform assessment; the meaning of actual value, market value, and fair market value; and the use of recent sales figures versus actual cost, less depreciation. In *Allegheny Pittsburgh Coal Company v. County Commission of Webster County, West Virginia*, 120 L Ed 2d 688 (1988), the U.S. Supreme Court invoked the equal protection clause in invalidating a local property tax assessment that employed current sales figures as the basis of worth because properties not recently sold were kept undervalued. Special assessments are attacked in court on grounds of their validity under charters and state constitutions, methods of factoring improvements, the size of the area to be assessed, and the legality of the assessment procedure. Assessors do not levy taxes; only the local legislative body can do that. Nor do assessors make the markets; they simply sample them.

Suggested Reading
International Association of Assessing Officers. *Property Assessment Valuation*. Chicago: IAAO, 1977.

Association of Community Organizations for Reform Now (ACORN)
A collection of local social action groups, each of which conducts research, organizes urban neighborhoods, and offers some aid to the urban poor. In some cities local ACORN organizations have actively promoted the homesteading of vacant, city-owned dwellings and worked to encourage neighborhood solidarity and community sentiment. *See also* MAXIMUM FEASIBLE PARTICIPATION; OUTSIDE INFLUENCE.

Significance ACORN has sought to fill a perceived void in representing the interests of urban residents. Concerned with social and economic problems on the one hand, ACORN has also seen city bureaucracies and decision makers as part of the problem of urban life. Local ACORN organizations have become involved in a variety of activities, from organizing marches on city hall to conducting studies of redlining by financial institutions and fighting large-scale redevelopment projects that destroy residential neighborhoods believed to be viable. These groups are reminiscent of Saul Alinsky's urban activist groups and continue the tradition of direct citizen involvement that had been institutionalized through the maximum feasible participation programs of the 1960s.

Suggested Reading
Borgos, Seth. "The ACORN Squatters' Campaign." *Social Policy*, vol. 15, no. 1 (1984), pp. 17–26.
Delgado, Gary. *Organizing the Movement: The Roots and Growth of ACORN.* Philadelphia: Temple University Press, 1986.

At-Large Election   Voting that embraces an entire political unit rather than being segmented into districts or wards. There are also mixed systems that combine single-member wards and at-large positions. At-large elections are favored by those who want candidates to know the issues of the whole community. Ward elections reflect greater concern for constituency needs. At-large elections favor majorities over minorities when both groups maintain cohesiveness. These elections depersonalize community politics and somewhat favor middle-class officials, who have more money to run for larger area office. At-large elections stress communitywide service delivery. *See also* BALANCED TICKET; PLUNK; REFORM GOVERNMENT; URBAN POLITICAL MACHINE; VOTER DILUTION CASES; WARD.

Significance   At-large elections are part of a fundamental package of reforms associated with antimachine politics. One impact is to make at-large officials more issue-oriented and less parochial representatives than ward-elected officials. Another impact is to allow for heavy recruitment of candidates from a few areas rather than ensuring broad spatial distribution on city commissions. Where minorities vote as a bloc, concentration in wards allows them some representation. There is some evidence that ward elections that produce black winners increase a feeling of black citizen identification with substate governments. In at-large elections, such minorities will remain losers unless they are able to participate in a slate that balances the ticket. At-large systems dilute minority blocs and may be a type of gerrymandering. Under the 1965 Voting Rights Act, two Illinois communities in the 1980s were forced by a federal district court to change from at-large to district elections because the minority black communities proved they had their power diluted by a white majority at-large system. This decision in Springfield affected only the city council, whereas in Danville it affected the school and park boards as well as the city council. The U.S. Supreme Court in *Thornburg v. Gingles,* 278 U.S. (1986), overturned a multimember North Carolina state legislative district on grounds it impaired the ability of black voters to elect their candidates. This ruling also was based on the Voting Rights Act of 1965. At-large city council elections are more common in communities of 25,000 to 250,000 and less so in major cities with populations greater than 500,000. The International City Management Association (ICMA) *Municipal Year Book* lists changes that occur in at-large electoral systems.

Suggested Reading
Bledsoe, Timothy. "A Research Note on the Impact of District/At-Large Elections on Black Political Efficacy." *Urban Affairs Quarterly*, vol. 22, no. 1 (1986), pp. 166–174.
Haselswerdt, Michael V. "Voter and Candidate Reaction to District and At-Large Elections: Buffalo, New York." *Urban Affairs Quarterly*, vol. 20, no. 1 (1984), pp. 31–45.
MacManus, Susan A. "City Council Election Procedures and Minority Representation: Are They Related?" *Social Science Quarterly*, vol. 59, no. 1 (1978), pp. 154–161. (Based on 243 central cities, the answer is that procedure is not significantly related to minority group representation.)
Packer, Mark. "Tracking the Count through a Political Thicket: At-Large Election Systems and Minority Vote Dilution." *Urban Law Annual*, vol. 23 (1982), esp. pp. 227–246.

Audit   An administrative approval (in preaudit) or monitoring (in postaudit) of monies spent by a government agency. Those who audit most often are part of the legislative branch of a government, which has responsibility to oversee the operations of the executive branch. At the federal level, the auditor is the comptroller general, who is appointed by the president, with the Senate's advice and consent, to a 15-year term to direct the General Accounting Office (GAO). State- and local-level auditors, also arms of the legislative branches, are elected or appointed. Governments at all levels are legally bound to conduct preaudits. Most municipalities contract out for postaudits to certified public accounting firms that specialize in this activity. *See also* CONTROLLER; CORRUPTION, GOVERNMENT.

Significance   In an attempt to impose greater rationality on government spending, regular pre- and postaudits of programmatic spending are important instruments of fiscal control. All public agency audits are open for inspection by the media or taxpayers. At the state and local levels of government, limited resources often restrict complete auditing procedures. As such, preaudits are required to authorize spending, but very few postaudits are conducted after the money has been spent by the executive branch agency. In more recent years, however, reduced federal funding to state and local governments and taxpayer demands for more efficient and effective programs have placed a greater emphasis on postauditing at all levels of government. A postaudit is considered a major technique for uncovering corruption such as skimming or diverting public funds.

Auditor   An elected or appointed official with responsibility for monitoring the expenditure of appropriated funds. In most cases, the auditor works for the legislative branch as a check on executive branch spending practices to determine agreement with legislative intent and authorization. In some states, the auditor is called the *comptroller*. However, in many cases, the term comptroller refers only to the individual or office that has postaudit responsibilities. At the local level, much of the auditing activity is restricted to a preaudit, in which a proposed executive expenditure is compared to legislative appropriations to determine conformity with prevailing law. The auditor for the federal government, the comptroller general, directs the General Accounting Office (GAO). *See also* AUDIT; CONTROLLER; COST-BENEFIT ANALYSIS.

Significance   The task of the auditor has become increasingly important during times of fiscal austerity and retrenchment. During the 1970s, taxpayers and concerned groups became more aware of public-sector spending and demanded greater fiscal accountability. While preaudits have been standard practice in most state and local governments for many years, these levels of government have begun to conduct much more postauditing since the early 1970s. In the political and policy struggles of the 1980s, proponents and opponents began using these evaluation studies to reinforce their respective positions about the merits of continued funding during times of scarcer resources. The use of cost-benefit analysis to justify continued spending or to support the reduction or elimination of program spending has been particularly common in environmental regulation and social welfare programs.

Suggested Reading
Davidson, Sidney, et al. *Financial Reporting by State and Local Government Units.* Chicago: Center for Management of Public and Nonprofit Enterprise, University of Chicago, 1977.
Municipal Finance Officers Association and Peat, Marwick, Mitchell & Co. *Study Guide to Governmental Accounting, Auditing and Financial Reporting.* Chicago: Municipal Finance Officers Association, 1974.

Authority, Public   A government corporation created by a local ordinance, or state or national statute, to build, operate, and maintain specific projects. Public authorities normally rely on fees generated by users of their facilities and are supervised by boards rather than a single executive. They have the power to borrow money (usually through revenue bonds), own property, condemn land, and tax, as well as impose fees. Although public authorities are wholly owned by a government, they have independent corporate status with the right to sue and be sued. Corporations formed by the national government include the Tennessee Valley Authority (TVA) and the U.S. Postal Service. Corporations formed by state and local governments more often are called authorities, and include many redevelopment authorities as well as those administering airports, hospitals, and other large public projects. By contrast, *school districts* and *special districts* are not considered public authorities because their revenues come from their own direct taxing power. *See also* DOWNTOWN DEVELOPMENT AUTHORITY; PORT OF NEW YORK AND NEW JERSEY AUTHORITY; PUBLIC-PRIVATE PARTNERSHIP; QUASI-PUBLIC; REVENUE IMPROVEMENT BOND; SPECIAL DISTRICT.

Significance   The history of public authorities goes back as far as sixteenth-century England, where they primarily were used to operate and pay for seaports and roads. In the United States, the first large-scale public authority was the Port of New York and New Jersey Authority, established in 1921 and created as an interstate compact between New York and New Jersey with the approval of the U.S. Congress. During the Depression, when many cities were unable to pay for public projects, authorities became an attractive alternative financing and administrative method for building infrastructure. The federal government encouraged the creation of public authorities by offering grants through its Public Works Administration and Reconstruction Finance Corporation (RFC) for urban projects that were self-financing. During the 1970s and 1980s, many urban development and redevelopment authorities were created to finance and build downtown areas or to develop specific projects within cities. These public authorities were empowered to borrow money against the specific development projects and therefore did not increase the municipality's general-obligation debt. Supporters of public authorities argue such entities are more efficient since general-purpose governments regulate their activities less than those of other government agencies. Critics caution against the reduced public access and accountability inherent in these organizations. In many cases, the literature on government corporations and public authorities makes little distinction between a "public authority" and the other manifestations of government enterprise: "corporation," "special district," and "commission."

Suggested Reading

Doig, Jameson W. " 'If I See a Murderous Fellow Sharpening a Knife Cleverly . . . ': The Wilsonian Dichotomy and the Public Authority Tradition." *Public Administration Review*, vol. 43, no. 4 (1983), pp. 292–304.

Henriques, Diana. *The Machinery of Greed: The Abuse of Public Authorities and What To Do about It.* Princeton: Woodrow Wilson School, Princeton University, 1982.

Walsh, Annemarie H. *The Public's Business.* Cambridge, MA: MIT Press, 1978.

B

Balanced Ticket   A list of electoral candidates selected by a party to accommodate a wide collection of racial, ethnic, or ideological groups. The goal of a balanced ticket is to organize a winning coalition by appealing to a diverse set of voters' loyalties. Among the elements that are balanced are age, sex, geographic section, religion, ethnicity, race, and ideology. Balanced tickets accomplish two major functions of political parties: to recruit candidates and to organize a popular government if elected. By creating a slate, the party guides the voters to a team approach that makes it easier to govern because many of the conflicting interests are directly represented in the government. The party reduces its costs of campaigning and demonstrates that it already has formed a consensus by brokering the cleavages within the community. *See also* BALLOT, SHORT; ETHNIC GROUP.

Significance   Balanced tickets also are known as fusion slates and unity tickets. In a parliamentary system, coalition building for a cabinet transpires after an election has sorted out the relative power of each bloc. In an American municipal election with a long ballot, the balanced ticket represents a preelection coalition. It is accommodation politics, also known as *quid pro quo* politics. The purpose of this diverse recruitment pattern is not just to showcase cooperation but to signal a willingness to give access to many groups. Reform governments thwart balanced tickets by creating a short ballot, which reduces the possibility of demonstrating this group appeal. It is not always an agreeable idea: New Orleans produced a "thug ticket" in the 1860s that was backed by organized crime. In New York City, tickets balance religious and ethnic groups so all three "I's" are represented: Italy, Ireland, and Israel. In Detroit, the Democrats particularly have to accommodate union ideological factions as well as ethnic groups. San Antonio from 1955 to 1975 was dominated by the Good Government

League (GGL), which produced a slate that co-opted the large Mexican-American community. Fiorello LaGuardia, mayor of New York in the 1930s and 1940s, often was called a one-man balanced ticket, since he had a Balkan background, Italian surname, Episcopalian religious affiliation, and partial Jewish descent. He sounded like a Democrat but had been a Republican congressman. In addition, he ran on an anti–Tammany Hall fusion slate for mayor.

Suggested Reading
Eldersveld, Samuel J. *Political Parties: A Behavioral Analysis.* Chicago: Rand McNally, 1964. Pp. 74–97 for Detroit's experience.
Johnson, David R., John A. Booth, and Richard J. Harris, eds. *The Politics of San Antonio: Community, Progress and Power.* Lincoln: University of Nebraska Press, 1983. Pp. 99–105 for the GGL.
Sayre, Wallace S., and Herbert Kaufman. *Governing New York City: Politics in the Metropolis.* New York: W. W. Norton, 1960, 1965.

Balkanization   The fragmentation of metropolitan areas into a maze of jurisdictions. The metaphor is based on the Balkans, a cluster of southeast European nations with diverse politics, economics, and cultures. Long organized arbitrarily into politically atomized units, the Balkans have been prevented by physical barriers from fully utilizing common resources. None of the Balkans has been able to dominate, and intergovernmental relations are often hostile. America's balkanized city jurisdictions similarly are a network of governments that often isolate resources from need, so that the tax base of one community may be more than sufficient for services, whereas an adjacent unit is resource-poor. Because land use and densities vary greatly among jurisdictions in the same metropolitan area, the types and levels of services differ dramatically. The anchor city seldom dominates the area. Among the top metropolitan areas, generally more than half the population lives outside the central city. *See also* COUNCIL OF GOVERNMENTS; HOME RULE; SUBURBANIZATION; TIEBOUT THESIS; TWO-LEVEL URBAN REORGANIZATION.

Significance   The extreme example of U.S. balkanization is Metropolitan New York, spread over 3 states, 22 counties, 5 boroughs, and more than 1,400 political units. Metropolitan St. Louis is spread over 2 states and some 470 units, and there is a 4-county Pittsburgh Standard Metropolitan Statistical Area (SMSA). As of the 1960 census, Greater New York's population, in excess of 16 million, had an overall ratio of one unit per 11,000 people, whereas Greater St. Louis's population, in excess of 2.3 million, converted to a ratio of about 1 unit per 5,000 people. Greater Pittsburgh's 1967 Census of Governments recorded 704 units, and in the 1972 Census of Governments, residents of the borough of Whitehall, a suburb, paid taxes or user fees to 17 tiers of general governments, districts, authorities, commissions, and regions. This means there are about 11 times more local governments for the New York metropolitan area and 4 times more local governments for the St. Louis metropolitan area than there are nations in the world. As the mother city, or metropolis, loses population and density, peripheral jurisdictions incorporate. There is no super-level to impose either consistent zoning districts or an areawide master plan. For most metropolitan areas, the only areawide body is the voluntary Council of Governments (COG), which serves as a clearinghouse for some information and as a contact for the national level, but by no means do COGs coordinate intergovernmental relations. Many of the newly formed units are overtly anti–core city. The small units do make access to decision makers easier for their relatively small number of residents. The central city serves as an anchor for select services such as entertainment, banking, and courts. The metropolitan area sprawls to the limits of in-place infrastructure. The core generally tends to have higher concentrations of blacks and lower-income residents, the periphery more whites and middle-income residents.

Suggested Reading

Goldfield, David R., and Blaine A. Brownell. *Urban America: From Downtown to No Town.* Boston: Houghton Mifflin, 1979.

Johnson, R. J. *The American Urban System: A Geographical Perspective.* New York: St. Martin's Press, 1982. Chap. 9.

Teaford, Jon C. *City and Suburbs: The Political Fragmentation of Metropolitan America, 1850–1970.* Baltimore: Johns Hopkins University Press, 1979.

Wood, Robert C. *1400 Governments: The Political Economy of the New York Metropolitan Region.* Garden City, NY: Doubleday, 1961.

Ballot, Short   An election format that presents a limited number of candidates to the voters. The short ballot is the opposite of the bed-sheet (or long) ballot, on which an extensive number of candidates and proposals is presented to the electors. *See also* BALANCED TICKET; ELECTIONS, TYPES OF; REFORM GOVERNMENT.

Significance   Most contemporary U.S. elections are on the short-ballot format. National elections and those in states such as Alaska, Hawaii, and New Jersey form the bastion of the short ballot. Long ballots are still frequently used in some counties and municipalities, notably within Louisiana. Although short ballots are less demanding for the voters, short-ballot voting remains an intellectually demanding exercise. In contrast, long ballots are often so lengthy that voters literally are unable to complete their ballots within the allotted time. The short-ballot movement was a progressive reform at the turn of the century in reaction to the excesses of Jacksonian democracy, which argued that a public office is a position of trust and thus requires direct public scrutiny. Reform advocates noted that voters' attention is limited and long ballots promote voter fatigue. Frequently on long ballots, voters do not get far enough to select candidates for lower-level positions. Further, long ballots invite machine politicians to balance interests, possibly to the detriment of the best available candidates. Clearly, the few candidate options on a short ballot raise the visibility for those remaining and increase their accountability to the electorate. On the other hand, a relatively long ballot allows attentive publics disproportionate power at the ballot box, simply because fewer voters bother to cast a ballot.

Banfield Thesis   A conservative argument, developed by Edward C. Banfield, that there is no general, unprecedented twentieth-century U.S. urban crisis, but only central-city and inner-ring-suburban problems. The thesis proposes that the bulk of those who live in metropolitan areas are better off in health and essential welfare than ever before. This progress is not a result of federal government intervention, especially that allotted for transportation and housing, but is a result of market forces. Only the intractable urban lower class has not benefited; its members are unable to defer gratification or wisely to use improved education, housing, and transportation facilities. Although there still is poverty and racial discrimination, it is decreasing. Many of the elements of the so-called urban crisis should not be changed, such as the decline of central business districts. There is only a series of interrelated, important but not serious issues that affect people's comfort and businesspeople's working conditions. The so-called urban crisis is so perceived because of our sense of rising expectations. If we had better historical perspective, we would not despair and say these problems are of crisis proportion. The thesis was developed by Banfield, a Harvard and University of Pennsylvania professor, in his widely circulated and debated 1970 book and its 1974 revision and expansion. Primarily a class analysis in historical perspective, the book focuses on what Banfield sees as the relatively small, unresponsive, and incorrigible lower class, which does not develop positive attitudes toward work, thrift, and long-term goals that would allow its members to rise above their perpetual squalor. *See also* MAXIMUM FEASIBLE PARTICIPATION; POVERTY LEVEL; URBAN CRISIS.

Significance   The Banfield thesis and supporting arguments represent an important and controversial attack on liberal political and social thought. Banfield debunks the belief that government should play an active role in the betterment of all groups, especially the lower class. The exact composition and scale of this group are never clearly specified, but the group is composed heavily of inner-city blacks. The thesis suggests there is an intractable residuum of the poor that will always be with us. Banfield's policy message is that it is inappropriate for government to attempt to reform a class that will not help itself. The Republican Nixon administration (1969–1974) cited this argument in justifying its lowered commitment to cities. From this line of argument came the corollary Nixon administration argument that cities should be treated with benign neglect.

Suggested Reading
Averch, Harvey A., and Robert A. Levine. "Two Models of the Urban Crisis: An Analytical Essay on Banfield and Forrester." Santa Monica, CA: RAND, 1970. RM-6366-RC.
Banfield, Edward C. *The Unheavenly City: The Nature and Future of Our Urban Crisis.* Boston: Little, Brown, 1968, 1970.
———. *The Unheavenly City Revisited.* Boston: Little, Brown, 1974.
Housman, Gerald L. *City of the Right: Urban Applications of American Conservative Thought.* Westport, CT: Glenview Press, 1982. Chap. 2. (An unsympathetic portrait of Banfield.)

Bankruptcy, Academic   A state-level receivership or state-imposed consolidation that follows review proceedings in which a local school board is found managerially insolvent or program-deficient. Academic bankruptcy statutes are also known as school takeover laws. Academic bankruptcy is analogous to a financial bankruptcy for a government in which the national courts take receivership and appoint a trustee in place of the regularly constituted authority. *See also* BANKRUPTCY, MUNICIPAL; DILLON'S RULE; FEDERALISM.

Significance   Academic bankruptcy statutes create a check on local malfeasance, fulfilling the principle of Dillon's Rule, which asserts that all substate units of government are products of and are accountable to the state. The statutes are a tool to ensure school board accountability. The academic standards of any one school district are not in the hands of that local community but, as a last resort, are state-imposed. This is in line with the theory of division of power. Six states have passed such statutes: Arkansas, Georgia, Kentucky, South Carolina, Texas, and New Jersey. Arkansas was the first to pass such a provision, under its Competency Based Education Action Act of 1983. The state did in fact threaten consolidation of districts. In 1989 the New Jersey education commissioner took over all 37 schools in the Jersey City system for failure to educate and because of the local board's creation of an environment of political patronage and cronyism. The Texas variant is particularly punitive in that it allows the state board of education to revoke a school district's accreditation and hold back all allocations.

Suggested Reading
Education Commission of the States (Denver, CO), the clearinghouse for these statutes, reports on them in *Education Week.*

Bankruptcy, Municipal   In federal statutory law, the proceeding invoked when a political subdivision, public agency, or instrumentality of a state voluntarily petitions the federal bankruptcy courts as a debtor under Chapter 9 of the Bankruptcy Reform Act of 1978. The statute delegates to the courts the authority to make decisions on repayment of debt. The municipality must be insolvent or unable to meet debt repayment schedules. The substate unit prepares a plan to adjust its debt repayment after it has been unable to negotiate directly with its creditors. After the court is petitioned and accepts the case, an order for relief is automatically issued, staying all creditors from other actions in any court. The court appoints a dispersing agent but cannot keep jurisdiction when administration of the plan is completed. Bankruptcy is exclusively a federal court matter. In state statutory law, there are legal proceedings, usually in a county trial court, that transfer responsibility for financial planning from elected officials to appointed receivers-conservators in order to reschedule debt payment to satisfy creditors and restore the government to solvency. Although the two procedures are similar, only units that undergo federal Chapter 9 proceedings are truly bankrupt. Some states have established a public debt commission to oversee state court–imposed repayment schedules in order to protect state creditworthiness and minimize any adverse impact from bond rating groups. In economics, bankruptcy is the inability to pay one's debts as they come due. General government insolvency cannot be treated like a private business debt, because the municipality has not been dissolved to satisfy creditors. There is an important jurisprudential issue regarding whether an insolvent, incorporated political community that has been successfully sued as an agent for an employee who has been found guilty of a tort has the option to revert to unincorporated status in order to avoid paying its court-assessed damages. *See also* BOND AND RATING SERVICES; FISCAL CRISIS; NEW YORK CITY BAILOUT; MUNICIPAL TORT LIABILITY.

Significance   Municipal bankruptcy is not only the result of default on payments, it is a voluntary petition by the local government to the national bankruptcy court asserting that it cannot work out a plan in direct negotiation with its creditors. It is a plea for federal judicial intervention to stay all other action and acknowledge its own inability to act. The municipal reorganization plan must be accepted by 51 percent of those holding interest in the municipality's debts. Appointed receivers take over for elected public officials. It is an option of last resort. State receivership proceedings exist but are uncommon. They signal that a community is persistently unable to balance its books and needs judicial intervention. Although financial crisis can be brought on by poor municipal budgeting, accounting, or reporting, the governor's office will usually step in with technical help either by providing personnel from its staff or by appointing a good-government group to supply experts. The noncontiguous Township of Royal Oak in Oakland County, Michigan, was in this position in the 1980s. Although county politicians urged that the unit be put into formal receivership, it never was, because to do so would adversely affect state-issued bonds. The Wayne County community of Ecorse, Michigan, also in the Detroit metropolitan area, underwent county-supervised receivership in 1987. The issues involved a rapidly deteriorating tax base because of plant closings and a persistent history of corruption. Cleveland, Ohio, formally went into default in 1978 on its obligations during the administration of Dennis J. Kucinich, becoming the first city to do so since the Great Depression of the 1930s. There were 31 Chapter 9 municipal bankruptcy filings from October 1979, when the new municipal bankruptcy law went into force, to March 1988. During the calendar year 1987, there were 6 municipal bankruptcies—5 in agriculturally depressed Nebraska and 1 in Arkansas. Most properly filed bankruptcies involve not general-purpose governments but sanitary districts and other single-purpose units.

Suggested Reading

Administrative Office of the U.S. Courts, Statistical Analyses and Reports Division. *Federal Judicial Workload Statistics*, published annually.

Bond, Kenneth W. "Municipal Bankruptcy under the 1976 Amendments to Chapter IX of the Bankruptcy Act." *Fordham Urban Law Journal*, vol. 5, no. 1 (1976), pp. 1–30.

King, Lawrence P. "Municipal Insolvency: The New Chapter IX of the Bankruptcy Act." *Duke Law Journal*, vol. 1977, no. 6 (1977), pp. 1139–1178.

Spiotto, James E. "Municipal Insolvency: Bankruptcy, Receivership, Workouts, and Alternative Remedies." Chap. 13 in M. David Gelfand, ed., *State and Local Government Debt Financing*, 2 vols. Chicago: Callaghan, 1986.

Swanstrom, Todd. *The Crisis of Growth Politics: Cleveland, Kucinich, and the Challenge of Urban Populism*. Philadelphia: Temple University Press, 1985.

Barrio   A neighborhood or community largely comprised of Spanish-speaking people or those with Spanish surnames. In Spanish, *barrio* literally means "district" or "ward." The barrio has a culture derived from a language that is distinct from the standardized English of the "gabacho," or dominant society. The largest U.S. barrio is East Los Angeles, where more than 500,000 Hispanics lived by the mid-1970s. Moreover, approximately one-quarter of Los Angeles County was Hispanic by 1989. Hispanics are served by a number of national, state, and local organizations, including the Mexican-American Legal Defense and Educational Fund (MALDEF) and numerous local outreach and community programs. As early as the 1960 census, more than 80 percent of people with Spanish surnames resided in central cities. By 1989, more than 20 million Hispanics lived in the United States, with more than half in California and Texas and 90 percent concentrated in nine states. *See also* ETHNIC GROUP; ETHNIC MEDIA; GHETTO; MIGRATION, URBAN.

Significance   *Barrio* tends to have a negative connotation, much like *ghetto*. Though the degree of residential segregation of Hispanics from white ethnics historically has been the lowest of all minority groups, neighborhoods of poorer Hispanics exist in most large cities. Barrios often have fallen to urban-renewal programs in the United States. In the past, controversy has occurred over use of the terms *Chicano* and *Hispanic*. *Chicano* was once a pejorative term, but militants in the late 1960s used it as a prideful definition of ethnic and cultural identification. By the late 1980s, Chicano once again had fallen into general disuse. It is forecast that Hispanics will replace blacks as the largest minority in the United States before the 2000 census, if not sooner.

Suggested Reading
Duran, Livie Isauro, and H. Russell Bernard. *Introduction to Chicano Studies.* New York: Macmillan, 1973.
Garcia, F. Chris, ed. *La Causa Politica: A Chicano Politics Reader.* South Bend, IN: University of Notre Dame Press, 1974.
————. *Latinos and the Political System.* South Bend, IN: University of Notre Dame Press, 1988.
Valdivieso, Rafael, and Cary Davis. "U.S. Hispanics: Challenging Issues for the 1990s." *Population Trends and Public Policy Series*, no. 17. Washington, DC: Population Reference Bureau, 1988.

Bay Area Rapid Transit (BART)   A 75-mile, high-speed commuter rail system that connects San Francisco, Oakland, and the surrounding communities in the San Francisco Bay region. BART consists of some 34 stations with stops averaging about two miles apart. First proposed in 1962, the BART system was meant to provide the latest rapid-transit technology. The original total of $1.5 billion in construction costs was financed by general-obligation bonds sold by the three counties that comprise the Bay Area Rapid Transit District—San Francisco, Alameda, and Contra Costa. *See also* MASS TRANSIT; URBAN MASS TRANSPORTATION ADMINISTRATION.

Significance   BART was intended to be the showcase rapid-transit system in a densely populated urban setting. However, the system has been viewed by many as a relative failure, at least in the first 15 years of its operation. Several problems occurred with the system as it began operating in 1974. Early mechanical failures and electronic malfunctions made the trains less reliable and convenient. Because the trains were intended to reach speeds of up to 70 miles per hour between stops, the stations were placed relatively far apart. Many stations were not within walking distance for potential commuters, and an undeveloped feeder-bus system discouraged suburban commuters from using the system. Average daily ridership on BART has reached only about half the original projections, and about half of all BART riders are former users of the bus system. Therefore, BART has fallen far short of its major goal of attracting large numbers of suburban commuters during its first years. The largest problem of BART ridership remains with a culture committed to the automobile, which appears fairly well insulated from high gasoline costs.

Suggested Reading
Hall, Peter. *Great Planning Disasters.* Berkeley: University of California Press, 1982. Chap. 5, pp. 109–137.
Zwerdling, Stephen. "Social Complexity and Technological Choice: The Bay Area Rapid Transit System." *Urban Law Annual,* vol. 8 (1974), pp. 97–120.

Bedroom Suburb   A non–central-city community (1) whose land use is dominantly residential; (2) whose tax base is dominantly nonindustrial and noncommercial; (3) whose population must commute out of the jurisdiction for work; and (4) whose economy is tied to a central city as opposed to being an independent, truly rural town. It is differentiated from the central city by lower density levels and a more family-centered life style. *See also* DEFINITION, OPERATIONAL; EXURBIA; LAND-USE CONTROL; POPULATION, DAYTIME AND NIGHTTIME; SUBURB.

Significance   *Bedroom suburb* is a commonly used but not a useful term in comparative urban analysis because it lacks specificity. It is employed casually; it is not operationalized by reference to a range of residential land uses. A more appropriately descriptive term is *residential community.*

Beltway   A limited-access circular expressway built around a city or other area of traffic congestion. Beltways were designed to alleviate heavy traffic volume from city centers by bypassing high-density areas. The complement of a beltway is a spoke or radially designed road that emanates from a common point, often a riverfront, ocean terminal, or central business district. Major beltway examples include Massachusetts Route 128 (I128) around Boston, Interstate 495 around Washington, D.C., and Interstate 820 around Fort Worth. *See also* INTERSTATE HIGHWAY SYSTEM; MULTINUCLEI MODEL.

Significance   Beltways comprise only about 2,500 miles of the interstate highway system, but they have made a major impact on city development because much post-1960s development has taken place where beltways form major intersections with older radial highways. These major built-up portions of the metropolis develop because of easy access for vehicles, relatively low-cost land, ample parking, and the long-term counterurbanism trend. Combined with major new infrastructure and annexation policies, satellite cities foster rapid growth. Shopping centers in particular develop in close proximity to beltways at junctions with conventional highways.

Suggested Reading
Sternlieb, George. *New Jersey Growth Corridors: Site Selection and Location Satisfaction.* New Brunswick, NJ: Transaction Books, 1987.
U.S. Department of Transportation and Department of Housing and Urban Affairs. *The Land Use and Urban Development Impacts of Beltways.* 4 vols. Washington, DC: Superintendent of Public Documents, 1980. GPO No. 050-000-00185-7.

Benign Neglect   A term used most notably in 1970 by Daniel Patrick Moynihan in reference to racial relations and the federal government's position on urban affairs. Benign neglect referred to the belief that tensions should be reduced, as they had been fueled, by extremists on both sides of the race issue. Moynihan, who was Richard Nixon's urban affairs adviser at the time, wrote in a memo that the nation had reached a time "when the issue of race could benefit from a period of 'benign neglect.'" *See also* BANFIELD THESIS.

Significance   Moynihan's use of the phrase "benign neglect" created substantial controversy when it became public. The term was used in a memo to President Nixon but was also circulated among cabinet members and then to their departments. The subsequent leak to the press emphasized "neglect," and this came to symbolize for many the lack of enthusiasm and support that the Nixon administration had for improving the plight of blacks. Most liberals condemned this revelation, but many conservatives felt the term was misunderstood by the press and the public. One of the earliest known usages of the term was made in 1839 by the earl of Durham, who was advising Queen Victoria on policy toward one of England's colonies—Canada. The earl wrote that Canada had prospered so much under a "period of benign neglect" that the queen should give the colony the authority to govern itself.

Biological Fallacy   A fallacious metaphor comparing a city to an organic entity that is born, grows, and dies in a predictable cycle. The term *biological fallacy* was coined by Geoffrey Scott in the early twentieth century. It applies to all attempts to compare urban areas to some form of life with an inherently limited life span.

Significance   The biological fallacy suggests that cities are born, not founded; grow, rather than increase in density, scale, and total population; and die rather than decline in importance as depopulation sets in and countermigration diminishes a city's economic base. The city is not a live oak tree, nor is a city crisis an urban plague. A city does not become sick and die, nor does it have a rebirth, a renaissance. Rather, a city may be repopulated and gain a new economic base. After the urban riots in the United States in 1967, critics of the central city called for a shroud, and pronounced the city dead. Those negative metaphors were questionable, as were the positive metaphors used to refer to the rebirth of downtowns. At some point analogies break down: The biological fallacy reflects the unjustified pessimism of those who unintentionally assume urban areas have organic lives.

Suggested Reading

Gordon, Mitchell. *Sick Cities: Psychology and Pathology of American Urban Life.* Baltimore: Penguin Books, 1965.

Herber, Lewis. *Crisis in Our Cities: Death, Disease, and the Urban Plague.* Englewood Cliffs, NJ: Prentice-Hall, 1965.

Jacobs, Jane. *The Death and Life of Great American Cities.* New York: Random House, 1961.

Robinson, Brian S. "On Meaning through Metaphor." *Annals of the Association of American Geographers,* vol. 72, no. 2 (1982), pp. 272–275; with a comment in reply, pp. 275–277.

Scott, Geoffrey. *The Architecture of Humanism: A Study in the History of Taste.* London: Constable, 1914, 1924.

Weimer, David R. *The City as Metaphor.* New York: Random House, 1965.

Black Panthers   The most militant and heavily armed organization of the black power movement in the United States. The Black
Panthers (formally the Black Panther Party) viewed their tactics of
direct and open violence as a strategy of black self-defense against the
white power structure. The Black Panthers were founded by Huey
Newton and Bobby Seale in the fall of 1966 at Merritt College in
Oakland, California. They formulated a ten-point program for black
liberation that included full employment, housing, education, the cessation of hostilities with police, and an end to the perceived railroad-
ing of blacks into prisons. At its height, party membership was
estimated at from 3,000 to 5,000, distributed among 40 chapters in
major U.S. cities. The Panthers officially disbanded in 1982. *See also*
BLACK POWER.

Significance   The Black Panthers became an important and feared
symbol of the black power movement. During the late 1960s and early
1970s, notable gun battles took place between Panthers and the police
in Berkeley, San Francisco, New York, Newark, and Chicago. Because
of these violent confrontations, Panthers became the target of massive
law-enforcement surveillance. In 1969, Federal Bureau of Investigation (FBI) Director J. Edgar Hoover announced that of all black
groups, "the Black Panthers without question represent the greatest
threat to the internal security of the country." A number of Panther
leaders, including George Jackson, Mark Clark, Fred Hampton, and
Bobby Hutton, eventually died in gun battles or police raids. By the
early 1970s, the party had split into two groups, with the more militant
wing headed by Eldridge Cleaver, who renamed this splinter the East
Coast Ministry of Self-defense. Leading the West Coast wing, Seale
and Newton began to work within communities, organizing programs
such as free medical care, sickle-cell anemia detection, free breakfasts,
and a food co-op. Seale also ran for mayor of Oakland in 1973,
narrowly losing to John Reading.

Suggested Reading
Blackstock, Nelson. *Cointelpro: The FBI's Secret War on Political Freedom.* New
        York: Random House, 1975. Chap. 4, "A Special Hatred for Blacks."
Cleaver, Eldridge. *Soul on Ice.* New York: Dell, 1968.
Davis, Angela Y. *If They Come in the Morning.* New York: Signet Books, 1971.
Pinkney, Alphonso. *Red, Black, and Green: Black Nationalism in the United States.*
        Cambridge: Cambridge University Press, 1976.

Black Power   A 1960s movement primarily involving militants of
the political left who became frustrated by the moderate approach of
the more traditional civil rights movement. Black power was meant to

unify black Americans both economically and politically. However, it was perceived by whites and some blacks as a philosophy of violence or, at best, an ambiguous term. Associated most often with Stokely Carmichael, then president of the Student Nonviolent Coordinating Committee (SNCC), and the Black Panthers, the term was publicly denounced by Martin Luther King, Jr., and established civil rights organizations such as the National Association for the Advancement of Colored People (NAACP). *See also* BLACK PANTHERS; NATIONAL ASSOCIATION FOR THE ADVANCEMENT OF COLORED PEOPLE.

Significance   Black power meant to give a new awareness, solidarity, and a sense of racial pride to blacks in the 1960s. Political self-determination and economic self-sufficiency seemed unattainable goals for blacks during this time, and to some the passive-resistance approach of the traditional civil rights movement seemed ineffective. By the spring of 1966, SNCC had officially changed its political platform from "civil rights" to "black power." Stokely Carmichael argued that part of black self-determination included the use of words by blacks for blacks—words that would provide a position of strength from which black Americans could be heard. During the late 1960s, other black groups such as the Black Panthers moved from a moderate position to a more militant strategy as they saw a white-dominated society unwilling to share in the benefits of a wealthy nation. Worldwide attention was given to black power during the 1968 Olympics in Mexico City, when black American athletes stood with clenched fists thrust into the air when the national anthem was played during their medal ceremonies. During the 1970s and 1980s, blacks were increasingly elected to state and local public office. However, the economic gap between whites and blacks did not close.

Suggested Reading

Barker, Lucius J., and Jesse J. McCorry, Jr. *Black Americans and the Political System*. Cambridge, MA: Winthrop, 1976.
Baughman, E. Earl. *Black Americans: A Psychological Analysis*. New York: Academic Press, 1971.
Carmichael, Stokely, and Charles V. Hamilton. *Black Power: The Politics of Liberation in America*. New York: Vintage Books, 1967.
Patterson, Ernest. *Black City Politics*. New York: Dodd, Mead, 1974.

Black Press (Afro-American Press or Negro Press)   A specialized mass medium written and distributed nationally and locally for a predominantly black readership. The first black newspaper began in New York City in the 1820s. The Chicago *Conservator* in the 1870s and 1880s was a major source of information for southern blacks who wished to migrate north; it gave its readership information on jobs and housing. It served as a vehicle for expression by blacks on racial injustice. Presently, the black press includes more than 300 outlets. Examples of limited-circulated metropolitan newspapers include the *Amsterdam News Weekly* of New York City, 1987 circulation, 35,000; the Chicago *Defender,* founded in 1905 and currently circulating 28,000 in its daily edition; and the weekly *Michigan Chronicle* of Detroit. The largest black newspaper was the Chicago-based *Muhammad Speaks* with a circulation of 700,000 in the 1960s and 1970s. Currently the largest black, paid-circulation, weekly newspaper is the New York City tabloid *Black American,* founded in 1962, with a circulation in excess of 170,000. The largest circulating black magazines are *Ebony, Jet,* and *New York Black Enterprise. See also* COMMUNITY PRESS; ZONED EDITION.

Significance   The black press is important to urban politics, because most blacks are city dwellers. The specialized press was conceived out of protest and defends but does not always control opinion in the black community. The black press serves as the eyes, ears, and voice of the black community. It is one of the institutional checks in the social system. Relying mainly on advertising for its revenue, the black press is organized nationally by the National Newspaper Publishers Association (NNPA) for marketing purposes to attract advertising targeted at urban blacks. They also issue annual merit awards and prizes. Many newspapers circulate the same weekly magazine. Readership is down from the high point reached just after World War II. The weekly black press serves as a farm team for tyro reporters, training and seasoning them before sending them to big metropolitan dailies and television networks. It serves as a source of society news, neighborhood events, and, to a limited degree, job listings. Litigation initiated by the Justice Department in the 1980s against dominantly white suburban communities that had prehire residency requirements provides the black press with suburban "classified ads." Consent decrees against white suburbs force these communities to post employment notices in newspapers outside the jurisdiction but within the metropolitan area, which has a substantial black readership. Examples of themes in the black press include photojournalism of abandoned buildings, editorials against drugs and in favor of staying in school, and opposition or support for local legalized gambling.

Suggested Reading

Brooks, Maxwell R. *The Negro Press Reexamined.* Boston: Christopher Publishing, 1959.

Gill, Kay, and Donald P. Boyden, eds. *Gale Directory of Publications,* 120th ed., 2 vols. Detroit: Gale Research, 1988. (Formerly *Ayer Directory of Publications.*)

Lowe, W. Augustus, ed. *Encyclopedia of Black America*. New York: McGraw-Hill, 1981, pp. 644 ff.

Myrdahl, Gunnar. *An American Dilemma*, Vol. 2, rev. ed. New York: McGraw-Hill, 1944, 1962. Chap. 42, "The Negro Press," pp. 908–924.

Ploski, Harry, and James Williams, comps. and eds. *The Negro Almanac*, 4th ed. New York: John W. Ley, 1983. Chap. 25, "The Black Press and Broadcast News."

Wilson, James Q. *Negro Politics: The Search for Leadership*. New York: Free Press, 1960. Chap. VI.

Wolseley, Roland E. *The Black Press U.S.A.* Ames: Iowa State University Press, 1972.

Blight   The unsightly and gray appearance of deteriorated or substandard living or working accommodations caused by inadequate maintenance. Blight also can be simply defined as a misuse of land that, if not checked by repairs, will lead to abandonment. Blight is an organic metaphor designating either a building or area. The end state of blight is "the death" of the building or area. It accumulates from a combination of private neglect and public failure to enforce building codes. Blight reflects a low quality-of-life index. It is defined in economic terms by some states. For example, Illinois lists blight as largely open areas "which, by reason of obsolete platting, diversity of ownership, deterioration of structures or site improvements, or taxes and special assessment delinquencies usually exceeding the fair value of the land, are unmarketable . . . for housing or other economic purposes," 67 1/2 Ill. Rev. Stat. Sec. 64. It is also defined in terms of the common-law concept of the police power. Michigan defines a blighted area as one "characterized by obsolescence, physical deterioration of structures therein, improper division or arrangement of lots and ownerships and streets and other open spaces, mixed character and uses of the structures, or any other similar characteristics which endanger the health, safety, morals, or general welfare of the municipality" (M.C.L. 125.72). *See also* ABANDONMENT; EXTERNALITY; SLUM; ZONING, AESTHETIC.

Significance   *Blight* is an inexact term that can be defined economically, legally, or administratively, depending on context. Local administrators for urban-renewal projects first made a factual determination that an area was so blighted as to constitute a slum, that the area should be condemned, the buildings razed, and the property put under eminent domain, all preparatory to redevelopment. Courts reserved the right to review local officials' determinations of blight. Blighted areas have high crime levels and many transient residents, and they make an adverse impact on adjacent neighborhoods. Although slum is defined in federal statutes, blight is not; it is often used as a simple negative connotation.

Suggested Reading
"Municipal Blight Declarations." *Urban Law Annual,* vol. 23 (1982),
    pp. 423–425.

Bliss Thesis   The proposition that the Republican party will win presidential elections only if it sets up organizations in every major city and appeals to urban minorities. The thesis is named after the GOP national chairman of the mid-1960s, Ray C. Bliss (1907–1987), who chaired a 1961 study on urban political organization. He championed a pragmatic, centrist politics that acknowledged the strategic implications of the Republicans being the minority party. To win in industrial states, it had to appeal to all Americans, most of whom, by 1960, lived in urban areas. The thesis asserted the Republicans could not afford to neglect the major cities, could not bypass urban ethnics, and could not focus on the sunbelt at the expense of the older, central cities in the snowbelt or rustbelt.

Significance   The Bliss thesis is predicated in part on the fact that many major U.S. central cities in the Northeast reached maximum populations in the 1950s. By the early 1960s, when Bliss delivered his report, both major political parties' managers read the census reports and realized a double demographic shift was under way (1) from the major, older cities to the suburbs, and (2) from the Northeast to the South and West. In 1960, Bliss was the Ohio State Republican Chairman for the Central and Executive Committee. He aided Richard Nixon in devising a strategy for an Ohio upset over John Kennedy, the only major northern industrial state Nixon won that year. The argument ran that the only nationwide election in the United States is for president, and the 13 (today 12) most highly populated states contain enough votes to carry the electoral college. Among them only North Carolina is without major cities. To win the presidency, one must appeal to the big cities in the big electoral states. Since central cities were becoming magnets for blacks and had long been first stops for recent ethnic arrivals, the GOP should focus on what had heretofore been conceded to the Democrats as their turf. This argument won in the national wing of the Republican party until 1980, when Ronald Reagan changed strategy and neglected the by-then black majorities in many of the cities in the northeastern quadrant. In 1988 Republican George Bush carried only 9 percent of the black vote.

Blockbusting   A strategy employed by real estate agents and speculators to force a decline in the price of houses in a neighborhood. The standard technique involves selling a housing unit to a black family or circulating stories among white homeowners that black families are moving into a segregated block or neighborhood. Subsequently, white homeowners who fear integration drop their selling prices, whereupon speculators quickly buy and then resell the houses for profit. *See also* KERNER COMMISSION; REDLINING; ZONING, EXCLUSIONARY.

Significance   Until the early part of the twentieth century, the black population of the United States was located largely in the rural South. With industrialization, a substantial migration of blacks to northern cities occurred, creating competition over jobs and living quarters. Segregated living patterns, as they occurred in central cities, then in many suburban areas, have been both a symptom and a continuation of racial tension and intolerance in the United States. Blockbusting had among its proponents both those genuinely interested in pursuing integrated living patterns and those primarily interested in making a profit from the fear this strategy seemed to generate. Federal antidiscrimination policies prohibited this activity, and in the 1960s, many states enacted their own statutes banning blockbusting. State sanctions also were imposed by most of these statutes, and a real estate agent found guilty of this infraction could have his or her license taken away. Some controversy remains about the causes of racially segregated living patterns, represented largely by those who feel that the market (ability to pay) is the determining factor and by those who feel that discrimination (both public and private) impedes free choice by racial minorities. Many antidiscrimination laws have been passed since the Kerner Commission found "two societies, one black, one white—separate and unequal," but some public and private housing policies reinforced segregation for many years. Though most of these practices are now illegal, zoning policies, redlining, restrictive covenants attached to housing deeds, racial "steering" by real estate agents, and many other practices have fostered segregated living patterns in the United States.

Suggested Reading
Heiman, Aba. "Nonsolicitation and Cease and Desist Orders against Real Estate Brokers in New York." *Fordham Law Review,* vol. 15, no. 3 (1986–1987), pp. 595–621.

Board of Assessment Appeal   A public hearing conducted by a quasi-judicial body composed of three or more members usually drawn from the assessment jurisdiction and commissioned to check on the completeness, accuracy, and uniformity of the tax rolls. In a few states the appeal process is conducted at the city and township level.

This board of review hears and decides appeals from property owners of the valuation of their land parcels and, in some cases, of their personal property. These appeal bodies are often prevented from making across-the-board adjustments; they must look at each parcel individually. The appeals procedure is determined by a combination of statute and court cases that prescribe meeting times and the basis on which they will determine whether the values are just and equal. Deliberations usually fall under the requirements of open-meeting acts. Minutes as well as the final tax rolls are open to public inspection in most cases. *See also* ASSESSMENT; TAX, REAL PROPERTY; TAX ABATE-MENT; TAX-EXEMPT PROPERTY.

Significance Having properly notified property owners of the right to appeal, the county board must meet and correct any errors in classification of land or its value before endorsing the final figures. The Board of Assessment Appeal in some states is an interim step in the preparation of final tax rolls. It comes after the assessor's notice and before any final appeal to the state-level tax tribunal and should be completed before the beginning of the next fiscal year.

Suggested Reading
Press, Charles. *Primer for Board of Review Members,* 3rd ed. East Lansing: Community Development Programs, Lifelong Education Programs of Michigan State University, 1982.

Board of Education The local or state policymaking body for public school education. The U.S. political system traditionally has vested most of the responsibility for primary and secondary public education with the local board of education. In most school districts, board members are elected; however, in some states, city councils may appoint board members. *See also* BANKRUPTCY, ACADEMIC; PUBLIC SCHOOL FINANCING CASES; SCHOOL DISTRICT.

Significance The local board of education has been a foundation of decentralized authority in U.S. education policy. Local school districts have been given taxing powers by their respective states, and spending for public education is usually the largest part of local expenditures. In more recent times, standards for education and a move toward centralizing funding for schools have brought federal and state governments into the arena of public education. School aid formulas in many states provide a minimum amount of spending per pupil for school districts unable to fund those levels because of a declining tax base. Curriculum standards, teacher certification, minimum number of days per school year, and school desegregation have all found substantial intervention by state and federal officials into education policymaking. Despite these trends toward greater centralization, much decision-making power continues with the local school board and its executive, the superintendent of schools. Hiring and firing decisions, salary negotiations, and some curriculum decisions still remain within the purview of the local board of education.

Bond, Municipal   A written certificate issued by local units of government in the process of borrowing funds to carry out activities beyond those that can be supported by current revenue. Municipal bonds take several forms, but cities generally enter into long-term obligations (where the loan is repaid over several years) for large capital projects and short-term obligations (with a repayment rate of up to a year) to pay for operating expenses. Two federal policies made during the 1980s influenced the ways in which municipal bonds were offered. The Federal Tax Reform Act of 1986 (266 U.S.C. 4221) distinguishes between "public purpose" bonds, which remained tax-exempt, and "private purpose" bonds, which are taxable unless specifically exempted. In addition, a 1988 U.S. Supreme Court decision in *South Carolina v. Baker* ruled that the federal government could require state and local governments to issue registered bonds, rather than tax-free bearer bonds, thus eliminating the federal tax exemption on the interest earned by municipal bond investors. *See also* BOND AND RATING SERVICES; BOND TYPES, MUNICIPAL; DEBT, MUNICIPAL; INCOME SOURCES, URBAN; INTERGOVERNMENTAL TAX IMMUNITY; MORAL-OBLIGATION BOND; TAX ANTICIPATION NOTE.

Significance   Cities often use municipal bonds to borrow large sums of money from private lending markets for their large-ticket capital projects. Their ability to repay these loans and their general creditworthiness are important to potential investors and lenders. Moody's and Standard and Poor's bond-rating services evaluate cities or public authorities that seek to borrow money for specific projects. The amount of money and the interest rate applied to a bond are primarily determined by current market rates and the credit rating that is established by these rating services. Many cities have substantial long-term indebtedness, both through general-obligation borrowing and from revenue bonds. Revenue bonds usually finance separate (and nonguaranteed) projects. By the mid-1980s, almost two-thirds of all municipal debt came from long-term borrowing. As state and local governments are forced to assume greater funding responsibility for services, the use of all types of municipal bonds likely will increase.

Suggested Reading

Advisory Commission on Intergovernmental Relations. *Understanding the Market for State and Local Debt.* Washington, DC: Government Printing Office, 1976.
Aronson, J. Richard, and John L. Hilley. *Financing State and Local Government.* Washington, DC: Brookings Institution, 1986.
Jones, L. R. "The WPPSS Default: Trouble in the Municipal Bond Market." *Public Budgeting and Finance*, vol. 4, no. 4 (1984), pp. 29–34.
Moak, Lennox L. *Municipal Bonds: Planning, Sales, and Administration.* Washington, DC: Municipal Finance Officers Association, 1982.

Bond and Rating Services   Private businesses that analyze and evaluate the credit of local governments. Many municipalities must seek a variety of long-term and short-term loans to provide public services or to support their infrastructure needs. Standard and Poor's and Moody's are the most common bond and rating services used by local governments. These firms also rate the creditworthiness of private businesses and public authorities, such as redevelopment authorities and public utilities, along with other public and private institutions that borrow money. The ratings for long-term debt obligations range from a high of "AAA" to a low of "D" in the Standard and Poor's system. The local governments receiving the highest rating generally are regarded as the best risks to lenders. As a consequence, more favorable terms and often larger loans can be available to those cities with the highest ratings. There has been some controversy over the evaluative criteria used by the rating services. *See also* REVENUE SURPLUS.

Significance   Municipalities operate under state constitutional and statutory restrictions on borrowing money. Borrowing is technically restricted to capital projects, for which long-term bonds usually are offered on the open market. Until recently, most of these bonds were general obligations, supported and legally guaranteed by the "full faith and credit" of the city's treasury. However, as cities began to experience general fiscal difficulties, some attempted "creative" borrowing that skirted constitutional restrictions. Many cities began to issue bonds that were not guaranteed, mostly in the form of revenue bonds. Revenue bonds borrow money against the projected income from a specific project, such as a hospital, utility plant, or redevelopment project, and therefore do not require the "full faith and credit" of the municipality. These nonguaranteed bonds are not subject to the restrictions on borrowing imposed by state constitutions. During the early 1980s, many cities had outstanding debts as large as their annual budgets, and in cities such as Los Angeles, the vast percentage of that debt was not guaranteed. By 1983, almost half (45 percent) of all municipal long-term debt in the United States was not guaranteed.

Suggested Reading

Farnham, Paul G., and George S. Cluff. "The Bond Rating Game Revisited: What Information Can Local Officials Use?" *Journal of Urban Affairs,* vol. 6, no. 4 (1984), pp. 21–38.

Marguette, Jesse F., R. Penny Marguette, and Katherine A. Hinckley. "Bond Rating Changes and Urban Fiscal Stress: Linkage and Prediction." *Journal of Urban Affairs,* vol. 4, no. 1 (1982), pp. 81 ff.

Peterson, John E. "Changing Fiscal Structures and Credit Quality: Large U.S. Cities." In Charles H. Levine and Irene Rubin, eds., *Fiscal Stress and Public Policy.* Beverly Hills, CA: Sage Publications, 1980.

Twentieth Century Fund. *The Rating Game: Report of the Twentieth Century Fund Task Force on Municipal Bond Credit Ratings.* New York: Twentieth Century Fund, 1974.

Bond Election   A referendum in which a legislature, board, council, or commission asks voters to approve long-term indebtedness, frequently for periods of 10 to 30 years, to construct infrastructure. In most states, bond elections must specify the maximum amount to be approved, the terms of repayment, and the specific project, such as street or highway construction, sewer, water treatment plant, public housing, or pollution-control equipment. Bond elections can be held in conjunction with other regularly scheduled elections or at special elections, where voter turnout tends to be much lower. *See also* REFER-ENDUM; USER FEE.

Significance   The most common bond election is to incur public debt for school capital improvements. Often approval is by a simple majority of voters. Some states impose a requirement of either a majority of all registered voters or 60 percent of those voting. This 60-percent requirement was challenged in a West Virginia case. Speaking for a majority, Chief Justice Warren Burger said an extraordinary-majority requirement is permissible under guidelines for equal protection of the law as long as all bond elections are held to the same standards. He declared, "There is nothing in the language of the Constitution, our history, or our cases that requires that a majority always prevail on every issue," *Gordon v. Lance,* 403 U.S. 1, at 6 (1970). The three-fifths requirement is justified since the burden for paying off the debt falls on generations not yet born. Many bond proposals are defeated by well-organized "antigroups." To avoid these confrontations, legislative bodies sometimes resort to creating or raising user fees or waiting until an emergency arises, an action that allows the body to bypass conventional electoral procedures. Other bodies parcel out work in amounts under the minimum amount requiring voter approval of bonds. Still other bodies anticipate capital projects by setting aside building improvement funds. Some home rule charters require simple ordinance approval of bond indebtedness.

Bond Types, Municipal   Categories of instruments of indebtedness entered into by local governments or their legal extensions. Though municipalities and their subdivisions borrow money through a number of specific categories, municipal bonds fall into two general types: general-obligation bonds and revenue bonds. General-obligation bonds are "guaranteed," in that they are backed by the taxing authority of a local government. Revenue bonds are not guaranteed and rely on the revenues generated by the specific project to repay the debtor. With the Federal Tax Reform Act of 1986, 266 U.S.C. 4221, investors divided municipal bonds into "public purpose" bonds, which continued to be tax-exempt, and "private purpose" bonds, which are taxable unless specifically exempted. The legal distinction between the two is based on the percentage of benefit a project will advantage private parties. More than a 10 percent benefit to a private party is considered private purpose. *See also* BOND, MUNICIPAL; BOND AND RATING SERVICES; INDUSTRIAL REVENUE BOND; TAX ANTICIPATION NOTE.

Significance   Municipal bond types vary in their attractiveness to investors. General-obligation bonds are the safest investment because repayment is guaranteed by the taxing powers of the municipality. They are also usually exempt from federal, state, and local taxes, and so are an attractive investment to high-income individuals and corporations. Because of these advantages, the return on investment tends to be lower than for other securities. Revenue bonds can take several forms and are most often administered by a separate public housing, hospital, airport, or redevelopment authority. Though most borrowing is for long-term, large-ticket items, short-term borrowing to cover operating costs is also allowed, usually through tax anticipation notes (TANs). Private bond-rating services, such as Standard and Poor's or Moody's Investor's Service, determine the security and value of municipal bonds and assign ratings for municipalities or their public authorities.

Borough   From the Old English, a town of a certain political status. (1) In New York City, one of five geographic units of government comprising the city since a reorganization in 1897. The boroughs also serve as county governments, in some cases with altered titles, thus:

Bronx County–Bronx, New York County–Manhattan, Queens County–Queens, Kings County–Brooklyn, and Richmond County–Richmond (Staten Island). Each borough elects its own president. The five boroughs are governed jointly by a strong mayor and council. (2) In Connecticut, New Jersey, and Pennsylvania, an incorporated town or village smaller than a city. (3) In Alaska, a unit of government since 1961 comparable in other states to a county, designed to achieve economies of scale while serving vast, sparsely settled spaces in the nation's largest and least populous state. *See also* NEW YORK CITY BAILOUT; REAPPORTIONMENT, CITY.

Significance   The five New York City boroughs represent a turn-of-the-century attempt by the legislature in Albany to consolidate yet decentralize an unprecedentedly large-scale city by retaining the five counties and giving them certain administrative functions, while relabeling them as subdivisions of the city and allowing them to elect their own borough presidents. These presidents are somewhat closer to the people than is the city mayor. The term *rotten borough* does not refer to any of the three definitions above, but to any incorporated area whose legislative representation is disproportionately large relative to its actual population. Rotten boroughs were effectively eliminated by reapportionment cases that began in the 1960s.

Suggested Reading
Harden, Donald H. "Sayre and Kaufman Revisited: New York City Government since 1965." *Urban Affairs Quarterly,* vol. 15, no. 2 (1979), pp. 123–145.
Sayre, Wallace S., and Herbert Kaufman. *Governing New York City: Politics in the Metropolis.* New York: W. W. Norton, 1960, 1965.

Borrowing Limit   A restriction imposed by state constitution or statute on the amount of money a local government may pledge to repay. Borrowing limits may differ with regard to long-term projects contained in a city's capital budget and to the short-term borrowing involved with a city's operating budget. Local borrowing limits can take various forms: ceilings on the amount of overall debt that can be outstanding, usually measured in relation to the value of a city's taxable property; approval by voters of bond authorization; and establishment of various debt-management principles and procedures. *See also* DEBT LIMIT, LOCAL; REVENUE IMPROVEMENT BOND; TAX ANTICIPATION NOTE; USER FEE.

Significance   Unlike the federal government, local governments usually have rigid borrowing and spending limits imposed on their budgets. Such budgetary control and management have been foundations of a rational budgetary process. Controls such as voter approval of general-obligation borrowing also help bring the budgetary decision-making process closer to average citizens. Many local governments, especially the larger industrialized cities experiencing fiscal crises during the 1970s, were forced to look for ways to circumvent the borrowing and spending limitations imposed by state constitution or statute. As revenues declined in these cities, the demand for services increased dramatically. This increased the need to borrow for the short term, as operating funds were depleted. The withdrawal of the federal government from many urban-aid programs also exacerbated these financial problems. Cities were required to reduce expenses through cutbacks and layoffs and to look for alternative means of raising money for both capital and operating expenses. The increased use of revenue bonds, whose debt is not applied to the general-obligation debt, and the increased use of user fees are two prominent examples of local attempts to skirt the borrowing limits.

Boss   The leader of an urban political party machine or a ward or labor union. Boss is most often used in a derogatory manner, as bossism and political machines are usually associated with centralized power and corruption. Bosses were most prevalent during the 1800s in the United States before the structural and procedural reforms of the Progressive Era eliminated most of the machines. Among the most noted machine bosses have been Richard Daley of Chicago, William Marcy Tweed of New York City, James Pendergast of Kansas City, and Frank Hague of Jersey City. None of this type of boss exists today, although some strong local political leaders resemble the old-style bosses. *See also* CORRUPTION, GOVERNMENT; PATRONAGE, URBAN; REFORM GOVERNMENT; TAMMANY HALL; URBAN POLITICAL MACHINE.

Significance   The boss of an urban political machine was not necessarily the elected mayor but typically held the patronage power upon which the machine rested. Bosses and machines were attacked largely because of the corruption associated with patronage, kickbacks, and the preferential treatment provided to businesses and citizens who supported the machine. New York's Boss Tweed Ring was considered among the most corrupt. Tweed diverted at least $30 million worth of public funds for the machine's private use. Tweed also routinely took at least 10 percent in kickbacks of all city construction contracts. While the graft and corruption of bosses and machines have been criticized universally, some observers have argued that machines performed certain necessary social, political, and economic functions in cities with vast numbers of immigrants in need of assistance and little support available from other sources. The adoption of various governmental welfare programs and at-large elections contributed to the demise of bossism in the United States.

Suggested Reading
Allswang, John M. *Bosses, Machines, and Urban Voters.* Baltimore: Johns Hopkins University Press, 1986.
Callow, Alexander B., Jr., ed. *The City Boss in America.* New York: Oxford University Press, 1976.
Rakove, Milton. *Don't Make No Waves, Don't Back No Losers: An Insider's Analysis of the Daley Machine.* Bloomington: Indiana University Press, 1979.
Riordan, William L. *Plunkitt of Tammany Hall.* New York: E. P. Dutton, 1963.
Royko, Mike. *Boss: Richard J. Daley of Chicago.* New York: E. P. Dutton, 1971.

Boundary   The limit of a territory that may contain a legal-political jurisdiction, a daily commuting area, a social group, an economic class, or a commercial trading area. In a metropolitan area there are many overlapping and conflicting governmental boundaries, marking areas ranging from municipalities to solid-waste collection districts. Some boundaries are specific and carefully defined, such as those recorded in cadastral surveys, whereas other boundaries demarcate nebulous or informally named areas such as Corktown, Downriver, or the gold coast. *See also* ASSESSMENT; BALKANIZATION; BOUNDED CITIES, TYPES OF; RESIDENT; ZONE, URBAN.

Significance   Urban dwellers are sensitive to multiple boundaries, many of which do not appear on conventional maps and go unrecognized by courts. All urban boundaries are artificial. Many are designated by survey lines or topographic features. Seldom are cities *truebounded,* that is to say with legal boundaries closely corresponding to the limits of the population. Zip code boundaries of the U.S. Postal Service do not recognize all political subdivisions. School attendance lines are often at odds with other taxing authorities because of consolidation. Local court districts often bracket together a host of cities, towns, townships, or school districts. Because of Supreme Court busing decisions, residency in units falling outside areas affected by integration orders became a major factor in white flight. Boundaries are often drawn up in a rush by city attorneys drafting incorporation papers before an adjacent community can prepare an annexation plan. Consequently, some boundaries may run irregularly through backyards and the middle of houses and may create enclaves. City boundary changes, whether by annexation, incorporation, or consolidation, must be viewed as actions that affect the interests of both the community and its residents. Insurance-imposed restraints on police activity limit or curtail hot pursuit outside some cities' boundaries. Fire departments also are constrained from fighting blazes just over their borders because of insurance limits or the failure of communities sharing a boundary to enter formally into a mutual aid pact. A major constraint on local physical planning is the failure of contiguous units to consult with each other on land-use designation for common boundaries. Most metropolitan residents think microspatially—that is, in terms of subdivision housing boundaries, school attendance districts, and the precincts and wards in which they vote and receive their public safety services.

Suggested Reading
Fleischmann, Arnold. "The Goals and Strategies of Local Boundary Changes: Government Organization or Private Gain?" *Journal of Urban Affairs*, vol. 8, no. 4 (1986), pp. 63–76.

Bounded Cities, Types of   Municipalities described by the spatial relationship between the legal boundaries of a local jurisdiction and the actual built-up area. (1) In a *truebounded* city, the extent of high-density land use and in-place infrastructure closely matches the legal jurisdiction. The city fringe is conterminous with the city's political limits. (2) In an *underbounded* city, urban sprawl reaches beyond the city's limits, and new development is going up without adequate public planning. Service delivery is spotty in the fringe area of an under-bounded city, but real estate taxes are very low. (3) In an *overbounded* city, annexation has locked in more land than is being used, defined either over the short run or according to a long-term master plan. *See also* ANNEXATION; BALKANIZATION; ENCLAVE; EXTRATERRITORIAL POWER; INFILLING.

Significance   No major American city will stay truebounded in the long run, because legal development of a city's jurisdiction lags behind suburbanization. This is an example of a relatively conservative legal-political system operating in a dynamic marketplace. New England towns embrace the built-up core plus the immediate rural hinterland; they are by definition overbounded. Overbounded cities possess vacant urban land. This may be zoned agricultural, raw land—i.e., unbuilt property—in small parcels surrounded by development, unbuildable sites, corporate reserves, speculation parcels, or industrial reserves. Combined, these vacant parcels constitute about one-fourth of the total land mass for 86 large U.S. cities. However, underbounded cities are the most prevalent in the United States. Older, larger central cities in the northeast and north-central regions are severely under-bounded. They are surrounded by separately incorporated suburbs, in some cases seven rings deep. State law usually prevents municipal units of the same type from annexing each other. Through careful public-policy manipulation by white elites, some southern cities remain underbounded so as to retain a white majority. Some of these cities face Justice Department challenges to their boundaries under color of the 1965 Voting Rights Act, which has been interpreted by the U.S. Supreme Court as embracing the effects of municipal annexation. The underbounded city may dilute minority voting by failure to annex fringe black settlements. Central-city black voting strength also may be diluted by wholesale annexation of fringe white suburbs.

Suggested Reading
Aiken, Charles S. "Race as a Factor in Municipal Underbounding." *Annals of the Association of American Geographers,* vol. 77, no. 4 (1987), pp. 564–579.
Northham, Ray M. *Urban Geography.* New York: John Wiley, 1975, pp. 364–374.

Broadacre City   A "think piece" urban plan that evolved in architect Frank Lloyd Wright's writing between 1901 and his death in 1959. He felt it captured the democratic potential of decentralized living in an economically reintegrated, low-density planned community. Broadacre City became a physical model representing four square miles in the United States of the mid-1930s. It was an amenity-filled environment in which Wright reacted to the highly compact city of the skyscraper. He rejected the city in favor of the county as the chief administrative unit. The design focused on the individual, the use of the commons, open space, mass participation in farming and gardening, environmentally clean industry, and educational structures. *See also* AMENITIES; GREENBELT; JEFFERSONIAN AGRARIANISM.

Significance   Wright wrote extensively about Broadacre City, especially after he forswore public lectures. As one of America's premier architects, he made a strong statement that the profession is better suited to laying out large-scale, integrated architectural space than designing discrete buildings. There must be reference to the larger physical environment and the uses to which buildings are to be put, not simply maximizing economies of scale, he said. Although the particulars of Wright's plan are now dismissed as useless and impractical, he did succeed in demonstrating the restrictive assumptions of designing a building out of context. His contribution to community planning was to bring attention to the natural environment of greenbelts and open spaces and the need to lay out new towns and whole recreation communities. Less successful than his contemporary,

Englishman Sir Ebenezer Howard (1850–1928), and the garden city movement, Wright did foreshadow shopping centers and recreation communities.

Suggested Reading

Cordon, Carrol. *Planned Cities: New Towns in Britain and America*, Vol. 55. Beverly Hills: Sage Library of Social Research, 1977.

Twombly, Robert C. "Undoing the City: Frank Lloyd Wright's Planned Communities." *American Quarterly*, vol. 24, no. 4 (1972), pp. 538–549.

Wright, Frank Lloyd. *The Living City*. New York: New American Library, 1958.

Brown v. Board of Education of Topeka, Kansas I, 347 U.S. 483 (1954); II, 349 U.S. 294 (1955)   Two landmark U.S. Supreme Court decisions, the first of which outlawed *de jure* racial segregation in all public school districts in the United States by overturning *Plessy v. Ferguson*, 163 U.S. 537 (1896). The second directed school districts to desegregate with "all deliberate speed." The majority of the Court argued that the legally sanctioned "separate but equal" facilities upheld in the *Plessy* decision violated the Fourteenth Amendment's guarantee of "equal protection of laws." *See also* BUSING; *DE FACTO* SEGREGATION; *DE JURE* SEGREGATION; DESEGREGATION.

Significance   The *Brown v. Board of Education* decisions were among the most important and controversial ever made by the U.S. Supreme Court. The unanimous decision by the Court concluded that separate facilities, even if they were equally funded, created a "stigma" for minorities. School desegregation came slowly in many states, and integration of school districts has been affected by other public-policy and social factors. During the 1960s, school desegregation was spurred as the federal government tied implementation to federal aid. Later Supreme Court decisions allowed busing of students within a unitary school district to achieve racial integration, most notably in *Swann v. Charlotte-Mecklenburg*, 420 U.S. 1 (1971). The *Swann* decision further approved remedies such as racial quotas and grouping noncontiguous school zones to remedy state-imposed school segregation. However, the high court later overturned lower court plans to implement compliance by cross-district busing in *Milliken v. Bradley*, 418 U.S. 717 (1974). In that case, the Court ruled federal courts could not impose busing across school district boundaries unless each affected school district was found to have practiced racial discrimination, or that district boundaries had been drawn to create racially segregated schools. This decision reaffirmed the concept and practice of neighborhood schools, even in the face of *de facto* segregation.

Suggested Reading
Kluger, Richard. *Simple Justice: The History of* Brown v. Board of Education *and Black America's Struggle for Equality.* New York: Knopf, 1976.
U.S. Commission on Civil Rights. *Twenty Years after* Brown. Washington, DC: Government Printing Office, 1975.
Walters, Raymond. *The Burden of* Brown: *Thirty Years of School Desegregation.* Knoxville: University of Tennessee Press, 1984.

Budget Types   There are two major categories of local public fiscal plans, namely capital and operating forecasts of revenues and expenditures. Capital budgets involve long-term, large expenditures usually financed by borrowing money. The expenditures can cover many years, and the debt acquired by such borrowing is normally not counted in the current fiscal year's accounting of deficits. The operating budget covers daily expenditures such as personnel costs, supplies, and smaller equipment. Usually, operating-budget outlays are exhausted within a single fiscal year. *See also* DEBT, MUNICIPAL; DEBT LIMIT, LOCAL; FISCAL YEAR.

Significance   Given the large amounts of funding usually required for capital projects, the methods of financing capital versus operating budgets are quite different. Capital budgets usually involve long-term borrowing, and state and local governments have strict procedures regarding borrowing and debt limits. These budgets also differ in the types of items purchased and often in the process of decision making required to approve and execute the budgets. However, in general practice, specific categories of spending, such as police, fire, parks and recreation, planning, and general government, may have both capital and operating-fund expenditures. In an attempt to provide greater policy control on spending, many cities have introduced rationalized budgeting plans, such as Zero-Based Budgeting (ZBB) or Program Planning Budgeting System (PPBS). These plans purport to offer greater understanding and more control of programmatic spending than can usually be realized by incremental, line-item budgeting techniques that sometimes hide overall program costs.

Suggested Reading
Burkehead, Jesse, and Paul Bringewatt. *Municipal Budgeting: A Primer for the Local Official.* Washington, DC: Joint Center for Political Studies, 1977.
Fisher, Ronald C. *State and Local Public Finance.* Glenview, IL: Scott, Foresman, 1989.
Lynch, Thomas Dexter. *Public Budgeting in America,* 2nd ed. Englewood Cliffs, NJ: Prentice-Hall, 1985.

Matzer, John, Jr., ed. *Practical Financial Management: New Techniques for Local Government.* Washington, DC: International City Management Association, 1984.

Municipal Finance Officers Association. *An Operating Budget Handbook for Small Cities and Other Governmental Units.* Chicago: MFOA, 1978.

Building Codes   Systematic compilation of regulations controlling construction standards usually adopted by reference by local civil jurisdictions. Congress has enacted a statutory building code, 42 U.S.C. 5401, covering mobile homes, more properly called manufactured housing, which factors in climatic needs relative to the location of product sale. In addition, there are four model on-site building codes: The American Insurance Association National Building Code, the International Conference of Building Officials (ICBO) Uniform Building Code, the Building Officials Conference of America (BOCA) Basic Building Code, and the Southern Building Code Congress Standard Building Code. ICBO is applied primarily in the western states, whereas BOCA is used in the Northeast and the Midwest. States may create model building codes. Cities with populations greater than one million usually write some of their own provisions to accommodate skyscrapers. Local codes are justified as a proper exercise of the state's police power over health and safety conditions. All building codes cover structural design and quality of material. Special codes cover electrical, mechanical, and plumbing standards. Codes touch on site plans and location decisions. The trend is toward performance codes rather than specification lists, allowing for more rapid diffusion of innovations. Most codes are updated through yearly council resolution. *See also* CERTIFICATE OF OCCUPANCY; FEDERALLY ASSISTED CODE ENFORCEMENT; MANUFACTURED HOME.

Significance   Because building codes are justified under the police power, which is a state-level prerogative, there is great variation in standards. Some states maintain a Bureau of Construction Code to assist localities. In addition to the need for localizing codes to account for energy requirements, there is also need for securing special performance in seismic-sensitive areas. If not regularly updated, codes can become burdensome to the construction industry and can crimp innovation. Codes are primarily designed for middle-class consumers; hence there is widespread noncompliance with codes in houses that have undergone filtering. Slum housing may never meet code standards, yet to demolish such homes is to destroy stock without providing alternative accommodations. Where cities attempt strict code enforcement, there is the opportunity for bribing code officials. Housing that is reconstructed to meet code for gentrifiers often causes rent increases beyond the means of original occupiers, thus creating displacement. Two major topics of code enforcement are recent staple political issues: Under what circumstances should potential for fire hazard force a city inspector to refuse a certificate of occupancy? Whose responsibility is it to oversee building inspection for such environmental problems as radon gas and asbestos fibers?

Suggested Reading
Brown, James Jay. "Building Codes and Construction Statutes in Missouri." *Urban Law Annual,* vol. 13 (1977), pp. 81–104.

Building Officials and Code Administrators International, Inc. (BOCA)   A nonprofit service organization, headquartered in Country Club Hills, Illinois. Since 1950 it has published the *BOCA Basic Building Code,* now published in three-year cycles, for general use in the United States and Canada. It develops performance-type codes that can be adopted by reference by local units. It covers building regulations from "street access" and "accessibility for the handicapped" to "ventilation" and "wall thickness." In addition it also issues codes for building mechanics, plumbing, fire protection, maintenance, and energy conservation. *See also* BUILDING PERMIT; HOUSING, MOBILE; SITE PLAN REVIEW.

Significance   BOCA's interests are both public and professional, and its chief activity is preparing model codes. It also provides technical information on specialty areas and enforcement. In those jurisdictions adopting the code, builders know in advance the standards to which they will be held by inspectors. The organization disseminates updates in between its triennial books with a bimonthly magazine written for specialists. The chief advantage of the organization is its rapid dispersal of innovations in building technology.

Building Permit   An administratively issued approval to erect any structure designed as a shelter or enclosure on a site, based on conformity with provisions of an ordinance. Before any work is done on location, a building permit is issued for a fee to cover all or most of the inspection costs. Permits are issued on the basis of written plans and specifications. The permit is waived if construction cost estimates are low enough. It is usually valid for a limited period, often six months. The site must be identified as belonging to the owner, as a permitted use for that land, and as conforming with floodplain restrictions. *See* *also* CORRUPTION, GOVERNMENT; CERTIFICATE OF OCCUPANCY; SITE PLAN REVIEW.

Significance   The building permit is justified as an exercise of the police power to regulate the community's health, safety, and welfare. Usually a city's own buildings are subject to the same restrictions as those of the private sector. This is the second stage in the public review procedure of a community's development. The first is site plan review; the third is issuance of a certificate of occupancy. To facilitate compliance, most communities adopt by reference the corpus of construction specifications established by the Building Officials and Code Administrators International, Inc. (BOCA) or some other code. Actual implementation of the permit system is controversial. It runs the gamut from inspection by American Institute of Architects (AIA) members and certified building officials to no on-site inspection whatsoever. City officials may increase construction costs by delaying approval; they can threaten to hold up rough inspection for minor infractions, or they can ignore and fail to record major infractions. At this point, bribes sometimes are paid by owners to facilitate construction schedules and close in structures before inclement weather arrives. Today many buildings are still erected without public inspection.

Busing   The transportation of public school students in order to achieve a racial balance in education. Busing became one of several actions approved by the U.S. Supreme Court in an attempt to mitigate *de facto* segregation. In the Court's *Brown v. Board of Education* I decision (347 U.S. 483, 1954), *de jure* segregation of school children was ruled unconstitutional, and school districts were instructed to desegregate "with all deliberate speed" (II 349 U.S. 294, 1955). However, the *Brown* decision did not address the problems of segregated living patterns and neighborhood schools. Therefore, full desegregation was not achieved, despite the legal elimination of state-mandated dual school systems. In 1971, the Court ruled that the Charlotte, North Carolina, school system was still segregated even though the state's legal requirement of segregation had been lifted (*Swann v. Charlotte-Mecklenburg Board of Education*, 402 U.S. 1, 1971). The busing of students ordered by a lower court was thus sustained. *See also* BROWN V. BOARD OF EDUCATION; COLEMAN REPORT; *DE FACTO* SEGREGATION; *DE JURE* SEGREGATION; DESEGREGATION; WHITE FLIGHT.

Significance   Busing met with considerable resistance in many parts of the country. Opponents often referred to it as "forced busing" to indicate their displeasure with such action. Although the *Swann* decision dramatically altered the way public education operated after 1971, the Court diluted busing's effect with its 1974 decision in *Milliken v. Bradley* (418 U.S. 717). In this case, the Supreme Court determined that a lower federal court could not require children to be transported across school district boundaries to achieve racial desegregation unless it had been proven that the boundaries were drawn to achieve segregated schools. This decision overturned an earlier decision by District Judge Stephen Roth involving the city of Detroit and 53 surrounding suburban school districts. Thus, the concept of neighborhood schools was upheld, despite evidence of the existence of *de facto* segregation. However, in later cases, the Court ruled affirmative policy must take place to achieve integration when decisions by officials to segregate intentionally could be identified (*Columbus Board of Education v. Penick*, 443 U.S. 449; *Dayton Board of Education v. Brinkman*, 443 U.S. 526, 1979). In addition the Court overturned a Washington State referendum that attempted to prohibit voluntary school busing (*Washington v. Seattle School District No. 1*, 458 U.S. 457, 1982).

Suggested Reading

Kelley, Jonathan. "The Politics of School Busing." *Public Opinion Quarterly*, vol. 38, no. 1 (1974), pp. 23–29.

Lupo, Alan. *Liberty's Chosen Home: The Politics of Violence in Boston*. Boston: Beacon Press, 1988.

Mills, Nicolaus, ed. *The Great School Bus Controversy*. New York: Teachers College, Columbia University, 1973.

Schwartz, Bernard. *Swann's Way: The School Busing Case and the Supreme Court*. New York: Oxford University Press, 1986.

Taylor, D. Garth. *Public Opinion and Collective Action: The Boston School Desegregation Conflict*. Chicago: University of Chicago Press, 1986.

C

Cable Franchise   The contractual power of a city or consortium of local units to grant to one or more bidders the right to wire a community for television reception. Cable television initially was known as Community Antennae Television (CATV) and was left largely unregulated by the Federal Communications Commission (FCC). Cities were free to ask for bids for an exclusive right to service an area with multiple-channel television and radio. City councils saw this as an additional revenue source. Since the 1984 Cable Communications Policy Act, 47 U.S.C. 521, cities have not been able to enforce agreed-upon price rates, because local contracts were preempted by the national level. *See also* FRANCHISE, GOVERNMENT; PUBLIC UTILITY; WIRED CITY.

Significance   By the late 1980s, more than half the nation's homes were wired for potential cable television reception, although about 40 percent of them had not elected the option. From its inception in the late 1940s in Mahoney City, Pennsylvania, cable television has increased to more than 5,000 municipal franchise holders, giving consumers a choice of broadcast networks or narrowcast channels. Bribes frequently have been associated with issuing cable television franchises. This was to be anticipated from literature on corruption that concluded it is during the capital-intensive phase of a city's history that most corrupt behavior takes place. Along with videocassette players and modem-connected computers, cable television is part of the major information revolution of the 1980s and 1990s. City contracts with franchisers are usually very difficult to break. Most cities are not using their dedicated channels to the fullest. The more public access provided to cities by cable companies, the more subscribers must pay for this service. Some California cities, notably Sacramento under court order, have broken the monopoly cable position on the grounds that cable is more closely akin to an electronic newspaper than a public franchise. With advances in microwave technology, it is possible to bypass wiring an area with coaxial cable by relying on direct relays of programs from satellites.

Suggested Reading
Powe, Lucas. *American Broadcasting and the First Amendment.* Berkeley: University of California Press, 1987.

Camouflaged Case Studies   Academic field studies of actual communities whose identities are disguised by using fictional names. Major examples of camouflaged studies in the United States include Yankee City (Newburyport, Massachusetts), studied by William Lloyd Warner in the 1930s and 1940s; Middletown (Muncie, Indiana), whose study was initiated by Robert S. and Helen M. Lynd in the 1920s and 1930s and continued by Theodore Caplow in the 1970s and 1980s; Elmtown, studied by August B. Hollinghead in the 1940s; Plainville, studied originally by Carl Withers in the 1940s and later by Art Gallaher, Jr., in the 1950s; and Regional City (Atlanta, Georgia), whose study by Floyd Hunter in the 1950s began a rash of community-power studies and was followed up in the 1960s by M. Kent Jennings. *See also* CASE STUDY; CHICAGO SCHOOL.

Significance   Camouflaged studies are a legacy of anthropology, in which the field-worker feels constrained from naming the community. In anthropology, a field-worker promises confidentiality to informants and in part executes this pledge by covering up the true identity of the location. According to the 1971 Statements on Ethics of the American Anthropological Association as amended through 1976, camouflaged studies are designed "to honor the dignity and privacy of those studied. That anonymity should be honored by others who should respect this decision, and the reasons for it by not revealing indiscriminately the true identity." Carl Withers went so far in his study of Plainville as to write under the pseudonym of James West. In many studies, the actual city name is one of the worst-kept academic secrets, and yet the author keeps up the charade in continuing to refuse to confirm its real identity. The canons of ethics of the national organizations in anthropology, sociology, or political science contain no ground rules for determining when a study should be camouflaged.

Suggested Reading
Caplow, Theodore, et al. *Middletown Families: Fifty Years of Change and Continuity.* Minneapolis: University of Minnesota Press, 1982. (Based on the Middletown III Project, 1976–1981.)

Gallaher, Art, Jr. *Plainville Fifteen Years Later.* New York: Columbia University Press, 1961.
Hollinghead, August B. *Elmtown's Youth.* New York: John Wiley, 1949.
Hunter, Floyd. *Community Power Structure: A Study of Decision Makers.* Chapel Hill: University of North Carolina Press, 1953.
Jennings, M. Kent. *Community Influentials: The Elites of Atlanta.* Glencoe, IL: Free Press, 1964.
Lynd, Robert S., and Helen Merrell Lynd. *Middletown: A Study in Contemporary American Culture.* New York: Harcourt, Brace, 1929.
————. *Middletown in Transition: A Study in Cultural Conflicts.* New York: Harcourt, Brace, 1937.
Warner, W. Lloyd, ed. *Yankee City,* abridged ed. New Haven, CT: Yale University Press, 1963.
Warner, W. Lloyd, et al. *Democracy in Jonesville: A Study in Quality and Inequality.* New York: Harper & Row, 1949, reprinted 1964. (Jonesville, Abraham, North Prairie, is Morris, Grundy County, Illinois.)
West, James. *Plainville, U.S.A.* New York: Columbia University Press, 1945. (West is a pseudonym for Carl Withers. The town was Wheatland, Missouri.)

Capital Expenditure   Money spent to purchase or improve a local government's assets, such as land, equipment, or buildings. Capital expenditures involve nonrecurring payments for projects lasting over an extended period of time. Local government budgets can be divided into two large categories: capital and operating budgets. Capital expenditures are often large-ticket items; financing such projects often involves long-term borrowing and can affect local debt restrictions. In addition, many cities give their planning departments responsibility for analyzing and evaluating the capital expenditure requests of various departments. *See also* DEBT LIMIT, LOCAL; REVENUE IMPROVEMENT BOND.

Significance   Capital expenditures have been increasingly financed through nonguaranteed revenue bonds rather than through municipal bonds guaranteed by the full faith and credit of the municipality. Since the late 1970s, increasing restrictions on taxing, borrowing, and spending have altered a city's flexibility in building capital projects. In most cases, revenue bonds are paid back by the revenues generated by the project itself, such as a bridge, tunnel, or hospital. Because capital projects are relatively long-lasting, citizens faced with the prospect of spending large amounts of money for future generations often oppose them. The early construction of infrastructure in the United States—sewers, roads, and bridges—saw considerable citizen resistance in the late 1800s and early 1900s. Less resistance was felt during the Depression, as many unemployed workers were put to work planting trees and building roads, bridges, canals, and dams through the

Civilian Conservation Corps. By the late 1980s, much of the infrastructure built during the 1930s had deteriorated, and a new generation of capital projects was being considered.

Suggested Reading

Aronson, J. Richard, and Eli Schwartz. *Management Policies in Local Government Finance.* Washington, DC: International City Management Association, Municipal Finance Officers Association, 1975.
Boness, A. James. *Capital Budgeting: The Public and Private Sectors.* New York: Praeger, 1972.
Steiss, Alan Walter. *Local Government Finance: Capital Facilities Planning and Debt Administration.* Lexington, MA: Lexington Books, 1978.
Wilkes, F. M. *Capital Budgeting Techniques.* New York: John Wiley, 1977.

Caretaker Government   An administration headed by an executive who will not initiate policy but is pledged to maintain services, preserve capital, and not raise taxes. Caretaker governments at the substate level normally exist because a vacancy was filled by a replacement who does not feel he/she has a mandate from the people to tamper with the *status quo.* No issue is felt to be so pressing that it cannot wait for the next chief administrator, fresh from an election victory. *See also* MAYOR, STRONG; STATE OF THE CITY ADDRESS; VACANCY IN OFFICE.

Significance   Caretaker governments at the municipal and county level usually result when a city or county executive has died, moved, or been removed from office for misfeasance, malfeasance, or nonfeasance. The interim leader generally is convinced that he/she should be noninnovative, or opts to defer to a successor who has explicit public support. However, in the name of providing only those services already on the ordinance books, caretakers have been known to create policy through administrative order by shifting personnel or stopping payment on in-place contracts. A caretaker in name need not be one in fact. Under true *status quo* leadership, any policy initiative shifts to department heads, the city council, or the corporation council. Caretaker administrations generally terminate with the next swearing-in ceremony.

Case Study   In social science research, an in-depth investigation of a single example. Individual cities have been the major single unit of case study analysis in urban research, because they provide accessibility to the researcher. In addition, the experiences of U.S. cities vary so considerably that it is difficult to develop generalizable theories about them. As a consequence, an overwhelming percentage of urban research has relied on the case study approach to understand the urban experience. The use of case studies is considered to be an example of inductive theory construction, seeking patterns or trends that may lead to universal or more generalizable principles. By contrast, the other major research approach is called deductive theory construction, which involves the development of hypotheses from theories and the testing of those hypotheses through empirical verification. Floyd Hunter's investigation of Atlanta, Georgia, and Robert Dahl's study of New Haven, Connecticut, are two classic examples of urban case study research on community power. Many studies attempting to replicate these community-power case studies have produced conflicting results and failed to resolve the dispute that came to the community-power forefront during the early 1950s. M. Kent Jennings reinvestigated Atlanta ten years after Floyd Hunter and concluded that power was much more dispersed and pluralistic than Hunter indicated. Conversely, G. William Domhoff's study of New Haven discovered a power elite, or community-power structure, in that city, in direct conflict with Dahl's findings. Even more complicated studies that attempted to compare power in several cities did not conclusively resolve the dispute begun by Hunter and Dahl. *See also* CAMOUFLAGED CASE STUDIES; CITY CLASSIFICATION; COMPARATIVE URBAN ANALYSIS; PERMANENT COMMUNITY SAMPLE; PLURALISM; REPUTATIONAL ANALYSIS.

Significance   Selecting the best method for understanding society, politics, and policy has been a traditional dilemma for social science researchers. The case study method has been most popular in urban research, largely because of the practical difficulties of comparing large numbers of cities. Such studies do provide some assistance in social science research, however. The findings of a case study may be quite relevant to other cities, other issues, or other phenomena in which one might be interested. Still, one of the lingering problems the case study presents is its lack of universality. The conclusions of a case study of New Haven or Atlanta may not hold true for any other cities. A researcher's findings in an analysis of a single policy issue may not hold true for any other issues, even in the same location or city. This problem of external validity has created many difficulties for urban researchers, who must attempt to translate their findings into more general trends and patterns. More recent studies of urban phenomena have attempted to use survey research over a broad sample of cities, such as Terry Clark's ongoing Permanent Community Sample and the study of urban structure, representation, and reform conducted by Susan Welch and Timothy Bledsoe.

Suggested Reading
Babbie, Earl. *The Practice of Social Research,* 4th ed. Belmont, CA: Wadsworth, 1986.
Dahl, Robert A. *Who Governs? Democracy and Power in an American City.* New Haven and London: Yale University Press, 1961.
Elazar, Daniel J., et al. *Cities of the Prairie Revisited: The Closing of the Metropolitan Frontier.* Lincoln: University of Nebraska Press, 1986.
Freeman, J. Leiper. "A Case Study." In John C. Wahlke and Heinz Eulau, eds., *Legislative Behavior: A Reader in Theory and Research.* New York: Free Press of Glencoe, 1959.
Hunter, Floyd. *Community Power Structure.* Chapel Hill: University of North Carolina Press, 1953.
Jennings, M. Kent. *Community Influentials: The Elites of Atlanta.* New York: Free Press of Glencoe, 1964.
Welch, Susan, and Timothy Bledsoe. *Urban Reform and Its Consequences: A Study in Representation.* Chicago and London: University of Chicago Press, 1988.

Categorical Grant   A part of the federal grants-in-aid system, with specific purposes defined by the grantor, leaving little discretion by the recipient over how the money will be spent or over the procedures used. There are four types of categorical grants: project, formula, formula/project, and open-ended reimbursement. Under project grants, money is distributed through variable grants for specific projects. Nongovernmental organizations—private, nonprofit, or profit-making agencies—could receive money under the project grants formula. Projects funded include those dealing with drug abuse, juvenile delinquency, bilingual education, and urban redevelopment. All four can be used only for a single program activity determined by the national government. *See also* COMMUNITY DEVELOPMENT BLOCK GRANT; FISCAL FEDERALISM; GRANT-IN-AID; URBAN DEVELOPMENT ACTION GRANT.

Significance   Beginning in the early 1800s, categorical grants are the oldest form of grants-in-aid and remain the most common form of federal aid to states and cities. Even with the increasing popularity of block grants, categorical grants continue to comprise about 75 percent of all grants-in-aid. By the mid-1980s, about $100 billion was made available for all grant programs annually. Historically, categorical grants have been used to encourage state and local governments to conform to certain standards of behavior: first, in promoting higher standards of service and administration during the 1920s and 1930s; later, in providing minimum standards and activity in such areas as civil rights and environmental programs. This argument over minimum standards versus local discretion remains a classic controversy of

American federalism. Income maintenance programs constitute the largest category of spending in the categorical grant system.

Suggested Reading

Gordon, George J., and Irene Fraser Rothenberg. "Regional Coordination of Federal Categorical Grants: Change and Continuity under the New Federalism." *Journal of the American Planning Association,* vol. 51, no. 2 (1985), pp. 200–206.

Saltzstein, Alan L. "Federal Categorical Aid to Cities: Who Needs It versus Who Wants It." *Western Political Quarterly,* vol. 30, no. 3 (1977), pp. 377–383.

Cemetery   Land set aside for interment of the dead in the ground, on the surface, or in mausoleums. Density of bodies in cemeteries sometimes reaches nearly 100,000 per acre. Authority of communities to set up, run, and regulate privately owned cemeteries is a traditional power, antedating the U.S. Constitution [*Laurel Hill Cemetery v. City and County of San Francisco,* 216 U.S. 358 (1919)]. They can be controlled at the state or local level under police power provisions for health and safety or under nuisance statutes and ordinances. Some communities prohibit cemeteries from within their jurisdiction entirely, such as San Francisco. The result is that nearby Colma is a virtual necropolis. However, courts have found against ordinances that prohibit cemeteries in cities. Cemeteries range in upkeep from abandoned to those maintained in parklike conditions under so-called perpetual-care agreements. Once established, cemeteries are very difficult to convert to another land use, as even the state has only limited power of condemnation, especially when permission for disinterment must be granted by a direct descendant. Under the National Cemeteries Act, 38 U.S.C. 1000 et seq. (1973), the Office of Memorial Affairs in the Department of Veterans Affairs maintains national cemeteries. *See also* LAND-USE CONTROL; MASTER PLAN; POLICE POWER.

Significance   An estimated 2 million acres in the United States are dedicated in perpetuity to cemeteries, much of the land in prime urban locations. In one community, Brooklyn, Ohio, 7 percent of the land is dedicated to cemeteries. Only for-profit cemeteries pay taxes, and they are a small percentage of the total. Most cemetery acreage is exempt from the tax rolls. Most states control cemeteries through a department of licensing and regulation or a cemetery commission and require the filing of annual accounts. Perpetual-care accounts, along with escrow accounts for vaults and plots, can run into millions of dollars per cemetery. Cemeteries are Locally Unwanted Land Uses (LULUs) and are thought to bring down adjacent land values. Yet, by tradition, most are located in residentially zoned neighborhoods. At the time of their creation, many cemeteries were located outside city boundaries, but with annexation these cemeteries now are surrounded by developed areas. In Boston, a cemetery has been converted into a botanical garden, and in Detroit, one cemetery's air rights are being used as an approach path for airplanes.

Suggested Reading

Jackson, Kenneth, and Camilo Jose Vergara. *Silent Cities: The Evolution of the American Cemetery.* Princeton, NY: Princeton Architectural Press, 1990.
Lehrer, Joseph D. "Cemetery Land Use and the Urban Planner." *Urban Law Annual,* vol. 7 (1974), pp. 181–197.

Census of Governments   An enumeration of all units of U.S. government taken at five-year intervals since 1957 as required by statute. The Census of Governments was taken approximately every ten years from 1850 to 1942. Conducted by the U.S. Department of Commerce, Bureau of the Census, it covers four major topics: government organization, taxable property values and assessment-sales price ratios, public employment, and government finance. The multivolume publication breaks down information over time, by region and population category within states, and by function. *See also* METROPOLITAN STATISTICAL AREA.

Table 1   Local Governments by Type, 1962–1987

TYPE OF GOVERNMENT	1962	1972	1982	1987
County	3,043	3,044	3,041	3,042
Municipality	18,000	18,517	19,076	19,205
Township	17,142	16,991	16,734	16,691
School District	34,678	15,781	14,451	14,741
Special District	18,323	23,885	28,588	29,487

Significance   The most widely used table from this enumeration is the total number of units. See Table 1, Local Governments by Type, 1962–1987. As of 1987, there were 38,938 general-purpose (county, municipal, and township) local governments and 44,228 limited-purpose (school district and special district) governments. Illinois has the most governments, with more than 6,000; Hawaii has the fewest, with fewer than 20. Special districts account for virtually all the increase in the number of governments in recent years; they increased by 10 percent from 1977 to 1987, now constituting more than 30 percent of all local government units. California, with more than 2,500, has twice as many special-purpose units as any other state. Colorado is second, with more than 1,000. Ninety percent of all special-purpose units perform only one function, the two most common of which are control of natural resources and fire protection. Not all units of government are included in some of the tables; a cutoff is used, such as only units of 2,500 population or more. Unlike most census material, the majority of the information in this series is not subject to confidentiality. These volumes are found in any government depository library under the call number C3.145/4.

Suggested Reading
U.S. Department of Commerce, Bureau of the Census, Data Services Division. *Factfinders to the Nation.* A serial, one of which is entitled "Statistics on Governments." C. 3.252.

Census of Housing   A survey of housing stock and units conducted by the U.S. Department of Commerce, Bureau of Census. The Census of Housing provides information on the quality and quantity of housing in the United States as part of the decennial census data-gathering effort. However, a number of other housing surveys are conducted more frequently. For example, market surveys and vacancy surveys are conducted quarterly, and the American Housing Survey is conducted every other year. *See also* CENSUS OF POPULATION; HOUSING STARTS.

Significance   The Census of Housing provides an important data base for government policymakers and private interests involved in housing. Such information reveals the nature and scope of problems associated with affordable housing, and the changes in America's housing stock make this census an important economic indicator. Producers of housing, building contractors, materials suppliers, and household goods manufacturers all use housing data for forecasting. Increases or losses in the number of housing units and vacancies influence locational decisions of retail businesses and help predict demands for energy supplies. Future needs for schools, water and sewerage facilities, highways, and many other services are determined in part by the Census of Housing.

Census of Population   A decennial enumeration of all people living in the nation by the U.S. Department of Commerce, Bureau of the Census, on April 1 of each year ending in zero. The Census of Population was first conducted in 1790 and currently inventories demographic information on more than 100 million housing units. Among the presently employed variables are age, citizenship, place of birth, race, sex, ethnicity, marital status, location by state and substate unit, employment status, occupation, language, and literacy. Some of the items have been counted since before the turn of the century. Historical studies are easily conducted through the publication of the Census Bureau entitled *Historical Statistics of the United States, Colonial Times to 1980*. The Census of Housing, conducted since 1940, is done at the same time as the population enumeration. Many of the other special censuses deal with economics, such as agriculture, construction, foreign trade, manufacturing, retail trade, wholesale trade, services, and transportation. There are also censuses of minorities and types of governments. Three of the major trend lines derived from the Census of Population are that (1) the nation's population is expanding absolutely, (2) there has been a dual shift from rural areas to metropolitan areas and from central cities to suburbs, and (3) the center of U.S. population has shifted from outside of Baltimore, Maryland, to outside of St. Louis, Missouri, between 1790 and 1990. *See also* CENSUS OF GOVERNMENTS; CENSUS OF HOUSING; CONSOLIDATED METROPOLITAN STATISTICAL AREA; COUNTERURBANISM; METROPOLITAN STATISTICAL AREA; POPULATION, DAYTIME AND NIGHTTIME; UNDERCOUNT.

Significance   The Census of Population is mandated by the U.S. Constitution in order properly to apportion the House of Representatives. Among major modern nations, the U.S. Census of Population is the longest-running and most reliable enumeration. The periodic inventory is conducted by an office that has been permanently in place since 1902. The two major instruments used in the 1990 head count were a 10-question short form and a 58-question long form. The decennial count is supplemented by special census counts that have been conducted since 1915 on an interim basis at the request and financial support of local governments. There are also monthly updates in the *Current Population Survey* (CPS). Census counts are used by national and state governments to compute billions of dollars of entitlement and revenue transfer payments. In some states, cities that increase in population are eligible for more liquor licenses. Schools use the data to project enrollments. When the census is coupled with state-level vital statistics on births, deaths, marriages, and divorces, it is possible to compute migration patterns, mobility, family size, and life expectancy. A special issue associated with the 1990 census was reliability and the amount of undercount. This is a major issue only because of the bureau's quality-control operations. The number of aliens, homeless, and Hispanics are all special topics under this heading. Census information is strictly confidential and cannot be revealed for 72 years. Beginning in 1990 the entire nation was broken down into census blocks for better microanalysis. Data are published in the form of tables, charts, graphs, maps, and discursive prose. They are available printed, on computer tape, on microfiche, and on information retrieval through DIALOG. Both time series and current information are available.

Suggested Reading
Anderson, Marge J. *The American Census: A Social History.* New Haven, CT: Yale University Press, 1988.
Eckler, A. Ross. *The Bureau of the Census.* New York: Praeger, 1972.
U.S. Bureau of the Census. *Statistical Abstract of the United States.* Washington, DC: Superintendent of Documents, annual.

Census Tract   A neighborhood-sized geographical unit designated by the Bureau of the Census to record social, demographic, and economic information. The entire United States is divided into census tracts. In urban areas, tracts are relatively small, usually containing between 3,000 and 6,000 people. This unit of analysis is the basis for much research, although a smaller unit of analysis is also available, called the *census block.* A census block normally includes only a few hundred households. *See also* CENSUS OF GOVERNMENTS; DEFINITION, OPERATIONAL; NEIGHBORHOOD.

Significance   A census tract is determined geographically, although some standardization prevails across all census tracts in terms of scale and population size. Tract boundaries usually are not changed over the years, since the Census Bureau seeks to compare long-term population trends. When areas increase dramatically in population, the Bureau normally splits the tract (for example, tract 001 becomes 001A and 001B) instead of renumbering it. Despite the popularity of census tracts for use in social research, other levels of Census Bureau aggregate data also are employed, such as counties, states, regions, and, of course, the nation as a whole.

Suggested Reading
U.S. Bureau of the Census. *Census Tract Manual,* various editions. Washington, DC: Government Printing Office, various dates.

Central Business District (CBD)   The central-city nucleus, in which are located government buildings, many financial services, and the convention and theater area. The CBD is the core of large-scale hotels and generally contains the tallest office buildings. The U.S.

Bureau of the Census defines CBDs as areas of high land value, traffic flow, and concentration of retail businesses, offices, theaters, hotels, and service establishments. Commonly known as downtown, or in Chicago, the Loop, it represents the first of Ernest W. Burgess's five concentric zones. It is the peak of land values and has the best access from the whole metropolitan area for both fixed-wheel transit and expressways. Although it has the highest daytime density, few people actually live in the CBD. It often has its own police precinct, and because of its important tax base it receives preferential treatment in police protection. In large cities it is represented by its own downtown Chamber of Commerce. CBDs have less retail and commercial trade than before the 1960s, as much of this activity has transferred to the suburbs. In smaller cities, the CBD also is the major retail and commercial focus. *See also* MULTINUCLEI MODEL; POPULATION, DAYTIME AND NIGHTTIME; SHOPPING CENTER; URBAN RENEWAL.

Significance   Many central business districts are in a protracted economic decline. The CBDs of some major cities have separate business associations, such as Central Atlanta Progress, to speak out on such matters as revitalization, transportation, improvements, and off-street parking. There is a general dispersion of activity outward to the many suburban centers because of improvements in transportation, advances in communication, and a desire for lowered densities and cheaper parking. The 1980 Census of Population and Housing listed CBDs by place of work, or daytime population. The 1982 Census of Retail Trade identified 456 CBDs in Standard Metropolitan Statistical Areas (SMSAs) or in any city with a population of 50,000 or more that met their economic guidelines. One major topic in the city councils of all central cities is the relative priority the CBD should receive versus the needs of the neighborhoods. In a few cities that have used urban renewal extensively, there may be a revitalized CBD with specialized shops and luxury apartments, as in Denver and San Francisco. Some cities, such as New Haven, took the opportunity to make over their CBDs. Revitalization of the CBD has been a major project in Pittsburgh's Golden Triangle, Atlanta's Peachtree Center, and Philadelphia's Market Square East. The CBD is normally the single largest factor in an area's cultural and entertainment life. Some CBDs overbuilt in the 1980s, resulting in excess office space, especially in Dallas and Houston, which suffered for a period from decreasing energy prices.

Suggested Reading
Friedman, Judith J. "Central Business Districts: What Saves Sales?" *Social Science Quarterly,* vol. 69, no. 2 (1988), pp. 325–340.

Robertson, Kent A. "Downtown Retail Activity in Large American Cities 1954–1977." *Geographical Review,* vol. 73, no. 3 (July 1983), pp. 314–323.
Stone, Clarence N. "Partnership New South Style." In Perry David, ed., *Public-Private Partnerships.* New York: Academy of Political Science, 1986.

Central City   The principal and most populated municipality within an urban area. The U.S. Department of Commerce, Bureau of the Census, calls it the largest city in population in a metropolitan area. It is also known as the anchor city or the mother city and contains the primary central business district. *Central counties* are defined by the census as those in which central cities are located. *See also* BANFIELD THESIS; BLISS THESIS; CENTRAL BUSINESS DISTRICT; CONCENTRIC ZONE MODEL; DIVESTMENT; SUNBELT.

Table 2   Top Ten Central Cities, 1986 Estimates

RANK	CENTRAL CITY	POPULATION	CENTRAL COUNTY	SECTION
1	New York City	7,260,000	Kings (Brooklyn)	Snowbelt
2	Los Angeles	3,360,000	Los Angeles	Sunbelt
3	Chicago	3,010,000	Cook	Snowbelt
4	Houston	1,730,000	Harris	Sunbelt
5	Philadelphia	1,640,000	Montgomery	Snowbelt
6	Detroit	1,090,000	Wayne	Snowbelt
7	San Diego	1,020,000	San Diego	Sunbelt
8	Dallas	1,000,000	Dallas	Sunbelt
9	San Antonio	910,000	Bexar	Sunbelt
10	Phoenix	890,000	Maricopa	Sunbelt

Significance   As of 1986, there were eight central cities with more than 1 million population, an all-time high for the nation. Of the top ten central cities, two were declining in population from 1968 to 1984, Philadelphia and Detroit. Six of the top ten central cities were in the sunbelt. Two of the top ten central cities are in California; three are in Texas. See Table 2, Top Ten Central Cities, 1986 Estimates. Most of the population growth in the older central cities is in the suburbs and exurbia. Most of these cities are surrounded by extant municipalities and cannot physically expand through annexation. Central cities themselves are not homogeneous, and public services are unevenly distributed among various neighborhoods. Chicago alone counts 76 community areas plus 2 enclaves. In many cases, the central city does not count for more than one-third of the total metropolitan population;

only in the sunbelt do central cities account for one-half of the area population. Among snowbelt examples, the central city is losing whites and gaining in minority groups, losing middle-class and gaining lower-class populations. These cities house a large share of the area's black and poor population, the less formally educated, and female-headed households. Many central cities are losing jobs at least as fast as residential population. Central cities, especially in the snowbelt, are bastions for the Democratic party and have been so since before the 1930s Depression.

Suggested Reading

Benton, J. Edwin, and Platon N. Rigos. "Patterns of Metropolitan Service Dominance: Central City and Central County Service Roles Compared." *Urban Affairs Quarterly,* vol. 20, no. 3 (1985), pp. 285–302.

Kennedy, Declan, and Margrit I. Kennedy, eds. *The Inner City.* New York: Halsted Press, 1974.

Marshall, Harvey H., and John M. Stahura. "The Growth and Decline of American Central Cities." *Journal of Urban Affairs,* vol. 4, no. 2 (1982), pp. 55–66.

Centralized Purchasing   A rationalized method of procuring goods and services for a government or organization. Centralized purchasing gives the task to a single office rather than have each city department buy for itself. This reduces waste and duplication. It often substantially reduces the net unit cost of items purchased in larger quantities. Such purchasing requires knowledge of supplies as well as skills in the laws regulating open and competitive bids, discounts, and quality control. *See also* COMPETITIVE BID.

Significance   Centralized purchasing became one element in the series of municipal reforms to come out of the Progressive Era. It was believed that fragmented purchasing practices lent themselves too easily to corruption and kickbacks. As municipal purchasing requirements grew, the task was seen as a professional function, with concomitant skills, training, and ethics. Despite the Progressive Era and more recent reforms, political pressures often are applied to favor certain contractors. Monitoring expenditures is accomplished more easily through a central purchasing agency. Centralized purchasing also can create administrative problems, as central offices are not always kept aware of the purchasing needs of the various offices within the government. Local-government purchasing departments often are given responsibility to control central services such as duplicating and mailing. In some cases, a number of municipalities have entered into joint purchasing agreements in an effort to save costs by buying bulk items such as road salt in large quantities.

Certificate of Need (CON)   A document required of a health facility if it proposes any substantial change of capital outlay that must be approved by a regulatory agency before permission is given for installation. CONs were first used in New York City in the 1930s by the privately controlled Health and Hospital Planning Council in order to limit the expansion of hospitals and other health facilities. *See also* CLOSING, HOSPITAL; MAXIMUM FEASIBLE PARTICIPATION; PUBLIC-PRIVATE PARTNERSHIP.

Significance   A certificate of need (CON) covers nursing homes, outpatient surgical facilities, and any outlay for buildings or major equipment involved in public health-care delivery. The purpose of CONs is to regulate bed capacity and control duplication of health services, the assumption being that containing health-care costs is better left to central planning rather than to market forces. The national government has had some role in determining the number of hospital beds since passage of the Hill-Burton Act, also known as the Hospital Survey and Construction Act of 1946, 42 U.S.C. 291. The idea of private planning spread to Detroit, Cleveland, and Toledo, where it was managed by Blue Cross in the 1960s. The second national government statute was the Comprehensive Health Planning Act of 1966, which fostered community participation in planning health facilities at the local, state, and national levels. In 1974 Congress modified the procedure with the National Health Planning and Resources Development Act, 42 U.S.C. 300. This required states to establish need reviews at the state level to be paid for by the Department of Health, Education, and Welfare (HEW). In 1974 the issue was also subject to federal legislation when Congress added federal funding for systematic CON reviews. This provision was repealed under the Reagan administration by P.L. 99-660, 1986. As of 1989, the number of participating states had fallen from 46 to 38, with other states threatening to terminate their CON procedures. Nevertheless, health-care costs are still among the leading causes for an increase in consumer spending, according to the Consumer Price Index (CPI). Private insurance providers, large companies with fringe packages, and government providers such as Medicare and Medicaid are all interested in plans that promise to reduce one of the nation's major runaway costs. Proponents of CONs contend that (1) marketplace solutions and experiments are too expensive, (2) adjustments in the free market would be too time-consuming, (3) types of review could be limited to fewer categories of facilities, and (4) the threshold amounts for new equipment review from multiple applicants for the same item should be expedited. Supporters also argue that an outside arbitrator is needed to ensure optimum distribution of facilities at the lowest cost to consumers, and that ensuring availability of health provisions in all communities, regardless of class or race, is too important to be left to the unbridled discretion of hospital boards and physicians. On the other hand, opponents of CON procedures contend planning (1) is arbitrary and not based on the latest demographic mobility and morbidity information, (2) dampens the spread of new technology and delays necessary new hospital construction in fast-growing communities, (3) is costly and creates a hospital bureaucracy that simply specializes in compliance, (4) results in too few applicants being turned down, and (5) in the long run is better regulated by open market forces than by artificially imposed limits on entry into the area.

Suggested Reading

Ehrenreich, Barbara, and John Ehrenreich. *The American Health Empire: Power, Profits and Politics.* New York: Random House, 1970. Chap. XIV, "Comprehensive Health Planning."
Shannon, Margaret A. "Certificate of Need: Where It Has Been and Where It Is Going." *Michigan Bar Journal,* vol. 67, no. 7 (1988), pp. 592–596.

Certificate of Occupancy (CO)   A document issued by a building department under authority of a building code that permits use of the property. The certificate of occupancy is the final stage in the public supervision of building construction. It begins with a site plan review and continues with a building permit. The CO stipulates that the premises meet all requirements of the code; if they do not, only a temporary occupancy permit is issued. In most jurisdictions the municipality has a limited number of days in which to grant or deny the CO. Thereafter the owner can appeal either within the city administration or to a local trial court. *See also* BUILDING CODES; CORRUPTION, GOVERNMENT; EXHAUSTION OF ADMINISTRATIVE REMEDIES; SITE PLAN REVIEW.

Significance   The certificate of occupancy is the most important document after clear title to the land. The owner has invested substantial sums in anticipation of moving in, and this document allows it. If the building inspector finds major structural faults, he can "red tag" it, signaling that the building is uninhabitable because it is unsafe. Some homes and businesses may not have a CO, and if a fire or structural collapse occurs, owners will have grave difficulty collecting insurance proceeds. A CO is issued for a specified use. Should the building undergo change of use, the owner must reapply for a CO, sometimes applying for a new site plan review. *Ipso facto* homeless squatters in abandoned buildings do not have a CO, and for that reason, as well as for breaking and entering, they can be evicted. There is always the temptation for owners or builders to pay off city inspectors to receive a CO on improperly constructed buildings.

Chamber of Commerce   A nationwide business organization that focuses on promoting the free market system. The Chamber of Commerce has state and local affiliates across the country, and many localities have a Junior Chamber of Commerce for younger, aspiring business leaders. Local Chambers of Commerce are usually active in promoting urban development and redevelopment and any policy that supports business investments in a state or community. In many communities, the local Chamber of Commerce has been the liaison between government and the private sector in negotiating and promoting private investment. Its primary targets traditionally have been government regulation of business, taxes, and welfare spending. *See also* GROWTH POLITICS.

Significance   The chamber is active in lobbying against excessive governmental spending at all levels. The chamber works closely with various public-private authorities and redevelopment agencies to identify and locate potential business sites and available public funding and to disseminate this information to its members. In many states, the chamber is a leading lobbying group and often has a well-funded Political Action Committee (PAC). Local Chambers of Commerce have been instrumental in incorporating suburban communities, in some cases to escape from central-city taxes and regulation.

Suggested Reading
Dinerman, Beatrice. *Chambers of Commerce in the Modern Metropolis.* Los Angeles: University of California, Los Angeles, Bureau of Government Research, 1958.
Logan, John R., and Harvey L. Molotch. *Urban Fortunes: The Political Economy of Place.* Berkeley: University of California Press, 1987.
Moch, Charles. "City Limits: Municipal Boundary Formation and Class Segregation." In William K. Tabb and Larry Sawers, eds., *Marxism and the Metropolis,* 2nd ed. New York: Oxford University Press, 1984.

Charter   The fundamental law of a city or county provided for by one or more state constitutional and statutory provisions. Charters are instruments given by the state so as to achieve better administration. Charters list the rights and obligations of the incorporated area, limiting the municipality or county's functions, especially with regard to taxing and borrowing. Both the manner and procedure for enacting ordinances are determined by charter. Authority to pass ordinances under charter must be explicit and construed strictly. Ordinances inconsistent with a charter are illegal. Only a formal charter amendment can properly change a charter. It cannot be accomplished by legislative resolution. Charter characteristics differ by state and may delegate various amounts of power depending upon the allowable degree of local discretion. *Home rule* charters are drawn up by the people themselves and confer more policy leeway on cities than state-drafted charters. Drafters of laws are substantially ambiguous regarding what units receive charters; the incorporating body is variously called a municipal corporation, a city, a public agency, or a public corporation. Charters are subject to the higher law of state and national constitutions, national statutes and state statutes of general applicability, and review by state and national courts. *See also* BOUNDED CITIES, TYPES OF; CITY CLASSIFICATION; EXTRATERRITORIAL POWER; HOME RULE; MUNICIPAL CORPORATION.

Significance   All local jurisdictions have a charter, whether formally written or contained in a series of fundamental constitutional and statutory provisions. As of 1987, 29 states allowed county home rule, but only slightly more than 75 charter counties were created. As many as one-fourth of metropolitan residents are estimated to live in unincorporated areas. Reasons for incorporation at a certain time are as diverse as wanting to get a liquor license (Florida), avoiding land-use regulations and building codes (Missouri), preempting a lucrative tax base so as not to share it with a larger population (Minnesota and California), and dodging a central city's high tax structure and bringing conventional urban services to an area that serves as a buffer between two large municipalities (Michigan). Charters cover both civil and criminal law. It is possible for a charter to supply no appeal procedure from local criminal law. Courts have upheld this nonappealable category of offenses. The proportion (A) Constitution is to (B) State as (C) Charter is to (D) City is partially valid in that both constitutions and charters are fundamental law. However, it ultimately breaks down, since constitutions are promulgated from below, whereas charters are promulgated from above in the name of the state. Charter revision or amendment is more frequent in cities than at the state or national level. *Reform charter* is simply another name for charter revision since a reform toward council-mayor equality in one city is called a reform toward a strong-mayor system in another. Petitions for charters can be withheld by the state if the requesting area fails certain tests of minimum population, density, or area.

Suggested Reading
Houghton, David G., and Helenan S. Robin. "City Charter Revisions: How Citizen Surveys Can Help." *National Civic Review*, vol. 74, no. 6 (1985), pp. 270–274.

Chicago School   The approach to urban studies used by the University of Chicago Department of Sociology. It focused on detailed, empirical field research and participant observation, using the South Side of Chicago as a natural laboratory, especially during the 1920s and 1930s. The Chicago School refers to the human ecology approach of the first department of sociology set up in a U.S. university (1892). The approach continued to be influential during the ground-breaking decades between the world wars and to a lesser extent through the 1950s. Among the major theoreticians, researchers, and writers of the school were Robert Park, Ernest W. Burgess, Louis Wirth, Harvey Zorbough, Robert Redfield, St. Clair Drake, William Foote Whyte, and Morris Janowitz. Among the topics studied were spatial distributions of land use (the concentric zone model), distributions of life styles (the gold coast and the slum), neighborhood communication patterns (ethnic and community press), racial groups by residency (Little Italy, Corktown, Black Bottom), and changing relationships over time (housing succession, community fact books, and recycling of churches). *See also* CASE STUDY; COMMUNITY FACT BOOKS; HUMAN ECOLOGY; SECTOR MODEL; SLUM.

Significance   Along with German sociologists from Heidelberg and Berlin, the Chicago School of Urban Sociology set the early tone for methodology and subject selection. In the strict sense of the term, it was not a school; not all members of the department subscribed to the same topical focus, methodology, or model. Contemporary analysis of the ethnic press, community press, and black press owe their origins to Park and Janowitz. With knowledge of the ecological fallacy and cross-cultural urban studies, many substantive findings of the school have been debunked or replaced, and Wirth's pessimistic view that cities *ipso facto* lead to increased social problems is now largely refuted. But the school's emphasis on research into ethnic groups, institutional change, and modes of communication remains. And its emphasis on systematic and objective field investigation is still a linchpin in all urban social science.

Suggested Reading
Harvey, Lee. "The Nature of 'Schools' in the Sociology of Knowledge: The Case of the 'Chicago School.'" *Sociological Review*, vol. 35, no. 2 (1987), pp. 347–369.
Short, James F., Jr., ed. *The Social Fabric of the Metropolis: Contributions of the Chicago School of Urban Sociology.* Chicago: University of Chicago Press, 1971. (Part of the Heritage of Sociology Series edited by Morris Janowitz.)

Smith, Dennis, ed. *The Chicago School: A Liberal Critique of Capitalism.* New York: St. Martin's Press, 1988. (Refers to the conservative orientation of the current era, not the earlier human ecology approach.)

Chinatown   An inner-city enclave in which ethnic Chinese live and work both voluntarily and because of racial segregation. U.S. Chinatowns exist in cities as diverse as Philadelphia, Boston, San Francisco, Chicago, and New York (in both Manhattan and Flushing, Queens). The earliest American Chinatowns on the West Coast were populated by migrant laborers forced into segregated housing. Later migration patterns were curbed by restrictive statutes. Many Chinatowns have their own community mayors and benevolent associations, and some have their own community newspapers. In New York City and Oakland, the communities have developed their own advocacy planning groups to protect their neighborhoods from other development efforts. *See also* BARRIO; COMMUNITY PRESS; ETHNIC GROUP.

Significance   Chinatowns are not analogous to other ethnic communities within the mosaic of large cities such as Corktown (Irish), the Barrio (Spanish), Little Sicily, or Greektown. Hispanics, Irish, Sicilians, and Greeks are racially Caucasian and assimilate easily into white society, whereas Chinese are identifiably different. As a consequence, Chinatowns have persisted longer than other ethnic enclaves. After a hiatus in immigration from the 1880s to the 1960s, Chinese again have begun entering the nation. It is estimated that 20 million overseas Chinese presently live in a worldwide diaspora. Large communities are divided by dialect, secret societies, and occupational clusters. Some of these newcomers move to the ethnic neighborhood for housing, assistance in finding work, and social life. Upper-class and professional Chinese are less likely than others to live in Chinatowns. In communities such as Houston and Detroit, most Chinese live scattered in the larger metropolitan area. As with Canadian cities, many new U.S. Chinatown developments are being financed by money originating in Hong Kong. Some of the older Chinese enclaves are being recaptured by gentrifying Caucasians.

Suggested Reading

Glick, C. E. *Sojourners and Settlers: Chinese Migrants in Hawaii.* Honolulu: University Press of Hawaii, 1980.
Kwong, Peter. *The New Chinatown.* New York: Hill & Wang, 1988.
Lai, David Chueyan. *Chinatowns: Towns within Cities in Canada.* Vancouver: University of British Columbia Press, 1988.
Lee, Calvin. *Chinatown, USA.* New York: Doubleday, 1965.

Nee, Victor G., and Brett DeBary Nee. *Longtime Californ': A Documentary Study of an American Chinatown.* New York: Pantheon Books, 1972, 1973.
Sung, B. L. *The Story of the Chinese in America.* New York: Collier, 1967.

Circuit Breaker   A program intended to protect taxpayers from overburden, usually from property tax. A circuit breaker normally limits property tax to a certain percentage of household income, thus preventing an "overload of taxes" in the same way an electrical circuit breaker prevents an overload in the house current. By 1984, more than 30 states had enacted circuit breaker programs. *See also* TAX, REAL PROPERTY; TAX EXEMPTION.

Significance   According to the Advisory Commission on Intergovernmental Relations (ACIR), there are three kinds of circuit breakers: basic, expanded, and general. Basic relief provides coverage to the elderly who own homes. Expanded coverage also includes elderly citizens who are renters. General relief covers all taxpayers who are considered overburdened by the established criteria. In most states, the circuit breaker is connected to the state income tax system. Other states use a sliding scale method, in which a certain fixed percentage of property tax is returned to taxpayers in each eligible income stratum. Money is returned through rebates on income tax liability, or straight refunds are given to those who exceed the predetermined threshold. The ACIR found that in 1984, approximately $1.4 billion in benefits was provided under the circuit breaker programs of participating states. In 1964, Wisconsin became the first state to adopt a circuit breaker program. Michigan's program returns the largest amount of money—about $540 million in 1981 alone.

Suggested Reading
Advisory Commission on Intergovernmental Relations. *Property Tax Circuit-Breakers: Current Status and Policy Issues,* M-87. Washington, DC: Government Printing Office, 1975.
Gold, Steven D. "Circuit Breakers and Other Relief Measures." *Proceedings of the Academy of Political Science,* vol. 35, no. 1 (1983), pp. 148–157.

Circulation Plan   A major component of a city master plan that proposes traffic patterns within the community and adjacent jurisdictions. Circulation plans deal primarily with vehicular traffic and to a lesser extent with mass and paratransit. Internal circulation plans focus on the effective designation of residential streets, collector streets, and throughways. General rules of the plan include anticipating traffic volume changes, protecting adjacent property values and scenic areas, coordinating flows with regional plans, deflecting traffic from residential streets, and maintaining acceptable aesthetic and noise-control standards. *See also* GRIDLOCK; INTERSTATE HIGHWAY SYSTEM; PRIVATE STREET; ROAD CLASSIFICATION; TAX, MOTOR FUEL.

Significance   City circulation plans have limited impact because existing land uses largely predetermine traffic density and patterns, and major and intermediate thoroughfares are usually in place before the circulation plan is adopted. A large number of transportation agencies must cooperate in a metropolitan area in order to develop an effective overall system. In addition to the local plan developed by a city planning body, recommendations and cooperation are needed from adjacent city, county, and intercounty highway commissions; Councils of Governments (COGs); and the state highway commission.

Suggested Reading

Bagby, D. Gordon. "The Effects of Traffic Flow on Residential Property Values." *Journal of the American Planning Association*, vol. 46, no. 1 (1980), pp. 88–94.
Cervero, Robert. *Suburban Gridlock*. New Brunswick, NJ: Center for Urban Policy Research, 1986.

Citizen Advisory Board   Either a permanent or *ad hoc* committee charged with offering opinions, support, and technical information to governmental bodies. Citizen advisory boards are composed of community influentials who represent a sector of the economy; are representatives of the press, organized labor, religious groups, women's groups, or retirees; or are selected for their special expertise and insight. Active at all levels and branches, they increase meaningful participation for the chosen few and add credibility as well as public support to the governmental unit requesting their input. The National Petroleum Council is the classic federal-level example. At the state level it is usually a governor's commission on revamping school finances or setting priorities in economic development. At the urban level Councils of Governments (COGs) routinely employ them for studying urban renewal projects, environmental pollution problems, or mass-transit financing. Universities and colleges assign curricular and financing tasks to such boards. Cities set them up to analyze whether or how best to institute business incubators or land banks. Citizen advisory boards differ from police review boards in that the latter serve as an outside, appointed disciplinary group with appellate-like responsibility. *See also* AD HOC BODY; GOAL SETTING; POLICE REVIEW BOARD.

Significance   The ultimate impact of a citizen advisory board is sometimes predictable from its membership: some will be potent because of the blue-ribbon people selected, whereas other panels will be but token acknowledgment by public leaders of the need for broad-based community support. Whereas some citizens are selected for their genuine ability, others are co-opted into a position by peer pressure. Many panelists will have extensive resources to contribute because they are supported by a major law firm, bank, newspaper, or public interest group (PIG). Panelists either are selected by public officials or have volunteered to represent major community interests such as the Chamber of Commerce or an urban coalition. Reputational analysis case studies amply demonstrate there is an ongoing communications network among such influentials that is well documented by sociograms. The short-lived urban observatory projects established in ten large and medium-sized cities in the 1960s and 1970s illustrate that citizen advisory boards are not influential enough to keep alive poorly funded programs.

Citizen-Initiated Contacting   A form of political participation in which the private individual asks local government personnel for a service. Citizen-initiated contacts became a major focus of urban political research when it was realized that urban governments are primarily service organizations. Voting may be the *sine qua non* of mass political participation, but it is a reactive and only sporadic action. When the citizen participates in the governmental process by asking for a service, he/she feels intensely about a situation. A related urban political literature on urban service delivery deals with citizen-initiated contacts from the bureaucratic perspective. Although clearly response time is an important consideration for police and fire departments, it does not capture the objective and subjective measurement of the citizen's reaction to the provision of the service. *See also* OMBUDSMAN, CITY; PARTICIPATION; STREET-LEVEL BUREAUCRAT; URBAN SERVICES.

Significance   Citizen-initiated contacts are a major form of participation. They went unstudied until the 1970s, when a burgeoning literature developed to examine how the recipient felt about the interaction. Empirical studies have uncovered unequal delivery but without any general discernible bias against racial minorities, ethnic groups, or specific classes. Individuals who feel well treated by street-level bureaucrats will have a higher sense of efficacy and perhaps a better sense of attachment to the community. People perceive that they are treated differently by the police in criminal as opposed to noncriminal matters. The most frequently encountered elected public official for most citizens is the clerk's office. The most serious complaints against city bureaucracies find their way to the office of the ombudsman or to a city council member.

Suggested Reading
Coulter, Philip B. *Political Voice: Citizen Demand for Urban Public Services.* Institute for Social Science Research Monograph Series 1. Tuscaloosa: University of Alabama Press, 1988. (Review of the contact behavior literature.)
Hero, Rodney. "Citizen Contacting and Bureaucratic Treatment—Response in Urban Government: Some Further Evidence." *Social Science Journal,* vol. 23, no. 2 (1986), pp. 181–187.
Sharp, Elaine B. "Citizen-Initiated Contacting of Government Officials and Socioeconomic Status: Determining the Relationship and Accounting for It." *American Political Science Review,* vol. 76, no. 1 (1982), pp. 109–115.

City   An imprecise term that describes a permanent human settlement large enough to house strangers, support a diverse and complex economic base, and serve as a communication center. Since "city" is not definitively established, various partial definitions are usually offered. Legally, in the United States, a city is a political jurisdiction that has been charted by a state or commonwealth, which represents that unit's highest urban classification in total population or assessed valuation. In the U.S. census, a city is an urban place with a population of 2,500 or more. Socially, a city is a human locus for specialized nonagricultural labor from which government and business emanate. Sociologist Louis Wirth of the Chicago School suggested in 1938 that, socially, "a city may be defined as a relatively large, dense, and permanent settlement of socially heterogeneous individuals." This frequently quoted definition of Wirth's has three major elements: scale, density, and heterogeneity. Economically, a city is a commercial center, the opposite of a village or a rural area. All cities perform a complex of functions; they are of some minimum population magnitude and serve a single economically integrated community. *See also* CENTRAL CITY; CHARTER; CONSOLIDATED METROPOLITAN STATISTICAL AREA; METROPOLITAN STATISTICAL AREA.

Significance   The 1920 U.S. census reported for the first time that a majority of citizens were city dwellers, and the 1980 census reported that city dwellers constituted approximately three-fourths of the U.S. population. According to the Census of Governments, the United States has about 17,000 cities, approximately 7,000 using the International City Management Association (ICMA) guidelines. Those who view the census demarcation of 2,500 as too low a threshold for a city sometimes prefer the 1980 Census Bureau urbanized area definition for a city: a central place and adjacent area with population of 50,000 or more. By that standard the United States consists of about 60 percent city dwellers. See Table 3, U.S. Cities Classified According to Population.

Table 3   U.S. Cities Classified According to Population

POPULATION GROUP	NUMBER	PERCENT	PERCENT OF TOTAL POPULATION
2,500 to 5,000	2,665	34	4.1
5,000 to 10,000	2,181	28	6.8
10,000 to 25,000	1,765	22	12.2
25,000 to 50,000	675	8	10.4
50,000 to 100,000	290	3	8.7
100,000 to 250,000	117	1	7.5
250,000 to 500,000	34	.004	5.4
500,000 to 1,000,000	16	.002	4.8
1,000,000 or more	6	.0007	7.7

Source: Statistical Abstract of the United States, 1988, 108th ed. (Washington, DC: Bureau of the Census, 1988), Tables 23 and 37.

Suggested Reading

Bairoch, Paul. *Cities and Economic Development: From the Dawn of History to the Present.* Chicago: University of Chicago Press, 1988.
Bookchin, Murray. *The Limits of the City.* New York: Harper & Row, 1974. (A Marxist-anarchist perspective.)
Hammond, Mason, et al. *The City in the Ancient World.* Cambridge: Harvard University Press, 1972. Chap. 2.
Mumford, Lewis. *The City in History: Its Origins, Its Transformations, and Its Prospects.* New York: Harcourt, Brace, 1961. (More than 600 pages of sweeping history.)
Pirenne, Henry. *Medieval Cities: Their Origins and the Revival of Trade.* Frank D. Halsey, trans. Princeton: Princeton University Press, 1925, 1952. Chap. 3.
Wirth, Louis. "Urbanism as a Way of Life." *American Journal of Sociology,* vol. 44, no. 1 (1938).

City Beautiful   A city planning movement exemplified by the contribution of Daniel H. Burnham's (1846–1912) plan to the World's Columbian Exposition of 1893, highlighted by aesthetic layouts for the Chicago civic center. The City Beautiful stressed wide boulevards, plazas, and spacious waterfront parks. The movement was preceded by the American park movement of the 1860s and 1870s, which was closely associated with Frederick Law Olmsted, Jr. (1822–1903), and his park systems for New York City (Central Park) and Brookline. The City Beautiful movement was a negative reaction to the early industrial city and a positive reaction to the wide-boulevard layouts by Houssmann in Paris for Napoleon III. Burnham's 1909 plan for Chicago was a prime example of the idea's success. *See also* GARDEN CITY; ZONING, AESTHETIC.

Significance   Critics of City Beautiful argued that planning could not be confined to the civic center and romantic boulevards while residential neighborhoods were being built to ever denser levels at the whim of speculators unfettered by zoning ordinances. Olmsted's most successful critic was Elbert Peets (1886–1968), who derided the park movement for an absence of creativity and uncritical, upper-class copying of British gardens. One of Burnham's most strident critics was Lewis Mumford (1895–1982), who called the partial planning process of City Beautiful advocates baroque, superficial, and cosmetic. The City Beautiful movement died out in response to the excesses of its proponents' demands for land and capital budgets while neglecting neighborhoods and the practical needs of the balance of the city.

Suggested Reading

Fein, Albert. *Frederick Law Olmsted and the American Environmental Tradition.* New York: Doubleday, 1972.

Hines, Thomas S. "The Paradox of 'Progressive' Architecture: Urban Planning and Public Building in Tom Johnson's Cleveland." *American Quarterly,* vol. 25, no. 4 (1973), pp. 426–448. (The group plan mall.)

Mumford, Lewis. *The City in History: Its Origins, Its Transformations, and Its Prospects.* New York: Harcourt, Brace, 1961. (For criticism of Burnham and the City Beautiful movement.)

Spreiregen, Paul D., ed. *On the Art of Designing Cities: Selected Essays of Elbert Peets.* Cambridge: MIT Press, 1968. (For criticism of Olmsted and the American park movement.)

City Classification   A ranking of incorporated substate areas by state constitution or state statute according to rational standards. Three ways of ranking communities for legal purposes are by function, by population, and by amount of discretion possessed by the local level. States create both single-function authorities and general governments. In turn, general governments are classed by population. Certain of these classes then are allowed either to organize into home-rule units or to remain as general governments with reduced discretion. *See also* COMPARATIVE URBAN ANALYSIS; HOME RULE.

Significance   City classification is a means of circumventing state constitutional provisions that require the state legislature to legislate by general law rather than by special act applicable to one or several cities. Among the reasons the state legally classifies cities, counties, townships, and villages are to provide aid formulas for state assistance, to establish the number of liquor licenses available to each unit of government, to designate different standards for annexation, to issue bonds, and to provide consideration for the problems peculiar to local units as diverse as simple hamlets and complex central cities. Cities cannot classify themselves, nor can they unilaterally modify their de-classification. The most commonly used standard for determining population is the decennial U.S. census, although some states allow for off-year and locally sponsored head counts. Except for California and Texas, all states that designate a class for "cities with more than 1 million residents" in fact are creating a category of one or none, an action that nevertheless meets state court standards of reasonableness. California and Texas each have two central cities in this limited class. City classification must be distinguished from comparative, empirical, urban studies that create *city typologies* for analytic purposes.

Suggested Reading
Winters, John M. "Classification of Municipalities." *Northwestern Law Review*, vol. 57, no. 3 (1962), pp. 279–304.

City Council   The legislative body of a city government. The powers of a city council vary considerably, depending on whether the city has home-rule status and on provisions of the city charter. Under commission plans or in mayor-council governments with a weak mayor, the council has administrative responsibilities as well as policy-making powers. Under council-manager governments or in strong-mayor plans, the council has legislative powers but little oversight ability. *See also* CITY MANAGER; COUNCIL-MANAGER GOVERNMENT; HOME RULE; MAYOR-COUNCIL GOVERNMENT; REFORM GOVERNMENT; SEPARATION OF POWERS; UNICAMERAL.

Significance   The city council form of government is structurally different from national policymaking institutions. In most cities, the council is unicameral. Beginning in the early 1900s, many cities adopted "reform government" forms, in which an appointed pro-fessional administrator, a city manager, directed the day-to-day tasks of the city. Many other reforms of the Progressive Era struck at the heart of city council structure, function, and representation. Nonpar-tisan at-large elections attempted to eliminate the influence that the partisan urban political machines held in many city council elections. Considerable research on city council representation was conducted during the 1970s and 1980s, some of which indicates that unreformed local governments are slightly more representative of their populations than are reformed governments. Still others have argued that cities and their policymaking bodies go through similar "life cycles." Councils exhibit certain characteristics and favor certain policies when they are new in contrast to when they mature. Council seats may be based on elections held at large, in districts, or in a combination of these two.

Suggested Reading

Landry, Lawrence D. "City Councils as Policy Makers: Myths that Destroy Effectiveness." *National Civic Review*, vol. 66, no. 11 (1977), pp. 553–557.

Lineberry, Robert L., ed. "Symposium: Does Reformed Government Make a Difference?" *Social Science Quarterly*, vol. 59, no. 1 (1978), pp. 117–177.

Lyons, W. E., and Malcolm E. Jewell. "Minority Representation and the Drawing of City Council Districts." *Urban Affairs Quarterly*, vol. 23, no. 3 (1988), pp. 432–447.

Waste, Robert J. *The Ecology of City Policymaking*. New York: Oxford University Press, 1989.

Welch, Susan, and Timothy Bledsoe. *Urban Reform and Its Consequences: A Study in Representation*. Chicago: University of Chicago Press, 1988.

City Manager   The primary administrative official of a municipal government. A city manager usually is a professionally trained, appointed administrative director, serving at the pleasure of the city council. The council-manager form of government became a popular reform beginning in the early 1900s, in response to the perceived corruption in many cities associated with urban political machines. Under the council-manager form of government, all policy is decided by the city council, but the day-to-day policy implementation is directed by the manager and the administrative staff. Most city managers belong to the International City Management Association (ICMA) and subscribe to its professional code of ethics and practices. *See also* COUNCIL-MANAGER GOVERNMENT; REFORM GOVERNMENT; URBAN POLITICAL MACHINE.

Significance   City managers and the council-manager form of government were strongly advocated by the "good government" groups of the Progressive Era. Dayton, Ohio, became the first large city (in 1914) to adopt the council-manager plan. Other reforms from this era include nonpartisan at-large elections and direct primary elections. Although the great excesses of urban political machines were checked to a large degree, the overall result of these reforms has been questioned. Some critics of these reforms claim that the changes did little more than shift the balance of urban power from the working class to the middle and upper classes. Others argue that city managers, while somewhat insulated from the most obvious aspects of city partisan politics, are nevertheless entangled in general city-level politics as much as elected officials. Considerable turnover exists for city managers, who average about five years before leaving or being dismissed. Critics of this system argue that city managers often become scapegoats for problems that elected city council members are unwilling or unable to face.

Suggested Reading

Newell, Charldean, and David N. Ammons. "Role Emphases of City Managers and Other Municipal Executives." *Public Administration Review,* vol. 47, no. 3 (1987), pp. 263–276.
Stillman, Richard J., III. *The Rise of the City Manager: A Public Professional in Local Government.* Albuquerque: University of New Mexico Press, 1974.
Vance, Mary. *City Managers: A Bibliography.* Monticello, IL: Vance Bibliographies, February 1987.
Wirth, Clifford J., and Michael L. Vasu. "Ideology and Decision Making for American City Managers." *Urban Affairs Quarterly,* vol. 22, no. 3 (1987), pp. 454–474.

City Political Profile   An in-depth study of one metropolitan area's history, geography, government, and politics. City political profiles are a variant on state government and politics profiles first made popular by V. O. Key in 1949 with a political study of southern states. The best in-depth city political profiles catalog a metropolis' historical background, physical setting, and intergovernmental relations, then focus on the area's legal structures and its major, recent public-policy battles. The profile covers the city's major decision makers—the elected, the appointed, and the self-anointed—as well as types and levels of public service delivery. City profiles do not forsake systematic analysis for richness of detail and idiosyncratic events. *See also* CASE STUDY; COMPARATIVE URBAN ANALYSIS.

Significance   City political profiles are an excellent entrance into a new city and provide clues to what should be studied in comparative and cross-cultural contexts. Among major examples for U.S. cities are reports on New Haven in 1961, Chicago in 1965, New York in 1965, San Antonio in 1983, and San Francisco in 1985. One multicity set of profiles from 1965 covers Atlanta, Boston, Detroit, El Paso, Los Angeles, Miami, Philadelphia, St. Louis, and Seattle. Among major examples of American states are reports on New Mexico in 1967, Kentucky in 1968, North Carolina in 1968, and Tennessee in 1975. Multistate and sectional profiles include Southern states in 1949, Border states in 1957, New England states in 1959, Midwest states in 1966, and Western states in 1969. One major systematic set of profiles of all states in the 1980s and 1990s is being published by the University of Nebraska Press. A major limit to profiles concerns whether or not the city or state is representative of the universe under study. Other limits are whether the categories selected for study correspond and whether the period covered is approximately the same as for others. This genre was most popular from the 1950s to the 1970s. Few full-fledged profiles were written in the 1980s. If authors insist on classifying a city as *sui generis,* the resulting study is of little value in systematic analysis. This was the case with two volumes written on London.

Suggested Reading

New Haven: Dahl, Robert A. *Who Governs?* New Haven: Yale University Press, 1961.

New York: Sayre, Wallace, and Herbert Kaufman. *Governing New York City.* New York: Russell Sage, 1965.

San Antonio: Johnson, David R., John A. Booth, and Richard J. Harris, eds. *The Politics of San Antonio: Community, Progress & Power.* Lincoln: University of Nebraska Press, 1983.

San Francisco: Scott, Mellier G. *The San Francisco Bay Area: A Metropolis in Perspective.* Berkeley: University of California Press, 1985.

Border states: Fenton, John R. *Politics in the Border States.* New Orleans: Hauser Press, 1957.

New England states: Lockard, Duane. *New England State Politics.* Princeton: Princeton University Press, 1959.

Midwest states: Fenton, John H. *Midwest Politics.* New York: Holt, Rinehart, 1966.

Western states: Jonas, Frank H., ed. *Politics in the American West.* Salt Lake City: Unviversity of Utah Press, 1969.

London as unique: Rasmussen, Steen Eiler. *London: The Unique City, I.* Cambridge: MIT Press, 1934. Two-part edition, 1974.

Foley, Donald L. *Governing the London Region: Reorganization and Planning in the 1960s.* Berkeley: University of California Press, 1972.

Civic Association   A voluntary organization active at the local level. Civic associations may be affiliated with national organizations that are concerned with public issues outside formal political party channels. Also known as civic voluntary organizations, civic associations are cataloged into various types such as service clubs like Rotary and Kiwanis, which usually have national affiliations. Business civic associations usually are not nationally affiliated. They include merchant improvement and taxpayers' associations. Good-government groups, also known as "goo-goos," include the League of Women Voters and Common Cause, both of which are nationally organized. National ethnic civic associations include the Arabic and Jewish antidefamation leagues. There are also local ethnic civic associations such as the Polish Century Club. Single-topic civic associations such as the Parent-Teacher Association (PTA) are loosely affiliated at the national and state level. *Ad hoc* civic associations organize around specific issues or personalities, often in reaction to another group that is actively altering the local political agenda, such as a neighborhood association opposing a crosstown expressway. *See also* AGENDA SETTING; LEAGUE OF WOMEN VOTERS; NATIONAL ASSOCIATION FOR THE ADVANCEMENT OF COLORED PEOPLE; NATIONAL URBAN LEAGUE; URBAN COALITION.

Significance   Civic associations often serve as training grounds for locally elected political offices. They generally are considered ineffective political actors because they lack many political resources and often refuse to join coalitions to press their views. Civic associations eschew controversy in order to keep their diversified memberships content. Civic associations have been studied in depth for particular cities and have been listed among a host of possible explanatory variables in the Permanent Community Sample studies. However, they have been generally left out of most community-power and urban sociology studies. Most of the major research on their role in urban politics was in the 1950s and 1960s.

Suggested Reading

Ackerman, Barbara. *You the Mayor? The Education of a City Politician*. Dover, MA: Auburn House, 1989. Chap. 7, "The Civic Association."

Rogler, Lloyd H. *Migrant in the City: The Life of a Puerto Rican Action Group*. New York: Basic Books, 1972.

Sayre, Wallace S., and Herbert Kaufman. *Governing New York City: Politics in the Metropolis*. New York: W. W. Norton, 1960, 1965. Chap. 13.

Zisk, Betty, Heinz Eulau, and Kenneth Prewitt. "City Councilmen and the Group Struggle." *Journal of Politics*, vol. 27, no. 4 (1965), pp. 633 ff. (San Francisco Bay Area communities.)

Clearinghouse   A location for the central exchange of information, often created as a cooperative in which all who contribute are allowed access without extra cost. As applied to government and politics, a clearinghouse is a consortium of institutions to collect, process, store, and retrieve information for a community of users; it is supported by member taxes, by a grant or mandate from a foundation, or by government. The first clearinghouse was established in London in the 1770s by bankers to facilitate processing claims on checks through a mutual institution. By the 1880s London had developed a central exchange for single-purpose charities. Two well-known clearinghouses sponsored by the national government are the Justice Department's Federal Bureau of Investigation Uniform Crime Reports and the Department of Education's Educational Resources Information Center (ERIC). The chief example of an urban clearinghouse was that mandated by the A-95 Review process of the Office of Management and the Budget (OMB); it required that Councils of Governments (COGs) in metropolitan areas receive, process, and store grant applications for all national government departments and agencies to ensure that Washington agencies would work with one spokesperson per metro area. Within the executive branch at the national and state levels are Offices of Management and Budget (OMBs) or Bureaus of Budget that serve as the president's and governors' clearinghouse on legislative bills. Regional Clearinghouse Review Committees (RC2s) are intergovernmental bodies empowered to provide advisory comments on such projects, plans, and programs as transportation capital-improvement programs (TIPs), areawide water-quality planning projects for wastewater treatment facilities, and some Environmental Impact Statements (EISs). Initially begun under A-95 Review procedures, the RC2 continues under its successor form, President Ronald Reagan's Executive Order 12372. Not-for-profit national clearinghouses on governmental matters include the International City Managers Association (ICMA) and National Association of Counties data bases on local-level personnel, finance, and service programs. The *ICMA Municipal Year Book* and *NACo-ICMA County Year Book* are their most important publications. The National Association of Clerks and Treasurers also serves as a clearinghouse for innovations and salary schedules. State-level clearinghouses include municipal leagues and township associations, especially in the form of libraries or archives. They are often the only organizations collecting charters and local ordinance codes. Some states maintain Bureau of Government libraries attached to public administration programs or political science departments to maintain archives on state elections, governmental structures, and budgets. Two academically sponsored clearinghouses for storage and retrieval of polling and social science survey research findings are The University of Michigan–based Inter-University Consortium for Political and Social Research and the Williams College Roper Center for polling results. A national clearinghouse for locating and reprinting periodical literature used in interlibrary loans is the Center for Research Libraries. *See also* A-95 REVIEW; CLERK; COUNCIL OF GOVERNMENTS; EDUCATIONAL RESOURCES INFORMATION CENTER.

Significance   Clearinghouses designed to collect, process, and retrieve governmental and political information are a twentieth-century
innovation. Among the advantages of clearinghouses are speed in
locating material, reliability in storing information (especially if it is
centrally processed), and convenience in obtaining material from one
location. Clearinghouses aid in dispersing innovations among members and, in the case of salary schedules, help standardize remuneration. Government clearinghouses *ipso facto* contain information in the
public domain, whereas university research clearinghouses work on
the assumption that information files are open to inspection and
verification. Allied to clearinghouses are *directories,* which also centrally collect information but usually publish it for sale outside the
cooperative format associated with a clearinghouse. One of the oldest
continuous clearinghouses of publicly available information of this
form in the United States monitors mass-circulation magazines and
newspapers. The *Ayer Directory of Publications* had been published since
1868 and is presently available as the *Gale Directory of Publications,*
120th ed., 1988.

Clerk   A substate elected or appointed official serving from county
to village level and responsible for a variety of functions revolving
around recording and recordkeeping. Clerks in the United States and
Canada trace back their lineage directly to the thirteenth century and
indirectly to biblical times. Among their functions are taking minutes
of meetings of governing bodies and acting as keepers of official
records and documents. Clerks promulgate rules and ordinances;
they receive summonses, register voters, and verify signatures on petitions. Normally a clerk is the chief election official and issuer of
licenses, including liquor permits in many instances. Clerks are often
partially responsible for preparing meeting agendas and budgets.
Clerks often serve as pension-fund managers and are the chief contact
persons for most residents who come to the municipal office. In some
states, clerks also provide vital statistics on births, marriages, and
deaths. *See also* PROMULGATE; TREASURER.

Significance   Clerks must be versatile in handling their many-
faceted functions in order to keep a community running smoothly.
In recognition of the need for adapting modern office-manage-
ment techniques to this venerable position, most states provide seminars and orientation sessions for clerks. They have been organized
nationally since 1947 and internationally since 1960. For those
who qualify, the International Institute of Municipal Clerks (IIMC),

headquartered in Pasadena, California, has issued certification credentials since 1965. The modern clerk presides over a computerized office, serving as official recorder of civic information and as formal remembrancer—a former title—of events and ordinances. Most communities require that a deputy clerk be cross-trained and available in the event the clerk cannot perform assigned duties, because the municipality cannot run without the office. Some estimate that up to three-fourths of the clerk's time is spent on intergovernmental relations, especially with the county or parish and the state level.

Closing, Hospital   A form of disinvestment in which a health-care facility goes out of business or moves out of a central city to a suburb or a more prosperous location. Hospital closings are part of the long-term process that has been depopulating central cities since the 1950s. It is closely related to housing abandonment and housing filtering as well as plant closings. Because most central cities are disproportionately populated by indigents and blacks, a hospital closing raises questions of class and race discrimination. Not-for-profit private hospitals argue that they must move to where "the people" are located; central-city advocacy groups counter that "the people" hospitals are talking about are those with proof of medical coverage. *See also* CERTIFICATE OF NEED; CLOSING, PLANT; DISINVESTMENT, URBAN; FISCAL CRISIS.

Significance   Hospital closings are an index of lowered density levels in the central city; there is a general relationship between hospital beds (the measure of hospital capacity) and the aggregate population of the service area. An exception to this rule is a specialty hospital with a very large service area. It is more important to know bed reduction levels than hospital reduction levels. The first comprehensive study of hospital closings nationally was conducted in 1987 by the Inspector General of the U.S. Department of Health and Human Services. These trends are monitored for the not-for-profit institutions by the American Hospital Association (AHA) and for the profit-sector hospitals by the Federation of American Hospitals (FAH). Detroit provides two illustrations that a private hospital closing is often really a hospital move: Detroit Providence Hospital became Southfield Providence in 1965, and Detroit Crittenton (closed 1974) became Crittenton Hospital of suburban Rochester in 1967. Some of the law on challenging hospital closings stems from the City of New York's decision to shut the publicly owned Sydenham and from the follow-up federal court of appeals case of *Bryan v. Koch, Mayor of the City of New York*, 627 F 2d 612 (1980). Although the federal district court upheld New York City's desire to shut the facility, precedents were set allowing patrons to challenge the move as a possible violation of Title VI of the 1964 Civil Rights Act, 42 U.S.C. 2000. The ground for the challenge is racial discrimination. An acute health-care facility is legally accountable under national guidelines by virtue of receiving some of its funds under the 1946 Hill-Burton Hospital Survey and Construction Act, 42 U.S.C. 291. The administration of a publicly owned hospital and the city in which it is located may have to carry the legal burden of proof that a closing is justified. The practical burden of inner-city patrons is to find comparable alternative facilities that are accessible and, in some cases, accept the uninsured. That is often impossible. The result is restricted access to adequate health care and a two-tier delivery system.

Suggested Reading
Cimkowski, Carol A. "Municipal Hospital Closings under Title VI: A Requirement of Reasonable Justifications." *Fordham Urban Law Journal*, vol. 9, no. 4 (1981), pp. 943–977.

Closing, Plant   A form of disinvestment in which a manufacturing or processing operation terminates operation, transfers to another location, is shut down for a protracted period, or is shut down after it has been consolidated with other operations. Plant closings are one sign that the U.S. economy is undergoing decentralization. Former urban rustbelt plants often transfer to rural locations in the sunbelt or outside the nation. Causes for plant closings are multifaceted and complex. They include union animus, the failure of unions to accede to corporate demands, corporate bankruptcy, technological advances making older facilities obsolete, failure of processors to penetrate nearby markets, failure of management to comply with mandated clean water and fresh air guidelines, and management's desire to consolidate operations because of plant underutilization. The closings cause severe hardships on employees in terms of lost severance and vacation pay, loss of retirement benefits, and emotional trauma from sudden unemployment. Closings also cause hardships on communities, especially if a plant represents a large part of the city's tax base. Negative externalities of plant closings include abandoned or mothballed buildings, increased unemployment claims, increased demand for social services, delinquent taxes, and, in extreme cases, abandoned homes. In turn, plant closings force suppliers to curtail local investment, producing a ripple effect through the local economy. As consumers leave, they affect retail trade patterns and levels of expenditure, making further inroads on local property tax collection. Particularly large-scale closings took place in the rustbelt when basic steel making was cut back. Youngstown, Ohio, and Pittsburgh became two symbols of permanent deindustrialization in the 1970s. *See also* CLOSING, HOSPITAL; DISINVESTMENT, URBAN; EXTERNALITY; POSTINDUSTRIAL CITY.

Significance   There are five interrelated governmental reactions to prospective and actual plant closings in the United States. First, the state Employment and Securities Commission distributes short-term unemployment compensation. Depending on context, there may be supplemental extended federal benefits. Second, if the plant closing was triggered by foreign trade competition, the Department of Labor can step in with trade adjustment assistance. Third, the state assists in placing workers in new jobs through employment services. Fourth, the Department of Commerce may contribute funds through its Economic Development Administration for Community and Business Development. Fifth, since 1988 Congress has required major firms with 100 or more employees to give workers and communities a 60-day notification of permanent closings or layoffs of longer than six months. There are substantial penalties for noncompliance by the firms. Because the United States has no national industrial policy, closings are treated as discrete events. Localities that extended subsidies to plants may have the right to a return on some of their equity if the enabling contracts so provide. Duluth, Minnesota, even sued one of its former corporate citizens when the plant exported tax-subsidized equipment to South Carolina. The U.S. Supreme Court has allowed Maine to mandate severance payments to employees of plant closings in *Fort Halifax Packing Co. v. Coyne*, 482 U.S. 1 (1987). Advocates of increased corporate responsibility argue that plants are public-chartered bodies that must share the public consequences of their private-sector capital decisions. Cities prepare budgets based on projections. Sudden plant closings toss public planning into turmoil. Cities are placed on the defensive by footloose corporations, because they may have financed infrastructure with 30-year bonds or 20-year tax abatements. Those who advocate the unfettered right to close plants argue that the free market allows firms to adjust to market conditions. This makes the whole system efficient. The central questions in the ideological debate are to whom and in what order a plant has obligations: to the shareholders, its workers, its suppliers, its customers, or the community in which it operates? If society has an interest in efficient use of capital formation by otherwise unencumbered firms, is there only a general social interest in the outcome, or is it geographic-specific?

Suggested Reading

Bluestone, Barry, and Bennett Harrison. *The Deindustrialization of America: Plant Closings, Community Abandonment, and the Dismantling of Basic Industry.* New York: Basic Books, 1982.

Buss, Terry F., and F. Stevens Debdurn. *Shutdown at Youngstown: Public Policy for Mass Unemployment.* Albany: State University of New York Press, 1983.
Duensing, Edward E., Jr. *Plant Closing Legislation in the United States: A Bibliography.* Monticello, IL: Vance Bibliographies, 1985.
Gordus, Jeanne Prial, Paul Jarley, and Louis A. Ferman. *Plant Closings and Economic Dislocation.* Kalamazoo, MI: W. E. Upjohn Institute, 1981.
Hamer, Andrew Marshall. *Industrial Exodus from the Central City: Public Policy and the Comparative Costs of Location.* Lexington, MA: D. C. Heath, 1973.
McKenzie, Richard B., ed. *Plant Closing: Public or Private Choices?* Washington, DC: Cato Institute, 1982.
Note. "Duty to Bargain about Termination of Operations." *Harvard Law Review,* vol. 92 (February 1979), pp. 768–780.
Perrucci, Carolyn C., et al. *Plant Closings: International Context and Social Costs.* New York: Aldine De Gruyter, 1988.
Staudohar, Paul D., and Holly E. Brown, eds. *Deindustrialization and Plant Closure.* Lexington, MA: D. C. Heath, 1986.
Way, Harold, and Carla Weiss, comps. *Plant Closings: A Selected Bibliography of Materials Published through 1985.* Ithaca, NY: ILR Press, 1988.

Closing, School   Part of the disinvestment process of central cities and mature suburbs in which public educational institutions are declared surplus. School closings are an inevitable part of the out-migration process. School closings are caused by lowered enrollment. In some rustbelt central cities, parochial school closings have outnumbered public school closings. School boards calculate closures based on current enrollments and microarea forecasts. Some third- and fourth-tier suburban school boards are building new schools concurrent with inner-city school closings. *See also* ABANDONMENT; CLOSING, HOSPITAL; CLOSING, PLANT; DISINVESTMENT, URBAN; FORECAST.

Significance   A school closing may be temporary, in which case the board of education retains title and simply mothballs the building or rents it out on short-term lease. If the closing is permanent, the board usually sells the building outright, though it may raze the building if it is in bad repair. Occasionally school boards will recommend consolidating districts if there is a drastic enrollment decline that appears permanent. The remaining school-age children must be bused to other locations. This becomes a major political issue as schools cease serving a single neighborhood and new boundaries must be set. Adaptive uses of closed schools include retirement homes, public and community centers, convalescent apartments, general office buildings, and mini-malls. These retrofitting projects conventionally are subject to zoning review as new site plans. School-appointed citizen advisory panels usually aid in the decision to close or mothball buildings.

Suggested Reading

Berger, Michael A., ed. "Managing Enrollment Decline: Current Knowledge and Future Application." Theme issue of *Peabody Journal of Education*, vol. 60, no. 2 (1983), pp. 1–119.
Colton, David, and Alan Frelich. "Enrollment Decline and School Closings in a Large City." *Education and Urban Society*, vol. 11, no. 3 (1979), pp. 396–417. (Case study of St. Louis.)
Larson, Martin A. *When Parochial Schools Close: A Study in Educational Financing*. Washington, DC: Robert B. Luca, Inc., 1972.

Code Enforcement   The power of a local government to inspect, evaluate, and enforce standards of publicly and privately owned buildings. Code enforcement has been used primarily to maintain health and safety standards of local housing stock. Building codes have been established to cover space requirements, electricity, plumbing, heating, and garbage disposal. *See also* BUILDING CODES; INSPECTION, BUILDING AND FOOD; ZONING.

Significance   Together with enforcement of zoning ordinances, enforcement of building codes is one of the most important powers of local government. The first building codes were established in New York City in the 1860s after a cholera epidemic devastated many residents of slum neighborhoods. Minimum standards or codes cover the entire range of a structure from building design to utility service, electricity, and sewerage connections. Actual enforcement of building codes remains a particular problem for most local governments. Inspection is often conducted only in response to specific complaints rather than through systematic scheduling. For buildings with absentee landlords, code enforcement sometimes leads to abandoned buildings; owners can make a profit only by reducing maintenance and repairs.

Suggested Reading

Symposium. "Code Enforcement: Issues and Answers for the 80s." *University of Detroit Journal of Urban Law*, vol. 60, no. 3 (1983).

Codes of Ethics   Self-policing guidelines of accountable behavior subscribed to by an organized occupational group. Also known as canons of professional conduct, codes of ethics are enumerations of values that members in good standing within an organization should use to guide themselves when predictable conflicts arise in the performance of their duties.

Significance   Actual codes have been formally adopted by such diverse groups as air-pollution-control workers, appraisers, arbitrators, assessors, and auditors through real estate brokers and urban and regional planners. Government employees at the national level, both civilian and military, work under codes written for them in statutes and administrative rules. The International City Management Association (ICMA) has had a code of ethics since 1924 and has revised it on five occasions. On the other hand, the American Society of Public Administration (ASPA) adopted a statement of principles only in 1981 and a code of ethics in 1984. The American Planning Association did not adopt its Statement of Ethical Principles until 1987. Most codes are not set up to be administered in any detail, although a few, such as those for physicians and lawyers, have elaborate boards of review to monitor possible unethical conduct. The extent to which codes influence the behavior of members varies with the profession, but without codes it is difficult to effect legal procedures for disaffiliating with a member who has been convicted of a felony while performing in a professional capacity. The most successful codes provide for an investigatory and enforcement mechanism to hold members accountable to group norms. A code of ethics is one of the preconditions for an occupation to call itself a profession.

Suggested Reading
American Planning Association. "Statement of Ethical Principles." *Planning*, vol. 53, no. 7 (1987), pp. 35–38.
Chandler, Ralph Clark. *Civic Virtue in the American Republic: Essays on Moral Philosophy and Public Administration.* Kalamazoo, MI: New Issues Press, 1987. (Chap. 12 on ASPA.)
————. "The Ethical Precepts of American Public Administration." In James L. Perry, ed., *Handbook of Public Administration.* San Francisco: Jossey-Bass, 1989.
Clapp, Jane. *Professional Ethics and Insignia.* Metuchen, NJ: Scarecrow Press, 1974. (Bibliography.)
Gonzalez, Lawrence A., and Philip C. Claypool. "Voting Conflicts of Interest under Florida's Code of Ethics for Public Officers and Employees." *Stetson Law Review*, vol. 15, no. 3 (1986), pp. 675–713.
Rohr, John A. *Ethics for Bureaucrats*, 2nd ed. New York: Marcel Dekker, 1989.

Coleman Report   A major study of U.S. education that argued black students attending primarily black schools had lower achievement scores and less ambition than black students (from similar backgrounds) who attended primarily white schools. This study, entitled *Equality of Educational Opportunity* and published in 1966, was directed by a Johns Hopkins University sociologist, James S. Coleman. The study led to the advocacy of busing as a tool to increase educational opportunities for black children. If *Brown v. Board of Education* tackled the legally sanctioned segregation of public schools, the Coleman Report and busing essentially addressed the problem of *de facto* segregation, which existed primarily in neighborhoods in the North. *See also* BROWN V. BOARD OF EDUCATION; BUSING; *DE FACTO* SEGREGATION; *DE JURE* SEGREGATION; WHITE FLIGHT.

Significance   Until this report was released, many people felt the problem of racial segregation rested primarily with the *de jure* segregation of the South. The Coleman Report found that segregated housing patterns and neighborhood schools produced equally adverse effects on educational opportunities for blacks. The Coleman Report faced serious opposition almost from the beginning. Many people did not want to hear that major differences in educational opportunities existed for minorities. Busing became one of the most hotly contested political issues of the late 1960s and early 1970s. Because of busing's unpopularity among many voters during its first years of implementation, many federal, state, and local candidates for elective office ran on an antibusing platform, whether or not they would be able to influence such plans. A series of Supreme Court cases soon addressed the issue of busing, most notably *Swann v. Charlotte–Mecklenburg Board of Education*, 402 U.S. 1 (1971), which upheld the use of busing plans and unitary school districts to remedy state-sanctioned segregation, and *Milliken v. Bradley*, 418 U.S. 717 (1974), which held that the Fourteenth Amendment did not require busing across school districts to achieve integration. One of the unintended consequences of busing in many cities has been "white flight," in which many white families moved to suburban areas or began sending their children to private schools. However, by 1979, a "second Coleman Report" was issued. In this second report, Coleman contended that one's home environment was more important than schooling as an influence on academic achievement. Further, he argued that the experience of busing as a vehicle for school desegregation had not worked in the ways his original research had indicated. Improvements in academic achievement among black students had not occurred in those cases studied during the late 1970s.

Suggested Reading

Coleman, James S. "Destructive Beliefs and Potential Policies in School Desegregation." In John W. Smith, ed., *Detroit Metropolitan City-Suburban Relations*. Dearborn, MI: Occasional Papers of the Henry Ford Community College, June 1979.
———. *Equality of Educational Opportunity*. Washington, DC: Government Printing Office, 1966.

Mosteller, Frederick, and Daniel P. Moynihan, eds. *On Equality of Educational Opportunity: Papers Deriving from the Harvard University Faculty Seminar on the Coleman Report.* New York: Random House, 1972.

Collective Bargaining   Negotiations over wages and working conditions between city or school management representatives and union representatives authorized to bargain for municipal or school district employees. About half of the states allow collective bargaining with teacher unions, but by 1975 most states allowed some form of collective bargaining for public employees. Until the 1960s, the creation of public employee unions and collective bargaining with governments were seen as violations of a government's sovereignty. The American Federation of State, County, and Municipal Employees (AFSCME) is the largest public employee union in the United States, with approximately 1 million members. *See also* AMERICAN FEDERATION OF STATE, COUNTY, AND MUNICIPAL EMPLOYEES; LOCAL MERIT SYSTEM; PUBLIC EMPLOYEE STRIKE.

Significance   Collective bargaining in the public sector has received resistance and criticism from many fronts. Much controversy over what issues may be negotiated and the legal right to strike has kept the debate alive in many states and cities. Even in Chicago, which has specific antistrike legislation, public school, fire department, and public transit employees all went on strike during 1980. Some state and local governments enter into mediation or even binding arbitration with public employee unions, usually with those that provide "essential services." Binding arbitration allows a settlement between labor and management to be imposed by an independent arbitrator to avoid the possibility of a strike. By 1986, about 40 percent of all state and local employees were unionized. Unionization has had effects on municipalities other than the specific budgetary implications of altered wages and working conditions. Unions have also affected the social, political, and personnel issues involving affirmative action and merit.

Suggested Reading
Bent, Alan E., and T. Zane Reeves. *Collective Bargaining in the Public Sector.* Menlo Park, CA: Benjamin-Cummings, 1978.
Gerhart, Paul F. "The Emergence of Collective Bargaining in Local Government." *Public Personnel Management,* vol. 9, no. 4 (1980), pp. 287–295.
Maier, Mark H. *City Unions: Managing Discontent in New York City.* New Brunswick, NJ: Rutgers University Press, 1987.

Methe, David, and James Perry. "The Impacts of Collective Bargaining on Local Government Services." *Public Administration Review*, vol. 40, no. 4 (1980), pp. 359–371.
Osigweh, Chimezie A. B. "Collective Bargaining and Public Sector Union Power." *Public Personnel Management*, vol. 14, no. 1 (1985), pp. 75–84.
Wellington, Harry H., and Ralph K. Winter, Jr. *The Unions and the Cities.* Washington, DC: Brookings Institution, 1972.

Combat Zone   A 70-acre site in Boston set aside in 1974 to concentrate and contain the location of adult theaters, strip joints, live adult entertainment, adult bookstores, and peep shows. Located adjacent to Chinatown and near the Boston Common in the central business district (CBD), the combat zone was accessible to conventioneers and easily patrolled by the police, who enforced health and safety ordinances. Boston's combat zone experiment ended in 1989, when the city approved redevelopment of the area. Although Boston's combat zone was not challenged in the U.S. Supreme Court, in Washington State, Renton's ordinance of restrictive zoning for adult motion-picture theaters has been. In the 1986 case *Renton v. Playtime Theatres,* 475 U.S. 41, the high court agreed that such activity could effectively be concentrated in about 5 percent of the land area of the city. Seattle also has opted to concentrate this activity into a single, visible zoned area in which "adult" is simply defined as prohibited to minors. A second approach to containing this form of vice is to force owners to secure special permits for operation. This is the option exercised in Indianapolis and Oakland, California. A third approach is to allow each county within a state to decide under local option whether to legalize prostitution and where the operation is to be allowed. This is the policy in Nevada, the only state to allow legal prostitution anywhere within its jurisdiction. A fourth approach is to scatter the activity by licensing operations only when they are substantially removed from other such businesses and any residence. New Orleans, Detroit, and New York City have taken this position. Detroit's ordinance was declared constitutional in *Coleman Young v. American Mini Theatres II,* 427 U.S. 50 (1976), two years after the start of the Boston combat zone. *See also* ZONING.

Significance   A combat zone is one diverse, recent policy response to a perennial issue in society: how to handle pornography and various forms of explicit entertainment. In a nation with a liberal interpretation of free expression, some adult entertainment must be accommodated. It can be regulated, however, through the police power and by the cities or counties within each state and commonwealth, especially under health and safety guidelines. The public costs associated with enforcing laws prohibiting prostitution amount to millions of dollars; these are dollars not being spent on solving violent crimes. This is also a land-use issue and hence governable under zoning ordinances. The present civil liberties posture of the U.S. Supreme Court finds it permissible to differentiate pornographic from other forms of expression on the basis of content and hence to treat such material differently from legitimate theaters and conventional bookstores and lounges.

Suggested Reading

Fee, Charles T., Jr. "Using Constitutional Zoning to Neutralize Adult Entertainment—Detroit to New York." *Fordham Law Journal*, vol. 5, no. 3 (1977), pp. 455–474.

Pearl, Julie. "The Highest Paying Customers: America's Cities and the Costs of Prostitution Control." *Hastings Law Journal*, vol. 38, no. 4 (1987), pp. 769–800.

Postawko, Edmund J. "The Conflict between the First Amendment and Ordinances Regulating Adult Establishments." *Journal of Urban and Contemporary Law*, vol. 30 (1986), pp. 315–331.

Weinstein, Alan C. "The *Renton* Decision: A New Standard for Adult Business Regulation." *Journal of Urban and Contemporary Law*, vol. 32 (1987), pp. 91–122.

Commercial Strip Development   A grouping of retail or commercial enterprises in a narrow band along major roadways or thoroughfares, usually near or beyond a city's limits. Commercial strip development, also known as "ribbon" or "string" development, usually allows each retail establishment some frontage on a major artery, thus giving the business greater street visibility. Businesses typically located in strip developments include automobile dealerships, gas stations, restaurants, and motels. Roadside malls offering diverse products and services have greatly increased in number. *See also* SECTOR MODEL; SHOPPING CENTER; TRAFFIC ANALYSIS; URBAN SPRAWL.

Significance   Commercial strip development substantially affects the patterns of land use in a community. Rather than concentrating business establishments within one area and building vertically, strip developments are most often low-rise structures. Highway construction patterns influence the location of these commercial and retail businesses. Much land speculation has occurred in local areas where the placement of the interstate highway system is being considered or where decisions regarding major state and county roads are still being debated. This linear development must be considered, in addition to the sector development that often occurs in communities. In some cases, businesses follow a major roadway beyond the city limits and become what urban geographers have called "interurban arterial businesses," since they form a growing link between cities. From an urban planning perspective, strip developments cause traffic flow problems. A number of major cities are known for the linear, rather than concentric, development that has tended to occur, most notably Los Angeles.

Commission Plan   A form of municipal government combining legislative and executive responsibilities first developed in 1901 in Galveston, Texas. The Galveston commission plan created a three-member panel to run the city, giving its members both administrative and legislative powers. Under this plan, a Board of Commissioners is directly elected by the voting population, then individual commissioners are given administrative responsibility over a specific municipal department, such as public works, finance, public safety, or parks and recreation. This form of government was created in response to a tidal wave that killed 6,000 people in Galveston, and the city felt an administrative commission could manage better during the crisis. *See also* COUNCIL-MANAGER GOVERNMENT; MAYOR, STRONG; MAYOR, WEAK.

Significance   The Galveston Commission plan was meant to carry the city temporarily through the aftermath of the tidal wave disaster. The combination of executive and legislative responsibilities inherent in a commission government allowed Galveston to recover from the disaster more rapidly. The plan proved popular enough that the city adopted a new charter in 1903 providing for a permanent commission government. Other cities followed in their adoption of the commission form after 1903, but this plan fostered inefficiency or too much corruption in some of the local governments, and most dropped the commission form. Each commissioner also had departmental loyalty, so budget meetings usually became political bargaining sessions, and no leader had budgetary responsibility for the city as a whole. Such political dynamics often gave excessive budgets to departments whose heads/commissioners were part of the ruling coalition and left those departments not represented by a commissioner in the coalition with paltry appropriations. More than 500 cities had this form of government at peak popularity. By 1988, a survey conducted by the International City Management Association found that of 176 commission plan cities that responded to the survey, 101 had populations less than 25,000. Portland, Oregon, and Tulsa, Oklahoma, remain the two largest cities with a commission form of government.

Suggested Reading
Rice, Bradley R. *Progressive Cities: The Commission Government Movement in America 1901–1920.* Austin: University of Texas Press, 1977.

Committee for Economic Development (CED)   One of several educational and policy-oriented organizations that represent the interests of large U.S. corporations. The Committee for Economic Development, with headquarters in New York City, was created in 1942 with the original purpose of providing analytical support for the business perspective on unemployment and the general issues associated with economic stability. It became an independent permanent organization in 1945. The CED researches and presents position papers on a variety of public-policy issues that directly concern the business community. For example, the CED has issued reports on urban poverty, regional growth, taxation as a particularly important fiscal policy, and the problems of inflation. *See also* CHAMBER OF COMMERCE; PUBLIC INTEREST GROUPS; THINK TANK.

Significance   The Committee for Economic Development has established a reputation of being a relatively objective research body presenting information to both public officials and the general population. In the past, it has been seen as both an arm of the "liberal" business community (it supported the Employment Act of 1946) and an objective think tank–like organization that provides credible research on a given topic. Many members of the CED's board of directors are representatives of the largest U.S. corporations, and many have been appointed to high-level positions in the federal government. At the time of great urban unrest during the tumultuous 1960s, the CED advocated that its member corporations take on a role of greater social responsibility and make more social investments.

Suggested Reading
Committee for Economic Development. *Improving Management of the Public Work Force: The Challenge to State and Local Government.* New York: CED, November 1978.
———. *Improving Productivity in State and Local Government.* New York: CED, March 1976.
———. *Modernizing Local Government.* New York: CED, July 1966.
———. *Reshaping Government in Metropolitan Areas.* New York: CED, February 1970.

Community   A network of people who share a sense of stability, order, and cohesion from interrelated daily life. A community uses a common language. Members feel a sense of inclusion by sharing values and responsibilities. Communities are not usually political units and may or may not be identified with a particular territory. *Community of place* suggests a close affinity to the idea of neighborhood, whereas *community of values* suggests the term need not be place-specific. A counterculture community located within the central city may be place-specific, whereas a community of scholars, Baptists, or Greek-Americans rests on shared values and not propinquity. Communities protect values through norms, whereas a polity protects its values through law enforcement. However defined, as place or shared values, community is viewed as a process. The dynamics of community demand that the collectivity must be born anew each generation. It is constantly developing or disappearing. Whereas a political unit enforces values by a bureaucracy, a community does so through inter-personal reinforcement. Community is personal, whereas governments are bureaucratic. Large-scale metropolitan areas with their high rate of mobility challenge the sense of belonging necessary for the maintenance of a community. A ghetto is not a community in the conventional sense; such areas are imposed by outside pressure. The nature of the modern metropolis makes it impossible to coordinate communities. They may generate intense intergroup conflict by their different life styles. Depending on the definition used, a neighborhood is a type of community. Others contend it is possible to distinguish between a neighborhood with cohesion and one with no developed sense of community. Communities may be spatially part of a city, an entire city, or several cities. *See also* COMMUNITY OF LIMITED LIABILITY; COMMUNITY PRESS; ETHNIC GROUP; HUMAN ECOLOGY; NEIGHBORHOOD; URBAN VILLAGE; ZONE, URBAN.

Significance   *Community* is one of the oldest and most basic terms in the study of society. It is also ambiguous. Urban studies have developed two traditions affirming both the territorial and transterritorial meaning. There is community as place and community as orientation. *Community* often is employed as a normative term, a feeling of belonging. It is also employed empirically to describe a network of self-identifying people. Community as a normative concept appeals to the entire political spectrum. Communists talk of communes, socialists and liberals of promoting communities unencumbered by the heavy-handed rule of oppressing groups. Conservatives stress the resurgence of community over mere formal government. Anarchists insist they alone are able to create true communities through the abolition of all government. Among the major themes of U.S. history is a sense of community gained, community lost, and community threatened by impersonal, complex, and large-scale bureaucracies. For many New Left advocates, the only meaningful participation transpires within the community, not within the state. When community is studied in specific cases, it is operationalized as being a network of people who share values by communication through local institutions. Thus sociograms, of who is talking to whom, and how often, are used to test for its existence and vitality.

Suggested Reading

Bernard, Jessie. *The Sociology of Community.* Glenview, IL: Scott, Foresman, 1973.

Connerly, Charles E. "The Community Question: An Extension of Wellman and Leighton." *Urban Affairs Quarterly,* vol. 20, no. 4 (1985), pp. 537–557.

Janowitz, Morris. *The Last Half-Century: Societal Change and Politics in America.* Chicago: University of Chicago Press, 1978. Chap. 8, "Residential Community."

Lyon, Larry J. *The Community in Urban Society.* Philadelphia: Temple University Press, 1987.

McWilliams, Wilson Carey. *The Idea of Fraternity in America.* Berkeley: University of California Press, 1973.

Swanson, Bert E. *The Concern for Community in Urban America.* New York: Odyssey Press, 1970. Especially Chap. 4.

Tönnies, Ferdinand. *Community and Society (Geimeinschaft und Gesellschaft).* Charles P. Loomis, trans. East Lansing: Michigan State University Press, 1957 (1887).

Warren, Rolan, ed. *Perspectives on the American Community: A Book of Readings,* 2nd ed. Chicago: Rand McNally, 1973.

Willman, Barry, and Barry Leighton. "Networks, Neighborhoods, and Communities: Approaches to the Study of the Community Question." *Urban Affairs Quarterly,* vol. 14, no. 3 (1979), pp. 363–390.

Community Action Program (CAP)   A project created by the Economic Opportunity Act of 1964 (42 U.S.C. 2701) to: (1) provide public services to the poor, (2) coordinate as well as encourage public and private funding to deal with poverty problems, and (3) encourage maximum feasible participation by those who were the targets of the various antipoverty programs. Community Action Agencies (CAAs), created to carry out the CAPs, most often were comprised of neighborhood activists independent of the city administration. The Community Action Program concept attempted to encourage feedback through citizen participation on local policy advisory boards or councils. *See also* ECONOMIC OPPORTUNITY ACT OF 1964; MAXIMUM FEASIBLE PARTICIPATION.

Significance   The concept of community action and "maximum feasible participation" by the clients of federal programs had its roots in the ideological left, which had identified urban problems as a major cause during the 1960s. Despite these origins, encouraging maximum feasible participation initially did not appear to be controversial. Critics of federal social programs argued that government had been unresponsive and ineffective. Once the program began, however, many city leaders felt threatened by community activists, who often demanded more reforms and greater authority. Federal funding for Community Action Programs eventually was eliminated under the Nixon administration, as was the Office of Economic Opportunity. Some versions of Community Action Programs remain at the local level, and they continue to encourage citizen participation.

Suggested Reading

Greenstone, J. David, and Paul E. Peterson. *Race and Authority in Urban Politics: Community Participation and the War on Poverty.* New York: Russell Sage, 1973.

Moynihan, Daniel P. *Maximum Feasible Misunderstanding: Community Action in the War on Poverty.* New York: Free Press, 1969.

U.S. Office of Economic Opportunity. *Community Action Program Guide.* Washington, DC: Government Printing Office, 1965.

Community Control   A direct form of political participation by citizens, in which neighborhood representatives have decision-making authority over selected public programs. The idea of community control centers on the question of decentralizing decision making to the neighborhood level. Community control has sought to make government bureaucracy and service delivery more accountable to the public. Initially advocated by citizen activists in the 1960s, community control gained some legitimacy when "maximum feasible participation" became mandated by the 1964 Economic Opportunity Act (42 U.S.C. 2701 et seq.). Among the programs that encouraged direct democracy were the federal urban renewal program, various federal antipoverty programs, local education programs, and in some cases, law enforcement. *See also* COMMUNITY ACTION PROGRAM; DECENTRALIZATION; MAXIMUM FEASIBLE PARTICIPATION; PARTICIPATION.

Significance   Community control gives power directly to average citizens, making it distinctly different from a decentralized form of government in which local elites have authority. Direct participation was advocated by the New Left and many black activists who felt clients of public programs should share power in determining the way programs were operating. However, power was decentralized in a variety of ways during the 1960s, 1970s, and 1980s. Some cities formed neighborhood advisory boards, some created little city halls, and still others formed neighborhood corporations. While much of the formal encouragement of direct participation was abandoned by President Richard Nixon, some Community Action Agencies have been retained into the 1990s.

Suggested Reading

Altshuler, Alan. *Community Control: The Black Demand for Participation in Large American Cities.* New York: Pegasus, 1970.

Fainstein, Norman, and Susan Fainstein. "The Future of Community Control." *American Political Science Review,* vol. 70, no. 3 (1976), pp. 905–923.

Fisher, Robert. *Let the People Decide: Neighborhood Organizing in America.* Boston: Twayne Publishers, 1984.

Katznelson, Ira. *City Trenches.* New York: Pantheon Books, 1981.

Morris, David, and Karl Hess. *Neighborhood Power: Returning Political and Economic Power to Community Life.* Boston: Beacon Press, 1975.

Zimmerman, Joseph F. *The Federated City: Community Control in Large Cities.* New York: St. Martin's Press, 1972.

Community Development Block Grant (CDBG)   Federal monies authorized by Congress through the 1974 Housing and Community Development Act (42 U.S.C. 5301). This act consolidated several urban categorical aid programs into one block grant. Community Development Block Grants apportion funding based on formulas that identify such factors as a city's population size, housing needs, and poverty levels. Funding also mandates that cities develop a comprehensive plan of development or redevelopment. *See also* DEMONSTRATION CITIES AND METROPOLITAN DEVELOPMENT ACT; HOUSING ACT OF 1949; HOUSING AND COMMUNITY DEVELOPMENT ACT OF 1974; URBAN RENEWAL.

Significance   The creation of the Community Development Block Grant constituted a part of the move away from categorical grants, which had funded specific projects, had strict guidelines of operation, and had required substantial reporting to the federal government. Block grants in general appealed to many state and local leaders who preferred the predictability of formula grants over the uncertainty of competing for categorical grants. Other advantages included reduced paperwork and greater local discretion over how money could be spent. In community development, state and local governments assumed much of the responsibility for programs, as well as added funding responsibilities. A wave of state and local community development agencies and such state and local programs as tax incentives followed the 1974 Housing and Community Development Act. Beginning in this period, the federal government withdrew from funding many urban programs, including Model Cities, urban renewal, and facilities for water and sewerage treatment.

Suggested Reading
Conlan, Timothy J. "The Politics of Federal Block Grants: From Nixon to Reagan." *Political Science Quarterly,* vol. 99, no. 2 (1984), pp. 247–270.
Dommel, Paul R., and Michael J. Rich. "The Rich Get Richer: The Attenuation of Targeting Effects of the Community Development Block Grant Program." *Urban Affairs Quarterly,* vol. 22, no. 4 (1987), pp. 552–579.
Wong, Kenneth K., and Paul E. Peterson. "Urban Response to Federal Program Flexibility: Politics of Community Development Block Grant." *Urban Affairs Quarterly,* vol. 21, no. 3 (1986), pp. 293–309.

Community Fact Books   Systematic compilations of social and physical data and statistics organized by metropolitan area; by civil jurisdiction, zip code, and administrative subunits; or by census tract. The books also are organized chronologically to allow for historical analysis. By frequently updating information between census reports, the books are made more valuable to local decision makers. Topics covered include demographics of age, race, sex, marital status, number of children, morbidity, and social status. Economic information includes auto registrations and family income. Public-policy items might cover traffic accidents and crime rates by Federal Bureau of Investigation (FBI) uniform reporting classification. Educational categories used are years of school completed and dropout rates. There might be political data on voting turnout, absentee ballot requests, and areas of party voting strength. Geopolitical information enumerates abandoned buildings, land use, zoning classifications, transportation corridors, and density. In public organizations, the material is compiled by planning and health departments and computer offices. Commercially, the fact books are developed by information-gathering firms in electronic information storage systems and sold as raw data or printouts processed for marketing surveys. These typically are commissioned by financial institutions and franchise operations to aid in determining locations for outlets and new markets. *See also* CENSUS OF POPULATION; CHICAGO SCHOOL.

Significance   Fact books originated with the University of Chicago School of Sociology in 1938, based on the 1930 census. The school produced four in a series, using consecutive censuses of population. That discontinued series on Chicago still is being developed, now in computer format as an electronic community fact book. Books also have been produced on Milwaukee, New York City, and Nashville. The Community Fact Books are used by civic and planning bodies to chart trends and frequencies. They are used by United Way and the Black United Fund (BUF), private, umbrella funding agencies. Academic researchers use them to plot neighborhood invasions, housing starts, land-use succession, and tax yields. Indices are created to produce social indicators that tip off planners to areas in incipient physical decline.

Suggested Reading
Choldin, Harvey N. "Electronic Community Fact Books." *Urban Affairs Quarterly*, vol. 15, no. 3 (1980), pp. 269–289.

Community of Limited Liability   In a modern urban society social relationships are neither simple (*gemeinschaft*) nor complex (*gesellschaft*) but are based on restrained commitments. An early Germanic conception of this principle was offered by Ferdinand Tönnies (1855–1936) and described changes in social relations when people moved from villages to large cities. Social relationships were transformed from intimate ties to indirect and bureaucratic ones. This early concept assumed that large urban areas destroyed close social bonds. However, in modern urban society, interpersonal contacts are not based solely on an impersonal "rule by desk," the literal meaning of bureaucracy. Because of family, financial, and emotional commitments to the home, modern urban man retains positive, albeit restrained, emotional attachments. *See also* COMMUNITY; NEIGHBORHOOD; WIRTH THESIS.

Significance   The term *community of limited liability* was coined by Morris Janowitz in his 1952 study of the Chicago community press based on his thesis that in a modern urban complex, individuals regulate the emotional capital they invest in their neighborhood. In other words, they impose on themselves a sense of a limited liability regarding what they owe their community. The concept of limited liability is borrowed from accounting. It suggests that if one loses an investment, the amount of loss is restricted. If the modern resident does not feel the community is serving his/her interests, he/she will withdraw by moving or eliminating most local interpersonal contacts. He/she stops voting, reading the paper, attending block club meetings. He/she goes into psychological exile without ever moving. In a large city, the immediate neighborhood can be of secondary importance. The concept received wide acceptance as an apt theoretical description of modern urban man's tenuous community ties.

Suggested Reading
Janowitz, Morris. *The Community Press in an Urban Setting: The Social Elements of Urbanism*, 2nd ed. Chicago: University of Chicago Press, 1952, 1967. Chap. 7.

Community Press   A weekly or biweekly newspaper addressing a general audience within a limited circulation area. The urban community press is published either for an urban zone within the central city or for one or more suburbs. An example is *The Citizen* of Hamtramck, a Detroit enclave. Founded in 1934, it publishes 28,000 copies once a week on Thursday, with ten employees. In addition to serving as the official newspaper for the enclave, it publishes approximately one-tenth of its 10 to 14 pages in Polish. There is still a hint of the older *immigrant press* in the paper, with its tradition of serving as a mediator and personalizer of information from the Anglo community to the ethnic subcommunity. *See also* OFFICIAL NEWSPAPER; ZONED EDITION.

Significance   The threshold for a flourishing urban community press appears to be a metropolitan area of about one million. This type of press is especially active in Los Angeles and Chicago, in contrast to New York City, which does not have a robust community-press tradition. The community press tends to have more readers per circulating area in the suburbs than in the central cities. Competition for readership comes from zoned editions of the daily metropolitan newspapers, the adjacent community press, and narrowcast cable television. This local press facilitates the spread of parochial political information and local advertising and serves as a bulletin board for community events. The greater the deconcentration of business districts in a metropolitan area, the greater the chance that a community press will find a receptive readership.

Suggested Reading

Janowitz, Morris. *The Community Press in an Urban Setting: The Social Elements of Urbanism,* 2nd ed. Chicago: University of Chicago Press, 1952, 1967.
Park, Robert E. *The Immigrant Press and Its Control.* New York: Harper, 1929.
Schroth, Raymond A. *The Eagle and Brooklyn: A Community Newspaper, 1841–1955.* Westport, CT: Greenwood Press, 1974.
Sim, John Cameron. *The Grass Roots Press: America's Community Newspapers.* Ames: Iowa State University Press, 1969.

Community Reinvestment Act   A federal statute passed to ensure that financial institutions regulated by the national government compile records on lending activity by area to make regulators aware of whether entire communities, including moderate- and low-income neighborhoods, are being properly served. With promulgation of detailed rules in the *Code of Federal Regulations,* national regulatory bodies keep tabs on the disparity between deposits and credit amounts approved by financial institutions. The regulators use that information to rate lending institutions and evaluate applications by deposit facilities to merge or acquire other institutions. The rating is a regulatory body's report card on how well financial institutions support their depository communities. *See also* DISINVESTMENT, URBAN; HOME MORTGAGE DISCLOSURE ACT OF 1975; REDLINING.

Significance   In 1977 Congress passed the Community Reinvestment Act (12 U.S.C. 2901 et seq.) after finding that redlining by lending institutions was not being curbed by the mere exposure of such activity. National regulatory bodies such as the Federal Reserve Board (the Fed), the Comptroller of the Currency, and the Federal Home Loan Bank Board now have power to grade depository institutions by an internal audit. If the banks accept deposits only for the purpose of shifting them out of the area, then they fail to meet the credit needs of the communities in which they are chartered. In fact, few banks are given unsatisfactory ratings. The ratings are considered confidential audit information, so their use is limited. Paying 5 percent interest on local deposits while lending only at 9 percent to out-of-state projects, for example, is a major form of disinvestment. So long as the lender has local applicants who can repay mortgages under sound banking operations, lenders have an affirmative obligation to keep resources in geographic proximity. Although not a well-known statute, the act gave local advocacy groups leverage over banks that wish to expand or merge.

Comparative Urban Analysis   The systematic study of urban areas by a variety of independent variables derived from or based on a classification system. *Intergenerational* comparative city analysis uses the same area over time, usually in three or more periods, often based on decennial census years. Sam Bass Warner did this for Philadelphia in the mid-1770s, the 1860s, and the 1930s. Olivier Zunz studied Detroit for the three census years of 1880, 1900, and 1920. Most comparative city analysis is conducted on an *intrasectional* or *intranational* scale. Daniel Elazar used the sectional scale in his study of the prairie cities. Finally, less often, comparative city analysis is conducted on an *international* scale, as Janet Abu-Lughod did in Arabic-speaking North Africa. Infrequently, comparative city analysis embraces some or all urban areas, working with cities in the first-world nations of the United States and its industrially developed allies, the second-world nations of the Union of Soviet Socialist Republics and its East European allies, as well as the third-world, or less developed countries (LDCs). The International Studies of Value in Politics Project covered four nations in North America, Asia, and Europe. Holistic comparisons are in an especially nascent phase of development. The most ambitious example was written in 1980 by Robert Fried and Francine Rabinovitz. There are six other overlapping disciplinary typologies employed in comparative analysis, each focusing on a host of variables. *See also* CITY CLASSIFICATION.

Suggested Reading

Abu-Lughod, Janet. "Developments in North African Urbanism: The Process of Decolonization." In Brian J. L. Berry, ed., *Patterns of Urbanism and Counterurbanism*. Beverly Hills: Sage, 1976, pp. 191–211.

Elazar, Daniel J., et al. *Cities of the Prairie Revisited: The Closing of the Metropolitan Frontier*. Lincoln: University of Nebraska Press, 1986. (Pueblo, Colorado, and three Illinois cities: Champaign-Urbana, Decatur, and Joliet.)

Fried, Robert C., and Francine F. Rabinovitz. *Comparative Urban Politics: A Performance Approach*. Englewood Cliffs, NJ: Prentice-Hall, 1980.

International Studies of Values in Politics Project. *Values and the Active Community: A Cross-National Study of the Influence of Local Leadership*. New York: Free Press, 1971.

Warner, Sam Bass, Jr. *The Private City: Philadelphia in Three Periods of Its Growth*, 2nd ed. Philadelphia: University of Pennsylvania Press, 1968, 1988.

Zunz, Oliver. *The Changing Face of Inequality: Urbanization, Industrial Development, and Immigrants in Detroit, 1880–1920*. Chicago: University of Chicago Press, 1982.

Comparative Urban Analysis, Demographic   U.S. studies of population primarily employing the census tract or some larger unit. These enumerations have been conducted decennially from 1790 to the present. (1) The most frequently used demographic variable is *absolute size* of the population. Many urban studies eliminate jurisdictions with populations of less than 2,500 or even 25,000. Large-scale urban areas are classed variously as conurbations, megalopolises, Standard Consolidated Statistical Areas, or giant cities. (2) *Race* also is used as a variable in such political studies as at-large versus district elections, or where communities are intentionally underbounded in order to discriminate against an identifiable group. (3) *Age* distribution of the population is another variable that can take on importance, especially in comparing first- and third-world cities. As of the 1980s, U.S. citizens had a median age greater than 30 years, in contrast to less than 15 years for some major third-world cities, such as Casablanca, Morocco. Retirement-oriented U.S. municipalities such as St. Petersburg, Florida, and Sun City, Arizona, also stand out in the charts. (4) *Housing* variables also are commonly employed, often in conjunction with other data used to calibrate a quality-of-life index in reference to density, occupancy per room, or age of the facilities. (5) *Race* often is combined with *housing* census information to analyze the rate and level of segregation patterns in metropolitan areas. (6-7-8) *Sex ratios,* *migration rates,* and *mobility rates* are other demographic variables. Sex imbalances in third-world nations sometimes herald a temporary migration cycle, stress in the hinterland in finding employment, or boom-and-bust cycles in city population patterns. Cities with mobility rates that differ substantially from national norms sometimes indicate very sedentary populations. In high-turnover cities, these factors might indicate a lack of local political commitment. *See also* CENSUS OF GOVERNMENTS; CENSUS OF POPULATION; COUNTERURBANISM; POPULATION, DAYTIME AND NIGHTTIME; QUALITY OF LIFE.

Suggested Reading
Aberbach, Joel D., and Jack L. Walker. *Race in the City: Political Trust and Public Policy in the New Urban System.* Boston: Little, Brown, 1973.
Berry, Brian J. L. *Comparative Urbanization: Divergent Paths in the Twentieth Century.* New York: St. Martin's Press, 1973, 1981.
Dogan, Mattei, and John D. Kasarda, eds. *The Metropolitan Era.* Vol. 1: *A World of Giant Cities.* Vol. 2: *Mega-Cities.* Newbury Park, CA: Sage, 1987.

Comparative Urban Analysis, Economic   Many early economic studies of cities focus on export activity, that is to say, what was made or done in excess of local consumption. (1) Many of these studies focus on some form of a fivefold economic activity index that catalogs cities according to their dominant export. These schema are organized into (a) primary activity, such as mining and agriculture; (b) secondary activity, such as manufacturing and construction; (c) tertiary activity, such as retail and wholesale goods sales, services, finance, and insurance, along with professional and governmental functions; (d) quaternary activity, such as producing, storing, retrieving, and consuming information; (e) quinary activity, consisting of making high-level private-sector decisions, such as functions based in world headquarters. (2) Economic geographers also organize cities by their dominant economic base, breaking communities into mining, manufacturing, commercial, financial, and transportation hubs/breakpoints. A more refined version of this is to catalog cities into those dominated by headquarters (New York City); those dominated by research, development, and engineering (the Research Triangle, North Carolina); those dominated by the production-industrial stage (Flint); those with entry ports (San Antonio and San Diego); and those with retirement centers (Tampa). Economic geographers also organize cities by the boom era during which they took on this economic base. Economists also list cities by their regional and national significance, the size of their hinterland, and the degree to which the city has a balanced or imbalanced economic base. *See also* POSTINDUSTRIAL CITY; TWIN CITIES.

Suggested Reading

Mollenkopf, J. H. *The Contested City*. Princeton: Princeton University Press, 1983.

Molotch, Harvey, and John R. Logan. "Urban Dependencies: New Forms of Use and Exchange in U.S. Cities." *Urban Affairs Quarterly*, vol. 21, no. 2 (1985), pp. 143–169.

Noyelle, T. J., and T. M. Stanback. *The Economic Transformation of American Cities*. Totowa, NJ: Rowman & Allanhead, 1984.

Comparative Urban Analysis, Geographic   Spatial studies of cities are organized around some of the most familiar and standard typologies. (1) *Population distribution* by work, residence, and recreation yields not only density studies but the parts of the metropolitan mosaic, such as the central business district (CBD); the central city with its various zones, enclaves, suburbs, polycentric business locations, urban fringe, and exurbia; and the daily urban commute (DUC). (2) *Microlevel* types include neighborhood and community studies, encompassing slums and urban renewal areas. (3) *Intermediate scale* analysis embraces such areas as the metropolitan region and the city-with-related-hinterland. (4) *Macrolevel* types include clusters of cities such as those along the Great Lakes or those extending along the East Coast from Washington, D.C., to beyond Boston, initially called Megalopolis by urban geographer Jean Gottmann. For more than 50 years geographers have developed rank-size relationships among cities within the same region. There is also voluminous literature on the functional classification of urban areas. These include administrative, cultural, defense, and ecclesiastical types along with the more familiar service, manufacturing, and commercial categories. Critics charge that these comparisons are prepared as an exercise in and of themselves, unrelated to any other theoretical purpose. *See also* CENTRAL BUSINESS DISTRICT; CENTRAL CITY; CONURBATION; DAILY URBAN SYSTEM; ENCLAVE; EXURBIA; LAND-USE CONTROL; MEGALOPOLIS; MULTINUCLEI MODEL; SUBURB; SUNBELT; URBAN SPRAWL.

Suggested Reading

Adams, John S., and Ronald Abler. *A Comparative Atlas of America's Great Cities: Twenty Metropolitan Regions*. Minneapolis: University of Minnesota Press, 1976. (Vol. 3 of the American Association of Geographers Comparative Metropolitan Analysis Project.)

Berry, Brian J. L., ed. *City Classification Handbook: Methods and Applications*. New York: John Wiley, 1972.

Berry, Brian J. L., et al. *Chicago: Transformations of an Urban System*. Cambridge, MA: Ballinger, 1976. (Also in the series of the AAG Comparative Metropolitan Analysis Project.)

Gugler, Josef, ed. *The Urbanization of the Third World*. New York: Oxford University Press, 1988.

Lowder, Stella. *The Geography of Third World Cities.* Totowa, NJ: Barnes & Noble, 1986.

Muller, Peter, et al. *Metropolitan Philadelphia: A Study of Conflicts and Social Change.* Cambridge, MA: Ballinger, 1977. (Also in the series of the AAG Comparative Metropolitan Analysis Project.)

Smith, Robert H. T. "Review Article on Functional Town Classification." *Annals of the Association of American Geography,* vol. 55, no. 3 (1965), pp. 539–548.

Yeates, Maurice. *The North American City,* 4th ed. New York: Harper & Row, 1990.

Comparative Urban Analysis, Historic   Temporal studies of more than one city or metropolitan area organized around a common theme of a region, era, scale, culture, or similar economic base. Most history is avowedly ideographic. It studies events *sui generis,* as discrete developments in order to gain understanding from only those circumstances. Comparative analysis, on the other hand, assumes a *nomothetic* position. Each case is to be studied as part of a class. Individual analysis must lead to generalizations. An early exception to the general rule of discrete city studies was the landmark account by Adna Weber, who systematically studied nineteenth-century urban demography, especially changing density and migration patterns in the rapidly industrializing portions of Europe and North America. But most U.S. urban history prior to 1953 is not *cliometric,* that is, based on careful measurement of historic data accomplished by application of appropriate statistical techniques, which in turn are amenable to comparison. In 1953, the American Historical Association section on urban history was formed, which has encouraged "the new urban history," based on greater empirical rigor. It is still most common for the contemporary historian to write on, say, Seattle with no intention of comparing it to other cities along the Pacific rim. Early twentieth-century comparative U.S. urban history is confined largely to the demise of the urban boss and his political machine and to the divergent paths that progressive reforms took in major cities. Since mid-century, however, there is a growing and sophisticated literature on comparative big-city mayors from the 1820s to the present, on patterns in industrial urbanization, and on the rise of cities in the South and West, as well as increasing industrialization. *See also* BOSS; CITY; REFORM GOVERNMENT; URBAN POLITICAL MACHINE.

Suggested Reading

Gilchrist, D. T., ed. *The Growth of the Seaport Cities: 1790–1825.* Charlottesville: University Press of Virginia, 1967.

Holli, Melvin G., and Peter d'A. Jones, eds. *Biographical Directory of American Mayors, 1820–1980.* Westport, CT: Greenwood Press, 1981.

McKelvey, Blake. *American Urbanization: A Comparative History*. Glenview, IL: Scott, Foresman, 1973.
Pred, Allan R. *The Spatial Dynamics of U.S. Urban Industrial Growth: 1800–1914*. Cambridge, MA: MIT Press, 1966.
Sale, Roger. *Seattle: Past to Present: An Interpretation of the History of the Foremost City in the Pacific Northwest*. Seattle: University of Washington Press, 1976.
Thornstrom, Stephen, and Richard Sennett, eds. *Nineteenth-Century Cities: Essays in the New Urban History*. New Haven, CT: Yale University Press, 1969.
Wade, Richard C. *The Urban Frontier: The Rise of Western Cities: 1790–1830*. Cambridge, MA: Harvard University Press, 1959.
Weber, Adna Ferrin. *The Growth of Cities in the Nineteenth Century: A Study in Statistics*. Ithaca, NY: Cornell University Press, 1899, 1963.

Comparative Urban Analysis, Political   Most political reports of whole cities are single and nonadditive studies. San Antonio is studied for its own importance, not because it is typical of any category or because the story produces an overarching model. Oliver Williams's classification for local governments dates only from the early 1960s. An exception to the conventional case study that justified its selection as representative of all urban areas, in categories as diverse as one-party dominance and percentage of white foreign-born, was Robert Dahl's 1961 account of New Haven. Yet New Haven is part of Connecticut, then the nation's wealthiest state. New Haven was governed by one of the nation's most competent mayors and was building, proportionate to population, the nation's largest renewal area. Daniel Elazar's four-city comparison, first published in 1970, is considered exceptionally rigorous. The study of local leadership in India, Poland, Yugoslavia, and the United States led by the University of Pennsylvania stands as the only in-depth, field-based comparative political study of first-, second-, and third-world nations. The two reports of giant cities edited by Robson and Dogan are largely descriptive and tentative, basing their comparisons on such problems as mass transit, management of migration influx, and the burdens of air and water pollution. The only ongoing intranational urban U.S. research based on both survey research and document analysis is headed by Terry Clark at the University of Chicago through his Permanent Community Sample. Most urban political studies are conducted on a particular area because the author lives in that area. *See also* CAMOUFLAGED CASE STUDIES; CASE STUDY; CITY POLITICAL PROFILE; COMMUNITY FACT BOOKS; PERMANENT COMMUNITY SAMPLE; PLURALISM; REPUTATIONAL ANALYSIS.

Suggested Reading

Deland, Robert T., ed. *Comparative Urban Research: The Administration and Politics of Cities*. Beverly Hills: Sage, 1969.

Goldberg, Michael A., and John Mercer. *The Myth of the North American City: Continentalism Challenged.* Vancouver: University of British Columbia Press, 1986.

Robson, William A., and D. E. Regan, eds. *Great Cities of the World: Their Government, Politics and Planning,* 3rd ed. Beverly Hills: Sage, 1954, 1957, 1973.

Sutton, Richard J., et al. "American City Types: Toward a More Systematic Urban Study." *Urban Affairs Quarterly,* vol. 9, no. 3 (1974), pp. 369–401.

Williams, Oliver P. "A Typology for Comparative Local Government." *Midwest Journal of Political Science,* vol. 5, no. 2 (1961), pp. 150–164.

Comparative Urban Analysis, Sociological   Human ecologists long have conducted comparative studies over time, focusing on community transformation. Survey research–oriented comparative studies may overcome some of the inherent limits of single case studies by incorporating a number of study sites. Researchers have developed two strategies: One is to select a Permanent Community Sample, as Terry Clark does. The second is to determine a most representative city for select categories, which is what RAND researchers did. Of the most highly populated 125 U.S. cities, they found Springfield, Massachusetts, the most representative; New York City, the best example of high density; Oxnard, California, the best example for fast growth; and Columbia, South Carolina, the best sample for southern cities. However, few non-RAND studies have taken heed of these best selections, and most sociological analysis is conducted neither on a regional scale nor with a balanced sample on the scale of Clark's 62 cities. The most enduring survey research site, the Detroit Area Study (DAS), has conducted a replication study only once and has never been programmed to conduct an intergenerational study. *See also* DETROIT AREA STUDY; HUMAN ECOLOGY; PERMANENT COMMUNITY SAMPLE; QUALITY OF LIFE; SOCIAL INDICATORS.

Suggested Reading

Clark, Terry N., comp. *Community Structure and Decision-making: Comparative Analysis.* Scranton, PA: Chandler, 1968.

Friedman, John, and Mauricio Salguero. "The Barrio Economy and Collective Self-empowerment in Latin America: A Framework and Agenda for Research." *Comparative Urban and Community Research,* vol. 1 (1988), pp. 3–37.

Keeler, Emmett, and William Rogers. *A Classification of Large American Urban Areas.* Santa Monica, CA: RAND Corp., 1973. R-1246-NSF.

South, Scott, and Dudley L. Preston. "The U.S. Metropolitan System: Regional Change, 1950–1970." *Urban Affairs Quarterly,* vol. 18, no. 2 (1982), pp. 187–206.

Walton, John, and Louis Masotti, eds. *The City in Comparative Perspective: Cross National Research and New Direction in Theory.* New York: Halsted Press, 1976.

Competitive Bid   A requirement that governmental purchasers find the lowest responsible price for goods and services. Competitive bids were instituted as one element of a rationalized budgeting process, in which procedures were established to avoid excessive charges, corruption, and waste. Under normal circumstances a local government advertises for bids per detailed specifications, accepts sealed offers, and publicly opens the bids. The contract or award is made to the lowest bidder for identical services or goods. Any alternative selected must be explained. *See also* CENTRALIZED PURCHASING; PUBLIC CONTRACT; SET-ASIDE.

Significance   Competitive bids became part of the reform movement of the early twentieth century, which attempted to eliminate the corruption associated with urban political machines. An open and competitive process was thought to reduce the possibility of bribery, kickbacks, and favoritism that had been common in many local-government contracting practices, whether or not it involved a local political machine. In addition, competition for the delivery of goods and services to the public sector was thought to provide the best quality for the lowest price, reducing governmental waste, maintaining smaller budgets, and theoretically minimizing taxes. In many smaller cities, towns, and counties, competitive bidding may be required only on large expenditures such as automobiles. Once a consulting planner, corporation counsel, or architect has been selected, additional work requested by the local government is not open to competition.

Comprehensive Employment and Training Act (CETA) (29 U.S.C. 801)   Federal legislation providing employment opportunities for unemployed adults. Later, the CETA program expanded to include unemployed youth and underemployed individuals to address both structural and countercyclical issues of unemployment. By 1978, the federal government was spending about $8 billion on various CETA projects. The CETA program provided that the federal government be the employer of last resort by directly creating temporary jobs for unemployed persons. These jobs were thought to provide the background and skills enabling program clients to make the transition to regular private-sector jobs. With its enactment in 1973, CETA replaced the Manpower Development and Training Act (MDTA) of 1962 (42 U.S.C. 2571). In turn, the Reagan administration advocated less direct public spending for jobs and more tax incentives for business. As a result, the Job Training Partnership Act (29 U.S.C. 1695) replaced CETA. *See also* UNDEREMPLOYMENT.

Significance   The Comprehensive Employment and Training Act carried forward the major goals of the Manpower Development and Training Act. However, political resistance to public-service employment grew during the late 1970s and produced many critics of CETA within the Reagan administration that took office in 1981. CETA, along with several other federal programs, provided for more local involvement in the provision of services. In many cases, CETA funding was passed through to state and local governments, which in turn contracted for services with nongovernmental agencies such as nonprofit community organizations. Theoretically, this brought federal money to its best use because community-based groups would be best able to identify qualified recipients. However, it provided an unaccustomed administrative role for state and local agencies because they were needed to monitor these nongovernmental groups, not actually to administer the programs themselves. Despite substantial political opposition to the CETA program by the 1980s, most of the evaluation studies have indicated that substantial net benefits were realized by CETA and the earlier Manpower Development programs.

Suggested Reading
Franklin, Grace A., and Randall B. Ripley. *CETA: Politics and Policy, 1973–1982.* Knoxville: University of Tennessee Press, 1984.
Mirengoff, William, and Lester Rindler. *C.E.T.A.: Manpower Programs under Local Control.* Washington, DC: National Academy of Sciences, 1978.
Morlock, Laura L., et al. "Long-Term Follow-up of Public Service Employment Participants: The Baltimore SMSA Experience during the 1970s." Baltimore: Johns Hopkins Health Services Research and Development Center, 1981.

Concentric Zone Model   A theory of urban land use that describes the city's land pattern as a series of five dynamic circular or semicircular rings of indeterminate width. The concentric zone model was postulated by E. W. Burgess in 1925 and was supplemented by two later theories: Hoyt's 1939 sector model and Harris and Ullman's 1945 multinuclei model. Thus, the theory also described city expansion. The first zone is the central business district (CBD). Zone two is in transition and represents a buffer between commercial and other land uses. Zone three contains the homes of working people, including the two-flat areas. Zone four is residential with both apartments and single-family dwellings. Zone five is the bungalow sector, including the suburbs and satellite towns. Some other areas transect the zones, such as the black belt, the residential hotels, and transportation

corridors. *See also* BOUNDARY; CENTRAL BUSINESS DISTRICT; HUMAN ECOL-
OGY; MULTINUCLEI MODEL; SECTOR MODEL; ZONE OF TRANSITION.

Significance   When Burgess postulated his theory (based on his
study of Chicago), he acknowledged that the concentric zone model
was an ideal type that generally described a large city's boundaries,
which were both definite and less obvious. Two major criticisms of the
model are that it does not account for an industrial zone and that it
does not adequately explain radial transportation lines with their at-
tendant sectors. The concept is generally suited in simplified form to
describe Chicago and select other U.S. cities.

Suggested Reading
Park, Robert E., Ernest W. Burgess, and Roderick D. McKenzie. *The City.*
    Chicago: University of Chicago Press, 1925. Chap. 2, pp. 47–62. (This
    is a reprint of a paper Burgess first delivered in 1923.)

Condominium Conversion   The process of transforming existing
apartment rental buildings into units for sale to individual owners.
Tenants' leases are terminated or not renewed. Notice of the condominium conversion project must be filed with state authorities and
brought under state guidelines or local ordinances. *See also* GENTRIFI-
CATION; HOUSING, CONDOMINIUM.

Significance   In July 1978, a Uniform Condominium Act (UCA)
was drafted by the National Conference of Commissioners on Uniform Laws. This draft became a model for state laws to address the
previous lack of legislation governing condominiums and conversion.
In 1980, West Virginia became the first to enact a state statute regarding condominium conversion modeled after this proposal. Included
in the model act are provisions for tenant protections, such as adequate notice of conversion and first right of refusal to current residents of the building to be converted. However, many renters cannot
afford the substantial increases in monthly payments the conversion
would demand. Many cities with increasing demand for housing and
with limited or no space for new construction have seen a tremendous
increase in condominium conversion. Since 1970, New York City,
Seattle, and Boston all have witnessed numerous conversions of apartment buildings into condominiums. In some cities, condominiums
have become a part of the gentrification process of certain neighborhoods, in which middle- and upper-income households are replacing
the low- to moderate-income households that previously had rented
the apartments.

Congress of Racial Equality (CORE)   A major civil rights organization founded in Chicago in 1942. James Farmer, a civil rights activist, was CORE's founder and first national director. CORE is considered to have pioneered the technique of using nonviolent direct action to promote civil rights, most notably in its organization of sit-ins and the Mississippi freedom rides in the 1960s. By 1968, CORE officially had endorsed the notion of "black power" and proclaimed itself a black nationalist organization. *See also* BLACK POWER; NATIONAL ASSOCIATION FOR THE ADVANCEMENT OF COLORED PEOPLE; NATIONAL URBAN LEAGUE.

Significance   The Congress of Racial Equality has become one of the dominant organizational forces of the civil rights movement in the United States. The original founders of CORE came out of a Christian pacifist tradition and sought to employ Gandhian nonviolence to the struggle against racism. After the U.S. Supreme Court prohibited segregation in bus and rail transportation and terminals in 1960 in *Boynton v. Virginia*, 364 U.S. 454, CORE sought to test the Court's decision and publicize the discrimination of southern transportation through the freedom rides. Riders went into the South, primarily Mississippi, in the spring of 1961. Considerable violence occurred, along with greater polarization between the federal and southern state governments over civil rights policy; there was also an increasing rift within the Democratic party in the South on the question of race. After the freedom rides, CORE became active with black voter registration in the South.

Suggested Reading
Eagles, Charles W., ed. *The Civil Rights Movement in America.* Jackson: University of Mississippi Press, 1986.
Meier, August, and Elliot Rudwick. *CORE: A Study in the Civil Rights Movement, 1942–1968.* New York: Oxford University Press, 1973.

Consolidated Metropolitan Statistical Area (CMSA)   A term reflecting a measure of urbanization used for statistical purposes by the U.S. Bureau of the Census, called a "Standard Consolidated Statistical Area" until June 30, 1983. A Consolidated Metropolitan Statistical Area consists of two or more Primary Metropolitan Statistical Areas (PMSAs) with a combined population of more than 1 million people. A PMSA is defined as a county or group of counties recognized locally for their relative independence within a metropolitan complex, or designated a metropolitan area as of January 1, 1980, with local opinion continuing to recognize the area as independent. As with the designation Metropolitan Statistical Area, the CMSA must be socially and economically integrated. *See also* ECUMENOPOLIS; MEGALOPOLIS; METROPOLITAN STATISTICAL AREA; METROPOLITIZATION.

Significance   The trend toward urbanization and then metropolitanization has been a significant demographic force in the United States. By 1980, more than 70 percent of the U.S. population was urban, though migration patterns revealed most of the population shifting to the suburbs and out of the central cities by the 1970s. In fact, out-migration has extended metropolitan boundaries and created even farther-ranging urban living patterns, in which chains of CMSAs or MSAs extend for hundreds of miles. This pattern produces what has been called a *megalopolis* by French urban geographer Jean Gottman. Urban planner Constantinos A. Doxiadis predicted that in the twenty-first century a worldwide network of urban areas will form an *ecumenopolis*. In 1986, the Census Bureau had identified 23 Consolidated Metropolitan Statistical Areas in the United States, including New York's metropolitan population of 18 million, Los Angeles's 13 million, and Chicago's 8 million.

Suggested Reading

Doxiadis, Constantinos A. *Urban Renewal and the Future of the American City.* Chicago: Public Administration Service, 1966.
Gottman, Jean. *Megalopolis: The Urbanized Seaboard of the United States.* New York: Twentieth Century Fund, 1961.
Hall, Peter. *The World Cities.* New York: World University Library, 1971.
U.S. Department of Commerce, Bureau of the Census. *Statistical Abstract of the United States: 1986.* Washington, DC: Government Printing Office, 1985.

Consolidation   Merging of incorporated governmental units of different levels with but one remaining successor organization. City-county consolidation refers to governmental unification of one or more cities with the surrounding county. It is called a *merger* when two jurisdictions of the same type join together. It is called *annexation* when a municipal corporation expands its territorial boundaries by absorbing adjacent unincorporated areas. Any land that later is split off from such an annexation is said to have been *detached*. A county that divides into two separate units is said to have been *partitioned* or split. *See also* ANNEXATION; CENSUS OF GOVERNMENTS; DETACHMENT; REFERENDUM; THREE-TIER REFORM; UNIGOV.

Significance   Complete consolidation between governmental units is a major structural reform. The most frequent consolidation in the twentieth century is by school districts. The rapid pace of mid-twentieth-century school consolidation was attributed largely to improved transportation that allowed for busing of students, combined with the rapid decline in rural school enrollments, which forced mergers to achieve economies of scale. Full *merger* of cities is so uncommon that Michigan records only two instances in its history, namely East Saginaw joining Saginaw in 1889 and Fordson joining Dearborn in 1929. Successful city-county consolidations have occurred throughout U.S. history. Major examples in the twentieth century occurred in 1904 between Denver and Denver County (Colorado); in 1907 between Honolulu and Honolulu County (Hawaii); in 1947 between Baton Rouge and East Baton Rouge Parish (Louisiana); in 1952 between Hampton and Elizabeth County (Virginia); in 1962 between South Norfolk and Norfolk County (Virginia); in 1962 between Virginia Beach and Princess Anne County (Virginia); in 1962 between Nashville and Davidson, and Davidson County (Tennessee); in 1967 between Jacksonville and Duval County (Florida); in 1969 between Indianapolis and Marion County (Indiana); in 1970 between Columbus and Muscogee County (Georgia); in 1974 between Lexington and Fayette County (Kentucky); in 1975 between Anchorage and Anchorage Borough (Alaska). Most twentieth-century city-county consolidation attempts have failed, however. Arguments favoring consolidation of any units include (1) a radical response to overcome the balkanized metropolitan mosaic of governments, (2) increasing efficiency through achieving economies of scale, (3) improved equity of services throughout the area, and (4) improved capacity to conduct comprehensive physical planning. Arguments opposing consolidation and favoring the *status quo* include (1) the local units lose their identity, (2) the majority control a minority, and (3) in the case of city-county consolidation, it allows former suburban units to dominate the old central city. Passage of consolidations usually requires an extraordinary majority, sometimes in each of the melding units; strong local leadership; a cooperative state legislature; and a campaign that demonstrates tax savings. Voter turnout in such referendums is not high and indicates a generally apathetic electorate.

Suggested Reading

Glending, Parris N., and Patricia S. Atkins. "City-County Consolidations" *ICMA Municipal Year Book,* vol. 47 (1980), pp. 68–72.

Gronouski, John A., and James L. Mercer. "A Consolidation Model: Austin/ Travis County, Texas." *National Civic Review,* vol. 76, no. 5 (1987), pp. 450 ff.

Harvard, William C., and F. L. Cortz. *Rural-Urban Consolidation: The Merger of Governments in Baton Rouge.* Baton Rouge: Louisiana State University Press, 1964.

Hawkins, Brett W. *Nashville Metro: The Politics of City-County Consolidation.*
Nashville, TN: Vanderbilt University Press, 1966.
Marondo, Vincent L., and Carl Reggie Whitley. "City-County Consolidation:
An Overview of Voter Response." *Urban Affairs Quarterly*, vol. 8, no. 2
(1972), pp. 181–203.
Martin, Richard. *Consolidation: Jacksonville–Duval County.* Jacksonville, FL:
Convention Press, 1968.
Mogulof, Melvin B. *Five Metropolitan Governments.* Washington, DC: Urban
Institute, 1972.
Rosenbaum, Walter A., and Thomas A. Henderson. "Explaining the Attitudes
of Community Influentials toward Government Consolidation." *Urban
Affairs Quarterly*, vol. 9, no. 2 (1973), pp. 251–275.

Constitution, State   The basic legal document for a state, always
written and announced in the name of the people. It establishes counties, cities, and sometimes townships. It distributes power, prohibits
some activities, and limits the role of government. The four states that
are technically commonwealths (Pennsylvania, Kentucky, Virginia,
and Massachusetts) also have constitutions. All original state constitutions have been amended substantially or replaced by new documents.
Substate units of government are the products of state constitutions or
state statutes, depending on how much authority is delegated to the
state legislature in the basic document. State constitutions stipulate
the types of government allowed and often classify cities by size and
by type of charter. They list the way land is to be incorporated, and
the types of partisan or nonpartisan elections allowed, as well as the
frequency and even the timing of elections. Constitutions usually list
conditions that merit recall elections and indicate whether there will
be initiatives and referendums. *See also* DILLON'S RULE; HOME RULE;
POLICE POWER.

Significance   State constitutions are the basic law to which all cities
and other substate units of government are subject. Although basic
laws should be brief and general, most state constitutions go into
detail. Their interpretation can be either liberal (favorable to innovation) or narrow (presumed to favor restraint by the state). Typically
state constitutions limit municipalities in the types of taxes they can
levy, tax ceilings, amounts that can be borrowed, and the length of
time for which those amounts can be borrowed. Constitutions usually
mandate certain functions to each level, set up the conditions in which
annexation and consolidation can take place, list the ground rules for
metropolitan functional coordination, and declare whether municipalities can go bankrupt. They may specify the beginning of the fiscal
year, the types of local budgets, and even the timing of public hearings. Not uncommonly, state constitutions specify whether there will be

local merit systems. In some states details of these items are left to legislative discretion; in other states they are spelled out. Model state constitutions suggest that detail is better left to statutes, but practices vary with the history of conflicts in each state and the politics of the most recent state constitutional convention.

Suggested Reading

Cornwell, Elmer E., Jr., Jay S. Goodman, and Wayne R. Swanson. *Constitutional Conventions: The Politics of Revision Processes in Seven States.* New York: Praeger, 1975.

Kincaid, John, special ed. "State Constitutions in a Federal System." *Annals of the American Academy of Political and Social Science,* vol. 496 (1988).

Shalala, Donn E. *The City and the Constitution: The 1976 New York Constitution's Response to the Urban Crisis.* New York: Citizens Forum on Self Government, National Civic League, 1982.

Consultant, Local Government A private or not-for-profit individual, firm, think tank, association, or bureau that serves as a source of policy advice in exchange for a fee. Consultants are outsiders whose function is to suggest an overall policy or to solve a specific problem but who are in a position neither to define the topic nor to implement the solution. This is because consultants do not hold a formal position of authority within the government. Unlike outside agitators, consultants are invited to participate in decision making and are under contract to be paid for advice rendered. Municipal bankruptcy receivers differ from consultants in that receivers have been handed authority temporarily to pay off creditors under court order. Also unlike consultants, court-appointed administrators taking superintending control of a public body such as a jail or school system temporarily substitute their judgment for that of the conventional supervisor or superintendent. *See also* ARBITRATION; ASSESSMENT; CORPORATION COUNSEL; OUTSIDE INFLUENCE; PLANNING, URBAN PHYSICAL.

Significance Elected politicians often have worked successfully with consultants by the time they are sworn into office. They have employed public opinion pollsters, direct mail campaign solicitation advisers, and campaign strategists. Successfully elected municipal officials thus are favorably disposed to employ short-term outside experts on specific assignment. Consultants may be asked to aid in defining a problem, to evaluate alternative courses of action for an identified problem, to evaluate costs and benefits, to suggest innovations, or to mediate agreements between labor and management in group contract bargaining. As issues become more technical and as cities wish to keep budgets low by contracting out for services for which they might otherwise use in-house employees, consultants' contracts become more common. There is not a large body of systematic empirical literature on consultants; however, five generalizations emerge. (1) Consultants are brought in to take attention away from elected officials and to neutralize controversial issues through the use of "neutral experts." (2) Private professional consultants seldom are brought in to resolve partisan debates; their advice is not predictable and may backfire. (3) High-prestige consultants who are perceived as neutral by the media and electorate can legitimize public-policy formation. (4) Criticism often develops if consultants misdefine their commission or fail to issue practical and cost-conscious advice. (5) Elected officials use consultants to buy time, to bury issues until after an election, or to deflect responsibility and mute their electoral accountability for unpopular decisions.

Suggested Reading

Kagi, Herbert M. "The Roles of Private Consultants in Urban Governing." *Urban Affairs Quarterly,* vol. 5, no. 1 (1969), pp. 45–48.
Sabato, Larry J. *The Rise of Political Consultants: New Ways of Winning Elections.* New York: Basic Books, 1981.
Szanton, Peter. *Not Well Advised.* New York: Russell Sage Foundation and Basic Books, 1981.

Consumer Price Index (CPI)   A statistical measure of changes in the cost of a fixed number of items commonly purchased by consumers in 91 urban areas. The Consumer Price Index figures are compiled on a monthly basis by the U.S. Bureau of Labor Statistics. The retail prices that make up the index are separated into seven major groups: food and beverages, housing, fuel and other utilities, medical care, transportation, apparel, and commodities and services. The index compares the cost of these designated goods and services in a given month or year with their cost in a predetermined base year. The Bureau of Labor Statistics compiles two sets of indices: CPI-U reflects the spending patterns of all urban households, and CPI-W is determined by the spending patterns of urban wage earners and those considered clerical worker families. Periodically, the Bureau of Labor Statistics changes its reference base years to account for inflation so that a common value of the dollar may be used for comparison purposes. In the past, the base periods have been 1957–1959 and 1968. In 1988, the CPI began using a reference base period of 1982–1984. *See also* HOUSEHOLD.

Significance   The Consumer Price Index is used to understand the inflationary or deflationary trends of the U.S. economy. It tends to emphasize the "purchasing power" of consumers, sampling approximately 400 goods and services, popularly called the "market basket," which can be purchased with a dollar across specified periods of time. Regular revisions of the CPI are made to account for the changes in the spending habits of consumers over time. The largest cities have samples taken on a monthly basis; other areas have their CPI published on a bimonthly, quarterly, or semiannual basis. The index also is used in labor contracts when unions are able to negotiate automatic pay increases, called cost-of-living adjustments (COLAs), during inflationary times. The index has also been applied to federal income tax brackets to eliminate "bracket creep," in which taxpayers face a higher marginal tax liability solely as a result of inflation. This is a much less severe problem with the 1986 federal income tax code, which has established two tax brackets of 15 and 28 percent.

Contracting Out   Supplying a governmental service through a private provider or another governmental unit. The opposite of contracting out is internal staff or line production. *Staff* refers to either supervisory or housekeeping services. Examples of housekeeping services include preparation of land-use plans or entry of computer data. *Line* refers to functions the city or county was established to perform, such as solid waste (garbage) collection or fire protection. Although most local governments determine what services are demanded and supply them in-house, it is always possible for the public body to monitor a service delivery by some external source, which may be intergovernmental, private, or a mixture of public and private. The most common line services contracted out are garbage pickup, street lighting, and supply of electricity. The most commonly supplied outside staff services are engineering and legal advice. Intergovernmental contracting out is more frequent among cities than privatization. Newer cities are more likely to use the device than those with established in-house personnel. Nonunionized public employers are more likely to use the option than strongly unionized shops. Cities in the western part of the nation are more amenable to the idea than cities elsewhere. The largest example of intergovernmental contracting out is the Los Angeles County Lakewood plan. The largest private supplier of fire services is the Arizona-based Rural/Metro Fire Protection Company. Other well-known private contractors include Waste Management, Inc., and Corrections Corporation of Nashville. *See also* CO-PRODUCTION; LAKEWOOD PLAN; PRIVATIZATION; PROPRIETARY FUNCTION; TIEBOUT THESIS.

Significance   Although it is not the main way in which cities conduct business, contracting out is a time-honored technique of local government in the United States. It is also practiced in such other nations as

Japan, Denmark, and Switzerland. Private contracts range from a year to 20 years, with options to break the pact available to the city from every six months to yearly. Arizona's Rural/Metro is not purely a private contract; the core of private fire fighters is supplemented with public employees. This would be an example of a mixed system. Rural/Metro covers more than 3,000 square miles and more than 100,000 residents with arrangements that range from limited to complete fire protection and fire prevention, on a basis that ranges from all-city to subscription. To ensure competition, some cities issue contracts to different providers by district, thus institutionally pitting two or more suppliers against each other, the better to gauge costs per unit. Arguments for contracting out include saving money, improving implementation of new technology, providing better services with lower start-up costs, keeping better control of information, and limiting the number of government personnel. The assumption is that competition between private and public providers will lower costs. There are also many disadvantages. These include lowering costs by busting unions; laying off those last hired, namely women and minorities; producing corruption-prone contracts; saving monies only in the short run before the supplier forces up costs at renegotiation time; and lowering the accountability of elected officials. In some states, specific functions are precluded by statute from being contracted out to the private sector. If costs are lowered for a service that is contracted out, there is no guarantee savings will be passed on to the city. They may be absorbed in profits, unless, as in the case of the Arizona fire contracts, the supplier is regulated as a public utility. Contracting out to private providers became an ideological issue during Ronald Reagan's presidency.

Suggested Reading

DeHoog, Ruth Hooland. *Contracting Out for Human Services*. Albany: State University of New York Press, 1984.

Ferris, James M. "The Decision To Contract Out: An Empirical Analysis." *Urban Affairs Quarterly*, vol. 22, no. 2 (1986), pp. 289–311.

Morgan, David R., Michael W. Hirlinger, and Robert E. England. "The Decision To Contract Out Services: A Further Explanation." *Western Political Quarterly*, vol. 41, no. 2 (1988), pp. 363–372.

Murin, William J. "Contracting as a Method of Enhancing Equity in the Delivery of Local Government Services." *Journal of Urban Affairs*, vol. 7, no. 2 (1985), pp. 1–10.

Stone, Clarence N., Robert K. Whelan, and William J. Murin. *Urban Policy and Politics in a Bureaucratic Age*, 2nd ed. Englewood Cliffs, NJ: Prentice-Hall, 1986. Chap. 22.

Controller   An appointed government officer at the national, state, or substate level whose functions are to establish accounts, supervise the budgetary process, and analyze expenditures for compliance. Special districts, especially schools, often appoint a controller, also known as a *comptroller,* an incorrect spelling of the same office introduced in English about 500 years ago. A controller serves as an internal check on the disbursement of accounts by others. *See also* AUDIT; AUDITOR; CORRUPTION, GOVERNMENT.

Significance   The controller is an organization's chief internal finance officer. In cities and universities the controller's job description will include some of the functions associated with office managers. The controller also is known as a director of accounts or director of finance and is usually a member of the Washington-based Government Finance Officers Association (GFOA).

Conurbation   A city-region or aggregation of a number of separate towns in England that have developed to their common boundaries or are linked by related businesses, industry, retail trade, or education and named after the most prominent unit or region. The large and unplanned area described contains rural land that might never be built up. It does not correspond with any single civil jurisdiction. The term was coined in 1915 by Patrick Geddes in his book *Cities in Evolution.* It was used in the 1951 and subsequent United Kingdom censuses. *See also* ECUMENOPOLIS; MEGALOPOLIS; METROPOLITAN STATISTICAL AREA.

Significance   The term is of value and in use in England to describe the seven conurbations of Greater London, West Midlands, West Yorkshire, South East Lancashire, Merseyside, Tyneside, and Central Clydeside. All seven recorded lower 1981 populations than they had in 1951, attesting to the decentralization of England's major urban centers in the last half of the twentieth century. The term has not caught on in North America, where the term *metropolitan area* is commonly used. The United Nations publications refer to *urban agglomerations.* The large U.S. conurbation of the urbanized northeastern seaboard from Boston to Washington, D.C., is more frequently described by Jean Gottmann's 1961 neologism *megalopolis.*

Suggested Reading

Cameron, Gordon C., ed. *The Future of the British Conurbations: Policies and Prescriptions for Change.* New York: Longman, 1980.
Freeman, T. W. *The Conurbations of Great Britain.* Manchester, England: Manchester University Press, 1959.

Copper Canyon   A relatively well-off residential section of a central city in which police (coppers), fire fighters, teachers, and other well-paid municipal officials live in order to conform with mandatory residence clauses in their contracts or the city charter. The alliterative phrase describes a neighborhood attracting municipal employees who would move to the suburbs if free to do so. *See also* RESIDENT.

Significance   There are copper canyons in all cities that have mandatory residency requirements. New York City does not have copper canyons because it does not impose a police residency requirement; in Chicago the copper canyon is situated in two northwest-side wards. The neighborhoods tend to be above the city average in value because the owners and renters make above-average salaries. Copper canyon precincts have high voter turnout and high absentee voter application rates. The owners also subscribe to local newspapers more frequently than the city average and in turn tend to be the focus of special marketing because of their above-average disposable incomes.

Coproduction   Citizen participation in the supply and delivery of city services. *Coproduction* is a recent social science term, coined by Vincent Ostrom at the University of Indiana in the 1970s. The concept developed from three academic sets of literature: participation, economic rational choice, and urban service delivery. There is no single agreed-upon definition. A broad version embraces all citizen activity, whether productive or counterproductive, that affects city services. A narrower definition limits coproduction to direct and positive citizen contribution and differentiates between coproduction and parallel production. Instances of individual commitments to coproduction occur when a citizen installs a home burglar alarm (which thwarts crime), serves as a candy striper at a hospital or as a volunteer school aide, works with the police youth officer, or voluntarily bundles solid waste for recycling. A resident who takes waste to the curb as opposed to having the collector walk to the sideyard is coproducing waste collection. If voluntarily done by most of the community, coproduction saves substantial public employee time. *Parallel production,* on the other hand, includes voluntary group activity, such as work on a committee to recodify a city's ordinances, neighborhood watch, neighborhood patrols, volunteer fire fighters, community cleanups of parks and rivers, and joining zoning boards, planning commissions, and *ad hoc* city bodies. *See also* PARTICIPATION.

Significance   Coproduction literature recognizes that citizen contributions are no substitute for the work of full-time municipal em-

employees but that an active citizen is usually a better informed, more politically active, and more cooperative citizen. Also, the theory behind coproduction is that much citizen participation goes unrecognized if it is not deliberately factored into the workings of a community. Empirical studies have investigated which communities have the most coproduction, and they are often those with wealth and leisure. Studies have also been done on which types of coproduction are most cost-effective. Coproduction does not necessarily lower city costs. Although the community may benefit from lower taxes, overall costs may go up because of the increased expenses for volunteer training and city employee liaison activity. One major consideration in evaluating the effectiveness of coproduction is under what conditions unions and department heads are actually reluctant to encourage coproduction. Not surprisingly, it appears to be when they perceive a job threat. When it works well, coproduction can be extremely effective. A recent example is the restoration of Bryant Park sponsored by residents of high-rise buildings adjacent to the New York Public Library and funded by private sources, which then drew immediate benefit from the change. Furthermore, in police protection, for example, coproduction can be costly and counterproductive if a neighborhood patrol turns vigilante.

Suggested Reading
Ahlbrandt, Roger S., and Howard J. Sumka. "Neighborhood Organizations and the Coproduction of Public Services. *Journal of Urban Affairs*, vol. 5, no. 3 (1983), pp. 211–220.
Brudney, J. L., and R. E. England. "Toward a Definition of the Coproduction Concept." *Public Administration Review*, vol. 43, no. 1 (1983), pp. 59–64.
Ferris, James M. "The Use of Volunteers in Public Service Production: Some Demand and Supply Considerations." *Social Science Quarterly*, vol. 69, no. 1 (1988), pp. 3–23.
Levine, Charles. "Citizenship and Service Delivery: The Promise of Coproduction." *Public Administration Review*, vol. 44, no. 2 (1984), pp. 178–187.
Percy, Stephen L. "Citizen Participation in the Coproduction of Urban Services." *Urban Affairs Quarterly*, vol. 19, no. 4 (1984), pp. 431–446. (The first of four articles in a minisymposium on coproduction.)
Schneider, Anne L. "Coproduction of Public and Private Safety: An Analysis of Bystander Intervention, Protective Neighboring, and Personal Protection." *Western Political Quarterly*, vol. 40, no. 4 (1987), pp. 611–630.

Corporation Counsel   An attorney-at-law who represents any incorporated government jurisdiction, such as an authority, city, or county. Municipal corporation counsels specialize in topics including annexation, bidding, contracts, Dillon's Rule, drafting ordinances, and zoning. They can be in-house advisers or on retainer in private law firms. Their advice, in theory, is confined to what the viable legal options are in any context, although in fact they try to keep clients out of trouble by anticipating problems. Theirs is not the only source of advice; mayors and city councils can solicit legal opinions from municipal leagues and township associations as well as formal attorney general opinions. Although some are appointed by the mayor, and some corporation counsels are elected, most are appointed by the city council. Many specialize in defending tort actions directed at municipal employees acting as agents of the government.

Significance   Corporation counsels are major decision makers in most city governments, suggesting what cannot be done or, alternatively, what actions carry a high risk of attracting difficult-to-defend suits. Usually they keep a low profile, and seldom are they portrayed in the media or in social science case studies. Their actual role is not merely that of a technical, neutral adviser. Their very selection is a political act. Many are conservative by training and political persuasion. Generally, they belong to a section of the state bar on municipal law and may be active in the National Institute of Municipal Law Officers, founded in 1935. Black corporation counsels may also be active in the National Conference of Black Lawyers, founded in 1968. Their line-item budgets can be major sources of cost overruns if they lose major actions; they can also provide savings by proposing precautionary actions. Turnover is an issue. Some counsels suggest that all such appointees are accountable primarily to the elected leaders who hired them and that they should therefore resign when a change in leadership occurs. Others advocate long tenure to ensure continuity. Like all attorneys, they are accountable to the canons of ethics of their own profession. Many use the position to try for judicial appointments as a career advancement.

Corruption, Government   A surreptitious perversion of public values for private advantage by an action deemed illegal, deviant, an improper allocation of resources, and/or immoral. The elements of corrupt government behavior include the facts that it is secret, that it is not sanctioned by the larger community, that it would be condemned if made public, and that the public interest is diverted for the benefit of a private individual or group. Examples of urban government corruption include payoffs, kickbacks, extortion, cover-ups of malfeasance, bribery, larceny, protection payments for not enforcing laws against illegal activity, voter registration fraud, illegal campaign contributions, multiple voting, and ballot box stuffing. There is no agreed-upon operational definition of corruption, but there are four common approaches to evaluating corruption. (1) Corruption is viewed as illegal. Public officeholders in any branch, whether elected or appointed, who violate their trusts or oaths are to be prosecuted for criminal violations of statutes, rules, and canons of ethics. Malefactors must be exposed and punished by fines, imprisonment, removal from office, and/or forfeiture of benefits. (2) Corruption is viewed as a social issue. Corruption is caused by environmental factors, and reform of bureaucratic institutions is required to remove incentives. There need to be more checks and balances, more exposure by the media and watchdog legislative committees, and clear statements that the government owns and will protect the commons. In this view, corrupt activity is endemic, and increased political participation alone defines public values. (3) Corruption is viewed as an economic issue in public policy. It is a matter of unrecorded reallocations in the marketplace. Corruption produces unknown costs and benefits without formal and open approval. Corruption is an exchange of goods and services representing an unspecified percentage of the gross domestic product that causes governmental inefficiency. Corruption may be either a major or minor reallocation and either beneficial or detrimental depending on how it affects the flow of goods and services. (4) Corruption is viewed as a moral issue and stands condemned. Wrongdoers and those who allow wrongdoing should always be exposed for putting the goals of the few ahead of the openly agreed-upon goals of the whole community. Corruption is always scandalous no matter its economic consequences. Antonyms of corruption include *honesty, public interest, efficiency, rationality,* and *ethical conduct. See also* AUDIT; OCCUPANCY PERMIT; REFORM GOVERNMENT; URBAN POLITICAL MACHINE.

Significance   There are no agreed-upon criteria for what constitutes corrupt behavior, of where to draw the line between permissible and illegal influence, or of a legal contribution versus an illegal payoff. There is little systematic and almost no comparative analysis of corrupt government behavior. Corruption has a negative connotation except in economic analysis, where it is simply a public-policy issue of an exchange of unknowable magnitude. We know only of corruption that has been exposed. Thus, there can never be an empirical answer to the question of how much government corruption exists relative to that in the private sector. Environmental factors cause corruption, such as paying off building inspectors to facilitate construction schedules, rigging bids based on insider information, arranging blackmail payoffs to unions that threaten delays or strikes, or extorting money to protect numbers racketeers from arrest or prosecution. Personal greed also causes corruption, such as wholesale stealing from the public treasury or skimming off funds when books are not properly audited. Corruption is an enduring issue of urban politics; its intensity appears to be cyclical. Corruption is especially high in the capital development cycle when the infrastructure of a city is put into place. Some cities appear to have more broad and systematic corruption than others. New York City has had proportionally more convictions for malfeasance over the years than San Francisco. Organized crime is active in services such as carting or waste hauling. The effects, or externalities, of corruption include eroded public confidence, lowered public support for tax and bond issues, increased cynicism about public officials, and a lowered sense of the legitimacy of governmental institutions. Where corruption is endemic to a city's mode of operation, no prosecutor or court system can stem it. There are degrees of corruption ranging from major scandal not supported by the public all the way to minor infractions that have public support because they facilitate access or speed service delivery.

Suggested Reading

Benson, G. C. S., et al. *Political Corruption in America.* Lexington, MA: D. C. Heath, 1978.

Gardiner, J. W., and D. J. Olson, eds. *Theft of the City: Readings on Corruption in Urban America.* Bloomington, IN: Indiana University Press, 1974.

Heidenheimer, Arnold J., Michael Johnston, and Victor T. Levine, eds. *Political Corruption: A Handbook.* Rutgers, NJ: Transaction Books, 1988.

Knapp Commission. *The Knapp Commission Report on Public Corruption.* New York: George Braziller, 1973.

Nfas, Tevfik, Albert C. Price, and Charles T. Weber. "A Policy-Oriented Theory of Corruption." *American Political Science Review,* vol. 80, no. 1 (1986), pp. 107–119.

Cost-Benefit Analysis   A method of evaluating policies or programs by quantifying in monetary terms the costs and benefits of those programs. A program could be recommended only if it showed a positive net benefit rather than a net cost. This method assumes a scarcity of resources and attempts to employ a systematic technique to assist decision makers in directing limited resources in the most cost-effective manner. *See also* EXTERNALITY; IMPACT ANALYSIS; URBAN IMPACT ANALYSIS.

Significance. Cost-benefit analysis began in earnest at the federal level during the 1960s. Concern over the federal deficit and the size of the budget led to the development of postprogram analysis as well as preprogram projections of federal policies. Further attempts to rationalize the federal budget have come in the form of Program Planning Budgeting Systems (PPBS) and Zero-Based Budgeting (ZBB). Under President Ronald Reagan, further efforts to reduce federal spending in many areas brought about greater use of cost-benefit analysis at the federal level. Critics of this type of analysis have argued that the social benefits of many programs or policies do not translate very well into monetary terms. Others have argued that the decision-making process is political at its heart (with bargaining, compromising, and partisan or philosophical considerations involved) and therefore not a rational process at all. At the state and local levels of government, very little systematic cost-benefit analysis is conducted, because these levels of government have neither the money nor the trained personnel to perform such analysis. Many state and local governments conduct a more simple cost analysis in an attempt to provide some minimal assistance with decision making.

Suggested Reading
Busson, Terry, and Philip B. Coulter, eds. "Policy Evaluation for Local Government: A Symposium." *Policy Studies Journal,* vol. 12, no. 2 (1983), pp. 273–385.
Hatry, Harry, et al. *Program Analysis for State and Local Governments,* 2nd ed. Washington, DC: Urban Institute, 1987.
Schofield, J. A. *Cost-Benefit Analysis in Urban and Regional Planning.* Winchester, MA: Allen & Unwin, 1987.

Council-Manager Government   A form of municipal government that vests policymaking powers with the city council but gives day-to-day administrative duties to a city manager who is usually professionally trained and who is appointed by and serves at the pleasure of the council. This form of government grew out of early twentieth-century Progressive Era reforms, which sought to curtail the corruption of urban political machine politics and the strong mayor–council form of government, which gave the mayor major policymaking and administrative powers. *See also* CITY MANAGER; COMMISSION PLAN; MAYOR, STRONG; REFORM GOVERNMENT; URBAN POLITICAL MACHINE.

Significance   The council-manager form of government has become the most popular system, particularly with medium-sized cities (25,000–500,000 population). Large cities have tended to retain a strong mayor system, because their populations are more heterogeneous, the number of interest groups is much larger, and their politics are more conflict-ridden. The largest cities with a city manager are San Diego, Phoenix, San Antonio, and Dallas. In each of these cities, critics have called for a strong mayor form of government to provide political accountability. Smaller cities often cannot afford to hire a city manager and most often have a mayor-council form of government. According to a 1988 study by the International City Management

Association (ICMA), about 35 percent of responding U.S. cities with populations greater than 2,500 have a council-manager form of government. Much controversy remains over the ability of city managers to maintain a distance from the political influences of a municipality. Most city managers have successfully avoided local partisan politics but have become substantially politicized as they initiate much local policy (rather than simply executing it) and as they become *de facto* political and policy leaders in their communities.

Suggested Reading

Booth, David A., ed. *Council-Manager Government 1940–1964: An Annotated Bibliography.* Chicago: International City Management Association, 1965.
Childs, Richard S. *The First Fifty Years of the Council-Manager Plan of Municipal Government.* New York: National Municipal League, 1965.
Svara, James H. "Mayoral Leadership in Council-Manager Cities: Preconditions versus Preconceptions." *Journal of Politics,* vol. 49, no. 1 (1987), pp. 404–409.

Council of Governments (COG)   A voluntary regional association that conducts research and provides technical assistance to its member local governments. A council of governments' policymaking body normally includes the major elected or appointed officials of its participating local governments. COGs were intended to deal with long-term planning concerns of a shared, regional nature. They do not have formal or enforcement powers *per se,* but many have assisted in the development of regional public transportation authorities, air and water quality control, community development, and shared purchasing arrangements. Funding for these associations normally comes from membership dues. *See also* A-95 REVIEW; NATIONAL CAPITAL PLANNING COMMISSION; THREE-TIER REFORM.

Significance   The first COG was formed in 1954 in the Detroit metropolitan region and was called the Supervisors Inter-County Committee (superseded in 1968 by the Southeast Michigan Council of Governments). Other COGs soon formed in the regions of San Francisco, Seattle, Los Angeles, Philadelphia, and New York City. Most large metropolitan areas now have COGs because federal grants since the mid-1960s have required regional planning and review before a city would receive funding. By 1970 there were more than 300 COGs in the United States, and all the nation's Metropolitan Statistical Areas (MSAs) have regional councils of some kind. In the 1980s, COGs began to adopt more entrepreneurial roles by becoming providers of services for local governments and acting as contractors for their members. Since COGs are voluntary associations, their effectiveness in fostering regional cooperation has been questioned.

Suggested Reading

Harmon, B. Douglas. "Council of Governments: Trends and Issues." *Urban Data Service*, vol. 1, no. 8. Washington, DC: International City Management Association, August 1969.

Marando, Vincent L. "Metropolitan Research and Councils of Governments." *Midwest Review of Public Administration* (February 1971), pp. 3–15.

Mogulof, Melvin B. "Metropolitan Councils of Government and the Federal Government." *Urban Affairs Quarterly*, vol. 7, no. 4 (1972), pp. 489–507.

Wikstrom, Nelson. *Councils of Governments: A Study of Political Incrementalism.* Chicago: Nelson-Hall, 1985.

Counterurbanism   The deconcentration of urban areas and especially central cities by the outward movement of people and jobs. Parallel to the absolute decline of population of most central cities, counterurbanism implies a revival of small towns and metropolitan areas with populations less than 500,000. The countertrend is also called *demetropolitanization.* It is based on both push and pull forces: pushing people out of densely populated cities and pulling them toward a rural renaissance. *See also* CENSUS OF POPULATION; GROWTH MANAGEMENT; OPTIMUM CITY; DENSITY, URBAN; POSTINDUSTRIAL CITY; SUBURBANIZATION.

Significance   American demographers and geographers noticed the counterurban trend in examining the 1970 census. Many of the larger and older central cities and Standard Metropolitan Statistical Areas (SMSAs) began losing population. The trend began with the Pittsburgh SMSA, according to the 1960 figures. As of the 1980 census, about 75 percent of the U.S. population lived in urban areas. The figure did not climb above that level. This reversed a long-term demographic trend line of growth in the big and medium-sized cities. A host of explanations has been offered, including the high costs of living in major cities and the lower costs associated with lesser scale. The diffusion of technology throughout the nation was another factor; transportation and communication were no longer justifications for increasing scale. As the nation's population grows older and more people retire, an increasingly important factor is the desire of people to get away from crime and other urban stress; these people tend to move to small towns or the smaller-scale metropolitan areas in the sunbelt. The countertrend away from major cities has been noted also in other advanced industrial nations. The 1990 census will reveal whether this countertrend has been sustained.

Suggested Reading
Berry, Brian J. L. "Urbanism and Counterurbanism in the United States." *Annals of the Academy of Political and Social Science*, vol. 451 (1980), pp. 13–20.
Berry, Brian J. L., ed. *Urbanism and Counterurbanism*. Beverly Hills: Sage, 1976.

County Administrator   The chief administrative officer of a county government. A county administrator can be elected (called a county executive) or appointed (called a county manager). Of the more than 3,000 counties in the United States, only about 150 have elected executives, including all 75 Arkansas counties, where the state legislature mandated "county judges" be given the role of executive. Most county governments have neither an executive nor a manager but still operate under a commission form in which the legislative body also serves as the administrative body. *See also* COMMISSION PLAN; COUNCIL-MANAGER GOVERNMENT; METROPOLITAN COUNTY; NATIONAL ASSOCIATION OF COUNTIES.

Significance   The county manager and county executive forms of government place considerable administrative powers within one office. Some county managers have more budgetary and appointive powers than others and thus can be considered "strong" or "weak" managers with respect to their formal powers. Hence, these county forms of government are analogous to the municipal forms of strong and weak mayor, council-manager, and commission plan. Strong county administrator governments remain in the minority, in part because of political resistance to change in many counties. Some states have constitutional prohibitions against an elected county executive.

Suggested Reading
National Association of Counties. *The County Year Book 1977*. Washington, DC: NACo and International City Management Association, 1978.

Crime   The commission of an act specifically prohibited and punishable by law, or failure to perform an act specifically required by law. Adults convicted of crimes can be punished by incarceration or other penalties, whereas a juvenile criminal can be brought under the jurisdiction of a juvenile court and either adjudicated as a delinquent or sent to an adult jurisdiction. Although law enforcement in the United States is decentralized among 16,000 city, county, and state agencies, information about crime is collected by the Federal Bureau of Investigation's (FBI) Uniform Crime Reports (UCR). These crime data are reported on a voluntary basis. Crimes considered "serious" are classified into eight categories: murder, forcible rape, robbery, aggravated assault, arson, burglary, larceny-theft, and motor vehicle theft. *See also* JUVENILE COURT; LAW ENFORCEMENT ASSISTANCE ADMINISTRATION; POLICE, PUBLIC; QUALITY OF LIFE.

Significance   Crime is one of the most thoroughly studied problems in the United States. Statistics on crime are used to determine public policy and law enforcement needs. Since the level of crime is a major factor in determining a city's "livability" for many people, judgments about the quality of life in individual cities and inevitable comparisons among cities are made in reference to the amount of crime reported by the UCR. In 1987, Detroit had the highest per capita murder rate in the nation; Miami, Florida, the highest robbery rate; Newark, New Jersey, the most vehicle thefts; and Gary, Indiana, the most arson. However, Fort Worth, Texas, had the most overall serious crime, followed by Tampa, Florida; Portland, Oregon; and Hartford, Connecticut. Recent trends in the study of crime have dealt with crime as it varies by geographic location and social organization or environment. The school of "critical criminology" views crime as an integral part of an inequitable legal system, with less-than-equal attention given to the pursuit of white-collar crime and the criminal behavior of the middle and upper classes. The "oral-ethnographic" tradition studies crime through interview techniques and is considered humanistic but perhaps policy-irrelevant. "Ecological analysis" investigates the social, economic, and physical environments of crime; drug culture studies examine the correlation between drugs and crime.

Suggested Reading

Heinz, Harvey, Herbert Jacob, and Robert L. Lineberry, eds. *Crime in City Politics*. New York: Longman, 1983.

Jackson, Pamela Irving. *Minority Group Threat, Crime and Policing: Social Contest and Social Control*. New York: Praeger, 1989.

Rush, George E. *The Dictionary of Criminal Justice*, 2nd ed. Guilford, CT: Dushkin Publishing, 1986.

Siegel, Larry J. *Criminology*, 3rd ed. St. Paul, MN: West Publishing, 1989.

Steel, Brent S., and Mary Ann E. Steger. "Crime: Due Process Liberalism versus Law-and-Order Conservatism." In Raymond Tatlovich and Byron W. Daynes, eds., *Social Regulatory Policy: Moral Controversies in American Politics*. Boulder, CO: Westview Press, 1988. Chap. 3, pp. 74–110.

D

Daily Urban System (DUS)   The tributary commuting area of an urban center. The daily urban system constitutes the actual commuting zone as opposed to any set collection of political jurisdictions. Commuting is defined as the transportation of people in their roles as employee and employer. The metropolitan or labor shed of a major city often crosses state and provincial boundaries. For example, Detroit's employee/employer hinterland radiates about 90 miles from the central business district (CBD) to cover parts of southeast Michigan, south-central Ontario, and northwest Ohio. New York City's DUS consists of southeast New York State, southern Connecticut, eastern Pennsylvania, and northern New Jersey. DUS is the largest-scale definition of an urban area. It is measured in terms of regular transportation flow and is employed in highway-use studies, transportation and land-use analysis, and marketing strategy. Smaller-scale transportation areas relate to magnet areas for shopping trips, recreation, and education. *See also* CONURBATION; EXURBIA; MASS TRANSIT; POPULATION, DAYTIME AND NIGHTTIME; TRAFFIC ANALYSIS; URBAN.

Significance   Great damage results from analyzing a metropolitan area by focusing on formal city and county boundaries to the exclusion of the Daily Urban System. Because of the interstate highway system, including ring roads, and widespread availability of private automobiles, urban cores serve as employment magnets for a vast area. In Detroit's case, this is approximately 25,000 square miles. Because the labor exchange system does not correspond to political jurisdictions, issues of city income taxes, proper census counts of people by time of day, and residency requirements become major political issues.

Suggested Reading
Doxiadis, Constantinos A. *A Concept for Future Development.* Vol. 3 of *Emergence and Growth of an Urban Region: The Developing Urban Detroit Area.* Detroit: Wayne State University Press, 1970.

***De Facto* Segregation**   A separation of racial groups in housing or education that is considered to have occurred as an accident or as a matter of personal preference. *De facto* segregation of neighborhood schools is the direct product of racially segregated neighborhoods but differs from *de jure* segregation in that no formal state or local action sanctioned such segregation. This commonly has been associated with segregation in the northern states. Busing has been used in some school districts to desegregate schools considered racially separate because of *de facto* segregation. *See also* BUSING; COLEMAN REPORT; *DE JURE* SEGREGATION; GHETTO; YONKERS-STYLE POLITICS.

Significance   *De facto* segregation, or segregated living patterns, in the United States has been caused by a number of factors: personal preference of home buyers, racial steering, the cost of homes, and zoning ordinances, among others. However, it has produced segregated neighborhoods and schools, considered a social negative by public-policy analysts. At the same time, courts have ruled that *de facto* segregation is not necessarily prohibited by the Constitution. Courts have ruled that busing across district lines is not required to achieve metropolitan school desegregation, and in school districts already made up of a large percentage of minority students, busing is seen generally as relatively ineffective.

***De Jure* Segregation**   A separation of racial groups sanctioned by law. *De jure* segregation is most often associated with the 17 southern and border states of the United States, in which racially separate facilities—schools, restaurants, housing, transportation, and other facilities—were required by state or local law. Such segregation in public schools was ruled unconstitutional in *Brown v. Board of Education of Topeka,* 347 U.S. 483 (1954). In 1955, in a continuation of the same case, the Court ordered all affected school districts to desegregate with "all deliberate speed," 349 U.S. 294 (1955). Later, segregation in privately owned places of public accommodation, such as hotels, motels, and restaurants, was prohibited by the 1964 Civil Rights Act and upheld by two companion cases heard in 1964 by the U.S. Supreme Court: *Heart of Atlanta Motel v. U.S.* (379 U.S. 241) and *Katzenbach v. McClung* (379 U.S. 294). *See also* DE FACTO SEGREGATION.

Significance   *De jure* segregation had been a way of life in southern states for many years before the 1954 *Brown* decision. The federal government had approved of such segregation with the Supreme Court's *Plessy v. Ferguson* case in 1896 (163 U.S. 537) allowing for separate facilities as long as they were considered equal. The difference between *de jure* and *de facto* segregation is an important legal distinction; action legally can be taken to eliminate the former but not necessarily the latter. Though normally associated with the South, a federal court more recently ruled that a northern school district (Ferndale, Michigan) that deliberately isolated a black neighborhood school was also considered a *de jure* segregated district and was thus required to desegregate.

Debt, Municipal   The total amount of money owed by a local government. As municipalities borrow money for operating expenses or capital projects, short- and long-term debt mounts. Although most states and cities operate under statutory or constitutional requirements to produce balanced budgets each year, long-term borrowing for capital projects usually is not counted against a city's annual budget figures. However, during the late 1970s and early 1980s, in a period known as the "taxpayers' revolt," many states and cities became subject to further limits on taxing and borrowing activities. *See also* AUTHORITY, PUBLIC; DEBT LIMIT, LOCAL; INCOME SOURCES, URBAN; REVENUE IMPROVEMENT BOND; TAXPAYERS' REVOLT.

Significance   Municipalities face many more restrictions on taxing, spending, and borrowing to fund debt than does the federal government. Municipal debt is limited by state constitution, or statute and/or municipal charter. Technically, each city in the United States must pass a balanced budget each fiscal year. However, cities must also build large projects for which capital must be borrowed. Cities have paid for these projects in several different ways: (1) on a pay-as-you-go basis; (2) with state and federal funding; (3) with general obligation bonds, backed by the full faith and credit of the municipality; and (4) with revenue bonds, repaid by the revenues generated from the project built. During the 1970s and 1980s, many cities could not afford to pay cash for even moderately sized projects and could no longer rely on state and federal financial assistance. State and local law limited the overall debt for general-obligation bonds, and many municipalities reached their limits. In addition, general-obligation borrowing, which requires approval from voters and can mean tax increases, was used sparingly in many cities. This left borrowing largely to revenue bonds, especially as municipalities established separate public authorities to incur the indebtedness. By the late 1980s, almost half of all municipal borrowing used revenue bonds.

Suggested Reading

Advisory Comission on Intergovernmental Relations. *Understanding the Market for State and Local Debt.* Washington, DC: Government Printing Office, 1976.

Aronson, J. Richard, and John L. Hilley. *Financing State and Local Governments,* 4th ed. Washington, DC: Brookings Institution, 1986.

Aronson, J. Richard, and Eli Schwartz. "Determining Debt's Danger Signals." *Management Information Service Reports,* vol. 8, no. 12. Washington, DC: International City Management Association, 1976.

Farnham, Paul G. "Impact of State Regulatory Activity on the Use of Local Government Debt." *Journal of Urban Affairs,* vol. 10, no. 1 (1988), pp. 63–76.

Debt Limit, Local   A statutory or constitutional restriction on the borrowing capabilities of a substate government. Greater budgetary controls at the state and local levels have established more stringent spending and debt limits on those governments compared to the federal government. The limits imposed on borrowing may be for a specified amount of money or derived by a formula that is usually based on assessed property valuation. *See also* BOND AND RATING SERVICES; FISCAL CRISIS; MORAL-OBLIGATION BOND; REVENUE IMPROVEMENT BOND; SPECIAL DISTRICT; TAX ANTICIPATION NOTE; USER FEE.

Significance   Many cities experienced a fiscal squeeze beginning in the 1970s, in which revenues declined, demand for services increased, and budgetary restrictions virtually handcuffed decision makers. State or local debt limits were among constraints placed on cities. As a consequence, many cities began to lay off employees and reduce services. Cities looked for revenue and payment alternatives such as user fees, privatization of some services, and use of revenue and moral-obligation bonds as over and against general-obligation bonds. Since the 1970s, larger, older, industrialized cities have experienced the biggest fiscal squeeze as demand for services increased dramatically, public employee payrolls increased, and the tax base dwindled. These cities tend to be in the vanguard of those that create special districts and redevelopment authorities, have instituted user fees, and use revenue bonds to circumvent local debt limits.

Decentralization   Dispersal of administrative services and political power to limited-scale districts within a city. Decentralization of authority most often is associated with public school operations, although it also is used frequently to diversify delivery of city hall services. It also refers to deconcentrating police offices below the precinct to the storefront level. Dispersal of people out of the metropolitan area is often called *counterurbanism.* Dispersal of people at lowered density levels but within the metropolitan area is called *multinucleation.* Dispersal of industry out of urban areas is called *disinvestment. See also* BOROUGH; COMMUNITY; MAXIMUM FEASIBLE PARTICIPATION; NEIGHBORHOOD; OPTIMUM CITY; URBAN VILLAGE.

Significance   Decentralization of administrative and political power has an ancient history, reverting back to the philosophic issue of the optimum scale for a polity. London is divided into more than 30 boroughs and New York City into 5 boroughs for some purposes. In an attempt to implement small-scale planning, New York City is divided into more than 60 planning districts. Phoenix is divided into 6 urban villages in order to break up the length of commuting and to give its residents a sense of community. Most attention to decentralization during the twentieth century stems from the urban riots of the 1960s and the New Left ideological reaction to the city as an impersonal place that fosters alienation and anomie because the average resident believes that he or she cannot participate meaningfully and does not feel effective or competent. New York City's local school boards, along with Detroit's and Chicago's regional school board reform, reflect a desire to broaden meaningful participation. In many instances, decentralization reforms have been superficial, with decisions about budget and personnel centrally retained. Militants who called for black power through community control in the 1960s were less likely to use that rhetoric when big-city black mayors and black-controlled councils won power. Most of the major writing on urban decentralization emanates from the 1960s and 1970s.

Suggested Reading

Fantini, Mario, and Marilyn Gittell. *Decentralization: Achieving Reform.* New York: Praeger, 1973. (Especially primary and secondary public school dispersion.)

Frederickson, George, ed. *Neighborhood Control in the 1970s: Politics, Administration, and Citizen Participation.* New York: Chandler Publishing, 1973.

Hambleton, Robin. *Policy Planning and Local Government.* Montclair, NJ: Allanhold, Osmun, 1978. Chap. 3, "Area Approaches."

Nordlinger, Eric A. *Decentralizing the City: A Study of Boston's Little City Halls.* Cambridge, MA: MIT Press, 1972. (Case study.)

Dedication   The selling, granting, donating, or devoting of all or selected property rights to privately held real property to a government for public use. Acceptance of the rights by some level of government is by formal resolution, by the spending of public monies on upkeep, or through use over time. Dedication is a voluntary act; condemnation and the use of eminent domain are the ways land is ceded by a private holder involuntarily. *See also* ABANDONMENT; EMINENT DOMAIN; GIFT TO GOVERNMENT; LAND CONSERVANCY; PRIVATE STREET.

Significance   More private land passes into public ownership through dedication than by eminent domain. The media rarely report a voluntary dedication. They make major news out of involuntary condemnation, because cooperation is less interesting than conflict. Dedication of land is usually an act in perpetuity. The state becomes responsible thereafter for maintenance. When land is dedicated to the public, liability also is shifted. Hence cities reduce exposure to lawsuits by allowing private roads. Because dedication adds costs each year to the budget, some municipalities have encouraged developers of subdivisions and condominiums to build roads to community specification but not to dedicate them. These roads are kept private, imposing maintenance costs on homeowner associations, while ensuring access to the general public. Major examples of dedications are for right-of-ways for streets, highways, alleys, parks, cemeteries, and schools. Developers are commonly asked to dedicate land for sidewalks, roads, and utility easements as a condition of acceptance at site plan review. One alternative to dedication of land for parks is creation of a nature conservancy. A dedication does not mean that all property rights are ceded to a government agency. The dedication of the right to build, for example, is becoming a common way to achieve a government's open space objectives.

Definition, Operational   A working explanation of a term or concept used in actual field measurement. Operational definitions translate stipulated definitions from the law or a general social theory into observable information. Working definitions often simplify the more elegant original definition in order to obtain available material that is cost-efficient. If general definitions are not easily translated into working definitions, substitute information such as an index or an indictor is employed. A black ghetto, for example, is defined operationally as any census tract with more than 50 percent blacks in a central city. The homeless may be defined as any person who does not give a permanent address to a drug center. Major decision makers in the community are reduced to 20 people whom a panel of experts (often unexplained) lists as major actors in city politics. *See also* CASE STUDY; DEFINITIONS, SOURCES OF.

Significance   Urban political and social studies have had a long history of simplifying complex definitions into much less subtle operations in order to conduct empirical studies. The major intellectual problem in this early and critical stage of research is ensuring that the collected information closely resembles the original concept as defined in the literature. It is difficult and time-consuming to collect data that represent the concept. Replication is not the issue, as the capacity to retrace the steps of an earlier study may simply verify a *non sequitur*.

Case studies conducted in the same city after a major lapse of time do not constitute a replication study; both actors and underlying political issues may have changed. The three major Middletown studies are not replication studies but rather a *panel study* of the same city over time. Operational definitions often are selected because of available information in the public sector, not because of a close fit to the original concept. There are several protocols for converting abstract definitions into working definitions. These include (1) ensuring that the original concept and not another, larger idea is being captured, (2) measuring a concept so that it can be reproduced in other studies, (3) collecting information that resists charges of being unreliable, and (4) employing indices that are free from cultural bias or intervening variables. This last protocol is especially important in comparative research. Examples of terms in urban studies that have not been converted into operational definitions by well-conceived working definitions include: (a) *Political participation.* Most of the empirical studies take a restrictive meaning, omitting violent actions and less conventional forms such as coproduction. (b) *Neighborhood.* Some studies substitute census tract information, assuming tract boundaries are the same or nearly the same as those of a neighborhood. (c) *Ethos.* The concept was never operationalized by its proponents to show a link between the original concept and collected data, and it has been largely dropped from urban studies. (d) *Reform government.* Many studies select three possible reforms to represent the type, assuming without proof that these are three litmus tests.

Suggested Reading

Bryant, Stephen. "The Dimensions of Reformism in Urban Policy Analysis." *Urban Affairs Quarterly,* vol. 12, no. 1 (1976), pp. 117–124.

Golembiewski, Robert T., William A. Welsh, and William J. Crotty. *A Methodological Primer for Political Scientists.* Chicago: Rand McNally, 1969. Chap. 6.

Massey, Douglas S., and Nancy A. Denton. "The Discussions of Residential Segregation." *Social Forces,* vol. 67, no. 2 (1988), pp. 281–315. (Proposed new five-part test replacing a single test.)

Rossi, Peter H. "Critical Methodological Issues in Research on Homeless Persons." *Research Methodologies Concerning Homeless Persons with Serious Mental Illness and/or Substance Abuse Disorders.* Washington, DC: National Institute on Alcohol Abuse and Alcoholism of the Public Health Service, 1987. Pp. 39–51. HE 20.8302:H75/2.

Definitions, Sources of   The origins of terms and their meanings that appear in local ordinances, administrative rules, and political dialogue. Rather than borrowing from one source for definitions, politics and law tap a host of resources. (1) National and state constitutions have contributed such technical terms as *taking,* meaning a permanent or temporary public condemnation of property, or *petitioning for a redress of grievances,* more commonly known as lobbying. (2) National and state statutes contribute terms such as *emergency evacuation, National Register,* and *public utility.* These terms do not have currency in all states, as each is tempered by particular administrative history. (4) National- and state-level common law contribute terms such as *inverse condemnation* and *easement.* These are subject to further refinement by the courts in later cases. (5) The national Office of Management and Budget (OMB) and its state counterparts have coined such terms as *A-95 Review, Standard Metropolitan Statistical Area (SMSA),* and *Metropolitan Statistical Area (MSA).* (6) Professional associations and trade groups add vocabulary. Planners stipulate as to what constitutes a *master or comprehensive plan.* Accountants specify what satisfies *acceptable auditing standards.* Bond-rating services establish the meaning of an *AAA rating.* Appraisers define *highest and best use.* Building code associations declare the meaning of *certificates of need* and *acceptable plumbing standards.* (7) Individuals also contribute to the neologisms of city politics and law. American political commentator Kevin Phillips added *sunbelt,* Greek planner Constantinos A. Doxiadis added *ekistics* and *ecumenopolis,* French geographer Jean Gottman contributed *megalopolis,* and Patrick Geddes of the United Kingdom contributed *conurbation. See also* CORPORATION COUNSEL.

Significance   Sources of definitions employed in urban politics and law are important elements in understanding political discourse. There is a lack of clarity in many political-legal terms: *resident* and *corruption* have multiple meanings. A few terms in urban politics and law are *ipso facto* weighted with negative connotations, such as *outside influence, slum, blight,* and *Locally Unwanted Land Use (LULU).* What is meant by *family* in zoning is unknown until placed in context. Some terms are based on a series of distinctions, such as *park*: It may be a recreation facility, an open space, a mobile home community, an industrial or research location, or a site for several schools. *Franchise* refers to either electoral power or the right to perform a service or use a name as authorized by the state or a business. Terms created by analogy are dangerous when taken literally, such as *triage,* borrowed from emergency medicine; *invasion, succession,* and *community,* all borrowed from ecology; and *academic bankruptcy,* an analogue of the more common financial bankruptcy. *Impact statements* may refer to judicial impact statements by the legislature, urban impact analysis once conducted by the national administration, or environmental impact statements (EIS) required by the Council on Environmental Quality (CEQ). Some commonly employed urban terms have no clear referent, such as *bedroom community* and *highway*. It is the responsibility of corporation councils to draft ordinances that will be understood by both lay community and courts. Consultants such as physical planners and accountants are responsible for the proper use of their specialized terms in ordinances and manuals. Journalists, sociologists, and political scientists need to employ carefully terms such as *gridlock, neighborhood, community*, and *reform government* in order to clarify political communication.

Deinstitutionalization   The process of releasing delinquent and dependent populations from large-scale institutions and returning them to the community at large. Deinstitutionalization, also known as mainstreaming, involves such groups as the mentally retarded, psychiatric patients, juvenile delinquents, and the elderly. In the twentieth century the movement began with the passage of the 1935 Social Security Act, which encouraged the elderly to live on their own. It increased in the 1950s with limited reductions in large-scale mental hospital facilities. It picked up momentum with the return of many developmentally disabled to communities in the 1960s. In an attempt to cut down on recidivism, juvenile offenders were taken out of the conventional criminal justice process and shifted into halfway houses. Some contend that people sent to group homes and halfway houses were not deinstitutionalized but only shifted from large to small institutions, an *institution* being defined as six or more supervised dependent people housed together. Others say the deinstitutionalized are those who are free of heretofore in-building treatment. The shift to outpatient status is the key element in the definitional disagreement. Reasons for deinstitutionalization range from humanitarian concern for those cooped up and mistreated, all the way to financial concerns that treatment on the outside is less or no more expensive. A major element in deinstitutionalization of mentally ill patients has been psychotropic drugs that allow for better behavior control. The self-help movement of the 1970s and civil libertarian concerns about unnecessary commitments were also contributing factors. President John Kennedy's plea for more attention to the mentally ill and passage in 1963 of the Community Mental Health Centers Act (42 U.S.C. 2681) sped up deinstitutionalization. Many of these dependent people returned to society were not well cared for in the communities, and they have clustered in large numbers in sections of the central city as homeless, living in transient quarters, wards of underfunded eleemosynary organizations. The question of whether or not the deinstitutionalized have had their safety nets preserved and their freedoms guarded is a major public-policy topic. *See also* GROUP HOME; HALFWAY HOUSE; HOMELESS; LOCALLY UNWANTED LAND USE; PRIVATIZATION; SAFETY NET.

Significance   Deinstitutionalization has been the dominant trend line in dealing with dependent populations in the United States in the 1980s and 1990s. Advocates call it humane and enlightened. Critics claim the state has abdicated responsibility for those needing support services. They note the idea of an *asylum* is that of a preserve or safe house for those in need, not a place set apart for the benefit of the community. Neither the finances to make the system operate at optimal levels nor the goodwill from the community have materialized. Opposition to treatment centers and placement of group homes restricts the program's effectiveness. Some of the homeless in large cities who are deinstitutionalized cannot cope with mainstream society. Critics say they should be returned to institutions. It is not clear whether those who live in shelters, foster care homes, and nursing homes have truly been deinstitutionalized or only reinstitutionalized in smaller units for the benefit of profit-making private enterprises.

Suggested Reading
Dear, Michael. "Psychiatric Patients and the Inner City." *Annals of the Association of American Geographers,* vol. 67, no. 4 (1977), pp. 588–594. (Ontario case study.)
Dear, Michael, and Jennifer Welch. *Landscapes of Despair: From Deinstitutionalization to Homelessness.* Princeton: Princeton University Press, 1987.
Fabricant, Michael. *Deinstitutionalizing Delinquent Youth.* Cambridge, MA: Schenkman Publishing, 1980. (Camouflaged case study of a Massachusetts city's implementation.)
Gronfein, William. "Psychotropic Drugs and the Origins of Deinstitutionalization." *Social Problems,* vol. 32, no. 5 (1985), pp. 437–454.
Lerman, Paul. *Deinstitutionalization and the Welfare State.* New Brunswick, NJ: Rutgers University Press, 1982.
Smith, Christopher J. *Public Problems: The Management of Urban Distress.* New York: Guilford Press, 1988. Chap. 5, "Deinstitutionalization of the Mentally Ill."

Demonstration Cities and Metropolitan Development Act (42 U.S.C. 3301)   A statute promoted by President Lyndon Johnson as a comprehensive, concentrated effort to improve the quality of urban life in communities. This legislation is popularly known as the Model Cities Act. The program provided funding and technical assistance to cities of all sizes to carry out a wide variety of programs. Originally, City Demonstration Agencies were created in 66 cities to administer the act's programs. Among those programs were slum clearance, the reduction of welfare dependence by city residents, reduction of crime, improvement of job opportunities, housing improvements and repairs, and upgrading of educational facilities. The act also emphasized that intergovernmental coordination was required to carry out these programs. The Model Cities program was replaced in 1974 by the Housing and Community Development Act and its Community Development Block Grant (CDBG) system. *See also* COMMUNITY ACTION PROGRAM; ECONOMIC OPPORTUNITY ACT OF 1964; NATIONAL URBAN POLICY.

Significance   The plight of U.S. cities became a major agenda item for the Johnson administration as it started its first full term of office. In 1965, Johnson created a new cabinet department called Housing and Urban Development (HUD). The next year Congress passed the Model Cities Act. Unlike the relatively independent Community Action Agencies created by the Economic Opportunity Act of 1964, the Demonstration Cities Agencies were an integral part of city administrations. Their programs were controlled by the city's political leadership.

Suggested Reading
Haar, Charles M. *Between the Idea and the Reality: A Study in the Origin, Fate, and Legacy of the Model Cities Program.* Boston: Little, Brown, 1975.
Kaplan, Marshall. *The Model Cities Program.* New York: Praeger, 1970.
U.S. Department of Housing and Urban Development, Office of Community Development Evaluation Division. *The Model Cities Program.* Washington, DC: Government Printing Office, July 1973.
Waldhorn, Steven Arthur, and Judith Lynch Waldhorn. "Model Cities: Liberal Myths and Federal Interventionist Programs." *Urban Law Annual* (1972), pp. 45–55.

Density, Urban   The degree of concentration of people per unit of land in local political units and built-up areas, expressed as people per acre, people per square mile, or people per square kilometer. U.S. density figures conventionally describe each unit's nighttime or residential population. On a *micro* scale, residential density rates often are limited by subdivision restrictions, along with land-use plans and zoning ordinances, to establish desirable levels of residences per acre. High-density settlements sometimes are defined as more than 50 persons or 15 dwelling units per net residential acre. Low-density settlements are defined as 24 persons or 6 dwelling units per acre. Business-district density levels are expressed in terms of setback requirements and height limits, thus encouraging or discouraging high-rise office buildings. Intermediate density levels often are created to encourage degrees of apartment/condominium/cooperative building concentration. Very low residential density levels economically discourage or prohibit the building of such infrastructure as water and sewer lines. Only low-density construction allows on-site septic tank construction. On a *macro* scale, density rates computed from decennial census counts of population and housing reflect (1) shifts of population from rural to urban areas (1790–1970), (2) shifts from central cities to suburbs (1950–1980+), and (3) lowered densities in major snowbelt cities and higher densities in major sunbelt cities (1970–1980). Cities experiencing rapid increases in absolute numbers and density levels are ripe for antigrowth or controlled-growth movements. See Table 4, 1980 Population Density and Rate of Change. *See also* CENTRAL BUSINESS DISTRICT; COUNTERURBANISM; GROWTH MANAGEMENT; OPTIMUM CITY; POPULATION, DAYTIME AND NIGHTTIME; ZONING, EXCLUSIONARY.

Table 4   1980 Population Density and Rate of Change (1970–1980) for the Ten Most Populated U.S. Central Cities (CCs) and Their SMSAs

RANK	CENTRAL CITY	CC DENSITY/ SQUARE MILE	POP. CHANGE	SMSA DENSITY/ SQUARE MILE	POP. CHANGE
1	New York City	23,416	−10.4	6,599	−8.6
2	Chicago	13,180	−10.8	1,908	1.8
3	Los Angeles	6,463	5.5	1,837	6.2
4	Philadelphia	12,413	−13.4	1,336	−2.2
5	Houston	2,869	29.3	430	45.3
6	Detroit	8,848	−20.5	1,105	−1.8
7	Dallas	2,250	7.1	357	25.1
8	San Diego	2,736	−25.5	442	37.1
9	Phoenix	2,437	35.2	165	55.4
10	Baltimore	9,835	−13.0	968	5.0
	318 SMSAs Average	3,001	.1	299	10.2

Source: U.S. Bureau of the Census, *Census of Population,* 1983, Part I, Chap. A, Vol. 1, Table 30, 1980.

Significance   Low-density urban residential zoning has been called exclusionary. Such practices have been the subject of extensive litigation, especially in *Southern Burlington County NAACP v. Township of Mt. Laurel,* I and II. Downsizing is planned reduction in density building levels. Building height restrictions designed to lower the density of San Francisco's central business district have been a major issue among land planners. The question of what constitutes an ideal or optimum urban density is discussed extensively in planning literature. Proper density levels calculated for land, exclusive of roadways, parks, parking lots, and water surfaces, range from Le Corbusier's 12,500 to Frank Lloyd Wright's 2,500+ people per buildable square mile. On the macro level, among the ten most populated central cities, snowbelt density levels went down between 1970 and 1980. For sunbelt cities in the top ten, density levels went up; thus there is a convergence among major central cites in overall density levels toward the overall 318 SMSA average of about 3,000 per gross square mile. The 1980 population density for the entire United States was 64 people per gross square mile. For the same period, state density per gross square mile varied from a high of more than 986 people for New Jersey to a low of 0.7 for Alaska.

Suggested Reading
Sussna, Stephen. "Residential Densities: A Patchwork Placebo." *Fordham Urban Law Journal*, vol. 1, no. 2 (1972), pp. 127–147.

Department of Housing and Urban Development (HUD)   A cabinet-level department of the federal government created in 1965. HUD was established by the Department of Housing and Urban Development Act (42 U.S.C. 3531). It administers a wide-ranging series of programs, including Community Development Block Grants, and a myriad of housing, rent subsidy, and home loan programs. HUD also has administered public housing, urban renewal, water and sewerage funding, Model Cities, and urban planning programs. The Public Housing Administration, the Housing and Home Finance Agency, the Federal Housing Administration (FHA), and the Government National Mortgage Association (GNMA) all had their operations consolidated under HUD in 1965. *See also* COMMUNITY DEVELOPMENT BLOCK GRANT; FEDERAL HOUSING ADMINISTRATION; GOVERNMENT NATIONAL MORTGAGE ASSOCIATION; HOUSING, PUBLIC.

Significance   Cabinet-level status for the Department of Housing and Urban Development was encouraged by both the Kennedy and Johnson administrations in the 1960s. The federal government's commitment to growing minority populations in cities was evidenced when Lyndon Johnson appointed Robert Weaver, a black former administrator of the Housing and Home Finance Agency, as HUD's first secretary. Other secretaries have included George Romney, Carla Hills, Patricia Harris, Moon Landrieu, Samuel Pierce, and Jack Kemp. HUD's budget authority declined under the Reagan administration, falling from $17.9 billion in fiscal year (FY) 1984 to $14.6 billion in FY 1987. A substantial portion of the total budget authority for HUD is spent through the Community Development Block Grant programs, with slightly more than $3 billion spent in each of the fiscal years between 1984 and 1987. In 1989, two scandals erupted over HUD programs and practices during Samuel Pierce's administration. One involved preferences given to certain contractors and developers for HUD project funding; the other arose over misuse of public-housing escrow accounts.

Suggested Reading

Fulton, William. "HUD at 20 Faces a Midlife Crisis," *Planning,* vol. 51, no. 11 (1985), pp. 12–18.

Journal Forum: "Looking Back at HUD." *Journal of the American Planning Association,* vol. 51, no. 4 (1985), pp. 461–483.

U.S. Government Manual, 1988–89. Washington, DC: Government Printing Office, 1989.

Weaver, Robert C. *Dilemmas of Urban America.* Cambridge, MA: Harvard University Press, 1965. (The Harvard University Godkin lectures of 1965.)

Depressed Area   A designation used by the federal government to determine the eligibility of an area for targeted grants, especially for economic development. A formula of distress using data on unemployment, housing deterioration, declining tax base, abandonment, and other factors determines a depressed area's eligibility for assistance. A depressed area is also known as an economically distressed area or a blighted area. The 1961 Depressed Areas Act is codified in 42 U.S.C. 250 et seq. Economic development programs such as Urban Development Action Grants (UDAGs) and Community Development Block Grants (CDBGs) have used eligibility formulas of economic distress to target funding to the neediest areas. *See also* COMMUNITY DEVELOPMENT BLOCK GRANT; SLUM; TAX ABATEMENT; TAX INCREMENT FINANCING; URBAN DEVELOPMENT ACTION GRANT.

Significance   The identification of Depressed Areas has been central to targeting federal funding. Since federal funding has been reduced or eliminated for many economic development programs, state and local governments often have applied similar formulas for determining the fund allocation. State-sponsored urban enterprise zones in New Jersey (N.J. Stat. Ann. 52: 27 H-60 et seq.) and Virginia (Va. Code 1950 §59.1-270 et seq.), for example, usually are designated on the basis of the unemployment rate and a declining tax base within the designated district. Other state economic development supports, such as tax abatements or tax increment financing, similarly require a finding of need and economic distress in most states. A depressed area is not to be confused with a *disaster area,* a designation of the Federal Emergency Management Agency after a calamity such as a flood, tornado, or oil spill.

Desegregation   The active removal of laws and policies that relegate races to certain areas, separate institutions, or unequal roles in society. Desegregation of public schools was required by the two U.S. Supreme Court decisions of *Brown v. Board of Education.* Desegregation can be contrasted with the more abstract concept of *integration,* connoting interracial harmony, acceptance, and cohesion, which cannot be mandated legislatively. In the United States, desegregation has been achieved; all laws requiring separation of the races have been abolished. *See also* APARTHEID; BLACK POWER; *BROWN V. BOARD OF EDUCATION* ; INTEGRATION, RACIAL; MELTING POT.

Significance   Desegregation has occurred with Supreme Court decisions and statutes that prohibit racial discrimination in employment, housing, transportation, and virtually all aspects of public life. However, the more personal and social practice of integration has remained elusive. Immigration has brought many races, cultures, and ethnic groups to the United States. Many groups have attempted to assimilate themselves into mainstream society, but the concept of the United States as a melting pot has lost favor with those seeking to maintain racial and ethnic identity.

Suggested Reading
Darden, Joe T., et al. *Detroit: Race and Uneven Development*. Philadelphia: Temple University Press, 1987.
Humphrey, Hubert H., ed. *School Desegregation: Documents and Commentaries*. New York: Thomas Y. Crowell, 1964.
Taylor, D. Garth. *Public Opinion and Collective Action: The Boston School Desegregation Case*. Chicago: University of Chicago Press, 1986.
Walters, Raymond. *The Burden of Brown: Thirty Years of School Desegregation*. Knoxville: University of Tennessee Press, 1984.

Detachment   Area legally removed from an incorporated municipality. Detachments often are triggered by a petition of area residents who are dissatisfied by services and tax rates. Detachments also result from a decision not to develop a parcel of land for a subdivision or shopping center. The jurisdictional status of land falls into several classifications. *Unincorporated* places have no formal government other than belonging in an undifferentiated fashion to a township or county. Once residents of an area have petitioned for *incorporation* as a village, town, or city, they have the right to *disincorporate*, revert to an unincorporated status. This usually transpires in quite small jurisdictions. Unincorporated places may also be *annexed* by an adjacent village, town, or city. The land passes into the already incorporated jurisdiction and is treated equally with the earlier existing unit. The term for the joining of equal units of government, such as two cities forming one, is properly a *merger*. When a city and county, two cities, or a city and a township join together, it is called *consolidation*. *See also* ANNEXATION; CONSOLIDATION; *MUNICIPAL YEAR BOOK* OF THE INTERNATIONAL CITY MANAGEMENT ASSOCIATION.

Significance   Detachment of land from a city is a sign that a parcel was not physically or politically integrated into the jurisdiction. Yearly total detachments amount to much less land than annexations. Major recent examples are all quite modest in population scale. In the 1970s, Little Rock, Arkansas, detached more than 30,000 people; North Las Vegas, Nevada, detached fewer than 10,000; and Topeka, Kansas, detached fewer than 8,000. In the 1980s, the only major example was Denver, which detached fewer than 3,000 people. The proper terms for boundary changes are not always adhered to by specialists, especially the distinction between merger and consolidation.

Suggested Reading
Miller, Joel C. "Municipal Annexations and Boundary Changes: 1980–1983." *1985 ICMA Year Book*, vol. 52, pp. 80–84.
Miller, Joel C., Frances Barnett, and Richard L. Forstall. "Annexations and Corporate Changes: 1970–1977." *1979 ICMA Year Book*, vol. 46, pp. 46–49.

Detroit Area Study (DAS)   An ongoing survey research project using a medium-sized sample of the 400+ respondents for the Detroit Tricounty Metropolitan Area from 1952 to the present. The DAS selects one or more annual projects conducted primarily by face-to-face interviews under faculty supervision with trained student fieldworkers. Housed in The University of Michigan Sociology Department in Ann Arbor—outside the study area—the project conducted 37 studies through 1989, including one replication project. It is the oldest ongoing area study using survey research in the United States. *See also* MIDDLETOWN; OAKLAND PROJECT; PERMANENT COMMUNITY SAMPLE; YANKEE CITY.

Significance   The Detroit Area Study has resulted in 18 books, 57 dissertations, and more than 300 chapters, articles, and monographs. Among the most specifically political research topics, along with the principal faculty participants, are the following: 1952, political behavior—Samuel J. Eldersveld; 1957, party leadership—Daniel Katz and Eldersveld; 1961, group influence on political behavior—Warren E. Miller and Donald E. Stokes; 1975, community life and politics— Thomas J. Anton and Bruce Bowen; 1979, metropolitan issues (including crime)—Colin Loftin; 1989, political participation—Steven J. Rosenstone. The study has not had the cumulative effect it might have had because the individual annual projects do not drive toward any single overview. Occasionally, survey results have been of value to political leaders, but the bulk of the sociological topics has not generally addressed pending items on community agendas. Study results are deposited for secondary analysis in The University of Michigan Inter-University Consortium for Political and Social Research.

Suggested Reading
Converse, Jean, and Erika Meyer. "The Detroit Area Study: A Record of Research Conducted by the Detroit Area Study 1951–1988." Ann Arbor: University of Michigan, 1988.
Duncan, Otis Dudley, Howard Schuman, and Beverly Duncan. *Social Change in a Metropolitan Community.* New York: Russell Sage, 1973.
Eldersveld, Samuel J. *Political Parties: A Behavioral Analysis.* Chicago: Rand McNally, 1964.
Schuman, Howard. "The Detroit Area Study after Twenty-five Years." *American Sociologist,* vol. 12, no. 1 (1977), pp. 130–137.

DIALOG™   A commercial, nationally available computerized bibliography bank with an extensive storage system that carries citations and abstracts of American urban government and politics, among many other topics. DIALOG, a public-access information storage and retrieval system, carries such sources as population bibliography, Educational Resources Information Center (ERIC), American Statistical Index (ASI), Public Affairs Information Service (PAIS), and Facts on File. *See also* EDUCATIONAL RESOURCES INFORMATION CENTER; LOGIN.

Significance   DIALOG is the most readily accessible general source for locating citations on many urban political topics among the many modern electronic networks available through computer technology. That information includes published monographs, journals, and national and state government documents, as well as unpublished reports delivered to conferences. Available through most libraries with telephone line interface to remote-location information banks, it is the information bank of choice for most first searches on urban political topics because of its wide coverage and modest cost. DIALOG outlets have printed thesauruses available that allow users to determine the appropriate controlled vocabulary to enter for the search. After selecting the data base and looking over the menu, a user selects the relevant topic. An example would be TRANSPORTATION, PUBLIC, and perhaps additional identifiers or cognate terms such as PHILADELPHIA and PITTSBURGH. Information stored on this entry is printed out in reverse chronological order, from most recent to past citations, allowing users to determine the cutoff of useful items.

Dillon's Rule   A principle of law promulgated by Iowa Judge John F. Dillon in *Municipal Corporations* (5th ed., 1911), which holds that municipal corporations are creatures of the state. Local governments can exercise only those powers the state expressly grants, those that are necessary or are fairly implied, or those essential to accomplish the local unit's purposes. When there is doubt concerning a municipality's capacity to act, it is to be resolved by courts in favor of the state and against the municipality. Those powers not explicitly delegated by the state constitution or statutes are reserved to the state because a city's relationship to a state is not analogous to the state's relationship to the national government. The federal analogy is false: Substate governments are not constitutionally grounded from direct power granted by the people. However, if the state grants home rule or local-option charters, then Dillon's Rule is less restrictive. The state legislature also may encourage local experimentation by explicitly overriding the rule as a basis for judicial construction. *See also* FEDERALISM; HOME RULE; POLICE POWER; STATE MANDATE.

Significance   Although at first applied strictly, Dillon's Rule is now not so much a judicial iron law as a general principle with qualifiers, foremost among them (1) whether the mode used by local government is reasonable and (2) how broad a scope of purpose the state gives local units. If the purpose is to promote the police power, then the local level has liberal leeway to experiment. In a wide-ranging, multistate review of Dillon's Rule as a canon of construction in Utah in 1980, that state's supreme court declared the rule inappropriate to strike down a local campaign-financing regulation in which the state granted general welfare power to municipalities. In this interpretation a broad reading of local discretion is necessary to ensure effective local management (*State of Utah v. Hutchinson*, 624 P. 2d 1116).

Disaster Designation   A formal finding by the president of either a "major disaster" or an "emergency." The disaster designation is based on a recommendation by the director of the Federal Emergency Management Agency (FEMA). By administrative rule, a governor applies to the national level for such a declaration, acknowledging that catastrophic events outstrip state and local response capabilities. Such events include hurricane, tornado, storm, flood, high water, wind-driven water, tidal wave, earthquake, volcanic eruption, landslide, mudslide, snowstorm, drought, fire, explosion, oil spill, or toxic-waste spill. Affected areas become eligible for federal relief coordination, including disaster housing, at no cost to victims. Those affected become eligible for individual and family grant programs (IFGs) and Small Business Administration (SBA) assistance. The federal government also supplies Community Disaster Loans to units that meet eligibility criteria. *See also* AGENDA SETTING; FEDERAL

EMERGENCY MANAGEMENT AGENCY; PLANNING, CONTINGENCY; SMALL
BUSINESS ADMINISTRATION.

Significance   Behind the news report of a formally declared disaster
is an important administrative process that begins when a mayor or
other local official requests the governor to petition the president for
federal help by way of a regional FEMA office. The national level then
coordinates relief efforts, including those by not-for-profit organizations such as the Red Cross. The federal statute authorizing intervention is the Disaster Relief Act of 1974, 42 U.S.C. 5121 et seq. It is
spelled out in administrative rules found in 44 CFR 205.33 et seq. If
the federal level does not agree that an event justifies intervention, the
state may decide special aid is justified and declare it a state disaster.
This allows the area to become eligible for state aid to homeowners
and businesses.

Suggested Reading
Casper, Dale E. "Municipal Disaster Preparedness: A List of Periodical Liter-
    ature, 1980–1984." Monticello, IL: Vance Bibliographies, Public Ad-
    ministration Series P 1802, 1985.
Chang, S. "Disaster and Fiscal Policy: Hurricane Impact on Municipal
    Revenue." *Urban Affairs Quarterly*, vol. 18, no. 4 (1983), pp. 511–523.
    (Case study of Hurricane Frederick.)

Disinvestment, Urban   The withdrawal or abandonment of private funds from the economic base of a city. Urban disinvestment has
meant the transfer of businesses and capital out of older, industrialized cities in the northern United States into suburban areas in the
same metropolitan areas, to the sunbelt, or completely out of the
country. *See also* ABANDONMENT; CLOSING, HOSPITAL; CLOSING, PLANT;
CLOSING, SCHOOL; FISCAL CRISIS.

Significance   Disinvestment has many causes, including global
macroeconomic trends that are well beyond the scope of local governments to control or influence. Other reasons for urban disinvestment
include rates of unionization and strike activity in an area; degree of
social upheaval, including crime, arson, and rioting; and the opportunity to build a new, technologically advanced facility. The ability of
footloose industry to move quite freely has put many cities at a relative
disadvantage as they attempt to attract private investment. Further,
many cities were forced to look to the federal government for financial
assistance, but federal aid to urban areas was greatly reduced under
the Reagan administration. With the withdrawal of federal assistance
from many urban programs beginning in the 1980s, cities were forced

to compete for business investment with much greater intensity by offering tax incentives and other local subsidies. Considerable controversy has emerged about the overall effects of such local subsidies, because many of these tax incentives further erode the local tax base. The consequences of urban disinvestment are severe for most cities. Some private disinvestment usually has a multiplier effect in higher unemployment rates, secondary business failures, abandonment, and a reduced tax base. Higher rates of unemployment create further demands on the public sector for services even though municipal revenues are declining.

Suggested Reading

Bensman, David, and Roberta Lynch. *Rusted Dreams: Hard Times in a Steel Community*. Berkeley: University of California Press, 1988.
Yago, Glenn H., et al. "Investment and Disinvestment in New York 1960–1980." *Annals of the American Academy of Political and Social Science*, vol. 495 (1984), pp. 28–38.

Displacement   Any involuntary residential or for-profit business or nonprofit organization dislocation. Displacement usually involves low-income residents forced to move because of urban renewal projects, gentrification, or public and private redevelopment projects. Physical displacement occurs when a landlord cuts off heat to a building, forcing tenants to leave. Economic displacement occurs when a landlord raises rent beyond the means of tenants, forcing them to move. Larger forces operating in a city can cause displacement. The economic redevelopment of a neighborhood and of specific residences may raise rents higher than tenants can afford. Sometimes states and cities use eminent domain powers to force residents to move because of a public project, such as construction of a highway. Displacement also could result from a private development project, such as a manufacturing facility. *See also* CONDOMINIUM CONVERSION; EMINENT DOMAIN; GENTRIFICATION; RELOCATION.

Significance   Urban displacement has been regulated for many years, at least since passage of post–World War II federal statutes providing for urban renewal programs. During the 1950s and 1960s, displacement of poorer tenants in many cities occurred as large public and private development projects replaced older, less expensive housing. Conversions to condominiums priced many tenants out of buildings, even though state and federal law requires that current tenants have a right of first refusal. Growing concern about compensation and proper procedures in dealing with displaced persons, as well as problems in providing relocation assistance under federal programs, prompted passage of the 1970 Uniform Relocation Act (42 U.S.C. 4601–4655). Implementation of the Uniform Act mandates substantial payments to displacees, and this has substantially limited redevelopment projects because of the high costs of relocation.

Suggested Reading

Eisinger, Peter K. *The Politics of Displacement.* New York: Academic Press, 1980.

Hartman, Chester, et al. *Displacement, How To Fight It.* Berkeley: National Housing Law Project, 1982.

Laska, Shirley Bradway, and Daphne Spain, eds. *Back to the City: Issues in Neighborhood Renovation.* New York: Pergamon Press, 1980.

Marcuse, Peter. "Gentrification, Abandonment, and Displacement: Connections, Causes, and Policy Responses in New York City." *Journal of Urban and Contemporary Law,* vol. 28 (1985), pp. 195–240.

Schill, Michael H., and Richard P. Nathan. *Revitalizing America's Cities: Neighborhood Reinvestment and Displacement.* Albany: State University of New York Press, 1983.

Sumka, Howard J. "Neighborhood Revitalization and Displacement: A Review of the Evidence." In Mark Baldassare, ed., *Cities and Urban Living.* New York: Columbia University Press, 1983.

Divestment   Stripping endowments, savings portfolios, and pension fund stock plans from private-sector institutions that invest in apartheid-controlled South Africa. In the context of state and local government policy, divestment is a moral statement of disapproval against white treatment of blacks and "coloreds." It is an attempt to apply economic pressure against U.S. companies conducting business there, either to pull out or overtly violate apartheid policy in treating their black employees. Divestment also describes investor approval of the outlawed African National Congress (ANC) party. Divestment is also an attempt to weaken the minority, repressive white regime. *See also* APARTHEID; SEPARATION OF POWERS; SISTER CITY PROGRAM.

Significance   Divestment has been a private as well as public response not only against the official South African apartheid laws but against the absence of U.S. confrontation on the issue. As of the late 1980s, 5 states and more than 20 cities and counties were divesting funds on either a binding or nonbinding basis. Some of these jurisdictions were refusing to conduct business with those U.S. corporations doing business in South Africa. Participating jurisdictions were articulating a liberal position in an attempt to influence foreign policy. In the United States such power is exclusively delegated to the national level. As with the sister cities program, the sanctuary movement, and nuclear-free-zone resolutions, subnational levels have found a way to make foreign policy statements, often at odds with national policy.

The constitutionality of such local foreign-policy actions has not yet passed U.S. Supreme Court scrutiny.

Suggested Reading
Walsh, Christine. "The Constitutionality of State and Local Governments' Response to Apartheid: Divestment Legislation." *Fordham Urban Law Journal,* vol. 13 (1985), pp. 767–800.

Downtown Development Authority (DDA)   A quasi-public agency created by a local government with state authorization and designed to promote, coordinate, and administer economic development in a city's central business district. Downtown Development Authorities usually have power to condemn land, borrow money, and plan economic development within their designated boundaries. *See also* AUTHORITY, PUBLIC; PUBLIC-PRIVATE PARTNERSHIP; QUASI-PUBLIC; URBAN DEVELOPMENT ACTION GRANT.

Significance   A vast number of economic development authorities have been created since 1975. Downtown Development Authorities were one element of the general trend of public-private partnerships established to help plan, finance, and execute the redevelopment of central business districts in many cities. States and cities were given most of the responsibility for local economic development as the federal government withdrew most of its funding for such programs. The intense competition for business investment that occurred in many states and cities resulted in many state and local policy incentives, including tax abatements, enterprise zones, and the creation of development authorities designed to engender cooperation between the public and private sectors. Federal policies reducing funding for local development and grants such as Urban Development Action Grants (UDAGs) encouraged the creation of locally established downtown development authorities beginning in the mid-1970s.

Dye Thesis   The assertion by political scientist Thomas R. Dye that a government's economic development is more important than its political system in influencing public policy. Dye developed his thesis using aggregate indices for state and local governments in the United States in the 1960s. His thesis attracted a great deal of retesting by commentators. In the most popular version Dye states that government output correlates closer to environmental than political variables. That is to say, factors such as wealth, white-collar employment, property values, and percentage of white population more closely account for what governments accomplish in the area of educational policy than do such considerations as the method of electing school boards, tax assessors, and the type of city government—whether re-formed or unreformed. Dye's analysis rests upon vast amounts of aggregate data, such as one policy area (education) for 67 large cities in relation to six environmental and six structural variables. In his 1965 book-length treatment, Dye employed 90 policy areas (health, welfare, corrections, recreation, taxation, etc.) for 48 states (Alaska and Hawaii were excluded because data were not available) in relation to four environmental and four structural characteristics. The de-grees of political competition and voter turnout were found to have less impact on policy than the environmental factors of degrees of urban-ism, amount of income derived from industrialization, per capita wealth, and years of completed education for adults. *See also* BANFIELD THESIS; MARXIST URBAN ANALYSIS; OPTIMUM CITY; REFORM GOVERNMENT.

Significance   Dye's thesis that economic factors weigh more heavily than political factors in determining public policy debunked the no-tion that competition and voter turnout are of greater importance. He felt that political machinery is best described as the process of facilitat-ing public demands into policy outputs rather than a cause of the policy itself. Dye's critics point to the impossibility of four variables carrying all the weight of "political factors" that possibly might make impact on policy. They acknowledge, however, the core of his asser-tion that economic influences on policy are stronger than any of the measured political factors at the local government level. Nevertheless, considerations of leadership, partisanship, and the type of govern-ment machinery do make some impact on the policies that emerge from cities. Dye adds that economic resources in cities must be viewed regionally as well, as there are clear differences between frostbelt and sunbelt cities regarding residential mobility, state of infrastructure repair, and capacity to respond to new circumstances.

Suggested Reading
Dye, Thomas R. *Politics, Economics, and the Public.* Chicago: Rand McNally, 1966.
———. *Understanding Public Policy,* 6th ed. Englewood Cliffs, NJ: Prentice-Hall, 1987. Chap. 12.
———. "Governmental Structure, Urban Environment, and Educational Pol-icy." *Midwest Journal of Political Science,* vol. 11, no. 3 (1967), pp. 353–380. (Sample of 67 cities.)
Robins, Barbara J. "Policy Outputs and Bureaucracy: The Roles of Need, Demand, and Agency Structure." *Urban Affairs Quarterly,* vol. 18, no. 4 (1983) pp. 485–509. (Bureaucratic-level analysis.)

Sharkansky, Ira, and Richard J. Hofferbert. "Dimensions of State Policy." Chap. 9 in Herbert Jacob and Kenneth N. Vines, eds., *Politics in the American States: A Comparative Analysis*, 2nd ed. Boston: Little, Brown, 1971.

E

Earmarked Fund   An expenditure specifically designated by a government for a particular purpose, as provided by constitution or law. Federal-level entitlements, such as Social Security, are one common example of earmarked funds. At the state level, gasoline tax revenues often are earmarked for road construction, generally on a shared basis with cities. State lottery revenues are often designated for education. *See also* LOTTERY; TAX, MOTOR FUEL.

Significance   At all levels of government, substantial portions of an annual budget are comprised of earmarked funds. For the federal government and some states, about half of the total yearly expenditures are earmarked. Earmarking has been used in the past to ensure "set-asides" for important constituent groups or to provide consistent revenues when required over an extended period. Because earmarking is required by constitution or statute, control by budgetary decision makers often is greatly reduced.

Easement   The property right that provides limited use to a non-owner of someone else's property. An easement typically allows an individual, a public or private utility, a government, or the general public specific access to a portion of a property. For example, a property owner who has no street front may have an easement arrangement with an adjoining property owner to allow access to the street. All public utilities secure easement rights to build their lines across otherwise private property. *See also* LANDLOCKED PROPERTY; LEASE-BACK; PUBLIC UTILITY.

Significance   An easement is a restriction on property rights, placing a limitation on the property owner's use of the land. Local govern-

170

ments have a secured right to construct and operate water and sewer lines across sections of private property. Property owners are therefore restricted from use of that portion of their land, because the easement permits the utility to have access for building, maintenance, or repairs. Local governments also have used easements as a tool for preserving open spaces or for limiting land use. The government may purchase an easement providing for bike paths.

Economic Base Analysis   A technique used to measure and evaluate the diversity and security of a community's manufacturing and financial activities. The economic base of a community consists of all activities that create income for a city. Economic base analysis is used to forecast the general economic growth of a city or region. An economic base that creates many exports, thus bringing in additional wealth, would suggest relative economic health for a city or region. In addition, this analysis is used to illustrate the economic difficulties some cities must face if they rely on only one industry as their base. *See also* CLOSING, PLANT; GROWTH POLITICS; URBAN CRISIS.

Significance   Economic base analysis is used to determine the strengths and weaknesses of a local economy, to forecast area economic trends, and to provide assistance to policymakers in planning economic development. An important element in economic base analysis divides a city's economic activities into basic (those that create goods and services for export) and nonbasic (those that create goods and services to be used within the community itself and not generating additional income). According to this analysis, basic industries are most important to a city's economic growth and vitality. Exports bring additional income, further encouraging investment and growth. Other data often are used, such as employment figures and population trends, to determine whether a local economy is importing or exporting goods and services or is essentially self-sufficient.

Suggested Reading
Glickman, N. J. *Econometric Analysis of Regional Systems: Explorations in Model Building and Policy Analysis.* New York: Academic Press, 1977.
Shah, Praful B. "Economic Base Studies." Chap. 20 in Frank S. So et al., *The Practice of Local Government Planning.* Washington, DC: International City Management Association, 1979, pp. 599–613.
Siegel, Richard A. "The Economic Base and Multiplier Analysis." *Urban Affairs Quarterly,* vol. 2, no. 2 (1966), pp. 24–38.
Ullman, Edward L., et al. *The Economic Base of American Cities.* Seattle: University of Washington Press, 1969.

Economic Development   In the context of urban politics, the attempt to attract investment within a government's jurisdiction. Some local governments have not focused on outside business investment exclusively, but emphasize locally initiated projects and efforts to diversify their economies. Economic development became a major policy focus in the mid-1970s. With the reduction of federal aid to cities, competition for business investment among states and cities increased substantially during that time. A wide variety of incentives has been offered to attract business investment. These include various combinations of tax abatements, tax increment financing, enterprise zones, and foreign trade zones. Although states and cities have long been involved, since 1974 increasing responsibility for financing urban economic development has shifted away from the federal government toward state and local governments. *See also* ENTERPRISE ZONE; HOUSING AND COMMUNITY DEVELOPMENT ACT OF 1974; TAX ABATEMENT; TAX INCREMENT FINANCING.

Significance   A combination of economic, political, and fiscal factors forced a major change in U.S. urban economic development by the early 1970s. Specific policies such as the 1974 Housing and Community Development Act provided for incentives to encourage private investment in cities, rather than a reliance on federal categorical or block-grant aid. In addition, later programs such as Urban Development Action Grants (1977–1988) required private investment as a precondition for public funding of urban development projects. President Ronald Reagan continued this greater emphasis on private investment over public aid, as he reduced federal antirecessionary aid to cities and called for cities to compete for residents, tourists, and investment rather than for federal grants. Many cities must compete with each other with one of the few devices they control—local taxes. Ironically, the actual effectiveness of tax incentives in attracting business investment has been questioned by many experts, and, for some cities, tax breaks may create greater revenue problems, at least over the short term.

Suggested Reading

Bingham, Richard D., and John P. Blair, eds. *Urban Economic Development*. Vol. 27, Urban Affairs Annual Reviews. Beverly Hills: Sage, 1984.
Doeringer, Peter B., et al. *Invisible Factors in Local Economic Development*. New York: Oxford University Press, 1988.
Harrison, Bennett. *Urban Economic Development*. Washington, DC: Urban Institute, 1974.
Stone, Clarence N., and Heywood T. Sanders, eds. *The Politics of Urban Development*. Lawrence: University Press of Kansas, 1987.
Luke, Jeffrey S., et al. *Managing Economic Development: A Guide to State and Local Leadership Strategies*. San Francisco: Jossey-Bass, 1988.

Economic Opportunity Act of 1964 (42 U.S.C. 2701, et seq.)   The major legislative foundation for the social programs associated with Lyndon Johnson's Great Society and the War on Poverty. The goal of the act was to alleviate, cure, and prevent poverty by overcoming its causes and by providing economic opportunities and community involvement. This act offered five basic opportunities: (1) to help under-privileged youth develop job skills and receive an education; (2) to enable communities to develop comprehensive plans to fight local poverty; (3) to assist farm workers in overcoming economic barriers; (4) to provide for volunteer programs so all Americans could help fight the War on Poverty; and (5) to establish a national headquarters for the War on Poverty—the Office of Economic Opportunity (OEO). The statute provided economic opportunities for a wide variety of people. Title I of the act established the Job Corps program, the Neighborhood Youth Corps, work training, and work study programs for young people. Title II provided for Community Action Programs and "maximum feasible participation," along with adult education programs and Project Head Start. Title III provided for direct loans to impoverished rural areas. Title IV established small-business loans and work experience programs. Title V created job training programs for families receiving AFDC. Title VI established the Office of Economic Opportunity and created the VISTA program. Title VII exempted recipients of antipoverty program funding from the Social Security Act, which required all public assistance to be considered in determining eligibility and the amount of public assistance to be received. *See also* COMMUNITY ACTION PROGRAM; HEAD START, PROJECT; MAXIMUM FEASIBLE PARTICIPATION; VOLUNTEERS IN SERVICE TO AMERICA; WAR ON POVERTY.

Significance   Motivated in part by concerns arising during John F. Kennedy's administration, Lyndon Johnson effectively forged a policymaking coalition to pass the Economic Opportunity Act of 1964 as a comprehensive national commitment to solving poverty. He brought the Office of Economic Opportunity directly within the Executive Office of the President to maintain close and direct contact with the progress of the programs created by the act. By fiscal year 1967, almost $2 billion was appropriated under the act's authority. However, Richard Nixon's election in 1968 brought about changes in the social programs of the federal government. He began impounding OEO funds in the early 1970s and attempted to dismantle the office by 1973. Initially saved by Congress and the courts, the OEO became the Community Service Agency in 1975. Project Head Start and the few remaining social-action programs of the Great Society were transferred to various other departments.

Ecumenopolis   A forecast of the twenty-second-century urbanized center and axis that will cover the inhabited earth as a network of built-up areas. The term was coined in the 1960s by Constantinos A. Doxiadis (1913–1975), the Greek civic designer. The etymology is Greek: "the one inhabited earth, universal" and "city." By that time there will be a breakdown in parochialism, and urban dwellers will recognize their economic and social interconnectedness. All urban residents will operate as one extended unit within a scale of 20 billion to 30 billion citizens. This is what the *dynopolis* or changing city will be in the long term. *See also* CONURBATION; EKISTICS; FORECAST; MEGALOPOLIS.

Significance   In the specialized vocabulary of the Ekistics Institute of Athens, the Ecumenopolis is tomorrow's city. It stresses continuous urbanization, further decline in rural population, an end to nationalism, development of international trade, and expanded economic interdependence. Ecumenopolis is the logical extension of Patrick Geddes's 1915 concept of *conurbation* to describe the dynopolis of the United Kingdom; of Jean Gottmann's 1960s concept of *megalopolis* to describe the urban complex along the northeastern seaboard stretching from Boston to Washington, D.C.; and of L. S. Bourne and R. D. MacKinnon's 1970s designation of urban central Canada along the northern shore of the Great Lakes, ranging from Windsor, Ontario, to Quebec City, Quebec.

Suggested Reading
Bourne, L. S., and R. D. MacKinnon, eds. *Urban Systems Development in Central Canada: Selected Papers.* Toronto: University of Toronto Press, 1972.
Doxiadis, Constantinos A., and J. G. Papaioannou. *Ecumenopolis: The Inevitable City of the Future.* New York: W. W. Norton, 1974.
Yeates, Maurice. *Main Street: Windsor to Quebec City.* Toronto: Macmillan of Canada, 1975.

Educational Resources Information Center (ERIC™)   An on-line data base coordinating 16 clearinghouses that collect and process information on education. ERIC is sponsored by the U.S. Department of Education's National Institute of Education. Information sources include select monographs, collections, select coverage of journal articles, policy papers, conference papers, and research reports. Many of the last three items were never published in referenced publications. The clearinghouses organize sources by author, title, subject, descriptors, and identifiers. After initial selection and abstracting, the sources are indexed, stored by acquisition number, and made available nationally for retrieval and distribution through either manual or computer recovery. Up to six descriptors are assigned to each source. A descriptor is a list of controlled vocabulary found through trial-and-error experience since 1966 to be appropriate for educational literature. There are currently more than 5,000 approved descriptor key terms, some of which, for example, are:

URBAN AREAS	URBAN EDUCATION
URBAN GEOGRAPHY	URBAN POPULATION
URBAN RENEWAL	URBAN TO RURAL MIGRATION
URBAN DEMOGRAPHY	URBAN ENVIRONMENT
URBAN PLANNING	URBAN PROBLEMS
URBAN SCHOOLS	URBAN TO SUBURBAN MIGRATION

Identifiers aid in searches. They are either proper names (such as a city) or concepts not yet certified as conventional descriptors. Complete documents are available on microfiche at more than 700 subscription libraries. Many of the reports also are available in paper. Two other parts of the ERIC system include Current Index to Journals in Education (CIJE) and Resources in Education (RIE). *See also* DIALOG; LOCAL EXCHANGE; LOGIN.

Significance   ERIC is the largest data base covering education, with more than 500,000 sources entered. This is in contrast to only 30,000 for LOGIN. Most sources are in English and confined largely to U.S. publications. Urban education entries are selected by the clearinghouse at Columbia University's Teachers College. It is an up-to-date system with relatively current input. Among audiences for the indexing and abstracting services are policymakers, researchers, and practitioners. Access costs are among the lowest of all data base systems.

Suggested Reading
Houston, James E. *Thesaurus of ERIC Descriptors,* 10th ed. Phoenix: Oryx Press, 1984.

Ekistics   The science of human settlements. Ekistics is the study of five interacting elements for all human settlements, viz., nature, man, society, shells (buildings), and networks (infrastructure). The term was coined in 1942 by Greek civic designer Constantinos A. Doxiadis (1913–1975). He took an interdisciplinary approach to land use, stressing the dynamics of communities and their patterned regularities, whether small-scale villages or urban areas of 10 million units called megalopolises. *Megalopolis* also is a Greek term, meaning a large urbanized area composed of several metropolitan areas, or mother cities. *See also* INFRASTRUCTURE; MASTER PLAN.

Significance   Ekistics is a holistic approach to physical city planning. It is also the name of a respected international journal focusing on contemporary and historical studies of cities in developed and developing nations. The largely architectural–physical layout approach has been applied to micro- and macroscale projects, from college campus master plans to long-term metropolitan projected growth patterns. With the concept's special orientation on physical layout (shells and networks), critics say the elements of man and society have been slighted. Doxiadis Associates' multimillion-dollar study of southeastern Michigan for Detroit Edison in the early 1970s was inaccurate in its projections of growth corridors and is largely unused.

Suggested Reading

Doxiadis, Constantinos A. *Action for Human Settlements*. New York: W. W. Norton, 1976.
————. *Building Entopia*. New York: W. W. Norton, 1975.
————. *Ecology and Ekistics*. Gerald Dix, ed. London: Elek Books, 1977. (Glossary, pp. xix–xxvii.)
————. *Ekistics: An Introduction to the Science of Human Settlements*. London: Hutchinson Publishing, 1968.
Doxiadis, Constantinos A., et al. *Anthropopolis: City for Human Development*. New York: W. W. Norton, 1974. (The "human city": glossary, pp. 372–375.)

Elections, Types of   Analysis of voting systems by ten major variables employed by psephologists, those who study elections. The ten dimensions of an election are: (1) The system's rules for winning, whether requiring a simple majority, extraordinary majority, plurality, or a proportional representation scheme. (2) The governmental level of the election, whether national, state, local, or a combination. (3) The stage of the election, whether primary or general. (4) The schedule for conducting the election, whether on-year (that is to say, a presidential contest), off-year in an even-numbered cycle, or off-year in an odd-numbered cycle. This also refers to whether the election is regularly scheduled or *ad hoc*. (5) The subject of the election, whether to fill one or more offices, a substantive referendum such as annexation, a bond issue, a recall, or, infrequently, a plebiscite. (6) The ballot type, whether partisan, nonpartisan, or a mixture of the two. (7) The ballot format, whether a short ballot focusing accountability on one or a few positions, or a long ballot in which multiple offices, initiatives, and referenda are presented to voters for resolution. (8) The geographic scale at which results are tabulated, whether at the subdivision, precinct, ward, or at-large level of a city. Subdivision elections are conducted for special assessment districts, precinct delegate elections for party representatives, and aldermanic elections for ward or at-large council positions. (9) The election's results, whether favoring acceptance or rejection of a proposal or bond issue; whether resulting in producing winners of the incumbents or challengers; and whether sustaining, deviating, dealigning, or, rarely, realigning the normal party vote. (10) The turnout, which is conventionally arrayed on a continuum of high, average, or low, expressed as a percent of registered voters or relative to similar past contests. *See also* AT-LARGE ELECTION; BOND ELECTION; NONPARTISAN ELECTION; OFF YEAR.

Significance   Empirical political science is probably most advanced in the study of elections. Yet most of this effort has been focused on national on-year plurality elections for partisan positions of high office, for which the turnout is as high as is ever obtained. Most urban political elections are off-year, nonpartisan, at-large events with low turnout. Local election types have not been studied exhaustively. Townships and school boards, for example, constitute more than 30,000 units of government in the United States. Combined, they represent the largest number of elective offices in the nation, yet they are not well studied.

Suggested Reading
Welch, Susan, and Timothy Bledsoe. "The Partisan Consequences of Non-partisan Elections and the Changing Nature of Urban Politics." *American Journal of Political Science*, vol. 30, no. 1 (1986), pp. 128–139.

Eleemosynary Group   A private-sector, nonprofit charity that supplements government welfare. Local religious groups, fraternal organizations, civic associations, benevolent associations, united funds, and humanitarian groups all aid needy individuals. Some charitable groups, such as the International Red Cross, have a broad global constituency. They provide such goods as shelter, food, and clothing and such services as substance-abuse counseling, job training, and medical and legal assistance. When dental, medical, and legal professionals donate time, it is often called *pro bono publico,* or for the public good. Frequently, professionals do not collect fees from indigents. *See also* HOMELESS.

Significance   The level of humanitarian activity is a function of both the public and the private sectors. The balance sheets for the two sectors are never totaled and no one knows the precise level of aid to the needy. Total charitable contributions exceed $55 billion a year. The U.S. Department of Agriculture distributes powdered milk, surplus butter, and honey, which are regularly supplemented in soup kitchens with 700 Club brown rice. The scale of private-sector philanthropy is large in relation to all charity, but figures are not kept for comparison of fiscal years and categories of giving. Federal and state governments encourage donations through favorable tax write-offs. Motives vary from tithing to wishing to act directly with the indigent. Some religious group activities, such as the Salvation Army soup kitchens and pantry stations, remain open year-round. Other organizations work on an *ad hoc* basis, responding to disasters. There is little coordination among private charities, even through such groups as United Way and Black United Fund (BUF). Public-welfare groups occasionally cooperate with private sources and refer clients when eligibility runs out or standards are not met. The dollar level of private giving varies over time: Costs of shelters for the homeless in northern cities change with the seasons and the level of unemployment as well as state enforcement of eligibility for residence in a mental institution. Absent these private charities, the dollar amount of welfare would be less, and the categories and number of persons receiving aid would change.

Suggested Reading

Akana, Paul. "Coordination with Private Agencies." Part of chap. 8 in Wayne F. Anderson, Bernard J. Frieden, and Michael J. Murphy, eds., *Managing Human Services*. Washington, DC: International City Management Association, 1977, pp. 243–254.

Weisbrad, Burton A. *The Nonprofit Economy*. Cambridge: Harvard University Press, 1988.

Emergency Employment Act of 1971   A federal statute that provided funding for state and local government public service jobs when the unemployment rate reached a certain threshold. The concept behind the Emergency Employment program was to make the government the employer of last resort by funding a "shelf of public works" projects. The Emergency Employment Act of 1971 (42 U.S.C. 4871–4883) operated between 1972 and 1974. It was replaced by the Comprehensive Employment and Training Act of 1973 (CETA) (29 U.S.C. 801 et seq.). *See also* COMPREHENSIVE EMPLOYMENT AND TRAINING ACT.

Significance   The Emergency Employment Act of 1971 was intended to provide temporary public service jobs to the unemployed. During its three-year life, it spent an estimated $2.3 billion and created about 200,000 jobs. It illustrated that local governments could create many worthwhile jobs in a short time. However, critics charged that vague and permissive eligibility requirements allowed local government officials to use the program for patronage to hire many nondisadvantaged individuals. Critics also argued the program had marginal effect on the lower-income, hard-core unemployed in the United States. Despite Democratic party support for public service jobs, many congressional Republicans and President Richard Nixon felt these were "make work" jobs and detracted from the private sector's ability to create permanent jobs. However, President Nixon signed the Emergency Employment Act of 1971 because the national unemployment rate had surpassed 6 percent, a relatively high rate at the time.

Suggested Reading

Baumer, Donald C., and Carl E. Van Horn. *The Politics of Unemployment.* Washington, DC: Congressional Quarterly Press, 1985.
Hallman, Howard W. *Emergency Employment: A Study in Federalism.* Tuscaloosa: University of Alabama Press, 1977.
Levitan, Sar A., and Robert Taggert. *The Emergency Employment Act.* Salt Lake City: Olympus, 1974.

Emergency Evacuation   Plans set up by managements of nuclear power plants in accordance with Federal Emergency Management Agency (FEMA) guidelines to move all people in a ten-mile radius out of jeopardy from any radioactive release in case of a nuclear accident. Emergency guidelines for nuclear power malfunctions are set up in *Code of Federal Regulations* 44 CFR 1.350. Initial-reactor-site criteria are established by the Nuclear Regulatory Commission (NRC), one of the Independent Regulatory Commissions (IRCs), in 10 CFR 100. Part of the emergency preparedness plan is a system of sirens to warn communities of a problem; also included is a set of transportation guidelines for local officials to follow in moving people out of danger. *See also* WRITE-DOWN.

Significance   Far from being an academic exercise, emergency evacuation procedures have been a major roadblock to nuclear reactor development in densely populated areas. In one of the largest write-offs of the twentieth century, Long Island Lighting Company (LILCO) closed its completed, $5.36-billion Shoreham nuclear power plant and sold it to the State of New York for a dollar, with the promise that the state regulatory commission would allow the company to pass construction costs on to consumers. This action occurred because it was thought to be impossible to create a viable emergency evacuation system. Neither the State of New York nor Suffolk County would take part in the emergency planning or emergency drills. A 1988 executive order allows federal officials to prepare emergency evacuation plans in the event local governments refuse to work with the utility. The Seabrook power plant in New Hampshire also was obstructed by the failure of neighboring Massachusetts communities to participate in emergency evacuation planning. If that plan fails, it also will represent a write-off of more than $5 billion. Local authorities in New York and Massachusetts argue it would be impossible to evacuate successfully during an actual radiation release. Proponents of nuclear power counter that relaxed NRC guidelines for radiation release would make evacuation of a densely populated area feasible.

Eminent Domain   The right of government to take private property for an immediate or long-term public purpose with due process and just compensation. There is no absolute right to private property under all conditions listed in either the national or state constitutions. The application of eminent domain is known as condemnation; it is one of the ancient prerogatives of the sovereign as a form of acquiring property for public purchase, along with voluntary purchase, dedication, and adverse possession. The power to condemn private land is listed in the national and state constitutions. It often is delegated to substate units such as municipalities and select special districts. It also can be provided for under color of statute, charter, ordinance, or resolution in various jurisdictions. *See also* DEDICATION; EASEMENT; INVERSE CONDEMNATION; POLETOWN; QUICK-TAKE LAW; TAKING.

Significance   Eminent domain cases make headlines because they are controversial, setting the state against the individual property owner. The basic concept is uncontested, but its application is often contested, regarding such issues as what constitutes an excessive taking, how protracted the proceedings should be, and what constitutes a fair market value or just compensation. In the last resort, just compensation is decided by courts determining what constitutes a fair market value. Eminent domain is used for clearing land in urban renewal projects; for creation of state ownership for highways, parking areas, and parks; and for gaining access to private lands by public utility lines.

Enclave   As used in political geography, a small-scale jurisdiction or area surrounded by a larger jurisdiction. Examples include the U.S. Guantanamo Base in Cuba, San Marino and the Vatican in Italy, Spanish Ceuta in Morocco, and British Gibraltar in Spain. Examples within the United States include Harwood Heights and Norridge, surrounded by Chicago; Norwood, St. Bernard, and Elmwood Place, surrounded by Cincinnati; Highland Park, surrounded by Dallas; Highland Park and Hamtramck, surrounded by Detroit; West University Place and Bellaire, surrounded by Houston; San Fernando, Culver City, and Beverly Hills, surrounded by Los Angeles; and the Village of Braetenahl, bounded on three sides by Cleveland and on the fourth by Lake Erie. An *exclave* is an outlying portion of a parent jurisdiction, completely surrounded by another unit's territory. West Berlin is an exclave of the Federal Republic of Germany.

Significance   Residents and citizens of the small-scale unit or enclave distinguish themselves from the surrounding unit. Enclaves often are set apart on some dimension, as with the relative wealth of Beverly Hills vis-à-vis Los Angeles, or the Polish ethnic community in Hamtramck vis-à-vis Detroit.

Endorsement, Municipal Political   Open support from a civic association or newspaper for a candidate or issue appearing on a local ballot. Municipal political endorsements are thought to be most effective when the electorate has little other information upon which to base decisions. A local election with many candidates running for the same office and no information from political parties is most likely to be affected by this cue-giving advice from so-called high-prestige associations. Many endorsements are based along predictable lines, such as a newspaper favoring conservative Republicans or a labor union tending to endorse Democrats. *See also* COMMUNITY PRESS; ETHNIC MEDIA.

Significance   There is little information beyond circumstantial evidence about the potency of municipal political endorsements. In the one empirical study on the topic, endorsements weigh the same in partisan and nonpartisan contests and in at-large versus single-member district contests. The ethics of newspaper editors can be brought into question; their endorsements often are based on cursory interviews by an editorial staff without any field experience concerning the community's problems and with no in-depth understanding of budget constraints. Candidates are more highly aware than the electorate that these endorsements are often examples of leadership by a largely self-serving and ignorant elite. There are no canons of ethics on this topic for newspaper editors to follow.

Suggested Reading
Coombs, Steven L. "Editorial Endorsements and Electoral Outcomes." In Michael Bruce McKuen and Steven Lane Coombs, eds., *More than News: Media Power in Public Affairs*. Beverly Hills: Russell Sage, 1981.

Stein, Lana, and Arnold Fleischmann. "Newspaper and Business Endorsements in Municipal Elections: A Test of the Conventional Wisdom." *Journal of Urban Affairs,* vol. 9, no. 4 (1987), pp. 325–336.

Enforcement Date   The time certain at which a government begins to administer a rule, ordinance, statute, charter, fee schedule, or directive. An enforcement date is also called an *effective date*. Depending on state constitution, state statute, and charter provisions, jurisdictions may apply provisions upon adoption; upon publication; after 30, 60, or 90 days; or at the beginning of the next fiscal year (FY). When fines or zoning are involved, there is usually a waiting period. *See also* CORPORATION COUNSEL; OFFICIAL NEWSPAPER; PROMULGATE.

Significance   Proper bill drafting entails beginning a statute or ordinance with an enacting clause stating the authority by which the rule is issued. The end of an ordinance should stipulate the beginning date of enforcement. When either is absent, it constitutes sloppy bill drafting and reflects adversely on the corporation counsel. Failure to announce a date explicitly invites litigation. Repealed ordinances usually cease to be enforced upon publication, unless otherwise stipulated. For a court, enforcement dates are called *execution dates* for judgments and decrees. Difficult-to-apply statutes and ordinances such as bottle return provisions may force the government to accommodate those affected with a year or more of preparation time. Actual enforcement of a new provision may be waived on advice of municipal administration or city council; a grace period of "looking the other way" also may be suggested. Controversial ordinances may be suspended immediately after passage, pending outcome of a test case. During the first months of a new ordinance, there is often only selective enforcement, as when breaking in new traffic controls. Some statutes were never meant for general enforcement, as in the case of literacy tests for voting, which were designed to discourage only certain minorities.

Enterprise Zone   An area of urban decay or blight containing businesses that are eligible for certain tax incentives and regulatory relief. Enterprise zones are designated by state governments, often by an agency within the state's department of commerce. The zone designations typically are based on a formula of economic distress. Businesses locating or relocating in an enterprise zone could be eligible for incentives such as credits against state corporate or business taxes. *See also* FOREIGN TRADE ZONE; SUPPLY-SIDE ECONOMICS.

Significance   Enterprise zones became one component of the Reagan administration's "supply-side" economics approach. Initially proposed in Congress in 1980 by Jack Kemp, the federal enterprise zone proposals encountered congressional opposition. Despite the delays at the federal level, at least 30 states adopted their own versions of enterprise zone legislation. The package of economic inducements offered by states and localities typically includes property tax reductions or abatements, low-interest loans, and sales tax exemptions for businesses that locate within the enterprise zones. These state initiatives reflect the trend toward more aggressive competition by states for urban economic development as the federal government began to withdraw its funding for these activities.

Suggested Reading

Bendick, Marc, and David W. Rasmussen. "Enterprise Zones and Inner-City Economic Revitalization." In George E. Peterson and Carol W. Lewis, eds., *Reagan and the Cities*. Washington, DC: Urban Institute Press, 1986.

Garoogian, Andrew. *Urban Enterprise Zones: A Selected Review of the Literature with Annotations: Bibliography 102*. Chicago: Council of Planning Libraries, 1983.

Gold, Steven D. *State Urban Enterprise Zones: A Policy Overview*. Denver: National Conference of State Legislatures, 1982.

Wilder, Margaret G., and Barry M. Rubin. "Targeted Redevelopment through Urban Enterprise Zones." *Journal of Urban Affairs*, vol. 10, no. 1 (1988), pp. 1–18.

Wolf, Michael Allan. "Enterprise Zones: A Decade of Diversity." *Economic Development Quarterly*, vol. 4, no. 1 (1990), pp. 3–14.

Environmental Impact Statement (EIS)   A report required of owners contemplating important capital expenditures for construction that will affect the human environment. An Environmental Impact Statement outlines the project's potential physical and biological effects in terms of the impact statement rules spelled out in 40 CFR 1500. The Environmental Impact Statement was established by the National Environmental Policy Act of 1969 (42 U.S.C. 4321 et seq.). Under Section 102, all contemplated major federal government construction requires the filing of a report. The same statute established the Council of Environmental Quality (CEQ), a part of the Executive Office of the President, to receive these reports in both a first draft and a final form. The final draft is an official document that may have to be defended in a court to determine whether or not there has been proper compliance. In addition to the federal policy, which is monitored through Federal Regional Councils, more than a dozen states and several cities have also passed mandatory EIS guidelines. State and local EIS orders may require private developers of substantial projects, such as shopping centers or subdivisions, to undergo review procedure. Under federal guidelines some private developments are required to write up EISs if the developer receives major federal funding. Examples of federally mandated environmental review projects include new office construction, highway construction, rapid-transit lines, airports, and harbor dredging. State and locally mandated EIS projects include construction of sanitary landfills, layouts for cemeteries, and nuclear waste dumps. *See also* ENVIRONMENTAL LEGISLATION; LOCALLY UNWANTED LAND USE; URBAN IMPACT ANALYSIS.

Significance   Environmental Impact Statements are a product of the second half of the twentieth century and reflect growing concern for humankind's often devastating effect on the landscape. EISs might better be labeled draft or final environmental statements because they call for not only impact assessment but calibration of unavoidable adverse environmental effects, assessment of alternatives to the proposed project, evaluation of long- and short-term consequences of the plan, and appraisal of any irreversible commitment of natural resources. The Council of Environmental Quality does not evaluate each impact statement but only acknowledges receipt of it. Initially, it was thought exposure of the information would be sufficient to make federal decision makers more sensitive to environmental issues and to give outside watchdog groups access to otherwise unavailable data. In fact, one major federal project was aborted because of an early filing, namely the cross-Florida barge canal, and others have been postponed as a result of late statement compliance or court challenges. Statewide EIS requirements, first initiated by California in 1970, require oversight of large-scale public and private planning by interdisciplinary review teams composed of physical, biological, and social scientists. Environmental Impact Statements have been transformed into a general public-policy device so that a legislature that creates a new category of crime might be forced to assess the *judicial impact* or *police manpower impact* of the proposed statute.

Suggested Reading

Bowie, Maryland, Committee for Environmental Quality. "The Role of Environmental Impact Statements in Local Government Decision Making." *Urban Lawyer*, vol. 6, no. 1 (1974), pp. 95–107.

Glickman, N. J., ed. *The Urban Impacts of Federal Policies*. Baltimore: Johns Hopkins University Press, 1980. (For a discussion of urban impact assessment.)

Taylor, Serge. *Making Bureaucracies Think: The Environmental Impact Strategy of Administrative Reform*. Stanford: Stanford University Press, 1984.

Environmental Legislation   Air, land, and water pollution control laws passed at the national, state, and local levels to protect the ecosystem and ensure healthy living conditions. Environmental legislation is generally separated into three major components. (1) National air pollution regulations include the 1955 Air Pollution Clean Air Act; the 1962 Clean Air Act; and the 1965, 1970, and 1977 Clean Air Act Amendments, all consolidated in 42 U.S.C. 1857; the 1967 Air Quality Act, 42 U.S.C. 1857; and the 1972 Noise Control Act, 42 U.S.C. 4901. Oregon was the first state to pass a state air pollution control act in 1952 (Ore. Rev. Stat. 1953 449 760). (2) National land pollution legislation includes the 1965 Solid Waste Disposal Act, 42 U.S.C. 6901; the 1970 Resource Recovery Act, 42 U.S.C. 3251; the 1976 Resource Conservation and Recovery Act, 42 U.S.C. 6901; and the 1980 Toxic Waste Superfund Act, 42 U.S.C. 9605. Oregon was also the first state to pass a mandatory recycling act in 1983. Since then Rhode Island, Oklahoma, and New Jersey also have passed mandatory recycling laws. Cities such as Philadelphia have also required recycling. (3) National water pollution control statutes have the longest history. Congress passed the Refuse Act in 1899, 33 U.S.C. 407, making it unlawful to dump garbage into navigable waters without a permit. Other national legislation includes the 1955 Federal Water Pollution Control Act as amended in 1972 and 1977, 33 U.S.C. 1251; the 1965 Water Quality Act, 33 U.S.C. 1151; the 1970 Water Quality and Improvement Act, 33 U.S.C. 1152; and the 1974 Clean Water Act, with amendments in 1977, 33 U.S.C. 1251. Because air and water are ambient and cannot effectively be regulated by local jurisdictions, much of the burden for passing restrictions on these forms of pollution passes to the state or national level. Localities that do not meet clean air standards can thus be cited under the 1970 Clean Air Act for failure to meet carbon dioxide and ozone levels. They can then be denied construction permits for new plants that emit more than a threshold level of the pollutants. Environmental impact statements also curb prospective large-scale polluters. Of the three types of environmental legislation, it is solid waste disposal that is most a local concern. Although major toxic landfills are largely the responsibility of the national Environmental Protection Agency (EPA) superfund, solid waste disposal planning is primarily a state, county, and local issue. Most local environmental legislation pertains to conservation zoning for floodplains, coastal plains, wetlands, stream banks, shore lands, and steep slopes. *See also* AMENITIES; ENVIRONMENTAL IMPACT STATEMENT; EXTERNALITY; LOCALLY UNWANTED LAND USE; SOLID WASTE MANAGEMENT.

Significance   Although there is no national industrial policy or national urban policy, since 1969 there has been a National Environmental Policy Act, 42 U.S.C. 4321 et seq. It sets up the Council on Environmental Quality as part of the Executive Office of the President and requires environmental impact statements. Major environmental pollution issues are most intensely felt in urban areas. With the exception of insecticide, fungicide, and pesticide pollution issues, which are largely rural in their impact, it is in cities that air is dirtiest, landfills are most taxed, and water is most polluted. The symbol of overburdened landfills came in 1987 with the tug *Mobro,* a garbage scow out of Islip, Long Island, New York, which traveled thousands of miles into the southern Caribbean searching for a location to dump its cargo. Should solid waste be handled through landfills, composting, incineration, recycling, or a combination of these techniques? Major issues include cost, safety to nearby residents, long-term leaching of water, and the effects of dioxins. As state-of-the-art control technology for any proper disposal system increases, so does the cost. Incinerators and sewage plants are two of the three largest environmentally related capital costs faced by most twentieth-century U.S. cities. Water purification plants constitute the third. All levels have experimented with solutions, from privatizing incinerator plants to charging a deposit on returnable containers. Cities limit or ban phosphates and bottom ash. A solution in one city, such as Saugus, Massachusetts, to encourage incinerators, is banned in other cities such as San Diego and San Francisco, California, and Lowell, Massachusetts.

Suggested Reading

Crenson, Matthew A. *The Un-politics of Air Pollution: A Study of Non-decision-making in the Cities.* Baltimore: Johns Hopkins University Press, 1971. (Based on case studies of Gary and East Chicago, Indiana.)

Kaiser, Edward, et al. *Promoting Environmental Quality through Urban Planning and Controls.* Washington, DC: U.S. Environmental Protection Agency, 1974. EP1.23/3:600/5-73-015.

Mendelker, Daniel. "Symposium: Law and Planning in the Environmental Decade." *Journal of the American Planning Association,* vol. 46, no. 2 (1980).

Palley, Marian Lief, and Howard A. Palley. *Urban America and Public Policies,* 2nd ed. Lexington, MA: D. C. Heath, 1981. Chap. 10, "Environmental Interdependence and National-Urban Policy Linkages."

Petulla, Joseph M. *Environmental Protection in the United States.* San Francisco: San Francisco Study Center, 1987.

Shirvani, H., and M. Stepner. "San Diego's Environmental Planning Ten Years Later." *Journal of the American Planning Association,* vol. 52, no. 2 (1986), pp. 212–219.

Wenner, Lottie M. *The Environmental Decade in Court.* Bloomington: Indiana University Press, 1982.

Ethnic Group   A people who by virtue of sharing a common cultural heritage form a subculture that distinguishes them from other groups in a society. Ethnic groups differ from *racial groups* in that race is genetically inherited and can be physically distinguishable. According to the 1980 census, the Irish are the largest group of white ethnics in the United States (40.2 million), followed by the French (12.9 million) and Polish (8.2 million). Hispanics make up the largest nonwhite ethnic group (14.6 million). *See also* BARRIO; CHINATOWN; MELTING POT; MIGRATION, URBAN; NEIGHBORHOOD.

Significance One of the most strongly distinguishing characteristics of society in the United States is the heterogeneous makeup of its citizens. Many white ethnic groups immigrated in the mid-1800s (primarily northern and western Europeans) and the late 1800s (primarily southern and eastern Europeans). During the early part of the twentieth century, blacks from the rural South moved north in great numbers. They and the bulk of the other groups came to the large industrialized cities of the Northeast and Midwest to work in manufacturing plants. The forces of ethnic pluralism pervade the political, social, and economic history of the United States. As a result, politics has been much more conflict-ridden and fragmented in the United States than in other industrialized nations. Ethnicity plays an important role in American voting behavior and has been strongly associated by some with urban political machines.

Suggested Reading
Allen, James Paul, and Eugene Turner. *We the People: An Atlas of America's Ethnic Diversity.* New York: Macmillan, 1988.
Bodnar, John. *The Transplanted: A History of Immigrants in Urban America.* Bloomington: Indiana University Press, 1985.
Maldonado, Lionel, and Joan Moore, eds. *Urban Ethnicity in the United States: New Immigrants and Old Minorities.* Urban Affairs Annual Reviews, vol. 29. Beverly Hills: Sage, 1985.
Parrillo, Vincent N. *Strangers to These Shores: Race and Ethnic Relations in the United States.* New York: Macmillan, 1985.
Pedraza-Bailey, Silvia. *Political and Economic Migrants in America: Cubans and Mexicans.* Austin: University of Texas Press, 1985.
Sowell, Thomas, ed. *American Ethnic Groups.* Washington, DC: The Urban Institute Press, 1978.
Wolfinger, Raymond E. "The Development and Persistence of Ethnic Voting." *American Political Science Review,* vol. LIX, no. 4 (1965), pp. 896–908.

Ethnic Media (United States) Non–English-language mass-communication outlets that disseminate information and entertainment by newspaper, radio, or television. *See also* BARRIO; BLACK PRESS; COMMUNITY PRESS.

Significance The ethnic media are produced and consumed primarily in the major metropolitan areas, which have long served as the first stop for immigrants. Many of these newcomers have no English proficiency and therefore need practical information in their native language. The second most frequently spoken language in the United States is Spanish. The United States is approximately the sixth-largest Spanish-speaking nation in the world with some 18 million speakers. The largest U.S. Spanish-speaking area is Greater Los Angeles, estimated at more than 4 million people. The New York metropolitan area has an estimated 3 million Spanish-speaking residents. The entire Commonwealth of Puerto Rico, the area President Gerald Ford suggested in his 1977 farewell address should become the fifty-first state, is Spanish-speaking. A New York City Hispanic has a choice of a newspaper, *El Diario*; three Spanish-speaking television outlets—Univision, Telemundo, and Univisa Satellite Communications; and the Spanish-voice FM radio station WSKQ. If an ethnic community is not large enough to support a full-time radio station, it often broadcasts over a voice-of-the-nations station or publishes an insert in a community press. Arabic, Armenian, Chinese, Irish, Italian, Korean, Polish, Portuguese, and Yiddish newspapers publish daily or weekly urban editions in the United States. For many of these ethnic newspapers, the major source of revenue is advertising, often from classified columns. An ethnic media audience often serves as a barometer of how rapidly and how well a foreign group learns English; the faster an ethnic group masters the host language, the less need there is for separate media. These foreign-language outlets serve as a transition between the old country and the host community. They thrive during periods of high immigration and slowly lose audience share as the second generation leaves the ethnic ghetto. All levels of government have had to cope with informing aliens of their rights and services. The U.S. Superintendent of Documents regularly issues select documents in Spanish and, to a lesser extent, other foreign languages. States publish maps in other languages, especially in Spanish along the Mexican border. Cities with major Spanish communities often designate a public library—*biblioteca de la gente*—for Spanish readers. Two major public-policy issues have developed from ethnic groups retaining their original languages. One has been the movement to declare English an official language. The second has been the need for Anglophones to adjust teaching methods to accommodate this pluralism. The U.S. Supreme Court in *Lau v. Nichols,* 414 U.S. 563 (1974), declared that under the 1964 Civil Rights Act (42 U.S.C. 2000), minority-language students are entitled to compensatory language instruction. One option has been to develop a curriculum in English as a Second Language (ESL). The other option is to develop a bilingual education curriculum, which provides instruction in two languages and cultural traditions simultaneously. The federal Bilingual

Education Act, 20 U.S.C. 880 et seq. (1975), provides partial federal funding for this option. Bilingual education strengthens the next generation's capacity to utilize such ethnic media as the Arabic press in Detroit, Chinese radio in San Francisco, Portuguese television and newspaper in Boston, and Spanish television in Miami.

Ethos Theory   The principle formulated by Edward C. Banfield and James Q. Wilson that identifies two opposing orientations to government that account in part for the existence of government structure and voter attitude toward policy issues. The ethos theory posits a *public-regarding* outlook characterized by customs and actions toward government that are magnanimous and holistic. People are said to look at abstract issues of law as general principles. The authors labeled this position the Yankee-White, Anglo-Saxon-Protestant, Jewish, and Black orientation and later changed the term to *unitary ethos*. In opposition to this theory was a second ethos, first described as a *private-regarding* orientation and later referred to as the *individualist ethos*. This outlook is centered on authority and a sense of personal obligation and loyalty to one's own group; it is characteristic of, for example, Irish, Italian, and Polish working-class immigrants. Banfield and Wilson posited that where the public-regarding unitary ethos prevailed, a city would adopt the three Progressive reforms of (1) council-manager with (2) nonpartisan elections in (3) at-large electoral contests. On the other hand, where the private-regarding or individualist ethos prevailed in the early twentieth-century city, governments would opt for the opposite three formats: (1) a mayor-council with (2) partisan elections (3) conducted in wards. The theory suggested that these three dimensions of urban politics were largely caused by ethnic composition. In fact, later empirical evidence found a very high correlation between the number of foreign-born, expressed in census figures, and the nature of local government structure. The theory also suggested that voting results and public-opinion polls revealed a positive correlation between public-interest topics and the Yankee public-regarding ethos. *See also* BANFIELD THESIS; ETHNIC GROUP; REFORM GOVERNMENT.

Significance   Ethos theory generated voluminous literature in political science and sociology in the 1960s and 1970s. By the late 1980s, there was not one favorable reference to ethos theory in an urban journal or urban political science textbook. The concept was attacked for being vague and pseudoscientific, for positing good-hearted Yankees against selfish immigrants, for confusing ethnic with class status, and, most seriously, for shifting operational definitions and never formulating what was being tested. The original formulation and subsequent empirical tests lacked clean cause-and-effect relationships and suffered from the ecological fallacy of positing individual behavior on the basis of precinct-level aggregate data. When regionalism was introduced into the equation, much of the variability was explained without recourse to a class-ethnic group ethos. The concept is now considered a social science conceptual failure.

Suggested Reading

Banfield, Edward C., and James Q. Wilson. *City Politics.* Cambridge, MA: Harvard University Press, 1965.

Eckert, William A. "The Applicability of the Ethos Theory to Specific Ethnic Groups and the Prediction of Urban Political Forms." *Urban Affairs Quarterly,* vol. 11, no. 3 (1976), pp. 357–374, and "A Reply to Plax," pp. 387–389.

Hennessy, Timothy M. "Problems in Concept Formation: The Ethos 'Theory' and the Comparative Study of Urban Politics." *Midwest Journal of Political Science,* vol. 14, no. 4 (1970), pp. 537–564.

Wilson, James Q., and Edward C. Banfield. "Political Ethos Revisited." *American Political Science Review,* vol. 65, no. 4 (1971), pp. 1048–1062.

———. "Public-Regardingness as a Value Premise in Voting Behavior." *American Political Science Review,* vol. 58, no. 4 (1964), pp. 876–887.

Ex Officio   From the Latin, by virtue of office or official title; responsibility to serve automatically on a body through holding another position. Mayors can serve *ex officio* on charter revision commissions, council members on committees reviewing audits, treasurers on retirement and pension boards, and clerks on records management committees. In some jurisdictions, prosecuting attorneys serve *ex officio* on halfway-house boards.

Significance   *Ex officio* membership strengthens informational transactions between boards and commissions. It forces liaison among decision-making bodies and makes public officials accountable for knowing about many facets of community life. To avoid ambiguity, the appointing authority often specifies whether the official has voting power. It is common for high-ranking *ex officio* members not to attend these meetings but to appoint deputies to do so.

Exaction   An order to a developer from a municipality that some facility, land, or in lieu thereof, some money, must be contributed to the community for a capital improvement prior to the issuance of a building permit. Exaction is also known as mandatory dedication, user impact fee, and linkage fee. In states that allow exaction, the practice is employed by cities to secure a predetermined amount of parkland for a housing development. If a master plan does not call for parkland in the area, the city may demand payment of money for other capital improvements that have an impact from the development. The U.S. Supreme Court in *Nollan v. California Coastal Commission*, 97L Ed 2d 672, one of the three "taking" cases decided by the high court in 1987, declared that exactions are allowable only when they relate to a specific purpose that is a legitimate part of the government's jurisdiction. Early examples of exactions, such as building low-income housing in exchange for being permitted to build a luxury hotel and installing a crosstown swimming pool, are probably impermissible under *Nollan*. On the other hand, requiring a builder to install a deceleration lane adjacent to a subdivision to ensure proper ingress and egress is acceptable. *See also* DEDICATION; EXTERNALITY; GROWTH MANAGEMENT; *ULTRA VIRES*; USER FEE.

Significance   Exactions are a 1990s metropolitan government technique based on earlier precedents. As early as the 1920s, some subdivision developers were required to install infrastructure within their area as a condition of securing a building permit. But these street, sewer, sidewalk, curb, and gutter improvements were within the project area. Exaction policy has now expanded from solely internal improvements to possible contributions external to the project investments. Texas state law allows cities to exact off-location capital improvements only if the facility is previously identified on a master plan. Only original costs can be imposed, not costs associated with repair or operation. California's Proposition 13, Massachusetts' Proposition 2½, and Michigan's Headlee Amendment make exactions a viable alternative to raising taxes to pay for capital expenditures associated with new growth. Municipalities have the leverage to withhold construction permits, a practice that some builders consider extortion. Some exactions have been successfully challenged in courts when plaintiffs have shown that the city is acting capriciously, that the off-site improvement is not related to the impact of the project, or that the exaction is disproportionate to the impact of the new construction. To avoid the argument of unfair impact fees, cities have devised *recapture agreements* in which the first area developer agrees to make necessary off-site improvements for the area. As later developers come in and reap the benefit of the initial improvement, they must pay the initial developer a prorated refund. The formula is made a matter of record so that future developers are aware of external cost repayments.

Suggested Reading

Babcock, Richard F. "Forward to Exactions: A Controversial New Source for Municipal Funds: A Symposium." *Law and Contemporary Problems*, vol. 50, no. 1 (1987).

Frank, James E., and Robert M. Rhodes, eds. *Development Exactions.* Chicago: American Planning Association, 1987.
Goetz, Edward G. "Office-Housing Linkage Programs: A Review of the Issues." *Economic Development Quarterly,* vol. 2, no. 2 (1988), pp. 182–196.
Kaiser, Ronald A., and James D. Mertes. *Acquiring Parks and Recreation Facilities through Mandatory Dedication—A Comprehensive Guide.* State College, PA: Venture Publishing, 1986. (Reviewed in *Urban Lawyer,* vol. 19, no. 19 (1987), pp. 761–765.)
Nelson, Arthur C., ed. "Symposium: Linkage Fee Programs." *Journal of the American Planning Association,* vol. 54, no. 2 (1988), pp. 197–224.

Executive Order 12372   A public policy proclaimed by President Ronald Reagan that was designed to reduce the number of federal programs mandated for review by regional planning councils under the A-95 process. The executive order eliminated most federal aid for substate regional planning. Under the Reagan order, review authority was given to the states. This change was in keeping with the administration's general aim to give a variety of programs back to the states. The A-95 Review directive, which was replaced by the executive order, lasted from 1969 to 1983. *See also* A-95 REVIEW; COUNCIL OF GOVERNMENTS.

Significance   Executive Order 12372 attempted to change the regional or metropolitan planning process in a fundamental way. This policy was intended to increase state power in metropolitan planning, but it also placed the funding burden on states if they wished to continue regional planning. President Reagan's initiative in eliminating regional planning support stemmed from his administration's belief that regional planning had accomplished its major goals. After the executive order, however, most of the Councils of Governments (COGs) with review responsibilities under A-95 continued those functions.

Suggested Reading
Council of State Planning Agencies. *The Promise of Partnership: A Status Report on Implementation of the President's Intergovernmental Consultation Initiative, Executive Order 12372.* Washington, DC: Council of State Planning Agencies, 1984.
Derthnick, Martha, with Gary Bombadier. *Between State and Nation: Regional Organizations of the United States.* Washington, DC: Brookings Institute, 1974.
Rothenberg, Irene Fraser, and George J. Gordon. "Out with the Old, In with the New: The New Federalism, Intergovernmental Coordination, and Executive Order 12372." *Publius: The Journal of Federalism,* vol. 14, no. 3 (1984), pp. 31–48.
Walker, David B. "Snow White and the 17 Dwarfs: From Metro Cooperation to Governance." *National Civic Review,* vol. 76, no. 1 (1987), pp. 14–27.

Exhaustion of Administrative Remedies   A common-law doctrine stating that no case will be accepted by a court when an administrative remedy is provided by statute or ordinance, except where excused. The requirement for exhaustion of administrative remedies dictates that relief first must be sought by way of rules and appeals before the court will act; otherwise the court will declare the case not yet ripe for review. Some administrative proceedings are optional, however, such as those that parallel civil rights action through federal courts to regain a job lost for racial reasons. The doctrine can be bypassed in emergencies when plaintiff can show that irreparable damage would be caused by administrative delay. In those circumstances, an equitable relief may be granted, pending further and fuller court review. *See also* QUICK-TAKE LAW.

Significance   The requirement for exhaustion of administrative remedies slows down the decision-making process by forcing potential litigants to pursue the bureaucratic process. Appeals from zoning variances may require argument at the zoning board of appeals. The same procedure applies to tax assessment appeals and appeals on just compensation in condemnation proceedings.

Experimental Housing Allowance Program (EHAP)   A ten-year Department of Housing and Urban Development (HUD) study of a rental supplement system for low-income families. The Experimental Housing Allowance Program study began in 1970 and involved more than 30,000 families at 12 sites across the country. The EHAP study sought to determine how rent supplements affected both demand and supply of better housing for low-income families. The study was spurred by the Nixon administration's interest in returning much of the federal government's Section 8 housing program to the private sector. The study followed the housing allowances given to selected families for a three- to ten-year period at a total cost of $160 million. *See also* HOUSING SUBSIDY; HOUSING, SECTION 8; SUPPLY-SIDE ECONOMICS.

Significance   The Experimental Housing Allowance Program sought to show the relative advantages of private-sector incentives versus direct public involvement in low-income housing. Because the housing allowance system allowed renters greater freedom to select where they wished to live and use their rent subsidies, supporters argued the program would stimulate greater private housing investment. The rent subsidy system sought to give greater freedom of choice to renters within certain ceilings and subject to eligibility requirements. The program also required landlords to maintain their buildings according to federal standards in order to be designated a public housing authority. In other areas, allowance payments were not tied to a housing quality requirement. The experience of renters able to demand improvements or relocate to housing that met those standards was not significant. Of the households that moved because their units failed to meet the quality standards, more than half relocated to units that also did not meet the established standards. Most of the early reports produced from the original EHAP study indicated that the program did not produce noticeable negative market effects in the form of inflated rental prices. However, later research revealed the allowance program increased rents for recipients and nonrecipients alike. Housing allowances did not produce obvious, positive market effects in the form of new housing construction or rehabilitation. In 1984, the Reagan administration eliminated the new construction component of Section 8, making it exclusively a rent supplement program.

Suggested Reading
Bradbury, Katherine, and Anthony Downs, eds. *Do Housing Allowances Work?* Washington, DC: Urban Institute, 1981.
Hartman, Chester. "Housing Allowances: A Critical Look." *Journal of Urban Affairs*, vol. 5, no. 1 (1983), pp. 41–55.
Struyk, Raymond J., and Marc Bendick, Jr., eds. *Housing Vouchers for the Poor: Lessons from a National Experiment.* Washington, DC: Urban Institute, 1981.
Zais, James P., et al. *Implications of Housing Allowance Evidence for the Section 8 (Existing Housing) Program.* Washington, DC: Urban Institute, 1977.

Externality   The concept of economics and public policy that recognizes certain costs (or benefits) fall outside a target group in the marketplace. Although they can be positive, externalities are usually regarded as public "bads" (as opposed to public "goods") and are an inevitable by-product of the productive process in a market economy. These by-products or costs are "external" to the market. Producers do not pay for producing these harmful by-products. For example, the pollution created by a corporation during its productive process is considered an externality. However, the public sector has often stepped in to control pollution generated by firms, or even public utilities, because this has been seen as important to the public at large. To the extent that corporations must alter their productive process (add pollution control devices, for instance), such costs must be recognized by the producer. *See also* LOCALLY UNWANTED LAND USE; PRIVATE SECTOR; PUBLIC SECTOR.

Significance   The arguments over what is considered proper involvement of the public sector in the private market have been fundamental to virtually all societies. In the United States, the mixed economy and limited-government traditions have allowed some governmental regulation of business activity. Over time, the government has tended to intervene in the market when the market has been unable or unwilling to provide public goods or prevent negative by-products. Many of these can be considered externalities of the market. Laws providing for pollution control, safety in the workplace, safe products and child labor laws all impose costs on the productive process that did not exist in the free market. As such, they are examples of government regulation of certain market activities that essentially internalize what had been an externality of the market.

Extraterritorial Power   As applied to municipalities, authority granted by states to control surrounding land or parcels outside corporate limits. Extraterritorial powers are of two types. The first includes police power functions in which residents outside but adjacent to the community are extended basic services, such as health protection, public safety, and land planning. An example is police patrolling beyond the city's limits. According to the 1963 Texas Municipal Annexation Statute, home-rule cities are surrounded by a ring of unincorporated territory. The width of the extraterritorial jurisdiction (ETJ) for planning purposes is a function of city population. The most populous jurisdictions have a five-mile radius reserved for future annexation. If small, non–home-rule cities wish to encroach on this domain, they first must secure the home-rule city's approval. The second type of extraterritorial power consists of proprietary functions in which the municipality owns property or provides a service outside its jurisdiction. Examples would be a city-owned camp outside the city border and processing sewage for adjacent municipalities. Less than half the states permit extraterritorial land-use planning. This allows for possible uncontrolled urban fringe development. *See also* CONSTITUTION, STATE; POLICE POWER.

Significance   About 35 states allow their political subdivisions some form of extraterritorial power. Extraterritorial police powers were challenged in the Alabama case of *Holt Civic Club v. Tuscaloosa*, 439 U.S. 60 (1978), on the ground of denial of equal protection of the law. Justice Rehnquist, speaking for a six-to-three court, found that the provisions of the state enabling statute served a legitimate purpose; it gave cities power to provide police, sanitary facilities, criminal jurisdiction, and licensing for businesses, trades, and the professions in a three-mile belt. In the case of Houston and Dallas, the extraterritorial jurisdiction is subject to annexation by action of mayor and council without a referendum by either the city residents or the targeted population. The ETJ serves as a surrogate land bank for future home-rule city expansion. Dearborn, in Wayne County, Michigan, publicly owns and operates Camp Dearborn in Milford Township, Oakland County, Michigan, as well as the Dearborn Towers apartment complex in Clearwater, Florida. These fall under the proprietary provisions of extraterritoriality. Although special districts sometimes are set up to supply metropolitan water service, many cities supply this service themselves beyond their borders in the name of economies of scale.

Suggested Reading

Gutman, Steven F. "Regulation without Representation: *Holt Civic Club."* *Urban Law Annual,* vol. 19 (1980), pp. 292–302. (Critical of the *Holt* holding.)

Maddox, Russell Webber. *Extraterritorial Powers of Municipalities in the United States.* Corvallis: Oregon State College, 1955. (Cited by Rehnquist in *Holt.*)

Thomas, Robert D. "Metropolitan Structural Development: The Territorial Imperative." *Publius: The Journal of Federalism,* vol. 14, no. 2 (1984), pp. 83–115.

Exurbia   Collectively, that prosperous area of acreage parcels located beyond suburban subdivisions and populated by upper- and upper-middle-class residents who commute to the suburbs and central city. The area is not serviced by typical urban amenities. Etymologically, the word *exurbia* derives from "out of" and "city." The term was coined in 1957 by Auguste C. Spectovsky. The sequence of space that radiates outward from the central business district (CBD) is (1) central city, then (2) suburbia, then (3) exurbia. Outside that area, in an arch surrounding the metropolitan area, is the true rural countryside not connected to the central city by commuters. In physical layout, exurbia is characterized by an absence of both curbs and sidewalks. It provides private, not public, recreation facilities such as swimming pools, tennis courts, and hunt clubs. The most characteristic building type is the shopping center, surrounded by ample, paved parking lots. *See also* GROWTH MANAGEMENT; METROPOLITAN STATISTICAL AREA; ZONING, EXCLUSIONARY.

Significance   Exurbia is the product of the automobile and the interstate expressway system, which allow for a manageable time-space ratio for the daily urban commute. It is designed for wealthier families who wish to live in small-scale towns, villages, townships, or unincorporated areas. Its large-parcel lots often have severe building restrictions that limit infilling and land splits. New York–area examples include Long Island's Northshore and Fairfield County, Connecticut.

Boston-area examples include Carlisle, Weston, and Wayland. A Detroit-area example is northern Oakland County. A Washington, D.C., metropolitan area example is Calvert County, Maryland. Property taxes are the primary source of government revenue; education and public safety are characteristically the two chief expenditure categories.

Suggested Reading

Herbers, John. *The New Heartland: America's Flight beyond the Suburbs and How It Is Changing Our Future.* New York: Times Books, 1986.
Spectovsky, Auguste C. *Exurbanites.* Philadelphia: Lippincott, 1957.

F

Fair Housing Title (Civil Rights Act of 1968, 42 U.S.C. 3601)
Title VIII of the Civil Rights Act of 1968 that attempted to promote open housing in the United States. The Fair Housing Title prohibited discrimination in the sale or rental of housing "to any person because of race, color, religion, or national origin." In addition, it prohibited discrimination in mortgage financing arrangements. This title is commonly referred to as the "Fair Housing Act," and it proclaimed that U.S. housing policy would "provide, within constitutional limitations, for fair housing throughout the United States." The general administration of all housing programs remained under the authority of the Department of Housing and Urban Development (HUD), which had been created in 1965. According to the Fair Housing Title, legal action against alleged violators of the fair housing provisions could be initiated by an individual citizen or the U.S. Attorney General's Office. The open housing provisions of the legislation were made effectively obsolete in June 1968 by the U.S. Supreme Court's decision in *Jones v. Mayer* (392 U.S. 409), which prohibited discrimination in the sale and rental of all housing. *See also* BLOCKBUSTING; HOUSING, OPEN; HOUSING, PUBLIC; RACIAL STEERING; RESTRICTIVE COVENANT.

Significance Discrimination against blacks in the housing market, in both renting and purchasing, had become a national scandal to many observers. Restrictive covenants, which prevented minorities from purchasing or renting housing, effectively closed many areas to blacks, particularly in suburban markets. The Civil Rights Act of 1968 was passed in the aftermath of Dr. Martin Luther King's assassination, but the housing portion was a weakened version of an earlier proposal supported by President Lyndon Johnson in 1966. Dr. King's 1966 open housing march in Chicago had brought the issues of racial segregation and discrimination from the South to cities in the North. However, a political backlash occurred with King's initiative in Chicago.

198

Even though a majority of all housing was covered under the Fair Housing Title of the 1968 Civil Rights Act, such practices as "racial steering" by real estate agents continue to reinforce *de facto* segregation, and racial discrimination in housing remains a problem in all regions of the country. Amendments to this legislation passed in 1974 expanded enforcement to include gender discrimination, and in 1988 to expand coverage to handicapped citizens and to increase enforcement provisions.

Suggested Reading
Kemp, Deborah. "The 1968 Fair Housing Act: Have Its Goals Been Accomplished?" *Real Estate Law Journal*, vol. 14, no. 4 (1986), pp. 327–343.
Lake, Robert W. "The Fair Housing Act in a Discriminatory Market: The Persisting Dilemma." *Journal of the American Planning Association*, vol. 47, no. 1 (1981), pp. 48–58.

Family   In law, a flexible term defined by statute and ordinance as relating to such conditions as marriage, households living as housekeeping units, and people related by blood and usually sharing the same last name. There is no definitive definition of family in the law. Various limits are placed on the institution relative to marriage licenses, public welfare, zoning, and insurance. Restrictive definitions of a family are employed by ordinance writers to limit residential areas to relatively small, nuclear family units of mothers, fathers, sisters, brothers, first cousins, and grandparents. The U.S. Supreme Court twice in the 1970s entered into the issue of defining family. In *Village of Belle Terre v. Boraas*, 416 U.S. 1 (1974), the court declared it acceptable for a municipality to define a family as those living in a single-family dwelling and related by blood, marriage, or adoption, with no more than a specified number of unrelated persons. The Court, speaking through Justice Douglas, reaffirmed that zoning is a legitimate exercise of the police power and that defining a family in a city ordinance is rationally related to the city's goal of eliminating traffic congestion and overcrowding. In *Moore v. City of East Cleveland*, 431 U.S. 494 (1977), just three years later, Justice Powell wrote for a divided court that produced six different arguments. In an opinion that represented only three other members, he stated that an ordinance's limited definition of a family is unconstitutional; it is an infringement on an individual's right to make decisions about how to live. Both the California and New Jersey supreme courts have disagreed with the *Belle Terre* restrictive family definition on state constitutional grounds. *See also* GROUP HOME; POLICE POWER; *VILLAGE OF EUCLID V. AMBLER*; ZONING, EXCLUSIONARY.

Significance   By limiting the size and scope of what constitutes a legitimate family, city councils and zoning boards have attempted to preserve certain middle-class ethics and property values. Prior to state and nationally imposed mandates to accept group homes, cities barred these communal homes under such laws. This engendered a classic confrontation between the civil liberties position that individuals should be able to live as they wish and the position that the community should have the power to impose societal norms.

Suggested Reading
Einbinder, Michael P. "The Legal Family: A Definitional Analysis." *Journal of Family Law,* vol. 13, no. 4 (1973–1974), pp. 781–802.
Madsen, RoJean. "Using a Flexible Definition of the Family in Social Services." *Journal of the American Planning Association,* vol. 49, no. 2 (1983), pp. 149–155.
Ritzdorf, Marsha. "Challenging the Exclusionary Impact of Family Definitions in American Municipal Zoning Ordinances." *Journal of Urban Affairs,* vol. 7, no. 1 (1985), pp. 15–26.
Rubin, Eva R. *The Supreme Court and the American Family.* New York: Greenwood Press, 1986.
Urban, Donald W. *"Moore v. City of East Cleveland:* Preserving Endangered Families." *Urban Law Annual,* vol. 15 (1978), pp. 337–349.

Federal Aid to Impacted Areas   Funding from the federal government to areas where the substantial presence of tax-exempt federal property has created a financial strain on the local public school system. The Federal Impacted Areas Aid Act (20 U.S.C. 236 et seq.), which began in 1950, was designed to help fill the revenue void that tax-exempt military installations had created in many school districts during World War II. The program allocates funding to affected areas for projects such as the construction and operation of public schools. Money for this federal initiative originally was appropriated under the auspices of the Federal Security Agency. *See also* CATEGORICAL GRANT; GENERAL REVENUE SHARING.

Significance   The Federal Impacted Areas Aid program was an outgrowth of postwar legislation that funded programs in areas affected by the federal government's defense work. Although technically considered a categorical grant, the impact aid money tends to be regarded by school districts as "no strings attached" money, with much the same local discretion over spending as has occurred with revenue sharing. Eligibility for this program has expanded considerably since 1950, largely because of effective lobbying by the National Association of Impacted Districts. Eligible beneficiaries grew from pupil dependents of military personnel to include students who were

Native Americans, children of any federal employee, all schools in Washington, D.C., schools hit by major disasters from natural causes, and any children living in federally subsidized public housing. Under President Ronald Reagan, the impact aid funding program was cut dramatically. During the 1970s and 1980s, the program was funded by as much as $1.1 billion and as little as $470 million.

Federal Emergency Management Agency (FEMA)   An independent national-level administrative organization that serves as a clearinghouse for disaster planning and relief operations as well as recovery assistance. FEMA was established in 1978 to coordinate national, state, and local efforts to deal with all natural and man-made emergencies. The first of five major line units is the Federal Insurance Administration, which aids localities in limiting flood damage. It also participates in insurance coverage for flood insurance, riots, and other civil disturbances. The second line agency is the U.S. Fire Administration, which maintains a national fire data center. Third is the Training and Education Directorate, which orients personnel to hazard mitigation. Fourth is the National Preparedness Programs Directorate, which develops plans to alleviate the impact of resource shortages in both peace and wartime. This includes preparing for any future gasoline shortage. Fifth is the State and Local Programs and Support Directorate, which administers the president's relief program when he declares an area a major disaster. Programs are administered through ten regional offices. Examples of emergencies include droughts, earthquakes, floods, hurricanes, hazardous waste spills, airplane crashes into densely populated areas, and nuclear meltdowns. *See also* EMERGENCY EVACUATION; PLANNING, CONTINGENCY.

Significance   FEMA is designed to work with disasters. It often prods uncooperative communities to anticipate a catastrophe. Such plans must be technically accurate, focused on coordinating efforts, easily understood by the participants, politically sensitive to the prerogatives of locally balkanized governments, and ever alert to the major role the mass media will play in the execution of any contingency plan. Flooding is the most frequently experienced emergency with which FEMA and the counterpart agencies must cope. It is estimated there are more than 6 million people living in dwellings built in designated floodplains. Many cities report that as much as half of their floodplain land is part of the built environment. Cities cannot manage flood control alone and must look to regional land-use management. Of the estimated 17,000 flood-prone U.S. cities, most are not in compliance with FEMA floodplain management criteria.

Suggested Reading

Foster, Harold D. *Disaster Planning: The Preservation of Life and Property.* New York: Springer-Verlag, 1980.

May, Peter. "FEMA's Role in Emergency Management: Examining Recent Experience." *Public Administration Review,* vol. 45, Special Issue (1985), pp. 40–48.

Platt, Rutherford H. "The Jackson Flood of 1979: A Public Policy Disaster." *Journal of the American Planning Association,* vol. 48, no. 2 (1982), pp. 219–231.

———. "Metropolitan Flood Loss Reduction through Regional Special Districts." *Journal of the American Planning Association,* vol. 52, no. 4 (1986), pp. 467–479.

Federal Home Loan Mortgage Corporation (FHLMC)   A federal agency involved in the secondary mortgage market, along with the Federal National Mortgage Association (FNMA) and the Government National Mortgage Association (GNMA). The FHLMC, or "Freddie Mac," was created in 1970 to purchase mortgages from commercial lending institutions that are part of the Federal Home Loan Bank system. This agency primarily purchases conventional mortgages, although it also buys Federal Housing Administration (FHA) and Department of Veterans Affairs (VA) loans. *See also* FEDERAL HOUSING ADMINISTRATION; FEDERAL NATIONAL MORTGAGE ASSOCIATION; GOVERNMENT NATIONAL MORTGAGE ASSOCIATION; HOUSING FINANCE AGENCIES.

Significance   The Federal Home Loan Mortgage Corporation actively buys and sells all types of home loans—conventional mortgages, FHA and VA loans, and loans made by the Government National Mortgage Association. In particular, Freddie Mac has been a substantial source of funding for condominium loans. Freddie Mac requires several standardized financial and accounting practices, such as specific documentation required in the Uniform Instrument. This is required for Freddie Mac participation, including loan applications, credit reports, and appraisal forms, along with the mortgage. More significantly, Freddie Mac established rigid regulations regarding the "due-on-sale" clause of a mortgage. This effectively eliminated the ability of home purchasers to assume extant mortgages at much lower interest rates than current market rates.

Federal Housing Administration (FHA)   A federal agency created by the National Housing Act of 1934 (48 Stat. 1246). The main purpose of the Federal Housing Administration was to stimulate housing construction during the period of the Great Depression by offering government-subsidized home mortgages to qualified individuals. The

FHA still insures a large percentage of home mortgages and allows the mortgagee to buy a house with a relatively low down payment. Under Title I of the Housing Act of 1934, the FHA began to make loans for home repair, thus attempting to address the problem of deteriorating housing during the economic downturn of the Great Depression. Various sections of Title II of the Housing Act provide funding for housing construction or home purchases. The FHA became part of the Department of Housing and Urban Development in 1965. *See also* FEDERAL NATIONAL MORTGAGE ASSOCIATION; GOVERNMENT NATIONAL MORTGAGE ASSOCIATION; HOUSING FINANCE AGENCIES.

Significance   The Great Depression created a substantial problem in housing in the United States. New housing starts plummeted from pre-Depression years, and money was unavailable to make basic repairs on existing housing stock. The Federal Housing Administration was created to help support the sagging housing industry by providing insurance for loans made to build new houses or to make permanent repairs to existing property. The FHA allowed borrowers to make down payments of as little as 5 percent of a home's cost, with loan periods of up to 30 years. This compares to the pre-Depression period, when conventional home mortgages required a down payment of 40 to 50 percent of the home's cost, with the repayment periods usually ranging from 6 to 11 years.

Suggested Reading
Bartke, Richard W. "The Federal Housing Administration: Its History and Operations." *Wayne Law Review,* vol. 13, no. 4 (1967), pp. 651–677.
U.S. Department of Housing and Urban Development. *Programs of HUD: 1987–1988.* Washington, DC: U.S. Government Printing Office, 1988.

Federal National Mortgage Association (FNMA)   A federal government agency that originally provided homeowner mortgage subsidies and loan guarantees for eligible applicants, called the secondary mortgage market. The FNMA, or "Fannie Mae," was created by congressional charter in 1938 to assume some risk, thus encouraging lenders to lend money and expand housing growth. In 1954, the activities of FNMA were divided into three parts by the Federal National Mortgage Charter Act (12 U.S.C. 1716 et seq.). These activities included secondary market operations, special assistance functions, and management and liquidation functions. With increased activities, some of the responsibilities of Fannie Mae were later given to the Government National Mortgage Association (GNMA), which is called "Ginnie Mae," and the Federal Home Loan Mortgage Corporation

(FHLMC), popularly known as "Freddie Mac." In 1970, Fannie Mae became a privately financed, for-profit corporation that primarily purchases mortgages from original lenders, using borrowed money and funding raised from the sale of its stock, which is listed on the New York Stock Exchange under the name of FNMA. By 1988, Fannie Mae held approximately $50 billion worth of home mortgages, making it the nation's largest mortgage underwriter. During the late 1980s, it helped to finance about 12 percent of all home mortgages. *See also* FEDERAL HOME LOAN MORTGAGE CORPORATION; FEDERAL HOUSING ADMINISTRATION; GOVERNMENT NATIONAL MORTGAGE ASSOCIATION; HOUSING, PUBLIC; HOUSING FINANCE AGENCIES.

Significance   During the Great Depression, public confidence in banks and other lending institutions plummeted considerably. Fannie Mae became part of Franklin Roosevelt's New Deal philosophy, in which the federal government began to intervene in the marketplace to support many private businesses and industries, in an effort to bolster the economy and resurrect the public's faith in it. Housing policy itself has changed considerably over the years. Earlier the federal government attempted to provide public housing for low-income families. However, dissatisfaction with public housing programs grew substantially among most groups, from builders and realtors to renting families. The Fannie Mae, Ginnie Mae, and Freddie Mac loan guarantees represent a shift from direct public subsidy to indirect support for home purchases. More recently, considerable controversy has emerged about the intended targets of support (urban, lower-income families) versus the actual beneficiaries of loan guarantees (suburban, middle-class families). Fannie Mae originally purchased VA and FHA loans at a discount but currently buys and sells conventional mortgages as well. Generally, Fannie Mae buys mortgages at market prices and in turn sells them in large blocks to institutional investors, such as insurance companies. In 1988, Fannie Mae, Ginnie Mae, and the FHA held a combined $825 billion in mortgages or mortgage-backed securities but had capital totaling only $6.5 billion.

Federalism   The two-level theory of decision making within a nation governed by a written constitution. Federalism is also known as division of power. In the United States, the national and state levels are the outcome of the Philadelphia Constitutional Convention's Great Compromise in 1787, also known as the Connecticut Compromise. It is associated with no one writer but rather with those who wanted to retain the former colonies as states but nevertheless wished a select, strong central government. Each level has independent authority over its jurisdiction. The national list of powers is delegated, such as those dealing with foreign relations. The states' jurisdiction consists of reserved powers, which are also known as police powers. Some powers are joint, or concurrent, such as the authority to tax. *See also* ADVISORY COMMISSION ON INTERGOVERNMENTAL RELATIONS; DILLON'S RULE; FISCAL FEDERALISM; GRANT-IN-AID; POLICE POWER; RESIDENT.

Significance   Federalism is generally considered the chief innovation made by this country in the art of statecraft. Division of power is designed to accommodate diversity, achieve efficiencies of scale, and ensure flexibility in finding answers to differing local or regional circumstances. It allows states to be laboratories for experiments, and it can put a premium on local initiative. It is also designed to give officials experience before being elevated to other levels. The key principle is that although both levels are independent and have their own grant of power from the people, they still coordinate their policies. With the same space having two governments, there is room for substantial conflict over turf. These inevitable conflicts are resolved ultimately by the U.S. Supreme Court, which serves as final arbitrator in state-national and state-state conflicts. Federalism, along with separation of power, are the two major structural techniques for allocating decision making in the United States. The two levels are not equal; there is national supremacy, according to Article VI, Paragraph 2, of the U.S. Constitution. There is no general federal police power, but on many issues, such as education, welfare, transportation, and health care, both levels spend substantial sums and issue policy guidelines. Division of power as a concept has changed over time with the progression of the nation from 13 to 50 states and from a largely agrarian former colony to a highly technological urban nation. The system puts a premium on cooperative intergovernmental relations; both levels work directly with the same problem and for the same people. Urban areas look to both their states and the national government for funds and information, the combination determined by constantly changing factors of personnel and partisanship. The states are represented at the national level *per se* in the U.S. Senate. The federal analogy, which compares the national Senate to state senates, is thus false. The U.S. Senate represents states, whereas state senates do not represent counties or districts but people in state senate districts. Hence, the only legislative chamber free from reapportionment along a one-person-one-vote formula is the U.S. Senate.

Suggested Reading
Advisory Commission on Intergovernmental Relations. "Local Government: Federalism's Workhorses." In Robert Jay Dilger, ed., *American*

Intergovernmental Relations Today: Perspectives and Controversies. Englewood Cliffs, NJ: Prentice-Hall, 1986. Chap. 7.

Anton, Thomas J. *American Federalism and Public Policy: How the System Works.* Philadelphia: Temple University Press, 1989.

Elazar, Daniel J. *American Federalism: A View from the States.* New York: Thomas Y. Crowell, 1966. Chap. 7.

Frug, Gerald E. "Empowering Cities in a Federal System." *Urban Lawyer,* vol. 19, no. 3 (1987), pp. 553–568. (The issue is devoted to essays on federalism.)

Nathan, Richard P., and Fred C. Doolittle and Associates. *Reagan and the States.* Princeton: Princeton University Press, 1987.

Federally Assisted Code Enforcement (FACE)   A funding program authorizing federal assistance to local governments in their attempts to regulate and enforce local housing code ordinances. FACE was a product of Section 117 of the Housing Act of 1965, which provided funding for a limited number of local enforcement activities, and the Housing and Urban Development Act of 1965, which required local code-enforcement programs as a precondition of receiving federal funds. Improvements such as street and lighting repairs, housing rehabilitation, and tree plantings were funded under this program. Most of these activities were replaced by provisions authorized under the Housing and Community Development Act of 1974. *See also* CODE ENFORCEMENT; HOUSING AND URBAN DEVELOPMENT ACT OF 1968; INFRASTRUCTURE.

Significance   Programs such as Federally Assisted Code Enforcement (FACE) were intended to encourage the maintenance and improvement of housing stock across the United States. Although the number of local code ordinances increased substantially during the mid-1960s and are now widely adopted, many observers have argued that the goals of FACE have not been met. The forces of the economy and the private housing market often have greater bearing than the law on the willingness of owners or landlords to repair and improve their housing. During periods when the local housing supply is low, code enforcement can create even greater shortages, because buildings that violate code are often closed. In addition, the quality of inspection, the uncertainty and variation in penalties, and the general lack of enforcement also have diluted the impact of housing code standards.

Filtering Theory, Housing   An economic argument suggesting that adequate housing stock is available to lower-income groups through a natural movement of residences from wealthier to poorer families. The filtering process occurs when housing surpluses exist and upper-income groups move to more desirable housing. Such a move leaves a residence available to those with lower incomes. With a housing surplus assumed to exist, theoretically the price of the vacated house drops. This downward movement continues until it finally reaches families at the lowest end of the income scale. Eventually the house is abandoned. But before then, all income groups are able to move into better housing that otherwise would not exist. *See also* ABANDONMENT; GENTRIFICATION; SECTOR MODEL; VACANCY CHAIN.

Significance The filtering or trickle-down theory of housing has been used to justify an emphasis on the construction of new housing for upper-income families, on the supposition that better housing thus would become available to all income groups down the economic ladder. This theory also has promoted the reduction or elimination of federal public housing programs by declaring that sufficient, adequate, and even improved housing is available for the lower-income groups who are traditionally the recipients of public housing programs. However, because the theory assumes the filtering process occurs during a housing surplus, its premise weakens when attempting to explain filtering during housing shortages. In addition, many other forces are at work that affect the demand for various types of housing. The migration of blacks to central cities during the twentieth century, a subsequent exodus by whites into surrounding suburban areas, and the more recent gentrification movement in many U.S. cities all have influenced the demand and price for housing stock. Filtering theory also has been associated with Homer Hoyt's sector model, which refers to the directional development of land-use patterns in cities. For example, if a city develops high-income housing along a river, there will be a tendency for that development to be maintained. In the St. Louis metropolitan area, those with higher incomes have tended to live west of the city; in Detroit and Seattle, they live to the north.

Suggested Reading
Blair, John P. "A Review of the Filtering-down Theory." *Urban Affairs Quarterly*, vol. 8, no. 3 (1973), pp. 303–316.
Downs, Anthony. "Key Relationships between Urban Development and Neighborhood Change." *Journal of the American Planning Association*, vol. 45, no. 4 (1979), pp. 462–472.
Marullo, Sam. "Housing Opportunities and Vacancy Chains." *Urban Affairs Quarterly*, vol. 20, no. 3 (1985), pp. 364–388.
Myers, Dowell. "Housing Allowances, Submarket Relationships, and the Filtering Process." *Urban Affairs Quarterly*, vol. 11, no. 2 (1975), pp. 215–240.

Weicher, John C., and Thomas G. Thibodeau. "Filtering and Housing Markets: An Empirical Analysis." *Journal of Urban Economics,* vol. 23, no. 2 (1987), pp. 21–40.

Fiscal Crisis   A turning point or critical moment in a process of governmental decisions on taxation, spending, and debt management, most centrally concerning the budget. Usually policy analysts speak of a federal fiscal crisis relating to decisions brought on by Congress. A federal monetary crisis pertains to the Federal Reserve Board's decisions on the availability of money, crimping inflation, or encouraging growth without sacrificing employment rates. An urban fiscal crisis cannot be separated from federal fiscal and monetary policy. Nonetheless, there are well-known warning signs of an impending crisis that might lead to the need for a bailout, even to a municipal bankruptcy: (1) In narrowly based city economies reliant on one major tax source, an impending plant closing or a cyclical major downturn in that sector's fortunes. (2) In most municipalities, largely reliant on property taxes for revenue, an increase in abandoned buildings or an influx of unpaid real estate taxes. (3) Warring between banks or other bondholders and a city's administration over impending bond defaults or low fund balances. (4) The failure of corporation counsel to defend a city against wrongful action suits, for which the city council does not set aside contingency funds to cover losses. (5) Persistently underfunded pension funds that are subject to class-action suits by retired public employees. (6) Persistent expenditures in excess of revenues. (7) The persistent floating of tax anticipation notes (TANs) to cover routine operating expenditures. (8) Mis-, mal-, and nonfeasance by treasurers and occasional ineptitude in posting accounts under the guise of shifting to a new ledger system, often blamed on improper software or delays in computer hardware. (9) Tax tribunal decisions that go against the community and in favor of major landholders, for which there was not ample time to build contingency funds. (10) Bond-rating services conventionally raise or lower municipal credit ratings incrementally. When they lower a city's rating several gradients at once, it may well mean they have read an auditor's caveats in a report or have uncovered threshold information on an impending shortfall. *See also* AUDIT; BANKRUPTCY, MUNICIPAL; NEW YORK CITY BAILOUT; URBAN CRISIS.

Significance   Fiscal crisis may lead to a default on bond payments, or to a long-term low rating by both major bond-rating companies, which in turn raises the future cost of borrowing. It may also lead to bankruptcy, in which the court substitutes its judgment for that of elected officials. There may be a cessation of long-term capital outlays and hence an end to any planned infrastructure renewal; there also may be copious, adverse media coverage. This would negate carefully orchestrated institutional advertising and progrowth campaigns designed to attract business into the area. The crisis may be caused by the private as well as the public sector. The 1970s Cleveland banks' distaste for the populism of Mayor Dennis J. Kucinich precipitated the default on the city's lighting operation.

Suggested Reading

Burchell, Robert, and David Listokin, eds. *Cities under Stress: The Fiscal Crisis of Urban America.* New Brunswick, NJ: Center for Urban Policy Research, Rutgers, the State University of New Jersey, 1961.

Levine, Charles, and Irene Rubin, eds. *Fiscal Stress and Public Policy.* Beverly Hills: Sage, 1980.

Martin, Jean K. *Urban Fiscal Stress: Why Cities Go Broke.* Boston: Auburn House, 1982.

Pohlmann, Marcus D. "Drawing in the Reins: Political Responses to Fiscal Crisis in American Cities." *Journal of Urban Affairs,* vol. 4, no. 3 (1982), pp. 51–64.

Poister, Theodore H., and Robert P. McGowan. "Municipal Management Capacity: Productivity Improvement and Strategies for Handling Fiscal Stress." *ICMA Municipal Year Book 1984,* Chap. D3, pp. 206–214.

Rubin, Irene S. *Running in the Red: The Political Dynamics of Urban Fiscal Stress.* Albany: State University of New York Press, 1982.

Weinberg, Mark. "The Urban Fiscal Crisis: Impact on Budgeting and Financial Planning Practices of Urban America." *Journal of Urban Affairs,* vol. 6, no. 1 (1984), pp. 39–52.

Fiscal Federalism   The financial relationship among the federal, state, and local governments. Fiscal federalism generally refers to the various grant-in-aid programs in which the federal government provides funding for programs administered at the state and local levels, as well as to the taxation policies of all governments. Overall, grant-in-aid funding programs have fallen into three broad types—categorical grants, block grants, and revenue sharing. *See also* CATEGORICAL GRANT; GENERAL REVENUE SHARING; INTERGOVERNMENTAL RELATIONS.

Significance   An associated term often used interchangeably with fiscal federalism is *cooperative federalism,* which can also include activities such as standards for training, operation, and procedure, in addition to funding. Federal grants-in-aid have been offered to states and local governments since the mid-1800s. One of the largest grant programs provided funding under the Morrill Land-Grant College Act of 1862, which authorized the federal government to give land to any state that would use it to create a college to teach agriculture and engineering. By the late 1980s, about $100 billion was being made available each year for the various categorical and block grant programs. In an effort to underscore innovation and change, each president since Richard Nixon has called his approach the "New Federalism," to emphasize new directions in fiscal policy. Under the Reagan administration, many federal grant programs were reduced or eliminated in an effort to take the federal government out of activities considered to be state or local responsibilities.

Suggested Reading

Advisory Commission on Intergovernmental Relations. *The Significant Features of Fiscal Federalism.* Washington, DC: ACIR, 1985.

Rosen, Harvey S., ed. *Fiscal Federalism: Quantitative Studies.* Chicago and London: University of Chicago Press, 1988.

Fiscal Year (FY)   A 12-month period, beginning at a given date, during which governmental revenues, appropriations decisions, and actual spending activities occur. The fiscal year is designated conventionally by the calendar year in which it ends. Many state and local governments have adopted the federal government's fiscal year of October 1 through September 30. This change occurred in 1977 after enactment of the federal Congressional Budget and Impoundment Control Act of 1974. Because many state and local governments have relied on federal grants-in-aid, their fiscal years also were altered to conform to the timing of federal budgetary activities. *See also* FISCAL FEDERALISM; GRANT-IN-AID; INTERGOVERNMENTAL RELATIONS.

Significance   The fiscal year, as opposed to the calendar year, represents the increased professionalization of governmental fiscal management. All budgetary decisions and recordkeeping were identified according to a cycle of revenues and expenditures that did not always conform to the calendar year. The conventional fiscal year of July 1 to June 30 reflected earlier appropriations and budgeting cycles employed by governments. The subsequent change in the fiscal year by the federal government, then by many state and local governments, underscores the fiscal dependency of state and local units on the federal government.

Suggested Reading

Burkhead, Jesse, and Paul Bringewatt. *Municipal Budgeting: A Primer for the Local Official.* Washington, DC: Joint Center for Political Studies, 1977.

Fluoridation Politics   A highly contentious local public-policy issue in U.S. politics from the 1940s through the 1960s regarding the desirability of adding fluorides into municipal water supplies to reduce the incidence of children's dental caries. The issue of fluoridation was debated emotionally in local referendums where it was often defeated, but more frequently debated in city councils, the state courts, and state legislatures. Advocates felt it was a legitimate exercise of the police power to protect part of the community through a preventive public health measure. Opponents, who had few medical personnel on their side, countered with arguments that it was enforced mass medication and an invasion of parental rights, that it was discriminatory in that it benefited only children, that it was used as rat poison in large dosages, that it was a plot by ALCOA, the aluminum company, to increase profits, and that it was an opening wedge to socialized medicine and an example of governmental interference in private lives. Because the topic was widely debated and drew otherwise dormant groups such as the Christian Scientists into political dialogue, it attracted a great deal of social science research. *See also* CASE STUDY; POLICE POWER; REFERENDUM.

Significance   About 60 percent of the U.S. population now lives in areas with water controlled for fluoride content. The United States leads the world in this form of preventive medicine. Fluoridation politics usually pitted dentists and other medical personnel, who were not well prepared for the political arena, against highly emotional opponents who used a barrage of counterarguments in heated campaigns. The electorate and city council members were largely ignorant of the issues and had difficulty filtering out the claims and counterclaims. In the long run, battles were generally won by the proponents in the city council elections. The claims for fluoridation were corroborated by the National Institute of Dental Research, a part of the National Institutes of Health (NIH), in a 1988 report that said children who use fluorides in water and toothpaste have substantially fewer cavities than other children. Current urban political texts largely ignore this rich literature, in part because one influential writer, John E. Mueller, reported that the issue was largely nonrepresentative of other urban public-policy issues.

Suggested Reading

Crain, Robert, et al. *The Politics of Community Conflict: The Fluoridation Decision.* Indianapolis: Bobbs-Merrill, 1969.

Hursh, R. D. "Annotation: Water Supply—Chemical Treatment." 43 ALR 2d 453–465, plus supplement service (1954) for a summary of legal aspects of statutes, ordinances, and administrative law.

McNeil, Donald R. *The Fight for Fluoridation.* New York: Oxford University Press, 1957.

Mueller, John E. "The Politics of Fluoridation in Seven California Cities." *Western Political Quarterly,* vol. 19, no. 1 (1966), pp. 54–67.

Forecast   That part of public-policy analysis that anticipates events or conditions through estimates of future outcomes. A forecast is prophecy based on partial empirical evidence. Forecasting differs from mere projection or extrapolation in that it can be a systematic study of the future. It often is based on a model that explicitly employs some base period, articulates a set of assumptions about change, anticipates new trend lines, and applies one or more methodologies to calculate events or conditions into some specified period. A simple projection, on the other hand, implicitly assumes that system relationships will remain the same and that policies will too. Forecasting is divided into long-term, medium-term, and short-term analysis. Ten years is often the conventional period for the beginning of long term, but it depends on the field. A five-year economics forecast generally is considered long term. Forecasting also is divided into large-scale and small-scale analysis, a single metropolitan area being small scale and international trends being large. Forecasting is differentiated by sponsorship as well. The national weather and census bureaus are examples of national public sponsorship. Most politically sponsored forecasts other than those involving defense are in the public domain. In addition to weather and population forecasts, urban areas make extensive use of forecasts for education, manpower, public health, utility growth, land-use planning, mass transit and transportation, water consumption, and solid waste disposal, as well as crime and housing. *See also* BUDGET TYPES; COST-BENEFIT ANALYSIS; INFRASTRUCTURE.

Significance   Forecasting is an aid to twentieth-century urban government decision making. Many levels are involved. School systems, county planning departments, and Councils of Governments (COGs) all forecast population trend lines to anticipate the need for new schools or school closings and the need for more subdivisions or control of abandoned buildings. Forecasting makes urban decision makers aware of dynamics and time spans longer than a fiscal year. Some state budget offices publish official population forecasts that must be used in local fiscal planning so that all civil jurisdictions make the same calculations. The U.S. Army Corps of Engineers calculates floods for 50- and 100-year scenarios, which then are used in calculating the portion of a valley that is unbuildable. Urban forecasts for passenger car and truck registrations from the 1950s are the basis of most urban interstate expressways in use in the 1990s. Transportation and land-use forecasts are generally rudimentary. Urban-fringe land values often begin to go up two decades before actual subdivision development. Anticipating urban decentralization and lower densities is a major goal of Councils of Governments. Social forecasting has had less success than scientific and technological projections. Much sociopolitical planning is surprise-insensitive. Improvements to forecasts are being made by paying attention to the development of the assumptions in the model, use of alternative scenarios, better baseline data, improved monitoring of forecasts for possible introduction of new variables, and interconnecting with other forecasts.

Suggested Reading
Asher, William. *Forecasting: An Appraisal for Policy-Makers and Planners.* Baltimore: Johns Hopkins University Press, 1978.
The Commission on the Year 2000 (Robert F. Wagner, Jr., Chair). *New York Ascendant.* New York City: n.p., 1987. (Economics, poverty, education, health, crime, housing, and transportation.)
Hudson Institute. "Final Report, Michigan Beyond 2000." Prepared for the Michigan State Senate, HI-3806-RR. Indianapolis, IN: Hudson Institute, 1985.
Hughes, Barry B. *World Futures: A Critical Analysis of Alternatives.* Baltimore: Johns Hopkins University Press, 1985.
Moyer, Reed. "The Futility of Forecasting." *Long Range Planning,* vol. 17, no. 1 (1984), pp. 65–72. (Nuclear power, electric consumption, computer capability, population and labor force, residential construction, and passenger car production.)
Spilerman, Seymour. "Forecasting Social Events." In Kenneth C. Land and Seymour Spilerman, eds., *Special Indicator Models.* New York: Russell Sage, 1975, pp. 381–403.

Foreign Trade Zone (FTZ)   A federally designated area of commerce that receives tax forgiveness. Foreign trade zones have been established in areas that often offer several tax incentives to induce business investment and location and are legally considered to be outside U.S. Customs territory (19 U.S.C. 81 a–u). Goods may enter a foreign trade zone to be stored, repaired, packaged, or combined with other products used in manufacturing activities. If the goods leaving the foreign trade zone are exported, no duty is paid. These zones are located in areas that usually are economically depressed, and such incentives are used with the belief that business investment would not otherwise occur within the designated area. By 1987, there were approximately 240 zones and subzones (single-firm manufacturing sites) in the United States. In 1970, there were fewer than 20 such zones. *See also* ENTERPRISE ZONE; SUPPLY-SIDE ECONOMICS.

Significance   Foreign trade zones were one example of the Reagan administration's supply-side approach to economic recovery. Rather than providing direct public-spending subsidies, the supply-side approach avoids public spending in favor of tax expenditures to encourage certain behavior. The tax forgiveness usually associated with foreign trade zones involves a waiving of taxes when a business imports parts from another country, puts those parts together to make a completed product, then exports the product to another country. Many U.S. companies have used foreign trade zones to import parts made in foreign countries, especially Japan, while avoiding customs duty charges. Much of the political debate over "domestic content" requirements in automobiles has stemmed from the use of foreign trade zones by automobile manufacturers with factories in the United States.

Franchise, Elective   The freedom or privilege of full membership in the state, as manifested by the granting of citizenship, which bestows the right to participate on equal terms in public affairs. The most frequently exercised example of elective franchise is voting in elections for public office, but it also encompasses voting on constitutions, participating in public forums, and serving on juries. To be given the freedom to participate is to be *enfranchised*; this is done by statute or constitutional provision. Residents of the District of Columbia were constitutionally enfranchised in 1961 in voting for president and vice-president. However, they still are denied the right to vote for representatives and senators. To have the privilege to participate taken away in part or totally is to be *disenfranchised* or *disfranchised*. Individuals may have their right to participate taken away for changing their citizenship; by "civil death," imposed in some states for conviction of major crimes; and in some states for being declared incompetent in a court of law. Partial disenfranchisement is caused by election fraud, uncorrected legislative districts in rapidly changing areas, gerrymandering, census undercount, and vote dilution that favors majorities who bloc-vote. The specific power to vote is referred to as the *suffrage*. A *suffragist* is an advocate of women's right to vote. This was first allowed statewide in Wyoming in 1870 and for municipal elections in Kansas in the 1890s. Nationally, the 19th Amendment ratified in 1920 enfranchised women. Courts have declared that groups of voters by ethnic or racial criteria (Hispanics and blacks, e.g.) may not have their votes diluted by imposition of at-large elections. *See also* AT-LARGE ELECTION; NONPARTISAN ELECTION; QUALIFICATIONS FOR OFFICE; VOTE DILUTION CASES; VOTING RIGHTS ACT OF 1965; WASHINGTON, DISTRICT OF COLUMBIA.

Significance   One of the major trend lines in U.S. politics for the past 200 years is the expanding franchise. The franchise was initially confined to propertied 21-year-old white males, who paid a poll tax and were literate and nonindentured (hence the phrase "free, white, and 21"). The elective franchise now approaches universal adult suffrage. Few believe complete universal adult franchise will ever occur, however; no one advocates franchise for aliens, felons, the severely developmentally disabled, and those who do not register to vote. Two major policy issues concerning the elective franchise in the 1980s were national supervision of voter registration for racial minorities, especially in the South, and underrepresentation of minority groups in representative bodies elected by at-large vote.

Franchise, Government   The privilege conferred by any level legislature to a corporation or individual to conduct business under a charter in the name of a public benefit. It is called a government franchise inasmuch as the public is the franchiser, as distinguished from a business franchise in which a for-profit organization allows another group called the franchisee to use a name, process, or service. Government franchises are never issued by an administrative body. Administrative bodies are allowed only to issue a *license,* which usually differs from a franchise in authorizing body, exclusivity, purpose, and duration. At the state and local levels, franchises are issued in the name of the public's health, safety, morals, welfare, or well-being—in short, under the police power. The charter cannot be sold or transferred without governmental approval. Franchises usually are issued for a limited period and are renewable. A franchisee must assume responsibility to serve all willing and able customers and cannot discriminate by limiting the amount of production. In turn, the government regulates the franchisee, ensuring a "reasonable rate of return" on capital investment. Since 1984 cities have not been able to regulate cable television rates. Government franchises usually are permitted to exercise eminent domain and to secure easements in order to function efficiently. Major local government franchise operations include transportation services such as light rail, bus, and taxi lines; public utilities with intensive capital investments, such as gas, water, cable, and electricity; parts of the public transportation roadbed, such as bridges, toll roads, and tunnels; and main-line municipal services, such as refuse collection and fire protection. *See also* CABLE FRANCHISE; CONTRACTING OUT; PRIVATIZATION; PROPRIETARY FUNCTION; PUBLIC UTILITY.

Significance   American urban governments have looked long at franchise arrangements as an alternative to direct government delivery of services or goods. With the fiscal stress of cities in the 1970s and 1980s, franchising became an alternative to reducing services, promoting coproduction (bringing in volunteers), creating fee schedules, and contracting out to other not-for-profit bodies, or privatization. Unlike business franchises, government charters always are interpreted strictly by courts to favor the franchiser, because the conveyance was created in the first instance to benefit the public at large and not for the aggrandizement of both parties.

Suggested Reading
Moore, Barbara H., ed. *The Entrepreneur in Local Government.* Washington, DC: International City Management Association, 1983.
Morgan, David R. "Municipal Service Delivery Alternatives." In Jack Rabin and Don Dodd, eds., *State and Local Government Administration.* New York: Marcel Dekker, 1985.

Freedom of Information Act (FOIA)   A federal or state statute that provides for public access to records held by executive branch agencies and departments. Most state laws follow the federal Freedom of Information Act (5 U.S.C. 552) of 1966, which opened up many federal agency records for public inspection. Some local governments have established similar ordinances that allow a citizen to request information from a city department. The rules regarding freedom-of-information recordkeeping, procedures for approving or denying requests, and exemptions vary from state to state. These are also known as "Open Records," "Right to Know," "Public Records," or "Open Government" laws.

Significance   Concern about control of information held by the executive branches of federal and state governments became evident by the 1960s. Freedom of Information laws can be considered part of the "good government" tradition that began in the United States in the late nineteenth century. Typical of state policymaking in general, considerable variation exists with regard to their implementation and the records and departments that are statutorily exempt from public inspection. Some states provide for inspection of local government records as well, but the wave of open records, open meetings, and general sunshine legislation has not reached local levels as much as the state level. Therefore, the availability of local executive branch documentation still depends primarily on the discretion of local officials.

Suggested Reading
Feinberg, Lotte E., and Harold C. Relyea, eds. "Symposium: Toward a Government Information Policy—FOIA at 20." *Public Administration Review,* vol. 46, no. 6 (1986), pp. 603–639.

G

Garcia v. San Antonio Metropolitan Transit Authority, **469 U.S. 528 (1985)** After less than a decade, the U.S. Supreme Court explicitly overturned *National League of Cities v. Usery* (1976), declaring that the Fair Labor Standards Act minimum-wage and overtime requirements applied to states and cities. *Garcia* revisited the issue of whether the U.S. Constitution's Commerce Clause allowed Congress to enforce pay scales on states and their subdivisions in their traditional functions. The highly split 5 to 4 high court opinion by Justice William Brennan stated that the distinction between traditional and nontraditional functions was unworkable. In the eight years between the *Usery* and *Garcia* decisions, the Court had been unable to forge any clear guidelines. The impositions at the national level of such standards on the transit authority violated neither state sovereignty nor the U.S. Constitution. *See also* NATIONAL LEAGUE OF CITIES V. USERY; PROPRIETARY FUNCTION; SEPARATION OF POWERS.

Significance The *Garcia* ruling narrowly established the dividing line between permissible national standardization and impermissible national interference with states. The traditional function test was found both inconsistent and unworkable, so the national high court pulled back on limiting Congress's powers. Brennan noted the increasing fiscal interrelationship of the national and state governments: As of 1982 it approached $100 billion in transfer payments. With one-fifth of state and local government appropriations originating from Washington, it was not surprising that the national level should have something to say about how the funds should be spent.

Garden City A self-contained, planned community with a minimum of 30,000 residents and a diversified economy nestled in a wide greenbelt; the community provides amenity-rich neighborhoods for low-density living and stresses physically healthy environments at home and work. The garden city movement was a reaction to the excesses of early industrial capitalism with its increased densities surrounding unhealthy smokestack factories. The prime mover of these ideas was Sir Ebenezer Howard (1850–1928), who wanted to stem the migration from the English and Welsh countryside into unhealthy central cities such as Liverpool, Birmingham, and London. He further differentiated between a *garden suburb*, which was an amenity-filled dependent city, and a *garden village*, which was a miniature dependent garden city with a single economic base attached to a larger central city for infrastructure and which lacked its own protective belt. Howard's ideas became a national and international movement, not always consistent with the founder's ideas, which stressed optimum scale, greenbelts, and public ownership or trust arrangements for most or all of the community's land. *See also* COUNTERURBANISM; GREENBELT; NEW TOWN; OPTIMUM CITY; URBAN SPRAWL.

Significance   Sir Ebenezer Howard's garden city ideal was a turn-of-the-century reaction to British industrialism. Actual garden city experiments were set up in Letchworth (1903) and Welwyn (1919). They were new towns that acknowledged the need for industry, as long as it was constructed on a modest scale in pleasant surroundings. Out of these projects came the genesis for present physical-planning professionals of the United Kingdom and the United States. There were two major limits that prevented the spread of the garden city movement. First, most new communities are not self-contained but privately planned and executed suburbs. Second, Howard's insistence on public ownership ran counter to the private-sector entrepreneurial American tradition.

Suggested Reading
Christensen, Carol A. *The American Garden City and the New Towns Movement.* Ann Arbor, MI: UMI Research Press, 1986.
Corden, Carol. *Planned Cities: New Towns in Britain and America.* Beverly Hills: Sage, 1977.
Fisher, Irving D. *Frederick Law Olmsted and the City Planning Movement in the United States.* Ann Arbor, MI: UMI Research Press, 1986.
MacFayden, Dugold. *Sir Ebenezer Howard and the Town Planning Movement.* Cambridge, MA: MIT Press, 1970.
Schaffer, Daniel. *Garden Cities for America: The Radburn Experience.* Philadelphia: Temple University Press, 1982.

General Revenue Sharing (GRS)   A federal funding program terminated in 1986 that passed money to the states, each of which took one-third of the money and distributed the remaining two-thirds to its cities. Unlike other federal transfers, General Revenue Sharing money could be used for virtually any legitimate governmental purposes. The General Revenue Sharing program became effective in 1972. The amount of GRS money made available to each state was determined by a fixed formula, based on federal taxes paid in each state. A certain amount then would be returned automatically to that state. The General Revenue Sharing program had a sunset provision attached to it, and although it was renewed in 1976 and 1980, the program was not renewed in 1986. *See also* GRANT-IN-AID.

Significance The strict guidelines imposed by federal categorical grants were attacked by states and cities as too restrictive. By the late 1960s, efforts to relax the spending guidelines produced two new federal funding programs—block grants and revenue sharing. This program has been closely associated with President Richard Nixon, and the idea for revenue sharing is attributed to Walter Heller, Nixon's chairman of the Council for Economic Advisors. During the 1970s, between $6 and $7 billion a year was provided to states and municipalities under general revenue sharing. During the 1980s, that amount decreased to about $4.5 billion each year. As in many other areas, the level of support assumed by different states to fill the void left by the federal government has varied considerably. Most cities used the monies for capital expenditures. Those that used them for operating revenue were in greater trouble when the program ended.

Suggested Reading
Caputo, David A., and Steven Johnson. "New Federalism and Midwestern Cities: 1981–1985." *Publius: The Journal of Federalism*, vol. 16, no. 1 (1986), pp. 81–95.
Dommel, Paul. *The Politics of Revenue Sharing*. Bloomington: Indiana University Press, 1974.
Juster, F. T., ed. *The Economic and Political Impact of General Revenue Sharing*. Ann Arbor: Survey Research Center, Institute for Social Research, University of Michigan, 1977.
Nathan, Richard P., and Fred C. Doolittle. *The Consequences of Cuts*. Princeton: Princeton University Urban and Regional Research Center, 1983.
Reagan, Michael D., and John G. Sanzone. *The New Federalism*. New York: Oxford University Press, 1981.

Gentrification The process of converting deteriorated residential areas of the central city into middle-class property use by displacing current owners and renters and physically improving the housing stock. *Gentrification* derives from the root *gentry*, people of good position or birth. The term was coined in the 1960s to describe the social upgrading of select London neighborhoods. The result is creation of middle- and upper-middle-class areas surrounded by other still deteriorated inner-city neighborhoods. The conversion is accomplished largely through private reinvestment, not by urban renewal. *Revitalization,* a broader term, refers to both redevelopment and renovation. The in-migrating gentry are predominantly white, whereas the displaced are black or recently arrived ethnics. It is a countertrend to the general population movement of whites to the suburbs and blacks into the central city. The white gentry are not primarily disenchanted ex-suburbanites but arrivals from other parts of the central city. As a movement, it is focused primarily on older central cities with brownstone houses that can be restored to their late-nineteenth-century grandeur. The movement is the opposite of counterurbanism. Explanations for gentrification by social scientists, mainly urban geographers and sociologists, range from social-cultural life style to demographic characteristics, along with economic interpretations of land use and underutilization of investment opportunities in housing markets. Some areas have used historic preservation designations to capture tax advantages. *See also* ABANDONMENT; DISINVESTMENT, URBAN; DISPLACEMENT; HISTORIC PRESERVATION; REDLINING; URBAN REVITALIZATION.

Significance   The scope of gentrification is small in comparison to the absolute decline in population in U.S. central cities since the 1950s. It does signal select restructuring of the well-built portions of communities situated on good transportation routes into the central business district. Although accounting for only a fraction of new housing and focused in the snowbelt, gentrification increases tax yield for cities experiencing the movement. Property values rise, as expressed in higher assessments. Central-city schools experience few new students; most gentrifiers either are empty-nesters or have not yet started families. This urban-core renaissance nets small-scale reinvestment but no citywide improvements, such as fewer homeless or increased consumer services. The gentry often are employed in downtown multinational corporation offices. They are often well-educated, low-budget families who are interested in the arts and who wish to be near the city's cultural center. Examples of gentrified neighborhoods include Society Hill in Philadelphia and Baltimore's Federal Hill. The same renovation spirit is taking place in Canada, in England, and on the European continent. When land values are low and property values are potentially high through renovation, a community is ripe for displacement. Two constraints to widespread gentrification are high inner-city crime rates and the availability of sufficient investment capital to accomplish the upgrading.

Suggested Reading
Beauregard, Robert A. "Politics, Ideology, and Theories of Gentrification." *Journal of Urban Affairs*, vol. 7, no. 4 (1985), pp. 51–62.
Henig, Jeffrey R., and Dennis Gale. "The Political Incorporation of Newcomers to Racially Changing Neighborhoods." *Urban Affairs Quarterly*, vol. 22, no. 3 (1987), pp. 399–419.
London, Bruce, Barrett A. Lee, and S. Gregory Lipton. "The Determinants of Gentrification in the United States: A City-Level Analysis." *Urban Affairs Quarterly*, vol. 21, no. 3 (1986), pp. 369–387.
Smith, Neil, and Peter Williams, eds. *Gentrification in the City*. Boston: Allen & Unwin, 1986.
Zukin, Sharon. "Gentrification: Culture and Capital in the Urban Core." *Annual Review of Sociology*, vol. 13 (1987), pp. 129–147.

Ghetto   A geographically distinct residential area that is highly segregated from other areas of the city by race, ethnic group, or economic class. "Upper-class ghettos," sometimes called "gilded ghettos," are a double contradiction: A ghetto is an area where residents are often impoverished. There are no voluntary ghettos. Exclusiveness is forced on ghetto residents by discrimination. Voluntary, geographical residential segregation is generally called a *colony*. The term *ghetto* derives from medieval Italian and originally referred to the Jewish quarter. In twentieth-century America, ghetto more broadly refers to any area of social isolation predominantly containing a subordinate minority. *See also* BARRIO; COMMUNITY; FILTERING THEORY, HOUSING; KERNER COMMISSION; SUCCESSION; URBAN VILLAGE.

Significance   A ghetto, defined as a segregated racial or ethnic community, may contain a combination of classes. Ghettos that are black, Latino (usually called barrios), Chinese (usually called Chinatowns), or Irish (usually called Corktowns) are financially diverse communities. On the other hand, a ghetto defined as a slum, a location of the lower class or underclass, is economically homogeneous. A ghetto in the economic sense has high unemployment, high transience, and high crime, whereas an ethnic ghetto may have stable family life and well-developed mutual support systems and be supportive of public schools. A ghetto defined economically was likely to have rioters in the 1960s, whereas a ghetto defined ethnically or culturally typically is a more stable residential area.

Suggested Reading
Downs, Anthony. *Urban Problems and Prospects*. Chicago: Rand McNally, 1970. Chap. 2, "Alternate Futures for the American Ghetto."
Forman, Robert E. *Black Ghettoes, White Ghettoes, and Slums*. Englewood Cliffs, NJ: Prentice-Hall, 1971.

Fusfeld, Daniel R., and Timothy Bates. *The Economics of the Urban Ghetto.*
    Middletown, CT: Wesleyan University Press, 1984.
Rose, Harold M. "The Development of an Urban Subsystem: The Case of the
    Negro Ghetto." *Annals of the Association of American Geographers,* vol. 60,
    no. 1 (1970), pp. 1–17.
Spear, Allan H. *Black Chicago: The Making of a Negro Ghetto 1890–1920.*
    Chicago: University of Chicago Press, 1967.
Ward, David. "The Emergence of Central Immigrant Ghettoes in American
    Cities: 1840–1920." *Annals of the Association of American Geographers,*
    vol. 58, no. 2 (1968), pp. 343–359.
Wilson, William Julius. *The Truly Disadvantaged: The Inner City, the Underclass,
    and Public Policy.* Chicago: University of Chicago Press, 1987.
Wirth, Louis. *The Ghetto.* Chicago: University of Chicago Press, 1928, 1956.

Gift to Government   A form of revenue derived from a charitable contribution of money or property. Gifts to governments may be directed to any level, including special districts. Most donations are in the form of real property, designed to enhance recreation parks, open space, sites for college buildings, easements for highways and public utilities, or historic preservation. The national government encourages such gifts and permits a major tax write-off if the grant is in perpetuity. It is common, however, for owners to retain a life interest in property on which they are presently living. *See also* DEDICATION; INCOME SOURCES, URBAN; LAND CONSERVANCY.

Significance   Gifts to government are not a major line item of public budgets. The recipient may turn down the donation if restrictive covenants that run with the contribution, such as keeping the land racially segregated, do not comport with public policy. But individual gifts of property often represent the largest source of land for parks and open spaces. As a *quid pro quo,* local units often agree to name the park, open space, or building after the benefactor. Tax-exempt institutions make gifts to cities for payments in lieu of taxes, or PILOT. Public schools receive large donations of equipment from corporations (for which the donor receives ample publicity and perhaps a laboratory in which to test its product). The corporation's timing is often related to a tax deadline or inventory control. Some cities allow taxpayers to check a box on their income tax form to forgo their tax rebates, automatically contributing the money to the general fund.

Goal Setting   An *ad hoc* form of community planning and consensus building through widespread citizen participation. In the goal-setting process, a public and private or a private organization alone studies, deliberates, and ultimately reports on which items ought to have the highest priority on the public agenda. The groups that study goal setting usually work in committees for a year or more, studying background papers and options before agreeing on those issues that most deserve public attention. Such bodies usually use small professional staffs and must be adequately funded in order to assemble background papers. Goals are usually formulated as performance standards, with due attention to political feasibility and relative cost-benefit ratios. If properly conducted, the goal-setting process is not dominated by any one interest group or economic sector. The group focuses on several interrelated issues that may or may not correspond to the agenda of local political party platforms. *See also* AGENDA SETTING; FORECAST; PARTICIPATION; PLANNING, STRATEGIC; URBAN COALITION.

Significance   State, county, and city goal-setting studies have been implemented since the 1970s. Typical state examples include reports entitled "Illinois 2000," "Hawaii 2000," and "California 2000"; city examples include the "New York City Commission on the Year 2000," the "Nashville Citizen Goals 2000," and "Goals for Greater Milwaukee 2000." Such bodies serve as a surrogate for the aggregation function usually associated with political parties. If well written, the goals will specify some monitoring group to follow through on recommendations. Well-researched reports are based on in-depth information gathering that forecasts demographic and economic events and potential crime behavior levels. Through general mission statements and suggested procedural changes, properly written reports make an impact on local legislative and executive processes.

Suggested Reading

Netzer, Dick, director. *Report from the Urban Research Center to the New York City Commission on the Year 2000.* New York: New York University Urban Research Center, 1986.

Smith, Frank J., and Randolph T. Hester. *Community Goal Setting.* Stroudsburg, PA: Hutchinson Ross, 1982.

Vogel, Ronald K., and Bert E. Swanson. "Setting Agendas for Community Change: The Community Goal-Setting Strategy." *Journal of Urban Affairs,* vol. 10, no. 1 (1988), pp. 41–61.

Gold Coast   A wealthy residential neighborhood with a pool of aristocratic leadership. This neologism was coined in 1929 by Harvey Zorbaugh (1896–1965) to refer to the prestigious residences of Chicago's North Shore along Lake Michigan. *See also* SLUM; ZONING, EXCLUSIONARY.

Significance   The *gold coast* is a diffuse descriptive term that has never been specifically operationalized. It is to be contrasted with its antipode, *slum*. Its original use was in a case study by Robert E. Park of the University of Chicago School of Urban Sociology, who noted that the term was intended to be generic and not to apply just to part of the lower north side of Chicago. The term does not refer to density (the original example has high-rise apartments and condominiums). Nor does it refer only to suburbs; the original example referred to the Social Register set, who lived within the city of Chicago proper.

Suggested Reading
Zorbaugh, Harvey Warren. *The Gold Coast and the Slum: A Sociological Study of Chicago's Near North Side.* Chicago: University of Chicago Press, 1929, 1976.

Government National Mortgage Association (GNMA)   A federal agency that is part of the secondary home mortgage market. The GNMA, or "Ginnie Mae," was created in 1968 as a division of the U.S. Department of Housing and Urban Development (HUD). Unlike the Federal National Mortgage Association (FNMA), or "Fannie Mae," Ginnie Mae is technically a corporation, but without capital stock. Its major functions include the operation of the special-assistance component of federally supported housing programs, in addition to the liquidation and management responsibilities formerly assumed by Fannie Mae. *See also* FEDERAL HOME LOAN MORTGAGE CORPORATION; FEDERAL HOUSING ADMINISTRATION; FEDERAL NATIONAL MORTGAGE ASSOCIATION; HOUSING FINANCE AGENCIES.

Significance   Ginnie Mae stimulates the housing market and encourages home ownership by acquiring high-risk or low-interest loans from mortgage lenders. Ginnie Mae purchases a mortgage and resells it at a discounted rate, thus providing a governmental subsidy to a home purchaser at a lower interest rate. Though GNMA loans are not a direct governmental obligation, Ginnie Mae's guarantees of securities purchased on the open market provide substantial funding used for financing home mortgages. All secondary mortgage market associations use mortgage-backed securities (MBS), in which pools of mortgages are brought together and sold as bonds. Pooling reduces risk and increases yield. The Ginnie Mae MBS combines Federal Housing Administration (FHA) and Department of Veterans Affairs (VA) mortgages. These various Ginnie Mae financial guarantees and securities have financed more than half of all FHA and VA mortgages in the United States. In fiscal year 1984, GNMA's budget totaled slightly more than $100 million for both mortgage-backed securities and mortgage purchases.

Grace Commission   An executive committee created formally by President Ronald Reagan on June 30, 1982, to find "waste" in the government, save tax dollars, and improve the efficiency of governmental service delivery. The Grace Commission was headed by J. Peter Grace, chairman and chief executive officer of W. R. Grace and Company, a multinational corporation with interests in consumer services, chemicals, and natural resources. President Reagan authorized the formation of the 161-member commission by issuing Executive Order 12369. Most of the commission's members were drawn from the corporate world. The commission investigated the federal bureaucracy for 18 months, had 36 separate task forces, and was staffed by more than 2,000 volunteers. The 47-volume final report of the Grace Commission was presented to President Reagan on January 16, 1984. *See also* PRIVATIZATION; PRODUCTIVITY; SUPPLY-SIDE ECONOMICS.

Significance   Part of the Reagan initiative against "big government," the Grace Commission attempted to present specific policy recommendations that would reduce federal involvement in a variety of issue areas. As a hand-picked presidential commission, the Grace Commission produced a ringing critique of waste within the bureaucracy but clearly placed the burden on Congress to solve the problems identified. In addition, many of the recommendations to save a claimed $424 billion over a three-year period would not have eliminated waste or inefficiency but would have cut specific benefits, such as Medicare payments. As a general rule, all new presidents have attempted to redistribute power to suit their own needs by attacking "waste" in government; this can garner public support for what are really political struggles.

Suggested Reading
Downs, George W., and Patrick D. Larkey. *The Search of Government Efficiency: From Hubris to Helplessness.* Philadelphia: Temple University Press, 1986.
Goodsell, Charles T. "The Grace Commission: Seeking Efficiency for the Whole People?" *Public Administration Review,* vol. 44, no. 3 (1984), pp. 196–204.
Kennedy, William R., Jr., and Robert W. Lee. *A Taxpayer Survey of the Grace Commission Report.* Ottawa, IL: Green Hill Publications, 1984.

Grant-in-Aid   Money paid by one level of government to another level to finance programs and services. By far the most common relationship has been federal money passed on to state and local governments (and to individuals through transfer payments). The earliest and still most common type of federal aid is the categorical grant. Other kinds include block grants and revenue sharing. *See also* CATEGORICAL GRANT; GENERAL REVENUE SHARING.

Significance   Although the great increases in federal grants occurred during the 1930s and 1960s, the grant-in-aid program started in the late 1800s. Even during the early years, it was apparent that the different levels of government needed to share the costs of various programs and services. As governmental activity in the economy and in social programs increased, the number of grants blossomed accordingly. Many observers pointed out that the federal government's use of grants during the twentieth century, especially the more restrictive categorical grants, was a major force in expanding the national government's power over the state and local levels. Supporters of this use of grants argue that federal standards were necessary to monitor and control the extreme variation in state implementation of social programs. These standards often forced state governments to follow federal law, because in some states money was being spent in discriminatory ways. By the 1980s, the Reagan administration adopted a more decentralized plan of delivering public programs, in which state and local government had more programmatic discretion but also received less federal aid to continue programs and services.

Suggested Reading

Stein, Robert M., and Keith E. Hamm. "A Comparative Analysis of the Targeting Capacity of State and Federal Intergovernmental Aid Allocations: 1977, 1982." *Social Science Quarterly*, vol. 68, no. 3 (1987), pp. 447–465.

Wright, Deil S. *Federal Grants-in-Aid: Perspectives and Alternatives*. Washington, DC: American Enterprise Institute, 1968.

Grantsmanship   A state and local governmental strategy that attempts to discover, apply for, and receive federal money from many different sources within the federal government. Grantsmanship has become an increasingly common practice among state- and local-level practitioners, particularly as federal funding became more scarce in the 1980s. As local governments develop greater skills in locating and receiving grants, efforts to reach other sources of funding, including foundations, nonprofit organizations, and educational institutions have become more popular. *See also* GRANT-IN-AID; INCOME SOURCES, URBAN.

Significance   Reduced federal funding to cities since the mid-1970s has created serious financial difficulties for many local governments. Falling revenues from property taxes have forced cities to look for new sources of funding. Grants of all kinds have become widely used to pay for programs and services that might have been reduced or eliminated. Unless these grants are based on a formula and are relatively predictable, most local governments fund these programs on a contingency basis, separate from the general fund. During the 1960s and 1970s, grantsmanship almost exclusively referred to a local government's quest for funding from the federal government. During the 1980s, the term has come to include the talent for finding a much wider variety of funding sources, particularly from the private sector. For those federal funding programs that have not been eliminated, many now require a minimum investment and commitment from the private sector, so funding requests now must cover many routes.

Suggested Reading
Bauer, D. G. *The "How To" Grants Manual.* New York: Macmillan, 1984.
Dilger, Robert Jay. "Grantsmanship, Formulaship, and Other Allocational Principles: Wastewater Treatment Grants." *Journal of Urban Affairs,* vol. 5, no. 4 (1983), pp. 269–286.
Hall, Mary S. *Getting Funded: A Complete Guide to Proposal Writing,* 3rd ed. Portland, OR: Continuing Education Publications, 1988.
Hebert, F. Ted, and Richard D. Bingham. "The City Manager's Knowledge of Grants-in-Aid: Some Personal and Environmental Influences." *Urban Affairs Quarterly,* vol. 7, no. 2 (1972), pp. 303–306.
Lauffer, Armand. *Grantsmanship,* 2nd ed. Beverly Hills: Sage, 1983.

Great Society   The term coined by President Lyndon B. Johnson to describe the America he hoped to mold through a broad spectrum of domestic legislative efforts. Johnson first used "Great Society" in an Ann Arbor, Michigan, speech May 23, 1964. The ambitious program was intended not only to "cut" poverty, but to "prevent" it. The Great Society became Johnson's symbol of presidential policy initiatives, akin to Franklin D. Roosevelt's New Deal, Harry Truman's Fair Deal, and John F. Kennedy's New Frontier. Many different policies and statutes were produced in the period between 1964 and 1968. The most notable legislation of LBJ's Great Society was the Economic Opportunity Act of 1964, which launched his "War on Poverty" program. Other laws dealt with fair housing, public housing, Model Cities, and federal aid to elementary and secondary education. Two cabinet posts also were created to head the Department of Transportation (DOT) and the Department of Housing and Urban Development (HUD). *See also* DEMONSTRATION CITIES AND METROPOLITAN DEVELOPMENT ACT; ECONOMIC OPPORTUNITY ACT OF 1964; WAR ON POVERTY.

Significance   The programs of the Great Society altered the relationship between the federal government and urban centers in fundamental ways. Under these programs, urban problems became part of the national agenda rather than problems to be dealt with only by states or individual cities. At the time, the Great Society represented a consensus among Americans to deal with poverty, enforce civil rights, and promote equal education opportunities. Although poverty programs were not new during the 1960s, the commitment to end and prevent poverty represented a substantial change. This was a time in which a nation could look at urban problems with a confidence that a "Great Society" could cure them. However, the escalating war in Vietnam in the late 1960s divided the Great Society and eroded confidence in the government. The new Nixon administration in 1969 proposed a new urban agenda, and many of the Great Society's programs were significantly reduced or eliminated.

Suggested Reading

Gettelman, Marvin E., and David Marmelstein, eds. *The Great Society Reader: The Failure of American Liberalism.* New York: Random House, 1967.
Gross, Bertram M., ed. *A Great Society?* New York: Basic Books, 1968.
Kaplan, Marshall, and Peggy L. Cuciti, eds. *The Great Society and Its Legacy: Twenty Years of U.S. Social Policy.* Durham, NC: Duke University Press, 1986.
Levitan, Sar A., and Rupert Taggert. "Great Society Did Succeed." *Political Science Quarterly,* vol. 91, no. 4 (1976–1977), pp. 601–618.
Murray, Charles. *Losing Ground.* New York: Basic Books, 1985.
Schwarz, John E. *America's Hidden Success: A Reassessment of Public Policy from Kennedy to Reagan,* rev. ed. New York: W. W. Norton, 1988.

Green River Ordinance   A local law named after one passed in Green River, Wyoming, in 1931, proclaiming door-to-door solicitation and selling without prior consent of the occupant to be *per se* a nuisance and making such activity subject to local criminal prosecution. Green River ordinances prevent what the Uniform Consumer Credit Code (UCCC) calls a home solicitation sale. These ordinances also have been justified as preventing fraud, because the solicitor may not have any permanent address. The U.S. Supreme Court upheld the validity of such an ordinance in *Bread v. City of Alexandria,* 341 U.S. 622 (1951). *See also* ORDINANCE; RESIDENT; SHOPPING CENTER.

Significance   Green River ordinances have been and are still on the books in hundreds of communities, in part encouraged by local businesses to limit competition, in part promoted by local Better Business Bureaus (BBBs) to stem the often-fraudulent door-to-door magazine salesman. Such salespersons also may be less stringently regulated through a local registration fee to control their whereabouts, thereby putting police on notice. Few supporters of itinerant peddlers and solicitors come to the rescue, espousing the right of free commercial speech. The major argument against Green River ordinances is the civil libertarian position that such activity may be regulated but should not be prohibited outright. A fine line on residency must be drawn between permissible local-community Girl Scout solicitation and impermissible solicitation by any outsider who might be canvassing unattended homes as targets for burglary. The issue of discriminating between residents and nonresidents is another form of the philosophical question of who should be allowed to use community parks and how large the civil polity should be: Should it be parochial or cosmopolitan? This is a question of how narrow or open an urban society should be.

Suggested Reading
Reynolds, Osborne M. " 'Green River Ordinances': Where Does the Burden Belong?" *Fordham Urban Law Journal*, vol. 11, no. 3 (1983), pp. 427–454.

Greenbelt   A band of protected open space in an urban area, designed to check urban sprawl by limiting or prohibiting development. A greenbelt is a form of land-use control that creates a buffer of open space around or within a metropolitan area. (1) As originally defined, a greenbelt initially was publicly owned or held in trust for the community. It was colored green on blueprints and was designed to surround garden cities as a protective zone against further growth in the new towns proposed by Sir Ebenezer Howard (1850–1928) and his garden city movement. Some of the belts were designated rural and some agricultural, some were part woodland, and some were to be used for recreation such as golf. London and Birmingham in the United Kingdom both had formally designated protective areas set aside. They were not uniform in width and were not necessarily contiguous. The original 1938 Greenbelt Act primarily preserved open space, whereas the 1947 Town and Country Planning Act overtly limited sprawl. The Town and Country Ministry administered the greenbelt program because planning for cities and adjacent areas was combined in Howard's conception of the garden city movement. The United States experimented with greenbelts through the Resettlement Administration of the 1930s in three communities: Greenbelt, Maryland; Greenhills, Ohio; and Greendale, Wisconsin. These greenbelts were undeveloped wooded areas designed to limit sprawl and provide recreation. The U.S. government withdrew support in 1950 from all three towns. Only one of the three has a semblance of a greenbelt remaining. (2) Today a greenbelt is any open space with no or low population density that cuts through or around part of a metropolitan area. It may be zoned for agriculture or park use, for example, and owned either by the community or privately. If owned privately, it is taxed at a low rate to keep it underdeveloped. *See also* GARDEN CITY; LAND USE CONTROL; URBAN SPRAWL.

Significance   Greenbelt is a nineteenth-century British idea that has not caught on in the United States because of the intractable issues of ownership and maintenance of the open space. It is questioned by the housing lobby as an extravagant use of space and by greenbelt owners as an inverse condemnation in which the government does not take land outright but refuses to allow for the highest and best use. Where it has been tried outside of the United Kingdom, as in the Tokyo area, it was not supportable in the face of development pressures. In the three U.S. cities cited, greenbelts were sold off to the private sector and largely exploited. There are two major reasons for the overall failure of the greenbelt idea as it was exported to the United States. First, the nation has a tradition of private ownership of urban land. (This is not true of rural land, as approximately one-third of the nation is controlled by various levels of government.) Second, greenbelts have had two contradictory purposes: as open space available to adjacent townspeople and as a barrier to city sprawl. Three examples of current U.S. greenbelts are Rock Creek Park in Washington, D.C.; Hines Park in Metropolitan Detroit; and the Cook County Forest Preserve system in Metropolitan Chicago.

Suggested Reading
Arnold, Joseph L. *The New Deal in the Suburbs: A History of the Greenbelt Town Program, 1935–1954.* Columbus: Ohio State University Press, 1971.
Munton, R. J. C. *London's Green Belt: Containment in Practice.* London: Allen & Unwin, 1983.
Nelson, Arthur. "An Empirical Note on How Regional Urban Containment Policy Influences an Interaction between Greenbelt and Exurban Land Markets." *Journal of the American Planning Association,* vol. 54, no. 2 (1988), pp. 178–184.
Osborn, Frederic J. *Green-belt Cities,* new ed. New York: Schocken Books, 1969.

Gridlock   Traffic congestion that makes movement virtually impossible on streets, highways, or airport roads. Gridlock is an extreme form of congestion and is a threat only in high-density urban centers, such as on Manhattan Island, New York. Urban planners have attempted to relieve traffic congestion by creating bypasses, business routes, and "ring roads" around heavily traveled streets. Some cities have installed traffic-control lights on freeway ramps to relieve rush-hour congestion. Despite increasing difficulties with traffic congestion, the costs to build and improve streets and highways are tremendous.

Federal surveys estimate that more than 60 percent of the 2.1 million miles of U.S. highways require some kind of improvement, as do almost 50 percent of the larger bridges in the country. *See also* INFRASTRUCTURE; MASS TRANSIT; TRAFFIC ANALYSIS.

Significance   The threat of gridlock is becoming an important policy issue for all levels of government. Central business district congestion, especially at times of peak use, remains a common problem in large cities. Unplanned, uneven economic development has created massive congestion in some suburban areas, especially where fast development has proceeded without a concomitant improvement and expansion of streets and highways. The costs to businesses have increased tremendously, as companies must wait longer than expected for materials, information, or people to arrive at their appointed destination. For example, in 1989, Los Angeles passed ordinances allowing the construction trades to begin work at 7 A.M. in order to keep prime-time deliveries from adding to already congested freeways and surface streets. Gridlock wastes fuel and time and is blamed for increases in employee fatigue and blood pressure. Despite attempts to solve the gridlock threat, reliance by Americans on the automobile remains at the heart of the traffic congestion problem.

Suggested Reading
Cervero, Robert. "Unlocking Suburban Gridlock." *Journal of the American Planning Association,* vol. 52, no. 4 (1986), pp. 389–406.

Group Home (Adult Foster-Care Home)   A community-based, communal living arrangement with 24-hour-a-day care for the mentally retarded and mentally ill. The U.S. Office of Human Development Services defines group homes as private facilities supplying year-round room, board, and supervision to residents, whom state governments designate as mentally ill or retarded. More than 90 percent of group home residents are on medication. In turn, most states supply a definition of adult foster-care facilities or some variant by statute, in reference to either social services or zoning. Some are also foster homes for patients with closed head injuries. The mentally retarded or developmentally disabled are those who function at a reduced intellectual ability and are unable to live in the mainstream of society without supervision. Most patients are classified as incapable of living on their own by certified mental health professionals in a court competency hearing. The U.S. Supreme Court, in the Texas case of *Cleburne v. Cleburne Living Center,* 473 U.S. 432 (1985), declared that it is rational public policy to treat the mentally retarded as an identifiable group with unique problems that state legislatures and city councils can address. Other courts have declared that the mentally retarded have rights to the least restrictive environment and that their segregation and concentration in asylums is a violation of equal protection rights. These groups cannot be barred from the community as long as they are not found to be dangerous to themselves or the community. Local zoning ordinances justified by the police power cannot exclude these community placement programs because overriding federal legislation allows them. *See also* HOMELESS; LOCALLY UNWANTED LAND USE; PRIVATIZATION; ZONING.

Significance   Group homes are a direct by-product of deinstitutionalization. Deinstitutional policies resulted from increased public awareness of the needs of the mentally retarded and mentally ill for more humane treatments, from improved medications that allowed the patients to be ambulatory, and from the national government's policy of reducing costs associated with large institutions. A major turning point was Congress's passage of the 1963 Community Mental Health Centers Act, 42 U.S.C. 2681, which opened the doors of big institutions to smaller and more cost-efficient community care units. This is the process of substantially lowering the size of large-scale and long-term asylum populations. The trend is toward small-scale— often 6 to 24 to a "home"—residential-based treatment using private accommodations. Living in the community, when combined with activity in a sheltered workshop, is better for patients and has been found to be cost-effective. These homes are LULUs (Locally Unwanted Land Uses) because adjacent neighbors fear reduced property values. However, some empirical studies of residential values have found the homes normally do not adversely affect nearby properties. At public licensing meetings, neighbors regularly resist these placements, but without success because of overriding state law. When residents go to court, they do not fare any better with arguments based on local deed restrictions. A major unresolved issue involves what constitutes excessive concentration of adult foster-care homes.

Suggested Reading

Architecture Research Construction, Inc. *Community Group Homes: An Environmental Approach.* New York: Van Nostrand Reinhold, 1985. (On-site research consideration.)

Dear, Michael. "Impact of Mental Health Facilities on Property Values." *Community Mental Health Journal,* vol. 13 (1977), pp. 150–158.

Feber, Stephen. "Market Segmentation and the Effects of Group Homes on Residential Property Values." *Urban Studies,* vol. 23, no. 6 (1986), pp. 519–526.

Ryan, Carey S., and Ann Coyne. "Effects of Group Homes on Neighborhood Property Values." *Mental Retardation,* vol. 23, no. 5 (1985), pp. 241–245.

Schonfeld, Robert L. "Five-Hundred-Year Flood Plains and Other Unconstitutional Challenges to the Establishment of Community Residences for the Mentally Retarded." *Fordham Urban Law Journal*, vol. 16, no. 1 (1987–1988), pp. 1 ff.

U.S. Department of Commerce, *Statistical Abstract of the United States*. Washington, DC: Superintendent of Documents, annual. (Lists the number of group homes or private facilities under the table "Residential Facilities for the Mentally Retarded.")

Growth Management   A public-policy position that advocates limiting further development of a community in favor of a *status quo* population or slow population increase controlled by the public sector. U.S. communities are forbidden from applying an antigrowth policy such as a moratorium on building, which could constitute a "taking under," *First English Evangelical Lutheran Church of Glendale v. County of Los Angeles*, 482 U.S. 304 (1987). Advocates of growth management want to keep newcomers out of their jurisdiction. Slow-growth policy has been proposed at city, county, and state levels. Proponents argue their community has absorbed all the jobs, residences, or automobile traffic the infrastructure can carry without degrading quality of life. Overcrowding requires stricter land-use controls and a cap on building permits per annum. This has been upheld in two courts. In *Golden v. Ramapo*, 285 N.E. 2d 291 (1972), the New York Court of Appeals found limits on building permits per year to be phased and orderly growth, constitutionally acceptable, and an example of foresighted planning. In *Petaluma v. Construction Industry Association*, 552 F. 2d 897 (1975), the U.S. 9th Circuit Court of Appeals upheld an annual building quota that considered aesthetics and class mix. Previously zoned industrial and commercial parcels can be "downzoned" from intensive use to residential use. Environmental degradation may come in the form of increased flooding; a loss of woodlands, wetlands, and farmland; decreased water quality; and more pollution. Overcrowded schools, caused by too rapid an influx of newcomers, can produce half-day sessions. Taxes generated by new firms and homes are insufficient to cover the high initial costs of constructing infrastructure. *See also* GRIDLOCK; GROWTH POLITICS; QUALITY OF LIFE; SUNBELT; TAX LIMIT; URBAN POLITICAL REGIME.

Significance   Growth management is more a suburban than a central-city issue and is advocated more frequently in burgeoning sunbelt communities than in the older, populated Northeast. Hawaii, Oregon, Maine, and Vermont have looked at these policies statewide. Princeton, New Jersey; Boulder, Colorado; Cape Cod, Massachusetts; Fairfax County, Virginia; and Orange County and Santa Monica, California, are typical locations where growth management is being advocated. It is very much the minority position. Most communities still use incentives designed to retain and promote their local economy. Techniques for discouraging growth are ample: They include adding on "linkage fees" or "impact fees" of thousands of dollars per house to defray costs of additional infrastructure. This is a payment to the community to account for the added public costs generated by the impact of the building. In 1987, San Francisco decreased the allowed size of new central business district (CBD) offices. Where allowed within the guidelines of tax limits, creating high tax levies may discourage new growth. Zoning land into large parcels and imposing high-cost building codes discourage all but the most affluent. Creating land preserves and zoning out all but single-family units reduce many builders' options. There are three major criticisms of the growth-management and slow-growth movement: (1) It adversely affects middle- and lower-class owners while having little impact on upper- and upper-middle-class residents. (2) Because population increase is taking place nationally, local growth-management policy simply shifts the overall growth problem to surrounding communities as an unforeseen externality. (3) The young are also adversely affected as they are the most mobile and the least likely to be able to afford the inflated prices for those few houses that come on the market.

Suggested Reading

Albrecht, Don E., Gordon Bultena, and Eric Hoiberg. "Constituency of the Antigrowth Movement: A Comparison of the Growth Orientations of Urban Status Groups." *Urban Affairs Quarterly,* vol. 21, no. 4 (1986), pp. 607–616.

Baldassare, Mark. "Predicting Local Concern about Growth: The Roots of Citizen Discontent." *Journal of Urban Affairs,* vol. 6, no. 4 (1984), pp. 39–50.

Bosselman, Fred P. "Growth Management and Constitutional Rights—Part I: The Blessings of Quiet Seclusion," and "Part II: The States Search for a Growth Policy." *Urban Law Annual,* vol. 8 (1974), pp. 3–32.

Downs, A. "The Real Problem with Suburban Anti-Growth Politics." *Brookings Review,* vol. 6, no. 2 (1988), pp. 23–29.

Kann, Mark E. *Middle Class Radicalism in Santa Monica.* Philadelphia: Temple University Press, 1986.

Levine, Robert A. "Growth Control: Some Questions for Urban Decisionmakers." Santa Monica: RAND, 1974. R-1419-NSF.

Lillydahl, Jane H., and Larry D. Singell. "The Effects of Growth Management on the Housing Market: A Review of the Theoretical and Empirical Evidence." *Journal of Urban Affairs,* vol. 9, no. 1 (1987), pp. 63–78.

Porter, Douglas R., ed. *Growth Management: Keeping on Target?* Washington, DC: Urban Land Institute, 1986.

Growth Politics   A public-policy position that advocates using state and local governments to encourage present industry to remain while inducing new businesses to locate within the jurisdiction. Most growth policies are predicated on the assumption that people follow jobs and that there will be a net in-migration if the job strategy is successful. Growth politics is boosterism, asserting that bigger is generally better; cities that do not grow are either stagnant or in decline. Birth is a better metaphor than death. Some jurisdictions discriminate in favor of encouraging services over goods production, and many draw the line between encouraging clean rather than smokestack industries. Success is measurable in terms of the decennial census: The population should go up. It is also measurable in terms of the annual government budget: Revenue should go up because of an enlarged tax base. Growth politics is prominent at the local level: Regional and even county or state figures are less important to boosters than city or township increments. *See also* ECONOMIC DEVELOPMENT; GROWTH MANAGEMENT; POLETOWN.

Significance   A majority of states, counties, and cities are closely associated with growth politics—often called the Chamber of Commerce mentality. Public-sponsored state and local techniques for promoting economic growth are legion. They include state-level right-to-work laws that attract antiunion businesses, the absence of plant-closing disclosure laws, and state Commerce Department product promotion. Additional incentives might be subsidized plant site location, placement in free-trade and enterprise zones, lax enforcement of building requirements, tax abatements, tax increment financing, waiver of building fees, favorable assessments, zoning variances, and land parcel sale at below-market cost from city land banks that have assembled and acquired the property. Other growth inducements provided to business include land offers to locate in commercial, industrial, and research parks; promises of low-cost, long-term loans; seed monies for new ventures; and, if all else fails, promises to acquire needed land under a quick-take law using eminent domain provisions while relocating any people or businesses that are in the way. One of the best inducements for growth is the development of high-quality education at all levels, primary and secondary as well as higher.

Suggested Reading
Elkin, Stephen L. *City and Regime in the American Republic*. Chicago: University of Chicago Press, 1987. (Chap. 3 is a political economy approach.)
Logan, John R., and Harvey L. Molotch. *Urban Fortunes: The Political Economy of Place*. Berkeley: University of California Press, 1987.
Molotch, Harvey. "The City as a Growth Machine: Toward a Political Economy of Place." *American Journal of Sociology*, vol. 82, no. 2 (1976), pp. 309–332.
Swanstrom, Todd. *The Crisis of Growth Politics: Cleveland, Kucinich, and the Challenge of Urban Populism*. Philadelphia: Temple University Press, 1985.

Gun Control, Local   An ordinance passed by a city council to prohibit carrying a handgun within city limits. Local gun control has passed in several U.S. municipalities, including Chicago, Oak Park, Evanston, and Morton Grove, all in Illinois. Other cities have had ordinances overturned when courts ruled that state penal codes prevailed over local ordinances, as occurred in 1982 in San Francisco. *See also* ORDINANCE.

Significance   Dissatisfaction with federal efforts to regulate handguns has spurred proposals for legislation at the state and local levels. Opponents, notably the National Rifle Association (NRA), argue that further controls curtail the use of weapons for sport, and that restrictions violate the constitutional right of citizens to bear arms. Yet the widespread use of handguns in criminal activity has continued to create support for those who wish to restrict handgun ownership and use. The use of a handgun in Robert Kennedy's assassination in 1968 and the attempt on President Ronald Reagan's life in 1981 renewed efforts of antihandgun groups. Emotions run high on this issue, and in response some cities have passed ordinances *requiring* homeowners to possess a handgun, as happened in Goreville and Pittsburgh, both in Illinois.

Suggested Reading
Note. "*Quilici* and *Sklar*: Alternative Models for Handgun Control Ordinances." *Journal of Urban and Contemporary Law,* vol. 31 (1987), pp. 341–372.

H

Halfway House   A community-based, minimum-security residence that acts as a transition between prison and parole for adult or
juvenile criminal offenders. Halfway houses provide some supervised
structure for prisoners removed from correctional facilities. Because
of prison overcrowding, the strategy of a halfway house became an
alternative to imprisonment, especially for youthful or first-time offenders. Vocational and personal counseling is often a major part of
the treatment for residents. In some states, these programs are called
"work release" or "education release," in which prisoners are allowed
to work or attend school during the day before returning to the
halfway house. The term of stay generally ranges from six weeks to
four months. Halfway houses serve four major groups of offenders:
(1) probationers who need some supervision; (2) inmates of gradual-
release programs who would benefit from a stepped integration into
society; (3) parolees needing assistance in mainstreaming back into a
community through employment and housing; and (4) parolees who
have served long sentences and still need some supportive services
from correctional authorities. *See also* DEINSTITUTIONALIZATION; GROUP
HOME; LOCALLY UNWANTED LAND USE; JAIL, LOCAL.

Significance   In 1954, the Reverend James G. Jones founded St.
Leonard's, the first halfway house, in Chicago. By the mid-1970s,
almost 400 halfway houses had been established in the United States.
Community-based transition residences also have been established by
mental health and substance-abuse programs for clients who no
longer require formal institutionalization but can benefit from a structured, supervised living arrangement. However, the establishment of
such residences has led to backlash in many areas from neighbors
concerned about the safety of their families and declining property
values. Such opposition is considered part of a larger movement,

called NIMBY or "Not in My Backyard," which has attempted to prevent land uses perceived as undesirable.

Suggested Reading
Duffee, David, and Robert Fitch. "Other Correctional Strategies on the Community Level." *An Introduction to Corrections: A Policy and Systems Approach.* Pacific Palisades, CA: Goodyear Publishing, 1976.

Head Start, Project   A comprehensive, neighborhood-centered program for children ages three to five who are living below the poverty level. Project Head Start is administered by the Administration for Children, Youth, and Families (ACYF), Office of Human Development Services, Department of Health and Human Services. This program began in 1965 after passage of the Economic Opportunity Act of 1964. Often regarded as a preschool program providing academic preparation for economically disadvantaged children, Head Start is far more comprehensive. This program also provides far-reaching health and dental care for participants. Head Start is as concerned about family and community life as about the individual child. Project goals include an emphasis on a child's social, emotional, and physical as well as cognitive development. Grant money is made available to schools, community action agencies, and nonprofit organizations to administer the programs. About two-thirds of all Head Start programs are located in urban areas. Administration of this program was transferred to the Department of Health and Human Services when the Office of Economic Opportunity (OEO) was disbanded by President Richard Nixon. *See also* ECONOMIC OPPORTUNITY ACT OF 1964; WAR ON POVERTY.

Significance   Project Head Start, once considered experimental, is a rare survivor from the War on Poverty era. By 1983, the program had served more than 8.5 million children, with almost a half-million recipients every year since. However, because of lack of funds and lack of awareness among parents, Head Start is reaching only about 20 percent of the children who qualify. Virtually every project office has waiting lists of children who wish to enter their local program. In part because the program was experimental, it has been the subject of many public and private evaluation studies. Evaluations have been somewhat mixed. One unexpected result was a long-term positive impact of the programs on their local communities. In many cases, the local Head Start program was credited with linking other community programs and organizations, such as schools, health services, and government agencies. In addition, it increased awareness in local governments of the needs of their poor. Though Head Start has received consistent bipartisan support in Congress, the program remains underfunded, and teachers and technical staff working in the program receive low wages, often without health or insurance benefits.

Suggested Reading

Lazar, Irving. *Summary: The Persistence of Preschool Effects.* Ithaca: Community Services Laboratory, New York State University College of Human Ecology at Cornell University, October 1977.

Mann, Ada Jo. *A Review of Head Start Research since 1969.* Washington, DC: George Washington University, 1978.

U.S. Department of Health and Human Services, ACYF. *The Impact of Head Start on Children, Families, and Communities: Head Start Synthesis Project.* Washington, DC: Government Printing Office, 1985.

Highest and Best Use   In real estate, an assumption that allows appraisers to estimate the top value land will bring in an exchange of ownership when optimally developed under present legal options and foreseeable short-term financing constraints. The highest and best use may well designate an alternative to that presently in existence. In theory, the concept takes into account a community's master plan, zoning districts, and deed restrictions, as well as the owner's profit maximization. The valuation is subject to market verification, possible challenges in courts, and counterclaims by planners. Synonyms for highest and best use include *maximum profit for the seller* and *probable development. See also* APPRAISAL; EMINENT DOMAIN.

Significance   Highest and best use is the assumption an appraiser makes when determining the value of a parcel of real estate. When government condemns private land, it must pay the owner. Just compensation is based on this standard. But the term has two elements that might work against each other: *Highest use* yields the real estate owner the best rent or return on investment, whereas *best use* suggests the development is compatible with the community's health, safety, morals, general well-being, and aesthetics. A private landowner's highest profit may conflict with the public's land plan and produce negative externalities for other private owners. For most privately held urban parcels, the highest and best use is residential, because that is the largest zone. Neither the planning nor the zoning board is established to maximize an individual entrepreneur's profits. These boards are established to calculate under law the community's land-use controls. Hence, *highest and best use* is an appraiser's term in market economics and is of little interest to community physical planners.

Suggested Reading
American Institute of Real Estate Appraisers. *Readings in Highest and Best Use.*
    Chicago: AIREA, 1981.

Hills v. Gautreaux, **425 U.S. 284 (1976)**   In an 8-0 ruling by Justice Potter Stewart, on an appeal from the Seventh Circuit Court of Appeals, the U.S. Supreme Court ruled on the question of whether the remedial order of a federal district court concerning scatter-site public housing could extend beyond Chicago's territorial boundaries. Gautreaux, one of the plaintiffs and a black man, initially brought suit in 1966 against the Chicago Housing Authority (CHA), claiming it had improperly restricted public housing sites to within the central city in order to limit the options for black families. Plaintiffs also charged that the Department of Housing and Urban Development (HUD) and its secretary, Carla Hills, had assisted the CHA in this strategy. At the trial level HUD was found guilty. At the Supreme Court level, *Gautreaux* was differentiated from the Detroit cross-school busing case of *Milliken v. Bradley,* 418 U.S. 717 (1974), and the Court noted there was no *per se* federal rule declaring that courts were prevented from ordering remedies beyond the boundaries of a city. The district court then ruled that about 9 percent of the public housing was to be scattered outside the central city of Chicago in the suburban housing market. *See also* BALKANIZATION; BOUNDARY; FAIR HOUSING TITLE; PRUITT-IGOE; *SOUTHERN BURLINGTON COUNTY NAACP V. MT. LAUREL* ; UNDER-CLASS; YONKERS-STYLE POLITICS.

Significance   The ruling in *Hills v. Gautreaux* was an attempt to open up the supply of public housing to people—mostly blacks—who qualified for public subsidies. The new supply area was a heretofore closed, white suburban market. With HUD's assistance, the CHA partially implemented the scatter-site housing order with a pilot project for several hundred *Gautreaux*-class families who were either living in inner-city public projects or on the waiting list. The relocated families, whom many felt were part of an underclass usually confined to high-rise projects, expressed general satisfaction with their new residences. However, after a decade, the Chicago-area federal district court, which had retained jurisdiction over the implementation, removed the CHA as administrator. There were court reviews in 1970, 1979, and 1982. By 1986 only about one-fourth of the 2,000-plus public housing family units were in existence. The judge appointed the Habitat Company, a private apartment manager, to build or promptly rehabilitate the additional 1,500 units. After a decade, the rule in *Gautreaux* was being honored nationally by only approximately one-third of the metropolitan housing agencies. *Gautreaux*, like the *Mt. Laurel* case and the *Brown* school desegregation case before it, dramatically illustrates the protracted politics of implementation of a contentious high court order.

Suggested Reading

Peroff, Kathleen A., et al. *Gautreaux Housing Demonstration: An Evaluation of Its Impact on Households*. Washington, DC: Superintendent of Documents, 1980.

Historic Area   A zone, designated by a government at any level, that contains unique or important artifacts that deserve special protection. A historic area or district designation may derive from artistic factors, architecture, engineering, or importance to American history or culture. If the area has been registered with the National Park Service of the U.S. Department of the Interior, it will be on the National Register of Historic Places. States also have their own lists, as do some cities. Michigan's first State Historical Commission, M.C.L.A. 399.1 of 1948, is typical, in both the period of its creation and its purposes. Once established, historic areas fall under stricter scrutiny than other parcels for urban renewal and site plan review. *See also* HISTORIC PRESERVATION; SITE PLAN REVIEW; ZONING.

Significance   The two major public advantages of historic area designation are to preserve examples of America's past and to encourage restoration using high standards of authenticity. The major private advantage is to give owners a tax shelter for restoration costs of up to one-fourth the value of the building, according to the 1981 Economic Recovery Tax Act, 26 U.S.C. 1. The major private disadvantages are that many owners do not want to receive the designation, because it may limit their options in renovating the property or changing the use of the property. An alternative to a historic area designation is a single-building designation. This allows for single-parcel preservation without encumbering adjacent properties. Road construction has been a major threat to several historic areas.

Suggested Reading

Anderson, Kenneth C. "Federal Aid Highway Project: The Historic Environment." *Highway and Urban Mass Transportation* (Fall–Winter 1973), pp. 18–21. (A publication of the U.S. Department of Transportation.)
Shull, Carol D. "Listing Your House in the National Register." *Historic Preservation* (November/December 1987), pp. 22 ff. (A publication of the National Trust for Historic Preservation.)
Wyckoff, Mark, ed. "Historic Preservation Issue." *Michigan Planner* (Spring 1981).

Historic Preservation   Protection and restoration of the nation's unique architectural, artistic, engineering, and cultural environment through creation of national, state, and local registries of historic places. Historic preservation has a long history in the United States, beginning with the national Antiquities Act of 1906, 16 U.S.C. 431. In 1916 the National Park Service Act, codified as 16 U.S.C. 1, was set up to administer and locate unique places that should be preserved as a public trust. The Historic Sites Act of 1935, 16 U.S.C. 461, followed. In 1949, Congress chartered the National Trust for Historic Preservation to preserve sites, buildings, and objects of national significance. This quasi-public body holds the trust account for more than 70 properties. It conducts an annual national convention, awards certificates to the best restoration projects, and publishes periodicals such as the bimonthly magazine *Historic Preservation* and the monthly newspaper *Preservation News*. The major current national statute is the National Historic Preservation Act of 1966, as amended in 1980, 16 U.S.C. 470. The act allows for matching grants to the states to set up inventories of eligible sites, and it provides the machinery for registering them. The 1981 Economic Recovery Act, 26 U.S.C. 1, extended investment tax credits for rehabilitation of certified historic structures. Certification is registered with the National Park Service of the U.S. Department of the Interior. *See also* GENTRIFICATION; HISTORIC AREA; ZONING, AESTHETIC.

Significance   Historic preservation is a worldwide movement. The United Kingdom, for example, has more than 400,000 buildings under protection. Holland, Belgium, and France have developed preservation districts. Under auspices of the United Nations Educational, Scientific, and Cultural Organization (UNESCO), there is a World Heritage List of almost 300 designations for such locations as Toledo, Spain, and Stonehenge in the United Kingdom. The U.S. National Register of Historic Places has more than 34,000 listings, not counting state and local designations. In 1965, the New York City Council passed its own Landmark Preservation Act. Examples of sites under the care of the National Trust for Historic Preservation include George Washington's Mount Vernon and Frank Lloyd Wright's suburban Chicago home and studio. Among whole villages that have been restored is Williamsburg, Virginia. The historic district of Charleston, South Carolina, was created in 1931. More than 80 percent of historic preservation commissions operate without full-time staff and generally rely for advice on local physical-planning departments. From 1976 through 1985, investors filed for more than $6 billion in investment tax credits. Some criticize these tax shelters as havens for the privileged. This is especially true of gentrifiers, who displace lower-class renters and owners in the central city by securing a historic designation and then refurbishing properties under a tax shelter. Cities also note that rehabilitation dollars come close to matching new-construction investment dollars, many of which benefit apartment and row-housing dwellers. Owners who have had their property designated as historic may not make major structural changes or raze their buildings without clearance from the registering authority. One major issue in all historic preservation is whether, in the name of progress, private individuals should be free to demolish the past. Even a high proportion of buildings on the National Register of Historic Places have been destroyed for want of funds to preserve them.

Suggested Reading
Datel, Robin E., and Dennis J. Dingemans. "Why Places Are Preserved: Historic Districts in American and European Cities." *Urban Geography*, vol. 9, no. 1 (1988), pp. 37–52. (Case study of five metropolitan areas.)
Fein, David B. "Historic Districts: Preserving City Neighborhoods for the Privileged." *New York Law Review*, vol. 60, no. 1 (1985), pp. 64–103.
Fitch, James Marston. *Historic Preservation: Curatorial Management of the Built World.* New York: McGraw-Hill, 1982. (Comparative approach.)
Mazey, Mary Helen. "An Overview of Historic Preservation in Belgium, The Netherlands, and the United States." *Journal of Urban Affairs*, vol. 7, no. 1 (1985), pp. 41–46.
Spearing, Mary. "Landmark Preservation: The Problem of the Tax-Exempt Owner." *Fordham Urban Law Journal*, vol. 3, no. 1 (1974), pp. 123–135. (Discusses the New York City Landmark Preservation Act.)
Suddards, Roger W. *Listed Buildings*, 2nd ed. London: Sweet and Maxwell, 1988. (United Kingdom registry of historical places.)

Home Mortgage Disclosure Act of 1975   A national statute that requires depository institutions such as commercial and savings banks, savings and loans, building and loans, and credit unions to publicize the location of approved home loans and purchases of mortgages by census tract or zip code. The disclosure act requires depository institutions to organize their loan activity for public inspection by dollar amount for the area in which it originated, whether within or outside the statistical area. Included in the tabulations by calendar year is information on loans to homeowners versus absentee landlords, and new construction versus home improvements. Enforcement is by the Federal Deposit Insurance Corporation, Comptroller of the Currency, and the Federal Reserve Board. *See also* COMMUNITY REINVESTMENT ACT OF 1977; FAIR HOUSING TITLE; REDLINING.

Significance   The Home Mortgage Disclosure Act of 1975 (12 U.S.C. 2801) was based on congressional hearings that found some metropolitan lending institutions were contributing to the decline of portions of their own marketing areas. Through a practice called redlining, the lenders were refusing to provide home financing. Congress's position is that although money should be mobile, lending institutions must be aware of their local base and, if necessary, be forced to be good institutional citizens. Some states also have mortgage disclosure and antiredlining statutes. The statute allows citizens and public officials to obtain information from lending institutions to determine whether they are fulfilling their obligations to serve the communities in which they are located. The act's assumption is that such visible discrimination, once exposed, will force lenders to change their practices. If not, depositors will shun the offending institution. Otherwise, the banks are simply collecting local monies and shifting the resource out of the area. This is deemed by Congress to be exploitation. The vicious cycle of declining maintenance and abandonment cannot be broken unless there is money available to improve local housing stock. But this act was only a modest first step in dismantling redlining. Disclosure alone did not require institutions actually to lend monies within their communities. This issue was addressed in 1978 with the Community Reinvestment Act.

Suggested Reading

Schafer, Robert, and Helen F. Ladd. *Discrimination in Mortgage Lending.* Cambridge, MA: MIT Press, 1981. (Critical of the act.)

Zipp, Elaine K. "Effect of Federal Home Mortgage Disclosure Act on Enforcement of State Disclosure and Antiredlining Statutes against Federal Financial Institutions." 57 ALR Fed 322–326.

Home Rule   A movement in a majority of states to allow local autonomy for select cities and counties in establishing their own charters and innovating in matters of local concern. The core idea of home rule is delegation of power for local affairs from the state to select substate jurisdictions. At state discretion, home-rule units are allowed to draft, approve, amend, and implement their own charters. Two subtypes of home-rule governments are those authorized to operate by constitutional dictate and those that operate under statutory guidance. A home-rule jurisdiction is free to innovate and does not need to ask permission of the state legislature. There is great variation in the measure of self-government, especially regarding tax limits and permitted revenue sources. *See also* CHARTER; DILLON'S RULE; PROPOSITION 13; STATE MANDATE; *ULTRA VIRES.*

Significance   Home rule creates local autonomy and limits the degree of state interference in local affairs. It is a general delegation from the state to its subunits, limited to specific fields, and subject to constant judicial interpretation. Because no two states have the same formal procedures, it is difficult to generalize; however, the thrust of home rule is to reverse the impact of Dillon's rule, which assumed that, in absence of a clear authorization, a substate level was powerless. In 1875 Missouri was the first state to offer home rule, and states in the 1960s were still drafting the conditions under which it could be offered. Special authorities are not granted home rule, and only those units with some threshold population are allowed to consider the option.

Suggested Reading

Anderson, William. "Resolving State/Local Governmental Conflict—A Tale of Three Cities." *Urban Law Annual,* vol. 18 (1980), pp. 129–152.

Leonard, Jane E. "Home Rule: Constitutionally Granted Planning and Zoning Powers vs. State Concern for Preservation of the Adirondacks." *Urban Law Annual,* vol. 16 (1979), pp. 389–403.

Levi, Julian H., Durward J. Gering, and Reed Groethe. "Application of Municipal Ordinances to Special Districts and Regulated Industries: A Home Rule Approach." *Urban Law Annual,* vol. 12 (1976), pp. 77–123.

Homeless   Those who lack adequate shelter, resources, and community ties. This definition was adopted in 1983 by the Alcohol, Drug Abuse, and Mental Health Administration of the U.S. Public Health Service. A broader definition includes all persons inadequately housed, living in another person's home, or precariously domiciled. A narrower definition includes all persons who do not rent or own conventional housing. A definition of homeless adopted in 1987 by the Department of Housing and Urban Development and promulgated in the *Federal Register* specifies an individual or family that does not have access to traditional or permanent housing but is capable of living independently within a reasonable amount of time, not to exceed one and one-half years. The homeless, also known as street people, often are treated as vagrants by local authorities. They survive in emergency shelters; motels and hotels; welfare hotels; on the street over heat grates; in subways, parked cars, and vans; on beaches; in abandoned buildings as squatters; and in jails. Causes of homelessness are complex, but among commonly listed reasons are lack of affordable housing, lack of adequate-paying jobs, loss of the "safety net," domestic violence, substance abuse, deinstitutionalization, underemployment, and loss of physical health. Reduction in the supply of public and trickle-down housing and cuts in federal social welfare during the 1980s also contributed. The number and type of homeless changed during the early 1980s, with a larger total destitute population and more women and families represented. The newer homeless do not have the same profile as skid row residents. Many are suffering from catastrophic illness, including AIDS. They are not covered by conventional hospitalization plans and are given only restricted access to public health care. *See also* BANFIELD THESIS; DEINSTITUTIONALIZA-TION; ELEEMOSYNARY GROUP; HOMELESS ASSISTANCE ACT; *IN REM* PROP-ERTY; POVERTY LEVEL; SAFETY NET; SKID ROW; UNDERCLASS; UNDERCOUNT; URBAN CRISIS.

Significance   The number of homeless is considered an epidemic and a national scandal by most commentators. Absent a consistent definition, there can be no definitive head count. The population is not easily subject to enumeration. The homeless are concentrated in cities but are also found in rural areas. When operationalized, their numbers range from a high estimate of 1.5 percent to a low of .15 percent of the adult U.S. population, from around 3 million people who are homeless for one night or more during a year to a low of 300,000. The largest concentrations appear to be in New York City, Los Angeles, and Chicago. Most short-term aid is provided by the private not-for-profit sector. Case studies on homeless populations have produced wildly inconsistent statistics but do give some indica-tion of high-frequency problems. They have the same median age of 34 as the general population. The incidence of alcoholics in case studies is as high as 86 percent of the total. The high estimate for drug abusers is 55 percent. In addition to these two substance-abuse classifications, mental health problems, especially schizophrenia, are associated with up to 72 percent. Personality and anxiety disorders account for as much as 21 percent of the homeless. Some people are in many of these overlapping categories. The homeless are not con-fined to central cities. However, urban and suburban residents have litigated against creation of shelters or more permanent housing stock in their neighborhoods. Advocacy groups for the homeless, on the other hand, have called for a "right to shelter." These are examples of LULUs, Locally Unwanted Land Uses. Some conservatives insist homelessness closely correlates with rent-control measures. Some lib-erals called the homeless Reagan's army, caused by cuts in Aid to Dependent Children, Housing and Urban Development housing re-ductions, Social Security insurance benefit curtailments, the end of the Comprehensive Employment and Training Act, and lowered levels of Medicare and Medicaid funding. In 1987, Ronald Reagan's penul-timate year in office, Congress passed the Stewart B. McKinney Homeless Assistance Act as a comprehensive measure, replacing the earlier *ad hoc* federal response consisting of the Homeless Housing Act of 1986 and ongoing Federal Emergency Management Agency (FEMA) and shelter programs. The National Homeless Union, an interest group, has staged takeovers on behalf of the dispossessed.

Suggested Reading

Bingham, Richard D., Roy E. Green, and Sammis B. White, eds. *The Homeless in Contemporary Society.* Newbury Park, CA: Sage, 1987.

Blasi, Gary L. "Litigation on Behalf of the Homeless: A Systematic Approach." *Washington University Journal of Urban and Contemporary Law,* vol. 31 (Winter 1987), pp. 137–142.

Burt, Martha, and Barbara E. Cohen. *America's Homeless: Numbers, Characteristics, and Programs That Serve Them.* Lanham, MD: The Urban Institute Press, 1989.

Dear, Michael J., and Jennifer R. Welch. *Landscapes of Despair: From Deinstitutionalization to Homelessness.* Princeton: Princeton University Press, 1987.

Erickson, Jon, and Charles Wilhelm, eds. *Housing the Homeless.* New Brunswick, NJ: Center for Urban Policy Research, 1986.

Hope, Marjorie, and James Young. *The Faces of Homelessness.* Lexington, MA: Lexington Books, 1986.

Rossi, Peter. *Without Shelter: Homelessness in the 1980s.* Boston: Unwin, Hyman, 1988.

Smith, Christopher J. *Public Problems: The Management of Urban Distress.* New York: Guilford Press, 1988. Chap. 11, "Home and Homelessness in the Postindustrial City."

Homeless Assistance Act   A congressional statute authorizing more than $600 million for fiscal year (FY) 1988 to provide aid to protect and improve the lives of those without access to conventional shelter. The full title is the Stewart B. McKinney Homeless Assistance Act of 1987, 42 U.S.C. 11311 et seq. Passed during the Reagan administration, it was designed to coordinate and maximize existing resources for poor people in need of housing. Specially targeted were the elderly (age 62 or older), veterans (Homeless Reintegration Project), handicapped (Supportive Housing Demonstration Program), families with children, and the deinstitutionalized with mental disabilities. Many homeless people fall into multiple categories. Most of the federal aid is coordinated by the Department of Housing and Urban Development (HUD). Smaller contributions are made by the Department of Health and Human Services, Federal Emergency Management Agency (FEMA), and the Departments of Defense, Labor, Education, and Veterans Affairs. Cities and counties apply for funds based on a needs statement, a local facilities inventory, and a program of matching funds. Each area must designate a coordinator. Both secular and religious not-for-profit institutions are eligible for funding. In addition to emergency food and shelter programs, the act calls for job training, literacy testing, food assistance, and location of permanent housing for the handicapped and families with children. The Comprehensive Homeless Assistance Plan (CHAP) and Transitional Housing Demonstration Program were designed to be short-term programs. *See also* HOMELESS; URBAN CRISIS.

Significance   The Stewart B. McKinney Homeless Assistance Act was the first major statute of its kind ever enacted. It was initiated by a congressman, not the Reagan administration, after substantial litigation had established partial judicial remedies. With the addition of surplus federal barracks and rehabilitation of some single-room-occupancy (SRO) hotels and motels, critics noted the total impact was far less than the growing need. State Departments of Public Health, Labor, Social Services, and Education coordinated efforts with city and county Community and Economic Development Departments to meet the crisis. Most short-term shelters such as Detroit's Coalition on Temporary Shelter (COTS) actually are operated by eleemosynary groups. Detractors called the bill a stop-gap proposal filled with quick-fix machinery that failed to get at the root causes of homelessness. Others said the law did not establish a national right of all people to overnight shelter. Finally, critics complain the law does not take into account adequately the high proportion of AIDS patients within the homeless population. Local governments need not apply for grants, and some elected officials exercised their discretion by buying bus tickets for their local homeless to other destinations. If the Community Development Block Grants (CDBGs) had not been cut off, detractors argue, this bill would have been partially unnecessary. Many homeless people are unaware of their entitlements to public services. Conservative opponents argue that the problem is a state-local issue, should not be bureaucratized by more government coordinators, and should be left to the private sector. The two major conservative victories on the bill were that it was made a demonstration program—that is to say, temporary—and that it was very modestly funded.

Suggested Reading

National Academy of Sciences. "Homelessness, Health, and Human Needs." Washington, DC: National Academy Press, 1988.

Reyes, Lila M., and Laura Dekoven Waxman. "The Continuing Growth of Hunger, Homelessness and Poverty in American Cities: 1987." Washington, DC: U.S. Conference of Mayors, 1987.

Solomon, Arthur P. *Housing the Urban Poor: A Critical Evaluation of Federal Housing Policy.* Cambridge, MA: MIT Press, 1974. (Pre–Homeless Assistance Act evaluation of housing.)

Household   A census and survey research term encompassing all persons who occupy the same housing unit. A household can be a family, a group of unrelated people, or an individual. Persons living in quartered housing on military bases or in college campus dormitories are not considered a household. Traditionally, the "head of household" is either the oldest adult living in a housing unit or the major income provider. Beginning with the 1980 census, *head of household* was replaced by the term *householder,* to indicate the first person in whose name the home is owned or rented. *See also* FAMILY.

Significance   The concept of a household as a unit of consumption and living is fundamental to understanding urban life. Urban policy-making depends substantially on the vast amount of data derived from interviews of urban households. Demographic and economic information relating to households is used to determine current needs and future trends. For example, the 1920 census determined that, for the first time, more than half of the U.S. population resided in urban areas. By 1980, the census found that of the nation's 29 million renter households, 86 percent were located in urban areas. The federal government, largely through the Commerce Department's Bureau of the Census, conducts surveys of households on a continuing basis. The Survey of Income and Program Participation (SIPP) interviews 20,000 households, following each sample for a period of two and one-half years, with results published on a quarterly basis in the *Current Population Report.* The Consumer Expenditure Survey (CES) contains extensive household expenditure data. The Current Population Survey (CPS) conducts a monthly poll of 60,000 households. Over time, the household has been designated the nation's basic consumer unit and survey research focus.

Suggested Reading
Sweet, James A., and Larry L. Bumpass. *American Families and Households.* New York: Russell Sage, 1988.

Housing, Condominium   An estate in real property consisting of an individual interest and a common interest. The individual interest in a condominium is held in the housing unit occupied, and an undivided common interest is held in "common areas" such as parking lots, stairwells, land, roofing, and central heating and cooling facilities. Unlike a rented apartment unit, each separate condominium housing unit is a legal entity that may be taxed, mortgaged, or have ownership transferred. *See also* CONDOMINIUM CONVERSION; GENTRIFICATION; HOUSING, COOPERATIVE; RENT CONTROL.

Significance   Condominiums have become a popular form of home ownership in areas where land is limited and housing demand has been high. Condominiums have become popular for commercial as well as residential use. Many urban planners have supported condominium development as a means for increasing the property tax base, because the aggregate taxes on separate condominium units in a building exceed the tax assessment on a single apartment building of the same size. In many urban areas undergoing revitalization, condominiums have brought young, middle- and upper-class residents back into cities by providing the tax advantages of home ownership in an urban setting. Thus, the conversion of apartment buildings into condominiums has been a vehicle for much of the gentrification in central-city areas. In 1975 the Department of Housing and Urban Development (HUD) conducted a study that found condominium conversion most likely to occur when all or most of the following factors were present in a city: (1) land for residential development is scarce; (2) single-family housing prices are high; (3) there are restrictive local growth policies; (4) tenants' rights laws have been passed or strong tenants' unions exist; (5) there is an adequate supply of good rental housing; (6) rent control exists or is likely to be implemented; and (7) there is no state or local legislation that controls or restricts conversion.

Suggested Reading
Dinkelspiel, John R., John Uchenick, and Herbert L. Selesnick. *Condominiums: The Effects of Conversion on a Community.* Boston: Auburn House, 1981.

Housing, Cooperative   A consumer housing enterprise, also known as a "co-op," which is owned and operated by its members on a nonprofit basis. Each member of the housing cooperative assumes ownership of a housing unit by purchasing shares in a cooperative corporation. The corporation holds title to the entire building. In exchange for stock, each member receives a proprietary lease that gives the member the right to occupy a specific unit of the building. Each stockholder pays a share of the corporate expenses, such as maintenance and property taxes. No rent is paid, but the unit is treated as personal property for tax purposes. When a unit is sold, the buyer is assigned the seller's stock.

Significance   Housing cooperatives in the United States began in New York City during the 1920s. New York State passed a law giving tax breaks for housing companies, but limiting their profits on investment. Labor unions, particularly the Amalgamated Clothing Workers Union (ACWU), have been especially active in the cooperative housing movement in the United States. Under the leadership of Sidney Hillman, the ACWU built a 2,600-unit cooperative in the Bronx. By 1927, 2,500 families had moved into the Amalgamated co-op. New York City became the leader and center of the cooperative housing movement and is headquarters of the United Housing Federation, the leading organization in providing expertise and technical support for nationwide cooperative-housing efforts. The federal government became involved in co-ops during the 1950s when the government transferred ownership of wartime housing projects to their residents. Although 95 percent of all U.S. cooperatives are in the state of New York, areas of the country with a history of a strong organized labor movement, such as Detroit, also have built housing cooperatives. In some cities, such as Boston, an effort to save medium- and low-income housing stock has resulted in the conversion of such units into cooperatives. The city allowed tenants to use their rent subsidies to purchase shares in a cooperative. This established home ownership and provided permanent low- and middle-income housing for residents who otherwise would not have had the opportunity for home ownership.

Housing, Mobile   A trailer type of residence, also known as a mobile home, that is generally not permanently attached to foundations or land. Mobile homes can be real property when affixed to land but are considered for taxation purposes to be personal property when mobile and not affixed to a permanent site. Although loans for mobile homes may be underwritten by the Federal Housing Administration (FHA) or the Veterans Administration (VA), financing is similar to loans for automobiles. *See also* HOUSING, PREFABRICATED OR TEMPORARY; PARK, MOBILE HOME; ZONING.

Significance   Mobile homes tend to exist in suburbs more than in the larger central cities. Limited space in central cities require high-rise, multiple-family structures rather than housing units that demand much more land per resident. Many cities restrict the creation of mobile home parks through various zoning ordinances. The fluctuations in demand and cost for more traditional housing have created parallel changes in the demand for mobile homes. Households unable to purchase the more conventional structure may find mobile homes an attractive alternative for their first home. Older individuals, often on fixed incomes, whose families have left the house, may no longer wish to live in the larger, more traditional house and may move into a mobile home.

Housing, Open   The elimination of racial discrimination in the housing market. Open housing became a cause of the civil rights movements of the 1950s and 1960s, in reaction to the use of restrictive covenants and other discriminatory practices that barred blacks and other minorities from many neighborhoods. During the 1960s, federal laws and policies sought to end housing discrimination. President John Kennedy issued Executive Order 11063, which prohibited discrimination in housing "owned, operated, or funded by the federal government," including all federal mortgage insurance programs. In 1968, the Civil Rights Act contained an open housing provision, Title VIII, commonly known as the Fair Housing Act (42 U.S.C. 3601 et seq.), which prohibited racial discrimination in most of the housing in the United States. Later that same year, the U.S. Supreme Court, in *Jones v. Mayer*, 392 U.S. 409 (1968), barred discrimination in all housing transactions, including single-family homes sold directly by the homeowner. Many states also passed similar statutes shortly after the national legislation. In some cases, state and local governments had already passed open housing proposals: Chicago, for example, did so in 1963. *See also* FAIR HOUSING TITLE; RACIAL STEERING; RESTRICTIVE COVENANT.

Significance   Open housing legislation became one of the major goals of civil rights groups. The first major battle for open housing was fought in Chicago in 1966. Although it had already passed an open housing ordinance five years before the federal Fair Housing Act, Chicago became a symbol of the problems of housing discrimination throughout the country. Martin Luther King came to Chicago in 1966 declaring that housing was the primary target of the civil rights movement, and stating that Chicago was to be an "open city." Racial discrimination in the United States often has been most obvious in the housing market. Despite numerous public policies prohibiting housing discrimination, more subtle forms of racial bias still intrude. *Racial steering,* for example, is a practice in which realtors direct minorities away from certain cities or neighborhoods and toward others, in an effort to prevent minorities from purchasing homes in still segregated areas. This illegal practice is often difficult to document, and the potential home purchaser may not realize steering is occurring. During the late 1980s, U.S. Department of Justice studies indicated that about four-fifths of all suits filed against real estate agents for alleged violations of the Fair Housing Act involved racial steering.

Suggested Reading

Anderson, Alan B., and George W. Pickering. *Confronting the Color Line: The Broken Promise of the Civil Rights Movement in Chicago.* Athens: University of Georgia Press, 1986.
Berry, Brian J. L. *The Open Housing Question: Race and Housing in Chicago, 1966–1976.* Cambridge, MA: Ballinger, 1979.
HUD Advisory Commission, Social Science Panel. *Freedom of Choice in Housing: Opportunities and Constraints.* Washington, DC: National Academy of Sciences, 1972.

Milgram, Morris. *Good Neighborhood: The Challenge of Open Housing*. New York: W. W. Norton, 1977.
Saltman, Juliet. *Open Housing: Dynamics of a Social Movement*. New York: Praeger, 1978.

Housing, Ownership vs. Rental   A legal distinction describing an individual's "tenure" classification with regard to residence. The primary forms of tenure in housing are renting, owner-occupied, and cooperative tenure. Home ownership can involve real estate transactions and financial infrastructure. *See also* IN REM PROPERTY.

Significance   Long a part of the American dream, home ownership has met various obstacles since 1980. Still, rising prices for houses and relatively high mortgage interest rates have kept many people from purchasing their own homes. Home ownership for 30- to 34-year-olds dropped from 59.3 percent in 1981 to 54.7 percent in 1985. The number of adults living with parents was higher in 1987 than it was for any other year since the 1950s. In 1987, the median cost for a house in the United States was $83,000 with a median down payment of $18,000 and $1,725 in closing costs; the median mortgage payment totaled 25 percent of the buyer's monthly income. Home ownership varies with urban and rural sectors of the nation. In 1980, 64 percent of the nation's households were homeowners. More rural households were homeowners than urban. In the northeast section of the country, only 54 percent of the homeowners were urban; 81 percent of the rural households owned their homes. Of the almost 29 million households across the nation that rented, 86 percent were urban; only 14 percent were located in rural areas.

Housing, Prefabricated or Temporary   Residential structures produced in large sections prior to delivery on a given site. Prefabricated walls and often entire rooms are produced in a factory before reaching the construction site. This method of housing production is cheaper and less time-consuming than the traditional method of building a home. *See also* HOUSING, MOBILE.

Significance   As housing construction costs increased during the 1970s, prefabricated housing became more popular, at least with developers. The costs of constructing conventional housing put new homes out of the financial reach of many families with low or moderate incomes. In 1986 almost one-quarter of the new-home building market consisted of manufactured homes. The National Association of Home Builders opposes the use of prefabricated, modular units in housing construction and has expended considerable lobbying efforts to restrict growth in the manufactured housing industry. However, in cities such as Los Angeles where the demand for inexpensive housing is extensive, public funding has been provided to build shelters for the homeless.

Housing, Public   Dwellings built by or for government to serve primarily low-income families. Construction of public housing units often has come in the form of high-density, multiple-family apartments called housing projects. Government housing efforts often have been two-pronged. First, funding has been made available to local housing authorities for the construction of new housing. Second, money also was made available for slum clearance and reduction of urban blight. The first government program to establish public housing came with the Housing Act of 1937. This act was in large part a response to the housing problems compounded by the Depression and the deteriorating condition of much of the housing stock in central cities. *See also* FAIR HOUSING TITLE; HOUSING ACT OF 1937; HOUSING ACT OF 1949; PRUITT-IGOE.

Significance   By the late 1930s, inadequate housing for many was seen as a major social problem, contributing to crime, poor health, and the breakup of families. However, public housing programs have been relatively controversial in the United States. High-rise and high-density public housing in such cities as New York, Chicago, and St. Louis has been a dismal failure in attracting and keeping tenants. Active lobbying groups have represented private real estate agents and building contractors who felt threatened by the intrusion of the federal government into the housing market. These private interests have lobbied heavily to retain a strong private-sector presence in all public housing programs and urban renewal plans. In all of the major housing legislation of the last 50 years, private-sector interests have been included either in programs for actual construction of housing units or in the financing arrangements. About 1 percent of the nation resides in public housing dwellings.

Suggested Reading
Aaron, Henry J. *Shelter and Subsidies: Who Benefits from Federal Housing Policies?* Washington, DC: Brookings Institution, 1972.
Connerly, Charles E. "What Should Be Done with the Public Housing Programs?" *Journal of the American Planning Association*, vol. 52, no. 2 (1986), pp. 142–155.

Friedman, Joseph, and Daniel H. Weinberg. *The Great Housing Experiment.* Urban Affairs Annual Reviews, vol. 24. Beverly Hills: Sage Publications, 1982.
U.S. Department of Housing and Urban Development. *Programs of HUD 1987–88.* Washington, DC: Government Printing Office, August 1988.

Housing, Rehabilitation   Restoration to an improved condition of existing residences. Housing rehabilitation also includes conservation of current structures. Rehabilitation programs can range from minor repairs to complete building revitalization. Federal funding, through Community Development Block Grants and the Neighborhood Opportunity Fund, is most often used for housing rehabilitation programs. *See also* BUILDING CODES; CODE ENFORCEMENT; COMMUNITY DEVELOPMENT BLOCK GRANT; URBAN HOMESTEADING.

Significance   As early as the 1800s, U.S. standards of housing were tied to notions of public health and welfare. Creation of housing codes arose from a concern over the public health implications of water contamination, rat and vermin infestation, fire hazards, and diseases. Local governments began to develop housing codes through planning and zoning regulations during the early part of the twentieth century. Title I of the 1934 Housing Act authorized the Federal Housing Administration to underwrite installment loans made by financial institutions that would finance repairs for individual homes. The Housing Act of 1954 required municipalities to adopt housing codes and building codes as part of the "workable" programs, as a condition for federal urban renewal funding. The 1974 Housing and Community Development Act restructured most of the federal housing grants program and eliminated the urban renewal program. However, the act funded local housing code enforcement activities through Community Development Block Grants. Under this program, communities could identify "neighborhood strategy areas" that were in decline and rehabilitate homes in these areas with federal funding. In addition to block grants, the other major source of funding for housing rehabilitation comes from Section 312 loans from the Department of Housing and Urban Development (HUD). Under Section 312, HUD makes rehabilitation money available directly to homeowners. Total outlay for Section 312 funding equaled $178 million in fiscal year 1987. These loans can be made to owner-occupiers of property, corporations, cooperatives, or urban homesteaders.

Suggested Reading
U.S. Department of Housing and Urban Development. *Programs of HUD 1987–88.* Washington, DC: Government Printing Office, August 1988.

Housing, Section 8   A low-income rental assistance program originally enabled under the 1937 Housing Act (42 U.S.C. 1437f), and
amended several times. Section 8 housing provides vouchers and
rental certificates to income-eligible renters who live in an approved
dwelling operated by a Public Housing Authority (PHA). Under Section 8, an eligible family pays 30 percent of its net income in rent to the
landlord, with the local public housing authority paying the difference
to meet the rental price. Because the rental dwellings must meet
building-code standards, landlords are encouraged to maintain their
buildings. This program replaced a "lease housing" program provided by Section 23 of the Housing and Urban Development Act of
1965. Under this program, about 2.2 million units were receiving
subsidies by the end of fiscal year 1987. *See also* EXPERIMENTAL HOUSING
ALLOWANCE PROGRAM; HOUSING SUBSIDY; PUBLIC HOUSING AUTHORITY.

Significance   Federal-government Section 8 housing has been the
most popular housing program for low- and very low income families.
Most local programs have long waiting lists of families seeking rental
assistance through Section 8. However, this program has had less
impact on public housing construction. In areas where developers and
builders normally would not profit from such construction, Section 8
has helped encourage the construction or maintenance of dwellings
for low- and moderate-income families. By the late 1980s, the general
increases in the cost of housing, gentrification, and urban redevelopment projects combined to make these dwellings more profitable on
the open market. In addition, the new building construction element
of this program was terminated in 1984, leaving Section 8 exclusively
a rental supplement program. Between 1986 and 1988, about 3,500
agencies owned and managed more than 1.4 million units of federally
assisted public housing in the United States. More than 2,000 agencies
administered over 850,000 Section 8 certificates and almost 115,000
Section 8 vouchers during that time.

Suggested Reading
Rosenthal, Donald B. *Urban Housing and Neighborhood: Turning a Federal Pro-
    gram into Local Projects.* Westport, CT: Greenwood Press, 1988.
Salins, Peter D., ed. *Housing America's Poor.* Chapel Hill: University of North
    Carolina Press, 1987.
U.S. Department of Housing and Urban Development. *Statistical Yearbook.*
    Washington, DC: Government Printing Office, annual editions.
Welfield, Irving. "American Housing Policy: Perverse Programs by Prudent
    People." *Public Interest,* no. 48 (1977), pp. 128–144.

Housing, Segregated by Race   The physical separation of whites
and blacks or other minorities in living patterns. Housing segregation,

as well as racial segregation of other public and private facilities, once was sanctioned legally in the United States. The "separate but equal" sanctions were dropped by the 1954 *Brown v. Board of Education I* case, but segregation in housing was not addressed specifically until 1968 in *Jones v. Mayer,* 392 U.S. 409. The U.S. Supreme Court explicitly prohibited racial discrimination in the sale or rental of real property. In the same year, Congress passed the Fair Housing Title of the 1968 Civil Rights Act. *See also* BROWN V. BOARD OF EDUCATION; DE FACTO SEGREGATION; DE JURE SEGREGATION; FAIR HOUSING TITLE; GHETTO; HOUSING, OPEN; INTEGRATION, RACIAL; WHITE FLIGHT.

Significance   Segregated living patterns in the United States have been explained by two sets of causes. First, it has been argued that people of similar races and ethnic backgrounds prefer to live in the same neighborhoods—that they choose to live in segregated areas. Second, responsibility has been fixed on racial discrimination in housing over the years, using such devices as restrictive covenants and exclusive zoning ordinances. Racial steering by real estate agents also has continued segregated housing patterns. Other forms of real estate practices include claims that there are no houses available. The Department of Housing and Urban Development and many state civil rights organizations have sent white and minority investigative teams to visit real estate agencies and investigate possible discrimination. In many states, violators face stiff fines and possible loss of their license. Some academic research has concluded that urban residents who live in integrated areas have a greater likelihood of developing more liberal racial attitudes, explained by what has been called the "contact hypothesis." This hypothesis argues that interracial contact reduces racial stereotypes and prejudices. In addition, each ethnic or racial subgroup develops a greater understanding and appreciation for the other's culture.

Suggested Reading

Galster, George C. "The Ecology of Racial Discrimination in Housing: An Exploratory Model." *Urban Affairs Quarterly,* vol. 23, no. 1 (1987), pp. 84–107.

Tobin, Gary, ed. *Divided Neighborhoods: Changing Patterns of Racial Segregation.* Newbury Park, CA: Sage Publications, 1987.

White, Michael J. *American Neighborhoods and Residential Differentiation.* New York: Russell Sage, 1988.

Housing Act of 1937 (18 U.S.C. 709, 1008–1010)   A federal statute that created the U.S. Housing Authority to provide loans to local housing authorities for the construction and management of low-income housing and for slum clearance. The act is also known as the Wagner-Steagall Housing Act, named after its cosponsors, New York Senator Robert F. Wagner and Alabama Representative Henry B. Steagall, both Democrats. The act also authorized construction of new dwellings to replace slum dwellings that were razed. This link between slum clearance and public housing construction created an important role for the federal government in community development. *See also* HOUSING, PUBLIC; HOUSING ACT OF 1949.

Significance   The Housing Act of 1937 became the first of President Franklin D. Roosevelt's New Deal programs specifically to address urban problems exacerbated by the Great Depression. It replaced a small public housing program that had operated under the Public Works Administration, created by the National Industrial Recovery Act. The 1937 Housing Act provided for federal funding and local administration of public housing. Considerable controversy erupted as some real estate agents and private builders saw these public housing programs as their competitors in the housing market. Because of intense lobbying, the 1937 Housing Act and those that followed in 1949 and 1968 allowed for substantial involvement of the private sector in programs that attempted to provide some form of housing for low- or middle-income families.

Suggested Reading
Keith, Nathaniel S. *Politics and the Housing Crisis since 1930*. New York: Universe Books, 1973.
U.S. Department of the Interior, National Resources Committee and Urbanism Committee. *Our Cities: Their Role in the National Economy*. Washington, DC: Government Printing Office, 1937.

Housing Act of 1949 (42 U.S.C. 1401 et seq.)   Landmark urban legislation that sought to create a comprehensive national housing policy. The Housing Act of 1949 was a product of concern about urban slums and residential blight in addition to worries about the deterioration in the central business districts of large cities in the United States. This act became the major impetus for the postwar urban renewal efforts in U.S. cities. Much like earlier housing legislation, this act sought to replace every demolished dwelling with a new dwelling. However, such reconstruction never took place. In the four-year period between 1967 and 1971, for instance, less than 50 percent of the half-million housing units demolished were replaced by new housing. *See also* EMINENT DOMAIN; HOUSING ACT OF 1937; HOUSING AND COMMUNITY DEVELOPMENT ACT OF 1974; URBAN RENEWAL.

Significance   For the first time, a national commitment was made by Congress to rebuild the nation's cities. The major drive toward an urban renewal program was established through the Housing Act of 1949. By the late 1940s, the combination of deteriorating central-city housing stock, expansion of urban slums, and the post–World War II housing shortage had created a housing crisis in the United States. Rather than simply building public housing projects, this act provided for a large-scale rebuilding effort. As was the case with provisions of the earlier Housing Act of 1937, this act provided for local administration of urban renewal and redevelopment and an active role for private real estate agents and developers to rebuild urban areas. For example, eminent domain (governmental purchase of private property for public purposes) became fundamentally redefined with the Housing Act of 1949 and its amendments in 1954. Government could still force an individual to sell his/her property under this act. However, that property could be turned over to private developers who could decide, within certain constraints, how to use the property. This act came under great criticism by the 1960s, as the urban renewal program became popularly known as "urban removal" because of its razing of housing and displacement of the poor and minorities, with very little rebuilding of housing units. The urban renewal provisions of the act were eliminated with the passage of the 1974 Housing and Community Development Act.

Housing and Community Development Act of 1974 (42 U.S.C. 5301)
A substantial revision in U.S. policy regarding urban redevelopment, housing, and urban aid programs. The Housing and Community Development Act (HCDA) consolidated seven community-development categorical-grant programs into one Community Development Block Grant (CDBG) program. This block grant system allowed greater discretion by local governments in how funding would be spent and tied federal funding to a formula based on a recipient government's population size, poverty rate, and housing needs. This act eliminated the urban renewal program but continued a variety of public housing and mortgage and rental subsidy programs established in earlier housing acts. During Ronald Reagan's presidency, less CDBG funding was available, although more local spending discretion was allowed. *See also* COMMUNITY DEVELOPMENT BLOCK GRANT; HOUSING ACT OF 1949; URBAN RENEWAL.

Significance   The Housing and Community Development Act of 1974 attempted to decentralize urban policymaking and reduce funding levels to local governments. As a requisite for funding, local governments were to establish three-year planning documents for development activities. In addition, the act required an annual Department of Housing and Urban Development (HUD) review of local programs. Critics argued that greater local discretion caused some cities to spend federal money in middle- to upper-income areas and not where the local need appeared the greatest. This argument about local control of decision making versus federal regulation of minimum standards has remained an important controversy in the federal grant-in-aid system. Most of the grants originally created under the Housing Act of 1949 were supplanted by this act. In addition to the urban renewal program, the 1974 act also eliminated the Model Cities program, Federally Assisted Code Enforcement (FACE), several demolition and housing rehabilitation grants, and the neighborhood facilities grants.

Suggested Reading
Gesmer, Ellen. "Discrimination in Public Housing under the Housing and Community Development Act of 1974: A Critique of the New Haven Experience." *Urban Law Annual,* vol. 13 (1977), pp. 49–80.

Housing and Urban Development Act of 1968 (42 U.S.C. 3901 et seq.) A federal statute that provided for government programs to subsidize housing purchases made by moderate- and low-income homeowners. The act increased the demand for home ownership and redistributed income at the same time. In addition to mortgage subsidies for families purchasing homes, rent subsidies became available to qualified renters. Because the act was intended to encourage the construction of new homes and rental units, the subsidies were available only for new or rehabilitated housing. *See also* ABANDONMENT; FAIR HOUSING TITLE.

Significance Despite the best intentions of the 1968 Housing and Urban Development Act, the mortgage subsidy program was unsuccessful in most cities. In some extreme cases, such as in Detroit, corruption arose when contractors built substandard homes, bribed government inspectors to approve the buildings, then quickly moved in unsuspecting buyers. Other problems arose. With very little money required for a down payment, families moved into homes they could not afford. Even with the subsidy, many low-income families could not meet the mortgage payments, especially if many repairs were needed to bring the structures up to code. Homeowners often abandoned their homes, because the mortgages were guaranteed by the federal government. The program was abolished under the Nixon administration, although rental subsidies still exist.

Housing Court A special division of the judiciary at the trial level in urban areas that focuses exclusively on conflict resolution relating to building-code enforcement, demolition, tenant eviction, and rent collection issues. Housing courts resulted from the realization that urban courts of general trial jurisdiction are not well equipped to deal with the laws of landlords and tenants, as well as related apartment-building issues. Housing courts are equipped to issue decisions on a case-by-case basis and generally do not consolidate cases. Assignment to hear such cases is usually considered undesirable by judges. Dockets are often crowded, too few courtrooms are assigned, and courts do not consider these cases a priority. Furthermore, judges often are ignorant of state statutory and case law, housing cases generate only nominal fees, and attorneys who take such cases are seldom among the highest-rated lawyers at the bar. *See also* BUILDING CODES; FEDERALLY ASSISTED CODE ENFORCEMENT; MEDIATION; NEIGHBORHOOD JUSTICE CENTER.

Significance   Urban housing courts are a product of twentieth-century judicial specialization and were designed better to dispense justice. In the 1970s in Chicago, eviction procedures each year represented nearly 9 percent of the city's rental units and numbered nearly 70,000 cases annually. One empirical study noted a landlord bias in the Chicago courts along with arbitrary procedure and delays in reaching decisions, both of which result in unnecessary complications for litigants. Traffic and housing courts are the two most likely locations for city residents to have contact with the trial-level judiciary. If most lay-persons' impressions are unfavorable, people will avoid using courts to resolve conflict. Housing courts seldom use fines against landlords for failure to maintain facilities according to code when enforcement is too lax. Adverse reaction to these weak judicial opinions includes rent strikes against select landlords, disrespect for courts generally, and a movement toward alternative dispute resolution. One technique used to keep the housing issue in front of the judicial machinery is the appointment of a housing ombudsman or a specially trained hearings officer. A second approach is the creation of neighborhood justice centers (NJCs), which use community laypersons promptly to resolve select issues, lower expenses, and minimize tension. A third possible method is binding arbitration and nonbinding mediation; they often are used to bypass the clogged and largely disrespected housing courts. On the other hand, when housing courts impose very stringent standards, housing stock often deteriorates and landlords abandon their property.

Suggested Reading
Scott, Randall W. "Housing Courts and Housing Justice: An Overview." *Urban Law Annual*, vol. 17 (1979). Special issue. (Boston, New York City, Hampden County [Massachusetts], Chicago, Pittsburgh, Los Angeles, Hartford, Buffalo, Indianapolis, and Detroit are discussed.)

Housing Finance Agencies   Organizations that provide a source of money to finance home mortgages. Housing finance agencies provide, to qualified purchasers, loans that represent the difference between the down payment and the purchase price of the house. Financial institutions that invest in mortgages include such thrift institutions as private mortgage companies, the secondary mortgage market of the Government National Mortgage Association (GNMA), Federal National Mortgage Association (FNMA), and Federal Home Loan Mortgage Corporation (FHLMC), as well as government lenders such as the Federal Housing Administration (FHA) and Department of Veterans Affairs (VA). *See also* FEDERAL HOUSING ADMINISTRATION; FEDERAL NATIONAL MORTGAGE ASSOCIATION; GOVERNMENT NATIONAL MORTGAGE ASSOCIATION.

Significance   Housing finance agencies have expanded their activities primarily since the post–World War II housing boom began. The mainstay of these agencies has been the traditional 30-year, long-term, fixed-rate mortgage, with savings accounts as their primary lending resource. This basis of the thrift industry also made mortgage lending vulnerable to a rapidly changing economy. The period from 1934 through 1986 witnessed the failures of almost 900 thrift institutions, three-fourths occurring after 1980. Such changes brought about a substantial reorganization of the mortgage lending industry since 1980. Many of the problems began during the 1970s, as savings institutions offered high-yield money market accounts, and the traditional savings account became much less popular with investors. Assumable mortgages at low interest rates were virtually eliminated after 1976, so new buyers had to borrow money at the much higher interest rates imposed during the late 1970s. As consumers avoided housing moves and purchases after 1976, adjustable- and variable-rate mortgages were developed. This opened up the mortgage market somewhat, because lenders could offer an initial low rate on a variable mortgage that would not have been available under the traditional fixed-rate loans, given the high interest rates of the time. This new system allowed more purchases of homes, but it put the largest portion of the overall American debt on the homeowner. In addition, lending institutions began to impose more initial charges on home buyers after 1980 by increasing closing costs; adding origination, loan discount, and buy-down fees; and generally requiring more up-front costs. These costs add up to as much as 5 percent of the total amount of the loan. There is also a Housing and Home Finance Agency, a federal agency authorized by the Housing Act of 1949 to help local governments eliminate blight and slums within their jurisdictions. This agency provides grants-in-aid to local governments to assist in assuming some of the write-down costs of land that has been cleared.

Suggested Reading
Boleat, Mark. *National Housing Finance Systems: A Comparative Study*. London:
    Croom Heim, 1985.

Housing Starts   A count of the number of new housing units on which construction has begun. Housing starts are an economic indicator of the amount of housing expected to be available in the near future and the strength of the nation's economy. For privately owned units, the start of construction is counted when the footings are set or excavation of the foundation begins. Starts for public housing are counted during the month of the contract award. Housing starts are published on a monthly basis by the Census Bureau and give statistical breakdowns of private and public housing starts, location inside or outside Metropolitan Statistical Area (MSA), location in a census region, and structure type. These data provide analyses of residential construction trends. *See also* COUNCIL OF GOVERNMENTS.

Significance   Housing starts are an important measure of economic activity in the United States. The housing construction industry is considered to be one of the most sensitive and vital indicators of the post–World War II economy. The numbers of housing starts peaked during the early 1970s, but they declined dramatically after the energy crisis of 1973 and continued their depressed levels through the first years of the 1980s. From 1980–1983, housing starts averaged fewer than 1.2 million units per year. High prices for houses and high interest rates for home mortgages have reduced the demand for new construction since 1975 and effectively eliminated the "American dream" of home ownership for many citizens. One of the functions of the regional Councils of Governments is to monitor housing starts within their metropolitan area. In the snowbelt states, housing starts are cyclical with the seasons. Across the entire country, they are responsive to the business cycle and fluctuate with the major trends in the Gross National Product.

Housing Subsidy   A transfer payment from government to a public or private body in keeping with the goal of increasing housing consumption. Housing subsidies can take the form of monetary grants and assistance through vouchers or certificates or through tax incentives that reduce the cost of one of the factors of housing: land, labor, management, or materials. The focus of government subsidy programs can be oriented toward either the demand or supply side of the problem and can be directed toward new, rehabilitated, or existing housing units. The general forms of housing subsidies can include land, construction, property tax abatements, mortgage financing, low-income rental assistance, and mortgage deductions on tax liability. *See also* DEPARTMENT OF HOUSING AND URBAN DEVELOPMENT; EXPERIMENTAL HOUSING ALLOWANCE PROGRAM; HOUSING, PUBLIC; HOUSING, SECTION 8; HOUSING ACT OF 1937.

Significance   In 1988, housing subsidy outlays from the Department of Housing and Urban Development (HUD) totaled almost $11 billion. Among the larger programs, those subsidies included about $8.6 billion under Section 8, $1.1 billion for public housing, and $780 million for the Section 235 and 236 assistance programs. Section 1 of the Housing Act of 1937 initiated subsidized housing designed to improve the living conditions of lower-income families and to stimulate employment in the construction industry. Housing policy in the United States often has attempted to balance government involvement with the powerful private interests that dominate the industry. Though the most direct examples of housing subsidies come in the form of vouchers, rent supplements, and public housing projects, the federal government provides substantial support to homeowners through federal income tax deductions of mortgage interest.

Suggested Reading
Bratt, Rachel G. "Private Owners of Subsidized Housing vs. Public Goals: Conflicting Interests in Resyndication." *Journal of the American Planning Association,* vol. 53, no. 3 (1987), pp. 328–336.
Varady, David P. "Indirect Benefits of Subsidized Housing Programs." *Journal of the American Planning Association,* vol. 48, no. 4 (1982), pp. 432–440.

Human Ecology   The study of communities in time and space through the analysis of the distribution of people, their residences, their occupations, and how these elements interrelate. Initially the field of human ecology was developed by Robert V. Park, Roderick McKenzie, and others associated with the University of Chicago School of Sociology. They borrowed their model from plant and animal ecologists who were interested in the interrelationship of the two biological kingdoms and of each to its environment. Human ecology is best viewed in an urban setting where there are large numbers of heterogeneous groups living in close proximity; as a result, most human ecology focuses on large cities. In one well-known formulation there are four major interrelated elements in the ecosystem of human groups: population, physical environment, technology, and social organization. Human ecology focuses on such issues as population density, residential patterns, vital statistics, immigration and emigration, land-use patterns and regional population shifts, comparative city size and function, the role of technology in transforming occupations, the development of the postindustrial city, stratification, and ethnic group inter- and intra-action. A central concern for human ecologists is locating "natural areas" within advanced cities in order to explain patterns of change. In early ecological studies, growth was a primary focus; however, population deconcentration from the 1950s on makes that concept important to human ecologists. The major findings for residential areas in North American cities focus on social stratification, ethnicity, segregation indices, and family status. *See also* BIOLOGICAL FALLACY; CHICAGO SCHOOL; INVASION; PARK THESIS; SUCCESSION; WIRTH THESIS.

Significance   Human ecology as a model for the study of urban affairs has passed through several intellectual phases. It is now considered an important theoretical approach to urban issues that focus on temporal, spatial, and dynamic elements of interdependent communities. Although not as prominent an approach as it was from the 1920s through the 1950s, human ecology claims its own journal and students in two academic fields, namely geography and sociology. It is still used as a model to study invasion and succession in residential neighborhoods. It assumes that there are periods of equilibrium between communities and other periods of cyclical change. Among the major concepts borrowed from plant and animal ecology are dominance, territoriality, competition, symbiosis (mutual dependencies that contribute to each community's existence), invasion, and succession. Critics of human ecology note that the approach pays little attention to the individual; does not anticipate physical planning; ignores or understates the roles of cultural values, political elections, and elected officials; and oversimplifies the urban mosaic by limiting itself to selected issues.

Suggested Reading

Hawley, Amos H. *Human Ecology*. New York: Roland Press, 1950. (The beginnings of neoecological theory.)
————. *Urban Society: An Ecological Approach*. New York: Roland Press, 1971.
McKenzie, Roderick. "The Ecological Approach to the Study of the Human Community." *American Journal of Sociology*, vol. 30, no. 3 (1924). Reprinted as Chap. 2 in James F. Short, Jr., ed., *The Social Fabric of the Metropolis*. Chicago: University of Chicago Press, 1971. (Classical ecological theory.)
Micklin, Michael, and Harvey M. Choldin, eds. *Sociological Human Ecology: Contemporary Issues and Applications*. Boulder, CO: Westview Press, 1984.
Perle, Eugene D. "Ecology of Urban Social Change—An American Example." *Urban Ecology*, vol. 7 (1982–1983), pp. 307–324.

Reissman, Leonard. *The Urban Process: Cities in Industrial Societies.* New York: Free Press, 1964, 1970, pp. 98–121. (Criticisms of both the original Park thesis and neoecological theory.)

Waste, Robert J. *The Ecology of City Policymaking.* New York: Oxford University Press, 1989. Contains a glossary.

Wilson, Franklin D. "Urban Ecology: Urbanization and Systems of Cities." *Annual Review of Sociology,* vol. 10 (1984), pp. 283–307.

Impact Analysis   A generic term that describes any study of the probable outcome of a change in policy. Impact analysis requires anticipation of events and an assessment of their benefit-to-cost ratio; it provides an alternative to discovery after the fact that a policy has significant and often negative ramifications. The first impact analysis was the Environmental Impact Statement (EIS) proposed in congressional testimony of the 1960s. Other examples include President Jimmy Carter's short-lived 1978 executive order on urban community impact analysis, economic impact studies based on the multiplier effect on the local economy, and state-imposed development guidelines for regional impacts of city plans. *See also* COST-BENEFIT ANALYSIS; ENVIRONMENTAL IMPACT STATEMENT; EXTERNALITY; URBAN IMPACT ANALYSIS.

Significance   Impact analysis is both a policy tool and a delay mechanism. Not all impact analysis is actually useful to decision makers. Sometimes it is completed only to comply with statutes or rules. Urban impact analysis did not outlive Carter's own administration. Florida statute requires local impact statements on regional spillovers. A Massachusetts Office of State Planning study in the 1980s suggested cities should analyze before-the-fact growth policies near their borders. Some legislatures are required to conduct a judicial impact analysis of the probable effects on court time for any proposed changes to civil and criminal codes.

Suggested Reading
Canter, Larry W., Samuel F. Atkinson, and F. Larry Leistritz. *The Impact of Growth: A Guide for Socio-Economic Impact Assessment and Planning.* Chelsea, MI: Lewis Publishers, 1985.
Cervero, Robert. "Unlocking Suburban Gridlock." *Journal of the American Planning Association,* vol. 52, no. 4 (1986), pp. 309–406. (Proposed traffic impact fee.)

Hunter, William J. "Economic Impact Studies: Inaccurate, Misleading, and Unnecessary." Policy Study No. 21. Chicago: Hartland Institute, 1988.

Impact Fee   A local government charge imposed on new developers designed to generate capital for infrastructure changes needed as a result of new construction. Also known as a development impact fee, it is a form of developer exactions, especially popular in California, Florida, Colorado, and North Carolina. It is used to pay for on- or off-site improvements in roads, intersection widening, transit facilities, sewer and water services, drainage systems, and recreational facilities, as well as libraries, parks, schools, and fire stations. Under the U.S. Supreme Court case of *Nollan v. California Coastal Commission*, 97 L Ed 2d 677 (1987), it is the local government's burden to demonstrate a direct statistical link, and not just a reasonable relationship between fees and the needed government improvements. *See also* EXACTION; GROWTH MANAGEMENT.

Significance   Impact fees were first suggested in the 1920s as a method of linking a developer's project to the community's on-site burden of supplying basic amenities such as roads, water, and drainage. With reduction in federal transfer payments to the states and the taxpayers' revolt against high property taxes, impact fees became a politically palatable but controversial revenue source. The fee schedules can be set by statute as in Texas, by ordinance as in Florida, or occasionally through negotiation as in California. The effect of the fee schedule has resulted in infilling, preservation of farmland, and an increased awareness by both builders and government of the relationship between growth and traffic circulation.

Suggested Reading
Nelson, Arthur C., ed. *Development Impact Fees: Policy Rationale, Practice, Theory and Issues*. Chicago, APA Planners Press, 1988.

In Rem **Property**   From the Latin, a legal term designating proceedings "against the thing," usually against property. The antonym of *in rem* is *in personam*, actions "against a person." In urban affairs, *in rem* property refers to city, state, or nationally owned property that the government possesses as the result of tax foreclosure. *In rem* property has often been abandoned by the owner, but there still may be tenants living in the facilities. Public takeover of heretofore private property exists in most major central cities when owners fail to pay taxes to the extent that foreclosure proceedings are initiated. *See also* ABANDONMENT; LAND BANKING; URBAN CRISIS.

Significance   In the late 1970s, the U.S. Department of Housing and Urban Development was the largest owner of property in Detroit through *in rem* actions against fraudulent landlords. It was estimated that New York City, especially the South Bronx, reluctantly held 150,000 *in rem* tenants with the city as landlord. *In rem* apartment properties constitute some of the most blighted housing in a community. The highest rate of *in rem* actions was in St. Louis in the early 1980s. In New York City in the mid-1970s, approximately 40,000 dwelling units a year were being abandoned. Cities and the national government have three conflicting goals when they become unwilling property owners: (1) They wish to sell the property to private interests and thus get the property back on the tax rolls. (2) They reluctantly become slumlords of last resort; if they force out the tenants, they have increased the numbers of homeless families. (3) They attempt to demolish buildings that do not meet code, thereby clearing land for possible renewal. Causes of *in rem* property include an owner's inability to find renters who can yield sufficient profits, a landlord's failure to find able buyers, the flight of residents from the area, the existence of rent controls that make the property unprofitable, the unwillingness of lending institutions to issue funds for capital improvements, and the failure of city inspectors to enforce building code compliance. As a rule, urban governments are slow to respond to the needs of remaining renters since government management mechanisms are cumbersome and not designed to fulfill the obligations of landlords.

Suggested Reading
Scherer, Andrew. "Is There Life After Abandonment? The Key Role of New York City's *In Rem* Housing in Establishing an Entitlement to Decent, Affordable Housing." *New York University Review of Law & Social Change,* vol. 13, no. 4 (1984–1985), pp. 953–974.

Income Sources, Urban   The origin of financial resources for U.S. local government units. Urban income sources for cities, towns, townships, special districts, and counties are diverse. They include (1) taxes, (2) bonds and notes, (3) transfer payments, (4) special assessments, (5) funds from proprietary services, (6) fees from services and franchises, (7) forfeitures and abandonment funds, (8) fines, (9) interest on investments and sinking funds, (10) lottery surplus, (11) surplus from property liquidation, (12) gifts and dedications, (13) grants, and (14) rents and leases. The first three categories in turn are subdivided into specific sources such as motor fuel tax, municipal income tax, personal property tax, real property tax, sales tax, and the single business tax. Bond and note types include revenue improvement bonds (RIBs), tax anticipation notes (TANs), capital improvement bonds, and industrial revenue bonds. Transfer payments derive from the national, state, and county level, some based on pass-through provisions and some based on such criteria as local road mileage or student attendance. In accounting, *revenue* is a narrower term than *income*. Revenue refers only to money received from external sources exclusive of such items as mutual aid payments, bonds, notes, and receipts from liquidation of property. *See also* BUDGET TYPES; DEDICA-TION; FISCAL CRISIS; FISCAL FEDERALISM; GIFT TO GOVERNMENT; *IN REM* PROPERTY; USER FEE.

Significance   In a period of taxpayers' revolts, urban governments have investigated a variety of income sources to reduce reliance on the property tax. In addition to improved tax collection, privatization, and reducing the expenditure ledger, local units have expanded their scope of income sources, especially from user fees, interest on investments, and liquidation of properties. Creative financing in part means tapping, for the first time, sources that are near the bottom of the list. Municipal budgets are not designed to account for income by source, hence the layperson does not see shifts in magnitude. Minor income sources receive publicity out of proportion to their importance. Multi-year audits are the most reliable tool for revealing relatively long-term shifts in urban government income patterns.

Suggested Reading
Mikesell, John L. *Financial Administration: Analysis and Applications for the Public Sector.* Homewood, IL: Dorsey Press, 1982. Part Two: Revenue Sources, Structure and Administration.

Incubator   A local economic-development program designed to promote largely indigenous, small-scale, start-up businesses. An inno-vation of the 1960s and 1970s, incubators are of three subtypes: those that promote new industry and assembly production, those that en-courage fledgling high-technology operations, and those that pro-mote small retail goods and service businesses. The justification for incubators stems in part from the high mortality rate of new busi-nesses that do not have adequate funding, proper management ad-vice, and auxiliary service support. These are all provided to some degree by the incubator, which aims to make the enterprise self-sufficient and capable of moving out even though the goal is for it to remain within the same community. To accomplish the nurturing role, incubators usually recycle a large building such as a factory or school by retrofitting it for a second use. *See also* PUBLIC-PRIVATE PART-

NERSHIP; SMALL BUSINESS ADMINISTRATION; SUCCESSION; URBAN DEVELOP-
MENT ACTION GRANT.

Significance Incubators are sponsored most frequently by city or
regional agencies as part of a broad-based strategy to improve the
local economy by fostering fledgling businesses. They are also sponsored by the Chamber of Commerce and other not-for-profit agencies, by universities as part of the spinoff of basic research and
development, by state agencies looking for new markets, and by private-sector corporations as a market for their services. Funding comes
in part from Community Development Block Grants (CDBGs) and
loans from the national-level Small Business Administration (SBA). In
addition to management advice and possible periodic review of the
businesses' accounts, incubators provide central services, such as
phone answering and computer centers. They often supply rent at
below-market rates. The municipality benefits from increased employment, a diversified tax base, and promotion of long-term economic viability. For a small initial investment, these innovation
centers, advanced technology groups, and home-grown economic
projects, as they are also known, might well reap better and larger
community rewards than would stem from a comparable sum paid out
in tax abatements or tax increment financing. Some of the jobs created
by the incubators are skilled and professional-level, but the bulk are
semiskilled and low-skilled positions. In urban economics, the *incubator hypothesis* states that the central city of a metropolitan area best
serves as the seedbed for new firms. This theory from the 1950s posits
that location within such an area is a major variable in the successful
nurturing of start-up firms.

Suggested Reading
Birch, David L. *Job Creation in America: How Our Smallest Companies Put the Most
People To Work.* Glencoe, IL: Free Press, 1987.
Campbell, Candace. "Hatching Small Businesses." *Planning,* vol. 50, no. 5
(1984), pp. 19–24.
Plosila, W., and D. Allen. "Small Business Incubators and Public Policy Impli-
cations for State and Local Development Strategies." *Policy Studies Jour-
nal,* vol. 13, no. 4 (1985), pp. 729–734.

Independent School District An organizational structure that has
total responsibility for providing local public education. Independent
school districts differ from dependent school districts in that the latter
are subsumed under the authority of a local county, municipal, or
town general government. Substantial consolidation of school districts
has occurred since World War II because of improved transportation,

more efficient administrative and fiscal organization, and demographic changes. In 1942, more than 100,000 independent school districts were operating in the United States; by 1982, there were approximately 15,000. *See also* CENSUS OF GOVERNMENTS; CONSOLIDATION; SCHOOL DISTRICT.

Significance   The independent school district has been the standard organizational tool for providing public education. While public education in the United States is a state-level function, it historically has been a local responsibility to operate. Overall, public education consistently has been the largest and most important of all local services. With fiscal difficulties occurring or increasing in many cities and states during the 1970s and 1980s, several states began to centralize school funding by guaranteeing a minimum per-pupil expenditure for each school district. These states included California, Florida, Kansas, Maine, Michigan, and Utah. In 1982, the states with the highest per-pupil expenditures were Alaska, New York, and New Jersey; the lowest per-pupil expenditures were recorded in Mississippi, Tennessee, and Arkansas.

Suggested Reading
Zeigler, Harmon, and M. Kent Jennings. *Governing American Schools: Political Interaction in Local Districts*. North Scituate, RI: Duxbury Press, 1974.

Industrial Revenue Bond (IRB)   A corporate certificate of indebtedness issued as a municipal bond used to finance selected industrial and commercial development during the 50 years from the Great Depression into the Ronald Reagan era. Industrial Revenue Bonds (IRBs) carry below-market interest charges (usually 2–3 percent) because the interest paid on them is exempt under federal income tax law. Revenue bonds do not involve general revenues and, therefore, need not be guaranteed by the municipality. They do not require voter approval, nor are they subject to a state-mandated debt limitation. *See also* BOND TYPES, MUNICIPAL; MORAL-OBLIGATION BOND.

Significance   Industrial Revenue Bonds were first used in 1936 by Mississippi to encourage economic diversification in the state's rural areas. Largely because of the costs borne at the federal level for these bonds, they were effectively rendered obsolete when changes in the 1986 federal tax laws eliminated the tax advantages to the underwriters of the bonds. Snowbelt states began to use IRBs increasingly, beginning in the 1960s, in an attempt to stem the flow of business to the sunbelt. Many city officials endorse their use because urban development projects presumably create jobs and increased tax revenues; therefore, they serve a public purpose. IRBs came under some criticism as unnecessary gifts to the private sector. Various social costs have been associated with the use of industrial revenue bonds: a dilution of the municipal bond market, excessive administrative expenses, and a reduction in federal tax revenues. In addition, critics argue that many of the projects using industrial revenue bonds were not properly targeted to the distressed urban areas that most needed investment.

Suggested Reading
Marlin, Matthew R. "Industrial Revenue Bonds at 50: A Golden Anniversary Review." *Economic Development Quarterly*, vol. 1, no. 4 (1987), pp. 391–410.
Pascarella, Thomas A., and Richard D. Raymond. "Buying Bonds for Business: An Evaluation of the Industrial Revenue Bond Program." *Urban Affairs Quarterly*, vol. 18, no. 1 (1982), pp. 73–89.

Infilling   Development of land that was bypassed in earlier stages of construction in a metropolitan area. Infilling takes place on vacant areas commonly known as raw land. Undeveloped parcels often are carried on assessment rolls at low valuations. This does not encourage owners either to sell or to develop them. Some of this land is kept by speculators, some as a land bank for later development by industry or public bodies. Many municipalities monitor the location and total acreage of their raw land. Planning agencies look at infilling as providing both potential opportunities and possible trouble spots because of the raw land's odd shape, drainage problems, small scale, or history of property tax arrearage. The opposite of infilling is urban sprawl. *See also* BOUNDED CITIES, TYPES OF; URBAN SPRAWL; WRITE-DOWN.

Significance   Infilling is a desirable strategy for a business that employs central-city workers at low wage rates. Near-in locations save workers transportation costs. Businesses that leapfrog to the metropolitan fringe discover they must compensate workers for the long "reverse commute." Infilling is most profitable for builders along suburban freeways. Some contractors are attracted to modest-scale, raw residential land, because they can get funding for these limited tracts. Physical planners encourage infilling as part of a public policy of enlightened growth management that saves on the energy costs of longer commutes. Near-in suburbs gain tax base from infilling at little extra cost, because most of the public infrastructure is already in place.

Suggested Reading
Anonymous. *Urban Infill: Its Potential as a Development Strategy*. Chicago: American Planning Association, 1981.

Erickson, R. A. "The Evolution of the Suburban Space Economy." *Urban Geography,* vol. 4, no. 2 (1983), pp. 109–114.
U.S. Department of Housing and Urban Development. *Urban Infill: The Literature.* Washington, DC: Superintendent of Documents, 1980.

Infrastructure   Literally, facilities that are below or within. *Infrastructure* is a collective term for man-made, permanent, basic physical facilities. Among the components of an urban infrastructure are public buildings such as fire stations, libraries, and schools. It includes the transportation systems of airports, railroads, highways, tunnels, bridges, culverts, subways, and sidewalks. Many waterworks are included, such as aqueducts, dams, water treatment plants, water towers, wastewater treatment plants, wells, and drain tiles. Utilities also are considered part of an infrastructure: cable networks, electrical power stations, supply grids and street lighting, gas lines, sewer lines, telephone systems, and water lines. Most components of the municipal infrastructure are publicly built and operated. There are, however, examples of privately owned elements of each type, from private toll roads to corporate-owned bridges and private airports. Housing is the major type of privately held infrastructure. Initial funding for the construction of infrastructure is usually a long-term project called a *capital expenditure.* Maintenance for infrastructure is covered by tolls and user fees, supplemented by subsidies and grants generated by taxes levied against the nonusing public. Public officials often prefer building new edifices to repairing extant facilities. When an infrastructure is privately owned and operated, it is regulated as a public convenience or necessity. Jurisdiction for building and maintaining urban infrastructure varies among all three levels: Most dam construction falls under the U.S. Army Corps of Engineers; interstate highways are funded by a national trust fund, and most local roads are maintained by state, county, or municipal road commissions; water supplies and sewage treatment plants usually are managed by municipal departments or special district authorities. *See also* CAPITAL EXPENDITURE; GROWTH MANAGEMENT; INTERSTATE HIGHWAY SYSTEM; URBAN RENEWAL.

Significance   Building and maintaining infrastructure are perennial topics of politics. Major examples include the San Francisco Bay Area Rapid Transit System (BART), the long-proposed Tunnel and Reservoir Project (TARP) for Metropolitan Chicago, and the Borough of Manhattan's water tunnels built through granite. Demands for large amounts of intergovernmental grants are designed to shift the burden from revenue bonds at one level to another level's general tax funds. Extending the length of the bond payback period is an attempt to shift the costs to a later generation on the assumption that it is future users who will reap the fruits of the facility. Few infrastructure projects are organized on a pay-as-you-go basis. Jurisdictions usually turn to the bond markets for funding. With increased borrowing costs in the 1980s, there was reduced investment in such public projects. Reduced federal grants under the Reagan and Bush administrations to pay for infrastructure repair shifted much of the responsibility to state and local units of government. This produced a major issue in national politics: What role, if any, should Congress play in addressing the deteriorating urban infrastructure? Estimates of the needs of the nation's major cities for the decade of the 1980s was calculated at more than $50 billion. Conservationists argue that it is better to rebuild the old-core city infrastructure with urban renewal projects than to convert agriculturally productive land on the urban fringe. Councils of Governments (COGs) could once curb new subdivisions by limiting new infrastructure, especially roads and water supplies. Economist John Kenneth Galbraith argued that an illiberal American civic community has deprived the public sector of an adequate and aesthetically pleasing infrastructure of the sort found in many European nations. Many economists argue there are optimum economies of scale for the use of in-place infrastructure, and both low and high densities produce added costs to the system: too low a density causes underutilization and spreads the costs among few users, whereas too high a density taxes in-place systems, causing frequent breakdowns through overloading. As residential lot size and frontage increase, so does the cost of infrastructure per dwelling. Low density levels increase infrastructure costs per unit so that acre parcels cost almost double the costs for half-acre lots.

Suggested Reading

Baker, Michael, ed. *Rebuilding America's Infrastructure: An Agenda for the 1980s.* Durham, NC: Duke University Press, 1984.

Hanson, Royce, ed. *Perspectives on Urban Infrastructure.* Washington, DC: National Academy Press, 1984.

Johnson, R. A., S. I. Schwartz, and S. Tracy. "Growth Phasing and Resistance to Infill Development in Sacramento County." *Journal of the American Planning Association,* vol. 50, no. 4 (1984), pp. 434–446.

Mudge, Richard R., and Susan Jakubiak. *Financing Infrastructure: Innovations at the Local Level.* Washington, DC: National League of Cities, 1987.

Real Estate Research Corporation for the Office of Policy Development and Research. *Urban Infill: Its Potential as a Development Strategy.* Chicago: American Planning Association, 1981.

Subcommittee on Economic Growth and Stabilization of the Joint Economic Committee, 96th Congress, 1st Session. "Deteriorating Infrastructure in Urban and Rural Areas." Washington, DC: Government Printing Office, 1979.

Initiative   A law passed pursuant to a petition circulated by the electorate and subsequently voted on at a general or specially called election. The initiative may be on any subject upon which the legislative body can pass a statute or ordinance. As with all legislative matters, due process must be followed in properly wording and circulating the proposal, filing it with the proper authority, and accomplishing the project in a timely manner so as to alert the clerk for the election. There is split authority regarding whether the successful local initiative is to be treated as an ordinary law and subject to later legislature-council revision and/or abrogation, or whether it is higher law not subject to legislative tampering because it is the direct voice of the people. Any initiative that attempts permanently to bind the legislature or council is voidable by the courts. The number of petition signers needed to validate the initiative varies from a set number to a percentage of those who voted for a particular office in a previous election. In some jurisdictions, legally eligible voters, not necessarily registered voters, are eligible signers. Initiative issues may involve establishing a new state constitution, constitutional amendment, or ordinance, or repealing one of these. All successful initiatives are subject to judicial review, as is any act of the legislature or council. *See also* REFERENDUM; REFORM GOVERNMENT; TOWN MEETING.

Significance   The initiative is a form of direct democracy favored by Progressive reformers. A major issue of the initiative is its enforcement date, which is established by the enabling legislation, by inclusion of a specific provision, or by the legislature or council during its drafting for submission to the people. Many local initiative topics are invalidated by the regular legislature, the clerk, or the courts as embracing more than one topic or covering a topic not fit for legislative determination. An initiative provides a last resort for groups wishing to bypass the conventional legislative process and go over the heads of elected officials directly to the people on such topics as growth management or maximum taxation levels. It is not needed in New England town meetings, because the annual meeting serves as a built-in, face-to-face initiative session. Initiatives cannot abrogate bonds already issued, cannot forever limit council formulation of budgets, cannot legislate administrative discretion out of existence, and cannot pass a resolution on taxes (because initiatives are the equivalent of statutes and ordinances), nor can a local initiative dissolve a charter, because that is the prerogative of the state. Local initiatives were designed by reformers to be instruments of occasional use and were not intended to be a daily tool; they are not a substitute for the conventional deliberations of state legislatures and city councils. At the state level, initiatives are used primarily in states west of the Mississippi.

Suggested Reading
Cronin, Thomas E. *Direct Democracy: The Politics of the Initiative, Referendum and Recall.* Cambridge, MA: Harvard University Press, 1989.
Magleby, David B. *Direct Legislation: Voting on Ballot Propositions in the United States.* Baltimore: Johns Hopkins University Press, 1984.
Price, Charles. "The Initiative: A Comparative State Analysis and Reassessment of a Western Phenomenon." *Western Political Quarterly,* vol. 28, no. 2 (1975), pp. 243–262.
Zimmerman, Joseph. "The Initiative and the Referendum: A Threat to Representative Government." *Urban Law and Policy,* vol. 8, no. 3 (1987), pp. 219–253.

Innovation Groups   A not-for-profit consortium of government and business, organized to serve as a clearinghouse and network system for new product application, information on new service delivery, and staff problem solving. Innovation groups are most active in ten states, including Florida (where the headquarters of the first one, established in 1980, is located in Tampa), California, and Texas. The groups bring together public agencies seeking ideas with private-sector corporations that may have solutions. Innovation groups serve as a liaison between the private sector and local government. They allow governments to avoid other cities' errors. They also spread the rate of innovation among jurisdictions within states and among regions of the nation. The groups eschew federal funding by relying on self-assessed dues contributed on the basis of population. *See also* CLEARINGHOUSE; PRIVATIZATION; PUBLIC-PRIVATE PARTNERSHIP; THINK TANK.

Significance   Innovation groups are funded and directed at the grass-roots level in an attempt to apply technological developments to urban problems. By applying the latest research, development, and engineering (RD&E), cities reduce construction and maintenance costs, lower liability, improve safety, and improve productivity. This diffusion of innovation is done without support from the National Science Foundation or the Department of Housing and Urban Development. Innovation groups feel there are excessive delays with federal sponsorship and excessive bureaucratization. The groups answer the question, "If we can put a man on the moon, why can't we repair a pothole?" Or, "If we can break the DNA code, why can't we control weeds?" In addition to product innovation and evaluation, the groups distribute information concerning computer software, personnel training techniques, and privatization experiments.

Suggested Reading
Bingham, Richard D. "Innovations in Urban Governments: A Preliminary Model." In Louis Massetti and Robert L. Lineberry, eds., *The New Urban*

Politics. Cambridge, MA: Ballinger Publishing, 1976. Chap. 6, pp. 135–144.

Bingham, Richard D., with Thomas P. McNaught. *The Adoption of Innovation by Local Government.* Lexington, MA: D. C. Heath, 1976.

Frendreis, John P. "Innovation: A Practice in Search of a Theory: Or So What Does All This Research Mean, Anyway?" *Journal of Urban Affairs,* vol. 5, no. 2 (1983), pp. 109–122.

Lambright, W. Henry. *Technology Transfer to Cities: Processes of Choice at the Local Level.* Boulder, CO: Westview Press, 1979.

Morley, David, Stuart Proudfoot, and Thomas Burns, eds. *Making Cities Work: The Dynamics of Urban Innovation.* Boulder, CO: Westview Press, 1980.

Walker, Warren E., and Jan M. Chaiken. "The Effects of Fiscal Contraction on Innovation in the Public Sector." Santa Barbara, CA: RAND, 1981. P-6610.

Yin, Robert. *Tinkering with the System: Technological Innovations in State and Local Services.* Lexington, MA: Lexington Books, 1977.

Inspection, Building and Food   A process of enforcing local ordinances dealing with the safety and quality of structures and food sold within a city's boundaries. Inspections are made to follow up specific complaints or to ensure continuing compliance. Building inspection is usually carried out by a local government's Building and Safety Engineering Department. Food inspection is normally a responsibility of a city's Department of Health. Inspectors monitor all aspects of food-service delivery, from storage and handling to vermin inspection. Local food inspection authority covers bars and restaurants, lunch wagons, and street vendors. Enforcement of a variety of building, safety, and health codes has created organizational difficulties for many cities. As a result, some cities have created a separate code enforcement department that coordinates all categories of health and safety enforcement. *See also* BUILDING CODES; BUILDING PERMIT; CODE ENFORCEMENT.

Significance   The functions of inspecting building and food are among the most basic forms of paternalism of local government. During the eighteenth and nineteenth centuries in the United States, city life was often hazardous. Residents lived with the constant threat of fire and disease, as well as inadequate plumbing and infrequent garbage removal. Epidemics such as smallpox, cholera, and yellow fever struck U.S. cities during the 1700s and 1800s. Chicago in 1871 and Seattle in 1898 experienced devastating fires, as did many other cities during this time. The demand for better services grew, and many local governments moved away from an *ad hoc,* volunteer system of service delivery (police and fire, for example) to the use of full-time, trained staffs. Water and sewerage systems were introduced during the early 1800s in New York and Philadelphia, and building and health codes were created for the safety of city residents. Later building codes included minimum standards for plumbing and electrical fixtures as well as structural safety and fire and rodent protection.

Suggested Reading

Glaab, Charles N., and A. Theodore Brown. *A History of Urban America,* 2nd ed. New York: Macmillan, 1976.

Korbitz, William E., ed. *Urban Public Works Administration.* Washington, DC: International City Management Association, 1976.

Warner, Sam Bass, Jr. *The Private City: Philadelphia in Three Periods of Its Growth.* Philadelphia: University of Pennsylvania Press, 1968.

Integration, Racial   Nondiscriminatory, equal participation and free association by all races in society. In contrast to *desegregation,* the term usually implies cohesiveness and harmony among persons of different races. Desegregation laws and policies, in eliminating compulsory and conventional separation of the races, often aim to promote a degree of racial integration, such as greater interracial tolerance in individual attitudes and in the norms of society as a whole. *See also BROWN V. BOARD OF EDUCATION ; DE FACTO* SEGREGATION; DESEGREGATION; HOUSING, OPEN; MELTING POT.

Significance   Social science research has investigated racial integration in the United States for many years. Early studies demonstrated a relationship between socioeconomic inequalities and segregation, prejudice, and discrimination. Some saw a vicious cycle in which white beliefs in the inferiority of blacks promoted segregation in employment and housing, thus creating an inferior economic status for many blacks. This status in turn reinforced white attitudes about black inferiority. In 1947, Kenneth B. Clark and Mamie Clark determined that black children were far less likely than white children to prefer dolls of their own race. This research concluded that racial identity and esteem were developed at an early age and that long-term stigmas evolved from segregation. Later studies of soldiers and homeowners determined that whites who had regular contact with blacks in integrated platoons or neighborhoods were much more likely to favor integration. These and other studies suggested that patterns of prejudice could be partially overcome by interracial contact. This "contact theory" became part of the basis for the 1954 *Brown v. Board of Education* decision, which mandated desegregated public schools. In the 1980s, researchers concluded that even though residential segregation declines as social standing improves, the higher socioeconomic status of blacks has little effect on their integration into mainstream neighborhoods. Moreover, a 1989 report released by the University of

Chicago claimed ten U.S. cities to be "hypersegregated"; that is, they are far more segregated than other urban areas. Using five dimensions of segregation, the researchers found nine snowbelt cities and one sunbelt city, Los Angeles, to be hypersegregated. Integration has been interpreted by some ethnic and minority groups as assimilation, or abdication of racial, ethnic, or cultural identity. Achieving a satisfactory balance between the goals of ethnic pride and racial integration is one of many difficulties in reaching interracial harmony among U.S. residents.

Suggested Reading

Denton, Nancy A., and Douglas S. Massey. "Residential Segregation of Blacks, Hispanics, and Asians by Socioeconomic Status and Generation." *Social Science Quarterly*, vol. 69, no. 1 (1988), pp. 797–817.

Dimond, Paul R. *Beyond Busing: Inside the Challenge to Urban Segregation.* Ann Arbor: University of Michigan Press, 1985.

Farley, Reynolds, Suzanne Bianchi, and Diane Colasanto. "Barriers to the Racial Integration of Neighborhoods: The Detroit Case." *Annals of the American Academy of Political and Social Science,* vol. 441 (1979) pp. 97–113.

Katznelson, Ira, and Margaret Weir. *Schooling for All: Class, Race and the Decline of the Democratic Ideal.* New York: Basic Books, 1985.

Molotch, Harvey L. *Managed Integration: Dilemmas of Doing Good in the City.* Berkeley: University of California Press, 1972.

Tobin, Gary A., ed. *Divided Neighborhoods: Changing Patterns of Racial Segregation.* Newbury Park, CA: Sage Publications, 1987.

Intergovernmental Cooperation Act of 1968 (42 U.S.C. 2701)   A federal statute that provided a major stimulus for metropolitan planning. The Intergovernmental Cooperation Act stated that, to the maximum extent possible, "all federal aid for development purposes shall be consistent with and further the objectives of state, regional and local comprehensive planning." This provision further strengthened metropolitan planning agencies, as it enabled the review agency to subordinate federal grants to the priorities and plans developed by that agency. *See also* A-95 REVIEW; DEMONSTRATION CITIES AND METROPOLITAN DEVELOPMENT ACT; PLANNING, URBAN PHYSICAL.

Significance   Under pressure from the federal government, localities were encouraged or forced to provide more comprehensive and rational public planning, often on a regional basis. This act, in addition to others, was drawn upon when the federal Office of Management and Budget (OMB) wrote Circular A-95, which required a process of review and comment by promoting intergovernmental planning for various federal development programs. Although A-95

Review was dropped by the Reagan administration during the 1980s, state governments took over much of the planning and coordinating functions formerly required by the federal review, and many of the state plans continued to follow the old review process fairly closely.

Suggested Reading
Haider, Donald H. *When Governments Come to Washington.* New York: Free Press, 1974.

Intergovernmental Personnel Act of 1970 (42 U.S.C. 4701)   A federal statute that sought to improve the training of state and local public employees, to define merit issues in public employment, and to improve intergovernmental cooperation in the administration of the federal grant-in-aid programs. The Intergovernmental Personnel Act (IPA) provided approximately $160 million in grants to state and local governments to improve their public personnel procedures and training. The IPA also included several merit principles: (1) recruitment, selection, and advancement of public employees based on ability, knowledge, and skills; (2) provision for adequate compensation; and (3) assurance of fair treatment of employees, regardless of race, gender, or political party affiliation. In addition, the IPA brought all federal merit standards under the jurisdiction of the Office of Personnel Management. Some of the merit principles of this act were amended in the Civil Service Reform Act of 1978 (5 U.S.C. 1101). *See also* LOCAL MERIT SYSTEM.

Significance   In addition to providing federal funds to train state and local officials, the Intergovernmental Personnel Act of 1970 encouraged temporary transfers between federal civil servants and state and local public employees. Between 1971 and 1977 almost 2,000 federal employees were transferred to state and local employment or to work in educational institutions and with Native American tribes. More than 2,600 employees from state and local institutions were transferred to federal agencies. The act was also the first comprehensive federal law regarding civil service merit since the enactment of the 1883 Pendleton Act. Although the law addressed many issues specific to federal personnel procedures, much of it sought to improve state and local procedures, especially as they affected intergovernmental relations in the administration of federal grants-in-aid. Under the Reagan administration in 1981, federal funding for state and local programs under the IPA was first reduced, then eliminated. Although many observers credited the IPA with strengthening state and local public personnel practices, the Reagan administration considered the

IPA another unnecessary intervention of the federal government in state and local affairs.

Intergovernmental Relations (IGR)   The fiscal, political, and administrative interaction of the federal, state, and local governments in the United States. It originated during the Depression as the federal government provided considerable funding to states and cities. The term tends to encompass the earlier term *fiscal federalism,* because it recognizes a greater interdependency among all types and levels of government in carrying out policy and programs. *See also* ADVISORY COMMISSION ON INTERGOVERNMENTAL RELATIONS; FEDERALISM; FISCAL FEDERALISM.

Significance   Intergovernmental relations were first officially referred to in a federal statute passed in 1953, an act creating the Kestnbaum Commission on Intergovernmental Relations (P.L. 83–109), and in a 1959 statute establishing the Advisory Commission on Intergovernmental Relations (ACIR). The pullback of the federal government during the Reagan and Bush administrations increased emphasis on state and local governments in funding and administering urban programs, and further altered the dynamics of intergovernmental relations.

Suggested Reading
Nice, David C. *Federalism: The Politics of Intergovernmental Relations.* New York: St. Martin's Press, 1987.
Wright, Deil S. *Understanding Intergovernmental Relations,* 2nd ed. Monterey, CA: Brooks/Cole, 1982.

Intergovernmental Tax Immunity   The mutual exemption of state and federal governmental operations and property from taxation. The issue of tax immunity in the United States was decided originally by the Supreme Court in *McCulloch v. Maryland,* 4 Wheaton 316 (1819). In that case, a Maryland state tax on the operations of the federal government's Bank of the United States was held unconstitutional through a broad interpretation of the elastic clause (Article 1, Section 8). Later court cases expanded the number of activities and agencies that were tax-exempt. In some situations, however, Congress may pay money in lieu of taxes (PILOT) in areas where there are extensive federal property holdings or activities, as it has done with its Aid to Impacted Areas program. However, in 1988, the U.S. Supreme Court ruled in *South Carolina v. Baker* that Congress may constitutionally require states and local governments to issue registered, rather than bearer (or coupon), tax-free bonds. State and local officials have argued that this ruling will put state and local public finance into the political arena at the mercy of the U.S. Congress. The Court decision upheld the federal sanction contained in the 1982 Tax Equity and Fiscal Responsibility Act (TEFRA). *See also* BOND, MUNICIPAL; FEDERAL AID TO IMPACTED AREAS; FEDERALISM.

Significance   A federated form of government provides for a division of power between the national and state governments. Fierce struggles over jurisdiction and authority have followed the changing dynamic of federalism in the United States since the original creation of the Articles of Confederation and through the enactment of the Constitution, the Civil War, and the various states' rights debates of the twentieth century. Intergovernmental tax immunity has provided some order to these struggles, eliminating undue interference by one government into the operations of another. The recent legal battle over tax-free bonds floated by state and local governments suggests a new era of intergovernmental reciprocal immunity. The *South Carolina v. Baker* decision specifically overturned an earlier Court ruling in *Pollock v. Farmers' Loan & Trust Company* (1895), which had determined that interest earned on state bonds was immune from federal taxation. By the end of 1988, state legislatures in Utah, South Carolina, and Oklahoma had enacted resolutions calling for a constitutional amendment to preserve tax immunity, either through a constitutional convention or by congressional initiative.

Interstate Highway System   A nationally sponsored roadway program designed to link all cities with populations of 50,000 or more in the 48 contiguous states. The Interstate Highway System was initiated under the Eisenhower administration as an extension of the 1944 Federal Aid Highway Act. The 42,900-mile system is funded by a grant-in-aid formula based on 90 percent federal contribution and 10 percent state monies. Slightly different formulas are used where funds are traded in and then diverted to other projects such as mass transit. To be completed in 1992, the system is supervised by the Federal Highway Administration of the Department of Transportation. From 1978 through 1983, governors and local authorities could petition the national level for *dedesignation* (the elimination of proposed routes) of highway plans, trading in the promised monies for diversions such as parks, other modes of transportation, and even construction of housing on the cleared land. The interstate system is based on high-level national design, construction, and maintenance standards. Not included in the system are *expressways,* which are high-volume highways with medians (dividers) that serve through traffic with generally limited access routes, as well as *freeways,* which are expressways designed for strictly limited access and usually connect to the interstate system. There are also *toll roads* and *turnpikes* (maintained by user fees), which meet interstate standards but charge tolls and thus are not eligible for federal funding. *See also* BELTWAY; DAILY URBAN SYSTEM; ENVIRONMENTAL IMPACT STATEMENT; INFRASTRUCTURE; MACHINE SPACE; RELOCATION.

Significance   Escalating costs and controversy caught up to the Interstate Highway System before it was finished. Initially designed to be finished by 1972, it was not completed because of protracted opposition from environmentalists and residential groups. The final 4 percent will cost about the same as the first 96 percent. It is the single largest civil engineering project in history. Although accounting for only 1 percent of all U.S. highways, it carries about 20 percent of all highway volume. From 1916, when the national level first promoted highways, until 1961, surface highways were the only mode of urban land transport promoted by the central government. The "freeway rebellion" broke out in 1958 over excess paving of land in urban areas, as a direct result of designs for San Francisco's Embarcadero Expressway. Several other city groups successfully fought the "asphalt lobby." Milwaukee stopped the Park Freeway West, Atlanta halted the Stone Mountain Freeway, and Memphis went all the way to the U.S. Supreme Court over I-40 in *Citizens to Preserve Overton Park v. Volpe,* 401 U.S. 492 (1971). Minneapolis fought the I-335, Boston fought the South West Freeway (I-95), and New Orleans put up a major battle over the Vieux Carre Expressway. Not all opposition groups succeeded, however; Dayton's I-675 and Richmond's I-95 beltways were dropped but were later refunded by Department of Transportation secretaries. The two most spectacular trust fund victories over community opposition involved six-lane projects: a 4.2-mile section of the Westway (I-478) in New York City and a 19.2-mile stretch of the Los Angeles Century Freeway (I-105). Both were delayed more than a decade by environmental lawsuits. I-696 in Oakland County, Michigan, was delayed two decades by municipal infighting. The interstate system has increased the daily urban commute area and encourages urban sprawl into exurbia. It has fostered multinucleation, especially along beltways, and has allowed suburbs to attract commuters from city central business districts (CBDs) with the promise of relatively short commutes.

Suggested Reading
Baumbach, Richard O., Jr., and William E. Borah. *The Second Battle of New Orleans: A History of the Vieux Carre Riverfront-Expressway Controversy.* Tuscaloosa: University of Alabama Press, 1981.

Gakenheimer, Ralph. *Transportation Planning as Response to Controversy: The Boston Case.* Cambridge, MA: MIT Press, 1976.
Goodman, Robert. *After the Planners.* New York: Simon & Schuster, 1971. Chap. 3, pp. 69–91.
Hebert, Richard. *Highways to Nowhere: The Politics of City Transportation.* Indianapolis: Bobbs-Merrill, 1972.
Leavitt, Helen. *Superhighway-Superhoax.* Garden City, NJ: Doubleday, 1970.

Invasion   Movement by a group or groups into a settled area, thus changing land use or type of resident. Invasion is the process of transforming (1) the function for which land is used or (2) the ethnic or racial composition of the land users. The term is used as a dynamic urban model by human ecologists. Unlike its use in international relations, this type of invasion does not involve the military and may be nonviolent. Urban invasion usually takes place over protracted periods and often ends in a succession of ethnic groups and *de facto* or *de jure* zoning changes. *See also* ETHNIC GROUP; FILTERING THEORY, HOUSING; GENTRIFICATION; GROWTH MANAGEMENT; SUCCESSION.

Significance   Invasion carries negative connotations to those who defend the *status quo.* Examples include subdivision developers who invade farmland. Group homes invade residential areas zoned R-1. Cluster-home developers invade areas of conventional, single-family, unattached residences. Industrialists and commercial developers invade the countryside at interstate highway access points. The goal of once common restrictive covenants was to prevent blacks and Jews from invading previously WASPish residential areas. Wealthy suburbanites who buy and remodel run-down inner-city homes are invading gentry who displace tenants driven out by price escalation. The decennial census records black invasion of central-city white census tracts; tax-roll assessments record the gentry's invasion and run-up of land values in formerly run-down central-city neighborhoods. Three standard tactics are used to block invaders. One is the practice of real estate agents steering "undesirables" to other locations along racial lines. The second is the legal attempt by present owners to prevent *in situ* "for sale" signs by barring them under the police power protection of aesthetic standards. The third is strict building-code enforcement, which constricts building-use invasion by forcing site plan review and expensive construction modifications. Invasions by extract resource firms, group homes, and public custodial institutions are labeled Locally Unwanted Land Uses (LULUs) and occasionally can be kept out by litigation under the pretext that the change is not the highest and best use of land. Completed invasions are called *successions.* Storefront churches often succeed an abandoned or failed bank. This type of succession is not to be confused with political succession, which is the transmission of rights to public office, as when one mayor succeeds another.

Suggested Reading
Hudson, James R. *The Unanticipated City: Loft Conversion in Lower Manhattan.* Amherst: University of Massachusetts Press, 1987.

Inverse Condemnation   In common law, a remedy in the form of a claim of deprivation of property without just compensation by the state. Plaintiffs in inverse condemnation cases have not physically had their land formally expropriated under eminent domain; rather, use of their land has been limited through state action. When the state invokes eminent domain, the process is called condemnation. When the private owner claims there has been an unjustly compensated condemnation, the policy is called inverse condemnation. Typical examples include the harm done to private land by governmental regulatory or nonregulatory action, such as the flooding of private property or the restriction of land use adjacent to an airport runway. *See also* EMINENT DOMAIN; IMPACT FEE; TAKING; ZONING, DOWN-.

Significance   Inverse condemnation is a controversial form of judicial relief that suggests a state has taken land without properly compensating the owner. Courts are asked to substitute their judgment for that of the political branches. Where it is found to exist, inverse condemnation is said to have reduced the property's value. Government has only to respond to and pay for actions resulting in outright denial of economic viability of property, *Argins v. City of Tiburon,* 447 U.S. 233 (1980). A celebrated early example of inverse condemnation was *Barron v. Baltimore,* 7 Peters 243 (1833), in which Baltimore was accused of ruining Barron's harbor by a dredging and filling operation.

Suggested Reading
Lazar, Lee A. "The Timeliness of Filing Inverse Condemnation Claims for Continuing or Repeated Injury to Land: The California Resolution." *Urban Law Annual,* vol. 12 (1976), pp. 309–318.
Northrup, Melinda. "Limiting the Availability of Inverse Condemnation as a Landowner's Remedy for Downzoning." *Urban Law Annual,* vol. 13 (1977), pp. 263–275.

J

Jail, Local   A place of incarceration under the administrative authority of a locally elected law-enforcement officer. A local jail differs considerably from a prison. Prisons house convicted criminals; jails hold those serving sentences for misdemeanors and those who have not been convicted of a crime but are awaiting trial and cannot make or have been denied bail. Prisons are operated and financed by state or federal government, whereas local jails usually are financed under the direction of a city or county board of commissioners. Although it is not known how many local jails are operating, it is estimated that by 1987 there were approximately 3,300 local jails in the United States, with an additional 13,000 local lockups, or temporary detention facilities. *See also* LOCKUP.

Significance   Most of the law enforcement burden, including the operation of jails, falls to local government. At any given time, local jails are holding about 250,000 inmates. In a given year, jails house more individuals than all state and federal prisons combined. Many local facilities are outdated, in poor repair, and overcrowded. State standards and federal court cases have improved conditions in recent years, especially with regard to overcrowding and recreational facilities. The many funding and civil rights issues raised with respect to local jail experiences have led in recent years to financial, administrative, and legal crises. Innovative techniques, such as work-release programs and electronic monitoring, have been implemented in many states and localities in an effort to avoid local jail overcrowding.

Suggested Reading
Advisory Commission on Intergovernmental Relations. *Jails: Intergovernmental Dimensions of a Local Problem.* Washington, DC: Government Printing Office, 1984.
"Symposium: Public Policy, Jails, and Criminal Justice." *Policy Studies Review,* vol. 7, no. 3 (1988), pp. 563–681.

Jeffersonian Agrarianism   The attitude of founding father Thomas Jefferson (1743–1826) favoring farmers as the basis of democracy and overtly expressing suspicion of the democratic virtues of cities. The Jeffersonian ideal was based on Greek and Roman theories that "Those who labor in the earth are the chosen people of God." Cultivators "are the most valuable citizens," whereas people who live in urban areas are "the instruments by which the liberties of a country are generally overturned." Jefferson hoped the United States would remain an agrarian republic, made up of yeoman farmers and only a limited manufacturing and trading class; he believed that a republic is not well served by corrupt city dwellers. He felt freemen remained true to limited government when they remained attached to their own land. *See also* WIRTH THESIS.

Significance   Jeffersonian agrarianism is a creed overtly hostile to cities, especially big cities. Jefferson's fidelity to rural ideals was matched by his wariness of cities, which he considered inherently corrupt. As an influential thinker, Jefferson worried about the new nation's possible loss of its agricultural social base to increasing urbanization. He envisioned that the stalwart republic might well be challenged if the population moved to the city. Despite the fact that Jefferson himself lived for a time in Williamsburg, Paris, and Washington, his hostility and suspicion toward large cities were keen and remain a part of U.S. culture to the present. Americans still sometimes reflect his bias in favor of pastoral culture and harbor a deep-seated suspicion of urban landscapes and city slickers.

Suggested Reading

Koch, Adrienne, and William Peden, eds. *The Life and Selected Writings of Thomas Jefferson.* New York: Random House, 1944. Quotations from his notes on Virginia, 1781, and a letter to John Jay, 1785.

Nash, Roderick. *Wilderness and the American Mind.* New Haven, CT: Yale University Press, 1967.

Peterson, Merrill D., ed. *Thomas Jefferson: A Reference Biography.* New York: Charles Scribner's Sons, 1986.

Rowin, Lloyd, and Robert M. Hollister, eds. *Cities of the Mind: Images of the City in the Social Sciences.* New York: Plenum Press, 1984.

White, Morton, and Lucia White. *The Intellectual versus the City: From Thomas Jefferson to Frank Lloyd Wright.* Cambridge,MA: Harvard University Press, 1962.

Job Corps   A residential job training and remedial education program created in 1964 by the Economic Opportunity Act (42 U.S.C. 2701 et seq.). In 1973, Title IV of the Comprehensive Employment and Training Act (CETA) authorized the Department of Labor to operate the Job Corps program. In addition to specific job training, the Job Corps helps to provide social and educational development for those who enroll. *See also* COMPREHENSIVE EMPLOYMENT AND TRAIN-ING ACT; ECONOMIC OPPORTUNITY ACT OF 1964; WAR ON POVERTY.

Significance   The Job Corps was one of the few federal urban social programs to resist massive spending cuts during the Reagan adminis-tration. Like Project Head Start, another social program holdover from the 1960s War on Poverty, the Job Corps earned bipartisan support because program evaluations concluded the program was successful in reaching its stated goals and in maintaining a favorable benefit-to-cost ratio. By the 1980s, the annual cost of the program reached approximately $600 million. It was annually enrolling about 100,000 participants in about 100 centers operated by private contractors.

Suggested Reading

Haveman, J., and L. Palmer. *Jobs for Disadvantaged Workers.* Washington, DC: Brookings Institution, 1982.
Mirengoff, William, and Lester Rindler. *CETA: Manpower Programs under Local Control.* Washington, DC: National Academy of Sciences, 1978.
Wholey, Joseph. "The Job Corps: Congressional Uses of Evaluation Find-ings." In Joseph S. Wholey, Mark A. Abramson, and Christopher Bellavita, eds., *Performance and Credibility: Developing Excellence in Public and Non-profit Organizations.* Lexington, MA: D. C. Heath, 1986.

Joint Center for Housing Studies of Massachusetts Institute of Tech-nology (MIT) and Harvard University   An urban research facility in Cambridge, Massachusetts, providing data, research, and consulta-tion for public and private organizations. The center was known as the Joint Center for Urban Studies from 1971 to 1989, and as of 1990 it had 22 full-time and 10 part-time researchers on staff. The center is an integral part of both Harvard and MIT. Its major fields of investi-gation over the years have covered the entire range of the urban experience, including government and politics, housing, transporta-tion, community development, education, public health, planning, demography, and voter attitudes. The center publishes books, mono-graphs, working papers, newsletters, and reports.

Significance   The Joint Center for Housing Studies is a prominent source of data concerning urban life and the social, economic, and demographic trends that affect urban living. Its reports are consid-ered highly credible and influential. The center's 1973 report, *Amer-ica's Housing Needs: 1970 to 1980,* was a widely read analysis concluding that more than 13 million U.S. citizens suffered from at least one form of housing deprivation, more than double the estimates of previous studies. In addition, the report argued that about 24 million housing units would be needed during the 1970s, more than 3 million more than previous studies had estimated. Through MIT's and Harvard's university presses, the center also has published such works as Banfield and Wilson's *City Politics,* Anderson's *The Federal Bulldozer,* and Glazer and Moynihan's *Beyond the Melting Pot.*

Suggested Reading

Anderson, Martin. *The Federal Bulldozer.* Cambridge, MA: MIT Press, 1964.

Apgar, William C., Jr., et al. *The Housing Outlook: 1980–1990.* New York: Praeger, 1985.

Baker, Kermit, and H. James Brown. *Home Ownership and Housing Affordability in the United States: 1963–1984. The 1985 Report.* Cambridge, MA: Joint Center for Housing Studies, 1985.

Banfield, Edward C., and James Q. Wilson. *City Politics.* Cambridge, MA: Harvard University Press, 1963.

Birch, David. *America's Housing Needs: 1970 to 1980.* Cambridge, MA: Joint Center for Urban Studies, December 1983.

Glazer, Nathan, and Daniel Patrick Moynihan. *Beyond the Melting Pot,* rev. ed. Cambridge, MA: MIT Press, 1970.

Pollakowski, Henry O., and John G. Edwards. "Life-Cycle Class, City Vintage, and the Probability of Suburbanization." *Working Paper W87-4.* Cambridge, MA: Joint Center for Housing Studies, 1987.

Joint Operating Agreement (JOA)   A contractual procedure allowed for under the Newspaper Preservation Act of 1970, 15 U.S.C. 1801, in which competing metropolitan dailies are exempted from antitrust laws and are allowed to combine their business operations while maintaining separate editorial and news reporting functions. Joint Operating Agreements permit two newspapers to operate a single facility for printing, distribution, advertising, and subscription in order to preserve a financially failing newspaper. *See also* COMMUNITY PRESS; ZONED EDITION.

Significance   Joint Operating Agreements are in force in 21 U.S. cities, including Miami, Seattle, Detroit, and San Francisco. For a JOA to be approved, the newspapers must demonstrate to a Justice Department administrative law judge that one of the two papers would fail unless allowed to merge business operations. If the law judge denies the appeal, it can be appealed to the U.S. Attorney General. The U.S. Supreme Court has not determined the constitutionality of JOAs, having tied at 4 in a 1989 Detroit newspaper case. Competing suburban dailies and the community press often oppose the request on grounds of unfair competition. In all cities where they operate, JOAs are profitable.

Juvenile Court   A specialized court with original jurisdiction over youthful offenders, normally those up to 18 years old. Juvenile courts act *in loco parentis,* or in place of parents, in an effort to provide youths another chance rather than punish them. There are more than 3,000 U.S. juvenile courts processing a total of about 1.5 million arrests annually. All states have juvenile codes and a separate court system to deal with minors. Juvenile courts usually come in contact with youths who commit the most serious crimes; communities seek to deal with most juvenile offenders by releasing them back to their parents or through community diversion programs. In more serious cases involving older youths, prosecutors may request the offenders be tried as adults. Most states have promulgated statutes that specify a minimum age at which an offender may be transferred to adult court (usually 14 to 17 years old), often for specific crimes (kidnapping, rape, or murder). *See also* CRIME; JAIL, LOCAL; MUNICIPAL COURT.

Significance   Juvenile courts traditionally have attempted to provide a "second chance" to minors. The juvenile justice system traditionally has been more forgiving of youthful offenders than adults. There are several differences between the juvenile and adult justice systems in the United States. More discretion tends to be used by police officers in formally arresting minors than in dealing with adults. Juvenile courts cannot send minors to county jails or state prisons. In addition, the criminal record of a juvenile is sealed upon reaching the age of majority. The Illinois State Legislature established the first juvenile court in the United States, called the Juvenile Court of Cook County, which opened in 1899.

Suggested Reading
Besharov, Daniel. *Juvenile Justice Advocacy—Practice in a Unique Court.* New York: Practicing Law Institute, 1974.
Ryerson, E. *The Best Laid Plans: America's Juvenile Court Experiment.* New York: Holt & Wang, 1978.
Siegel, Larry J., and Joseph J. Senna. *Juvenile Delinquency: Theory, Practice, and Law,* 3rd ed. St. Paul, MN: West Publishing, 1989.

K

Kerner Commission   A blue-ribbon panel created to investigate the causes of the urban riots of the 1960s. Formally called the National Advisory Commission on Civil Disorders, this panel was chaired by Illinois Governor Otto Kerner. The Kerner Commission was created by President Lyndon Johnson's Executive Order 11365 on July 29, 1967, after urban riots had occurred in the Watts neighborhood of Los Angeles (1965), in Newark (1967), and in Detroit (1967). The 11-member commission traveled across the country holding hearings and conducting interviews. It employed a professional research staff of more than 30. The commission's report, released February 29, 1968, found that the major factors leading to urban violence were police-community relations, segregation and generally inadequate housing, and high unemployment among urban blacks. An update of this report on urban affairs was conducted by a second "Kerner Commission" panel that studied urban problems 20 years later. This second panel included some of the same members as the original and reported its findings February 29, 1988. These findings indicated that although some improvements had been made in the state of urban minorities, there were "quiet riots" occurring in the nation's cities. These took the form of persisting unemployment, poverty, crime, and continued segregation in housing and schools. *See also* AD HOC BODY; POLICE REVIEW BOARD; RIOT.

Significance   The Kerner Commission's report raised considerable controversy. The blame for the urban unrest of the 1960s was placed squarely on the hostility and ignorance of the white population and on public and private institutional racism. A number of specific programs were created after the report's release, among them vigorous hiring of minority police officers in many cities, the establishment of police-community relations programs, and open housing programs. However, many of the problems identified by the Kerner Commission

292

remain. The updated report released in 1988 stated that racism was still a critical problem, but some of the panel members disagreed about its importance. Among the improvements cited were the emergence of a black middle class, the election of black officials in many cities, and increased job opportunities for blacks in previously segregated workplaces. At least two follow-up reports also were issued, both sponsored by the Urban Coalition and chaired by two members of the original Kerner Commission, Democratic Senator Fred Harris (Oklahoma) and Republican Mayor John Lindsay (New York City). These two reports, conducted in 1969 and 1971, pointed out small improvements in the plight of urban blacks, but the tone of each report was quite pessimistic. Each report concluded that for the foreseeable future, American cities are likely to have a majority of poor black or minority residents, and cities probably will face severe fiscal problems or even bankruptcy.

Suggested Reading

Harris, Fred R., and John V. Lindsay. *The State of the Cities: Report of the Commission on the Cities in the 70s.* New York: Praeger, 1972.

Report of the National Advisory Commission on Civil Disorders. New York: New York Times Company, 1968.

Urban America, Inc., and the Urban Coalition. *One Year Later: An Assessment of the Nation's Response to Crisis Described by the National Advisory Commission on Civil Disorders.* New York: Praeger, 1969.

Ku Klux Klan (KKK)   A white-supremacist secret society founded in Tennessee in 1865 in reaction to Civil War reconstruction and revived in Georgia in 1915. The KKK is often a violent organization that resorts to intimidation. All of the Klans are based on bigotry and a series of antipositions: antiblack, anti-immigrant, anti-Jewish, anti–Roman Catholic, anti-Mormon, and antigay. The highly ritualistic Klan society employs an extensive alliterative terminology and symbolically uses the color white.

Significance   The KKK has shifted targets throughout its many phases. It has been especially active in the South and Southwest but has had periods of electoral activity as far north as New York State, where it was outlawed as a threat to the public welfare. The ban was upheld by the U.S. Supreme Court in *New York ex. rel. Bryant v. Zimmerman,* 278 U.S. 63 (1928). Often called a hate organization, the KKK appeals to the violent tradition of America. It has long been under FBI surveillance and was listed as a subversive organization by the U.S. Attorney General. However, it has often been aided by police passivity or outright cooperation. The various KKK organizations are highly authoritarian and are still active in such northern states as Idaho and Michigan, where they have bombed buses and churches involved in integration. In recent years, the KKK has sought to get its message across by a somewhat more sophisticated approach, but its basic negative ideology remains. Always associated with Christianity, it especially appeals to blue-collar males who favor a direct and physical approach to public issues.

Suggested Reading

Alexander, Charles C. *The Ku Klux Klan in the Southwest*. Lexington: University of Kentucky Press, 1965.

Chambers, David M. *Hooded Americanism: The History of the Ku Klux Klan*. Durham, NC: Duke University Press, 1987.

Jackson, Kenneth T. *The Ku Klux Klan in the City: 1915–1930*. New York: Oxford University Press, 1967.

Wade, Wyn Craig. *The Fiery Cross: The Ku Klux Klan in America*. London: Simon & Schuster, 1987. Book Three: 1930–1987, pp. 257–403.

L

Lakewood Plan   A comprehensive interlocal agreement under which the County of Los Angeles supplies services by contract in variable quantities to more than 25 California cities. When Lakewood, California, incorporated in 1954, it created a quasi-market arrangement by selecting the county to provide virtually all its major services except local land-use planning. Because the county received its revenue from the city or specially created taxing authorities, the residents benefited from economies of scale. In turn, the California contract cities maintained an option to cancel services. Law enforcement from the sheriff is the kingpin service. When a conflict arises between the contracting cities and the sheriff's department, the sheriff is favored under a clause written into the contracts. This is analogous to the supremacy clause built into the U.S. Constitution. In all, more than 75 cities contract for one or more services. More than 25 cities have opted for most of the bundle of 20 services offered. There are more than 1,500 contracts in force over the county. The contracting cities vary in population from less than 1,000 to more than 100,000. *See also* BALKANIZATION; CONTRACTING OUT; TWO-TIER LOCAL GOVERNMENT.

Significance   The Lakewood Plan has not been imitated as a form of intergovernmental relations for central supplying of services. There are, however, some parallels in St. Louis County, Missouri, and Stockholm, Sweden. The California area uses very large-scale operations; for example, the original sheriff's station in Lakewood, as of the late 1980s, served almost 250,000 people in six cities from one location. The Lakewood Plan is popular with residents and is stable, with few contracts being broken and few private companies outbidding the public supplier. The County Board of Supervisors and city administrators engage in bargaining and adjust procedures within the general master contracts. Regional cooperation in land-use management is negligible; each city develops its own master plan, and communities vary from industrial enclaves (City of Industry and Santa Fe Springs) to residential suburbs (Rolling Hills has all private roads). Many of the cities that incorporated in the 1950s under the Lakewood Plan did so to preserve their tax base and exclusive class orientation. This example of multiple general- and limited-function public decision-making bodies is parallel to the myriad of government authorities from boroughs to villages found in most balkanized metropolitan areas in the United States.

Suggested Reading

Cion, Richard M. "Accommodation Par Excellence: The Lakewood Plan." In Michael N. Danielson, ed., *Metropolitan Politics: A Reader*, 2nd ed. Boston: Little, Brown, 1971. Pp. 224–231.

Hoch, Charles. "Municipal Contracting in California: Privatizing with Class." *Urban Affairs Quarterly*, vol. 20, no. 3 (1985), pp. 303–323.

Miller, Gary J. *Cities by Contract*. Cambridge, MA: MIT Press, 1981.

Shoup, Donald C., and Arthur Rosett. "Fiscal Exploitation by Overlapping Government." In Werner Hirach et al., eds., *Fiscal Pressure on the Central City: The Impact of Commuters, Nonwhites, and Overlapping Governments*. New York: Praeger, 1971. Chap. 4, pp. 241–304.

Sonenblum, Sidney, John J. Kirlin, and John C. Ries. *How Cities Provide Services*. Cambridge, MA: Ballinger, 1977.

Land, Raw   A subclassification of vacant property that has not been developed by infrastructure such as roads and water or sewer lines. In addition to raw land, the other classification for vacant property is *improved* or *developed*. Many cities have classified some of their land as zoned for agriculture use: Those parcels that are fenced or graded and planted are not raw but developed for that use. Raw land may or may not be readily available for building, depending on its zoning status. Surfaces covered by water, dedicated to greenbelts, or declared environmentally sensitive are not truly raw land, because they would not be available later for building. Raw land is properly advertised as unplatted, never-built-upon acreage having a topography suitable for potential building sites. *See also* INFILLING; INFRASTRUCTURE; LAND, VACANT URBAN; LAND BANKING.

Significance   Raw land attracts speculators who hold it in large-scale units awaiting future use, hoping it will be planned, intensely developed, and not used for agriculture. The term often is applied indiscriminately to any vacant land. But refined, developed vacant land is worth much more, being available in the short run for building. The cost of raw land is largely a function of market-anticipated growth and the availability of the two key elements of infrastructure, namely, paved roads and utilities. Raw land may not be parceled into landlocked units. The ability of the raw land to perk—that is to say, to accommodate septic tanks—is the *sine qua non* for later development if sewer lines do not come into the area.

Land, Vacant Urban   A classification of property on which there are no buildings and the designated function of which is not being achieved. Vacant urban land can be differentiated from *open space,* which is dedicated to greenbelts, recreation fields, or agriculture. Vacant land is organized into two subclasses: raw land, on which there is no infrastructure; and developed land, on which refinements have been made, ranging from grading and drainage to placement of public utilities. Obviously, not all vacant land sells for the same amount; developed land is worth substantially more than raw land. Cleared urban renewal land costs more than never-built-upon land, unless the displaced property has been written down by a public authority to make it more attractive. *See also* INFILLING; INFRASTRUCTURE; LAND, RAW; PUBLIC UTILITY.

Significance   Vacant urban land constitutes on average about one-fourth of all the acreage of U.S. cities with populations of more than 100,000. About three-fourths of vacant urban land is buildable by local zoning standards. Vacancy rates vary from about one-tenth of land in major cities to more than one-third in cities of 100,000. This rate also varies by region and population. Some buildable vacant parcels are remnants that have been skipped over, some are being held in reserve by government and private institutions, and some are owned by individual speculators. Most city and county planning departments monitor their vacant land and periodically inventory it. Municipalities buy vacant parcels, consolidate them into desirable sale parcels in a land bank, and seek to attract industrial developers. The more vacant residential land in a city, generally the lower the population density recorded by the decennial census. In most cases, vacant land that is infilled yields higher property tax collections with little extra public-capital improvement. The more infilling of vacant urban land, the less need there is for urban sprawl on the metropolitan fringe.

Suggested Reading
Carlson, Cynthia J., and Robert J. Duffy. "Cincinnati Takes Stock of Its Vacant Land." *Planning,* vol. 51, no. 11 (1985), pp. 22–26.
Northam, Ray M. *Urban Geography.* New York: John Wiley, 1975, pp. 364–370.

Land Banking   Acquisition and ownership of urban property by a public body for future use. Land banking by government removes taxable property from the tax rolls. The purposes of land banking are to control future development, limit sprawl, capture the increasing increment of land values, fashion the pace of construction, and assemble large parcels so as to be able to bid on major development sites for such projects as a new government building or an automotive plant. Land banking in Canada, especially active in the prairie provinces of Alberta and Saskatchewan, must be used substantially for residential construction, according to the National Housing Act of 1954, Chapter 23. Land banking in Milwaukee is designed primarily for future industrial development. Milwaukee's modest industrial land bank was authorized in 1960 and first implemented in 1964. *See also* GROWTH MANAGEMENT; LAND, VACANT URBAN; TAX EXEMPTION.

Significance   Urban land banking is analogous to the rural U.S. Soil Bank Act of 1956 (7 U.S.C. 1801 et seq.) in that both are designed to set aside parcels of land for future use while temporarily removing the land from its present activity. The major difference between the two programs is that urban land banking requires government ownership, whereas rural soil banking maintains private ownership through federal payments to the cultivator in exchange for a promise that the farmer will forgo current cultivation. Although land banking is used in Canada and Sweden, it is not as actively employed in the United States, where the tradition is for the government to sell land to current user-owners. Some property held in urban land banks is purchased or acquired at a tax sale, some is acquired by dedication or negotiated sale, and some is acquired under condemnation proceedings. Actively developed land banks are examples of municipalities pursuing a growth policy rather than passively waiting for entrepreneurs to fashion land-use decisions. The largest land bank based on former industrial properties was arranged in 1988 when the Allegheny County Industrial Development Authority in Metropolitan Pittsburgh was deeded 360 acres of riverfront property after the closing of a steel mill on the site. The arrangement was atypical in that the steel company continued to pay taxes on the land's assessed value but also claimed the right to later partial compensation when and if the land was resold to a private developer. Urban land banking is usually conceived as a relatively short-term holding, likely to expire after 5 to 15 years.

Suggested Reading

Fisherman, Richard P., and Robert D. Gross. "Public Land Banking: A New Praxis for Urban Growth." *Case Western Reserve Law Review*, vol. 23, no. 1 (1972), pp. 897–975.
Harr, Charles. "Wanted: Two Federal Lovers for Urban Land Use—Land Banks and Urbank (excerpts)." In David Listekin, ed., *Land Use Controls:*

Present Problems and Future Reform. New Brunswick, NJ: Center for Urban Policy Research, 1974, pp. 365–379. Chap. 23.

Maier, Henry W. *Challenge to the Cities: An Approach to a Theory of Urban Leadership.* New York: Random House, 1966. Chap. 5.

Stoebuck, William. "Suburban Land Banking." *University of Illinois Law Review,* vol. 1986, no. 3 (1986), pp. 581–607.

Land Classification   A typology of land areas designed to perform one of two major functions: (1) to create in law a set of permitted uses by way of zoning districts or (2) to compile an analytic set of land categories empirically derived from surveys and organized into an overall model that explains the patterns of all land within the universe of investigation. As a normative typology, land classification is zoning. This system may have any number of small-scale districts, ranging from less than a dozen in a homogeneous, small-scale community to many score in a highly populated, heterogeneous city. Among the more common designations in zoning are Public Property (PP), Agricultural (A), Business (B), Residential (R), Parking (P), Office (O), and Industrial (I). In turn, most zoning ordinances further refine categories such as R-1, Single-Family Residential with no more than a certain number of houses per acre; R-2, with greater density; and R-M, Residential Multiple. As an empirical typology, land classifications are based on the physical properties of the soil, its yields, or its surface and subsurface uses by man. Because urban usages constitute less than 5 percent of the earth's surface, schemes focus on rural patterns. Land often is classified as covered by water, forest, used for pasture and grazing, barren, used for recreation, exploited for mineral deposits, or used for transport, commercial and industrial, and residential purposes. The three most frequently used urban land classifications are the concentric zone, sector, and multinuclei models. Physical planners do not use a standardized land classification system. Each city, county, parish, or New England town is free to employ its own system. Other variables used in land classification besides soil types and use patterns include density, ownership (on cadastral maps), and transportation networks (hinterlands). *See also* CONCENTRIC ZONE MODEL; LAND, VACANT URBAN; MULTINUCLEI MODEL; SECTOR MODEL; ZONING.

Significance   Systematic land classification is peculiar to the late twentieth century. Zoning was a western European innovation of the 1870s, especially in Sweden and Germany. New York City was the first jurisdiction to adopt zoning, and Euclid, Ohio, a suburb of Cleveland, was the village against which a U.S. Supreme Court test case was brought in 1926. The concentric zone model was devised in 1925 to account for Chicago's development; the sector model was devised in 1939 to account for more than 140 other American cities; and the multinuclei model was developed in 1945 to explain lapses in the first two models. All land classification systems are more sophisticated today as a result of two technologies; aerial photography and remote sensing on the one hand have aided systematic data collection, and computers and coding systems have developed rigor heretofore unthought of. There is no uniformity in zoning districts among cities or states, nor is there an agreed-upon single land classification system in use among urban geographers or urban planners. Comparative land-use studies often are based, therefore, on noncomparable information. Vacant land in one system may be raw land, barren land, or open space in another system. Computer-Aided Design and Drafting (CADD) maps used by counties, Councils of Governments (COGs), and some states are revolutionizing maps created to a common scale. These land-use models can be drawn to the same scale for large areas to designate property lines (cadastral maps), utility lines (infrastructure), and land cover (geobotanical maps). The Michigan Land Information Exchange (MLINX) is automating on the state level.

Suggested Reading

Bollens, Scott A., and David R. Godschalk. "Tracking Land Supply for Growth Management." *Journal of the American Planning Association,* vol. 53, no. 3 (1987).
Morris, Joe. "Computer Mapping the Infrastructure." *American City and County,* April 1987, pp. 50–53.

Land Conservancy   A private, tax-exempt, and not-for-profit corporation that protects endangered species and insulates from development such ecologically sensitive areas as rivers, marshes, forests, and open spaces. It is also known as Nature Conservancy. Land conservancies acquire property by donation, by purchase, and through easement. Operating costs are paid for by tax write-off contributions and membership dues. Some of the land is kept in a totally natural condition; some supports limited developments, such as access bridges, paths, and ponding; and some, such as Central Park in New York City, is extensively landscaped. *See also* PUBLIC-PRIVATE PARTNERSHIP.

Significance   The best-known land area held by a conservancy is Central Park in the Borough of Manhattan. The largest, with more than 1.5 million acres, is the internationally organized Nature Conservancy. Not all states allow a tax shelter for such privately held land.

This land later can be deeded with the public's permission to urban or state park systems. Land conservancy is less common than private preserves, which are deeded to cities with permanent restrictions for easement and improvements. Conservancy is part of a private-public land ownership network designed to ensure open space and a natural heritage. In rural areas, such groups as Ducks Unlimited and the National Audubon Society often control more ponding and wetland area in flyways than does the state itself. In urban areas, floodplains can be held by these groups, even preventing construction and sometimes public access to these unpredictable lands. The three chief advantages of private land preserves are that (1) a natural heritage of unique, rare, or special conditions is preserved for residents; (2) the group can act to buy land with much greater dispatch than its government counterpart; and (3) donors and sellers receive local and federal tax advantages. The chief disadvantages are (1) future conflicts with preserved land may arise as a community grows and changes; (2) the land so designated might have been developed and put on the property tax rolls in a manner sensitive to the environment; and (3) such lands are taken off the property tax rolls, albeit the adjacent lands' value is thereby enhanced.

Suggested Reading
Nature Conservancy Magazine, vol. 39, no. 1 (1989).
New York City Department of Parks and Recreation and Central Park Conservancy. *Rebuilding Central Park: A Management and Restoration Plan.* Cambridge, MA: MIT Press, 1986.
Smith, Robert J. "Special Report: The Public Benefits of Private Conservation." In Council of Environmental Quality, *Environmental Quality, 1984.* (15th annual report.) Washington, DC: Superintendent of Public Documents, 1984. Pp. 364–429.

Land-Use Control   A generic term to describe public or private guidelines for present and future property development. The national government owns one-third of the nation's land and manages it mostly through parks, forests, grasslands, and Defense Department bases. The other two-thirds of the land is privately owned. It is administered primarily at the local and state levels through zoning and subdivision controls. All states have passed plat acts governing the breakup of land into small parcels; many states have set up park and forest preserves, and those adjacent to major waterways have established Coastal Zone management at national government insistence. In all states, such conflicts are resolved on a case-by-case basis. There are numerous public tools for controlling land. They generally fall into three broad groups: guiding initial use, guiding reuse, and public ownership of land. In addition to zoning ordinances, condominiums, and subdivision restrictions, there are historic preservation codes, quotas on building permits, moratoriums on new construction, preservation of agricultural land, and creation of greenbelts and land banks. Three common purposes for controlling land are (1) protecting the health, safety, and aesthetics of the community (the police power), (2) properly managing the environment, and (3) protecting real estate values and promoting the highest and best use. *See also* BUILDING CODES; EMINENT DOMAIN; GREENBELT; LAND BANK; MASTER PLAN; PLANNED UNIT DEVELOPMENT; ZONING.

Significance   Most land-use controls have been preempted by the public sector at the local and state levels. Local land-use controls must conform to state guidelines. Local opposition to group homes, for example, is overridden by state statutes mandating their acceptance. The United States came late to using land-use controls: New York City, in 1916, was the first to pass a general zoning ordinance. It was not until 1926 that the U.S. Supreme Court constitutionally sanctioned zoning. Critics say zoning is too piecemeal and not concerned enough with the big picture outside each balkanized unit's own borders. Many communities have not developed a master plan that explains and puts the zones into context. Also, there is a single-ordinance orientation in most municipalities: A historical preservation district is examined by city councils out of the context of the local master plan or Councils of Governments (COGs) regional plan. Zoning ordinances allow for many exemptions on hardship grounds, and critics maintain that too many special allowances are dispensed. Once land-use controls are in place, administration is not an exact science; for example, someone must determine the carrying capacity of the land, where the coastal zone begins, or whether the topographic features demand fewer or no building permits. Street-level bureaucrats in controlling land use must determine what constitutes an environmentally sensitive area or whether a parcel is mostly or only incidentally in the floodplain.

Suggested Reading

Godschalk, David R., et al. *Land Supply Monitoring: A Guide for Improving Public and Private Urban Development Decisions.* Boston: Oelgeschlager, Gunn & Hain, 1986.
Nelson, Robert H. *Zoning and Property Rights: An Analysis of the American System of Land-Use Regulation.* Cambridge, MA: MIT Press, 1977.
Wengert, Norman. "Land Use Policy." In Stuart S. Nagel, ed., *Encyclopedia of Policy Studies.* New York: Marcel Dekker, 1983. Chap. 27.

Landlocked Property   Any land parcel that does not have immediate access to a road. The term is based on an analogy with landlocked nations, which do not have access to the sea. Landlocked property cannot be developed, because ingress and egress depend upon passing over someone else's private land. *See also* LAND, RAW.

Significance   Many states and municipalities have passed statutes and zoning ordinances that absolutely prohibit creation of landlocked property, because to do so is to create a parcel that is contrary to public policy and cannot be developed to its highest and best use. The owner of such property is at the mercy of contiguous lot owners for access and would be forced to sell the land at below-market levels for attachment to a neighboring unit. If a landlocked parcel exists at the inception of a zoning ordinance, it can be declared nonconforming, and the state or municipality may force an elimination of the condition, through either consolidation of parcels or creation of a permanent easement.

Law Enforcement Assistance Administration (LEAA)   A federal agency created in 1968 by Title 1 of the Omnibus Crime Control and Safe Streets Act (5 U.S.C. 5108; 42 U.S.C. 3334 et seq.). In part a response to the urban riots of the 1960s, the LEAA was designed to provide federal assistance to state and local governments for a variety of law enforcement activities. The Safe Streets Act charged the LEAA with (1) encouraging state and local governments to adopt comprehensive law enforcement plans based on their specific needs; (2) allocating grants to state and local governments to improve their law enforcement responsibilities; and (3) supporting research and development of crime reduction, detection, and prevention, as well as the apprehension of criminals. Encouraging the creation of State Planning Agencies (SPAs), LEAA provided planning and action block grants to states and cities, with certain entitlements reserved for major cities and urban counties. By the mid-1970s, the ineffectiveness of LEAA programs was criticized by the Office of Management and Budget and such groups as the Twentieth Century Fund. The agency was terminated in 1982. *See also* CRIME; POLICE, PUBLIC.

Significance   The LEAA-sponsored programs were typical of intergovernmental relations in the 1960s and 1970s. Federal funding was made available through block grant assistance, with some federal standards and guidelines imposed on state and local spending. LEAA allowed states and cities to develop their own law enforcement priorities but required governments to submit their plans to LEAA for approval before implementation. The research and development element of the act attempted to encourage innovation but also to bring a minimum set of crime prevention and detection practices to all jurisdictions in the country. A wide variety of law enforcement programs was funded under LEAA's authority. Computerized recordkeeping systems, purchase of communications systems for police, officer training programs, and crime-fighting equipment were all expenditures funded through LEAA. During the first eight years of the LEAA, more than $5 billion was allocated to state and local governments.

Suggested Reading

Twentieth Century Fund. *Law Enforcement: The Federal Role, Report of the Task Force on the Law Enforcement Assistance Administration.* New York: McGraw-Hill, 1976.

U.S. Congress, House Committee on Government Operations. *Block Grant Programs of the Law Enforcement Assistance Administration, Twelfth Report.* House Report, no. 92-1072, May 1972.

League of Women Voters   A national organization of volunteers, headquartered in Washington, D.C., and established with the stated objective of promoting informed political participation at all levels of government. The League of Women Voters grew out of the suffragette movement and was first proposed in 1919 by Carrie Chapman Catt. Her idea was that the league would be a vehicle for the enfranchisement of women in every state and would encourage women to give service in gratitude for their political independence. The league was to be nonpartisan and nonsectarian. It is organized at the national, state, and local levels. Its strength is at the local level, where there are more than 100,000 members in more than 1,100 chapters nationwide. Adding contributors to the number of members, total league support is approximately 250,000. Among the league's activities are voter registration drives, distribution of voters' guides, candidates' nights, and publication of league studies on public-policy issues. It sponsored presidential debates from 1976 to 1984. It is known for its studies of individual state, county, and city governments.

Significance   The name of the organization, League of Women Voters, is a misnomer; men have been members since the 1970s. Critics claim it is not strictly neutral. The league backs specific policies and lobbies for and against legislation at the national and state levels. For example, at the national level it supports a strong Clean Air Act and a welfare reform package and opposes protectionist trade legislation. By sponsoring get-out-the-vote projects and registration drives, the league encourages new voters. Defenders point out the league does not endorse specific candidates or parties. Most observers would label the league a "goo-goo," a good-government group. The league is more concerned with local issues than is Common Cause, another good-government group. Some league leaders go on to elected partisan office after having developed their leadership skills within the group. The league has evolved over the decades. Originally concerned mainly with the study of issues, it is now equally concerned with action (lobbying) at the national, state, and local levels. In earlier years, the league tended to operate alone. Now it frequently joins with other interest groups in filing *amicus curiae* briefs or lobbying in peak associations. Its debates and studies sometimes are funded partially by foundations, corporations, and even government agencies.

Suggested Reading
The National Voter. League of Women Voters of the United States, 1730 M
     Street, NW, Washington, DC 20036.

Lease-back   The sale of real or personal property whereupon the buyer conveys the property back to the seller under specific terms. Although lease-back is used by private individuals or businesses for tax purposes, local governments use lease-back arrangements to acquire land and control land use but not necessarily to occupy the property. A public agency may purchase a tract of land, then lease it to a private individual with an open-space requirement in keeping with the approved public plan for the area. *See also* EASEMENT; LAND BANKING; LAND-USE CONTROL.

Significance   Lease-backs have been used by local governments as a way of controlling land use while acquiring some additional income. For example, the Cook County Forest Preserve in Illinois has used lease-back to maintain open-space requirements. Other local governments have used easements in an attempt to expand and control land use. These scenic or conservation easements have been used by public agencies for specific functions such as bike paths. They may also be simply restrictive, enabling the government to prohibit the occupier of the property from using the land for certain purposes. Washington, D.C., and Monterey, California, are other examples of governments that have used conservation or scenic easements.

Suggested Reading
Vallee, William L., Jr. "Sale-Leaseback Transactions by Tax-Exempt Entities
     and the Need for Congressional Guidelines." *Fordham Urban Law Journal*, vol. 12, no. 2 (1983–1984), pp. 349–381.

Levittown   New suburban developments named after the Levitt family of builders on the east coast of the United States in the immediate post–World War II era. Levittowns in New York, Pennsylvania, and New Jersey were all built on large parcels of suburban land by mass-production methods for middle-income and largely younger, white residents. The first large-scale Levittown built in the late 1940s was on Long Island in Nassau County, New York, and is now part of Hempstead. The second Levittown was built in Bucks County, Pennsylvania, and is known by its four jurisdictional names of Tullytown, Falls Township, Middletown, and Bristol. Each of these Levittowns had a 1980 population in excess of 60,000. The third large Levittown is located in Burlington County, New Jersey, where voters elected to return the area to its original name of Willingsboro. With a population of more than 20,000, it is the smallest of the three developments. The first Levittown is a suburb of the New York metropolitan area. The latter two are in the Philadelphia metropolitan area. *See also* ADULT-ONLY COMMUNITY; BEDROOM SUBURB; NEW TOWN; SUBURB.

Significance   Levittowns exist in the three U.S. northeastern seaboard locations plus one each in Puerto Rico and France. All were preplanned suburban communities that included prepared infrastructure for transportation, utilities, schools, shopping centers, recreation, and community centers. They were financially successful, something not true of later preplanned communities such as Reston, Virginia, or Columbia, Maryland. Levittowns were *turnkey operations,* that is to say, the builder prepared all elements of the physical community and turned over finished products to the community for ownership and maintenance. Often satirized as a symbol of suburban drabness and conformity, early Levittowns' residents were in fact quite content with their new communities and satisfied with their environment. One major shortcoming to all three northeast coast Levittowns was their racial exclusiveness.

Suggested Reading
Gans, Herbert J. *The Levittowners: Ways of Life in a New Suburban Community.* New York: Columbia University Press, 1982. Originally issued in 1967.
Popenoe, David. *The Suburban Environment: Sweden and the United States.* Chicago: University of Chicago Press, 1977. (Levittown, Pennsylvania, case study.)

Lobbying by Cities   Asserted, articulated, felt needs interjected at any stage of the governmental decision-making process by local units of government. Lobbying by cities is directed at other cities and local units, the state, and especially the national government. This activity is not confined to the legislature but includes courts, the bureaucracy, and the executive office. Lobbying is not confined to demands articulated by private groups; it also embraces governments petitioning other governments. Lobbying is a communication process. It is both outgoing and incoming information, that is to say, intelligence collection. One of the earliest and largest urban lobbies is the U.S. Conference of Mayors, which represents the nation's biggest cities. Smaller-size units are represented by the National League of Cities. Cities also lobby Washington individually. Liaison officers, as lobbyists are sometimes called, long have represented individual cities such as Long Beach, Oakland, San Francisco, and Los Angeles. Urban lobbying is a part of intergovernmental relations. When operating alone, a city is often asking for special consideration. When working within a coalition, it typically is asking for general awareness of city problems. At the national level, city lobbyists focus on the House and Senate Banking and Currency Committee, the Department of Housing and Urban Development (HUD), and the Department of Transportation (DOT). Many states have set up city affairs bureaus within the governor's office to handle the special needs of large urban areas. *See also* GRANTSMANSHIP; NATIONAL LEAGUE OF CITIES; STATE-MUNICIPAL AFFAIRS OFFICE; U.S. CONFERENCE OF MAYORS.

Significance   All lobbying is constitutionally protected under color of the First Amendment right to petition the government for redress of grievances. Lobbying by cities is simply information gathering and distribution conducted by substate levels. One of the most important goals of city lobbying is to keep decision makers at other levels aware of the special urban needs that arise from high density and larger populations. Because about 70 percent of the nation lives in places designated urban, this seems simple; however, many legislators and civil servants need reminding. In the systems approach, lobbying is initially an input, but as the loop of policy continues, it is also a feedback mechanism. All lobbying, including that done by cities working alone or in concert, is regulated by four formal techniques: (1) registration-identification-publicity statutes, (2) tax incentives and disincentives, (3) legislative, newspaper, and executive agency investigations, and (4) court reviews, especially of lobbying based on written contracts. The impact of lobbying is also limited by three informal techniques: (1) well-educated and high-quality legislators who can discount information, (2) counterinformation supplied by committee staff and legislative reference services, and (3) countervailing pressure from other interests, including those that are rural-based.

Suggested Reading
Farkas, Suzanne. *Urban Lobbying: Mayors in the Federal Arena.* New York: New York University Press, 1971.

Haider, Donald H. *When Governments Come to Washington: Governors, Mayors, and Intergovernmental Lobbying.* New York: Free Press, 1974.

Pelissero, John P., and Robert E. England. "State and Local Governments' Washington 'Reps'—Lobbying Strategy and President Reagan's New Federalism." *State and Local Government Review,* vol. 19, no. 2 (1987), pp. 68–72.

Smith, John W. "Regulation of National and State Legislative Lobbying." *University of Detroit Law Journal,* vol. 43, no. 5 (1966), pp. 663–693. (Definition here from p. 663.)

LOCAL EXCHANGE™   An information storage and retrieval network sponsored by the National League of Cities (NLC), the International City Management Association (ICMA), the Government Finance Officers Association (GFOA), and others. LOCAL EXCHANGE provides several substate government data bases for elected officials, line departments, and staff budget and finance personnel. The best-known service is updated information from the NLC's *Urban Affairs Abstracts,* which is also available in weekly, semiannual, and annual printed form. *See also* DIALOG; EDUCATIONAL RESOURCES INFORMATION CENTER; LOGIN; WIRED CITY.

Significance   LOCAL EXCHANGE is the most recent of the local government on-line electronic information services. Parts of it originally were available on LOGIN. Like LOGIN, it offers electronic mail, in which communities and government libraries are able to send information and inquiries. It is also an electronic bulletin board that updates information, such as the status of legislation, and provides the latest guidelines on government accounting. LOCAL EXCHANGE has a smaller data base than ERIC or DIALOG. Some of its services duplicate conventionally printed material.

Suggested Reading
Minter, Nancy L., ed. *Urban Affairs Abstracts,* vol. 18, nos. 1–52 (1988). Washington, DC: National League of Cities.

Local Merit System   A procedure of recruitment, retention, and promotion of public employees based on objective testing, computation of scores, and ranking of candidates. Local merit systems were established during the municipal reform period of the early 1900s to combat the patronage abuses associated with urban political machines. *See also* AFFIRMATIVE-ACTION PROGRAMS; PATRONAGE, URBAN; REFORM GOVERNMENT; URBAN POLITICAL MACHINE.

Significance   Local merit systems were created to circumvent the political or partisan influence involved in many local hiring practices

during the late 1800s. Virtually all large U.S. cities instituted personnel merit procedures. Less formal influences remained in some cities,
but other cities covered only a percentage of their employees under
the merit system, leaving the remainder to patronage. Ironically, the
merit system itself has encountered substantial criticism. Under most
merit systems, the public employment work force was overwhelmingly
white and male. Supporters of representative bureaucracies argue
that merit, as it currently operates, should not be used exclusively to
hire and promote employees. Beginning in the 1960s, many large
cities added residency requirements for police and fire officers and in
some cases for all city employees. In addition, federal policies regarding equal employment, civil rights, and affirmative action forced
changes in the merit personnel procedures of local governments. The
Supreme Court's ruling in *Griggs v. Duke Power,* 401 U.S. 424 (1971),
required that employment examinations be job-related. In many
cases, local governments as employers were found to discriminate.
Most cities with populations of more than 25,000 have a separate
personnel department staffed by officers specially trained in the many
facets of employment, promotion, retirement, and reductions in force
(RIFs). Overall, local personnel practices operate in a complex environment of bureaucratic and partisan politics, public employee
unions, merit plans, and affirmative action programs that reflect both
federal and state legislative and judicial policy.

Suggested Reading
Eisinger, Peter K. "Black Mayors and the Politics of Racial Economic Ad-
    vancement," In Harlan Hahn and Charles H. Levine, eds., *Readings in
    Urban Politics: Past, Present, and Future,* 2nd ed. New York: Longman,
    1984.
Gottfried, Frances. *The Merit System and Municipal Civil Service: A Fostering of
    Social Inequality.* Westport, CT: Greenwood Press, 1988.
Stein, Lana. "Merit Systems and Political Influence: The Case of Local Govern-
    ment." *Public Administration Review,* vol. 47, no. 3 (1987), pp. 263–271.

Locally Unwanted Land Use (LULU)   A term coined by physical
planners to describe capital projects that are needed in an area, even
though local residents wish to see them located elsewhere. A LULU is
also often opposed by a Not in My Back Yard (NIMBY). The projects
are long-term dedications of land that are politically unsatisfactory,
although physical planners may have selected a site for some public
economy involving topography, air quality, transportation, or
drainage. These projects are especially contentious, often drawing
irate audiences when their locations are publicly debated. *See also*
EXTERNALITY; ZONING.

Significance   The very nature of a LULU is a major negative externality that is offensive to those who own property, live, work, or recreate nearby. Examples of LULUs include site placement for power-generating plants (whether coal-fired or nuclear), hazardous and radioactive waste facilities, landfills, sewer and solid waste processing plants, jails, prisons and juvenile correction facilities, sand and gravel pits, cemeteries and crematoriums, group and foster homes, Intensive Livestock Operations (ILOs), and solid waste incinerators. Other examples include: mobile home parks, shelters for the homeless, military and police firing ranges, airports, ammunition depots, and Department of Public Works (DPW) marshaling yards. Although deemed to be needed by society at large, LULUs are individually in conflict with the particular neighborhoods for which they are intended. Proposed projects threaten adjacent property values and may lower revenue generated from property tax levies. They are sometimes fought as zoning infractions. Opponents argue that local land use already is preempted by higher and more desirable development. Because LULUs cause emotional arguments, resolution often is postponed while more benefit-cost analysis studies are conducted. Final decisions are elevated to higher administrative jurisdictions or to the courts in class-action suits. LULUs are often sited in neighborhoods with little political clout. Two arguments for the existence of some LULUs are the securing of a more stable, local job base and willingness to sell out to the project at higher prices. The term *LULU* also may be construed as a corruption of "in lieu of." As such, it is a payment made by a nonprofit institution such as a university to a city for municipal services rendered in lieu of tax payments. It is also used in legislative parlance to refer to lump-sum reimbursement for out-of-pocket expenses in lieu of detailed expense vouchers.

Suggested Reading

Ducsik, Dennis W. "Citizen Participation in Power Plant Siting: Aladdin's Lamp or Pandora's Box?" *Journal of the American Planning Association,* vol. 47, no. 2 (1981), pp. 154–166.
Lake, Robert W., ed. *Resolving Locational Conflict.* New Brunswick, NJ: Center for Urban Policy Research, 1987.
Pearlman, Kenneth, and Nancy Wait. "Controlling Land Use and Population Near Nuclear Power Plants." *Washington University Journal of Urban and Contemporary Law,* vol. 27 (1984), pp. 9–69.

Lockup   A short-term detention facility operated by city or township police rather than the county sheriff. Unlike a jail, a lockup normally houses offenders for no more than 48 hours and detains only pretrial offenders. Those detained in lockups who cannot post bond within the 48-hour period are then normally transferred to a county jail. *See also* JAIL, LOCAL; POLICE, PUBLIC; SHERIFF.

Significance   Like county jails, lockups vary considerably in size. While larger urban areas may have many cells, smaller jurisdictions may have only one or two cells. Some cities or townships have none at all. Lockups provide several advantages for local police as well as the offender. First, they give police ready access to a prisoner for interrogation. Transportation of the offender to a local court may be easier from the local lockup than from the county jail. Attorneys, families, and friends are closer and easier to contact from the lockup than a jail. There is controversy over the quantity and quality of services and care for lockup prisoners. Because offenders are housed for very short periods of time, little emphasis is placed on inmate programs, particularly counseling services that inmates may need during their first few hours of incarceration.

Suggested Reading
Duffee, David E. *Corrections: Practice and Policy.* New York: Random House, 1989.

LOGIN™   An acronym for Local Government Information Network, a data base sponsored by Control Data Corporation of Minneapolis. LOGIN has been in existence since the late 1970s and as of the late 1980s had more than 35,000 entries or information units on topics ranging from abandoned houses and auxiliary police forces to zoning ordinances. New information is incorporated from such sources as *Journal of Housing, Journal of Property Management,* and *Zoning News.* Its most important sources of information within each document are Selectors, Brief Text, and Contact. The Selectors field contains the keywords, such as self-insurance/risk management. The Brief Text is a case study of a specific institution that encountered a problem, noting its response and the results. Contact refers to a person to write/phone for follow-up information. To secure cooperation from municipalities, the system creates an incentive for proposing new ideas by reducing the cooperating city's access costs. *See also* DIALOG; EDUCATIONAL RESOURCES INFORMATION CENTER; LOCAL EXCHANGE.

Significance   LOGIN is part of modern electronic networking brought about by computer technology. In addition to conventional journal synopsis, LOGIN offers two valuable research/reference features: First, the case studies are usually not available in any other printed form. Second, LOGIN serves as an electronic mail network that allows a member-subscriber to solicit ideas from other subscribers for late-breaking ideas not yet loaded into the system, such as how other jurisdictions are handling safe houses for AIDS patients. It is a major source for discovering innovations. LOGIN preserves research that might well become lost in a typical library paper search. Any city may be a user. In many locations, Councils of Governments (COGs) serve as clearinghouses by subscribing for all their members, thus lowering user costs. (A larger and much older system is available for education information storage and retrieval. Called Educational Resources Information Center [ERIC], it is sponsored by the U.S. Department of Education, Office of Educational Research and Improvement, and has been in existence since 1965. In addition to on-line inquiries at a low cost per minute of use, its summary annual index volumes are widely available at participating libraries in paper form, and the reports themselves are widely available on microfiche.) LOGIN's two closest commercial data base competitors are LOCAL EXCHANGE™ and DIALOG™. The latter is available from DIALOG Information Services, Inc., of Palo Alto, California, which offers a wide variety of data bases, including ERIC, providing a multidisciplinary approach to international journal and conference literature. Access is by keyword, author, performing agency, or journal name.

Lottery   A form of legalized gambling in which numbers (also called "lots") or games are sold in the form of tickets to provide revenue for state governments. Lotteries usually are organized in three variations. Some states offer an "instant game," which is a version of tic-tac-toe with immediate verification of winning. A "daily" game features 3- or 4-number combinations. The third form of betting is most often called a "lotto," in which players pick a 6-number combination out of a possible 40 or more. Depending on the overall numbers, the odds for winning a lotto game are between 7 and 12 million to 1. *See also* INCOME SOURCES, URBAN.

Significance   Government-sponsored lotteries date back to the seventeenth century in America, when English colonizers sold lots to provide financing to help establish the colony in Virginia. By the late 1600s, most county governments used lotteries to finance schools and for general government purposes. Lotteries were also used to help found Harvard, Yale, Princeton, and most of the universities now in the Ivy League. The Continental Congress sponsored a five-million-dollar drawing to finance the Revolutionary War. Between 1790 and 1860, 24 of the then 33 states held lotteries to fund infrastructure and capital improvements. An antilottery reform movement in combination with the Civil War ended almost all of the government lotteries by the late 1800s. In the most recent era, New Hampshire (1963), New York (1967), and New Jersey (1971) were the first states to introduce the modern lottery. By 1989, 28 states and the District of Columbia had government-sponsored lotteries, although constitutions in a few states, such as Alabama, Mississippi, and Louisiana, still prohibited lotteries. Despite their increased use by states, opposition comes from some religious groups over the moral question of a government's involvement in gambling. Moreover, other critics argue lotteries exploit the poorest segments of the population, especially the urban poor. Although studies have not reached a consensus regarding who plays, most have found that the urban poor use a significantly larger proportion of their budgets for lottery ticket purchases. Public administrators argue that lotteries are an inefficient method of raising revenue. Conventional taxes cost 1 to 2 cents per dollar to collect, whereas lotteries cost up to 75 cents per dollar of revenue. Prizes average between 40 and 50 percent of gross receipts; administration and promotion average 15 to 20 percent. About half the states with lotteries place net income into their general funds. Others earmark net income for education, transportation, local government use, or other special funds. In several states, a fixed percentage of lottery revenues is earmarked for education, as in New York (45 percent) and Michigan (41 percent in 1988). However, their education budgets also are fixed, so if lottery revenues increase, the state cuts back on school funding from general sources. In sum, larger lottery revenues end up going to other programs instead of education. Despite the recent use of lotteries, a number of states have regulated and taxed pari-mutuel gambling at horse and dog race tracks for many years.

Suggested Reading

Curry, Bill. "State Lotteries: Roses and Thorns." *State Legislatures,* vol. 10, no. 3 (1984), pp. 9–16.

Heffner, Judy. "Legalized Gambling in the States: Who Really Wins?" *State Legislatures,* vol. 7, no. 8 (1981), pp. 6–16.

Hersch, Philip, and Gerald S. McDougall. "Voting for 'Sin' in Kansas." *Public Choice,* vol. 51 (1988), pp. 127–139.

Sternlieb, George, and James Hughes. *Atlantic City Gamble.* Cambridge, MA: Harvard University Press, 1984.

M

Machine Space   Territory primarily used by equipment and for the use of which humans have second or no priority. The term was coined in the 1960s to refer to land parcels that were largely alienated from human use by a technologically advanced society. By far the largest machine space in a city is automobile territory, which may take up as much as 70 percent of the downtown surface of such large cities as Detroit and Los Angeles and more than 50 percent of such medium-sized cities as East Lansing, Michigan. Included in machine space for the automobile are expressways, surface streets, alleys, parking facilities, and all businesses that service vehicles. Railroad beds, highways, and airport runways represent only the most actively used portion of the transportation system: Parking lots, railroad marshaling yards, and airplane hangars must be added to the total of transportation-used space. Machine space for modern factories includes tooling areas, storage areas, egress and ingress roads, cooling and heating spaces, and loading ramps. Many highly polluted rivers represent machine space used as a source of coolant, for transportation, and as an effluent dump. *See also* CENTRAL BUSINESS DISTRICT; PRIVATE STREET.

Significance   Machine space reduces the amount of land dedicated to human, open, or agricultural use. There has been adverse reaction to the high portions of urban areas dedicated to machines. Advocates of open space call for automobile-free areas, partially closed-off streets, and more efficiently designed parking areas. Highways and streets are also the locus of more deaths in the twentieth century than all officially declared U.S. wars. Machine space is portrayed most dramatically in specially designed maps that delimit areas for which the highest priority is equipment, especially vehicles.

Suggested Reading
Horvath, Ronald J. "Machine Space." *Geographical Review,* vol. 64, no. 2 (1974), pp. 167–188.
Marx, Leo. *The Machine in the Garden.* New York: Oxford University Press, 1964.
Moudon, Anne Vernez, ed. *Public Streets for Public Use.* New York: D. Van Nostrand Reinhold, 1987.

Magnet School   An educational program designed to comply with court-ordered school desegregation by voluntarily attracting students to innovative school curricula. A magnet school draws from the entire school district by offering appealing and seemingly advantageous educational programs, such as music, art, drama, computers, or the Montessori method. These programs have overcome to some degree the previous plans to desegregate schools by busing or other compulsory means. Magnet plans vary: a few special schools may be established, or an entire districtwide program of magnets can exist. Publicity campaigns are used to encourage parents to enroll their children in a school outside of their own neighborhood. Students who apply to these programs are placed according to the racial makeup required by the courts and according to available space. School districts receive funding for these programs through Federal Magnet School Grants. *See also BROWN V. BOARD OF EDUCATION.*

Significance   Magnet schools produce a more palatable alternative to busing as a means of desegregating schools. It allows for voluntary parental choice and creates incentives for parents to send children to other than a segregated or racially imbalanced neighborhood school. However, in many school districts, the former black schools were closed in order to induce black student movement into predominantly white schools. Exceptional and better schools were created to attract white students, while still providing students of color with their formal right to equal education. The effect of this plan is to offer more attractive, improved, innovative, and nonstandard programs to one group in order to provide "equal" educational opportunities to another group.

Suggested Reading
Henig, Jeffrey. "Choice, Race and Public Schools: The Adoption and Implementation of a Magnet Program in Montgomery County, Maryland," *Journal of Urban Affairs,* vol. 11, no. 3 (1989), pp. 243–259.
Metz, Mary Haywood. *Different by Design: The Context and Character of Three Magnet Schools.* New York: Routledge & Kegan Paul, 1986.

Mandatory Land Dedication   Requirement by a local government, based on state enabling legislation, that a subdivision developer must deed land for a public park as a condition of plat approval. If the statute allows for negotiation, and if the developer wishes to bypass such a mandatory land dedication, the city may accept a fee in lieu of the dedication. The amount of land to be dedicated is computed as a percentage of the overall development or based on a formula related to the number of residential units. *See also* DEDICATION; GIFT TO GOVERNMENT; PARK, RECREATION; POLICE POWER; PRIVATE STREET.

Significance   What began in the 1930s as governmental requirements for developers to deed public streets and public utility easements expanded in the 1960s in some states to mandatory land dedication for public parks. Parks are used in proportion to the proximity to the residence: Remote parks seldom are visited, whereas nearby facilities are used often. Thus, there is a clear need for locally available facilities. If the subdivision development does not lend itself to one, or if there are already ample proximate facilities, it is preferable for the city to be flexible and site the facility elsewhere in the community. All parks are justified in their development under the general police power of promoting the health and well-being of residents. States have split on the constitutional standards of mandatory dedication. The requirement met constitutionality in the California case of *Associated Home Builders of Greater East Bay, Inc. v. City of Walnut Creek,* 484 P. 2d 606 (1971). In Michigan, the same practice was held illegal in *Ridgemont Development Co. v. City of East Detroit,* 100 N.W. 2d 301 (1960).

Suggested Reading
Note. "Impact Fees: National Perspective to Florida Practice; A Review of Mandatory Land Dedications and Impact Fees That Affect Land Development." *Nova Law Journal,* vol. 4, no. 1 (1980), pp. 137–186.

Manufactured Home   A residence constructed in a factory before being moved to a particular site on its own wheels and chassis. A manufactured housing unit formerly was called a *mobile home*. However, fewer than 5 percent ever were moved from their original sites, and in 1980, Congress adopted the term *manufactured home*. In 1976, Congress authorized the Department of Housing and Urban Development (HUD) to administer a nationwide building code specifically for manufactured housing, called the National Manufactured Home Construction and Safety Standards. In addition, federal underwriting agencies, the Federal Housing Administration (FHA) and Department

Map   317

of Veterans Affairs (VA), have special foundation requirements and financing arrangements for manufactured housing. *See also* BUILDING CODES; HOUSING FINANCE AGENCIES; PARK, MOBILE HOME; RESTRICTIVE COVENANT.

Significance   Manufactured housing became more popular as housing costs increased during the 1970s and 1980s. In 1987, about one-quarter of all new single-family homes sold in the United States were manufactured homes. Many communities have restricted the use of manufactured homes through governmental zoning ordinances and restrictive covenants. However, some courts have ruled that the zoning restrictions on manufactured housing are an improper use of the police power. Manufactured housing can be designed as modules, that is, first built in sections and assembled later. Modular homes are built to state and local building codes. A manufactured home usually is financed as personal property rather than real property. Manufactured homes usually are not appraised, as are on-site homes, and maximum loan amounts usually are determined by using a markup to the manufacturer's wholesale price, plus itemized options.

Suggested Reading
Manufactured Housing Institute, in Cooperation with the Federal Trade Commission's Office of Consumer & Business Education. *How To Buy a Manufactured Home*. Arlington, VA: Manufactured Housing Institute, March 1986.

Map   A graphic presentation of geographic information on a flat surface according to an established scale. Maps present select information at some specified time according to some projection and direction point, conventionally north. Properly drawn maps include a key for symbols. All maps are partial spatial representations in two or three dimensions, with the X and Y axes representing latitude (north-south) and longitude (east-west), and the Z axis representing relief or altitude (elevation). Maps can be drafted to be proportionate or intentionally distorted. They are used to designate past, present, or future land use, boundaries, central and peripheral areas, seats of government, districts and subdivisions, ownership, and rights-of-way. On a very small scale, a map is often known as a plan. Scale represents the ratio of a map to actual ground distance. *See also* MAP, CADASTRAL; MAPS, TYPES OF.

Significance   All maps are subjective. They are symbolic and selective abstractions and represent only some of the information at the expense of omitted data. Maps are used to show spatial distributions and relationships. They are abstractions and only as reliable as the ground information upon which they are based. Aerial photographs are used as maps, especially when identified, scaled, dated, and highlighted to show select patterns. Hydrographic maps are usually known as charts. Mapmakers, or cartographers, can display either continuous or discontinuous distributions of either events or items. By far, governments are the biggest makers of maps and employ the most cartographers. The government needs maps for public-purpose functions such as taxing and land ownership records, and for public-improvement planning. As planning tools, maps are normative projections and do not always record past or present conditions. Comparability between maps depends upon consistency of scale and control for period of coverage.

Map, Cadastral   A specialized graphic showing property boundaries by political jurisdiction on a small scale, often 1/2,500. In some jurisdictions, cadastral maps are updated annually to reflect lot splits as authorized by legally appointed authorities such as planning agencies. In conjunction with the map, taxing authorities maintain a cadastral survey, which records present ownership, value, and land description. The survey is updated daily in jurisdictions that have their tax rolls keyed into computers. Land parcels are usually not recorded by common mailing address but by some systematic grid locator, such as the widely used Sidwell system. The term *cadastral* derives from the French *cadastre,* which was an official register of land units subject to territorial-based taxes. *See also* MAP; MILLAGE.

Significance   Modern cadastral maps reflect surveyed or demarcated property lines. Against this plotted lot or parcel acreage, millage is levied. In those few cases where urban land has not been surveyed, boundary limits are posted by reference to rivers, trees, or fences. Unfortunately, riverbeds change, trees die, and fences are torn down. Accurate ownership maps are the *sine qua non* of planning and zoning, for without them public policies are based on hearsay. Both cadastral maps and surveys are open to public inspection and are published. They are of use to physical planners, title insurance companies, real estate brokers, and the buying public.

Maps, Types of   Various representations in graphic form of parts of the earth's surface. In addition to the conventional road map, there is a variety of other maps often used in land-use planning and urban politics generally. These include base maps, cadastral maps, cento-graphs, choropleth maps, contour and topographic maps, dot maps, isometric maps, land-use maps, official maps, soil maps, and zoning maps. *See also* MAP, CADASTRAL.

Significance These are the 11 types of maps commonly used in physical planning and urban politics. (1) *Base Map:* Depiction of basic features that provides the outline for additional information such as outer boundaries, streets, and prominent physical features. These are useful in plotting overlays of other data, such as social or economic distributions, and are of particular use to physical planners. (2) *Cadastral Map: See* separate entry. (3) *Centograph:* Pictorial representation of central tendencies through space, displaying mean or mode centers, such as the graphic center of the United States (South Dakota) or of North America (North Dakota) or the population center of the United States for the 1980 census (Missouri). (4) *Choropleth Map:* Also known as a shaded map. Depiction of an area demarcated by natural and political divisions colored by frequency or rate, such as crime frequency, racial or ethnic composition, or percentage of home ownership. (5) *Contour Map:* Depiction of elevation by lines connecting all points of the same height. A *Topographic Map,* or *topo,* is a representation of a portion of the earth's ground surface. Among its many uses in urban planning, it portrays floodplains, which allows planners to calculate buildable areas. (6) *Dot Map:* Depiction of relative frequency of a variable by use of symbols such as dots, squares, or glyphs. These indicate occurrence of events or objects, e.g., specific location of crimes by category, by precinct, or by year. (7) *Isometric Map:* Spatial representation of distribution rates or occurrences depicted by lines connecting the same or similar weight. Examples include density of ethnic groups, new construction zones depicted by number of housing starts, areas of high incidence of cancer, and population density zones differentiated by 5 percent gradients. (8) *Land-Use Map:* Graphic portrayal of areas as large in magnitude as the nation or as small as a county or township indicating present categories of utilization, ranging from various types of agriculture to urban usage. *See also* LAND CLASSIFICATION. (9) *Official Map:* Map formally approved by a civil jurisdiction that is published or publicly available and presentable as conclusive evidence in court regarding locations and boundaries. It depicts certified boundaries, public lands, dedicated easements, and prospective land use. It may be used as a base map. (10) *Soil Map:* A graphic depicting distribution of surface and subsurface composition by gradient; water content; capacity to perk; sand, gravel, or shale content; and compacting characteristics. Soil maps are often prepared by the U.S. Department of Agriculture, Soil Conservation Service, or by a private engineering consultant. They are useful to planners in determining buildable areas, floodplains, and mud-slide zones. (11) *Zoning Map:* A land-use map depicting permissible land uses, assuming a Euclidean zoning system. If the jurisdiction employs flexible zoning, the map designates broad categories of possible use. This type must be updated periodically, subject to granted variances in the Euclidean zoning scheme and new construction in the case of the flexible system.

Suggested Reading

Abler, Ronald, and John S. Adams, eds. *A Comparative Atlas of America's Great Cities: Twenty Metropolitan Regions.* Vol. 3 of the Contemporary Metropolitan Analysis Project. Minneapolis: University of Minnesota Press, 1976.

Johnson, R. J., Derek Gregory, and David M. Smith, eds. *The Dictionary of Human Geography,* 2nd ed. Oxford: Blackwell, 1986.

Stamp, Sir Dudley, and Audrey N. Clark, eds. *A Glossary of Geographical Terms.* London: Longman, 1979.

Marxist Urban Analysis   The application of Marxist theories to explain urban social, economic, and political development. Following the major tenets of Karl Marx (1818–1883), Marxist urban analysis places cities within a more general economic and historical context. Therefore, Marxist urban analysis examines cities primarily as sites of economic production (of goods and services) and social reproduction (consumption behavior). In this sense, cities serve as spatial units in a larger system where class structuring and conflict unfold as dynamic processes in capitalist development. Some neo-Marxist theorists have focused on the role of the state (government) in urban development. They ascribe to the state and its urban administrative apparatus, the local state, two major tasks: (1) facilitating economic development and (2) mediating class conflict within the urban context. Along with the Chicago "human ecology" school, political regime analysis, and neoclassical economics, the Marxist approach represents an important normative and empirical inquiry into the urban question. Differences in emphasis and analysis exist between the various camps of Marxist and neo-Marxist thought. *See also* CHICAGO SCHOOL; URBAN POLITICAL ECONOMY; URBAN POLITICAL REGIME.

Significance   In order to investigate cities, Marxist urban analysis first requires an understanding of the society's mode of production, that is, its economic stage in history. In the United States, that economic stage is capitalism. Capitalism in turn creates its own set of classes: the owners of capital and those who sell their labor and produce the goods and services. In general, the state makes policies that assist the owning class with capital accumulation. The state also maintains a social order and environment in which profits can be made without dramatic change or conflict. Specifically, the local states make policies that financially assist private entrepreneurs through tax abatements, loans, subsidies, favorable financing mechanisms, tax exemptions, enterprise zones, infrastructure improvements, and other direct financial support. Secondly, local states act as a buffer between the classes to reduce class conflict and provide a stable work force ready and available to produce the surplus value from which profits are taken. Included in the mediating policies are various education and job training programs that give workers necessary job-related skills. According to this analysis, unemployment, worker's compensation, and welfare policies keep the working class from challenging the social and economic relations between the two classes. These devices provide greater stability for capital accumulation and legitimize the political *status quo*. However, the two major roles of the state ultimately contradict each other and produce a "fiscal crisis" of the state, with the systemwide contradictions focused largely in the local state. The major contributions of Marxist urban analysis have included an analysis of socioeconomic class, class conflict, and the mediation of conflict by government, a political economy perspective that recognizes the uneven economic and social impacts of the market, as well as the notion of uneven urban development within cities, among cities of the United States, and among nations in a world capitalist system.

Suggested Reading

Bluestone, Barry, and Bennett Harrison. *Capital and Communities: The Causes and Consequences of Private Disinvestment.* Washington, DC: Progressive Alliance, 1980.

Castells, Manuel. *The Urban Question: A Marxist Approach.* Cambridge, MA: MIT Press, 1979.

Fainstein, Susan, et al. *Restructuring the City: The Political Economy of Urban Redevelopment,* rev. ed. New York: Longman, 1986.

Gottdiener, Mark. *The Decline of Urban Politics: Political Theory and the Crisis of the Local State.* Beverly Hills: Sage Publications, 1987.

Harvey, David. *Social Justice and the City.* Baltimore: Johns Hopkins University Press, 1973.

Jackson, Peter, and Susan J. Smith. *Exploring Social Geography.* London: Allen & Unwin, 1984.

O'Connor, James. *The Fiscal Crisis of the State.* New York: St. Martin's Press, 1973.

Smith, Michael Peter, ed. "Structuralist Urban Theory: A Symposium." *Comparative Urban Research,* vol. 9, no. 2, 1983.

Smith, Michael Peter, and Joe Feagin, eds. *The Capitalist City.* Cambridge, MA: Basil Blackwell, 1987.

Tabb, William, and Larry Sawers, eds. *Marxism and the Metropolis.* New York: Oxford University Press, 1978.

Mass Transit   A system of transporting large numbers of people in a metropolitan area from one point to another. Mass transit routes and schedules are prearranged and fixed. Densely populated urban centers are best suited for mass transit systems, which can offer transportation services to a substantial number of passengers, and reduce automobile-generated air pollution. A mass transit system typically uses subway, elevated train, commuter rail, buses, or some combination. *See also* BAY AREA RAPID TRANSIT; PARATRANSIT; TRAFFIC ANALYSIS; URBAN MASS TRANSPORTATION ADMINISTRATION.

Significance   Mass transit systems ideally provide quick, inexpensive, and convenient transportation to a highly concentrated population. In many cities where substantial air pollution is created by automobiles, mass transit has become an increasingly valued part of city life. Successful systems are those that terminate in a single location where there is a concentration of employment opportunities, such as the Chicago loop. However, critics of mass transit argue many systems are inefficient, dangerous, and unpredictable in their operations. In addition, overcrowding, noise, filth, and crime are associated with some systems. Mass transit is viewed as unfair competition by private-sector interests, such as automobile manufacturers and taxicab operators. Furthermore, poor or nonexistent mass-transportation systems in cities such as Detroit and Los Angeles have been justified by claiming their population densities are insufficient to support a mass transit system. Despite massive support for the automobile, the U.S. Congress has encouraged mass transit by providing research and planning funds through the Urban Mass Transportation Act of 1964.

Suggested Reading
Cohen, James K. "Capital Investment and the Decline of Mass Transit in New York City, 1945–1981." *Urban Affairs Quarterly*, vol. 23, no. 3 (1988), pp. 369–388.
Plant, Jeremy F. "Beyond the Beltway: Urban Transportation Policy in the 1980s." *Journal of Urban Affairs*, vol. 10, no. 1 (1988), pp. 29–40.
Schofer, Joseph L., ed. "Symposium: New Departures for Urban Transportation." *Urban Affairs Quarterly*, vol. 19, no. 2 (1983), pp. 147–216.
Taebel, Delbert A., and James V. Cornhels. *The Political Economy of Urban Transportation*. Port Washington, NY: Kennikat Press, 1977.
Wachs, Martin, ed. "Symposium: Emerging Themes in Transportation Policy." *Journal of the American Planning Association*, vol. 48, no. 3 (1982), pp. 291–350.
Weiner, Edward. *Urban Transportation Planning in the United States: An Historical Overview*. New York: Praeger, 1987.

Master Plan   A comprehensive guide and policy statement designed to influence future land-use and capital improvement decisions, projecting present values from baseline information. A master plan is a blueprint rationally developed for the future community, free from the particulars of immediate crises. Developed by the early Greeks, master plans long have had two opposing traditions. One assumes the plan is a finished and static document. The other describes planning as an ongoing and occasionally adjusted statement of values. Both approaches are designed for the long run. The baseline study conventionally includes a set of maps compiled to some consistent scale. It lists current land use by type. It also lists a current census of population and traffic circulation patterns. This yields density information as well as current construction technology for support structures and transport. Conventionally, the plan's elements include population trends for mortality, fertility, and migration as well as age, sex, and manpower needs. Other elements are traffic circulation patterns, recreation needs, community facilities and service needs, capital improvements, redevelopment plans, and utility layouts. Most plans explicitly state goals and objectives for each element. To be effective, the plan discusses implementation, foremost of which is through zoning decisions. A city with a formally adopted long-term plan is easier to defend in a court action where some zoning decision is in dispute. Master plan scales can be as small as a college campus or as large as a conurbation. Master plan results are presented in maps and graphics and with discursive prose. *See also* GROWTH POLITICS; TRAFFIC ANALYSIS; ZONING.

Significance   Because there are two opposing master plan traditions, no one definition will suffice. One assumes constant technology and a fixed set of land uses. The other is dynamic and requires periodic updating. All master plans are compromised by later technology and changes in goals and objectives. The long-term agenda of a community is in its master plan. It expresses desirable land uses, proper densities, and the correct mix of public and private control over land. Some urban areas formally adopt a plan. More commonly, master plans are informal documents, never aired in public hearings, never published, and not on file with a county planning department. Some communities voluntarily prepare plans; others do so to comply with state mandate. Some states, such as Florida under the 1985 Growth Management Act, mandate that every county and city must have an approved master plan in place to ensure that local facilities can handle population influx. Errant communities that cannot calibrate their projected level of service may have their state aid formula reduced by the supervising state-level municipal affairs office. Major examples of implemented master plans include such new towns as Columbia, Maryland, Reston, Virginia, and Washington, D.C. Since much planning is technical, it is done generally by professional staffs, either in-house or by consultants. Private developers must be mindful of master plans if they are to be overall, effective public-policy land-use guidelines.

Suggested Reading
Chapin, F. Stuart, Jr. *Urban Land Use Planning,* 3rd ed. Urbana: University of
    Illinois Press, 1979. Chap. 9.
Cornish, Robert, et al. "Notes on the Master Plan." *Planning,* vol. 53, no. 9
    (1987), pp. 16–23.
Lorenzen, Leo. "Old Faithful." *Planning,* vol. 53, no. 9 (1987), pp. 11–14.

Maximum Feasible Participation   A federal initiative that sought to establish a variety of participatory devices for citizens directly affected by public policy. Maximum feasible participation was mandated under the Economic Opportunity Act of 1964, which allowed for the creation of citizen advisory committees in the antipoverty program. Under this mandate, Community Action Programs (CAPs), Community Action Agencies (CAAs), and urban renewal authorities could be created to influence federal urban policies without working through established local institutions and officials. *See also* COMMUNITY ACTION PROGRAM; ECONOMIC OPPORTUNITY ACT OF 1964.

Significance   Maximum feasible participation sought to promote more direct ties between federal antipoverty programs and the recipients of those programs. In response to the urban protests of the 1960s, the federal government sought to address some of the criticisms community leaders were leveling—primarily the lack of citizen representation and input on decision-making bodies that were implementing urban poverty programs and urban renewal policy. At the same time, the "participatory democracy" initiatives of the New Left supported the call for greater citizen participation in federal urban-aid programs. A bureaucratic enfranchisement of citizens occurred, permitting residents to influence directly the manner in which agency missions or program objectives were implemented. Congress began to limit the autonomy of these groups, and with the shift from categorical to block grants, city officials enjoyed greater discretion over spending, while no further federal funding was allocated to staff these neighborhood groups. Under the Nixon administration, the parent funding agency for the CAAs, the Office of Economic Opportunity (OEO), was eliminated, and most of the antipoverty programs were turned over to other agencies. After 1974, the CAAs became highly dependent on their own city halls for funding, influence, and survival.

Suggested Reading
Moynihan, Daniel P. *Maximum Feasible Misunderstanding: Community Action in the War on Poverty*. New York: Free Press, 1969.

Mayor, Strong   The chief executive officer of a local government, usually exercising considerable administrative, appointive, policymaking, and veto powers. Strong-mayor systems are most common in larger cities. Some urbanists have distinguished between strong and weak mayors by investigating leadership styles or roles, regardless of whether they serve in a strong- or weak-mayor system. For example, former Chicago Mayor Richard J. Daley and Los Angeles Mayor Tom Bradley have been considered "strong mayors" in technically weak-mayor systems. *See also* MAYOR, WEAK; MAYOR-COUNCIL GOVERNMENT; REFORM GOVERNMENT; URBAN POLITICAL MACHINE.

Significance   Despite some criticisms leveled at this form of government, the strong-mayor system itself was a "reformed" system of local governing. Municipal reformers of the early twentieth century associated the corruption of political machines with a weak-mayor system that allowed too much independence and political entrepreneurship among department heads. The strong-mayor system brought overall budgetary control to the mayor's office and gave the mayor considerable appointive powers in selecting department heads. Substantial debate has emerged over whether urban political machines prosper more under a strong- or weak-mayor system of government. While early wisdom suggested weak-mayor systems were too susceptible to machine dominance, later arguments have suggested strong-mayor systems have become the base of support for more contemporary machines, particularly as used by black mayors. Further revisionist research has most recently suggested that even nineteenth-century political machines coincided with the centralization of formal mayoral powers, not with the weak-mayor forms of government.

Suggested Reading
Ferman, Barbara. *Governing the Ungovernable City: Political Skill, Leadership and the Modern Mayor*. Philadelphia: Temple University Press, 1985.
Good, David L. *Orvie: The Dictator of Dearborn*. Detroit: Wayne State University Press, 1989.
Holli, Melvin. *Reform in Detroit: Hazen S. Pingree and Urban Politics*. New York: Oxford University Press, 1969.
Holli, Melvin G., and Peter d'A. Jones, eds. *Biographical Dictionary of American Mayors, 1820–1989*. Westport, CT: Greenwood Press, 1981.
Nelson, William E., Jr., and Philip J. Meranto. *Electing Black Mayors: Political Action in the Black Community*. Columbus: Ohio State University Press, 1977.

Pressman, Jeffrey L. "Preconditions of Mayoral Leadership." *American Political Science Review*, vol. 66, no. 2 (1972), pp. 511–524.
Preston, Michael B., Lenneal J. Henderson, Jr., and Paul Puryear, eds. *The New Black Politics: The Search for Political Power*. New York: Longman, 1982.
Svara, James H. *Official Leadership in the City: Patterns of Conflict and Cooperation*. New York: Oxford University Press, 1989.

Mayor, Weak   The chief executive officer of a local government, generally exercising few powers compared to the city council and key department heads. The mayor may be elected directly by the voters or, in some cases, selected from and by the city council. Most present weak-mayor systems exist in smaller cities. Under this governing system, the mayor presides over the city council or serves as a ceremonial executive and often has limited or no veto power and budgetary authority. Decisions concerning specific departmental budgets and procedures are often left to the city council. In some systems, especially in commission-style governments, department heads may be elected directly by the voters. In virtually all weak-mayor systems, the office of mayor is a part-time job. *See also* CITY COUNCIL; COUNCIL-MANAGER GOVERNMENT; MAYOR, STRONG; URBAN POLITICAL MACHINE.

Significance   The weak-mayor form of government was attacked by municipal reform groups in the early 1900s because it was thought to be more vulnerable to machine politics than the strong-mayor system. However, it has been argued that the very consolidation of power in the mayor's office, as mandated by reformed city charters, allowed a number of machines to flourish. Baltimore, Boston, New Orleans, Cleveland, and Denver are among the cities that saw the power of the machine grow with the adoption of a strong-mayor form of government. Overall, the general demise of the weak-mayor form can be traced to its association with political machines, its lack of accountability to voters, the growing need for strong political leadership to deal with increasingly complex problems, and its greater likelihood for inefficiency and duplication of government services.

Suggested Reading
Greer, Ann L. *The Mayor's Mandate*. Cambridge, MA: Schenkman, 1974.
Kotter, John, and Paul Lawrence. *Mayors in Action: Five Approaches to Urban Governance*. New York: John Wiley, 1974.
Merton, Robert K. *Social Theory and Social Structure*. New York: Free Press, 1968.
Rhyne, Charles S. *Mayor: Chief Municipal Law Executive*. Washington, DC: Local Government Operations Project, 1985.
Ruchelman, Leonard I., ed. *Big City Mayors: The Crisis in Urban Politics*. Bloomington: Indiana University Press, 1969.
Swanstrom, Todd. *The Crisis of Growth Politics: Cleveland, Kucinich and the Challenge of Urban Populism*. Philadelphia: Temple University Press, 1985.

Mayor-Council Government   A form of local government in which an elected mayor serves as the chief executive and an elected city council serves as the legislative body. Mayor-council governments can have either a strong-mayor or weak-mayor system. For the most part, the larger cities in the United States tend to have strong-mayor governments, smaller rural communities have weak-mayor governments, and the middle-sized cities have council-manager governments. *See also* COUNCIL-MANAGER GOVERNMENT; MAYOR, STRONG; MAYOR, WEAK; SEPARATION OF POWERS; UNICAMERAL.

Significance   Despite the major differences between strong- and weak-mayor systems, the mayor-council form of government illustrates the traditional separation of governmental powers in the United States. Many of the earliest forms of urban government favored the weak-mayor system because of the fears of executive abuses that were notorious during the colonial period. However, weak-mayor systems later became associated with political patronage and the corruption of urban political machines. Under the weak-mayor system, department heads and council members often had considerable budgetary and hiring powers that led to many corrupt machine practices. In many weak-mayor systems, voters use the long ballot to elect treasurers, city attorneys, and city clerks. With the reform impulse still strong among some small- and middle-sized cities, weak-mayor–council governments have been replaced by the council-manager form of government.

Suggested Reading
Caraley, Demetrios. *City Government and Urban Problems.* Englewood Cliffs, NJ: Prentice-Hall, 1977.
Ferman, Barbara. *Governing the Ungovernable City: Political Skill, Leadership, and the Modern Mayor.* Philadelphia: Temple University Press, 1985.
Hain, Paul, F. Chris Garcia, and Judd Conway. "From Council-Manager to Mayor-Council: The Case of Albuquerque." *Nation's Cities,* vol. 14 (October 1975), pp. 10–12.
Kotter, John P., and Paul R. Lawrence. *Mayors in Action: Five Approaches to Urban Governance.* New York: John Wiley, 1974.

Mediation   A form of third-party conflict resolution designed to solve problems extrajudicially. Mediation is both a reactive, case-by-case process and an anticipative technique that brings together parties in conflict to negotiate a long-term solution. Although long associated with dispute settlements for families and international disputes, it also is used in local- and state-level politics. Examples of mediated settlements are as diverse as town-gown disputes and conflicts over water use. Mediators long have been associated with labor-management dispute resolution: The Federal Mediation and Conciliation Service was founded as an independent agency in 1947. Some local, non–labor-related mediation is fostered by the American Arbitration Association (AAA) through its Community Dispute Services, established in 1968. States including Delaware, Florida, Colorado, Minnesota, and Hawaii have established mediation services. Unlike arbitration, which is written into contracts and supplies third-party problem solvers who write their own decisions, mediation is a process of bringing interested parties informally to a *forum*. In labor arbitration, the parallel terminology is the *table*. Mediators find it especially important to establish a working relationship with all members of a dispute before bringing the principals together to the forum to frame the major issues. The goal is to have the principals develop and execute an *accord*. The mediator does not impose a *settlement*, as in arbitration. Most mediation is voluntary, although some issues in environmental law now require mediation before formal litigation. *See also* ARBITRATION; HOUSING COURT; NEIGHBORHOOD JUSTICE CENTER.

Significance   Mediation is an alternative to traditional litigation. Litigation is more formal, more costly and adversarial. Mediation stresses direct contact between those involved in the dispute and fosters a more cooperative solution than would be imposed by a jury or judge in a bench trial. The process would be resisted by public administrators, who want more formal due process standards, especially discovery and cross-examination. One well-documented example of a mediated urban solution was the placement of the crosstown Interstate 30 Expressway in Fort Worth, Texas. Although the case already was in litigation, the mediated solution won all the major participants' approval and was accepted by the courts. The mediation took two years, cost more than $70,000, and involved 14 participants in protracted negotiations. Locating hazardous-waste treatment facility sites also lends itself to mediation procedures. Mediation works best with issues that have been well developed, rather than those in the early stages of a dispute.

Suggested Reading

Amy, Douglas J. *The Politics of Environmental Mediation.* New York: Columbia University Press, 1987.
Auberbach, Jerold. *Justice without Law: Resolving Disputes without Lawyers.* New York: Oxford University Press, 1983.
Laue, James H., ed. "Using Mediation To Shape Public Policy." *Mediation Quarterly,* vol. 20 (1988), pp. 1–118. Bibliography.
Negotiation Journal, vol. 1, no. 1 (1985).
Sullivan, Timothy. *Resolving Development Disputes through Negotiations.* New York: Plenum Press, 1985.

Megalopolis   From the Greek for "very large city," an ancient term applied by French geographer Jean Gottmann in 1961 to the contemporary, built-up urban and suburban band stretching for more than 500 miles along the Atlantic, from New Hampshire in the north to Virginia in the south, and inland to the Appalachians. It encompassed 10 states, 117 counties, and over 38 million people as of the 1960 census. Megalopolis is the most densely populated portion of the United States. The area cuts across rural interludes to represent a unique and disorderly array of intense land uses. Originally, megalopolis was the cradle of industrialization. As that function shifted to the Midwest and South, commerce and management functions grew. It is the most affluent area in the world when compared to similar populations. It is the best educated, best housed, and best serviced by modern infrastructure. With only 300 years of history, the area is a relative newcomer among the major world urban complexes. The chief identifying characteristic of megalopolis is a high concentration of a wide diversity of activity, from advertising to commerce, government, and trade. *See also* CONURBATION; ECUMENOPOLIS; EKISTICS; MUL-TINUCLEI MODEL.

Significance   The main nucleus of megalopolis is New York City. The area also contains Boston, Philadelphia, Baltimore, and Washington, D.C. *Megalopolis* is also used as a generic term for any large, built-up urban area, but in reference to the eastern seaboard conurbation, the term was designed to restructure traditional definitions and point to the East Coast ganglion of governments. A key ingredient of megalopolis is the extraordinary pressure put on land use. In stressing this, Gottmann prophetically anticipated the importance of the anti- and slow-growth movement, the need to plan land use in larger units than cities and counties, and the interrelated nature of policy arenas. He wrote of the "polynucleated metropolitan" area, now generally referred to as the multinucleated metropolis. He did not anticipate the rapid decline of the snowbelt or the rise of the sunbelt starting in the 1960s, in large part because he did not write on the comparative development of megalopolis in relation to the balance of the nation.

Suggested Reading

Doxiadis, C. A. "The Prospect of an International Megalopolis." In Mason Wade, ed., *The International Megalopolis*. Toronto: University of Toronto Press, 1969. Chap. 1, pp. 30–39.

Gottmann, Jean. *Megalopolis: The Urbanized Northeastern Seaboard of the United States*. Cambridge, MA: MIT Press, 1961.

———. *Megalopolis Revisited: 25 Years Later*. College Park: University of Maryland Press, 1987.

Von Eckardt, Wolf. *The Challenge of Megalopolis: A Graphic Presentation of the Urbanized Seaboard of the United States.* New York: Macmillan, 1964. (Based on the original study of Jean Gottmann. Also sponsored by the Twentieth Century Fund, it was written to make Gottmann's findings more accessible to the general reader.)

Melting Pot   A term used to describe the United States as the great repository and assimilator of the various ethnic groups that have immigrated to this country. At times, the term is used descriptively. The melting pot is most often used prescriptively to suggest that assimilation is an ideal or goal. With the great increase in ethnic and racial pride in recent years, the term has been viewed with some derision. Some minority groups have felt the dominant majority has tried to "whitewash" their ethnicity and the variety of cultures present in the nation. Most minority groups have attempted to strike a balance by making great strides to "become Americans," while retaining a pride and a sense of history about their origins. In the past, a few separatist groups have made attempts to break entirely from the majority society and culture. *See also* BLACK PANTHERS; BLACK POWER; ETHNIC GROUP; MIGRATION, URBAN; NATIONAL ASSOCIATION FOR THE ADVANCEMENT OF COLORED PEOPLE.

Significance   The United States is among the world's most pluralistic countries, a melting pot for immigrants from many different nations. Though we nominally think of White Anglo-Saxon Protestants (WASPs) as the "majority" group in this country, such is not the case. This group was merely the first of many different ethnic groups to migrate to what became the United States. The waves of immigrants that followed—African-Americans, southern and eastern Europeans, Hispanics, Asians, and many others—became generally known as "ethnic" or "racial" groups or minorities in the eyes of the dominant culture. As one policy approach to assimilating these later immigrants, mandatory public education was instituted during the 1800s to teach these newer arrivals "proper" values in addition to basic skills. Despite conflicts that have arisen over competing cultures and values, the United States indeed has been a melting pot of sorts—witness the multitude of second-, third-, and fourth-generation citizens who can count several identifiable ethnic branches in their family tree.

Suggested Reading
Allen, James P., and Eugene Turner. *We the People: An Atlas of America's Ethnic Diversity.* New York: Macmillan, 1988.
Glazer, Nathan, and Daniel Patrick Moynihan. *Beyond the Melting Pot,* 2nd ed. Cambridge: MIT Press, 1970.
Zangwill, Israel. *The Melting Pot.* New York: Macmillan, 1909.

Metropolitan Area   A geographic location usually comprising a large central city and its surrounding suburbs, which are socially and economically integrated. By the 1980 census, approximately 70 percent of the U.S. population lived in metropolitan areas. After 1983, the Bureau of the Census used the term *Metropolitan Statistical Area (MSA)* to designate those areas determined by a formula of population size, density, and conditions of economic and social integration among its local governing units. In 1986, there were 332 MSAs. *See also* CENSUS OF GOVERNMENTS; CONSOLIDATION; COUNCIL OF GOVERNMENTS; COUNTERURBANISM; METROPOLITAN STATISTICAL AREA; METROPOLITIZATION; MIGRATION, URBAN.

Significance   The urbanization of the United States into metropolitan areas has come in several stages. Large numbers of immigrants created relatively large central cities during the mid- to late 1800s. By 1920, more than half of the U.S. population lived in cities. However, the migration trend more recently has been toward decentralization, that is, from central cities to suburbs. Therefore, urbanists now speak of "metropolitanization," to account for the population shift of a metropolitan area into outlying suburban communities. These demographic shifts raise several important policy questions. One has been the dilemma faced by individual local governments in providing service delivery and engaging in problem solving of large social issues such as pollution, transportation, and crime. A number of organizational or structural responses have been devised in an attempt to deal with these problems, which transcend local government jurisdictions. City-county consolidations, regional Councils of Governments, intercommunity partnerships, and multijurisdictional agencies have all been offered as answers to provide coordinated, efficient, and effective services to metropolitan areas.

Metropolitan County   A primary administrative subdivision of a state, located within a Metropolitan Statistical Area (MSA). The U.S. government defines counties as "metro" or "nonmetro," distinguishing between those located within or outside the boundaries of a Metropolitan Statistical Area. By governmental definition, a metropolitan county must have a central city (or contiguous cities) of 50,000 or more people, including those adjacent counties that are socially and economically integrated with the central county. *See also* CENSUS OF governments; CONSOLIDATION; METROPOLITAN STATISTICAL AREA; MIGRATION, URBAN.

Significance   Increases in the number of metropolitan counties during the past 30 years vividly illustrates the general pattern of urbanization in the United States. Of the 3,042 counties in the country, about 336 were considered to be metropolitan in 1987. In 1985, the United States was considered to be about 78 percent metropolitan, an increase from approximately 70 percent in 1980. For grant-in-aid purposes, a metropolitan county designation provides certain entitlements. For example, the Community Development Block Grant (CDBG) programs allocate funding to metropolitan counties. Urbanization has given way to suburbanization and counterurbanism. Such population shift has forced metropolitan areas to adopt various schemes to ensure service delivery. City-county consolidations and regional governments have been used in many areas. Others have simply adopted a functional consolidation of services, in which the already-established county government assumes various service responsibilities—for example, transportation, water supply, sewage, and some social services. Many metropolitan-area politicians favor functional consolidation, because it does not require any major structural changes, as would be required by city-county consolidations.

Suggested Reading
Grauby, Barbara H., and Wasserman, Natalie. "Profiles of Individual Counties." *County Year Book 1978.* Washington, DC: National Association of Counties and International City Management Association, 1978.

Metropolitan Statistical Area (MSA)   The official Office of Management and Budget term for an urbanized area. A Metropolitan Statistical Area designation is used by the U.S. Bureau of the Census to describe any city with a population of 50,000 or more, in conjunction with surrounding counties with predominantly urban populations. An MSA signifies a high degree of social and economic integration in a metropolitan area. The term was *Standard Metropolitan Statistical Area (SMSA)*; the Census Bureau dropped "Standard" from nomenclature on June 30, 1983, and slightly altered the formula for determining an MSA. The federal government also uses the term *Consolidated Metropolitan Statistical Area (CMSA)* to signify a large metropolitan complex (more than 1,000,000 population) within which individual components of 100,000 or more people exist. These individual components are termed *Primary Metropolitan Statistical Areas (PMSAs)*. *See also* CONSOLIDATED METROPOLITAN STATISTICAL AREA; METROPOLITAN AREA; METROPOLITIZATION.

Significance   The Census Bureau divides the entire country into metropolitan and nonmetropolitan areas for statistical purposes. By the 1980 census, approximately 75 percent of the U.S. population lived in MSAs. Urbanization of the United States remains a strong force, despite substantial out-migration from central cities since 1970. The strong economic, social, and political interrelationships between central cities and surrounding suburbs, as well as the interaction among contiguous counties, is reflected clearly by the Metropolitan Statistical Area and Consolidated Metropolitan Statistical Area figures identified by the Census Bureau. Some MSAs and CMSAs cross county and state boundaries, especially in the Northeast. In 1986, the Census Bureau identified 332 Metropolitan Statistical Areas.

Suggested Reading
Federal Committee on Standard Metropolitan Statistical Areas. "The Metropolitan Statistical Area Classification." *Statistical Reporter*, no. 80-3 (December 1979).
U.S. Bureau of the Census. *Statistical Abstract of the United States*. Washington, DC: Government Printing Office, annual editions.

Metropolitization   The process of creating areawide service delivery of governmental functions that were initially carried on by separate urban jurisdictions. In order to overcome the inefficiencies of many fragmented cities, governments have created metropolitan coordinating procedures and service delivery of *line* functions in the community. Metropolitization may relate to library, police, fire, emergency medical, water, sewer, and refuse collection services. *Staff* functions, such as hospital need surveys, flood planning, highway design, nuclear accident emergency preparedness, and sewer and water line mapping, do not constitute metropolitanization; they are defined as support duties and are generally handled by county planning agencies, Councils of Governments (COGs), or special districts. *See also* BALKANIZATION; CONSOLIDATION; COUNCIL OF GOVERNMENTS; SOLID WASTE MANAGEMENT; THREE-TIER REFORM.

Significance   Metropolitization is a compromise between rigid separation of city services and structural consolidation of service delivery departments at the all-urban level. Libraries coordinate services by sharing and lending privileges, specializing in collection areas, and informing each other of serial and monograph holdings. In the Detroit area, for example, this is performed by the Southeast Michigan League of Libraries (SEMLOL). As a result, public libraries are often no longer free-standing buildings but are part of an integrated supply and delivery system. Two of the earliest forms of metropolitization were water delivery and refuse disposal. In part, diminishing available space for waste disposal has forced area coordination. Police and fire services are often among the last to be metropolitanized, because mutual-aid pacts often stir jealousies between the ranks of professionals and volunteers or between police and police-fire departments organized as public safety organizations.

Middletown   A camouflaged urban case analysis of Muncie, Indiana (population 35,000), studied initially between 1925 and 1927 and again in 1935 by Robert S. Lynd and Helen M. Lynd. Middletown has continued to be a locus of social science team research and was restudied by Caplow et al. 50 years later. The Lynds' two major volumes were published in the 1920s and 1930s, just ahead of the Warner team accounts of Yankee City. Both teams explicitly used anthropological field methods. The Indiana studies focused on the daily life and values of the largely homogeneous white, Protestant community. Subjects of research included social mobility, social stratification, and the role of institutional religion. *See also* CAMOUFLAGED CASE STUDIES; CASE STUDY; YANKEE CITY.

Significance   The Middletown studies are influential reports on the dynamics of social values in a single community. The Lynds used baseline information from the 1890s to calibrate the rate and types of change in the community. Thus, with the follow-up Middletown III study of the 1980s, the studies cumulatively represent nearly 100 years of empirical field material, in part based on standardized tests and participant observation. Middletown of the 1980s has increased to 80,000 and thus is still a modest-scale urban location. The greatest value of the Middletown studies lies in their information on change and continuity in one community. They contribute a historical dimension to what is often ahistoric social research. There are two common criticisms of the studies: One is that Muncie is never demonstrated to be a microcosm for the nation's other cities. The ability to generalize to other areas is problematic. The second is the anthropological academic tradition out of which the Lynds worked. It largely stressed apolitical issues. Hence, race relations were a major omission in the first two studies.

Suggested Reading

Caplow, Theodore, et al. *Middletown Families: Fifty Years of Change and Continuity*. Minneapolis: University of Minnesota Press, 1982.
Lynd, Robert S., and Helen Merrell Lynd. *Middletown: A Study in Contemporary American Culture*. New York: Harcourt, Brace, 1929.
———. *Middletown in Transition: A Study in Cultural Conflicts*. New York: Harcourt, Brace, 1937.
Stein, Maurice R. *The Eclipse of Community: An Interpretation of American Studies*. New York: Harper & Row, 1960. Chap. 2, "The Lynds and Industrialization in Middletown."

Migration, Urban   Originally, the nineteenth-century mass movement of individuals and groups into the northeast and midwest American urban centers. During the initial migration pattern, northern and
western Europeans arrived during the early and mid-1800s; eastern
and southern Europeans came to the United States during the late
1800s and early 1900s; later in the twentieth century followed rural
whites, Hispanics, and blacks. These migration patterns have greatly
affected urban life and politics, including the great economic and
political growth and decline of urban centers, the rise and fall of
urban political machines, and the urban fiscal and social crises of the
1960s and 1970s. *See also* ETHNIC GROUP; METROPOLITIZATION; URBAN
CRISIS; URBAN POLITICAL MACHINE.

Significance   Urban migration patterns have shaped fundamentally the contours of American life. The concept of "push-pull migration" generally is recognized as the major cause of global demographic
movement. A migrant is pushed by economic deprivation and pulled
by the perception that a new location will remedy that deprivation.
Political, social, and economic upheavals in European countries
pushed first the English, Irish, and Welsh to the United States, primarily during the early and mid-nineteenth century; this period was followed by the immigration of Poles, Italians, Germans, and other
eastern and southern Europeans. The movement of black Americans
came in two stages: first a general movement from rural to urban
counties in the South after the Civil War, then from the South to
northern cities after World War I. In 1910, 90 percent of blacks living
in the United States still lived in the South. However, the two world
wars created a demand for industrial labor in the North, and mecha-
nization of southern agriculture displaced large numbers of rural
southern blacks from tenant farming and the wage-labor agricultural
work force, forcing their migration into cities. The more recent U.S.
migration patterns have shown a movement out of large, central cities
into surrounding suburbs, so the urbanization era has been replaced
by suburbanization, metropolitanization, and counterurbanism. In
addition, a large influx of Asians and Hispanics migrated into some
central cities in the 1970s and 1980s.

Suggested Reading

Frey, William H. "Migration and Depopulation of the Metropolis: Regional
    Restructuring or Rural Renaissance?" *American Sociological Review*,
    vol. 52, no. 2 (1987), pp. 240–257.
Handlin, Oscar. *The Newcomer: Negroes and Puerto Ricans in a Changing Metropo-
    lis*. New York: Doubleday, 1962.
Hartman, David W., ed. *Immigrants and Migrants: The Detroit Ethnic Experience*.
    Detroit: Wayne State University Press, 1974.
Long, Larry. *Migration and Residential Mobility in the United States*. New York:
    Russell Sage, 1988.

Ward, David. *Cities and Immigrants: A Geography of Change in Nineteenth-Century America*. New York: Oxford University Press, 1971.

Millage   A rate of taxation on personal and real property. One mill yields $1 against $1,000 of assessed value *per annum*. One mill is one-tenth of a cent. Millage rates are established after the assessor sets the annual value of property. Hence, millage is expressed for one fiscal year (FY). In democratic theory, millage is to be set by elected representatives (city councils, township trustees, boards of selectmen, county commissions, etc.). However, the state legislature may mandate a function to be performed by the local level and direct that it be paid by local revenue. Both national and state courts can set millage for a stipulated function by taking superintending control over a public agency in litigation properly arising before it. In 1987, Kansas City, Missouri, had taxes raised by a federal judge to pay for school desegregation. Also in 1987, in Hamtramck, Michigan, a county judge forced a 15-mill increase to pay for delinquent city employee cost-of-living payments. In the rare instance of a city falling into bankruptcy, the receiver sets millage with court supervision. Millage rates may be adjusted automatically in some states by statute or constitutional provision. This is triggered by an index such as the Bureau of Labor Statistics Consumer Price Index (CPI) so as to hold down overall yields (e.g., the Headlee Amendment of Michigan). State constitutions can set maximum millage rates. Local charters may limit the allowable millage unless raised for a limited time by an ordinary or extraordinary majority in a referendum. Even larger property burdens are allowed for special assessments where these have been defined as not constituting a general tax. *See also* ASSESSMENT; TAX ABATEMENT; TAX LIMIT.

Significance   Millage is levied against the assessed value of property. This is called an *ad valorem* tax. Because states differ markedly in assessment standards—from 100 percent of value down to 10 percent of value—comparing millage rates among states is unsound. It is equally unsound to compare rates within the same state over the years unless corrected for abatement programs and state-equalized assessment changes. Residential suburbs without appreciable industrial or commercial tax base must spread millage primarily over private housing. Opposition in some states to mobile home parks stems in part from the low yield secured by conventional millage rates. City budgets largely dependent on industrial millage are highly vulnerable to major dislocations by these firms if they close or declare bankruptcy. Actual revenue yield from millage is computed by the following formula:

Assessment (corrected for exemptions and abatements)
× *millage*
= gross yield
− collection costs
− arrearage
− tax tribunal decisions favoring owners
− abandoned property taxes never collected
+ recovery from sheriff's tax sales
+ *late payment* fees and interest
= net yield (figures available three to four years
   after the close of the FY books)

Moral-Obligation Bond   A tax-exempt bond issued by a state authority or municipality and backed by a state legislature's promise to repay. The obligation is moral, rather than legal, since in certain situations a standing state legislature may not obligate future legislatures to appropriate the funds required to repay the debt. *See also* BOND, MUNICIPAL; DEBT, MUNICIPAL; REVENUE IMPROVEMENT BOND.

Significance   A moral-obligation bond is backed by a state legislature if the primary debtor, such as a municipality, defaults on the bond issue. However, repayment of a long-term debt extends well beyond the session of the legislature that has promised to underwrite the obligation. Any promises to pay after the session ends would require another decision by the state legislature that convenes later. This type of bond differs from a general-obligation bond, which has the full faith and credit of the municipality's property tax revenues, and a revenue bond, which repays its debt through revenues generated by the project built with the funds borrowed.

Suggested Reading
Jones, Richard M. "The Future of Moral Obligation Bonds as a Method of Government Finance in Texas." *Texas Law Review*, vol. 54, no. 2 (1976), pp. 314–335.

Moratorium   Temporary suspension by a government of all or a select category of construction permits. A moratorium serves as a period of delay during which a public body may not issue approval for new buildings or repairs. Originally, moratoria were issued by the state to suspend debt collection temporarily. Cities employed construction moratoria in the 1970s and 1980s. In five states during the 1980s, hospital review agencies prevented new hospital construction in anticipation of completing an areawide hospital-needs inventory. *See also* CERTIFICATE OF NEED; GROWTH MANAGEMENT; INVERSE CONDEM-NATION; TAKING.

Significance   Moratorium on new construction was a frequent public policy pursued by governmental bodies against private property owners until the late 1980s. A builder in the process of exhausting administrative remedies in a city bureaucracy cannot judicially complain that the delays amount to a temporary taking under the Fifth Amendment provision, which prohibits the state from taking private property without just compensation. But in *First English Evangelical Lutheran Church of Glendale v. County of Los Angeles, California,* 482 U.S. 304 (1987), the court held governments are barred from forcing owners of land to bear public burdens while the state decides whether to take the property permanently. If regulation goes "too far," courts will make the state pay the landholder for the temporary taking. Builders working under a moratorium while the legislature decides what to do with property have a judicial remedy if they can prove there has been an inverse condemnation. But there may be no judicial recourse under some circumstances: (1) If the state is phasing-in a building program of a limited number of permits a year. (2) If a sign company falls under a billboard phaseout program. (3) If a hospital is under an areawide study to determine future service needs.

Multijurisdictional Agency   A federally supported metropolitan- or regionwide special district established to coordinate, plan, and implement service delivery across several local boundaries. Multijurisdictional agencies (MJAs) generally cannot sell bonds or impose taxes, but they operate with public funds and serve specific areas. The federal government has encouraged MJAs through various funding programs that require metropolitan coordination and planning. For example, A-95 Review requirements, regional council requirements for some Department of Housing and Urban Development programs, and transportation and criminal justice planning all have mandated the creation of multijurisdictional agencies. Examples of MJAs would include Comprehensive Health Planning Councils, Air Pollution Control Agencies, and Community Action Agencies. *See also* A-95 REVIEW; COMMUNITY ACTION PROGRAM; CONSOLIDATION; COUNCIL OF GOVERN-MENTS; METROPOLITIZATION; SPECIAL DISTRICT.

Significance   Multijurisdictional agencies have received federal support to cope with the larger social problems that transcend local government boundaries. Like Councils of Governments, city-county consolidations, mutual aid pacts, and intercommunity partnerships, MJAs recognize the need to address the problems of environmental protection, crime, transportation, and service delivery on a regional or metropolitan scale. For the most part, there has been a general recognition that the various problems that make up the "urban crisis" cannot be addressed adequately by a single local government. Regional cooperation has been the most common answer, although it has taken several organizational forms, from Councils of Governments through city-county consolidation to multijurisdictional agencies.

Suggested Reading
Mogulof, Melvin B. "Federally Encouraged Multijurisdictional Agencies." *Urban Affairs Quarterly*, vol. 9, no. 1 (1973), pp. 113–131.

Multinuclei Model   A theory of urban growth and land use in Anglo North America holding that the built-up portion of the environment accommodates many work centers other than the central business district around which families work and are oriented. The multinuclei model was first formulated by Chauncy Harris and Edward Ullman in 1945. The model is also known as the galactic metropolis, the multicentered urban region, and the variegated network. The multinodal system can be focused around retail, wholesale, port, or residential activity and has been operationalized as any location within the metropolitan area with 5,000 or more employees. For the 1977 census of manufacturing, Boston had 34 suburban nucleations, Pittsburgh 8, and Chicago and Los Angeles–Long Beach 44 each. The original Harris-Ullman formulation stressed four functions: a common occupation and related infrastructure, propinquity of activity, the separation of noncompatible activity, and historical explanation of location based on favorable location costs over already-established centers. Clearly, rail/highway/port facilities are a key to the multicentered city. The process can be a planned effort to disperse density, as in Toronto, where the Planning Department has established ten nuclear centers in all, including St. Clair, Eglinton, York, and Islington. Or, more commonly, the process can be the result of private-sector investment decisions. Means of measuring multinucleation include population density, convention space, hotel/motel rooms, retail sales space, parking spaces, and total employment in a single, recognized census category. *See also* BALKANIZATION; CONCENTRIC ZONE MODEL; CONURBATION; GROWTH POLITICS; HUMAN ECOLOGY; SECTOR MODEL.

Significance   The multinuclei model is a characteristic urban form in the postindustrial era, with its emphasis on white-collar employment, modern telecommunications, regional shopping malls, and mature expressway system. It explains the lowered-density central city with its disinvestment and new businesses reestablished in suburbia or exurbia. As a model, Harris and Ullman's approach avoids the specificity of actual nodes, because the nuclei appear to be located along major transportation lines. A multinucleated metropolitan area has major ramifications for energy costs, should prices for gasoline and heating fuels substantially increase. For many workers, commuting time actually is shortened by multiple centers; for others it is increased. Prime examples of multinucleated cities include Los Angeles, Phoenix, Houston, and Dallas. All three theories of urban space—concentric, sector, and multinucleated—apply to a greater or lesser extent in various North American cities. None by itself is an adequate model to describe urban growth and land use.

Suggested Reading

Berry, Brian J. L., and John D. Kasarda. *Contemporary Urban Ecology*. New York: Macmillan, 1977.
Erickson, Rodney A. "The Evolution of the Suburban Space Economy." *Urban Geography*, vol. 4, no. 2 (1983), pp. 95–121.
———. "Multinucleation in Metropolitan Economies." *Annals of the Association of American Geographers*, vol. 76, no. 3 (1986), pp. 331–346.
Haines, Valerie A. "Energy and Urban Form: A Human Ecological Critique." *Urban Affairs Quarterly*, vol. 21, no. 3 (1986), pp. 337–353.
Harris, Chauncy D., and Edward L. Ullman. "The Nature of Cities." *Annals of the American Academy of Political and Social Sciences*, vol. 242 (November 1945), pp. 7–17.
Ostrom, Vincent, Charles M. Tiebout, and Robert Warren. "In Defense of the Polycentric Metropolis." *American Political Science Review*, vol. 55, no. 4 (1961), pp. 831–842.

Municipal Assistance Corporation (MAC)   "Big MAC" is one of several institutions created to supervise New York City's finances after the near-bankruptcy of the city in 1975 (N.Y. Public Authorities Law, Consol. Laws Chap. 43A Sec. 3030 et seq.). The MAC is an independent public corporation authorized to sell municipal bonds for the city and to revamp the city's accounting procedures. Still operating in 1990, MAC originally was charged with oversight of the city's finances only from 1975 to 1985. MAC is not confined to New York City. It became overseer of finances when Yonkers, New York, was threatened with bankruptcy through failure of its city council to comply with a federal district judge's escalating contempt fines. *See also* FISCAL CRISIS; NEW YORK CITY BAILOUT; YONKERS-STYLE POLITICS.

Significance   The Municipal Assistance Corporation was the first of several organizations created by the State of New York to deliver New

York City from the verge of bankruptcy. As part of the massive over-haul of New York's finances, the state converted the city's sales tax into a state tax, the funds of which would be available to MAC for debt repayment but were insulated from city control. Because New York City received financial support from a consortium of private banks, the federal government, and the state, financial power in the city shifted to three centers after 1975. One is the Municipal Union–Financial Leaders organization, a coalition of private banks and mu-nicipal employee unions that helped bail out the city. The second center of financial power rests with the U.S. Treasury, the Fiscal Con-trol Board (FCB), and MAC. These creditor and monitor agencies are among the most powerful of the three groups, since they most directly control the city's finances and economic health. The third center of power rests with the mayor's office, revitalized since Abe Beame's mayoral administration of 1974 to 1977. Ed Koch, who held the New York City mayor's office from 1977 to 1989, made local economic development a top priority, thus resurrecting some confi-dence in the office.

Suggested Reading
Shefter, Martin. *Political Crisis/Fiscal Crisis.* New York: Basic Books, 1987.

Municipal Corporation   A legal designation given to a local gov-ernment by the state that enumerates the local government's rights and responsibilities as an incorporated body. Municipal corporations are established by a charter to carry out various public services such as police and fire protection. A municipal charter establishes the govern-mental structure, its functions, and permitted financing methods. While municipal corporation powers entitle local governments to pro-mulgate civil and criminal ordinances affecting their own jurisdic-tions, their very existence and authority is retained by the state. This is true even though in many cases, such as New York, Boston, Detroit, St. Augustine, and Los Angeles, cities predated the creation of their states. *See also* CHARTER; DILLON'S RULE; HOME RULE.

Significance   Because cities have no U.S. Constitutional standing, their creation as municipal corporations rests on the discretion of their state governments and they have only those powers granted to them by their states. Through the early twentieth century, courts tended to interpret local powers rather narrowly, beginning most notably with Dillon's Rule. More recently, state legislatures have given general-law cities powers and autonomy similar to those given to home-rule cities. However, states still authorize different classes of charters in which cities have more or less autonomy in making policy.

Most supporters of local discretion advocate home-rule charters, in which the state grants wide authority to a city to promulgate its own operating rules and to exercise those legislative powers not specifically prohibited. In other cases, cities are prohibited from taking action unless the state explicitly allows it.

Municipal Court   A trial-level bench established and financed by a city to hear cases largely involving persons accused of violating municipal ordinances and state and local traffic laws. In smaller cities, most cases tried in a municipal court are minor criminal offenses, such as parking violations. For the most part, such courts deal only with criminal, not civil, matters. In larger urban areas, the municipal court may serve as an arraignment court for felonies in addition to hearing misdemeanors. Larger cities also may establish separate specialty court facilities, such as Traffic Court, Housing Court, or Juvenile Court, to handle those cases exclusively. Judges are often assigned on a permanent basis in order to develop some expertise in hearing those specialized cases. *See also* HOUSING COURT; JUVENILE COURT.

Significance   All states establish their own state court systems, which may include a separate trial-level municipal court, even in larger urban jurisdictions. Despite the variation across the states, most municipal courts rarely deal with matters other than misdemeanors, and most of these cases involve traffic or parking violations. Many cities do not choose to create a municipal court even if they have state authorization. In these cities, alleged municipal violations are heard by the lowest-level state court. In many smaller cities, a justice of the peace (JP) remains the lowest level justice official, dealing primarily with traffic violations. Because many JPs are not legally trained, and this system led to some corruption, cities in some states have begun to abolish the position. Most larger urban centers no longer have a justice-of-the-peace system.

Suggested Reading
Dolbeare, Kenneth M. *Trial Courts in Urban Politics: State Court Policy Impact and Functions in a Local System.* New York: John Wiley, 1967.
Jacob, Herbert. *The Frustration of Policy: Response to Crime by American Cities.* Boston: Little, Brown, 1984.

Municipal Tort Liability   The legal responsibility held by local governments over the actions of their employees. The extent of municipal tort liability historically has been unclear. In early cases, local governments were considered immune from legal action, because civil suits could not be brought against any level of government without its consent, due to the concept of "sovereignty" of government. A number of recent U.S. Supreme Court cases have expanded the scope of municipal liability, especially in antitrust and civil rights violations. In *City of Lafayette v. Louisiana Power & Light Co.,* 435 U.S. 389 (1978), the Court ruled local governments could be held liable in antitrust suits. Moreover, private individuals or organizations can be sued if they were acting in conjunction with a local government that allegedly violated antitrust laws. Later, the Court held a municipality subject to liability for constitutional violations of civil rights. In *City of Canton, Ohio v. Harris,* 103 L Ed 2d 412 (1989), the Court ruled the municipality was negligent by giving police officers and shift commanders discretion to summon medical assistance for individuals, without giving those officers any special training to help them assess the need for medical care. The Court held the right to medical attention was guaranteed under the due process clause of the Fourteenth Amendment, and the city acted to deprive a citizen of those rights by failing adequately to train its officers. *See also* HOME RULE; PROPRIETARY FUNCTION.

Significance   Generally speaking, the tort liability of municipalities is quite limited. State laws vary in the extent to which they allow individuals to sue municipalities for alleged wrongful activity by government employees. However, as governments became more involved in activities historically left to the private sector, the public-private distinction became less clear. In some cases, state laws have allowed individuals to sue municipalities over proprietary functions (transportation, for example) assumed by governments. In addition, individuals may sue states or cities over alleged violations of federal law. In *Maine v. Thiboutot,* 448 U.S. 1 (1980), the U.S. Supreme Court ruled that a citizen could sue the state for the alleged denial of benefits available under the Social Security Act. In a case involving a mandatory maternity-leave policy, *Monell v. Department of Social Services, New York City,* 436 U.S. 658 (1978), the Court ruled municipalities may be held liable when their policies violate a person's constitutional rights. Municipalities have been sued for anticompetitive policies, zoning decisions, adopting urban renewal plans, denying building permits, and many other municipal policies. Some of these cases have not reached litigation because many of those policies were made because of a specific state-government authorization. However, home-rule cities, with general rather than specific state authorization, may be more subject to liability lawsuits after these Supreme Court decisions.

Suggested Reading
Schnapper, Eric. "Civil Rights Litigation after Monell." *Columbia Law Review*,
    vol. 79, no. 2 (1979), pp. 213–266.

Municipal Year Book of the International City Management Association (ICMA)   An annual reference book of statutes, trends, statistics, and general information relating to local governments in the United States. The *Municipal Year Book* is published by the International City Management Association and uses expert academic contributors and practitioners from across the country. *See also* NATIONAL ASSOCIATION OF COUNTIES; PUBLIC INTEREST GROUPS.

Significance   As part of its efforts to lobby on behalf of local governments and to improve urban management, the ICMA disseminates a wide variety of research and data on local governments through the *Municipal Year Book.* Much of the data reported each year is derived from survey research of cities in various categories, which provides current knowledge of local experiences and trends. The research provided has a high level of reliability, and the *Year Book* publishes annual surveys on boundary changes, the salaries of local officials, an extensive bibliography, and a list of research associations and local governments.

Suggested Reading
International City Management Association. *Municipal Year Book.* Washington,
    DC: ICMA, annual editions.
National Association of Counties and the International City Management
    Association. *County Year Book.* Washington, DC: NACo and ICMA,
    1975–1978.

Mutual-Aid Pact   A form of local intergovernmental relations in which two or more governments sign a formal agreement to assist one another under specified conditions. The mutual-aid pact is a form of joint exercise of power and usually serves as a standby agreement that supplements individual city service provision. It is called bilateral when two cities, counties, or other units sign the pact; it is multilateral when three or more are involved. Ongoing multilateral local cooperation is generally called metropolitization of the function. Purely one-purpose informal liaison between cities is *ad hoc* cooperation. With the complexity of equipment, the need for specialized training, and the cautious attitude of risk-management providers, *ad hoc* cooperation is on the wane. If a county supplies a service to cities and villages on a contract basis, it is called a type of Lakewood Plan. If a single function is provided by a special district, it is a structural reform and is delivered by a public authority. In the rare instance where a host of functions are structurally transferred to a higher level, it is called metropolitan government. Consolidation of staff functions, such as grant application review and land-use planning assigned to an areawide body, is usually conducted by a Council of Governments (COG). *See also* AUTHORITY, PUBLIC; COUNCIL OF GOVERNMENTS; LAKEWOOD PLAN; METROPOLITIZATION; MULTIJURISDICTIONAL AGENCY.

Significance   A mutual-aid pact is a relatively simple form of intergovernmental agreement that overcomes some of the effects of balkanization. It does not require any structural rearrangement. Mutual-aid pacts yield improved economies of scale. That is to say, the unit experiences increased productivity for the same cost or has a lower per-unit cost. Mutual-aid pacts often become agenda items after a major crisis such as a multialarm fire, riot, earthquake, volcano, flood, or blizzard. It is the most widely exercised form of interlocal cooperation. The pacts are entered on an indefinite basis, renewed after a specified number of years, or brought to an automatic end by a sunset provision unless renewed in advance by consent of all parties. All states allow for some form of agreement among local units, but occasionally only *horizontal intergovernmental relations* are allowed between units of the same legal status, such as Class A city with Class A city, county with county, or township with township. *Vertical intergovernmental aid pacts* between township, village, borough, and parish are often more useful because the problem being addressed prevails in a variety of legal settings. The most frequent type of mutual-aid pact is for police or fire backup protection. The protocols may require a set number of units or personnel to respond upon request. The pact may also call for maintenance standards, common training, or even the purchase of complementary equipment. A major drawback to greater use of mutual-aid pacts is professional jealousies: fire fighters refuse to cooperate with public safety officers who are cross-trained or with volunteer units that are thought to have lower training standards. Where these issues are overcome, whole urban counties such as Macomb in metropolitan Detroit are covered by one mutual-aid fire agreement.

Suggested Reading
Frieden, Bernard J. *Commission Findings and Proposals: Challenge to Federalism.* Washington, DC: Advisory Commission on Intergovernmental Relations, 1966. Y3.Ad 918.

N

NAACP Legal Defense and Educational Fund, Inc. (LDF)   An organization founded in 1940 by the National Association for the Advancement of Colored People (NAACP) as a separate, tax-exempt, fund-raising organization. The Legal Defense Fund was created because the NAACP was lobbying for antilynching laws during the 1930s and therefore could not be considered a tax-exempt organization. Although the general public assumes legal actions taken by the NAACP regarding civil rights cases originate from one organization, the general-membership NAACP and the LDF are distinct bodies. The NAACP tends to focus its efforts on education and lobbying, with its court litigation directed toward local-level problems. The LDF focuses primarily on cases with the potential of establishing Supreme Court doctrine on civil rights. The Legal Defense Fund was begun in New York City. Its charter director was Thurgood Marshall, who later became a U.S. Supreme Court justice. In 1989, the LDF raised $8.1 million, none from governmental sources. *See also* BROWN V. BOARD OF EDUCATION; NATIONAL ASSOCIATION FOR THE ADVANCEMENT OF COLORED PEOPLE.

Significance   The NAACP Legal Defense and Educational Fund, Inc., has participated in virtually every important civil rights case to come before the U.S. Supreme Court since 1940. Not only did the LDF sponsor argument in the 1954 *Brown v. Board of Education* case, it was responsible for many of the landmark civil rights and civil liberties cases arising from the 1960s during the second decade of the Warren Court era. Legal Defense Fund cases have expanded rights in the following areas: the right to be represented by counsel even if indigent; the right to a jury representative of one's peers; the freedom from coerced confession; the right to vote in primary elections without racial discrimination; the right to peaceful protest; and the right to buy and sell a home free from racially discriminatory restrictive

346

covenants. In addition to litigating cases, the LDF monitors the implementation of Supreme Court decisions and takes positions on federal judicial appointments.

Suggested Reading

Armstrong, Scott, and Bob Woodward. *The Brethren.* New York: Simon & Schuster, 1979.
Division of Legal Information and Community Service, NAACP Legal Defense and Educational Fund, Inc. "It's Not the Distance, 'It's the Niggers.'" New York: NAACP LDF, 1972.
NAACP Legal Defense and Educational Fund, Inc. *1987–1988 Annual Report.* New York: NAACP LDF, 1988.

National Association for the Advancement of Colored People (NAACP)   The oldest and largest civil rights organization in the United States, with national membership of more than 500,000 distributed among 22,000 local chapters. The NAACP's major objective is encouraging racial integration through education and lobbying. The organization's national headquarters is located in Baltimore, with active branches addressing local concerns. The NAACP has worked toward implementing the national civil rights acts in the areas of housing, employment, voting, schools, transportation, and recreation. The organization publishes a monthly magazine, *Crisis. See also* NAACP LEGAL DEFENSE AND EDUCATIONAL FUND; NATIONAL URBAN LEAGUE.

Significance   The NAACP has worked actively toward civil rights for minorities since its formation in New York City in 1909. Its membership and activities grew tremendously after World War I, when many southern blacks migrated to cities in the North. The NAACP has been the most prominent organization in defining the civil rights objectives and agenda for the United States. Among its greatest lobbying efforts have been the 1957 and 1964 Civil Rights Acts, the 1965 Voting Rights Act, and the 1968 Civil Rights Act, which included the Fair Housing Title. Traditionally a moderate voice for minority rights and black empowerment, the NAACP disassociated itself from the black power movement during its 1966 national convention. In the era of New Federalism, the organization did not change roles, but became more significant as a local-level watchdog of civil rights. The NAACP is legally separate from the NAACP Legal Defense and Educational Fund, Inc., which was established in 1940 by the NAACP, but became a self-sustaining entity active in influencing national civil rights doctrine through U.S. Supreme Court decisions.

Suggested Reading

Finch, Minnie. *The NAACP: Its Fight for Justice.* Metuchen, NJ: Scarecrow Press, 1981.

Kellogg, Charles Flint. *NAACP: A History of the National Association for the Advancement of Colored People.* Baltimore: Johns Hopkins University Press, 1967.

Meier, August, and John H. Bracey, Jr., general eds. *Papers of the NAACP, Parts 1–9.* Frederick, MD: University Publications of America. (35mm microfilm, various dates.)

National Association of Counties (NACo)   An organization composed of management-level policymakers that conducts research and represents county officials on national policy matters. NACo was founded in 1935, with headquarters in Washington, D.C. The organization is considered one of the "Big Seven" Public Interest Groups (PIGs) and has a permanent research and clerical staff of approximately 50. About 2,100 of some 3,100 U.S. counties are members. NACo provides educational conferences, workshops, resource sharing, and publications for its member counties and officials. The organization has 15 affiliate organizations that parallel the functional organization of county government. *See also* PUBLIC INTEREST GROUPS; U.S. CONFERENCE OF MAYORS.

Significance   Beginning in the 1930s, the increasing role of federal funding in local government affairs caused local and state officals to become more active politically. Many Public Interest Groups, such as NACo and the U.S. Conference of Mayors, were founded during the Depression. NACo provides research and reference support for its members, and it staffs several policy committees that are important to county officials. Areas covered by NACo research committees include community development, employment, environment and energy, health and education, criminal justice and public safety, and social welfare. Between 1975 and 1978, NACo and the International City Management Association (ICMA) jointly published an annual *County Year Book,* with data on U.S. counties and county officials. Since 1978, information on counties has been included in the ICMA's *Municipal Year Book.*

Suggested Reading

International City Management Association. *Municipal Year Book.* Washington, DC: ICMA, annual editions.

National Association of Counties. *County Year Book.* Washington, DC: NACo and ICMA, 1975–1978.

National Association of Housing & Redevelopment Officials (NAHRO)   A professional organization of individuals and public

agencies involved in community redevelopment, housing construction, and rehabilitation. The association proclaims as its goal the provision of a decent home and a suitable living environment for all
Americans. NAHRO was founded in 1933, and was originally called
the National Association of Housing Officials. Headquartered in
Washington, D.C., NAHRO had approximately 7,500 members in
1987, with a budget of approximately $3 million. The organization
conducts research, operates a Technical Services Department, and
lobbies on issues involving community redevelopment and housing.
In addition, NAHRO publishes the *Journal of Housing* and the *NAHRO
Monitor. See also* HOUSING, PUBLIC; URBAN DEVELOPMENT ACTION GRANT.

Significance   The National Association of Housing & Redevelopment Officials has endorsed housing and redevelopment programs
during its half-century history. Its current position is to support public
and private cooperation in the creation of suitable housing and revitalized communities. NAHRO supported the Urban Development Action Grant (UDAG) program during UDAG's ten-year existence, and
has long supported senior citizen and public housing programs. The
organization recognized the need for increased state and local involvement in community redevelopment, but by 1984 had recommended at
least four federal initiatives to support state and local governments in
their redevelopment efforts. One, NAHRO endorsed the continued
allocation of Community Development Block Grants to enable local
communities to conserve and upgrade their neighborhoods. Two, it
recommended a public works investment grant program to allow local
governments to improve their infrastructure. Three, it proposed new
housing allocations for rehabilitation of current housing and construction of new units. Four, it advocated major reinvestment programs, along the same principle as UDAGs, for all cities, to allow them
to make long-term investments in support of economic development
projects. NAHRO's 1989 legislative agenda recommended a $3.5 bil-
lion appropriation to revitalize public housing stock, encouraged programs to eliminate drugs in public housing projects, advocated
increased funding to build and rehabilitate rental housing, urged
increased reauthorization of Community Development Block Grant
and Urban Development Action Grant funding, and supported programs for community and neighborhood preservation.

National Capital Planning Commission   An appointive regional
body for the Washington, D.C., metropolitan area serving as a
clearinghouse of information on coordinating development, physical
planning, and projecting the impact of the national government's
capital program and personnel needs on the area. The National Capital

Planning Commission (NCPC) jurisdiction extends to the 10-square-mile district, the two counties of Montgomery and Prince George's in Maryland, and the four counties of Arlington, Fairfax, Loudoun, and Prince William in Virginia. It is an atypical Council of Governments (COG) in that it was established by Congress with the National Capital Planning Act, 40 U.S.C. 71 et seq., in 1952. The commission is composed of 12 appointed and *ex officio* members. Its comprehensive physical planning includes transportation and open space protection. It also serves as a regional review body for other units of governments, similar to the A-95 Review requirement issued by the Office of Management and Budget. *See also* COUNCIL OF GOVERNMENTS; PLANNING, URBAN PHYSICAL; WASHINGTON, DISTRICT OF COLUMBIA.

Significance   The National Capital Planning Commission is unique to the Washington, D.C., metropolitan area because it was imposed by Congress on the planning region before the movement became popular in other areas on a voluntary basis. The commission has problems peculiar to its location because the tax base is primarily only one sector, the national bureaucracy. The NCPC has not been very successful in either developing an areawide circulation pattern or coordinating development with Fairfax County, Virginia, which is interested in a growth-management program, or with adjacent Baltimore and its Metropolitan Regional Planning Council.

Suggested Reading
U.S. Government Archives. *The United States Government Manual.* Washington, DC: Superintendent of Documents, 1989.

National Industrial Policy   Federal statements of explicit long-term economic goals that articulate the rational expectation of the country toward various sectors in basic manufacturing, articulated through specific objectives relating to productivity, rate of expansion or contraction, worldwide competitiveness, and use of natural resources. There is no explicit national industrial policy in the United States. There is only an implicit policy in the tax laws, various statutes on industrial bailout programs for corporations such as Lockheed and Chrysler, and hands-off attitudes toward loss of jobs in the sunset industries of basic steel making and automobile assembly. During the national recession of 1981–1982 there were many congressional attempts to pass bills on the subject. Some states, such as Rhode Island, attempted to institute statewide industrial policies. That project failed to win in a 1984 statewide referendum. Regional attempts also have been made, as in northern Minnesota. *See also* BELTWAY; GROWTH MANAGEMENT; INCUBATOR; NATIONAL URBAN POLICY.

Significance   With the failure to adopt a national industrial policy and with only little more success at the state level, some metropolitan regions have forged a local industrial policy. This differs from the more common economic development planning in going beyond recruiting firms and inducing already-located plants to remain. Local industrial policy is based on rational calculation regarding the region's economic base, comparative advantage in transportation costs, available natural resources, most productive work force, and potential markets. The local policy cultivates a select sector or sectors with incubators and increased Research, Development and Engineering (RD&E) funding through local colleges and universities. The local policy invests seed monies in start-up concerns derived from local pension funds. The process assumes that market forces work in somewhat random ways and that governments have the right to formulate the mix and magnitude of industries in their communities.

Suggested Reading

Goldstein, Harve A., ed. "Symposium: The State and Local Industrial Policy Question." *Journal of the American Planning Association,* vol. 52, no. 3 (1986), pp. 262–318. (Extensive bibliographies.)

Iacocca, Lee. *Iacocca: An Autobiography.* New York: Bantam Books, 1984. Chap. 28.

Rodberg, Leonard S., and William K. Tabb. "What We Learn from the Industrial Policy Debate." *Social Policy,* vol. 17, no. 3 (1987), pp. 27–33.

Scipes, Kim. "Industrial Policy: Can It Lead the U.S. Out of Its Economic Malaise?" *New Labor Review,* no. 6 (1984), pp. 27–53. (A Marxist interpretation.)

National League of Cities (NLC)   The largest U.S. lobbying organization representing municipal government, with more than 1,300 direct member communities. Through its 49 state municipal league members, the National League of Cities indirectly represents more than 16,000 cities in the United States. Formerly called the American Municipal Association, the NLC was founded in 1924 as a reform-oriented coalition of ten state municipal leagues; in 1964, the name was changed. The National League of Cities maintains a full-time research and lobbying staff in Washington, D.C. This staff monitors and lobbies legislative and bureaucratic offices that may affect local-level issues. The NLC also commissions studies on various problems that might affect its membership, especially taxation and revenue proposals. Until 1977, only state municipal leagues could be direct NLC members. After that date, the league opened up direct membership to any general-purpose local government. While NLC membership includes cities of all sizes, in 1989 in excess of 75 percent of all direct member communities had populations less than 50,000. *See also* GARCIA V. SAN

ANTONIO; LOBBYING BY CITIES; LOCAL EXCHANGE; *NATIONAL LEAGUE OF CITIES V. USERY*; PUBLIC INTEREST GROUPS; U.S. CONFERENCE OF MAYORS.

Significance   Early in the twentieth century, cities of all sizes realized the need for effective lobbying at the federal level, because federal funding became so important during the Depression. The National League of Cities is considered to be one of the "Big Seven" Public Interest Groups (PIGs), which also includes the U.S. Conference of Mayors, the National Governor's Conference, the Council of State Governments, the National Association of Counties, the National Legislative Conference, and the International City Management Association. Most of these groups have been active in lobbying for federal-funding programs to states and cities. The National League of Cities' Board is served by five standing policy committees: Finance, Administration, and Intergovernmental Relations; Energy, Environment, and Natural Resources; Community and Economic Development; Transportation and Communications; and Human Development. The NLC publishes *Nation's Cities Weekly*, a weekly summary of urban-related journal articles called *Urban Affairs Abstracts*; a number of local government official directories; and numerous books and monographs on housing, energy and environment, local finance, and human services. In 1976, the NLC became a key litigant in a dispute involving the application of the Fair Labor Standards Act to local government employers and employees. The U.S. Supreme Court, in *National League of Cities v. Usery*, 426 U.S. 833 (1976), ruled five to four that local governments were not required to pay federally mandated minimum wages to its employees. This ruling was overturned in 1985 by *Garcia v. San Antonio Metropolitan Transportation Authority*, 469 U.S. 528. In conjunction with the International City Management Association and Public Technology, Inc., the NLC offers an electronic-mail bulletin-board system, and a computerized data base service called LOCAL EXCHANGE™.

Suggested Reading
National League of Cities. *The National League of Cities Handbook: A Guide to Services and Participation*, 2nd ed. Washington, DC: NLC, December 1987.

National League of Cities v. Usery, 426 U.S. 833 (1976)   A case arising from several states and cities through their association, the National League of Cities, against the Secretary of Labor, asking for nonenforcement of 1974 congressional amendments to the 1938 Fair Labor Standards Act, which extended minimum wages and maximum hours for employees of states and their subdivisions. Losing at the federal district court, the National League of Cities appealed to the U.S. Supreme Court, asking for the amendments to be declared unconstitutional. By a 5–4 vote, with Justice Rehnquist writing, the majority found that federally imposed wage restraints would impermissibly interfere with the integral functions of those governments. The states and cities temporarily won the right to be exempt from nationally imposed wage-and-hour mandates. The court noted overburdensome effects on cities, which would have to pay more to fire fighters, police, and sanitation, public health, and parks and recreation workers. The majority's opinion and reasoning were based upon the congressional amendments' potentially crushing burden on the discretion of the sovereign states within the federal system. *See also* FEDERALISM; *GARCIA V. SAN ANTONIO* ; STATE MANDATE.

Significance   *National League of Cities* was a short-lived, significant departure from the Supreme Court's long-standing support for cooperative federalism and from other cases that relied on the interstate commerce clause to justify national mandates. Although private enterprise had to comport with national standards, states and their subunits were exempt from paying for what Congress declared to be threshold working conditions. After nine years, the U.S. Supreme Court reversed itself and applied the minimum wage and overtime requirements of the Fair Labor Standards Act to public mass-transit authorities. Justice Blackmun's decision in *Garcia v. San Antonio* (1985) was an explicit overruling of this case.

National Municipal League   A private, professional, reform and educational organization established in 1900 by representatives of citizens' reform groups, with headquarters in New York City. The league formed in large measure as a response to the urban political machines that grew to prominence during the mid- and late 1800s in the United States. The league has worked actively to promote a model state constitution and model city charter, seeking to standardize local government organization and permit home rule for municipalities. This organization publishes the *National Civic Review. See also* HOME RULE; LOBBYING BY CITIES; URBAN POLITICAL MACHINE.

Significance   The National Municipal League was quite typical of reform-minded groups of the Progressive Era. Through its model city charter the league advocated such reforms as the institution of a city manager, merit system of local employment, and nonpartisan, at-large elections. The league also opposed immigration and supported the

Immigration Act of 1921, which set quotas on the "newer" immigrants arriving from southern and eastern Europe. The league argued these immigrants were largely responsible for the creation of urban political machines, and therefore sought to restrict their numbers.

National Urban League   A voluntary, nonpartisan organization whose goals are to end racial segregation and discrimination in the United States. The National Urban League was founded in 1910. By 1987, it had approximately 50,000 members, with a support staff of 2,500 employees. There are 113 local affiliates in 34 cities plus 4 regional offices. The league works primarily toward identifying and ending institutional racism and providing direct service programs to minorities in employment, education, housing, health, and many other social-service areas. Specific programs include the Black Executive Exchange, economic development, and projects attempting to reduce teenage pregnancy. Through its Seniors in Community Service, it increases senior citizen activity. The league also conducts extensive social research and publishes several periodicals—the *Urban League News,* the *Urban League Review,* and the annual *State of Black America.* Headquartered in New York City, the league has had recent annual budgets of more than $20 million, of which approximately $16 million come from the federal government for the administration of existing federal programs. *See also* NATIONAL ASSOCIATION FOR THE ADVANCEMENT OF COLORED PEOPLE.

Significance   The National Urban League is one of the oldest nongovernmental organizations involved in providing social services and promoting civil rights for black Americans. Originally called the "National League on Urban Conditions among Negroes," the league initially sought housing for the large number of migrants who came to New York City during the early 1900s. Long involved in the traditional areas of housing, health care, employment, poverty, social welfare, and economic development, the league identified five specific areas needing special attention during the late 1980s and beyond. Those areas were teenage pregnancy, female heads-of-households, crime by blacks against blacks, citizenship responsibility, and education.

Suggested Reading
Dancy, John C. *Sands against the Wind.* Detroit: Wayne State University Press, 1966.
Parris, Richard, and Lester Brooks. *Blacks in the City: A History of the National Urban League.* Boston: Little, Brown, 1971.

National Urban Policy   Those governmental decisions in the United States taken as a whole at the central level that have an intended or unintended effect on cities and metropolitan areas. The 1965 enabling section of the Department of Housing and Urban Development (79 Stat. 667) notes that as a matter of national purpose there should be sound development of the nation's cities and urban areas. Despite this statutory goal there is no explicit national-level urban policy. In the 1970s, one-third of some cities' revenue consisted of intergovernmental transfer payments from national and state levels. This was as much a condition of grantsmanship, lobbying, and bargaining as one of systematic financial support. Direct national-local relations increased in frequency and financial importance during both the New Deal of Franklin Roosevelt and the Great Society of Lyndon Johnson. But in a federal system cities are the products of states and have only a secondary relationship with the center. Some states, such as North Carolina, have carefully worked out balanced-growth policies; others, such as Ohio, have no semblance of a state-level policy toward major cities. The phrase "National Urban Policy" began to gain its present currency during Richard Nixon's administration, where it was discussed by his Urban Affairs Council. From 1972 to 1978, presidents issued biannual reports under the auspices of the Urban Growth and New Community Development Act of 1970, 42 U.S.C. 4502. But no coherent set of policy directives, including the once-touted urban impact analysis, ever emerged. In 1978 President Jimmy Carter promised a national urban policy called *A New Partnership to Conserve American Cities,* but no major legislation passed during his tenure. Presidents Ronald Reagan and George Bush dismantled most aid to cities under domestic fiscal-austerity programs and tax cuts, turning over responsibility for cities to the states or the local units themselves. Bush has tended to follow the Reagan lead in matters of national urban policy. *See also* A-95 REVIEW; BANFIELD THESIS; CLOSING, PLANT; FEDERALISM; GRANTSMANSHIP; JEFFERSONIAN AGRARIANISM; NEW YORK CITY BAILOUT; STATE MANDATE.

Significance   In the United States, there is no coordinated urban policy, national transportation policy, or industrial-manufacturing policy. However, there is a national environmental policy. A specific urban topic is placed on the agenda, usually because of a crisis, with little thought to calculations of equity or efficiency. The national level imposes a series of uncoordinated standards on municipalities, such as antidiscrimination laws, environmental impact statement requirements, and aesthetic controls in the form of limiting billboards along interstates. Local compliance is largely ensured by the threat of withheld grant monies. The largest national-level effect does not come from the Department of Housing and Urban Development (HUD) but from the sum total of other programs that have place-specific impact such as transportation decisions on highways, beltways, and transit and paratransit systems. Other programs involve concentrating federal employment in the Washington, D.C.–Virginia–Maryland area, subsidizing new housing construction through the tax code, as well as government-backed mortgages. Department of Defense contracts for military procurement have regional impacts, largely favoring cities in the sunbelt and along the two coasts. Federal bailouts of Lockheed, Chrysler, Penn Central, and New York City also have effects on specific cities. The long-term net result of national-level policy, because of the importance of highway construction and subsidies to new home building, has been to favor suburbs. Whatever national policy emerges is directed not so much at metropolitan areas, where approximately two-thirds of Americans live, but at functionally specific crises. National policy is driven more by private-sector decisions, both corporate and family. During the Reagan and Bush era, little thought was given to coordination of the needs of cities and suburbs.

Suggested Reading

Gelfand, Mark I. *A Nation of Cities: The Federal Government and Urban America 1933–1965*. New York: Oxford University Press, 1975.

Goldsmith, William W., and Harvey M. Jacobs. "The Impossibility of Urban Policy." *Journal of the American Planning Association*, vol. 48, no.1 (1982), pp. 53–66.

Mills, Edwin S. "Non-urban Policies as Urban Policies." *Urban Studies*, vol. 24, no. 6 (1987), pp. 561–569.

Morrison, Peter A., et al. *Recent Contributions to the Urban Policy Debate*. Report 2394-RC. Santa Monica: RAND, 1979.

Stowe, Eric L. "Defining a National Urban Policy: Bureaucratic Conflict and Shortfall." Chap. 6 in Donald B. Rosenthal, ed., *Urban Revitalization*, Urban Affairs Annual Reviews, vol. 18. Beverly Hills: Sage Publications, 1980.

Tabb, William K. "The Failures of National Urban Policy." In William K. Tabb and Larry Sawers, eds., *Marxism and the Metropolis*. New York: Oxford University Press, 1984. Chap. 2, pp. 255–269.

Vance, Mary. *Urban Policy: A Bibliography of Material Published 1980–1984*. Public Administration Series, Bibliography P 1730. Monticello, IL: Vance Bibliographies, 1985.

Vaughan, Roger J., Anthony H. Pascal, and Mary E. Vaiana. "Federal Urban Policies: The Harmful Helping Hand." In Irving Louis Horowitz, ed., *Policy Studies Review Annual*, vol. 5. Beverly Hills: Sage Publications, 1981, pp. 456–468.

Warren, Charles R. *A Comparative Analysis of the States and Urban Strategies*. Washington, DC: Department of Housing and Urban Development, 1980.

Neighborhood   A small-scale section of a city, town, or village demarcated in terms of either people or place, or both, and distinguishable from adjacent locations. Planners and sociologists differ in their
understanding of a neighborhood, its boundaries, and its total population. Neighborhoods usually are defined by residents but may be
demarcated by developers or designated by city community and economic affairs departments. The national urban renewal program of
1954 required all cities requesting funds to map the location of their
neighborhoods. By whomever defined, neighborhoods are areas
where informal, face-to-face interaction transpires because of both
propinquity and the sharing of common interests in the same infrastructure and essential services. These common interests include public roads, parks, school districts, police and fire precincts, and branch
library patronage boundaries. Part of living in a neighborhood is
sharing common levels of amenities, local business services, and religious institutions. *See also* BOUNDARY; COMMUNITY; COPRODUCTION; ETH-
NIC GROUP; HUMAN ECOLOGY; PARTICIPATION; PRECINCT; STABILIZATION.

Significance   There is no definitive meaning for *neighborhood,* but it
tends to have positive connotations. Since the 1920s in urban social
planning, it also has referred to a *neighborhood unit.* This is an area that
accommodates people who live in similar homes, share common primary schools, patronize the same everyday stores, and, above all,
utilize a single traffic circulation pattern. In new-town planning for
the United Kingdom, neighborhood units range from 5,000 to 10,000
and average close to 6,000 people. "Neighborhood" has been used in
urban administration policy analysis to designate separate, small-scale
clusters. Sociologists define neighborhoods as networks that possess
similar socioeconomic conditions, such as a slum or a gold coast. Or
they have similar ethnic and racial composition, such as Chinatown,
Corktown, Little Sicily, the Barrio, or Black Bottom. It is possible for
a neighborhood to have no sense of a community of interests. Some
observers thus argue that neighborhood organizations may be devoid
of a sense of community and should not be made the basis of decentralized policymaking. On the other hand, some commentators use
neighborhood and *community* as interchangeable terms. Neighborhoods
are posited as existing by the media when they do not in fact have a
common history. For example, "Poletown" in Detroit and Hamtramck
was the area in which the General Motors Cadillac assembly plant was
constructed. It had validity as a neighborhood only insofar as it was
the place undergoing quick-take eminent domain proceedings. Using
a biological metaphor, the University of Chicago Human Ecology
School of Sociology focused on natural areas that others would term
neighborhoods. Its researchers particularly stressed neighborhood

dynamics through periods of invasion, succession, and reestablished stabilization. Continuing the metaphor, city councils often ask about the "viability" of neighborhoods before deciding whether to contribute more city services. If found moribund, a neighborhood will be adjudged beyond the scope of a "triage" response. Most residents' cognitive map of the metropolis is focused on their own neighborhood. Hence, most projects aimed at encouraging participation focus on voluntary, grass-roots work. The Community Development Block Grant project took this tack. Neighborhood participation in local charities, club politics, and civic associations is a function of many factors. Especially important are length of residency, home ownership, racial homogeneity, and socioeconomic status (SES). Sociologists have created typologies (integrated or parochial; defended or defeated) to clarify the wide array of neighborhoods. In empirical studies, the term *neighborhood* often is forced onto a procrustean bed, being defined as a census tract or transportation zone, because information is readily available for those units.

Suggested Reading

Carmon, Naomi, ed. "Symposium on Neighborhood Policy and Practice." *Policy Studies Journal*, vol. 16, no. 2 (1987–1988), pp. 263–392.

Crenson, Matthew A. *Neighborhoods: Their Place in Urban Life*. Beverly Hills: Sage Publications, 1984.

Downs, Anthony. "Some Changing Aspects of Neighborhoods in the United States." *Urban Law and Policy*, vol. 6 (1983), pp. 65–74.

Haeberle, Stephen H. "People or Place: Variations in Community Leaders' Subjective Definitions of Neighborhood." *Urban Affairs Quarterly*, vol. 23, no. 4 (1988), pp. 616–634.

Keller, Suzanne. *The Urban Neighborhood*. New York: Random House, 1968.

O'Brien, David J., and Lynn Clough. "The Future of Urban Neighborhoods." In Gary Gappert and Richard V. Knight, eds., *Cities in the 21st Century*. Vol. 23 of Urban Affairs Annual Reviews. Beverly Hills: Sage Publications, 1982. Chap. 13, pp. 232–248.

Olson, Philip. "Urban Neighborhood Research: Its Development and Current Focus." *Urban Affairs Quarterly*, vol. 17, no. 4 (1982), pp. 491–518. ("Community" and "neighborhood" used interchangeably. Extensive bibliography.)

Silver, Christopher. "Neighborhood Planning in Historical Perspective." *Journal of the American Planning Association*, vol. 51, no. 2 (1985), pp. 161–174. (Extensive bibliography.)

White, Michael. *American Neighborhoods and Residential Differentiation*. New York: Russell Sage, 1987.

Neighborhood Justice Center (NJC)   A community-based program for dispute resolution that avoids more formal and expensive court procedures. Neighborhood justice centers, also known as community justice centers, were begun in the 1970s as an alternative for dealing with disputes between parties who know each other. The centers are either independent and community-based, or attached to one or more court systems in a city. The more informal procedure of these centers emphasizes negotiation and mediation. By 1988, there were almost 200 neighborhood justice centers, handling anywhere from a few hundred cases a year to almost 30,000. There are centers in at least 43 states. Prominent examples are located in Columbus, Atlanta, San Francisco, Chicago, Honolulu, and Dorchester, Massachusetts. *See also* COMMUNITY CONTROL; DECENTRALIZATION; HOUSING COURT; MEDIATION.

Significance   Neighborhood justice centers were an innovative response to the rising costs and number of court cases. Early funding came from foundations and the federal government. After the federal grants ended, the centers turned to such alternative sources as local governments, the United Way, and private contributors. Some centers also have begun to charge nominal fees for services. Most cases involve family members, landlords and tenants, employees and employers, or local consumers and merchants. The cases can be either criminal or civil. Most clients are low-income. Most disputes are resolved through mediation, and the centers often have dozens of trained volunteer mediators. Although some of the centers have large staffs, three-fourths have fewer than four staff members.

Neighborhood Movement   A coalition of loosely organized, locally based, and locally focused nonprofit citizens' organizations that foster grass-roots participation. The contemporary neighborhood movement has been active since the late 1950s, when neighborhood-based organizations (NBOs), block clubs, club politics, or community associations, as they are variously called, caught the attention of social commentators. The New Left stressed local organizations for working-class neighborhoods to encourage people to take control of their own lives. The right stressed local voluntary organization as the antithesis of centralized, bureaucratized government. Although the movement has application to any neighborhoods, including those in suburbia, it has been identified especially with inner-city, working-class neighborhoods as a way of fighting shrinking service levels, opposing drug houses, revitalizing the housing stock, combating crime, challenging group homes, and promoting cooperatives. Into the late 1980s, Saul Alinsky still was invoked as an example of a successful community organizer and outside agitator. The tradition lives on through the neighborhood development organization (NDO), which works on urban revitalization in lower-income areas. *See also*

ASSOCIATION OF COMMUNITY ORGANIZATIONS FOR REFORM NOW; COPRO-
DUCTION; NEIGHBORHOOD; ECONOMIC OPPORTUNITY ACT; OUTSIDE INFLU-
ENCE; PARTICIPATION.

Significance   The neighborhood movement promotes the democratic values of political mobilization and community solidarity. It
develops a sense of personal efficacy and promotes a concrete orientation to the needs of the city. However, citizens' organizations have
high membership turnover. Many of the organizations wax and wane
as viable entities. Empirical studies stress the severe limitations of
community groups because of underfunding; most decision making is
rooted at higher levels in urban society. A large portion of the time of
any grass-roots organization is taken up with funding, including grant
application writing and contacting such groups as the United Fund or
Black United Fund (BUF). Studies indicate that those that are structurally well organized and have low leadership turnover command
more resources and are more likely to be heard by other groups, city
hall, and higher levels of government.

Suggested Reading

Lenz, Thomas J. "Neighborhood Development: Issues and Models." *Social
    Policy*, vol. 18, no. 4 (1988), pp. 24–30. (NDOs.)
Milofsy, Carl. "Neighborhood-Based Organizations: A Market Analogy." In
    Walter W. Powell, ed., *The Nonprofit Sector: A Research Handbook*. New
    Haven, CT: Yale University Press, 1987. (NBOs.)
Mitchell, Stephen A. *Elm Street Politics*. New York: Oceana Publications, 1959.
Morris, David, and Karl Hess. *Neighborhood Power: The New Localism*. Boston:
    Beacon Press, 1975.
O'Brien, David J. *Neighborhood Organization and Interest Group Processes*. Prince-
    ton: Princeton University Press, 1975.
Rich, Richard C. "A Political-Economy Approach to the Study of Neighbor-
    hood Organizations." *American Journal of Political Science*, vol. 24, no. 4
    (1980), pp. 559–592.
Schoenberg, Sandra Perlman, and Patricia L. Rosenbaum. *Neighborhoods That
    Work: Sources for Viability in the Inner City*. New Brunswick, NJ: Rutgers
    University Press, 1980.
Susser, Ida. *Norman Street: Poverty and Politics in an Urban Neighborhood*. New
    York: Oxford University Press, 1982.

Neighborhood Watch   A form of coproduction in which citizens
participate in crime prevention and apprehension through mobile
watch programs, surveillance, and escorting services. Coproduction is
any voluntary contribution to a government activity. Neighborhood or
community watch programs are a response by concerned residents to
high street-crime rates and the inability of police to cope alone with
the issue. Most watch programs are supervised by a community rela-

tions division of the city police department to ensure that they do not turn to vigilante activity. *See also* COPRODUCTION; PARTICIPATION; POLICE, PRIVATE.

Significance   Neighborhood watch programs are strictly an urban residential reaction to street crime. In "communities of limited liability," volunteers feel they are aiding the understaffed regular police force. Although not well trained, they supplement both public and private police. All three services operate mobile patrols through some residential parts of suburbs and central cities. Participants tend to be better educated than national norms and feel they have a personal commitment to their community, in part because of a financial stake in their homes.

Suggested Reading
Rohe, William M., and Stephanie E. Greenberg. "Participation in Community Watch Programs." *Journal of Urban Affairs,* vol. 6, no. 3 (1984), pp. 53–66.

New Town   Any large-scale, relatively self-sufficient, self-governing community that is centrally pre-planned, is designed with a balanced economy, and provides for a diverse population, integrating residential with industrial, commercial, retail, recreational, and civic facilities. The antonym of *new town* is *organic community,* one that simply develops to whatever scale and density are forged by the independent market. New towns are self-regulated to a maximum scale, density, and overall population. They also are based on prearranged construction schedules, often called phases. New towns differ from subdivisions in their scale, autonomy, balanced land use, and economic independence from preexisting cities. Commentators differ about whether to categorize retirement and recreational communities as new towns. New towns may be sponsored by the government, the private sector, or a combination of the two. One sponsor must act as principal developer. Twentieth-century new towns in both the United Kingdom and the United States are indebted to the pioneering works of Sir Ebenezer Howard and the Garden City movement. The earliest U.S. example was Radburn, New Jersey, founded in 1928. Under Franklin D. Roosevelt's 1935 Emergency Relief Act, the national level experimented with three new towns called greenbelt communities — Greenbelt, Maryland; Greenhills, Ohio; and Greendale, Wisconsin. The Atomic Energy Commission (AEC) sponsored Los Alamos, New Mexico; Oak Ridge, Tennessee; and Richland, Washington. The Tennessee Valley Authority (TVA) built Norris, Tennessee; Boulder City,

Nevada, also was federally sponsored. In 1968 Congress passed Title IV of the Housing and Urban Development (HUD) Act, 42 U.S.C. 3901, which established the New Communities Act. In 1970, this was modified by Title VII of the HUD Act, called the Urban Growth and New Community Development Act, 42 U.S.C. 4501. Under these programs, the national level funded many nascent projects, such as Flower Mound, Texas, and Jonathan, Minnesota. In the Nixon-Ford era, HUD cut off all funding, accepted no more applications, foreclosed on the seed money projects, and canceled all further involvement. Some of the projects had developed into modest-scale communities, such as Forest Park South, Illinois, with a population of about 6,000. The major new American communities since the 1950s were sponsored by private developers on large parcels, namely Irvine Ranch, California; Columbia, Maryland; Las Colinas, Texas; and Reston, Virginia. Columbia is confined to a population of about 30,000 and Reston to about 20,000. The only major example of a federally funded U.S. new town remains Washington, D.C. Some new towns, such as Battlement Mesa, Colorado, were victims of the collapse of shale oil production in the aftermath of the energy crisis of the 1970s. *See also* BROADACRE CITY; CIRCULATION PLAN; GARDEN CITY; GREENBELT; GROWTH MANAGEMENT; LEVITTOWN; OPTIMUM CITY; PLANNED UNIT DEVELOPMENT; TRAFFIC ANALYSIS; WASHINGTON, DISTRICT OF COLUMBIA.

Significance　　New towns in the United Kingdom date back to the 1909 Housing and Town Planning Act. This was substantially rewritten in the 1946 New Towns Act. With more of a concern for regional development and preservation of agriculture and with centralized commitment, projects in the United Kingdom have been a major but not unqualified success. The opposite is the case in the United States. The key to successful American new towns has been large land acquisition, targeted in growth corridors in proximity to good transportation. Private developers have been more successful than public efforts. The local level plays a critical role in attracting infrastructure funding through tax-exempt interest rates. Excluding recreational communities, estimates place the number of U.S. new towns at about 120. The major advantages of new towns are prevention of urban sprawl and reduction of commuter travel. New towns serve as a natural laboratory for social planning and technological innovation. Those residents most attracted to the towns are young, white, middle-class, and upwardly mobile. The best future for new towns in the United States is in growth corridors on beltways near major, established metropolitan areas that can cultivate a broad-based economy and appeal to both a residential and a business population.

Suggested Reading

Clapp, James A. *New Towns and Urban Policy: Planning Metropolitan Growth.* New York: Dunellen Publishing, 1971. (Chap. 3 on definitions.)

Corden, Carol. *Planned Cities: New Towns in Britain and America.* Beverly Hills: Sage Publications, 1977.

Miller, Zane L. *Suburb: Neighborhood and Community in Forest Park, Ohio, 1935–1976.* Knoxville: University of Tennessee Press, 1981.

Murray, William A. "New Communities: In Search of CIBOLA—Some Legislative Trails." *Urban Law Annual,* vol. 12 (1976), pp. 177–219.

Nicoson, William. "Institutional Innovation in New Towns: The Dual Developer Concept." *Fordham Urban Law Journal,* vol. 4, no. 1 (1975), pp. 65–89.

Osborn, Frederick, and Arnold Whittick. *New Towns: Their Origins, Achievements and Progress,* 3rd ed. Boston: Routledge & Kegan Paul, 1977. (Analysis of 28 new towns in the UK since 1946.)

Rubenstein, James M. *The French New Towns.* Baltimore: Johns Hopkins University Press, 1978.

Steiner, Frederick. *The Politics of New Town Planning: The Newfields, Ohio Story.* Athens: Ohio University Press, 1981. (Case study of a failed new town.)

Whelan, Robert K. "New Towns: An Idea Whose Time Has Passed?" *Journal of Urban History,* vol. 10, no. 2 (1984), pp. 195–209.

New York City Bailout   A 1975 plan developed to save New York City from bankruptcy. The near-default and subsequent bailout of the city symbolized the urban fiscal crisis that many municipalities faced during the early 1970s. By that time, the scale of New York's municipal debt was staggering. Almost $13 billion was needed in 1975 just to deal with short-term loans, cope with cash-flow needs, and finance minimum services and required capital projects. Because the city was unable to deal with its financial problems and private banking consortia could not finance such a large amount of debt, the State of New York took the lead in creating a plan to rescue the city. The plan included federal and state funding, as well as substantial state-level decision-making authority over the city's finances. *See also* FISCAL CRISIS; MUNICIPAL ASSISTANCE CORPORATION; URBAN CRISIS.

Significance   The bailout of New York City illustrated many of the political and economic problems facing large urban centers during the 1970s. At a time when demand for city services continued to grow, federal funding to cities decreased dramatically. The energy crisis of 1973 further exacerbated the fiscal problems that New York City was experiencing. Because the city has symbolized the best and worst of large U.S. urban centers, its near-bankruptcy brought many political, economic, and social issues to a head. Critics of New York's administration felt that the city's problems were mostly of its own making; they warned that a bailout would merely encourage mismanagement in other municipalities. Supporters who favored assistance to the city argued that difficulties in the nation's most highly populated city obligated support by both the federal and New York State governments, especially because many of the city's fiscal problems were not the fault of the city itself, nor could those problems be solved by the city alone.

Suggested Reading
Benjamin, Gerald, and Charles Brecher. *The Two New Yorks: State-City Relations in the Changing Federal System.* New York: Russell Sage, 1989.
Shefter, Martin. *Political Crisis/Fiscal Crisis: The Collapse and Revival of New York City.* New York: Basic Books, 1987.

Nonconforming Use   A zoning term designating land that on the date the zoning ordinance became effective was and continues to be employed for a function not subsequently allowed by law. To be legally nonconforming either all or part of the land must be employed for a prohibited use by that date. Nonconforming use cannot be made retroactive. To allow the nonconforming use to continue, the zoning board may issue a *special variance* or the ordinance may issue a *blanket variance*. The variance is issued to preserve the constitutionality of the overall zoning law. To do otherwise would make the nonconforming use an implied government taking and deprive the nonconforming use owner of his or her rightful benefit of the land. Such land may be grandfathered into the code and allowed to stand so long as the use does not change. Zoning ordinances may provide that nonconforming uses can also be phased out after a reasonable time, such as 30 years. *See also* TAKING; VARIANCE; ZONING CLASSIFICATION.

Significance   A nonconforming use does not shield a user-owner from other police power regulations affecting health, safety, morals, and general welfare. For example, a used car lot in a residentially zoned area must comport with ordinances that regulate hours of business and types of visual barriers. A drive-in theater located within a residential area can be regulated with regard to its use by patrons according to time. After passage of a city's first zoning ordinance, it is possible for close to half of all land to be nonconforming. Legal nonconforming uses run with the land and are not affected by changing ownership. Nonconforming use issues are some of the most frequently litigated zoning questions.

Nonpartisan Election   A ballot in which candidates for office are prohibited by law from being identified by party affiliation. The opposite of *nonpartisan* is *party column,* sometimes called the Indiana-type system, in which all candidates are identified by the party that nominated them. An office block ballot stresses the position and may or may not allow party affiliation. Some elections are mixed, with the council selected nonpartisan and executives designated by party. In Chicago, for instance, the mayor is elected on a partisan ballot at the same time that aldermen are selected on a nonpartisan ballot. *See also* OFF YEAR; REFORM GOVERNMENT.

Significance   Nonpartisan elections were part of the progressive reform movement at the turn of the century. Most common nonpartisan positions are judges (17 of 33 statewide systems), school boards (about 85 percent), and municipal officials (about 75 percent), including such major jurisdictions as Atlanta, Dallas, Detroit, Denver, Houston, Phoenix, San Antonio, and Seattle. All the county elections in California and Wisconsin are nonpartisan. The original intent was to curb the influence of political machines, including their bosses, and hence eliminate corruption. In the 1980s Republicans were the chief beneficiaries of this reform, because Democrats dominated central-city partisan elections at higher levels. Good-government groups, also known as "goo-goos," also fill the vacuum left by the absence of the major parties. The argument for nonpartisan elections is that there is no Republican or Democratic way to collect refuse, only a technically efficient way. In the attempt to separate administration from politics, it is assumed that municipal services are administered equitably by class and section of the community, a fact challenged by the service delivery literature. Wealthy candidates are favored by this reform; in the absence of party cues, candidates with the most financial resources can achieve the highest name recognition. Not all cities with nonpartisan ballots are in fact fully free of partisanship, because parties may act behind the scenes. Also, nonpartisan candidates may have campaigned as partisans at another level in previous contests.

Suggested Reading

Hawley, Willis D. *Nonpartisan Elections and the Case for Party Politics.* New York: John Wiley, 1973.
Welch, Susan, and Timothy Bledsoe. "The Partisan Consequences of Nonpartisan Elections and the Changing Nature of Urban Politics." *American Journal of Political Science,* vol. 30, no. 1 (1986), pp. 128–139.

Oakland Project   A University of California at Berkeley liaison with the city of Oakland from 1965 to 1973, designed to render service to officials and the community based upon participant observation and policy analysis. The Oakland Project allowed Professor Aaron Wildavsky to train his graduate students in lifelike situations. Graduate students worked in particular departments and developed new theories in public administration, such as implementation of intergovernmental programs. Oakland became a case study for urbanologists. *See also* CASE STUDY; CHICAGO SCHOOL; PERMANENT COMMUNITY SAMPLE.

Significance   The Oakland Project was a valuable experience for the city in that it benefited from expertise, which would have cost substantial amounts if it had been supplied by conventional consultants. The University of California also gained from the experience by using the city as an urban laboratory and fulfilled three of its missions: research, service to the community, and teaching. Six books and a host of articles came out of the project. Oakland is not included as one of the 62 cities in the University of Chicago Permanent Community Sample (PCS). Along with New Haven, Connecticut, where some of the California political scientists studied, Oakland is overrepresented in the professional literature, relative to its population.

Suggested Reading
Kramer, Ralph M. *Participation of the Poor: Comparative Community Case Studies on the War on Poverty.* Englewood Cliffs, NJ: Prentice-Hall, 1969. Chap. 4, "Community Case Study of the Oakland Economic Development Council."
Levy, Frank S., Arnold J. Meltsner, and Aaron Wildavsky. *Urban Outcomes: Schools, Streets, and Libraries.* Berkeley: University of California Press, 1974.

Meltsner, Arnold J. *The Politics of City Revenue.* Berkeley: University of California Press, 1971.

Pressman, Jeffrey L. *Federal Programs and City Politics: The Dynamics of the Aid Process in Oakland.* Berkeley: University of California Press, 1975.

Pressman, Jeffrey L., and Aaron Wildavsky. *Implementation: How Great Expectations in Washington Are Dashed in Oakland.* Berkeley: University of California Press, 1973.

Thompson, Frank. *Personnel Policy in the City: The Politics of Jobs in Oakland.* Berkeley: University of California Press, 1975.

Occupancy Permit   An approval by a local code official, in writing and kept on file, verifying that a building or structure complies with the type of construction and uses for which it was intended. The complete Building Officials and Code Administrators' (BOCA) national building code term for occupancy permit is *certificate of use and occupancy.* In addition to certificates for new buildings, code officials also issue permits for altered structures, changes in use, and temporary occupancy. An occupancy permit is the final stage in the public review procedure for a new building. After successful completion of a final building inspection, an owner makes formal application for a certificate of use and occupancy. Code officials usually have ten days or one work week either to issue or to deny the permit. Denials can be appealed to a court if no other administrative remedies are available. If weather or press of a move require it, landscaping may be postponed even if there are drainage problems. The owner may be required to post a performance bond to ensure that work will be completed. *See also* ABANDONMENT; CORRUPTION, GOVERNMENT; GENTRIFICATION.

Significance   Failure to secure an occupancy permit has major ramifications in case of a later fire or injury suit. Owners are vulnerable to liability if they did not conform to government standards. Squatters generally are removed from abandoned buildings under color of trespass; but if they claim to be homesteading, they could be removed for failure to secure an occupancy permit. Because many buildings were grandfathered into a zoning code as nonconforming at the time of the ordinance's passage, any subsequent change in use gives the code official administrative discretion to deny the new use. Over time, any city has buildings that need to be retrofitted for a second and third use, from one industrial classification to another, from commercial to storefront church, or from warehouse to marginal commercial development. The city's chief control over this private-sector land-use change is its power to withhold occupancy permits. It also gives inner cities leverage over remodeling standards by the gentry. This new wave of in-migrants must conform to building codes upgraded from the more lax standards in use during the period of initial construction. A nearly completed structure represents a large investment to the mortgage holder. Any delay in securing the occupancy permit causes strains. This may tempt the owner or city official to a bribe in order to secure the permit.

Off Year   A 12-month calendar period in which there is no presidential election. *On years* are presidential election periods in a cycle of every four years in multiples of four relative to the year 2000. National off-year elections are on a cycle of two years in an even-numbered sequence at four-year intervals in which all the House of Representatives and one-third of the Senate are elected. Less than one-fifth of municipal elections are set to correspond with the on-year cycle. *See also* AT-LARGE ELECTION; ELECTIONS, TYPES OF; NONPARTISAN ELECTION; REFORM GOVERNMENT.

Significance   Off-year elections produce lower voter turnout than on-year contests. This is because off-year contests generally are less convenient for the voter. Off-year elections focus on local issues and candidates; this was the thinking of the progressive reformers who proposed it. National and sometimes even state political coattails are not factors because there is no other contest at that election.

Official Newspaper   A designated, general serial publication in which a local unit of government, under a constitutional, statutory, or charter requirement, promulgates competitive bids, ordinances, and other legal advertisements, such as public meetings, resolutions, and notices of elections. Official newspapers are usually printed in sheet form and circulated within the community. They may be sold or circulated free. They may be published weekly, biweekly, or more frequently. The jurisdiction making the announcement must acknowledge itself as the originator and sponsor. *See also* CLERK; PROMULGATE.

Significance   An official newspaper announcement puts a resident on notice that an ordinance has been passed and will be enforced on a date certain. Absent this announcement, the resident has not been duly notified, and ignorance of the law becomes an excuse. Open deliberations are only as available to public inspection as the government makes them by announcing their times and places. The thrust of sunshine statutes is to make the public aware that government is not operating in *executive session,* that is to say, closed to the public. Any governmental meeting that is subject to the rays of sunshine statutes but is not properly announced in an official newspaper can be voided later by a court of law. Payment of official government notices is a major source of revenue for many local newspapers. A city's threat of taking its publication business to a competitor can be used by politicians to solicit better news coverage.

Ombudsman   Originally, a Scandinavian-designed, legislatively sponsored, civilian complaint office that conventionally reports to the legislature. The Swedish term for representative or delegate is *ombud*. The city or county ombudsman office in the United States was designed to receive and act on the complaints of residents about their dissatisfaction with public services in their jurisdiction. Some states have opened an office of the ombudsman either to hear complaints against state-level public administrators or specifically to hear complaints by businesses having problems securing state permits or complying with state-mandated regulations. Two of the earliest ombudsman offices were at the county level in Nassau County, Long Island, New York, and Maui County, Hawaii. There is at least one joint city-county ombudsman, in Dayton–Montgomery County, Ohio. King County, Washington, formerly shared one with Seattle. Uncompromised U.S. city ombudsman offices exist in such cities as Anchorage, Alaska; Berkeley, California; Jamestown and New York City, New York; and Wichita, Kansas. Newark's ombudsman was established by ordinance, whereas in Michigan, Detroit's ombudsman was created by charter. Typically, the office hears complaints, investigates those felt to warrant such action, and proposes either remedial individual or *pre facto* overall action. Its forte is in correcting administrative, not policy, grievances. The annual ombudsman report summarizes activity by volume, complaint type, and disposition. Detroit's annual report carefully notes a pattern of complaints over the years, citing the persistence of resident grievances about such problems as refuse collection, abandoned vehicles, and abandoned buildings.

Significance   The city and county ombudsman is a movement whose time appears to have passed. Most of the ombudsmen were created in the 1960s after initial defeats in such cities as Philadelphia, New York, and Washington, D.C. An ombudsman must be an impartial investigator responsible to the legislature and free to make recommendations about both the particular participating incident and overall procedure. Surrogates for the ombudsman include neighborhood city halls, civilian complaint review boards for police, the legislative aides of state and national legislators, private newspaper and electronic media troubleshooters, and Better Business Bureaus. There are also ombudsmen in hospitals, prisons, universities, and state government.

Suggested Reading

Angus, William H., and Milton Kaplan. "The Ombudsman and Local Government." In Stanley V. Anderson, ed., *Ombudsman for American Government.* Englewood Cliffs, NJ: Prentice-Hall, 1968.

Caiden, Gerald E., ed. *International Handbook of the Ombudsman: Evolution and Present Function,* 2 vols. Westport, CT: Greenwood Press, 1983.

Hyman, Drew. "Citizen Complaints as Social Indicators: The Negative Feedback Model of Accountability." *Ombudsman Journal,* no. 6 (1987), pp. 47–64.

Rowat, Donald C. *The Ombudsman Plan: Essays on the Worldwide Spread of an Idea.* Toronto: McClelland and Stewart, 1973.

Open Space   Any land under public or private ownership upon which there is minimal above-ground development or none at all. Open space is not a single land-use category; rather, it encompasses arboretums, beaches, cemeteries, floodplains, forest preserves, greenbelts, hunting preserves, recreational parks, wetlands, and wilderness areas. As a matter of public policy, open spaces have several interrelated purposes, including protecting the environment, ensuring aesthetics, affecting crime rates, controlling density, managing growth, and accommodating outdoor recreation. *See also* CEMETERY; GARDEN CITY; GREENBELT; LAND, RAW; LAND, VACANT URBAN; LAND BANKING; LAND CONSERVANCY; PARK, RECREATION.

Significance   Open space has a value to urban dwellers, because it represents a pause in the bustle of urban life. However, maintaining open space and paying for it through taxes will always be major issues. Devices used to achieve open space include purchase, private deed restrictions, public easements, exactions from developers, land banking, planned unit developments (PUDs), state-level land-use laws (as developed in Oregon, Maine, and Vermont), and, most commonly, zoning classification.

Suggested Reading

Foresta, Ronald A. "Comment: Elite Values, Popular Values, and Open Space Planning." *Journal of the American Planning Association,* vol. 46, no. 4 (1980), pp. 449–456.

Platt, Rutherford H. *Open Land in Urban Illinois: Roles of the Citizen Advocate.* DeKalb: Northern Illinois University Press, 1971.

Shomon, Joseph James. *Open Land for America: Acquisition, Safekeeping, and Use.* Baltimore: Johns Hopkins University Press, 1971.

Wagenlander, James F. "The Urban Open Space Game." *Urban Lawyer,* vol. 6, no. 4 (1974), pp. 950–976.
Whyte, William H. *The Social Life of Small Urban Spaces.* Washington, DC: Conservation Foundation, 1980.

Optimum City   The best or most favorable size and type of local government. The question of what constitutes the optimum city is as old as classical Greek political thought and, for more than 2,500 years, has encompassed two issues. The first is the ideal population for city life. The second is the most desirable distribution of power for both the mass and the elite in governing such a community. The classical Greek answer of Plato was a *polis,* or city-state, which it is estimated consisted of about 30,000 citizens (as opposed to residents). The *polis* was governed by a republic with widespread public awareness and broad public participation. *See also* BROADACRE CITY; GROWTH MANAGEMENT; NEW TOWN; URBAN CRISIS.

Significance   There has been a twentieth-century revival of interest in the optimum population size and density for a city. Architect Frank Lloyd Wright in the 1920s pondered the proper size community, its density, and leadership style in his extensive writings on Broadacre City. Otis Dudley Duncan and Amos Hawley, two sociologists, wrote about size and economies of scale in the 1940s and 1950s. Political scientist Robert A. Dahl in the 1960s and 1970s was in favor of a city with a population range from 50,000 to 2,000,000 in order to maximize quality of life in terms of meaningful political participation and useful political socialization. The range also captures the economies of scale for such urban amenities as museums and libraries. Smaller populations, such as villages, do not nurture enlightened political participation because outcomes are trivial and factions develop. On the other hand, larger population concentrations such as conurbations and Consolidated Metropolitan Statistical Areas (CMSAs) do not allow for any other than the most limited form of voting. Advocates of optimum population scale favor either antigrowth or slow-growth positions and the planning of new towns with population caps and density restrictions.

Suggested Reading
Dahl, Robert A. "The City in the Future of Democracy." *American Political Science Review,* vol. 61, no. 4 (1967), pp. 953–970.
Dahl, Robert A., and Edward R. Tufte. *Size and Democracy.* Stanford, CA: Stanford University Press, 1973.
Duncan, Otis Dudley. "Optimum Size of Cities." In Paul Matt and Albert Reisse, eds., *Reader in Urban Sociology.* Glencoe, IL: Free Press, 1951.

Hawley, Amos. "Metropolitan Population and Municipal Government Expenditures in Central Cities." *Journal of Social Issues,* vol. 7 (1951), pp. 100–108.
Rogers, Andrei, and Jeffrey G. Williamson. "Migration, Urbanization, and Third World Development: An Overview." *Economic Development and Cultural Change,* vol. 30, no. 3 (1982), esp. pp. 477–481. (Overurbanization.)

Ordinance   A government rule passed at a substate level by a county commission, township board, or city or village council. The analogue of an ordinance for the national and state legislature is a statute. Ordinances are based on the police power, a common-law concept designed to promote the public's health, safety, morals, welfare, well-being, or aesthetics. As local public rules, ordinances must be passed in open meetings and announced in a publication such as an official newspaper, the contents of which must always be available for public inspection. When organized systematically, ordinances become part of a code. Ordinances must go into effect on some designated enforcement date after being published, although actual enforcement may be delayed to accommodate the public. An ordinance can impose either criminal or civil penalties but must in either instance specify an enforcing office. *See also* ENFORCEMENT DATE; POLICE POWER; PROMULGATE.

Significance   Not all local units are sanctioned to adopt the same types of ordinances. Home-rule cities have wider discretion in passing ordinances than do legislatively chartered cities. The state may also differentiate a city's capacity to pass ordinances based upon city size. Ordinances are low in the hierarchy of laws and must comport with city charter provisions and state statutes as well as the state constitution. An ordinance that once was deemed permissible may later be revoked and that power transferred to another level by the state legislature, because it is the state alone that has the general power to define the boundary of the police power. It is the responsibility of the judiciary to review actual conflicts of law that arise as cases, or controversies between ordinances and higher levels of law. In each decision, the court will decide in favor of the higher law over the ordinance if the higher level preempts the field. Local units also can pass *resolutions,* which may cover such topics as setting a tax rate or passage of a budget. Resolutions are used for implementing ministerial functions for short-term purposes. Topics covered by ordinances include direct commands of conduct, laws governing regulations of conduct for businesses and households, and land-use plans.

Outside Influence   An individual or group that is not a member of a local community and that agitates for a new political agenda or attempts to polarize the community. Such people or groups often use confrontation and fear to keep the heat on a highly publicized issue. These hell-raisers—or, more neutrally, "activists"—encourage conflict and high levels of publicity, intending to disrupt the prevailing power base with tactics such as boycotts, trespassing, sit-ins, or even stock-proxy wars with community-based corporations. When used by insiders, the term is assumed to be pejorative, because they assume that only homegrown policy is legitimate. Those opposed to outside influence call it *radical,* a term suggesting extremism, with a tendency toward violence and irrational demands.

Significance　　Many leaders and groups fall within this umbrella designation as an outside influence, and in fact the groups often generate their attack from another community. They counter that in a democracy every group has protected free speech and right to peaceable assembly. ACORN, Association of Community Organization for Reform Now, indeed uses confrontational tactics on behalf of the poor and dispossessed. The most celebrated example was Saul Alinsky, a CIO organizer with John L. Lewis in the 1930s. Alinsky became a community organizer in Chicago's Back of the Yards and Woodlawn neighborhoods; he was also a gadfly in Oakland, California, and in Rochester, New York, against Eastman Kodak. There are also radical American architects who believe in "advocacy planning" on behalf of the poor and disfranchised against central business districts (CBDs), institutionally sponsored city planners, and real estate speculators. Radical planners typically stress the city as polluter and as institutional racist in its promotion of urban renewal and interstate highway construction projects that may destroy viable ethnic settlements.

Suggested Reading
Alinsky, Saul. *Reveille for Radicals.* New York: Random House, 1969.
———. *Rules for Radicals: A Practical Primer for Realistic Radicals.* New York: Random House, 1971.
Bailey, Robert, Jr. *Radicals in Urban Politics: The Alinsky Approach.* Chicago: University of Chicago Press, 1972, 1974.
Lancourt, Joan E. *Confront or Concede: The Alinsky Citizen Action Organizations.* Lexington, MA: Lexington Books, 1979.
Reitzes, Donald C., and Dietrich C. Reitzes. *The Alinsky Legacy: Alive and Kicking.* Greenwich, CT: JAI Press, 1987.

P

Paratransit   Forms of urban transportation provided by small, non–fixed-wheel vehicles designed to meet individual needs through flexible scheduling and routing. Paratransit is primarily provided by the private sector, although public transportation authorities sometimes supply components. Examples include route-deviated bus and minivan service, limousine, share-ride taxi, dial-a-ride bus, and car pooling. *See also* MASS TRANSIT.

Significance   Urban mass transit in the United States accounts for less than 3 percent of passenger miles traveled. Well-coordinated paratransit feeds into mass-transit systems like capillaries off veins and major arteries. Most paratransit services are equipped for the special needs of the handicapped, thus providing precious mobility to an otherwise homebound ridership. Often the elderly are serviced also by paratransit. To be effective, the system often needs coordination from a transit authority, a major employer, or a service group, as in the case of servicing convalescent homes and senior citizens.

Suggested Reading
Kirby, Ronald F., et al. *Para-transit.* Washington, DC: Urban Institute, 1974.

Park, Industrial   A tract of land that is planned and zoned for light manufacturing, warehousing, and allied functions. Industrial parks are confined to those *industrial districts* — or industrial estates, as they are known in the United Kingdom—that feature environmental amenities. These amenities usually include low-density, single-story construction with substantial setbacks, maintained landscaping, and centrally provided security. Well-planned industrial parks limit both parking and outside storage. The key element in a park's location is access to transportation. Early examples were clustered around the

374

railroads. Those built more recently developed around interstate expressways and air terminals. With the advent of just-in-time delivery techniques, suppliers have had to keep larger inventories available near their major customers, increasing the number of industrial parks adjacent to final assembly plants. About 70 percent of industrial parks are privately owned and managed for a profit. In some cases, after a park is subdivided, parcels may be sold to individual companies. In addition to several not-for-profit parks, some are owned by public authorities or city agencies and designed to promote and direct local growth. There are many other types of urban parks, including educational parks, office parks, recreational parks (the original type), research parks, and mobile home parks.

Significance   Industrial parks first were developed in the United Kingdom and the United States in the late 1890s. Most of the development in industrial parks came after World War II. Every state except Wyoming presently has at least one designated industrial district. Most do not utilize all their land; hence parks functionally serve as land banks. They are underbounded and were developed in part to anticipate long-term industrial development. The largest urban industrial park in the United States is the Almonaster-Michoud Industrial Corridor, covering approximately 12,000 acres in New Orleans. Only Michigan, through its Department of Commerce, certifies industrial parks through a rating system based on factors such as infrastructure, transportation links, and in-place amenities. The major advantage of industrial parks is that they do not leave industrial plant location to chance. Parks come equipped to offer industries a complete package of services, from in-place roads, utilities, and buildings to properly zoned land and adequate vehicular parking. One impact of industrial parks has been to decentralize industry, especially the clean, so-called footloose, small-scale units. They have fled central cities and located in suburbs or the urban fringe on less expensive land. Those parks located near residential areas serve to shorten the commute for some employees. Metropolitan Chicago has more than 350 industrial parks, most in the suburbs. The five-county Detroit metropolitan area has only 23 certified industrial parks meeting guidelines of the Michigan Industrial Development Association and State Department of Commerce. Interested builders and developers are organized by the National Association of Industrial and Office Parks (NAIOP). Since 1970 they have published *Development*, a quarterly magazine, from their Arlington, Virginia, headquarters. Industrial parks are not appropriate locations for heavy industry with very large-scale operations because they take up all of an assembled site and are not concerned with parklike amenities.

Suggested Reading
Marak, Robert J. "The Biggest Industrial Park of All." *Planning,* vol. 48, no. 5 (1982).

Park, Mobile Home   A location where two or more manufactured homes may rent space offering utility connections for long-term occupancy on a dedicated parcel. Mobile home parks are also known as trailer courts, mobile home villages, and mobile home tracts. Mobile homes are more properly known as manufactured homes. The antonym of all these is *immobile housing.* Most modern manufactured homes are transported to a site on axles, set up on blocks, and rarely moved thereafter. Mobile homes, on the other hand, can be moved by large equipment. Manufactured homes are differentiated from modular homes that are prefabricated, moved to a location on separate trailers, and fastened permanently to a foundation. Recreation vehicles are self-propelled. Building codes appropriate for immobile homes are inappropriate for mobile homes. Modular homes often meet a third type of code standard for construction. Mobile homes on-site can be regulated under local police powers regarding health and safety standards and can be set apart physically in their own enclosures with greater density levels, as close as 20 feet apart. States regulate the maximum size of a mobile home that can be towed on a public road to some limits such as 14 feet wide by 80 feet long. On-site they may measure 28 feet wide by 80 feet long when two units are assembled. The federal government has set standards for safety under the National Mobile Home Construction and Safety Act of 1974, 42 U.S.C. 5401. A *trailer campground,* on the other hand, is a location for short-term sojourns, limited to some maximum period such as 30 or 90 days. *See also* BUILDING CODES; MANUFACTURED HOME; ZONING CLASSIFICATION.

Significance   Mobile home parks are controversial because they do not usually yield the same tax that would derive from immobile home construction. Many states tax the owner of the park land on which the mobile home sits along with any amenities but not the homes themselves, which yielded a sales tax when purchased. Most states recognize mobile home parks as a rational land-use category and allow for their enumerated inclusion and licensing in a master plan. Most cities that have tried to prohibit mobile homes *per se* have had their ordinances voided as overbroad and arbitrary. Mobile homes constituted about 10 percent of all new U.S. home construction as of the late 1980s. They are often starter houses for young families. Landlords typically charge rent on the mobile home park site. With an insufficient land supply in many urban areas, landlords are in a position to gouge homeowners unless regulated by ordinance or state statute. Some communities that are free of mobile homes achieved that status by simply having platted land so expensive that it was not feasible for developers to consider the option. Cities that impose minimum home size effectively discourage mobile homes being set up on individual platted subdivision lots. They are thus indirectly prohibited. Every state has copious litigation on mobile home parks, from questions of outright prohibition to challenges of individual homes. There has been a long tradition of resistance from adjacent residential lot owners trying to preserve their low density, their tax base, and their perceived aesthetic standards. Owners of immobile homes manipulate zoning standards and other police power regulations for their advantage.

Suggested Reading

Berry, Rita L. "Restrictive Zoning of Mobile Homes: The Mobile Home Is Still More 'Mobile' than 'Home' under the Law." *Idaho Law Review*, vol. 21, no. 1 (1985), pp. 141–164. (The author opposes exclusionary mobile home parks and favors viewing mobile homes as manufactured homes.)

Park, Recreation   Any open area designated for public use. Recreation parks usually contain some landscape or ornamentation and some amenities such as outdoor furniture. In U.S. law, parks are defined as either enclosed or demarcated and open to the public for their health and well-being. Previously known as squares or commons, recreation parklands are exempt from property tax as being of general community benefit. Not all parks are owned and maintained by a unit of government; some are held in individual trusts or as a land conservancy. Large park tracts removed from urban areas and maintained by the Department of the Interior or the Department of Agriculture are known as national parks, national forests, and grasslands. Parks are found in all sizes, from vest-pocket scale to vast waterfronts, parkways, riverbanks, floodplains, pedestrian ways, and nature paths. Parks are created by voluntary dedication, city acquisition, condemnation, urban renewal, or historic designation. *See also* AMENITIES; CITY BEAUTIFUL; MACHINE SPACE; QUALITY OF LIFE.

Significance   Recreation park land acquisition and maintenance are low priorities in cities confronted by a fiscal crisis. Patrolling parks consumes more police time than other types of comparable urban land-use acreage. Yet open spaces with the amenities of fresh air and light are important to most urban dwellers, who often are confined most of the day to high-density interior environments. Open space is considered a major public asset. A well-landscaped park system for every community was the goal of the prominent early American landscape architect Frederick Law Olmsted. Open admission to all is considered a democratizing influence of city parks. Park utilization is directly related to proximity, so that placement of parks adjacent to population concentrations is as important as park design, maintenance, and police surveillance. Cities situated on waterways have two options for using their waterfronts: either they can face the water and encourage general public access, or they can plan commercial uses of the waterfront for shipping and discourage public access. The national government assists local communities with park development through Army Corps of Engineers–designated floodplain land, upon which permanent buildings are often barred. In the 1960s and 1970s, the Department of Housing and Urban Development aided cities in securing land through the Open Space Land Act for recreation and nonorganized outdoor use, 42 U.S.C. 1500 et seq. The Department of the Interior, Bureau of Outdoor Recreation, and the National Seashore Recreation Areas program have preserved public access to large-scale open spaces near urban areas. Most of the responsibility for urban parkland acquisition and maintenance falls on substate levels. Because as much as half of some central business district land consists of machine space, it is not so much the amount of open land that is important but the fact that it is specifically dedicated to human use for renewing the human spirit.

Suggested Reading

Cranz, Galen. *The Politics of Park Design: A History of Urban Parks in America.* Cambridge, MA: MIT Press, 1982. (1850–present.)

Gold, Seymour M. *Recreation Planning and Design.* New York: McGraw-Hill, 1980.

Hecksher, August, with Phyllis Robinson. *Open Spaces: The Life of American Cities: A Twentieth Century Fund Essay.* New York: Harper & Row, 1977.

New York City Department of Parks and Recreation and Central Park Conservancy. *Rebuilding Central Park: A Management and Restoration Plan.* Cambridge, MA: MIT Press, 1986.

Park, Research   An area set aside for multiple-tenant facilities that focus on pure and applied science. Most research parks are affiliated with universities. They are often concerned with basic understanding or technological transfer in medicine, aerospace, computers, or defense. Tenants are interested in Research, Development, and Engineering (RD&E). The forerunner of today's research park was Menlo Park in West Orange, New Jersey (presently located in Edison Township), where inventor Thomas A. Edison worked. Examples of such parks include Research Triangle Park in Triangle Park, North Carolina; Stanford Research Park in Palo Alto, California; and Northwestern/ Evanston Research Park in Evanston, Illinois. *See also* GROWTH POLITICS; INCUBATOR; POSTINDUSTRIAL CITY; PUBLIC-PRIVATE PARTNERSHIP.

Significance   Research parks are a twentieth-century innovation, first developed in the 1960s. They are primarily established to nurture clean economic growth associated with well-paying white-collar employment. Many research facilities are abetted by local economies through tax abatements and property tax exemptions. These advantages are offered in anticipation of later multiplier effects that may establish a new tax base analogous to what computer chip manufacturing did for Silicon Valley in California or computer research has done for the ring road around Boston. With manufacturing jobs diminishing in the United States, it is better for cities and universities to spawn new technology than to foster smokestack industry. The parks are nationally organized by the Association of University Related Research Parks. There are also a few freestanding facilities. Of more than 50 examples in operation in the late 1980s, half of all tenants were directly involved in R&D, with many other tenants servicing those positions. Many industrial parks are not located in urban areas (as was the case with Menlo Park), because many university sponsors are not located in substantial-sized central cities.

Suggested Reading
Farley, John, and Norman J. Glickman. "R&D as an Economic Development Strategy: The Microelectronics and Computer Technology Corporation Comes to Austin, Texas." *Journal of the American Planning Association*, vol. 52, no. 4 (1986), pp. 407–418.

Park Thesis   An analysis holding that the modern city is best viewed as an environment in which a variety of communities interact and relate to their physical environment. The Park Thesis is named for American sociologist Robert Ezra Park (1864–1944), who took his Ph.D. in Germany in 1904 and borrowed Ernest Haeckel's ecological model of the study of plant and animal communities. Park asserted that individuals function primarily as members of various groups and largely have a spatial sense of community. Park eventually headed up the University of Chicago School of Human Social Ecology. His approach treated individuals primarily as parts of collectivities. Thus, he stressed community, invasion of one group by another, dominance, segregation, succession, territoriality, and zones of transition. He is best known for his theory that race relations are based on a cycle of competition, conflict, accommodation, and finally assimilation. He referred to spatially specific areas as subcommunities or natural areas; in the parlance of plant ecology, these correspond to niches. *See also* CHICAGO SCHOOL; COMMUNITY; COMMUNITY FACT BOOKS; HUMAN ECOLOGY, INVASION; SUCCESSION; ZONE OF TRANSITION.

Significance   The Park Thesis was a spatially based analysis of group behavior in an ever-changing city. Urban ecologists studied the internal forces of community and neighborhood and the external competition of groups within the same confined environment. In addition to the symbiotic relationships of communities, Park stressed that what makes human environments unique is their capacity to communicate with other groups as well as with their own community; hence the emphasis on the migrant press, the black press, and the neighborhood press from later Chicago-trained sociologists. Few students of urban areas employ human ecology today because it has not proved particularly fruitful in understanding race relations, public-policy formulation, or the role of political forces, such as political parties and legislatures. Human ecology is apolitical and largely devoid of insight into economic forces. Many of the individual Park-inspired studies involve the *ecological fallacy*; that is to say, they make statistical inferences about individuals, assuming the average/median/mode in an area is indicative of individual behavior, when in fact specific individuals are arrayed across a continuum of positions. Location may or may not have played a role in their behavior.

Suggested Reading

Entrikin, J. Nicholas. "Robert Park's Human Ecology and Human Geography." *Annals of the Association of American Geographers,* vol. 70, no. 1 (1980), pp. 43–58.
Goist, Park Dixon. "City and Community: The Urban Theory of Robert Park." *American Quarterly,* vol. 23, no. 1 (1971), pp. 46–59.
Raushenbush, Winifred. *Robert E. Park: Biography of a Sociologist.* Durham, NC: Duke University Press, 1979.
Young, Gerald L., ed. *Origins of Human Ecology.* Stroudsburg, PA: Hutchinson Ross Press, 1979.

Participation   Actions of the mass of citizens who attempt to influence or support government policies and political processes. Urban participation embraces all those activities of the mass, as opposed to elites, that make an impact on local politics and government. *Urban,* as opposed to *rural,* is an independent variable in participation studies by sociologists and political scientists. The amount of participation is greatest in communities with high-status residents who feel well integrated into their neighborhoods. Ethnic neighborhoods with strong community cohesion often have high participation despite low status. Direct participation of the electorate is possible in New England town meetings. Coproduction, or joint rendering of urban services, is a direct form of participation, as are urban protest events and riots. But most mass-citizen participation is indirect through voting for others. The community power literature of the 1950s and later was in part an analysis of how much power the mass had in governing cities. The New Left ideological emphasis on maximum feasible participation was another element in demanding greater mass action. The study of citizen-initiated complaints is yet another form of inquiring into community mass action. *See also* CITIZEN ADVISORY BOARD; CITIZEN-INITIATED CONTACTING; COPRODUCTION; ELECTIONS, TYPES OF; MAXIMUM FEASIBLE PARTICIPATION; OMBUDSMAN, CITY; OPTIMUM CITY; TOWN MEETING.

Significance   Participation is one of the major elements in political theory. From earliest Greek thought to the present, the question of the optimum city has resolved itself into two questions: What is the ideal type of structure in which people can meaningfully participate? and What is the ideal scale or population size that encourages participation? Direct participation in New England town meetings was ruled out as a viable option for most cities as their population increased past 5,000. In the 1950s and 1960s, political scientists concentrated on national voting as the *sine qua non* of mass political participation, slowly increasing the ambit of their perception of participation to include other conventional forms such as campaign work, service on boards, and running for office. Even unconventional participation forms such as protests were added to the continuum of political participation. Constructive participation as a desirable goal is a major concern holding together such divergent groups as the League of Women Voters, advocacy planning architects, Old Leftists in the mold of Saul Alinsky, and New Leftists. Since most residents find the community most directly relevant to their lives, participation will typically have the greatest meaning at the community, suburban, or urban level.

Suggested Reading
Conway, M. Margaret. *Political Participation in the United States*, 2nd ed. Washington, DC: Congressional Quarterly Press, 1990.
Edwards, John N., and Allan Booth, eds. *Social Participation in Urban Society.* Cambridge, MA: Schenkman Publishing, 1973.
Hutcheson, John D., Jr. "Citizen Representation in Neighborhood Planning." *Journal of the American Planning Association*, vol. 50, no. 2 (1984), pp. 183–193. (One of three participation articles in the issue.)
Kramer, Daniel C. *Participatory Democracy: Developing Ideals of the Political Left.* Cambridge, MA: Schenkman Publishing, 1972.

Milbrath, Lester W., and M. D. Goel. *Political Participation: How and Why Do People Get Involved in Politics?* 2nd ed. Chicago: Rand McNally, 1977. (A synthesis of empirical findings.)

Nagel, Jack H. *Participation.* Englewood Cliffs, NJ: Prentice-Hall, 1987.

Thomas, John Clayton, ed. "Symposium: Citizen Participation and Urban Administration." *Journal of Urban Affairs,* vol. 5, no. 3 (1983).

Patronage, Urban   Favors bestowed by local government and political officials as a political reward. Patronage is not conducted in the public interest but as a personal right of the grantor. It is synonymous with favoritism. Narrowly defined, patronage is the power of elected and political party officials to fill appointed positions with their supporters. The patron is usually an elected official; the employee becomes the client. Broadly defined, patronage is the power to reward those who contribute to the party with inducements, whether in the form of salaried jobs, contracts, or symbolic awards. Patronage is also known as the spoils system and was at its height at all government levels in the nineteenth-century era of the party boss and local machines. It was based on the assumption that to the victor belongs the spoils. If patronage is defined narrowly, then a distinction is made with *preferments,* the prerogative accruing to elected office to dispense advantages, such as steering public business to selected law, architectural, and planning firms. Some county executives and mayors have the prerogative to appoint lobbyists, cable television boards, and special assessors. Trial judges use patronage in many systems through discretionary appointment of receivers, guardians, and overseers. *See also* BOSS; REFORM GOVERNMENT; SET-ASIDE; URBAN POLITICAL MACHINE.

Significance   However defined, patronage was the *sine qua non* for the maintenance of machine politics. It cemented loyalty by maximizing votes in hopes of material reward. Patronage allowed bosses to control line bureaucracies. In the early twentieth-century era of progressive reforms, patronage declined but did not disappear. Major reasons for the eclipse include creation of the civil service system, competitive and open bidding, union contracts forbidding layoffs based on partisan litmus tests, and case law. Two of the most important cases were decided by the U.S. Supreme Court. In the Cook County Chicago sheriffs' case of *Elrod v. Burns,* 427 U.S. 347 (1976), the high bench prevented the firing of employees below the policy-making level based on partisan grounds. In *Branti v. Finkel,* 445 U.S. 507 (1980), the court extended the reasoning to prevent elected officials from removing assistant public defenders based on tests for partisan loyalty. What remains of patronage in most urban American areas is a form of symbolic dispensation in which elected officials appoint party faithful to blue-ribbon boards with no or only nominal honoraria. In the broad meaning of patronage, small insurance contracts are exempt from competitive bids and hence available for use as patronage. Mayors and councils with substantial set-aside contract provisions use those provisions for rewards, provided they are not subject to qualified, lowest-bidder provisions.

Suggested Reading

Banfield, Edward C., and James Q. Wilson. *City Politics.* Cambridge, MA: Harvard University Press, 1965. Chap. 11, "Reform."

Johnson, Michael. "Patrons and Clients, Jobs and Machines: A Case Study of the Uses of Patronage." *American Political Science Review*, vol. 73, no. 2 (1970), pp. 385–398. (Case study of CETA jobs in New Haven, Connecticut, a practice that ended with the termination of CETA.)

Sorauf, Frank J. "State Patronage in a Rural County." *American Political Science Review*, vol. 50, no. 4 (1956), pp. 1046–1056. (Case study of Center County, Pennsylvania, a practice which largely ended in the early 1970s.)

Sorauf, Frank J., and Paul Allen Beck. *Party Politics in America*, 6th ed. Glenview, IL: Scott, Foresman, 1988. Chap. 4.

Pension Fund Politics   Policy decisions that determine fringe benefit contributions by local governments, funding levels in anticipation of actual payouts, and levels of pension benefits relative to current compensation. Pension fund politics focuses on collective bargaining decisions that have a delayed impact on the local government's budget. Not all pension funds are well monitored or require annual public reports. Decisions to allow early-retirement incentives can negate the integrity of otherwise secure programs. An increased city contribution to a pension fund costs the present administration little in current expenditures. *See also* DIVESTMENT; FISCAL CRISIS; NEW YORK CITY BAILOUT; SINKING FUND.

Significance   More than 10 million local employees are covered by government pension funds into which billions of tax dollars have been invested. As much as one-fifth of a city budget may be accounted for by contributions to pension funds. The funds may be invested in conservative treasury notes or in higher-risk stocks. Empirical studies have found most cities responsibly adding to investment pools relative to future drawing levels based on reasonable market return rates and anticipated fringe package negotiations. However, some pensions are underfunded for mechanical reasons dealing with poor investment management, improper actuarial assumptions, inadequate disclosure regulations, or unanticipated early vesting rights. Political reasons for underfunding are heavily based on the expediency of increasing pension levels in present contracts that will not come due until the next official is in office. Major signs of fiscal strain in a budget are underfunding of either pensions or sinking funds. Major underfunding has been an issue in New York City and Los Angeles. In the Detroit enclave of Hamtramck, a federal judge took control of the city budget to mandate adequate pension funding levels in order to compensate for past neglect. One of the major sources of corruption in the Central States Teamsters Union has been tampering with pension funds. So far, this has not occurred in a major city's fund. Some pension funds may not invest in stocks of corporations that do business with apartheid-dominated South Africa because of divestment laws. Public employee pensions are not covered by Title IV of the Employee Retirement Income Security Act, 29 U.S.C. 1301 et seq. The Pension Benefit Guaranty Corporation only guarantees private plans.

Suggested Reading

Ferris, James M. "Funding Local Public Employee Pensions: One City's Tale." *Journal of Urban Affairs*, vol. 6, no. 3 (1984), pp. 67 ff. (Los Angeles's fire and police funds.)

Love, James Packard. *Economically Targeted Investments: A Reference for Public Pension Funds.* Sacramento, CA: Institute for Fiduciary Education, 1989. (Sponsored by the Ford Foundation, this is a short summary of the issues involved in social investments with retirement funds.)

Webster, Charles, and Ellis Perlman. "Employee Retirement as a Growing Urban Problem." *Journal of Urban Affairs*, vol. 6, no. 1 (1984), pp. 53–67.

Permanent Community Sample (PCS)   A sample of 62 U.S. cities, ranging in population from New York City down to communities of 50,000 and representing 22 states and all regions. The sample cities have been studied since 1967 by the National Opinion Research Center (NORC) of the University of Chicago. The permanent sample began as 51 cities, augmented by information on parent counties. It later was enlarged to the present size. This large undertaking was funded by the National Science Foundation. It contains two major types of information: material collected from printed sources, such as the census, and completed field-staff interview schedules. Cities sampled are proportionate in size to places of residence of the U.S. population as a whole, so as not to bias the sample in favor of small communities. The six most highly populated central cities are included, along with many suburbs and some freestanding smaller communities. The PCS thus generates consistent economic, social, and political information that addresses policy issues over time. Examples of studies include those on city structure and decision-making style, the role of communities in responding to group demands, and the level and severity of city fiscal stress. Not all principal investigators are affiliated with the University of Chicago. Data analysis is sophisticated and sensitive to measurement error. The 62 PCS cities are:

1. Akron, OH	32. Manchester, NH
2. Albany, NY	33. Memphis, TN
3. Amarillo, TX	34. Milwaukee, WI
4. Atlanta, GA	35. Minneapolis, MN
5. Baltimore, MD	36. New York, NY
6. Berkeley, CA	37. Newark, NJ
7. Birmingham, AL	38. Palo Alto, CA
8. Bloomington, MN	39. Pasadena, CA
9. Boston, MA	40. Philadelphia, PA
10. Buffalo, NY	41. Phoenix, AZ
11. Cambridge, MA	42. Pittsburgh, PA
12. Charlotte, NC	43. St. Louis, MO
13. Chicago, IL	44. St. Paul, MN
14. Cleveland, OH	45. St. Petersburg, FL
15. Clifton, NJ	46. Salt Lake City, UT
16. Dallas, TX	47. San Antonio, TX
17. Detroit, MI	48. San Diego, CA
18. Duluth, MN	49. San Francisco, CA
19. Euclid, OH	50. San Jose, CA
20. Fort Worth, TX	51. Santa Ana, CA
21. Fullerton, CA	52. Santa Monica, CA
22. Gary, IN	53. Schenectady, NY
23. Hamilton, OH	54. Seattle, WA
24. Hammond, IN	55. South Bend, IN
25. Houston, TX	56. Tampa, FL
26. Indianapolis, IN	57. Tyler, TX
27. Irvington, NJ	58. Utica, NY
28. Jacksonville, FL	59. Waco, TX
29. Long Beach, CA	60. Warren, MI
30. Los Angeles, CA	61. Waterbury, CT
31. Malden, MN	62. Waukegan, IL

See also CASE STUDY; CHICAGO SCHOOL; COMPARATIVE URBAN ANALYSIS; PLURALISM; REPUTATIONAL ANALYSIS.

Significance   The Permanent Community Sample overcomes the weakness inherent in any case study: the possibility of analyzing an atypical city. Yet the PCS does not forfeit the benefits of case study detail for the greater rigor of quantitative work because the NORC follows up annually with updated information and field tests in select cities. For example, the NORC did fieldwork in South Bend, Indiana, and Waukegan, Illinois, to verify aggregate information. Hundreds of reports, including many books, have been based on the PCS. Information goes beyond the anecdotal to the generalizable assertion. It allows ten or more dependent variables to be analyzed in one study with directly comparable research in true comparative fashion. Information on the PCS is available from the National Opinion Research Center, 1155 East 60th Street, Chicago, Illinois 60647-2799.

Suggested Reading
Clark, Terry Nichols, and Lorna Crowley Ferguson. *City Money: Political Process, Fiscal Strain, and Retrenchment.* New York: Columbia University Press, 1983. (App. 1 details the PCS.)

Planned Unit Development (PUD)   A discretionary land-use control that permits clustering of residential, commercial, or industrial functions, created to achieve environmentally sensitive designs and open or parklike spaces. PUDs were created in the 1960s as an alternative to the more rigid Euclidean zoning. Model PUD laws were written by the Urban Land Institute in 1964 and by the American Society of Planning Officials in 1974. They are allowed overtly in more than ten states and are in use without formalities in others. PUDs replace zoning board reviews and master plan processes with administrative-builder bargaining. Most PUDs apply to five acres or more and stress mixed land use with flexible separation of use boundaries. Findings of fact, design standards, traffic studies, and density concessions all enter into this surrogate for conventional zoning. *See also* INFILLING; ZONING.

Significance   PUDs are a flexible response to the rigid land-use categories set up by Euclidean zoning. Conventional zoning must accommodate change also, and hence zoning boards issue variances. Compatible land-use mix is still ensured by PUD governmental review. Developers save money on land costs, and cities attempt to avoid tracts of overly homogeneous housing. Variants on PUDs include Planned Industrial Developments (PIDs), Planned Unit Residential Developments (PURDs), Special Use Districts (SUDs), and Planned Commercial Districts (PCDs). Small-scale PUDs promote infilling in older suburbs and central cities by making land more attractive to developers. PUDs supplement conventional zoning; they do not replace the need for master plans and land-use designations.

Suggested Reading
Dugan, John M. "Memphis Cottons to PUD." *Planning*, vol. 47, no. 1 (1981), pp. 19–22.

Moore, Colleen Grogan. *PUDs in Practice.* Washington, DC: Urban Land Institute, 1985.

Procos, Dimitri. *Mixed Land Use: From Revival to Innovation.* Stroudsburg, PA: Dowden, Hutchinson & Ross, 1976.

Sternlieb, George, et al. "Planned Unit Development Legislation: A Summary of Necessary Conditions." *Urban Law Annual,* vol. 7 (1974), pp. 71–200. (p. 74 contains alternative definitions from Illinois statute and California case law.)

Planning, Advocacy   Systematic advance preparation of counterproposals in land use by professionals on behalf of a disfranchised group or community of limited resources, in contradistinction to an official agency proposal. Advocacy planning was a product of the 1960s, when land design specialists realized that city-sponsored and large, corporate-favored schemes frequently ran counter to the needs and interests of those living in the area. Typically, advocates work for reduced wages or for free, performing their tasks *pro bono publico,* for the public good. This was part of a movement encompassing alternate budgeting (counterbudgets) as well as antiestablishment land-use plans (advocacy planning), which pitted consultants on both sides of such controversies as the national budget priorities and local highway expansion proposals. It culminated symbolically in a counterinauguration at the opening of the second Nixon administration (1973). *See also* CODES OF ETHICS; PLANNING, URBAN PHYSICAL; UNDERCLASS; YONKERS-STYLE POLITICS.

Significance   Advocacy planning derived from the realization that official proposals are vested interests, often favoring major developers at the expense of the lower or underclass. When physical planners and architects realized they were espousing the racist cause of whites in the 1970s in Yonkers, New York, by keeping minorities isolated in one section, some professionals concluded there should be a pluralism of views expressed. Advocacy planners invoke the American Institute of Planners' Canons and Rules of Discipline, which demand that members primarily serve the public interest and that they exercise independent professional judgment. Likewise, when highway design teams in Boston realized the disruption that crosstown expressways caused to urban communities in the name of rationalized transportation, some backed off from the official plan and advanced counterproposals to save viable communities from displacement.

Suggested Reading
Benson, Robert S., and Harold Wolman, eds. *The National Urban Coalition Counterbudget: A Blueprint for Changing National Priorities 1971–1976.*

New York: Praeger, 1971.
Blecher, Earl M. *Advocacy Planning for Urban Development.* New York: Praeger, 1971. (Note: Both the counterplanning and advocacy planning books were published the same year by the same house.)
Davidoff, Paul. "Advocacy and Pluralism in Planning." *Journal of the American Planning Association,* vol. 31, no. 4 (1965), pp. 331–337.
Goodman, Robert. *After the Planners.* New York: Simon & Schuster, 1971.
Heskin, A. D. "Crisis and Response: A Historical Perspective on Advocacy Planning." *Journal of the American Planning Association,* vol. 46, no. 1 (1980), pp. 50–63.
Krunholtz, Norman, and Janice Cogger. "Urban Transportation Equity in Cleveland." In Barry Checkoway and Carl V. Patton, eds., *The Metropolitan Midwest: Policy Problems and Prospects for Change.* Urbana: University of Illinois Press, 1985. Chap. 10, pp. 211–228.

Planning, Contingency   An attempt to establish guidelines to cope with the uncertainty and risk that result from natural or man-made disasters. Contingency planning is assigned conventionally to a civil defense or emergency preparedness office. It is designed to coordinate such first-response groups as police, fire, public works, and hospital facilities. Management techniques in such planning include coordination of tasks, establishment of priorities, crowd control, prevention of looting, and preparing a common voice for statements to the media. Among common natural disasters that can be planned for are blizzards, earthquakes, floods, hurricanes, tornadoes, and volcanoes. Common man-made disasters include nuclear-plant meltdowns, air crashes into urban areas, natural gas explosions, and gasoline shutdowns. *See also* AGENDA SETTING; EMERGENCY EVACUATION; FEDERAL EMERGENCY MANAGEMENT AGENCY.

Significance   On paper, most cities and counties have formal disaster plans, although they often are given low priority. Once an emergency strikes, there is no assurance the communities will learn from their experiences. The national government is set up to respond to such local disasters through the Federal Emergency Management Agency (FEMA). Academic analysis is conducted at the University of Delaware Disaster Research Center. The United States of America responds to foreign disasters through the U.S. Foreign Disaster Assistance Program.

Suggested Reading

International Journal of Mass Emergencies and Disaster, vol. 1, no. 1 (1983).
Karetz, Jack D., and Michael K. Lindell. "Planning for Uncertainty: The Case of Local Disaster Planning." *Journal of the American Planning Association,* vol. 53, no. 4 (1987), pp. 487–498.

Meyer, Michael D., and Peter Belobaba. "Contingency Planning for Response to Urban Transportation System Disruptions." *Journal of the American Planning Association,* vol. 48, no. 4 (1982), pp. 454–465.
Quarantelli, E. L., ed. *Disasters: Theory and Research.* London: Sage Publications, 1978.
Wright, J. D., and Peter H. Rossi. *Social Science and Natural Hazards.* Cambridge, MA: Abt Books, 1981.

Planning, Focal-Point   A form of physical planning in which large-scale developments are coordinated by a lead governmental agency through a common forum. Focal-point planning brings together all parties—public and private—concerned with a building project that is regulated by a series of overlapping jurisdictions. Instead of securing approvals serially, the developer can do so in a batch. Examples of national agencies involved in coordinated efforts include the Army Corps of Engineers, Federal Emergency Management Agency (FEMA), and the U.S. Department of the Interior Fish and Wildlife Service. State-level units include departments of natural resources and state highway planning agencies. Regional bodies include floodplain districts, Councils of Governments (COGs), and school districts, especially if tax deferrals are involved. City-level bodies include zoning and planning boards and public-private corporations. Three examples where focal-point planning has worked are the Nevada-California multipurpose Tahoe Regional Planning Agency, the New York Adirondack Park Agency, and the San Francisco peninsula San Bruno Mountains conservancy. *See also* BALKANIZATION; GROWTH MANAGEMENT.

Significance   Focal-point planning is able to reconcile with much greater dispatch the permits and approvals needed for major developments. At the same time, public interests are well represented by direct dealings with developers' plans. This form of coordination is not well advanced in most balkanized metropolitan jurisdictions, where, for example, circulation plans often cannot be discussed until floodplain approval has been secured, being contingent on both local planning and zoning approval, which awaits an Environmental Impact Statement (EIS). Growth-management advocates favor focal point planning because it focuses attention on the project and strengthens public interest positions through mutual reinforcement. Developers favor it because it potentially expedites the process of securing all approvals. Major opponents of focal-point planning are advocates of the *status quo* who use the seriatim approval approach to gain repeated delays.

Suggested Reading
Marsh, Lindell L. "Using Focal-Point Planning for Land-Use Decisions." *Practical Real Estate Lawyer,* vol. 1, no. 3 (1985), pp. 57–66.

Planning, Social   Long- and short-term, public and private, systematic advance preparation for the noneconomic needs of individuals and groups. Social planning is sometimes labeled *social engineering,* a term that carries strong negative connotations. As a denotation, it describes activities at every level of American government including the national Social Security program, which is a forced-contribution insurance system for the elderly, survivors, and the disabled. Another example of national social planning is Project Head Start, an early education-enrichment program. Creation of scattered-site public housing is another. Insofar as the national income tax intentionally redistributes income, it, too, is a form of social planning. Local social planning has long been an unintended aftermath of physical planning. This was based on the assumption of physical determinism that once the built environment improved, social pathologies would diminish because of improved amenities and aesthetics. Major current examples of local social planning are zoning ordinances and school attendance boundaries, topics that are closely interrelated. Decisions about where to house the developmentally disabled and halfway house ex-convicts are other examples. Two of the major physical-planning decisions with well-known social ramifications are whether to encourage or manage population growth and whether to promote public transit. There is no sharp division between social and physical planning. Snob zoning keeps out most minorities and all lower-class residents. Interdistrict metropolitan busing integrates schools. Balkanized suburbanization predictably creates fiscal disparities between school districts. Social planning often hides behind the names of "efficiency standards" and "neutral" physical-planning decisions. *See also* CITY BEAUTIFUL; COMBAT ZONE; DEMONSTRATION CITIES AND METROPOLITAN DEVELOPMENT ACT; GROWTH MANAGEMENT; NEW TOWN; PLANNING, ADVOCACY; *SOUTHERN BURLINGTON COUNTY NAACP V. MT. LAUREL* ; ZONING.

Significance   Charges of social planning or "social engineering" are serious attacks on local programs when leveled by ideological conservatives. Other critics argue that social planning is inherent in modern, paternalistic government. There is little consensus about the proper role of the local community in promoting the social equality (leveling) of races, ethnic groups, or classes. One reason for large-scale eleemosynary activity in the United States is the reluctance of many Americans to champion overtly the state as a proper instrument in promoting family planning. A major social-planning issue of the 1990s is optimum population scale and the desirability of having that population relatively stable in terms of class and race composition. To many, for a city council to look the other way on the issue of adult entertainment is preferable to the option of openly creating a combat zone. Professional physical planners are aware that their proposals are not ethnically neutral. Most, however, profess that their institutional patrons' middle-class values carry acceptable social ramifications.

Suggested Reading

Bolan, Richard S. "Social Planning and Policy Development." Chap. 18 in Frank S. So et al., *The Practice of Local Government Planning*. Washington, DC: International City Management Association, 1979, pp. 521–551.
———. "Social Planning and Policy Development in Local Government." Chap. 4 in Wayne F. Anderson et al., eds., *Managing Human Services*. Washington, DC: International City Management Association, 1977, pp. 85–127.
Coleman, Alice. "The Social Consequences of Housing Design." In Reian Robson, ed., *Managing the City: The Aims and Impacts of Urban Policy*. Totowa, NJ: Barnes & Noble, 1987. Chap. 7.
Dyckman, John W. "Social Planning in the American Democracy." In Ernest Erber, ed., *Urban Planning in Transition*. New York: Grossman Publishers, 1970.
Frieden, Bernard J., and Robert Morris, eds. *Urban Planning and Social Policy*. New York: Basic Books, 1968. Part I: Approaches to Social Planning.
Gans, Herbert J. "Regional and Urban Planning: Planning, Social." In David L. Sills, ed., *International Encyclopedia of the Social Sciences*. New York: MacMillan, 1968, pp. 129–137.
Rein, Martin. "Social Planning: The Search for Legitimacy." In Daniel Patrick Moynihan, ed., *Toward a National Urban Policy*. New York: Basic Books, 1970. Chap. 18, pp. 206–237.

Planning, Strategic   Top management decision making designed to maximize conditions by adapting the organization to its changing, competitive environment. Strategic planning was initiated by the military, which, by definition, has the most hostile environment in which to operate. It was also developed as an approach by the private-capital sector, most especially by General Electric in the 1950s and 1960s. It differs from conventional master planning in that the focus shifts from internal efficiency and rational-comprehensive decision making to external probable and possible trends. Strategy refers to decisions made by generals, chief executive officers, and, by extension, mayors. As applied to urban politics it is long-term and citywide in scope. The sequential process assumes a mission statement or other given goals, a carefully developed set of forecasts about extraterritorial or external events, and a capacity to implement plans in order to counter threatening events. *See also* FORECAST; GOAL SETTING; PLANNING, URBAN PHYSICAL.

Significance   Strategic planning is a twentieth-century U.S. innovation that promotes long-term flexible and reactive goal setting. After being developed by the private sector for more than two decades, by the 1980s it was adopted in half the states, primarily as a technique to foster select economic growth. For example, Delaware's Office of State Planning and Coordination uses strategic planning in criminal justice, economic development, environmental management, and infrastructure maintenance and design. Because strategic planning embraces several approaches, it is practiced differently in the several cities, most of which are highly populated. Two chief advantages are said to be a holistic and long-term orientation to both internal and external forces. Critics point out the U.S. private sector is backing off from strategic planning's heavy staff orientation. It had useful but limited application for cities such as San Francisco and Albany, both in the 1980s. The process is said to produce a conservative, progrowth bias but neglects the bargaining process with its questions of equity and redistribution.

Suggested Reading

Bryson, John M. *Strategic Planning for Public and Nonprofit Organizations: A Guide to Strengthening and Sustaining Organizational Achievement.* San Francisco: Jossey-Bass, 1988.
———. "Symposium: Strategic Planning." *Journal of the American Planning Association,* vol. 53, no. 1 (1987), pp. 6–69.
Harmon, Keith, and Charles R. McClure. *Strategic Planning for Sponsored Project Administration: The Role of Information Management.* Westport, CT: Greenwood Press, 1985.
Kemp, Roger L., ed. *America's Cities: Strategic Planning for the Future.* Danville, IL: Interstate Printers and Publishers, 1988.
Swanstrom, Todd. "The Limits of Strategic Planning for Cities." *Journal of Urban Affairs,* vol. 9, no. 2 (1987), pp. 139–157.
Walter, Susan, and Pat Choate. *Thinking Strategically: A Primer for Political Leaders.* Washington, DC: Council of State Planning Agencies, 1984.

Planning, Urban Physical   Systematic preparation through rational decision making of land use in accord with legal guidelines, local public objectives, and areawide conditions. Urban physical planning is concerned with all public and private land use from housing and industry through open space and transportation. In the United States the private sector performs many small-scale planning functions through developers. Public planning is carried on by both in-house staff and outside consultants. Activities range from the practical aspects of checking for zoning conformity and subdivision controls through idealistic designs such as Frank Lloyd Wright's Broadacre City. Most technical planning is conducted by specially trained personnel, many of whom are members of the American Institute of Planners (AIP) or are certified on state registries. Policy planning functions are often conducted by boards or commissions composed of laypersons who report to the city council, or less often by planning departments that report to the city manager or mayor. Typical issues with which planners deal include demographic trends, economic base studies, infrastructure analysis, and implementation of planning through zoning ordinances, along with environmental and historic preservation. *See also* CITY BEAUTIFUL; EKISTICS; FORECAST; MASTER PLAN; PLANNING, STRATEGIC; ZONING.

Significance In the United States formal government physical planning is vastly less important than market forces in affecting the profile of the city's built environment. Most professional planners offer advice to elected officials accountable to the electorate. Physical planning is sponsored at the city, county, Council of Governments (COG), and state levels. Such planning cannot be divorced from politics because paper plans must be forged into working projects through such implementation tools as zoning, site plan review, issuance of building permits, and linkage agreements. Physical planning is grounded in traffic circulation patterns, recognition of topographic features, design of major amenities such as water and drainage, and the local political and judicial climate. Planners spend time on such activities as zoning and subdivision review, policy planning, economic development, urban design, environmental planning, demographic analysis, and housing studies and consulting. The functions physical planners want to perform include such activities as coordinating balkanized government decisions, serving as a liaison between developers and the community, designing urban spaces, and social advocacy on behalf of the poor and disfranchised. This is also called *advocacy planning*. The liberal critique of physical planning is that it is too entrenched in defense of the *status quo* and that it is ineffective in promoting minority causes and long-run thinking. On the other hand, the conservative critique of physical planning is that it improperly interferes with the supply and demand of the marketplace and violates rights vested in owners to dispose of their property for the highest and best use. In addition to formal training in civic design graduate schools, physical planners often have a background in architecture, law, civil engineering, and geography.

Suggested Reading
Altshuler, Alan A. *The City Planning Process: A Political Analysis.* Ithaca, NY: Cornell University Press, 1965.

Blowers, Andrew. *The Limits of Power: The Politics of Local Planning Policy.* Elmsford, NY: Pergamon Press, 1980.

Dluhy, Milan J., and Kan Chen, eds. *Interdisciplinary Planning: A Perspective for the Future.* New Brunswick, NJ: Center for Urban Policy Research, 1986.

Goodman, William, and Eric Freund, eds. *Principles and Practices of Urban Planning.* Washington, DC: International City Managers Association, 1968.

Morgan, David R. *Managing Urban America: The Politics and Administration of America's Cities.* North Scituate, MA: Duxbury Press, 1979. Chap. 10, "City Planning," pp. 260–293.

Rabinovitz, Francine F. *City Politics and Planning.* Chicago: Aldine Publishing, 1969. (Six-city analysis of physical planners.)

Scott, Mel. *American City Planning since 1890.* Berkeley: University of California Press, 1971.

Whittick, Arnold, ed. *Encyclopedia of Urban Planning.* New York: McGraw-Hill, 1974. (Comparative approach.)

Plunk   In an election, to vote for fewer candidates than the law allows in multiple-seat contests for the same office. Plunking is also known as *bullet voting.* Both share a common etymology of shooting or hitting a small target. In an extreme form, the elector votes for only one candidate on the entire ballot. In a less extreme case, the elector votes for one or fewer candidates than allowed and then passes on to make selections in other contests. Examples of plunking involve city council races and judicial contests with two or more seats to be filled.

Significance   An elector can plunk in a primary, runoff, or general election. The practice is most common when an entire board or council is simultaneously running at large. By voting for only one person, citizens are not expressing hostility against the other partisans or factions. They are simply using a voting tactic that aids their candidate by lowering the number needed to become a winner. Racial minorities and ethnic groups voting in large city elections for city council use the technique to help their own group's candidate.

Pluralism   A descriptive and prescriptive theory of power distribution and policymaking that argues political power is fragmented and widely distributed among a number of competing interest groups. The term is derived from the assumption that many plural elites, rather than a single power elite, determine urban public policy. The theory of pluralism has existed in some form for many years, but is most closely associated with Robert A. Dahl's 1961 publication of *Who Governs?*, a case study of decision making and power in New Haven, Connecticut. Using survey research data, census information, personal interviews, and participant observation, Dahl's team of researchers contended that, while different groups and individuals had different degrees of power, no one interest was able to dominate New Haven politics over an extended period. This case study was hailed as a direct refutation of the power elite studies conducted by Floyd Hunter, Robert and Helen Lynd, C. Wright Mills, and others. These power elite studies employed a "positional" or "reputational" method, as they equated power with positions assumed to be powerful, and they identified power holders by asking knowledgeable people about who wielded local political power. Though these power studies were conducted in U.S. cities, many attempts have been made to generalize to the national level. These national-level studies have included several different methods of approaching the study of power.

The controversy over power and its degree of distribution is based on how researchers have defined "power" and on the methods used to determine who wields it. Researchers who tend to be pluralists traditionally have been trained as political scientists. They emphasize decision-making processes and equate power with "influence." This method of inquiry has been termed "decisional," as compared to the "positional" or "reputational" analysis of Hunter, the Lynds, and other anthropologists and sociologists. Dahl's researchers investigated three issues in New Haven that they felt would shed the most light on the exercise of power in the city. The three issues were selected for their controversial natures, since it was felt these would reveal more about the political process. Dahl chose the issues of urban redevelopment, public education, and the partisan political nomination process. Both normative and empirical volumes have been written that claim to find support for pluralism or the power elite theories, or even for a separate theory such as the neo-Marxist perspective called structuralism.

The major tenets of pluralism are as follows: (1) Power is defined as influence in the decision-making process. (2) No one individual, group, or like-minded set of interests is able to dominate an issue area over an extended period of time. A group powerful on one issue will not be able to transfer that power to another issue. (3) Power is widely fragmented and distributed among interest groups and voters, which reflects the fragmentation of our policymaking institutions. (4) The average citizen can participate in the political process in meaningful ways through expression of public opinion, membership in an interest group, or by voting. The theories of power distribution in the United States first sought empirical verification through analyses of power in cities. Robert Dahl's pluralist conclusions about New Haven politics followed earlier studies of Atlanta, New York City, and a variety of individual small cities or clusters of cities around the nation. Later studies have attempted to account for various changes in city structure, demographic changes, and economic changes, each of which has affected power within cities. One study investigated the substantial changes in New York City's decision-making process after the state and federal governments stepped in with their 1975 joint bailout to avert the bankruptcy of the city. Other studies found that cities have become ungovernable, largely due to the excessive demands by too many interest groups that can effectively control "islands of power" within a city. This *hyperpluralism* identified in American cities is not so much a refutation of pluralism as it is a more recent report covering perceived changes in cities since the mid-1960s. Theodore Lowi (1967), Douglas Yates (1977), Frederick Wirt (1974), and Donald Haider (1979) are among the many researchers who have taken this approach. Robert Lineberry and Ira Sharkansky (1978) suggested the urban bureaucracy, as a third force in addition to business and political leaders, must be taken into account when investigating political power in a city. *See also* AGENDA SETTING; CASE STUDY; REPUTATIONAL ANALYSIS.

Significance   After more than 30 years of research and discussion, no conclusions have emerged between Dahl's and Hunter's backers. Many works that followed the initial power studies have sought to refine the original arguments or correct alleged methodological errors. Peter Bachrach and Morton Baratz argued that Dahl oversimplified power by ignoring non–decision-making power and agenda setting in a community. These "two faces of power" create a bias within the political process that limits the scope of issues to more or less "safe" concerns and restricts the alternative solutions to a narrow range of socially and politically acceptable choices. The voluminous work on "subgovernments" also has criticized Dahl's original assumption that a balance of power exists within the political system, at least at the national level. *Subgovernments,* or iron triangles, can effectively dominate policymaking for an extended period of time through control of the distributive policy process. A subgovernment system includes a dominant interest group or set of like-minded groups, along with the relevant committee or subcommittee members or their staffs, and bureaucratic agencies that implement the particular policy. The tobacco, oil, and defense procurement and contracting industries all have been used as examples of subgovernments at the national level of policymaking. At the local level, many observers point to unethical or illegal arrangements between elected officials and local businesses, particularly in highway contracting or solid-waste disposal.

Suggested Reading
Bachrach, Peter, and Morton S. Baratz. *Power and Poverty.* New York: Oxford University Press, 1970.

Clark, Terry N. *Community Power and Policy Outputs.* Beverly Hills: Sage Publications, 1973.

Crenson, Matthew. *The Un-politics of Air Pollution: A Study of Non-decision Making in the Cities.* Baltimore: Johns Hopkins University Press, 1971.

Dahl, Robert A. *Who Governs? Democracy and Power in an American City.* New Haven, CT: Yale University Press, 1961.

Haider, Donald. "Sayre and Kaufman Revisited: New York City Government since 1965." *Urban Affairs Quarterly,* vol. 15, no. 2 (1979), pp. 123–145.

Hawley, Willis D., and Frederick M. Wirt, eds. *The Search for Community Power,* 2nd ed. Englewood Cliffs, NJ: Prentice-Hall, 1974.

Jennings, M. Kent. *Community Influentials: The Elites of Atlanta.* Glencoe, IL: Free Press, 1964.

Rose, Arnold M. *The Power Structure: Political Process in American Society.* New York: Oxford University Press, 1967.

Waste, Robert. *Community Power.* Beverly Hills: Sage Publications, 1988.

Yates, Douglas. *The Ungovernable City: The Politics of Urban Problems and Policy Making.* Cambridge: MIT Press, 1977.

Poletown (Detroit, Michigan)   An area in east-central Detroit that became the site for the General Motors (GM) Detroit/Hamtramck assembly plant. The term *Poletown* refers to the large Polish-American population that lived in this area before construction of the plant. The GM facility was completed in 1981 and produces the luxury models of the Buick, Oldsmobile, and Cadillac (B-O-C) divisions of General Motors. *See also* ENCLAVE; QUICK-TAKE LAW.

Significance   The construction of the GM plant in Poletown was the largest industrial-renewal project in U.S. urban history and represents one of the most important issues and symbols of urban redevelopment during the 1980s. The entire process whereby GM decided to build on 450 acres in a densely populated area of Detroit encompasses all of the major issues in the most recent phase of urban redevelopment policymaking in the United States: the competition by cities over business investment; the emerging importance of public-private authorities; increased state and local financing of private business projects; and publicly funded and executed site assembly and preparation and improvement of infrastructure prior to construction. The city's acquisition and demolition of homes, churches, local businesses, schools, and hospitals within one year, despite some neighborhood opposition, was upheld by the Michigan Supreme Court in *Poletown Neighborhood Council v. City of Detroit,* 410 Mich 616 (1981). The court ruled that even though this project would clearly benefit a private party, the overall project satisfied the public-purposes provision of eminent domain and economic development laws, since it would create jobs and bring investment into an economically distressed community. The long-term results for Detroit have been mixed, however. Only half of

the 6,000 projected jobs were created, and many of those were transfers from other plants. By 1987, the plant's second shift was laid off
indefinitely.

Suggested Reading

Fasenfest, David. "Community Politics and Urban Redevelopment: Poletown,
    Detroit, and General Motors." *Urban Affairs Quarterly*, vol. 22, no. 1
    (1986), pp. 101–123.
Jones, Bryan D., and Lynn W. Bachelor, with Carter Wilson. *The Sustaining
    Hand: Community Leadership and Corporate Power.* Lawrence: University
    Press of Kansas, 1986.
Wylie, Jeanie. *Poletown: Community Betrayed.* Urbana: University of Illinois
    Press, 1989.

Police, Private   Nongovernmental law enforcement organizations
in both the profit and not-for-profit sectors that function independently but in cooperation with public police agencies. Private police,
also known as "rent-a-cops," perform such diverse services as security,
protection, traffic control, investigation, detection, and guarding.
Most states require private police to be incorporated and to register
with some bureau responsible for licensing and regulation. The same
city neighborhood may be patrolled by as many as three police systems: public, private, and neighborhood watch. Private police do not
have the same limits on jurisdictional boundaries that local public
police units must obey. They operate both in uniform and in plain-
clothes. They are usually organized as paramilitary units. Many private police operations cooperate with public counterparts; some limit
their liaison activity and do not share information. Major examples of
nationally organized private police organizations include Brinks, Inc.,
the National Automobile Theft Bureau, and the Pinkerton Agency.
See also COPRODUCTION; NEIGHBORHOOD WATCH; POLICE, PUBLIC; PRIVA-
TIZATION; PUBLIC SAFETY, DEPARTMENTS OF.

Significance   In some urban jurisdictions there are as many as three
times more private police than their public police counterparts.
In many urban areas private security guards write more parking tickets than the public police because "rent-a-cops" are often assigned
to the city's largest parking structures and lots. Private police personnel are generally not as well trained or as well disciplined as their
public counterparts. They are generally paid low wages, have higher
turnover, and do not have the same opportunities for in-service training. Private police recruited from among retired public-duty officers
may be as well trained as conventional forces, but they are neither as
young nor as agile. "Rent-a-cops" are not accountable to the public by

way of a departmental chain of command and *ipso facto* are more organized for efficiency and profit and less concerned with public welfare. Yet they reduce taxes by shifting the burden of salaries to private businesses or to public institutions that pay for them out of increased fees and tuition. A major unresolved public-policy issue is under what conditions a city should ask an institution—whether it be a fast-food restaurant, college, or hospital—to take responsibility for its own security and thereby shift costs from all taxpayers to institutional overhead.

Suggested Reading
Germann, A. C., Frank D. Day, and Robert R. J. Gallati. *Introduction to Law Enforcement and Criminal Justice*, rev. ed. Springfield, IL: Charles C. Thomas, 1981. Chap. VIII, "Private Police and State Agencies."

Police, Public A governmental law-enforcement agency whose functions include prevention, detection, and investigation of crime as well as incarceration of criminals. Unlike the situation in most other nations, law enforcement by public police in the United States is highly decentralized. Three-fourths of all police officers serve under local jurisdiction, and all police jurisdictions are independent of each other with separate law-enforcement agencies at the local, county, state, and federal levels. At the local level, agencies performing law-enforcement duties can include city police departments, sheriff's departments, publicly financed campus police, and officers under the jurisdiction of transit, bridge, port, public housing, and special district authorities. In 1986, more than 12,000 city, county, and state police agencies employed more than 475,000 officers and 150,000 civilians. In some cases, state police may perform local criminal code enforcement in patrolling unincorporated areas or in assisting local police departments. Though decentralized, law-enforcement agencies cooperate in compiling crime statistics through the Uniform Crime Reports published by the Federal Bureau of Investigation. *See also* CRIME; GUN CONTROL, LOCAL; KERNER COMMISSION; POLICE, PRIVATE; POLICE REVIEW BOARD; PUBLIC EMPLOYEE STRIKE; PUBLIC SAFETY; STREET-LEVEL BUREAUCRAT.

Significance Professionalization of local public police forces in the United States increased substantially during the first part of the twentieth century. Over time, many public-policy issues have been raised regarding crime and law enforcement. After the Kerner Commission Report was released in 1968, concern over police-citizen relations resulted in calls for increased minority employment in law enforcement, the creation of police-community relations agencies, and citizen review boards of police behavior. During the 1960s and 1970s, public-employee unionism affected local employment and budgetary policy and played a mixed role in affirmative-action programs for minority employment in local police and fire departments. The 1970s also saw an increased investigation of the behavior of police officers as "street-level bureaucrats," those public employees having direct contact with citizens and with considerable discretion in interpreting public policy. During the late 1970s and early 1980s, budgetary cutbacks in many cities increased the demand for consolidation of police and fire work into departments of public safety. By the late 1980s, many police departments were calling for substantially larger budgets to hire more officers and purchase automatic or semiautomatic weapons to keep pace with the resources of many criminals.

Suggested Reading

Davis, Kenneth Culp. *Police Discretion.* St. Paul, MN: West Publishing, 1975.

Germann, A. C., et al. *Introduction to Law Enforcement and Criminal Justice.* 29th printing. Springfield, IL: Charles C. Thomas, 1981.

Goldsmith, Jack, and Sharon S. Goldsmith, eds. *The Police Community: Dimensions of an Occupational Subculture.* Pacific Palisades, CA: Palisades Publishers, 1974.

Grimshaw, Roger, and Tony Jefferson. *Interpreting Policework, Policy and Practice in Forms of Beat Policing.* Boston: Allen & Unwin, 1987.

Skolnick, Jerome H., and Thomas C. Gray, eds. *Police in America.* Boston: Little, Brown, 1975.

Slovak, Jeffrey S. *Styles of Urban Policing: Organization, Environment, and Police Styles in Selected American Cities.* New York: New York University Press, 1986.

Wilson, James Q. *Varieties of Police Behavior, The Management of Law and Order in Eight Communities.* Cambridge: Harvard University Press, 1968.

Police Power   A common-law concept, nowhere definitively defined, allowing the sovereign to rule on behalf of the community. In the United States, where localities are the product of state creation, the police power resides in plenary form at the state level and is allocated to localities at the pleasure of the authors of the state constitution or statutes. In the absence of state constitutional provision, police powers are vested in the state legislature. There is no general, federal common-law police power. The conventionally enumerated elements of the police power include but are not limited to regulations and services exercised on behalf of the community's health, safety, morals, welfare, and well-being. Other elements of the police power relate to maintaining the public's peace and sense of aesthetics. A private business affected by a public interest is subject to regulation under the police power as a public utility. Home-rule cities generally have more discretion in enforcing police powers than do legislatively chartered municipalities. The generalization in Dillon's Rule, holding that a police power not explicitly allocated is denied to the locality, is negated in part in the case of home-rule communities. Challenges about whether a locality is properly exercising a police power are appealable to the local legislature in the first instance, then to the state legislature, and most commonly to a state court. The state legislature may abrogate the authority of a locality to exercise a police power. That power then may be transferred to another level or branch or retained by the state legislature for its exclusive use. Court challenges to improper exercise of local police power usually are brought under the complaint that a local unit of government has acted *ultra vires,* beyond the proper scope and authority of its office. *See also* DILLON'S RULE; HOME RULE; PUBLIC UTILITY, TAKING; *ULTRA VIRES* ; ZONING.

Significance   Most local services and regulations are justified under color of the police power and cover the alphabetical gamut from alcoholic beverage controls (delegated to the states under the Twenty-first Amendment), building codes, curfews, demolition of dangerous buildings, environmental regulations, food inspection, garbage pickup, hotel regulation, indecent exposure laws, junkyard location, and so on, all the way to weed abatement, X-rated movie house location, yard-sale controls, and zoo site ordinances. Local and state police enforce portions of the police power, but so do the local building inspector, health nurse, and planning board. There is a fine line separating permissible public regulation of private property under the police power from impermissible public taking of private property without just compensation. There is an equally fine line between protected First Amendment free exercise of rights and state abridgment of those rights under the police power. The general proposition is that all five First Amendment rights are relative, not absolute, and are limited by the needs of the community to determine their proper exercise according to time, place, and manner. In both taking and First Amendment exercise issues, it is generally the courts that are asked to draw the line according to the facts of a particular case.

Police Review Board   A panel of citizens acting as mediators, investigators, and monitors of local police activity. Most police review boards are advisory in nature, with little or no actual power. *See also* DECENTRALIZATION; KERNER COMMISSION; LAW ENFORCEMENT ASSISTANCE ADMINISTRATION; POLICE, PUBLIC.

Significance   Police review boards were one reaction to the urban riots of the 1960s. Much criticism was directed at local police forces, which were often dominated by whites who were accused of brutality.

The increasing percentage of blacks moving into larger cities made the predominantly white police forces appear to be "occupation armies." In the aftermath of the riots, the Kerner Commission called for increased minority hiring and the creation of outreach programs to improve police-community relations. However, some research has concluded that police-community relations programs, especially in larger northeast and north-central cities, were often among the first to lose funding when police departments lost Law Enforcement Assistance Administration (LEAA) funding, and during the cutback period that many cities faced during the 1980s.

Suggested Reading

Hudson, James R. "Police Review Boards and Police Accountability." *Law and Contemporary Problems,* vol. 36, no. 4 (1971), pp. 515–538.

Kahn, Ronald. "Urban Reform and Police Accountability in New York City: 1950–74." In Robert L. Lineberry and Louis H. Masotti, eds., *Urban Problems and Public Policy.* Lexington, MA: D. C. Heath, 1975.

Steel, Brent S., and Nicholas P. Lovrich. "Police-Community Relations Programs in U.S. Cities: Did They Survive the Termination of LEAA and the Fiscal Crisis of the 1980s?" *American Journal of Police,* vol. 7, no. 1 (1988), pp. 53–80.

Politics   Actions, topics, or events over which the community exercises power. Politics is the public's business. In law, political questions refer to those topics over which the courts will not exercise judgment because they properly belong to the political branches, the legislature, and the executive. See *Luther v. Borden,* 7 Howard 1 (1848), and *Baker v. Carr,* 369 U.S. 186 (1962). In ethics, political issues refer to those values over which the larger community passes binding judgment in contrast with issues over which individuals exercise volition. In religion, the political realm refers to those things that belong to Caesar, to current worldly matters, and not the spiritual and permanent. In common discourse, politics concerns groups that have gone public with their concerns. In the United States, politics is the art of the possible. It is the activity of political parties. Thus, politics, in part, is a line-drawing contest delimiting private from public matters. For example, the right to drink alcohol before passage of the Seventeenth Amendment was private. As of 1919, it became a national public issue and was prohibited. In 1933, it was made a state-level public issue to be allowed or prohibited, or even passed down to the county or township for the exercise of a local option. Prohibition *politicized* a heretofore private issue, which later was partially *privatized.* The reverse process occurred over abortion. The several states had long politicized the issue by prohibiting or severely regulating the practice, whereas after 1973 in *Roe v. Wade,* 410 U.S. 113, the practice was partially privatized. *Public politics* is distinct from private politics of the church or office. Investing retirement funds in stocks is *above politics* and a matter of net return for some, while for others it is an issue of divesting funds in corporations that operate in apartheid South Africa. In many jurisdictions, local officials are elected on a nonpartisan ballot because they are not dealing with the political and partisan issues of the higher levels. People who have no political orientation whatsoever, amounting to about 1 percent of the total population, are called *apolitical.* Their actions, however, may have serious political overtones. The term *power politics* is redundant, because once an issue is in politics, it will be resolved by power plays. Politics is often synonymous with that which is self-serving; however, politics can also mean pursuit of the public interest. *See also* FEDERALISM; OUTSIDE INFLUENCE; POLICE POWER.

Significance   Politics is composed of compromise, conflict, and consensus. Those who define politics as the art of the possible stress compromise. Politics defined as factional fighting stresses conflict. Politics defined as consensus building among pluralistic communities stresses accommodation. From the mayor's chair, two community associations differing over the need for a new road are in conflict. From the position of the association leader, the community association represents consensus. Both are correct and partial views. Structural functionalists focus on interest-group articulation and political party opinion aggregation. System analysis focuses on formal decision making, the environment in which this transpires, and the inputs of demands and supports, along with the outputs of acts and decisions. System analysis also refers to feedbacks and communication loops. Political scientists conventionally break politics into process and policy outcomes. Most of this literature is process-oriented. Elections are to process as issues are to policy. The process/policy dichotomy is artificial; policy cannot be divorced realistically from the process by which it is created. No process transpires without attachment to some substance. Urban politics, in comparison to national politics, is characterized by small geographic scale. Urban American politics is conducted at the substate level and is largely centered on the proper exercise of the police power. Urban political units operate within a limited tax base and are dependent on a restricted economic base. The two major structural elements of urban American governmental politics are division of power, or federalism, and a form of separation of power, or functions distributed among branches. Urban American politics operates under national and state government constitutions and statutes with a limited agenda. Hence, urban politics emphasizes transfer payments, intergovernmental relations, and the mobility of jobs and population.

Suggested Reading
Crick, Bernard. *In Defense of Politics*. Chicago: University of Chicago Press, 1962.
Swanstrom, Todd. "The Limits of Strategic Planning for Cities." *Journal of Urban Affairs*, vol. 9, no. 2 (1987), esp. pp. 151–153.

Population, Daytime and Nighttime   Two complementary measures of a community's inhabitants, based on the number who utilize it as a place of work and the number for whom it is their place of residence, respectively. Work-force population is associated with the day and has been measured by the Bureau of the Census only since the 1970 census, whereas population has been measured officially since 1790 by one's nighttime residence. It is at one's nighttime location that one votes, and it was for this reason that the census was originally mandated by the U.S. Constitution. If urban Americans worked in the same political jurisdictions where they resided, the issue would not be so important, but there is a great deal of work-related mobility among balkanized jurisdictions. Residential suburbs are often called bedroom communities, emptying out each workday for the daily urban commute (DUC). Employing suburbs supply jobs for the commuters. Within a central city, the central business district (CBD) by definition has a larger daytime than nighttime population, and so do the centers in the multinucleated metropolitan area. *See also* BEDROOM SUBURB; CENSUS OF POPULATION; CENTRAL BUSINESS DISTRICT; COMPARATIVE URBAN ANALYSIS.

Significance   The convention in the United States has been to emphasize the nighttime population, because citizenship, residence, and place to vote are associated with location of home. In other systems, such as Yugoslavia, where the workers' cell is the place of voting, a daytime population count is more significant. Japan officially calculates both daytime and nighttime figures. Planners cannot anticipate infrastructure needs, however, without knowing both daytime and nighttime levels. In fact, most suburbs are places of both work and residence, and the combinations range widely along the continuum. More people in metropolitan areas appear to commute out of their jurisdiction than work within it, suggesting the importance of the issue. Nighttime population counts are used to determine some aid formulas. A city might record a substantial population loss and intergovernmental aid decrease when in fact it houses more daytime people than ever. Some U.S. multinucleated centers have a ratio of two or more to one; that is to say, there are twice as many people who work in the area as live there. The two populations are markedly similar in many suburbs but may be substantially different in terms of race and social status. The daytime and nighttime populations in Detroit's New Center area differ markedly on both dimensions. Types of police activity and expenditures for highways and sewers will differ between a dominantly residential and a dominantly commercial or manufacturing population. Some cities will change their population ratio over time. For example, Southfield, Michigan, began as a dominant residential suburb in the 1950s, but, with the shift of office buildings out of Detroit, the area became a dominant employing community by the 1970s.

Suggested Reading

Breese, G. W. *The Daytime Population of the Central Business District of Chicago.* Chicago: University of Chicago Press, 1949.

Gottman, Jean. *The Coming of the Transactional City.* College Park: University of Maryland Institute for Urban Studies, 1983. Chap. 3.

Gust, Avery M. "Nighttime and Daytime Populations of Large American Suburbs." *Urban Affairs Quarterly,* vol. 12, no. 1 (1976), pp. 57–82.

Schnore, L. F. *The Urban Scene.* New York: Free Press, 1965.

Port of New York and New Jersey Authority (Port of New York Authority, PNYA)   Created on April 30, 1921, it was one of the first part-public, part-private organizations established in the United States. The PNYA was the first quasi-public authority to serve an area involving more than one state. It is governed by a 12-member board of commissioners, six each of whom are appointed for six-year terms by the governors of New York and New Jersey. Like all public authorities, the Port of New York Authority membership comprises representatives from both the public and private sectors. The Authority has power to build, purchase, or operate any terminal or transportation facility within the Port District, which covers an area of 25 miles within each state. While it cannot tax, the Authority has powers to borrow money for the construction of specific projects within its jurisdiction. The PNYA was established by an interstate compact between New York and New Jersey, and operates several projects of joint interest to the two states. Examples include the World Trade Center, the various bridges and tunnels that connect the two states, and the three major New York City–area airports: LaGuardia, John F. Kennedy, and Newark. The PNYA also performs economic analyses and forecasting for the New York City metropolitan region. It is one of the few "multipurpose" authorities that exist in the United States. Most public authorities are created for a single purpose—one bridge, one tunnel, or one airport. Public authorities in general have been in existence since at least seventeenth-century England, which created thousands of authorities, most notably the Port of London Authority. *See also*

CENSUS OF GOVERNMENTS; INFRASTRUCTURE; PUBLIC-PRIVATE PARTNER-SHIP; QUASI-PUBLIC.

Significance   The Port of New York Authority grew tremendously under the directorship of Austin Tobin and the stewardship of Robert Moses, chief architect of many New York City public projects. The PNYA typifies the experience of public authorities, with their ability to borrow money separate from the city's borrowing powers, and the greater insulation from public scrutiny that the authorities provided for policy decision. The PNYA did not borrow money for any projects until 1925 and did not expand its operations in any major ways until the 1930s, when the Great Depression hit cities particularly hard. By the 1980s, the budget of the PNYA was larger than the budgets of some state governments. In the early years, all public authorities created by interstate compact needed approval from Congress, because such agreements were perceived as potential power threats by states against the federal government. However, public authorities now are created for many different purposes (economic development, hospitals, utilities) through authorization by state governments and have become a major adjunct of local government activity.

Suggested Reading

Bard, Erwin W. *The Port of New York Authority*. New York: Columbia University Press, 1942.

Caro, Robert A. *The Power Broker*. New York: Knopf, 1974.

Doig, Jameson W. "Coalition-Building by a Regional Agency: Austin Tobin and the Port of New York Authority." In Clarence N. Stone and Heywood T. Sanders, eds., *The Politics of Urban Redevelopment*. Lawrence: University Press of Kansas, 1987, pp. 73–104.

Walsh, Annemarie Huck. *The Public's Business: The Politics and Practices of Government Corporations*. Cambridge: MIT Press, 1978.

Postindustrial City   An urban area in the advanced stages of capitalism characteristic of the late twentieth century, based upon an emerging social and economic system with decreasing emphasis on manufacturing. Postindustrial cities specialize in the service fields including transportation, recreation, trade, research, government, the professions, insurance, and real estate. The term was coined by Daniel Bell in two essays in 1967. The preindustrial era focuses on the *primary* occupations of agriculture, mining, and fishing. The industrial era specializes in *secondary* occupations associated with manufacturing. The postindustrial era will focus on the *tertiary* services and *quaternary* occupations that are centered on information acquisition, storage, processing, and exchange. Bell selected 1956 as a symbolic beginning in the United States for the postindustrial era. That was the first year white-collar employment exceeded blue-collar employment. The industrial era is characterized by the dynamic private firm. The post-industrial era, according to Bell, will focus on the generator of new knowledge, the university. Postindustrial problems will focus on such issues as the building of global markets and large-scale technical planning. Cities that rapidly adapt to the new order will encourage new technology, foster the building of headquarters for multinational corporations, and promote higher education. *See also* CLOSING, PLANT; DISINVEST-MENT, URBAN; FORECAST; INCUBATOR; PARK, RESEARCH; WIRED CITY.

Significance   Bell's original formulation predicted the emergence of a postindustrial society. The city that is to prosper in such an era must adapt to the new distribution of jobs and land use. Population densities will be lower. Sunbelt cities that offer more research parks and encourage high-tech businesses in computers, aerospace, and defense will prosper most. If one accepts the theory, it encourages the national level into a *laissez-faire* response, allowing economic problems to work themselves out in a free marketplace. Northern cities would lose heavy industry to overseas locations without governmental interference. There are two major criticisms of the postindustrial thesis. One stresses the vague nature of the concept as it applies to what will actually replace the industrial society and city. The other notes that although the nation has shifted labor out of agriculture and basic manufacturing, it has not shifted away from farming or manufacturing. It has only become more technologically efficient. The United States will still depend on the comparative advantage of its agricultural and manufacturing to finance its balances of payments with creditor nations in the forthcoming global economy.

Suggested Reading

Bell, Daniel. *The Coming of Post-industrial Society.* New York: Basic Books, 1973.
Birnbaum, Norman. *Toward a Critical Sociology.* New York: Oxford University Press, 1971. Chap. IV, "Is There a Post-industrial Revolution?" pp. 393–415.
Cohen, Stephen S., and John Syzman. *Manufacturing Matters: The Myth of a Post-industrial Economy.* New York: Basic Books, 1987.
Scott, A. J. "Industrialization and Urbanization: A Geographical Agenda." *Annals of the Association of American Geographers,* vol. 76, no. 1 (1986), pp. 25–37.
Sjoberg, Gideon. *The Preindustrial City: Past and Present.* New York: Free Press, 1960.

Poverty Level   A measure of an individual's or a family's bare subsistence or minimally acceptable standard of living. Measures of the poverty level usually are given in "absolute" terms. Absolute poverty conventionally is defined by a minimum level of income for an urban family of four. The figures are adjusted annually to account for inflation. In 1959, the poverty level for an urban family of four was considered to be $2,973 (with a U.S. poverty rate of 22.4 percent); in 1970, the poverty level was $3,970 (with about an 11 percent rate). The 1979 figure was $7,412 (approximately 11 percent rate); in 1985, it was $10,989 (14 percent rate). Poverty levels for the United States are published annually by the U.S. Census Bureau in the *Current Population Report*. Relative poverty is a measure of income distribution in a given society. *See also* POVERTY PROGRAMS; WAR ON POVERTY.

Significance   High absolute-poverty levels or rising levels of relative poverty measures have demanded attention from policymakers to investigate the possibility of governmental action to alleviate the perceived causes of poverty. Measuring the poverty level itself has become a political battle, because many arguments have surfaced regarding what assets should be counted in determining eligibility for social programs. However, for many years standard measures have been used to determine the general income equality of societies. A society that has perfect income equality would find that the first 20 percent of households in the population would hold 20 percent of a society's income, the first 40 percent would hold 40 percent of the income, and so on. Social scientists employ a geometrical device called the Lorenz Curve and its Gini coefficient to determine the level of equality in the distribution of income. A Gini coefficient of 0 would mean perfect income equality existed, and a coefficient of 1.0 would indicate perfect inequality. The Gini coefficient for the United States is about .40, roughly that of most western European countries.

Suggested Reading
Albert, Vicky N. *Welfare Dependence and Welfare Policy*. Westport, CT: Greenwood Press, 1988.
Berkowitz, Edward, and Kim McQuaid. *Creating the Welfare State: The Political Economy of Twentieth-Century Welfare Reform*, 2nd ed. New York: Praeger, 1988.
Sidel, Ruth. *Women and Children Last: The Plight of Poor Women in Affluent America*. New York: Penguin Books, 1987.

Poverty Programs   Income maintenance assistance through cash or in-kind support provided by governments to alleviate poverty. Poverty programs can be classified into several types. One includes programs that are income transfers but do not require "means testing," in which recipients usually have made prior contributions. Social Security is the major income-transfer program that does not have an income eligibility requirement. Though Social Security is not normally considered a poverty program, it is an income maintenance program. Other programs in this category include Medicare and unemployment compensation. Another type of program involves income transfers with an income eligibility requirement. In this category are Aid to Families with Dependent Children (AFDC), Supplemental Security Income (SSI), and General Assistance (GA). An additional type of program includes in-kind assistance programs such as food stamps, food commodities distribution, housing, medicare, and free school lunches. *See also* ECONOMIC OPPORTUNITY ACT OF 1964; GREAT SOCIETY; POVERTY LEVEL; WAR ON POVERTY.

Significance   American governmental participation in poverty programs came from the application of English poor laws in the American colonies. Though the prevailing thought during this time was that aid to the poor encouraged dependency, several states began early programs for those in need. In 1863, Massachusetts established a state Board of Charities. In 1911, Missouri and Illinois enacted "Mothers' Aid" laws for mothers of children left fatherless. Forty out of 48 states had established aid-to-mothers laws by 1926, and over half the states provided aid to the aged by 1933. The Industrial Revolution brought many changes to the United States, including not only the expansion of cities, but urban slums, disease, and poverty. The federal government established many programs in the early twentieth century, but most poverty programs typically provide for shared financing between the federal and individual state governments. Studies conducted in the 1970s and 1980s indicated an increasing "feminization" of poverty, in which about half of all families in poverty have a female head of household. In 1985, 34 percent of all female-headed households lived in poverty.

Suggested Reading

Danziger, Sheldon H., and Daniel H. Weinberg. *Fighting Poverty: What Works and What Doesn't.* Boston: Harvard University Press, 1987.

Harrington, Michael. *The New American Poverty.* New York: Holt, Rinehart, 1984.

Heineman, Ben W., Jr., et al. *Work and Welfare: The Case for New Directions in National Policy.* Washington, DC: Center for National Policy, 1987.

Levitan, Sar. *Programs in Aid of the Poor for the 1980s.* Baltimore: Johns Hopkins University Press, 1980.

Melzer, Milton. *Poverty in America.* New York: William Morrow, 1986.

Plotnick, Robert D., and Felicity Skidmore. *Progress against Poverty.* New York: Academic Press, 1975.

Precinct   (1) A minor administrative subdivision, the smallest scale of electoral politics, which serves as the neighborhood polling place. (2) An administrative subdivision in a large city serving as a unit for police and fire administration and containing one major station and possibly some ministations. (3) The lowest level of political party organization that corresponds with the boundaries of the electoral precinct. As an election unit, a precinct is set up to conduct and report vote totals to a clerk, who is legally accountable for overall administration. As a police and fire unit, a precinct is a subdivision of a citywide operation that is broken into manageable scale and assigns precinct commanders who report to a citywide chief. As a political unit, a precinct elects a captain or committee person who is clustered with others into a city or town or, in larger metropolises, into wards. In turn, these captains are delegates eligible to attend higher-level party organizations, represent presidential hopefuls, and, in well-disciplined party systems, get out the vote at election time. *See also* AT-LARGE ELECTION; BLISS THESIS; ZONE, URBAN.

Significance   Precinct boundaries are not fixed for all time. They can be amended by administrative action because of population decline or expansion. Most electoral precincts contain fewer than 1,000 registered voters and one polling place. There are more than 170,000 nationwide. Police and fire precincts contract or expand in scale as the level of activity warrants; ironically, as population declines in a central city and the number of abandoned buildings increase, the frequency of fire runs may increase rather than decrease. Party precincts follow whatever contour the electoral precinct takes. Some electoral precincts with high turnout attract more day-of-the-event campaign workers. Those precincts that consistently vote for winners are called *bellwether* or *indicator precincts* and are canvassed by parties in order to anticipate trends. Politically well-organized precincts provide get-out-the-vote campaigns, check off voters as they come to the polls, encourage absentee voting, and supply poll watchers to guard against irregularities. Many precincts are not organized well enough even to fill their positions: This is especially true of Republican precinct captains in central cities that are heavily Democratic-controlled. In most states, machines and paper ballots are sealed formally by the clerk or a representative after the count to await certification by the board of canvassers or a timely recount on a precinct-by-precinct basis. Absentee ballots usually are counted not at the precinct but on a separate tally board.

Private Sector   The portion of the national economy comprising all those activities and functions that are part of the "free enterprise" system. However, there is no "pure" private sector that is totally free from government supervision. The boundary between the public and private sectors has often changed, as in the case of public-private partnerships making urban redevelopment policy. In addition, all private property is subject to planning and zoning by way of the police power. All "free enterprise" business is subject to multiple taxes and government regulation. *See also* DYE THESIS; PRIVATIZATION; POLICE POWER; PUBLIC-PRIVATE PARTNERSHIP; PUBLIC SECTOR; QUASI-PUBLIC; SUPPLY-SIDE ECONOMICS.

Significance Some of the earliest research on American urban politics has attempted to explain the role of the private sector in urban policymaking and the general relationship between the public and private sectors. Community power studies using reputational analysis found that the private sector had a major, even a predominant, influence in overall urban policymaking. With an emphasis on urban economic development, most urbanists, regardless of personal political perspective, recognize the major role the private sector plays in urban politics and policymaking. Much urban research focuses on macroeconomic influence and the degree to which local governments can control their own economic fate. Paul Peterson's influential *City Limits* argues that the pursuit of business investment and the general economic context of cities impose severe limits on local policymakers, leaving elected officials to decide on "allocative" rather than the more important "developmental" policies. Peterson's market theory of urban politics reveals an economic determinism similar to some of the neo-Marxist theories, which argue the private sector has created various urban crises in its quest for profit-making. Private-sector decisions dominate and leave urban policymakers with the task of reacting to the excesses of private decisions.

Suggested Reading

Elkin, Stephen L. "Twentieth Century Urban Regimes." *Journal of Urban Affairs*, vol. 7, no. 2 (1985), pp. 11–28.
Jones, Bryan D., and Lynn W. Bachelor. *The Sustaining Hand: Community Leadership and Corporate Power*. Lawrence: University Press of Kansas, 1986.
Kantor, Paul, with Stephen David. *The Dependent City: The Changing Political Economy of Urban America*. Glenview, IL: Scott, Foresman, 1988.
Molotch, Harvey, "The City as a Growth Machine: Toward a Political Economy of Place." *American Journal of Sociology*, vol. 82, no. 2 (1976), pp. 309–332.
Peterson, Paul. *City Limits*. Chicago: University of Chicago Press, 1981.
Smith, Michael P., ed. *Cities in Transformation: Class, Capital, and the State*. Beverly Hills: Sage Publications, 1984.
Swanstrom, Todd. "Semi-sovereign Cities: The Political Logic of Urban Development." *Polity*, vol. 21, no. 1 (1988), pp. 83–110.

Private Street   Any thoroughfare owned and maintained by an individual, association, or nongovernmentally incorporated body, allowing access to more than one residence or business but generally open to persons other than those who own the road. Private streets often are designed and built to minimum construction standards of cities or counties. Many streets originally built by developers to unacceptable standards remain private because public bodies will not accept their dedication in below-par condition. They are identified by stylistic signage or "Residents Only" signs. *See also* HOUSING, CONDOMINIUM; INFRASTRUCTURE; PRIVATIZATION; ROAD CLASSIFICATION.

Significance   Distribution of private streets varies, depending upon whether they are banned or encouraged by state or local general government jurisdictions. The trend is toward building more private streets in condominium and cluster-home development. Thus, cities are freed of an ongoing overhead cost as well as the initial capital expenditure. This reduces the need for issuing public infrastructure bonds and the need to levy taxes or special assessments for maintenance. Some states also free the city of liability for accidents that occur as a result of improper construction or care. The local unit usually secures by deed restriction both ingress for public service vehicles and easement for utilities. In those states with highway trust funds, private roads are excluded from the formula for distributing grants based on the number of miles of roadway within their jurisdiction.

Privatism   An American value system that suggests actions should take place in the marketplace and that public goals will result from the free interplay of individual pursuits. The term *privatism* was first coined in 1958 by Sam Bass Warner, Jr., in his book on the history of Philadelphia. He described the focus on individual and family and the search for personal wealth, with community interest emerging from the sum of these concerns. In practical terms this meant land development was the result of profit-making private enterprise. Public schools were simply an extension of private schools; civic improvement in waterworks was not allowed to redistribute wealth from the successful to the poor by subsidizing tie-ins for all. Early American cities shunned direct public-service delivery in favor of such devices as subscription and nonregulated services. Privatism was based on an open society that allowed all migrants access to the system, widespread prosperity, and individualized work habits. Large corporate businesses were not yet prevalent. *See also* JEFFERSONIAN AGRARIANISM; NATIONAL URBAN POLICY; POLICE POWER; PRIVATIZATION.

Significance   According to Warner, privatism is one of the values most relevant to understanding urban American culture. Early U.S. cities were largely the unplanned result of private market forces. Building codes, the constitutionally sanctioned zoning ordinance, and the spread of infrastructure to all urban residents were not the dominant trends until well into the twentieth century. One manifestation of privatism was opposition to public housing on the grounds that it did not allow for a profit motive. Vouchers for schools and housing subsidies are contemporary examples of privatism. Championing privatization is also a form of modern privatism. The prize-winning thesis of Warner has had independent verification as an apt description of values in American cities well into the 1930s. However, the thesis can be criticized for not incorporating the countertrend of robust use of the police power on behalf of the community's needs. Warner does not suggest whether any city politicians were championing the larger public interest.

Suggested Reading

Barnokov, Timothy K., Daniel Rich, and Robert Warren. "The New Privatism, Federalism, and the Future of Urban Governance." *Journal of Urban Affairs*, vol. 3, no. 4 (1981), pp. 1–14.

Bennett, Larry. "Privatism and Housing Policy in the United States." *Urban Law and Policy*, vol. 6 (1983), pp. 169–184.

Gluck, Peter R., and Richard J. Meister. *Cities in Transition: Social Changes and Institutional Responses in Urban Development.* New York: New Viewpoints, 1979. (Uses the thesis as one of two movements in nineteenth- and twentieth-century urban history.)

Savitch, H. V. *Urban Policy and the Exterior City: Federal, State, and Corporate Impacts upon Major Cities.* New York: Pergamon Press, 1979.

Warner, Sam Bass, Jr. *The Private City: Philadelphia in Three Periods of Its Growth,* 2nd ed. Philadelphia: University of Pennsylvania Press, 1958 and 1968.

Privatization   The process of government paying for a service by contracting for it through a nonpublic supplier in the not-for-profit or profit sector. The privatization process is not, however, the same as contracting out a service, because one unit may simply shift the delivery to another governmental unit. The government's role is confined to selecting the provider, determining the level of activity, financing the service, and overseeing the delivery. Urban examples include shifting from in-house to outside and profit-motivated engineering services, refuse collection, department of public works duties, wastewater treatment, and jail and janitorial services, as well as medical and social services. *See also* CONTRACTING OUT; CORRUPTION, GOVERNMENT; LAKEWOOD PLAN; SELF-INSURANCE.

Significance   *Privatization* is a new term for an old process. The major example of privatization in U.S. history occurred during the eighteenth and nineteenth centuries. The national government gave away and sold more than 250 million acres from the public domain to homesteaders and railroads. Civil engineering and landscape architectural services, along with planning, consulting, and surveying agencies, have been supplied for centuries by outside experts. Arguments for privatization include saving monies on salaries, fringe packages, and retirement costs; reducing the size of personnel departments and supervision costs; and creating a smaller payroll. It gives the appearance of a leaner budget, especially if financing the service is shifted from a tax to user fees. It allows the private sector to compete for profits from whatever economies of scale are available through bulk purchases. An argument against privatization is the lack of proof that the private sector can provide a service for less without busting unions. It is a conservative ideological reaction usually not backed by cost-benefit analysis. It is not always possible to find competitive bids. Public accountability may suffer unless carefully preserved. Standardized service delivery may be a difficulty. Open bids deteriorate into negotiated bids when there is no competition. The maximum use of these privately directed services currently available has now potentially increased to more than 10 percent of a city's budget if the city were to contract out for wastewater treatment, Department of Public and Works (DPW) services, and refuse collection. Phoenix uses private contracts for security, DPW functions, and operation of the public landfill. The potential for rigged bids means corruption could increase with privatization. Case law is unsettled on stipulating the limits of privatization. In the absence of case law, in Michigan the attorney general has issued an opinion that jails may be privately built but not privately operated. Few states allow private jails to operate. There are no guidelines on establishing standards for profits of the supplier. Once private bidders win a contract, they may assume it is a long-term alternative to public delivery. The initial bid winner has built-in advantages over other bidders in later rounds, because it has proprietary audits that it need not share with challengers. Productivity studies do not support the argument that private sources are inherently superior to public delivery. New York City and Rochester, New York, saved revenue when they canceled printing and trash collection contracts. For-profit firms may be more cost-effective only at the expense of union jobs. The opposite of privatization is nationalization. There is a countertrend to privatization in the movement toward self-insurance; in this process, the local units take away privately sponsored insurance coverage in favor of lower-premium insurance through a public consortium.

Suggested Reading

Hanke, Steve H., ed. "Prospects for Privatization." *Proceedings of the Academy of Political Science*, vol. 36, no. 3 (1987).

Lave, Charles A., ed. *Urban Transit: The Private Challenge to Public Transportation*. Cambridge, MA: Ballinger, 1985.

Miller, John R., Christopher R. Tufts, and Harry P. Harty. "Privatization Crossfire." *National Civic Review*, vol. 77, no. 2 (1988), pp. 100–117.

Peck, Janet Rothenberg, ed. "Symposium: Privatization: Theory and Practice." *Journal of Policy Analysis and Management*, vol. 6 (1987).

Savas, Emanuel S. *Privatization: The Key to Better Government*. Chatham, NJ: Chatham House, 1987.

———. *Privatizing the Public Sector: How To Shrink Government*. Chatham, NJ: Chatham House, 1982.

Productivity   The relationship of overall output to the level of expenditure. Improved local government productivity yields more service at no increase in tax or bond expenditure. Local government services often amount to 70 percent or more of total budget outlays. However, productivity also applies to any production of goods, as from a municipal water or electric corporation or other public utility. Some of these goods have been labeled proprietary. To be productive, government pursues *efficiency* of output per employee per hour and *effectiveness* in expending revenue for services and goods for residents. Paternalistic government supplies services such as compulsory education, restaurant health inspection, and water fluoridation. The state mandates these services as being of value to all citizens, whether or not they were explicitly demanded by voters. Responsive local governments also supply discretionary services and goods based on interest group and voter demands as expressed through the political process. *See also* INNOVATION GROUPS; POLICE POWER; PRIVATIZATION; PROPRIETARY FUNCTION; PUBLIC ULILITY; TIEBOUT THESIS; URBAN SERVICES.

Significance   It has never been the primary goal of government to achieve the highest possible productive standards. The local level aims to promote justice, equity, equality, and domestic tranquility. Productivity is subordinant to statecraft. In most cases, it is inappropriate to compare public- and private-sector productivity standards. Local governments do not produce profits or always eschew losses. It is impossible to produce a cost-benefit model for, say, educational excellence, physical security, or aesthetic ambience. Productivity is not a goal in and of itself. Rather, it is an instrument for achieving freedom, justice, or equity. Low productivity, like corruption, is a condition to be avoided, not a prime value pursued for its own sake. With caution, proprietary functions can be compared with private, for-profit counterparts so long as adjustments are made for such factors as subsidized services, differing depreciation schedules, and tax payments by the private sector. Public utilities also do not promote maximum productivity, as they are established to provide a good no matter the marginal cost of production. A major topic in late twentieth-century U.S. local politics is whether, once a service or good has been decided upon as a governmental responsibility, the supplier should be in the for-profit sector. Many political conservatives assert that the private sector should always be promoted. Political liberals disagree, saying that productivity gains are achieved largely at the cost of breaking unions and limiting services to economically marginal consumers. *Performance* should not be equated with productivity. Performance relates to overall policy outcomes and is conventionally measured by comparing cities or nations.

Suggested Reading

Committee for Economic Development. *Improving Productivity in State and Local Government.* New York: CED, 1976.

Fried, Robert, and Francine Rabonowitz. *Comparative Urban Performance.* Englewood Cliffs, NJ: Prentice-Hall, 1980.

Morgan, David R. *Managing Urban America,* 3rd ed. Pacific Grove, CA: Brooks/Cole, 1989. Chap. 7, "Productivity Improvement and Cutback Management."

Poister, Theodore H., and Robert H. McGowan. "Municipal Management Capacity: Productivity Improvement and Strategies for Handling Fiscal Stress." *Municipal Year Book 1984.* Washington, DC: International City Management Association, 1984. Chap. D3, pp. 208–214.

Schultze, William A. *Urban Politics: A Political Economy Approach.* Englewood Cliffs, NJ: Prentice-Hall, 1985. Chap. 7, "Conflict over Urban Performance."

Washnis, George J., ed. *Productivity Handbook for State and Local Government.* New York: John Wiley, 1980.

Promulgate   To announce publicly, to publish or post where everyone can view an announcement. Local governments in the United States must officially proclaim ordinances so that the public is informed. Only after a law is promulgated is ignorance of the law no excuse. The official publication of a new law includes announcement of an enforcement date. Many local government jurisdictions also require advance notice of public meetings. Among items that must be promulgated are notification of forthcoming elections, location of polling places and posting of certified results, the last day to register or vote by absentee ballot, and bids for government contracts over a set threshold. Other topics covered by mandated promulgations include summaries of audited year-end budgets, changes in fee schedules, and notification of the right to appeal tax assessments. These announcements appear in one of the local presses, which is designated an official newspaper, with general circulation in the affected area. Such information is required to be available for public viewing at the seat of government, and copies of ordinances must be available for sale to the public. This tradition of circulating information stems from Roman times: "Promulgate" is derived from the Latin *promulgare*, to make public. The symbol of the revolutionary colonies was the Philadelphia Liberty Bell, the instrument used preceding public announcements. *See also* ENFORCEMENT DATE; OFFICIAL NEWSPAPER.

Significance   Promulgations are the cornerstone of an open society. An informed citizenry is a precondition for democracy, and that information is disseminated in part through public announcements. Local clerks customarily are assigned responsibility for preparing and paying for public announcements in a timely manner and in proper form. Failure by government to comply with statutory guidelines is grounds for courts to nullify results, including overturning contracts. Since *Mullane v. Central Hanover Bank and Trust Co.*, 339 U.S. 306 (1950), notice by publication has been insufficient for certain classes of state action that "affect an interest in life, liberty, or property protected by the Due Process Clause of the Fourteenth Amendment." This includes action on trust funds, because the conventional promulgation is only "an advertisement in small type inserted in the back pages of a newspaper" (id. at 315). The higher standard was extended to state sale of land for back taxes in *Mennonite Board of Missions v. Adams*, 462 U.S. 791 (1983).

Proportional Representation (PR)   An at-large election system in which voters make several selections in multimember electoral districts by indicating numerical preference next to each candidate for whom they wish to vote. To win, candidates must get a quota of votes according to a formula that stipulates the lowest number of votes to qualify. Any winning candidates who have "surplus" votes then have them transferred to second and third choices, who might thereby qualify for office. The single transferable vote system is also known as the Hare plan, named after Thomas Hare, an Englishman who developed the formula in his book *A Treatise on the Election of Representatives, Parliamentary and Municipal*, first published in the 1850s. PR is in use at the national level in many foreign nations, including most of Latin America, all of Western Europe except France and the U.K., plus such new democracies as Israel and Japan. It has not caught on in the English-speaking world. *See also* AT-LARGE ELECTION; REFORM GOVERNMENT; WARD.

Significance   Proportional representation has been used by 25 U.S. cities for council elections, first in Ashtabula, Ohio, from 1915 to 1929. It was also used in other Ohio cities, including Cincinnati from 1926 to 1957, Cleveland from 1921 to 1931, and Toledo from 1934 to 1949. It was used in conjunction with the Bucklin preferential voting plan in Boulder, Colorado, from 1917 to 1947; in Worcester, Massachusetts, from 1949 to 1960; and in New York City from 1937 to 1947. The only U.S. city still using it is Cambridge, Massachusetts, where it was first adopted in 1940. Since 1969, the New York State legislature imposed PR on the New York City school board elections to ensure minority group representation. The first and chief advantage is that it allows for majority rule while accommodating minority interests at the electoral level in proportion to their strength at the polls. Second, it discourages the coattail effect and forces candidates for boards, councils, and commissions to run on their own merit. Third, it avoids gerrymandering, as all elections are conducted at large. The first and major disadvantage is that its workings are complex and not grasped by a majority of the electorate. Second, it encourages third and fourth parties by rewarding them rather than forcing them to amalgamate into one of the two major groups. Third, it is successful in promoting minority candidates who would not have won in a winner-take-all system. PR's most celebrated philosophic proponent was John Stuart Mill. For years the National Municipal League suggested PR in its model charter. It was still being championed for local use by American political scientist Joseph Zimmerman in the 1970s, but its day as a viable, fundamental reform of the American urban political process is past.

Suggested Reading
Straetz, Ralph A. *Politics in Cincinnati.* New York: New York University Press, 1958.
Zimmerman, Joseph F. *The Federated City: Community Control in Large Cities.* New York: St. Martin's Press, 1972. Chap. IV.

Proposition 2¹/₂   A tax-limitation initiative passed in 1980 by voters in Massachusetts. Proposition 2¹/₂ required property taxes to be limited to 2¹/₂ percent of a community's assessed valuation. Any subsequent increases could not exceed 2¹/₂ percent annually. The proposition forced local Massachusetts governments to cut their budgets by a total of over $357 million in 1981. Between 20,000 and 25,000 state and local public employees accordingly lost their jobs after 1980. *See also* BOND AND RATING SERVICES; PROPOSITION 13; TAX LIMIT; TAXPAYERS' REVOLT.

Significance   Proposition 2½ represented both the positive and negative aspects of the taxpayer revolts of the 1970s and 1980s. The state had been popularly called "Taxachusetts," because of its high tax burden compared to other states. While grass-roots taxpayer activity forced greater fiscal austerity on public expenditures, the tax limit measure produced many negative effects that were not considered by supporters. For example, Proposition 2½ did not exempt money for the repayment of local debt. As a result, bondholders had no guarantee bonds would be repaid. Bond ratings of many Massachusetts communities were suspended, making it impossible to float new bonds for public works or capital projects. A large majority of new bonds since 1981 have been revenue bonds, because general-obligation bonds have been more difficult to sell. For those cities able to restore a bond rating, most were at a lower level, increasing their borrowing costs. In addition, user fees have increased dramatically, especially for water and sewerage services.

Suggested Reading

Greiner, John M., and George E. Peterson. "Do Budget Reductions Stimulate Public Sector Productivity? Evidence from Proposition 2½ in Massachusetts." In George E. Peterson and Carol W. Lewis, eds., *Reagan and the Cities*. Washington, DC: Urban Institute, 1986.

Ladd, Helen, and Julie Boatright Wilson. "Who Supports Tax Limitations: Evidence from Massachusetts' Proposition 2½." *Journal of Policy Analysis and Management*, vol. 2, no. 2 (1983), pp. 256–279.

Susskind, Lawrence E., and Jane Fountain Serio, eds. *Proposition 2½: Its Impact on Massachusetts*. Cambridge, MA: Oelgeschlager, Gunn & Hain, 1983.

Tvedt, Sherry. "Enough Is Enough: Proposition 2½ in Massachusetts." *National Civic Review*, vol. 70, no. 10 (1981), pp. 527–533.

Proposition 13   A tax-limitation initiative passed by voters in California in 1978. Proposition 13 was the first and most notable of the statewide "taxpayer revolts" that arose in the late 1970s and early 1980s. This initiative was promoted initially by Howard A. Jarvis, director of the United Organization of Taxpayers, who had tried to put the tax-limitation issue on the California ballot three times before 1978. More than 1.2 million signatures easily qualified Proposition 13 for the ballot, and the initiative passed by a 2–1 margin. The proposition had three major provisions: (1) it established a 1 percent maximum tax on the fair market value of property, thus reducing current taxes by almost 60 percent; (2) it limited increases in property assessments to 2 percent each year; and (3) it required a two-thirds vote of the California legislature to create any new state tax that might

SUBSTITUTE FOR LOST LOCAL REVENUES. *See also* INITIATIVE; PROPOSITION 2¹/₂; TAX LIMIT; TAXPAYERS' REVOLT.

Significance   Proposition 13 fired the first shot in the taxpayers' revolt. There were several reasons behind the popularity of the initiative. One, California property values and, therefore, taxes had been increasing at unprecedented rates. Two, overall taxes made California residents among the most highly taxed in the nation. Three, the state had a $5 billion surplus in the late 1970s. Four, the state legislature failed to pass a tax-relief bill in its previous sessions. These factors set the stage for general taxpayer animosity and frustration. Also on the ballot was Proposition 8, a legislative proposal that would have based future state- and local-government expenditures on a formula of general economic growth. It did not reduce government spending and would have replaced some lost local tax dollars with state revenues. Proposition 8 was defeated 53 to 47 percent by the voters. Proposition 13 has been considered the classic revolt by average taxpayers because the issue used the statewide initiative process. Many of the state's major political leaders and organizations opposed the initiative. Proposition 13's impact on local government services has been severe. Numerous studies indicate local governments and school districts have been hurt tremendously by their inability to raise revenues. The quality of education and local service delivery plummeted. Some school districts, such as San Jose, were forced to declare bankruptcy. Many local governments have turned to alternatives such as impact or user fees and large-scale borrowing through revenue bonds to raise lost revenues.

Suggested Reading
Chapman, Jeffrey I. *Proposition 13 and Land Use: A Case Study of Fiscal Limits in California.* Lexington, MA: Lexington Books, 1980.
Mushkin, Selma J. *Proposition 13 and Its Consequences for Public Management.* New York: Norton, 1979.
Oakland, William H. "Proposition 13—Genesis and Consequences." *Policy Studies Review Annual,* vol. 3 (1979), pp. 547–564.
Orr, Daniel. "Proposition 13: Tax Reform's Lexington Bridge?" *Policy Studies Review Annual,* vol. 3 (1979), pp. 573–583.
Schwadron, Terry, ed. *California and the American Tax Revolt: Proposition 13 Five Years Later.* Berkeley: University of California, 1984.

Proprietary Function   Any governmental function or activity that is primarily designed and run for profit and is not associated with a conventional public activity supported by taxes and fees. It also refers to the same type of function in a nonprofit organization. The definition is so labeled in either a state statute or by a state common law.

Justice Frankfurter in the 1945 case of *New York v. United States,* 326 U.S. 572 at 583, refused to use the proprietary versus governmental function distinction in denying tax exemption for a state-owned mineral water bottling operation, calling these "untenable criteria." If a government performs a businesslike function and persistently runs a loss or deficit, this may mean it is simply a subsidized conventional activity. States are likely to make the final determination on a case-by-case basis. *See also* MUNICIPAL TORT LIABILITY.

Significance The opposite of a proprietary function is a conventional line operation, that is to say, one the organization was designed to perform. Whether a particular activity is proprietary is likely to be determined for two purposes. One reason is to determine whether the government function is immune from suits. In some states, conventional line functions are immune from litigation, whereas proprietary functions are an exception to the general rule that governments can do no wrong in the eyes of the law. The second reason is to determine whether a government not-for-profit operation, free from paying taxes, presents unfair competition to private businesses in the same marketplace. Laissez-faire advocates in the Reagan administration were particularly sensitive to this unfair business competition. Major examples of local government proprietary enterprises include municipal electricity companies, state-owned liquor stores, and city bus lines and hospitals. Minor examples include state-owned university bookstores, public museum gift shops, and map counters at the county planning commission.

Suggested Reading
Brams, Marvin R., James Taylor, and Young-Doo Wang. "The Tax Equity Effects of the Substitution of Municipal Electric Profits for Property Taxes." *Journal of Urban Affairs,* vol. 5, no. 1 (1983), pp. 141–150.

Pruitt-Igoe (St. Louis, Missouri) A public-housing project built in 1955 and demolished in 1972–1973. The Pruitt-Igoe Project originally was considered a model of high-density, high-quality public housing. The project consisted of 33 buildings, each 11 stories high. However, living conditions deteriorated, and many families moved out of the project, with other families unwilling to fill the vacancies. By 1971, 75 percent of the housing units were unoccupied. After several attempts to revitalize and rehabilitate the buildings, officials had the project torn down. *See also* HOUSING, PUBLIC.

Significance The Pruitt-Igoe Project came to symbolize the worst of public housing in the United States. Cost-cutting construction measures—eliminating landscaping, not painting the cinder-block galleries, leaving steam pipes uninsulated—made the project much less suitable for living. Poor maintenance, crime, and vandalism also combined to create a poor living environment. As working families moved out, they were replaced by families on welfare, making expenditures for maintenance and security even more difficult. The project had been designed originally for a mixed population, but by 1965, the project was inhabited almost entirely by black families with female heads of households. Less than 10 percent of the residents were male, most of them elderly. Pruitt-Igoe raised many questions about the high-rise public housing program in the United States. Even though there always has been greater demand for subsidized housing than units available, the actual living standards of public housing came under criticism from both liberals and conservatives, both of whom brought the entire public housing program into question. This led to a gradual move away from direct public housing programs, toward much larger private-sector involvement in providing housing for low-income families. Some housing in the 1980s has been privately built, then operated by the public sector. Other programs include governmental subsidy of low-income families who simply live in privately owned buildings. Ironically, when Pruitt-Igoe was first built, it was intended to be segregated—Pruitt was built for black residents, Igoe for whites. After the U.S. Supreme Court outlawed segregation in public housing, Pruitt-Igoe became an integrated housing project.

Suggested Reading
Rainwater, Lee. *Behind Ghetto Walls: Black Families in a Federal Slum.* Chicago: Aldine Publishing, 1970.
Meehan, Eugene J. *Public Housing Policy.* New Brunswick, NJ: Rutgers University Press, 1975.

Public Contract   A legal agreement between a government and a supplier or vendor to provide a service or good in exchange for an established price. Public contracts were subject to considerable corruption before the reforms of the early twentieth century were established. Contracts usually require open and competitive bidding by potential suppliers or vendors. Internal and external audits are also conducted in an effort to monitor governmental expenditures in general. *See also* AUDIT; COMPETITIVE BID; CORRUPTION, GOVERNMENT; PRIVATIZATION; SET-ASIDE.

Significance   For many years, the process of deciding on suppliers for public contracts was conducted in relative secrecy. Kickbacks and favoritism for building and road construction, repairs, and other services often were involved in the contracting decisions made by city governments during the 1800s. Excessive costs applied to many agreements also allowed public employees, elected officials, or contractors to skim substantial sums of money from a contract for private gain. Although exceptions have occurred, procedures such as competitive bidding, auditing of budgets, and public disclosure of decisions generally have reduced corruption. Public contracting became a more controversial and important issue during the 1980s relative to two prominent factors affecting public decision making and service delivery. First, many local and state governments considered privatization of a number of services formerly performed by public-sector employees. Second, the U.S. Supreme Court ruled in 1989 that city contracts that provide for set-asides for minority businesses are unconstitutional without proof of specific past discrimination of minorities in contract awards. At least 190 local governments had established programs for minority contracting by the time of the *Richmond* decision.

Suggested Reading
Mushkin, Selma J. "PPBS in City, State, and County: An Overview." *Innovations in Planning, Programming, and Budgeting in State and Local Governments.* Washington, DC: Subcommittee on Economy in Government of the Joint Economic Committee, Government Printing Office, 1969, pp. 1–14.

Public Employee Strike   A work stoppage or job action taken by workers in government or public organizations such as hospitals. In most states, strikes by public employees are illegal. Because of this restriction, many public employees seeking wage increases or improvements in working conditions have resorted to unofficial job actions such as "blue flu," in which police officers call in sick. Of the 5,535 work stoppages in the United States in 1977, only 413 were by public employees. However, public-employee strikes often have a greater scope than private-sector strikes, because work stoppages by police officers, fire fighters, sanitation employees, teachers, or nurses can directly and immediately affect the lives of many city residents. *See also* AMERICAN FEDERATION OF STATE, COUNTY, AND MUNICIPAL EMPLOYEES; ARBITRATION; COLLECTIVE BARGAINING; LOCAL MERIT SYSTEM.

Significance   Labor relations between governments and their employees have changed substantially since World War II. Old concepts of governmental sovereignty forbade public employees to negotiate with governments, let alone strike. However, the acceptance of union representation and collective bargaining undercut the sovereignty argument, and many public-employee unions became more militant during the 1960s. While public-employee strikes are still illegal in most states, many governments have not taken the extreme action of arresting striking employees. Occasionally, however, employees, and more often their union leaders, have risked serving jail time. Short of walking a picket line, public employees often favor other tactics designed to increase their bargaining power or publicize their plight. Social workers and other street-level bureaucrats with heavy caseloads sometimes engage in work slowdowns, called *work-to-rule*. Formal procedures are followed literally, drastically reducing productivity and destroying the routine and pace of the normal workday.

Suggested Reading

Berube, Maurice R., and Marilyn Gittell, eds. *Confrontation at Ocean Hill–Brownsville*. New York: Praeger, 1969.
Stieber, Jack. *Public Employee Unionism: Structure, Growth, Policy*. Washington, DC: Brookings Institution, 1973.

Public Housing Authority (PHA)   A local agency that uses a variety of methods to develop and operate housing for lower-income families. Under one method, the PHA receives proposals from private developers, selects the best proposal, and purchases the completed project from the developer. The local PHA also can acquire a site, then request competitive bids, thus acting as its own developer. Finally, a PHA is free to purchase existing housing and, if necessary, rehabilitate it. *See also* EXPERIMENTAL HOUSING ALLOWANCE PROGRAM; *HILLS V. GAUTREAUX*; HOUSING, SECTION 8; HOUSING SUBSIDY.

Significance   Public Housing Authorities have become the local implementers of public housing programs in the United States. Under the Reagan administration, more encouragement was given to private-market initiatives in housing, including the development of a voucher plan to allow renters to select their own best rental arrangement with eligible landlords. Eligibility is determined by the Department of Housing and Urban Development (HUD). HUD authorizes the creation of local PHAs, which can include private individuals. Despite the efforts of the federal government to provide access to decent and affordable housing to low-income families, some PHAs have discriminated against minorities, as demonstrated by the Chicago Housing Authority in the *Hills v. Gautreaux* case, 452 U.S. 284 (1976).

Suggested Reading

Bratt, Rachel G., Chester Hartman, and Ann Meyerson. *Critical Perspectives on Housing*. Philadelphia: Temple University Press, 1986.

DeBorger, Bruno. "Alternative Housing Concepts and the Benefits of Public Housing Programs." *Journal of Urban Economics,* vol. 22, no. 1 (1987), pp. 73–89.

Public Interest Groups (PIGs)   The seven organizations that represent various local- and state-level public institutions and officials. The "Big Seven" PIGs include the U.S. Conference of Mayors (USCM), the National League of Cities (NLC), the International City Management Association (ICMA), the National Association of Counties (NACo), the National Governor's Association (NGA), the National Conference of State Legislators (NCSL), and the Council of State Governments (CSG). Most of the Big Seven have headquarters in Washington, D.C., and all use the lobbying, grant writing, and technical expertise of "a Man in Washington" office, which provides assistance to these groups in dealing with the federal government. Except for the ICMA and the CSG, these PIGs are active in lobbying at the federal level on such issues as general revenue sharing, federal grants-in-aid, social welfare programs, taxation issues, and many intergovernmental matters. *See also* LOBBYING BY CITIES; NATIONAL ASSOCIATION OF COUNTIES; THINK TANK; U.S. CONFERENCE OF MAYORS.

Significance   The creation of many Public Interest Groups points out the increasing importance of the grants-in-aid system in U.S. intergovernmental relations. Because federal policy directly began to affect cities and their budgets in major ways during the 1930s, a number of local- and state-level lobbying and educational groups formed around this period. Grantsmanship skills and direct lobbying have been among the most important skills and activities promoted by these organizations. However, beginning in the early 1970s, declining federal involvement in funding urban projects and services produced a different strategy among many of the organizations. States and cities looked more toward private investment and funding or sought to develop alternative revenue sources, such as user fees. Many governments also were forced to reduce costs through layoffs, cutbacks, and privatization of some urban services. In addition to the "Big Seven" groups, a number of other organizations have called themselves, or are called, "public interest groups," including the Government Finance Officers' Association (GFOA) and the National Association of Housing and Redevelopment Officials (NAHRO).

Suggested Reading

Berry, Jeffrey. *Lobbying for the People.* Princeton, NJ: Princeton University Press, 1977.
Stanfield, Rochelle. "The PIGs: Out of the Sty, into Lobbying with Style." *National Journal* (August 14, 1976), p. 1137.

Public-Private Partnership   A cooperative effort between governmental and profit-oriented representatives to implement certain urban policies, typically development or redevelopment projects. Public-private partnerships were created largely because of the perception that the public sector imposed excessive taxes while remaining ineffective in solving urban economic problems. Reduced federal aid to cities, taxpayers' revolts, and "supply-side" economics all have played a role in encouraging greater private-sector involvement in urban economic development. The specific manifestation of these efforts includes quasi-public agencies such as redevelopment authorities (RDAs) or downtown development, authorities (DDAs). These bodies have representatives from both the public and private sectors and usually have legal authority to condemn and raze land, levy taxes, and borrow money. *See also* DOWNTOWN DEVELOPMENT AUTHORITY; PORT OF NEW YORK AND NEW JERSEY AUTHORITY; QUASI-PUBLIC; PRIVATE SECTOR; PUBLIC SECTOR.

Significance   Across the 200-year history of the United States, the provision of many urban services initially had been assumed by the private sector in areas such as water supply, waste disposal, and fire protection. For many years, the urban-renewal programs were a product of substantial private investment and cooperation with government agencies. With the increasing forces of urbanization and industrialization, the scope of public-sector responsibility for service delivery increased dramatically. However, by the mid-1970s, a general antigovernment sentiment had grown, along with resistance to higher taxes and a belief that government spending was wasteful. The supply-side approach endorsed by the Reagan administration placed federal mandates on private-sector initiatives in urban redevelopment policy as a precondition for several of the remaining federal urban-aid programs. Urban development action grants (UDAGs) (1977–1988), for example, required private investment (of 20 percent of the total cost) in an urban project as one qualification to receive grant funding. In addition to economic development, other targets for public-private partnerships have included providing housing, developing minority enterprise, strengthening community institutions, and improving the environment. Because of these initiatives, the distinction between public versus private delivery of urban services has become less obvious in recent years. In addition, critics have argued that this move toward more direct private power in urban public policy has led to an "urban corporatism" in which large businesses make important planning and development decisions, but remain publicly unaccountable.

Suggested Reading
Colman, William G. *State and Local Government and Public-Private Partnerships: A Policy Issues Handbook*. Westport, CT: Greenwood Press, 1989.

DeSeve, G. Edward. "Financing Urban Development: The Joint Efforts of Governments and the Private Sector." *Annals of the American Academy of Political and Social Science,* vol. 488 (1986), pp. 58–76.

Fosler, R. Scott, and Renee A. Berger, eds. *Public-Private Partnership in American Cities: Seven Case Studies.* Lexington, MA: D. C. Heath, 1982.

Weaver, Clyde, and Marcel Dennert, eds. "Symposium: Public-Private Partnership for Economic Development in the Pittsburgh Region." *Journal of the American Planning Association,* vol. 53, no. 4 (1987), pp. 430–477.

Public Safety   Combined local police and fire departments in which officers are cross-trained for both duties. Public safety departments became popular during the 1980s as local governments sought to cope with fiscal problems by reducing the largest items in their budgets—personnel costs. These cutbacks have been fought by police and fire personnel in many cities, both in the courts and through local political activity. *See also* POLICE, PUBLIC.

Significance   Public safety consolidation has taken different forms in different cities. Sometimes the integration of the two departments is administrative only. In other cases, cities have a partial consolidation of duties in which a police patrol car is equipped with fire-fighting equipment and officers check for fire hazards as they perform their traditional law-enforcement duties. In still others, usually limited to small and medium-sized cities, a fuller integration of duties occurs as officers are trained to perform both police and fire-fighting tasks. Of the larger cities, Fort Lauderdale, Florida, has consolidated its police and fire departments into a single department of public safety. In cities where such consolidation has met substantial resistance, other efforts to cut costs have been developed. Miami, Florida, for example, has hired civilians to handle nonenforcement tasks, such as general nonemergency complaints, that would normally occupy regular law-enforcement officers.

Suggested Reading

Barnett, James H. *A Study of Police and Fire Department Integration in Selected Cities of North America.* Grand Forks: Bureau of Governmental Affairs, University of North Dakota, 1973.

Cholst, Kenneth. "Police-Fire Merger: A Preimplementation Analysis of Performance and Cost." *Journal of Urban Affairs,* vol. 9, no. 2 (1988), pp. 171–188.

Public-School Financing Cases   A series of decisions in state and national courts deciding the constitutionality and statutory legality of discrepancies in funding between wealthy and less well-off school districts. More than a dozen states have had their school financing formulas reviewed, starting with California in 1971. That state's supreme court found the system unconstitutionally violative of both national and state equal-protection clauses in *Serrano v. Priest*, 487 P. 2d 1241 (1971). The New Jersey supreme court two years later found that state's public-school financing plan violative of the state's educational rights clause in *Robinson v. Cahill*, 303 A 2d 273 (1973). However, that same year the U.S. Supreme Court decided *San Antonio Independent School District v. Rodriguez*, 411 U.S. 1 (1973), declaring that public compulsory education is not a protected federal right. The high court deferred to the states and localities, which have the responsibility for making policy and raising most revenues. New York's highest court decided *Levittown v. Nyquist*, 439 N.E. 2d 359, in 1982, finding the state school-aid formula constitutional, albeit very unevenly distributed. Buffalo, New York City, Rochester, and Syracuse unsuccessfully argued in briefs that large cities have special problems providing equal funds to students because of their other public-service burdens, the extra costs associated with big-city living, higher student absenteeism, and a higher frequency of students with special needs. Arizona, Colorado, Connecticut, Idaho, Maryland, Ohio, Oregon, Texas, Washington, West Virginia, and Wyoming all have had court challenges to their public-school funding formulas. *See also* BALKANIZATION; BANKRUPTCY, ACADEMIC; BOUNDARY; COLEMAN REPORT; SCHOOL DISTRICT; TAX, REAL PROPERTY.

Significance   Public-school financing cases take on a high priority because school taxes represent the single largest government expenditure for most communities. In every state public schools are funded by a combination of state and local taxes with more affluent school districts having available substantially more revenue than the poorest districts. If the state legislature does not act to redistribute revenues, taxpayers bring suits to accomplish the objective through alternative access points. As long as there are balkanized jurisdictions within a metropolis with residence linked to class, there will be political challenges in various forms to correct and preserve those fiscal disparities. Courts have split into three answers: (1) It is a political question and jurists should defer to the political branches. (2) The financing formulas are inequitable on either equal-protection grounds or state education aid formulas. (3) The formulas pass judicial scrutiny. The issue will continue to be debated in many forms, especially by legislatures and courts.

Suggested Reading
Guthrie, James W., ed. *School Finance Policies and Practices*. Cambridge, MA: Ballinger, 1980.

Public Sector   The government and its legal extensions. The public sector would therefore include a wide range of activities, policies, and programs, carried on independently of the private sector. The distinction between public and private sectors often has been blurred with the advent of quasi-public organizations and public-private partnerships. *See also* DOWNTOWN DEVELOPMENT AUTHORITY; ECONOMIC DEVELOPMENT; POLICE POWER; POLITICS; PRIVATE SECTOR; PRIVATISM; PRIVATIZATION; PUBLIC CONTRACT; PUBLIC-PRIVATE PARTNERSHIP; QUASI-PUBLIC; SUPPLY-SIDE ECONOMICS.

Significance   The constitutional, legal, social, and political relationships between the public and private sectors have been changing constantly. The U.S. Constitution has addressed many of the general issues of providing for a limited government that also serves the public good, honors the freedoms of its citizens, and protects the rights of individuals. U.S. history illustrates an ever-shifting boundary between what has been considered "public" and "private." The issue of civil rights protections for minorities and women once was considered a private matter, but now is public. Once the matter becomes a public issue, a new set of rules over process and behavior often prevails. For example, private organizations establish their own rules of membership. However, a "private" organization, the Junior Chamber of Commerce (Jaycees), had enough public impact to be considered "public" by the U.S. Supreme Court and was prohibited from discriminating against women in its membership. Privately owned businesses are prohibited from discriminating by the 1964 Civil Rights Act if they are places of public accommodation or have a public presence through a reliance on interstate commerce (*Heart of Atlanta Motel v. U.S.*, 379 U.S. 241 [1964] and *Katzenbach v. McClung,* 379 U.S. 294 [1964]). Conversely, the Court also has determined that state political-party organizations are "private" and can set their own rules about delegate selection, thus ending the open primary in most states. The well-being of large corporations conventionally has been a private matter, but the federal government has loaned millions of dollars to Chrysler Corporation and Lockheed Corporation as public concerns. Most public utilities and the numerous urban economic development projects since the 1970s are viewed as having public purposes and substantial public involvement. The question of right to an abortion has gone from a public matter to a hybrid issue of private choice with some public involvement, and in a 1989 Supreme Court case, the "publicness" of the issue again was raised in *Webster v. Reproductive Health Services,* 106 L Ed 2d 410. Privatization, the movement toward using the private sector to carry out responsibilities formerly assumed by government, has become a popular battle cry during the 1980s and 1990s. Indeed, privatization has occurred, particularly at local levels, as governments have: (1) contracted out services, such as garbage collection, transportation, sewerage facilities, and jails; (2) used vouchers, especially for education and housing; and (3) deregulated certain industries in which government previously barred competition.

Suggested Reading

Bozeman, Barry. *All Organizations Are Public: Bridging Public and Private Organizational Theories.* San Francisco: Jossey-Bass, 1987.

Brettler-Berenyi, Eileen. "Public and Private Sector Interaction Patterns in the Delivery of Local Public Services." *Governmental Finance* (March 1980), pp. 3–9.

Bruggink, T. H. "Public versus Regulated Private Enterprise in the Municipal Water Industry: A Comparison of Operating Costs." *Quarterly Review of Economics and Business,* vol. 22, no. 1 (1982), pp. 111–125.

Edmunds, S. W. *Basics of Private and Public Management.* Lexington, MA: D. C. Heath, 1978.

Fisk, Donald, Herbert Kieseling, and Thomas Muller. *Private Provision of Public Services, An Overview.* Washington, DC: Urban Institute, May 1978.

Fottler, M. D., and N. A. Townsend. "Characteristics of Public and Private Personnel Directors." *Public Personnel Management,* vol. 6, no. 3 (1977), pp. 250–258.

Hawley, W. D., and D. Rogers, eds. *Improving the Quality of Urban Management.* Newbury Park, CA: Sage Publications, 1974.

Lindblom, Charles E. *Politics and Markets.* New York: Basic Books, 1977.

Perry, James L., and K. L Kraemer, eds. *Public Management: Public and Private Perspectives.* Palo Alto, CA: Mayfield, 1983.

Public Utility   In institutional economic theory, a good or possibly a service that is produced for purchase by the entire community and whose price is determined by government in lieu of free-market forces. In public law, a public utility is contrasted to a private right. Public utilities must serve all who can pay, because the good or service is fundamental. Economically, a public utility is placed neither in the private market nor in the public sector; it is in between. It is an attempt to identify the provider in terms of supplying a good or service in which all consumers have a special interest. By supplying fundamental wants, the provider accepts a special status in exchange for restraints on service levels, prices, and long-term planning. In turn, utilities receive a protected or favored return on investment. The restraint on service consists in providing a supply level without delay and up to capacity, not wholly dependent on marginal profitability. In exchange, the whole economy avoids wasteful duplication. Because all public utilities are highly capital-intensive, investors would not enter the market unless assured of a protected rate of return. Legally, in the

United States, a public utility is a category of business conducted as a public calling and vested with a public or community interest. The major U.S. Supreme Court case discussing this property "clothed with and affected by a public interest" was the Granger case of *Munn v. Illinois,* 94 U.S. 113 (1877). Chief Justice Waite contrasted property that is *juris privati* only with property that is *juris publici,* or property open to use by a whole community, such as highways and bridges, and thus subject to special state control. Public utilities have special obligations to the community and can be specially controlled under the police power. Whether defined economically or legally, a public utility is not a fixed category of firms, for that may change with technology and legislative determination of public policy. Rather, a public utility is a concept that some domestic activities are set apart because of their fundamental importance and hence subject to special community supervision. *See also* EASEMENT; INFRASTRUCTURE; POLICE POWER; PROPRIETARY FUNCTION; PUBLIC SECTOR; QUASI-PUBLIC.

Significance   Major categories of public utilities in the United States include (1) transportation; (2) communication; (3) power, heat, and light; and (4) water supply. Transportation was the subject of the landmark *Munn* case, which dealt with grain elevators that stood in "the very gateway of commerce and taking toll from all who pass." Street railroads, interstate railroads, and pipelines viewed as common carriers are other examples. Communication includes the postal service, telephone, telegraph, and cable, but not radio-relayed telephonic communication. Power, heat, and light include electricity, gas, and steam generation. Water service includes potable water and sewers. In Arizona, the privatized fire-fighting company is regulated by the state public utilities commission. It is a fallacy to define a public utility in terms of its being a regulated business, because there is a long history of cities owning public utilities, and *ipso facto* regulation must be by a third party. It is equally a fallacy to define a public utility by focusing on monopolistic or oligopolistic producers, because select utilities such as telephone and gas have entered increased regulated competition because of technological advances. A public utility is characterized by its capacity to be granted an easement, because all utilities must gain access lines and routes to deliver their product. It is also a fallacy to define a utility in terms of dampened competition. The essence of a public utility has changed fundamentally since the 1960s, when the Federal Communications Commission opened up telephone lines to competition. All states and territories in the 1910s and 1920s established public service commissions to regulate some of the utilities. Since their inception, cities have regulated select utilities, such as waterworks and sewage plants. The first national independent regulatory commission was the Interstate Commerce Commission, established in 1887. The trend is toward more national regulation at the wholesale level for utilities, with continued state-level retail regulation, except for water utilities, which usually are controlled locally. States and localities that regulate or own outright a utility conduct their operations under the police power for the community's health, safety, morals, and well-being. A modern urban area is partially defined as an amenity-rich locus of well-run and widely available public utilities.

Q

Qualifications for Office   Requirements imposed by constitution, statute, or charter that must be fulfilled in order to be legally eligible to run for or hold an elected position. (1) The most important and long-standing qualification for office is citizenship. (2) Residency within the jurisdiction is also widely required of local positions. (3) Most local elected positions require the candidate to be a registered voter. (4) In those states that allow or mandate local partisan elections, the candidate must be a registered partisan and not an independent. (5) Age is a common qualification both nationally and frequently in the states. Minimum age can also be imposed at the local level. (6) Past criminal status is also relevant. Convicted felons forfeit the right to vote and hold public office under conditions of a civil death. (7) Governments also impose a one- or two-term limitation on running for the same office, thus preventing experienced leaders from running again. (8) By statute or attorney general opinion, dual officeholding is proscribed, thus eliminating a village official from concurrently holding township office. (9) Cities may disallow a seated official from running for another elected position without resigning the first office. (10) In some states, school board candidates have had to prove property ownership in order to be certified. *See also* RESIDENCY REQUIREMENT; RESIDENT.

Significance   Running for and holding elected public office is a privilege and not a fundamental right. Thus, governments impose qualifications for office. The major function of political parties is to recruit well-qualified candidates for office. The state reduces the party's burden by limiting the field of eligibles before the party locates the most attractive and available person. Age restrictions apply to lower limits: There are no known upper age limits. The rationale is that the community deserves mature leaders. Residential restrictions ensure familiarity and relevant experience. States do not impose any

433

minimum intellectual ability. Both the institutionalized and deinstitutionalized developmentally disabled living in asylums and group homes in most states are eligible to register and run for office. Challenges to allegedly unqualified candidates occur at the preelection stage addressed to the official who certifies candidates for the ballot, or at the postelection stage addressed to a court of competent jurisdiction. There is no statute of limitations on challenging unqualified elected officials. They can be removed from office at any time a qualification is not met.

Quality of Life   The social condition of well-being, as measured by quantified rankings of environmental factors and personally perceived elements, calibrated either separately or jointly. There is no agreement about what elements should be included in a quality-of-life measure. As few as 4 variables are included in some studies (transportation, economy, health, and education), and as many as 17 are included in others (climate, crime rate, housing, wealth, social pathologies, culture, communication, etc.). This has invited intercity comparisons using number of library patrons as a gauge of cultural institutions. However, libraries also lend video games, function as surrogate latchkey programs, and accommodate the homeless, making the comparisons attenuated. Hence, the rankings are subjective evaluations using quantified indicators. Some quality-of-life studies also use subjective measures such as "How would you rate this house as a place in which to live?" and "How would you rate your neighborhood as a place in which to live?" Quality-of-life studies are conducted on the national, state, and county levels. Most are on the city level. Only a few from the 1980s are at the subcity or neighborhood level. Most studies employ a simple linear additive model to arrive at a single ranking. Lists of the best states and cities for living conditions developed from these indicators praise and blame jurisdictions based on the number of infant deaths, hospital beds, physicians, and nurses, all per 100,000 population. *See also* CITY CLASSIFICATION; COMMUNITY FACT BOOKS; SOCIAL INDICATORS.

Significance   H. L. Mencken, editor of the *American Mercury* magazine, was the first to write a quality-of-life article (in 1931) on the worst state in the United States. Mississippi was the worst; Massachusetts the best. In 1975 Arthur Louis of *Fortune* magazine wrote an article for *Harper's* on the quality of life in the 50 most populous U.S. cities. Newark was the worst, St. Louis the penultimate, Seattle and Tulsa the best. The journalistic tradition of intercity comparisons is now a literary genre. In 1987, Yuba City, California, was selected the worst in one study; St. Louis County, Missouri, was singled out as the worst in another study. One author who has computed quality-of-life scores for U.S. and foreign cities used 29 tables for American cities on land, climate, and the physical environment, but when assessing foreign cities reduced the tables to seven, only six of which were common to both studies. There are no protocols on variables, measurements of those variables, definition of elements within the quality of life, inclusion of objective versus subjective standards, or methods for aggregating rankings. Quite often cities do not publish comparable information. This produces voids in the comparison. At the micro scale, intracity quality-of-life studies have identified disadvantaged areas that point to a confluence of factors. This allows the analyst to identify distressed neighborhoods in need of public-policy attention.

Suggested Reading

Berger, Marc C., Glen C. Blomquist, and Werner Walddner. "A Revealed-Preference Ranking of Quality of Life for Metropolitan Areas." *Social Science Quarterly*, vol. 68, no. 4 (1987), pp. 761–778.

Bloomquist, Glenn C., Mark C. Berger, and John P. Hoehn. "New Estimates of Quality of Life in Urban Areas." *American Economic Review*, vol. 78, no. 1 (1988), pp. 89–107.

Dahmann, Donald C. "Assessment of Neighborhood Quality in Metropolitan America." *Urban Affairs Quarterly*, vol. 20, no. 4 (1985), pp. 511–535.

Johnston, Dennis F. "Toward a Comprehensive 'Quality-of-Life' Index." *Social Indicators Research*, vol. 20 (1988), pp. 473–496.

Liu, B. C. *Quality of Life Indicators in United States Metropolitan Areas: A Statistical Analysis*. New York: Praeger, 1976.

Louis, Arthur M. "The Worst American City: A Scientific Study To Confirm or Deny Your Prejudices." *Harper's* (January 1975), pp. 67–71.

Marlin, John T., and James S. Avery, with Stephen T. Collins. *The Book of American City Rankings*. New York: Facts on File Publications, 1983. (100 large U.S. cities.)

Marlin, John T., Immanuel Ness, and Stephen T. Collins. *Book of World City Rankings*. New York: Free Press, 1986. (105 cities worldwide.)

Pacione, Michael. "Quality of Life in Glasgow: An Applied Geographical Analysis." *Environment and Planning A*, vol. 18, no. 6 (1986), pp. 1499–1520.

Swanson, Bert E., and Ronald K. Vogel. "Rating American Cities: Credit Risk, Urban Distress and Quality of Life." *Journal of Urban Affairs*, vol. 8, no. 1 (1986), pp. 67–84.

Quasi-public   In U.S. law, resembling a government but differing in substantive ways from a formal state or one of its subunits. Quasi-public also is known as quasi-government: The term refers to the gray area between distinctly legitimate governing entities that have constitutional powers derived from the people by way of a constitution, and the private sector. "Private" refers to those affairs to which government cannot directly reach and over which the individual has discretion. Public necessarily implies coercion. The dividing line between the two realms changes over time, as when state legislatures declared every abortion a matter of public policy and hence proscribed, and later when the U.S. Supreme Court declared in *Roe v. Wade* that having an abortion in the beginning of a pregnancy is initially a private matter. The line between public and private organizations is also indistinct. At the national level, the Federal National Mortgage Association, "Fannie Mae," is labeled quasi-governmental. At the state level, political parties, public utilities, and regulated professional associations are called quasi-public. At the municipal level, community associations and public-private corporations are considered quasi-public. *See also* POLITICS; PRIVATE SECTOR; PUBLIC-PRIVATE PARTNERSHIP; PUBLIC SECTOR; PUBLIC UTILITY.

Significance   Quasi-public bodies raise the issue of the improper delegation of legislative power to private groups. Modern urban U.S. communities experiencing fiscal distress, if not crisis, have encouraged formation of community associations in new subdivisions. These incorporate with a board of directors empowered to regulate members, with rules that are enforceable in courts. Based on common ownership, the board has coercive powers to levy fees, much as councils levy taxes to supply some of the same services for the balance of the community. Neighborhood civic associations, on the other hand, are voluntary bodies without common property; they cannot petition courts to enforce dues and fee schedules. Public-private partnerships likewise form a blurred line between the two realms; industrial parks or incubator projects with some public capital or public supervision must meet government standards of due process and equal protection. The community association of Radburn, New Jersey, a new town, was accused of establishing a "private government" through contracts enforceable in court. "Private government" is an oxymoron; it translates into a quasi-public organization. Insofar as the American Arbitration Association (AAA) is employed in binding, compulsory public-employee–management disputes, it too is quasi-public.

Suggested Reading
Hyatt, Wayne S. "The Community Association as a Business and Quasi-governmental Organization." *Practical Real Estate Lawyer*, vol. 1, no. 2 (1985), pp. 89–95.

Quick-Take Law   In eminent domain proceedings concerning heretofore privately held land, the immediate vesting of ownership in the government. Quick-take laws are established by state statute to facilitate public acquisition of individual parcels that otherwise might take years to assemble. If the issue is litigated, courts must still find that there is a public necessity for the taking. The just compensation provision of the taking then is negotiated or litigated after the fact without permitting an individual property owner to delay consolidation of a large parcel through protracted judicial maneuvering. *See also* EMINENT DOMAIN; POLETOWN; TAKING.

Significance   Original impetus for the quick-take law was a desire by public authorities for immediate ownership of urban renewal land in order to demolish it or, less commonly, to refurbish it without administrative delay. This often was followed by more delays in courts, sometimes amounting to as much as five years. The most celebrated and, critics would say, infamous use of the quick-take law was in Detroit and Hamtramck, Michigan, in the 1980s. After General Motors gave them a deadline for producing clear title to a built-up portion of the two cities, the local governments complied in a matter of months through expediting condemnation proceedings on the largest urban renewal parcel in U.S. history. In the media and by its detractors, the project was called Poletown. By its proponents, the same project was known as Central Industrial Park. Upon state supreme court review, the two cities were exonerated for the taking on the grounds of alleviating unemployment.

Suggested Reading
Jones, Bryan D., and Lynn W. Bachelor, with Carter Wilson. *The Sustaining Hand: Community Leadership and Corporate Power.* Lawrence: University Press of Kansas, 1986. Chap. 8.

R

Racial Steering   The practice by real estate agents of directing potential home buyers to particular areas for the purpose of maintaining racially segregated neighborhoods. Steering also could include the practice of showing minority families only undesirable houses in a certain city in a surface effort to comply with the law but discouraging those families from purchasing a home in that area. Racial steering is illegal under the Civil Rights Act (Fair Housing Title) of 1968 (25 U.S.C. 1341). In some cases, real estate agents may purposely direct home seekers to a certain neighborhood and thus change the racial makeup of the area and thus make a profit on the panic selling that may occur. This practice, also illegal, is called *blockbusting. See also* BLOCKBUSTING; FAIR HOUSING TITLE; REAL ESTATE AGENT; YONKERS-STYLE POLITICS.

Significance   Racial steering, while illegal, can be quite subtle. Home seekers without complete knowledge of different areas may not know when steering takes place. Many states monitor real estate agents to try to detect steering practices. The usual investigation utilizes Civil Rights Commission employees posing as couples interested in purchasing a home. The couples are called testers and are white as well as black. They have virtually identical interests and financial profiles. If there is a pattern of home offerings in certain neighborhoods, steering can be proved. Reports by the U.S. Department of Justice indicate that more than 80 percent of all suits filed against real estate agents for alleged violations of the Fair Housing Title involve racial steering practices.

Suggested Reading
McRae, Teresa L. "*Havens Realty Corp. v. Coleman*: Extending Standing in Racial Steering Cases to Housing Associations and Testers." *Urban Law Annual*, vol. 22 (1981), pp. 107–134.

Real Estate Agent   An individual authorized to act on behalf of another in the sale, purchase, or transfer of real property. All states require real estate agents to be licensed. The state licensure requirements usually include successful completion of specific educational courses, passing a written examination, and payment of the prescribed fees. Realtor™ is a registered trade name whose use is restricted to members of state and local real estate boards affiliated with the National Association of Realtors (NAR). Realtors operate under a code of ethics of the National Association as well as state-mandated licensure requirements. The National Association of Realtors has approximately 1,850 local boards. *See also* BLOCKBUSTING; RACIAL STEERING; ZONING, EXCLUSIONARY.

Significance   Housing opportunities for many minorities in the United States have suffered from unethical and illegal practices by some elected city officials, sellers, and real estate agents. Activities such as blockbusting, exclusionary zoning, and restrictive covenants have all restricted full access by minorities to housing in the United States. The activities of real estate agents are now heavily regulated by the federal, state, and local levels of government. Fair housing laws prohibit agents from refusing to sell, show, or rent a property because of race, religion, sex, or national origin. While most real estate agents abide by the law and a professional code of ethics, some still practice forms of discrimination, such as racial steering or falsely claiming that a house is no longer available for sale.

Suggested Reading

Galster, George, Fred Freiberg, and Diane L. Houk. "Racial Differences in Real Estate Advertising Practices: An Exploratory Case Study." *Journal of Urban Affairs,* vol. 9, no. 3 (1987), pp. 199–216.

Hughes, Everett Cherrington. "The Growth of an Institution: The Chicago Real Estate Board." Chap. 3 in James Short, ed., *The Social Fabric of the Metropolis: Contributions of the Chicago School of Urban Sociology.* Chicago: University of Chicago Press, 1971. (This classic was written in 1927 and 1928.)

Reapportionment, City   Reassignment of seats in legislative bodies based on decennial census counts so as to conform to the equal-protection clause of the U.S. Constitution's Fourteenth Amendment. City reapportionment is tied to the general issue of equitable distribution of representatives at all levels. The reapportionment revolution began with *Baker v. Carr,* 369 U.S. 186 (1962), when the high court declared the judiciary had jurisdiction over the subject, that the litigants in the *Baker* case had standing to sue in their individual capacity, and that the issue was not a political question but a matter of equal protection of the law. Two years later, the revolution continued with *Westbury v. Sanders,* 376 U.S. 1 (1964), which established congressional district standards for fair representation. Justice Black declared, "As nearly as is practicable one man's vote in a congressional election is to be worth as much as another's." The same year in *Reynolds v. Simms,* 377 U.S. 533, the high court established state legislative district standards. In *Avery v. Midland County, Texas,* 390 U.S. 474 (1968), the U.S. Supreme Court extended the principle of equality of representation to units of local government, including cities, towns, and counties. However, the Court refused to apply the principle to special districts in *Hadley v. Junior College District of Metropolitan Kansas City, Missouri,* 397 U.S. 50 (1970), or *Salyer Land Co. v. Tulare Lake Basin Water Storage District,* 410 U.S. 719 (1973). The Court made its greatest single impact on city reapportionment by declaring the New York City's chief governing body violative of equal protection standards in *Board of Estimate of the City of New York v. Morris,* 103 L Ed 2d 717 (1989). The board was the most important policymaking legislative body in the nation's largest city. *See also* AT-LARGE ELECTION; BOROUGH; VOTER DILUTION CASES.

Significance   City reapportionment refers both to reestablishing legislative fairness of representation between urban and rural areas and to fair allocation of seats within local units of government. The urban-rural readjustment occurred first, primarily in the 1960s. Through reapportionment based on the 1970 census, the state and national legislatures equitably mirrored population shifts. City reapportionment lagged behind, because there were other issues. These related to at-large versus district formats and borough structures, in which some aldermen were elected at large and others were to be distributed within each of the boroughs. The U.S. Supreme Court declared mixed at-large/borough district systems permissible in *Dusch v. Davis,* 387 U.S. 112 (1967). But the Fourteenth Amendment's equal-protection clause was not the only peg on which these cases were decided. The Voting Rights Act of 1965 prohibited local malapportionment based on discrimination against groups. These were voter dilution cases that predicated voting as a communal concern.

Suggested Reading
Baker, Gordon E. *The Reapportionment Revolution: Representation, Political Power, and the Supreme Court.* New York: Random House, 1955, 1966. Chap. 4, "Metropolitan America: New Dimensions of Rural-Urban Conflict."

Recall   A special election to determine whether one or more named elected officials should be removed from office or continue until their term expires. If the candidates are recalled, there may be a simultaneous replacement election. For some jurisdictions, a charter may specify the successor. There are no recall elections for federal officials, but in some states, positions from governor through school board members may be challenged. The election is held after certified petitions by some specific number of electors are secured, often accompanied by a short statement as to why the incumbent deserves recall. The justification for recalls is based on the theory of accountability between regular elections by voter approval or disapproval on grounds of incompetence, corruption, or lack of voter support over policy. Recall provisions are spelled out in constitutions, statutes, or home rule charters. *See also* REFORM GOVERNMENT; VACANCY IN OFFICE.

Significance   Recall elections are allowed in 14 states for both state and local positions and in another 15 states only for local elected offices. Los Angeles was the first major city to adopt the recall in 1903; Oregon was the first state in 1908. Both are in the West, suggesting the early lead of this region in adopting the Progressive reform package of techniques for more direct democracy. The threat of a recall may be as potent as its exercise. The most frequent cause of successful local recalls is a charge of criminal malfeasance. Three issues that commonly trigger recall drives, even if they do not muster enough signatures, are votes on abortion, on raising taxes, and on racially integrating public facilities. North Dakota and Arizona are the only two states to have recalled a governor. Mayors in Los Angeles, Seattle, and Detroit have been recalled, as have members of city councils, but the most commonly recalled officials are school board members. Although Alabama has no recall provision to remove elected officials, citizens can institute a civil impeachment trial in a state circuit court. If found guilty, an official is removed from office and faces separate criminal charges. The current list of states using the recall is found in the annual *Book of the States,* Lexington, KY: Council of State Governments.

Suggested Reading
Cronin, Thomas E. *Direct Democracy: The Politics of the Initiative, Referendum and Recall.* Cambridge, MA: Harvard University Press, 1989.
Price, Charles M. "Electoral Accountability: Local Recalls." *National Civic Review,* vol. 77, no. 2 (1988), pp. 118–123.

Receivership   In federal municipal bankruptcy law, the condition of appointing a fiduciary of the court as a minister to receive and preserve the local government's assets in lieu of the duly elected or appointed public officials. Receivers also are appointed to restructure the public body's finances. The receiver's goal is to restore a balanced ledger and to be discharged so as to return power to conventionally selected leadership or, in rare circumstances, to dissolve the municipal corporation or special district with dispatch by disposing of all assets to creditors. Also, in both federal and state litigation concerning large institutions such as prisons, schools, and public authorities, a receiver is a parajudicial officer appointed by a judge to supervise judicial decrees and formulate policy to bring the public institution into compliance. Examples of such receivers in the 1970s and 1980s include court-appointed supervisors for the Alabama state prisons, South Boston High School, the City of Ecorse, Michigan, and the Boston Housing Authority. *See also* BANKRUPTCY, ACADEMIC; BANKRUPTCY, MUNICIPAL; YONKERS-STYLE POLITICS.

Significance   Federal municipal bankruptcy receivers are appointed on the basis of disinterest and skill, like any other federal bankruptcy receiver. In other cases, appointment of a court receiver is a last resort, being the most intrusive form of judicial intervention into public affairs. The courts will use this device only when contempt proceedings and the levying of fines—no matter how confiscatory—will not achieve the same end. Appointing a receiver amounts to a bench determination that the political process is incapable of remedying a problem and the democratic process is not working to protect basic interests. To preserve assets, prevent waste, and modify procedures injurious to health and civil rights, the court determines an outsider must be brought in and made judicially accountable. Judicial self-restraint limits the use of receivers to those instances where the judge is willing to supervise the institution extensively and continue to hear complaints from bypassed officials. Such actions also herald a breakdown in the capacity of legislative bodies to respond to legal challenges. Receivers are more likely to be appointed for proprietary functions rather than for general governments; they also are likely to be appointed after protracted litigation.

Suggested Reading
Bryan, Mitchell. "An Outlook on the Use of Receivers in the Implementation of Institutional Reform: *Perez v. Boston Housing Authority.*" *Urban Law Annual*, vol. 21 (1981), pp. 255–271.

Redlining   The practice of drawing a boundary, or a "red line," around a map area considered to be a bad investment for mortgage, insurance, or loan companies. One consequence of this practice is that lenders refuse to issue loans, even to qualified buyers, because of the geographic location of the property. Though contemporary redlining does not involve red pencils to mark out areas where investment will be avoided, zip-code designations often are used to classify poor-risk areas. A variety of federal, state, and local restrictions has made redlining practices illegal. However, some housing lenders continue such activities through new tactics, such as taking longer to complete appraisals, requiring higher down payments, charging higher interest rates and closing costs, and demanding more stringent loan qualifications than would be required in areas considered better investment risks. *See also* ABANDONMENT; COMMUNITY REINVESTMENT ACT OF 1977; DISINVESTMENT; HOME MORTGAGE DISCLOSURE ACT OF 1975.

Significance   In some cities, redlining practices have altered substantially the home ownership and the housing stock of many neighborhoods. A 1977 study by the *St. Louis Post-Dispatch* determined that only 5.6 percent of all mortgage money lent by the city's banks went to finance property within the city itself. In 1986, Detroit's seven largest mortgage lenders made no more than 8.9 percent of their total metropolitan-area loans in the city. In Washington, D.C., the figure was less than 12 percent. The practice of redlining has raised many questions concerning the proper role of public and private institutions in building, financing, and improving the nation's housing stock. While the 1968 Civil Rights Act prohibits redlining based on a neighborhood's racial makeup, lenders often cite a wide range of risks in a certain area, thus avoiding the charge of racial discrimination. Many local-government officials have argued that redlining promotes disinvestment, a withdrawal of resources and services from declining areas, which leads to abandonment of housing and general urban decay. Lenders have argued that disinvestment and decay cause them to avoid unreasonable risks. For many years, the Federal Housing Administration (FHA) required that its insured properties be located in neighborhoods that were "economically sound." By the mid-1960s, that requirement was dropped. Many of a city's houses in declining areas have been insured almost exclusively by the FHA, since private lenders have refused to accept the perceived risks of investment. Some of the information about redlining practices came to light only because of disclosure requirements under the Equal Credit Opportunity Act of 1974 and the Home Mortgage Disclosure Act of 1975.

Suggested Reading

Schafer, Robert. *Mortgage Lending Decisions: Criteria and Constraints.* Vols. I and II. Cambridge: Joint Center for Urban Studies of the MIT and Harvard University, December 1978.
Squires, Gregory D., and William Velez. "Insurance Redlining and the Transformation of an Urban Metropolis." *Urban Affairs Quarterly,* vol. 23, no. 1 (1987), pp. 63–83.

Taggert, Harriet Tee, and Kevin W. Smith. "Redlining: An Assessment of the Evidence of Disinvestment in Metropolitan Boston." *Urban Affairs Quarterly*, vol. 17, no. 1 (1981), pp. 91–107.

Referendum   A form of direct democracy in which a legislative measure requires voter approval by some specified majority before it is enforced. A referendum differs from another form of direct democracy, the initiative, in that voters are called on to accept or reject a legislatively drafted proposal. With the initiative, both drafting and passage are by the people. The mechanics for submitting the petition to the council and for voting on the measure may be different from those specified for an initiative drive. Both forms were championed by the Progressive Movement as part of a reformed government. The referendum was designed to lessen the power of the machine by widening mass political participation. Both direct-democracy forms differ from a New England town meeting in that they are not debated and voted in a face-to-face assembly. A referendum must affirm some idea; it cannot simply come out against an idea unless it repeals an ordinance. Referenda cannot substitute for administrative discretion, nor generally can they repeal emergency ordinances. *See also* BOND ELECTION; FLUORIDATION POLITICS; INITIATIVE; REFORM GOVERNMENT.

Significance   As of 1988, 39 states required or allowed local referenda. They are used in some form in 49 states. It is estimated there are 10,000 or more referenda conducted annually. They are or have been especially important to public-policy formulation in annexations, bond issues, open-housing ordinances, proposals to build water and sewer systems, and measures to fluoridate municipal water supplies. In *James v. Valtierra*, 402 U.S. 137 (1971), the U.S. Supreme Court upheld a California state constitutional amendment requiring a referendum on publicly sponsored, local, low-income housing. The United States is one of the few democracies never to have used a national referendum. Congress may propose a referendum to decide the future of Puerto Rico in the early 1990s. Although referenda have not been studied systematically at the local level, several generalizations emerge. Turnout is generally lower than for on-year elections. It is possible for a minority of the total electorate to win in a referendum, as it is in a general election as well. Turnout is the highest when combined with an on-year election. As with other types of elections, turnout is a function of both race and class, with blacks and lower socioeconomic classes underrepresented at the polls. Most voters typically do not clearly understand the issues or know which groups have endorsed each side. The "anti" voters are often better organized, attested to by the large number of defeated referendums.

Suggested Reading

Butler, David, and Austin Ranney, eds. *Referendums: A Comparative Study of Practice and Theory.* Washington, DC: American Enterprise Institute, 1978. Especially Chap. 4.

Cronin, Thomas E. *Direct Democracy: The Politics of the Initiative, Referendum and Recall.* Cambridge, MA: Harvard University Press, 1989.

Hahn, Harlan, and Sheldon Kamieniecki. *Referendum Voting: Social Status and Policy Preferences.* Westport, CT: Greenwood Press, 1987.

Hamilton, Howard. "Direct Legislation: Some Implications of Open Housing Referenda." *American Political Science Review,* vol. 64, no. 1 (1970), pp. 124–137.

Magleby, David B. *Direct Legislation: Voting on Ballot Propositions in the United States.* Baltimore: Johns Hopkins University Press, 1964.

Shepard, W. Bruce. "Participation in Local Policy Making: The Case of Referenda." *Social Science Quarterly,* vol. 56, no. 1 (1975), pp. 55–70.

Reform Government   A municipality structured to reflect the urban Progressive Movement goals of reduced corruption, increased efficiency, and greater responsiveness to the electorate through more popular political participation. The Progressive Movement, which fostered reform governments, began in the 1890s. It advocated a package of structural changes that could break the hated urban party machine and better represent values of middle-class and mainstream business America. Major components included (1) direct primaries, which bypassed smoked-filled rooms, and (2) the direct democracy devices of the initiative and referendum. It sometimes included (3) the right to recall elected officials and replace them with others before the next scheduled election. Three of the most important reforms called for (4) at-large elections to bypass ward bosses, (5) nonpartisan elections to bypass corrupt political parties, and (6) the council-manager form of government, first adopted in 1912 in Sumter, South Carolina. (7) The short ballot, with its greater accountability, was a popular reform. Allied with it were (8) small, unicameral city councils of five to nine members, also designed for direct accountability. (9) Reformers championed off-year elections in order to focus attention on local issues and differentiate them from state and national contests in even-numbered years. Progressives called for purity at the ballot box through (10) the Australian ballot, which was not only filled out in secret but was printed at government expense. Progressives also advocated (11) increased appointive powers for the mayor, without city council consent, in order to make that office more accountable, (12) civil service reform at the local level to improve professional management and strengthen codes of ethics, (13) overlapping terms of office designed to avoid the possibility that one issue in one election would produce a landslide and hence total turnover in elective office,

(14) elections that required a simple majority and, if necessary, runoff elections to promote democratic choice, (15) nominal or no remuneration for city council duties on the grounds that a public office is a public trust and should be sought as a civic duty, and (16) home rule, which focused attention on local innovation and the city's capacity to decide its own level of taxation and bond indebtedness. For a long time, (17) proportional representation was connected with the movement. First adopted in 1915 in Ashtabula, Ohio, it never caught on. *See also* AT-LARGE ELECTION; HOME RULE; NONPARTISAN ELECTION; PROPORTIONAL REPRESENTATION; RECALL; REFERENDUM; PRODUCTIVITY; URBAN POLITICAL MACHINE.

Significance   No city adopted all the Progressive Era reform government ideas; some major cities such as Chicago were left largely untouched by the era. Cleveland and Toledo, Ohio, on the other hand, were forerunners in the movement, in part because of the leadership of Mayors Tom L. Johnson (1901–1909) and Samuel "Golden Rule" Jones (1901–1903). The reforms reduced but did not eliminate corruption. They did lower public spending and affect participation levels. The most conspicuous but unsuccessful Progressive reform was proportional representation, which remains operative in only one American city—Cambridge, Massachusetts—and one school system—the New York City Board of Education. Many of these structural features are built into the American city fabric of today. When used in aggregate data research by urban scholars, these 17 components are reduced to 3, namely, at-large elections, nonpartisan ballots, and the presence of a city manager. There are obvious limits to how well these three truly represent the reform tradition.

Suggested Reading
Clark, Terry Nichols, and Lorna Crowley Ferguson. *City Money: Political Process, Fiscal Strain, and Retrenchment.* New York: Columbia University Press, 1983. Chap. 9 and App. 5.
Hennessy, Timothy M. "Problems in Concept Formation: The Ethos 'Theory' and the Comparative Study of Urban Politics." *Midwest Journal of Political Science,* vol. 14, no. 4 (1970), pp. 555–557. (A critique of this simplification as a type concept.)
Lineberry, Robert L., and Edmund P. Fowler. "Reformism and Public Policies in American Cities." *American Political Science Review,* vol. 61, no. 3 (1967), pp. 701–716.
Lyons, William. "Reform and Response in American Cities: Structure and Policy Reconsidered." *Social Science Quarterly,* vol. 59, no. 1 (1978), pp. 118–131.

Registrar of Deeds   A county or local official who records and maintains titles and liens against property. A registrar of deeds, sometimes known as a recorder of deeds, may be appointed or elected. One nationwide survey found that more than 90 percent of the registrars of deeds were elected. Terms of office ranged from two to six years, with most serving for four years. Because the office is administrative rather than policymaking in nature, many students of local government advocate that it be appointive and combined with the office of clerk.

Significance   In many states and localities, the registrar of deeds system for recording property titles has been established to simplify sales and transfers and to protect interests of buyers and sellers. An examination of the public records of a property, called a title search, is ordered by a mortgage lender (at the borrower's cost) to determine whether there are liens or encumbrances on the property in question. The search usually is performed by a title or abstract company. Statutory fees or transfer taxes often are imposed upon the recorded documents.

Relocation   The forced movement of property holders or residents from an area due to a change in land use. Most typically, homeowners and renters are forced to relocate because of a public-works project, such as a freeway, or a private economic development project, such as a manufacturing plant. Owners of property acquired for any project that uses federal funding are compensated under the rules and procedures established by the Uniform Relocation Assistance and Real Property Acquisition Policies Act of 1970 (42 U.S.C. 4601–4655). The Office of Community Planning and Development of the Department of Housing and Urban Development establishes the policies and procedures for treatment of displaced persons, and monitors their relocation to ensure proper treatment under the law. *See also* EMINENT DOMAIN; DISPLACEMENT; POLETOWN.

Significance   Relocation of individuals and businesses has been a common by-product of development since the wave of federal public-works programs in the 1930s. Relocation continued with the urban-renewal programs begun under the 1949 Housing Act. Most recently it has involved displacement caused by private economic-development projects, such as the Poletown General Motors Assembly plant in Detroit. Federal courts have held that relocation benefits are available only to those who are directed to vacate their property because of federal acquisition of that property, not for those who somehow are displaced in an indirect way by federal programs.

Suggested Reading
Buie, Debra A. "The Uniform Relocation Act: Eligibility Requirements for Relocation Benefits—*Young v. Harris.*" *Urban Law Annual,* vol. 19 (1980), pp. 207–227.

Rubenstein, James M. "Relocation of Families for Public Improvement Projects: Lessons from Baltimore." *Journal of the American Planning Association,* vol. 54, no. 2 (1988), pp. 185–196.

Rent Control   A ceiling placed by local ordinance on the amount of rent a landlord may charge tenants. Though the laws vary with each city, many rent-control ordinances allow for specific, limited increases in rents annually. In some cities, such as New York City, rental units are designated either as rent-control or "rent stabilization" buildings. By contrast, rent stabilization allows for additional increases in rent for specific reasons, subject to guidelines imposed by local rules. In 1989, various forms of rent control were in place in about 200 municipalities, mostly in California and New Jersey. Many of the nation's largest cities—New York City, Boston, San Francisco, Los Angeles, and Washington, D.C.—provide for some form of rent control. Other major cities, such as Philadelphia, Detroit, and New Orleans, have no rent-control provisions. *See also* HOMELESS.

Significance   Rent control has become an issue in the urban centers of the United States, as the problem of homelessness has generated increasing public concern. Every winter, the mass media carry stories of homeless urban citizens, particularly those who live in cold climates. However, rent-control ordinances date as far back as 1949 in New York City, where about two-thirds of all apartments are covered by rent control or stabilization. Supporters of rent control argue that poor residents virtually are prevented from locating affordable, decent housing in cities that have low vacancy rates and a housing market that favors landlords. Critics of rent control argue such ordinances drive away builders and that ultimately all new housing stops. Landlords lose their incentive properly to maintain buildings. If neglected too long, the structures must ultimately be demolished. By 1988, 15 states had established laws prohibiting their cities from establishing rent-control ordinances. Also in 1988, the U.S. Supreme Court upheld a San Jose, California, rent-control law with its 6–2 decision in *Pennell v. San Jose,* 99 L Ed 2d 1. This decision has been seen as making it harder to overturn similar rent-control ordinances in other cities.

Suggested Reading
Bartelt, David W., and Ronald Lawson. "Rent Control and Abandonment: A Second Look at the Evidence." *Journal of Urban Affairs,* vol. 4, no. 4 (1982), pp. 49–64.
Kaish, Stanely, "What Is 'Just and Reasonable' in Rent Control?" *American Journal of Economics and Sociology,* vol. 40, no. 2 (1981), pp. 129–137.

Rent Strike   A direct-action tactic used by a tenant organization to force a change in rental conditions by withholding rent payments. In a rent-strike action, the rent monies normally are placed in an escrow account to demonstrate goodwill. Rent strikes evolved out of the larger consumer movement of the 1960s and most often occur in tight housing markets such as revitalized downtown neighborhoods or college campus markets, in which increases in rents often conflict with the relatively low incomes of the tenants. Issues that have mobilized tenants have included rent control, building safety and maintenance, attempts to convert buildings to condominiums, eviction procedures, raising rents disproportionate to the costs of building improvements, and alleged landlord "arson for profit." *See also* CONDOMINIUM CONVERSION; HOUSING, COOPERATIVE; HOUSING COURT; RENT CONTROL.

Significance   Rent strikes have brought to the general public an increased awareness of the rights of renters. In the eyes of the law, the landlord-tenant relationship traditionally has weighed heavily in favor of the property owner. The law has long imposed on the tenant an obligation to pay rent. Any failure to pay rent gave a tenant no legal protection. Renters are similar to many consumers in that they are relatively difficult to organize for collective action. The transient nature of the renter population often has made organizing more difficult. The oldest tenant organization is New York City's Metropolitan Council on Housing, formed in 1959 and active in the city's "Co-op City" complex. Another, the New Jersey Tenants' Organization, was formed in 1969 and had over 80,000 dues-paying members by the early 1980s. This organization was instrumental in promoting the strongest tenant-landlord laws in the country and was active in supporting candidates for state and local elections. In 1980, Santa Monica, California, saw the election of several pro-tenant candidates for the city council backed by the Santa Monicans for Renters' Rights. The city has strong rent control and condominium conversion ordinances, and it has actively negotiated housing linkage agreements with developers who wished to build in the city.

Suggested Reading
Brill, Harry. *Why Organizers Fail: The Story of a Rent Strike*. Berkeley: University of California Press, 1971.
Lipsky, Michael. *Protest in City Politics: Rent Strikes, Housing and the Power of the Poor*. Chicago: Rand McNally, 1970.

Reputational Analysis   A method of understanding power and its distribution. Reputational analysis of community power is most often associated with the *Middletown* studies of Muncie, Indiana, by Robert and Helen Lynd, and Floyd Hunter's study of Atlanta, *Community Power Structure*. This analysis is considered "reputational" since its method emphasizes interviews with presumed "knowledgeables" who are asked which citizens of a community have the reputation for being influential or powerful. Reputational analysis is associated with positional analysis, in that researchers of power also have determined which positions within a community are influential, then conclude that the holders of such positions have power. While the initial reputational studies involved power within specific communities, later scholars, such as C. Wright Mills in *The Power Elite* (1956), attempted to use a similar technique to investigate the national power structure. The major competing theory of power distribution is called pluralism, and it too was a product of a community power study, Robert Dahl's investigation of New Haven, Connecticut, *Who Governs?* (1961). Many studies done since the 1950s attempt to determine who wields power in cities and across the nation. Generally, disciplinary training has led political scientists to use a decision-making analysis and to conclude that pluralism is most accurate in describing power, while sociologists tend to emphasize the reputational analysis and conclude a class and power structure exists, dominated by a power elite.

While Floyd Hunter's reputational method of analysis has incurred considerable criticism, his application of this method to the community power structure was academically revolutionary. Hunter had worked as a fund-raiser for the United Service Organizations (USO) during World War II. As he traveled from city to city, his job required that he quickly find individuals who were able to raise money and "get things done" in that city. Consequently, he had considerable experience locating community leaders, whether they were elected officials, business executives, or heads of major community organizations. The most practical and direct method for determining these civic leaders was to ask people to name individuals within the community who could get things accomplished. Hunter's camouflaged case study of power in Atlanta, which he called "Regional City," essentially used the same technique, asking people who they thought had power, why those individuals had power, and how they used it. Lists of community leaders were developed from among members of local ogranizations and from newspaper articles. A panel of knowledgeable people was asked to screen the original list of 175 power holders; that list was reduced to 40 leaders considered the most influential. From personal interviews of the 40, Hunter developed his analysis of Atlanta's power holders. Because this group dominated the city's economy, lived in the same wealthy neighborhoods, and belonged to the same social clubs, Hunter concluded that Atlanta operated under a "power structure." Most surprisingly, only 4 of Hunter's final 40 influentials were public officials. The rest were leaders in the business world. The tenets of the reputational analysis are as follows: (1) Power is defined as having the reputation for being able to get things done in a community. Those who control the economic resources in a community tend to be the most powerful. (2) A culture of leadership exists, in which the powerful tend to live in the same neighborhoods, belong to the same social clubs, and interact socially on a regular basis. (3) Power is structured; that is, the same individuals and families tend to hold power over a long period. In addition, those with power tend to dominate a wide variety of issue areas. (4) The power elite is relatively insulated from outside influences, and average citizens are unable to be meaningful participants in the decision-making process. *See also* CAMOUFLAGED CASE STUDIES; CASE STUDY; MIDDLETOWN; PLURALISM; YANKEE CITY.

Significance   Much of the difference between pluralists and power elite theorists rests with their different definitions of *power*. The term is so elusive to social scientists that no real consensus has been reached. Researchers originally chose to study power by conducting case studies of single communities from the 1920s to the 1970s. Studying single cities had certain advantages. Individual jurisdictions are more accessible and are small enough to make a complex investigation more manageable. Reputational analysis is criticized because it is not sufficiently systematic, relies on the opinions of a small group of individuals, and promotes a conspiracy theory that empirically cannot be proved.

Suggested Reading

D'Antonio, William V., and Eugene C. Erickson. "The Reputational Technique as a Measure of Community Power." *American Sociological Review*, vol. 27, no. 3 (1962), pp. 362–376.

Domhoff, G. William. *Who Really Rules?* Santa Monica, CA: Goodyear, 1978.

Dye, Thomas R. "Community Power Studies." In James A. Robinson, ed., *Political Science Annual*. Vol. 2. Indianapolis: Bobbs-Merrill, 1970.

Ewen, Lynda Ann. *Corporate Power and Urban Crisis in Detroit*. Princeton: Princeton University Press, 1978.

French, Robert Mills. *The Community: A Comparative Perspective*. Itasca, IL: F. E. Peacock Publishers, 1969.

Hawley, Willis D., and James H. Svara. *The Study of Community Power: A Bibliographic Review*. Santa Barbara, CA: ABC-CLIO, 1972.

Hunter, Floyd. *Community Power Structure*. Chapel Hill: University of North Carolina Press, 1953.

———. *Community Power Succession: Atlanta's Policy-makers Revisited*. Chapel Hill: University of North Carolina Press, 1980.

Lukes, Steven. *Power: A Radical View*. London: Macmillan, 1974.

McConnell, Grant. *Private Power and American Democracy*. New York: Vintage Books, 1966.

Parenti, Michael. "Power and Pluralism: A View from the Bottom." *Journal of Politics,* vol. 32, no. 3 (1970), pp. 501–530.
Presthus, Robert. *Men at the Top.* New York: Oxford University Press, 1964.
Trounstine, Philip J., and Terry Christensen. *Movers and Shakers: The Study of Community Power.* New York: St. Martin's Press, 1982.

Residency Requirement   A regulation mandating that a class of individuals live or move into a jurisdiction as a condition of holding office. A residency requirement ties daytime occupation to nighttime residency. The position may be elected, appointed, or open to competitive employment. Such regulations are based on state statutes that allow cities to set qualifications in city or county ordinances, executive orders, or Civil Service Commission administrative rules. Courts make a distinction between *durational residency,* which refers to a waiting period before an individual is eligible for a right or benefit, and *continuing residency,* which mandates that an individual who obtains a position must move in and remain within the municipality. In *Shapiro v. Thompson,* 394 U.S. 618 (1969), the U.S. Supreme Court limited the durational requirement of welfare recipients to 30 days' residency. Durational residency also properly applies to obtaining various licenses, voting, and qualifying for special tuition rates. Residency requirements have racial implications. In the late 1980s, the U.S. Justice Department started action against suburbs that had durational residency ordinance requirements effectively blocking minorities and especially blacks from competing against whites for local government employment. They won consent orders against such cities as Cicero, Illinois, and Warren, Michigan, opening up job eligibility to blacks and other minorities living in nearby central cities. The national level argued that suburbs were artificially depleting the available metropolitan job market. In turn, black politicians in predominantly black inner cities favor residency restrictions to reduce the competition for their constituents. *See also* COPPER CANYON; FEDERALISM; RESIDENT.

Significance   A residency requirement increases the chance for a local individual to gain employment at the expense of the whole area's community employment pool. By narrowly proscribing availability, it also limits the municipality in finding and hiring the most qualified person. Arguments for residency requirements, on the other hand, include reducing local unemployment, establishing a staff familiar with local conditions and needs, and finding staff and line personnel who can respond rapidly to an emergency by living in close proximity. The city also benefits from the multiplier effect of funds spent locally. In the case of police, requiring off-duty officers to live within the community may have a deterrent effect on crime. Most cities with populations greater than 250,000 have continuing residency rules. Courts have been unable to reach a consensus on durational residency rules, frowning on long-term requirements of three or five years but splitting on the wisdom of year-long residency as a prerequisite for running for office. In fact, residency requirements for appointed public positions are not administered uniformly; exceptions are made and special permissions granted, and only some employees are subject to dismissal for failure to comply. Central-city public employee unions oppose residency requirements, whereas some suburban public employee unions favor them as a means to keep most of the labor pool from competing for jobs. The practical effect of *de facto* white suburban communities establishing residency rules is to keep their public employees all or nearly all white.

Suggested Reading

Eisinger, Peter. "Black Mayors and the Politics of Racial Economic Advancement." In Harlan Hahn and Charles H. Levine, eds., *Readings in Urban Politics*, 2nd ed. New York: Longman, 1984, pp. 249–260.

Hager, Connie M. "Residency Requirements for City Employees: Important Incentives in Today's Urban Crisis." *Urban Law Annual*, vol. 18 (1980), pp. 197–222.

Myers, Ross S. "The Constitutionality of Continuing Residency Requirements for Local Government Employees: A Second Look." *California Western Law Review*, vol. 23, no. 1 (1986), pp. 24–41.

Resident   One who legally has adopted a place of habitation and has qualified after a waiting period for rights and privileges under state law. One who accepts the duties and obligations of the jurisdiction, for example, may be required to be domiciled to qualify for a divorce or probate an estate. A state can establish residency requirements to vote and be eligible for elected public office. Residency generally is determined by a two-part test. First, a resident is one who expresses intent to domicile within a jurisdiction. Second, the intent must be manifested by living or incorporating or doing substantial business within the jurisdiction. Where intent and outward manifestation are in conflict, residency status may be in question. Tax status follows from having residence. Residency is also a requisite for naturalization and citizenship. Labor union contracts or charters may require one to be a resident or to become a resident in order to work for a local unit of government. Residents qualify for lower tuition and for favorable treatment in obtaining hunting and fishing licenses. A resident may be eligible for hospitalization at county expense, for workers' compensation, or public welfare benefits that a nonresident cannot receive. A *resident alien* is one who has permission from the

Immigration and Naturalization Service (INS) to live permanently in the country and who has obtained a "green card" attesting to that status. *See also* FEDERALISM; SET-ASIDE.

Significance　　*Resident* is one of the most ambiguous terms in the common law. It has a restricted or enlarged meaning depending upon context. The term has caused substantial litigation. For nearly all purposes, a person may be a resident of only one state and local jurisdiction at a time. It has been variously defined by constitution, statute, charter, the courts, and in contracts. Since the Fourteenth Amendment of 1868, there has been a clear definition of a citizen: "All persons born or naturalized in the United States, and subject to the jurisdiction thereof, are citizens of the United States and of the state wherein they reside." When this clause was interpreted by the U.S. Supreme Court in the *Slaughterhouse* cases, 83 U.S. 36 (1873), the Court declared, "There is a citizenship of the United States, and a citizenship of a state, which are distinct from each other, and which depend upon different characteristics or circumstances in the individual." Justice Miller went on to write that "a citizen of the United States can, of his own volition, become a citizen of any State of the Union by a bona fide residence therein." In this context, state citizenship simply means being a state resident. On the other hand, *citizen* and *resident* are not necessarily synonymous. Citizenship attaches to a constitutional level, whereas residency attaches to a substate level. If a citizen is one who has the rights and privileges to receive protection from a state and who owes allegiance to a state, then there is dual citizenship in the United States because of federalism. In turn, a resident is one who lives in a substate jurisdiction such as a county, township, village, or city, according to some waiting period. One political implication of residential status is favorable treatment by private contractors on city-financed construction projects. Cities are permitted to mandate the hiring of a quota of residents. This quota, or set-aside, survived a constitutional challenge in *White v. Massachusetts Council of Construction Employers*, 406 U.S. 204 (1983). Another implication is that in some states cities can tax nonresidents who work in a jurisdiction without extending to them the right to vote.

Restrictive Covenant　　A written agreement limiting the use and occupancy of real property. Restrictive covenants are private agreements, in contrast to public zoning ordinances. These private agreements are written into the instruments of real property, such as deeds and leases. Municipal-owned property sold to individuals also may include restrictive covenants in order to limit use. Though covenants theoretically bind all future owners, some include a specific expiration date or length of time specified by state law. Restrictive covenants used for racial discrimination purposes were declared unenforceable by the U.S. Supreme Court in *Shelly v. Kraemer,* 334 U.S. 1 (1948), and *Hurd v. Hodge,* 334 U.S. 24 (1948). *See also* LAND-USE CONTROL; ZONING.

Significance   Restrictive covenants are often associated with racial discrimination. They also have been used to limit land use beyond the police power given to communities in their zoning authority. Urban planners have encouraged the use of restrictive covenants by developers to facilitate additional objectives of land-use control that lay beyond the scope of public zoning restrictions. Examples include minimum square footage for houses, side yard setbacks, height limits, and prohibition against fences. The Federal Housing Administration (FHA) still encourages the use of restrictive covenants to maintain neighborhood quality. Some local restrictive covenants limit the ability of developers to install manufactured homes in certain subdivisions. Houston, which has no zoning ordinance, requires private restrictive covenants as a prerequisite for issuing building permits. The Texas legislature has enacted law allowing cities without zoning ordinances to sue for violations in restrictive covenants, thus giving covenants force of law. Critics have questioned the constitutionality of this, alleging unlawful delegation of legislative authority to nongovernmental parties. Others argue that covenants without zoning or master plans constitute control without planning. In general, covenants have been used by local governments to complement zoning with a form of "contract zoning," in which municipalities rezone an individual parcel of land in exchange for a land restriction.

Suggested Reading
Bradburn, Norman N., Seymour Sudman, and Galen L. Gockel. *Side by Side: Integrated Neighborhoods in America.* Chicago: Quadrangle Books, 1971.

Revenue Improvement Bond (RIB)   A directly marketed local government debt issue that bypasses bond-rating services as well as underwriters and is sold in small denominations. RIBs also are known as citizen bonds, because they generally are purchased by local residents and not through brokers, in units substantially smaller than the conventional $5,000 amount. Rather than the local unit receiving one check from the principal bond-placement office for the value of the bonds, minus fees and commissions, these bonds are sold by the local government from its offices and through its own advertising promotion. *See also* BOND, MUNICIPAL; BOND AND RATING SERVICES.

Significance   RIBs are vehicles for debt management approved in concept by the research center of the Washington, D.C.–based Government Finance Officers Association (GFOA). Advantages include saving the local unit overhead costs, because the bonds are discounted and have no coupons to redeem. They are affordable to the small, local investor who otherwise might not have enough capital accumulated for the larger conventional denominations. By adding a put option, the bondholder is assured of an early redemption, because there is a weak secondary market. RIBs generate goodwill and positive publicity for the local government by direct contact with nontraditional investors. Disadvantages include an inability to market the bonds out of state because they do not necessarily comply with other states' security laws. Most important, they are confined to relatively modest offerings in comparison to the million-dollar placements available only through major brokerage houses. Fort Worth, Texas, has prepared literature on its experience with the bonds.

Revenue Surplus   Extra funds available to a government above short-term expenditure levels as taxes become due. Because tax yields are seasonal, a revenue surplus is considered desirable for governments so available capital exceeds need. Revenue surplus funds are a necessary part of a government's budget to avoid cash flow difficulties such as payless paydays for government employees. Surpluses usually give a government three- and six-month cushions until the next taxes become due. *See also* INCOME SOURCES, URBAN; SINKING FUND; TAX ANTICIPATION NOTE.

Significance   The notion of revenue surplus illustrates the fiscal problems facing governments that collect property tax money once each year. With balanced budgets, state and local governments project to spend no more than they generate in revenues, but many factors affect revenue amounts and spending patterns of governments. In an effort to smooth over the unpredictability of revenue generation, local governments have resorted to techniques that assure revenues will be available to pay for daily operating expenses. Many cities borrow money based on future tax receipts, called tax anticipation notes (TANs). Under the standards established by the American Institute of Certified Public Accountants (AICPA), governments are required to declare publicly the surplus and deficit status of each fund contained in the budget. In certain systems, a surplus of more than a three-month cushion of capital to meet fiscal year obligations might indicate tax rates should be reduced. Whereas many cities have operated under considerable fiscal stress during the 1970s and 1980s, some of the nation's wealthier municipalities boast regular surpluses, and strict auditing should help determine local action regarding such surpluses.

Suggested Reading
Mikesell, John L. *Fiscal Administration.* Homewood, IL: Dorsey Press, 1982.

Riot   In statutory and common law, unlawful conduct by an assembly of three or more people who are disturbing the peace, who have been told to disperse, and who threaten to destroy property or take life. In general usage, a riot is an unplanned form of collective domestic violence. There is no recorded usage of the term *rural riot*. The distinction among a riot, a rebellion, and an insurrection is not clear. What contemporaries called the Boston Massacre of 1770 is now called a riot. Race riots can be between blacks and whites, reds and whites, Chinese and whites, or other racial groups. The New York City draft riots of 1863, during the Civil War, placed Irish-Americans against blacks who were not being drafted to fight for their fellow blacks. The Detroit events of 1919 were race riots. Because they did not pit blacks against whites, the 1967 Detroit disturbances are more properly called riots by whites and blacks, despite the fact they are popularly regarded as race riots. The 1943 so-called Zoot-Suit Race Riots in Los Angeles pitted Mexican-Americans against largely Anglo military personnel. It is difficult to draw the line between permissible and protected assembly and impermissible, nonpeaceable assembly that is not protected by the First Amendment. Courts make such distinctions after the fact, based upon determination of the proper time, place, and manner of exercise. Riots often are investigated after the fact by executive agencies or *ad hoc* commissions, such as the Kerner Commission of 1968 or the Walker Commission Report on the Chicago Police Riot of the same year. Seven guidelines conventionally used to diagnose riots after the fact include assessing whether they were (1) spontaneous or planned by insiders or outsiders; (2) driven by irrational or rational behavior; (3) used by a few leaders or amounting to a form of mass behavior; (4) a single event or an ongoing *modus operandi*; (5) a statement of moral indignation, immoral activity, or amoral events; (6) a plea for separate status, pleas for access to the system, or actions by those who felt their relative deprivation from the good life; and (7) events designed to overturn the *status quo*, events that should modify access to the power structure, or events that should have no bearing on the future power structure. *See also* AGENDA SETTING; BLACK POWER; KERNER COMMISSION; PARTICIPATION; URBAN COALITION; URBAN CRISIS.

Significance   Riots are among the most widely studied events in urban politics. They are a staple of urban British and American history. "To read one the riot act" is a phrase derived from a 1714 British statute that required a constable to read a notice to disperse before arresting those deemed improperly assembled. The U.S. riots of the 1960s produced a flood of research into their causes and consequences. Many of the findings were keyed to researchers' left, center, or rightist ideological persuasion. Right-of-center explanations focused on conspiracy theories. The post-1967 Congress responded by making it a federal offense to cross a state boundary with the intent of creating a riot. Left-of-center analysis tended to emphasize the role of the underclass, concluding that riots were a precursor of more widespread dissatisfaction with the capitalist system. Centrists, especially in the Johnson and Nixon administrations, stressed the need for "law and order." They largely denied that there were any major curable causes outside of inadequate police protection. Hence, Congress passed the Safe Streets Act, which provided cities with improved police equipment through the Law Enforcement Assistance Administration (LEAA). The mass media performed many *postmortems* about their own possible role in fanning the fires through overvivid reporting. Specific ameliorative efforts derived from the 1960s riots included the creation of urban coalitions and federally sponsored riot insurance for inner-city residents and businesses through the Federal Emergency Management Agency (FEMA). The riots exacerbated white flight from select central cities and became an index of the seriousness of the urban crisis. The January 1989 riots in Miami, Florida, were a reminder that rioting was not just a problem of the 1960s.

Suggested Reading

Boskin, Joseph, ed. *Urban Racial Violence in the Twentieth Century,* 2nd ed. Beverly Hills: Glencoe Press, 1976.
Davis, Terry. "The Forms of Collective Racial Violence." *Political Studies,* vol. 34, no. 1 (1986), pp. 40–60.
Feagin, Joe R., and Harlan Hahn. *Ghetto Revolts: The Politics of Violence in American Cities.* New York: Macmillan, 1973.
Fine, Sidney. *Violence in the Model City: The Cavanagh Administration, Race Relations and the Detroit Riot of 1967.* Ann Arbor: University of Michigan Press, 1989.
Hofstadter, Richard, and Michael Wallace, ed. *American Violence: A Documentary History.* New York: Random House, 1970.
Manheim, Jarol B., and Melanie Wallace, comps. *Political Violence in the United States 1875–1974: A Bibliography.* Garland Reference Library of Social Science, vol. 8. New York: Garland Publishing, 1975.
Sears, David O., and John B. McConahay. *The Politics of Violence: The New Urban Blacks and the Watts Riot.* Boston: Houghton Mifflin, 1973.
Smith, John W., and Lois H. Smith. "First Amendment Freedoms and the Politics of Mass Participation: Perspective on the 1967 Detroit Riot."

Chap. 1 in Richard A. Chikota and Michael C. Moran, eds., *Riot in the Cities: An Analytical Symposium on the Cause and Effects*. Rutherford, NJ: Fairleigh Dickinson University Press, 1968–1970, pp. 13–72.

Waskow, Arthur I. *From Race Riot to Sit-in: 1919 and the 1960s: A Study in the Connections between Conflict and Violence*. Garden City, NY: Doubleday, 1966.

Road Classification   Typology of highways and streets according to function, financing, ownership, or traffic count. Governments maintain an elaborate system of classifying roads to determine liability and responsibility for maintenance. Functional classification of roads includes expressways, main arteries, secondary or collectors, and residential or local streets. Traffic lights and parking are forbidden on those higher on the list, whereas traffic signs and limited parking are allowed on the local or residential streets. Speed limits are determined by ownership, location, and function. Financing categories include the national interstate highway system, the major state-owned arteries, county-owned and maintained roads, municipal-maintained streets, and privately owned and maintained streets. Ownership is classified according to general governments, such as a state, by toll road authorities, or by private corporations owning toll ways and bridges. Traffic counts are taken regularly on most thoroughfares by direction, date, and hour to calibrate patterns and anticipate wear levels. *See also* INFRASTRUCTURE; INTERSTATE HIGHWAY SYSTEM; MACHINE SPACE; PRIVATE STREET; TRAFFIC ANALYSIS.

Significance   Road classification is one of the most important aspects of local government budgeting because of the immense costs involved in land acquisition, initial construction, and maintenance. Budgets for roads are technical financial plans. The typology is not uniform across the states. Few citizens understand that their daily commute may take them across highways, streets, roads, and alleys owned and operated by six different levels of government (national, state, authority, county, township, and municipal), as well as private corporations and private condominium associations. With those involved in traffic accidents increasingly filing litigation based on improper maintenance—for bridge repair, shoulder grading, and chuckhole maintenance—liability issues become a paramount budget concern.

Rule of Contiguity   A guideline for permitting city boundaries to be altered so as to avoid creating a jurisdiction that is separated into unconnected parcels. Contiguity means to be connected or adjoining. When states allow cities to alter their size through annexation, consolidation, or detachment, statutes may provide that such changes are valid only if the resulting incorporation is a single entity. Unincorporated areas adjacent to the city may, however, produce a pattern of enclaves.

Significance   In the highly balkanized metropolitan mosaic of U.S. cities, the rule of contiguity limits cities from becoming more of a patchwork. Breaks caused by a river, lake, or limited-access expressway are generally allowed even if this means a city must cross into another jurisdiction to service part of its own territory. Michigan law, which allows portions of townships to incorporate as cities, has resulted in three noncontiguous Detroit-area units: Brownstown Township to the south and Royal Oak Township along with West Bloomfield Township to the north. Whichever piece does not have the township hall is called "little orphan acres." Residents complain that they feel left out. In some states a city may be allowed to annex a desirable piece of outlying land through the long lasso, that is to say, through an extended, narrow corridor such as a road right-of-way that is attached at the end to a large parcel.

S

Safety Net   A group of federal poverty programs that collectively provide a subsistence standard of living. The safety net concept was a part of President Ronald Reagan's initiative in reducing welfare spending for social programs. The safety net was meant to save those families who were the most deserving—the "truly needy." *See also* HOMELESS; POVERTY LEVEL; POVERTY PROGRAMS; UNDERCLASS.

Significance   The imagery of the safety net was intended to divert some of the criticism leveled at President Reagan for his massive welfare-program cuts. Defenders stated that federal programs would be more effective because they were better targeted, and only those who truly needed assistance would receive it. For example, the income eligibility limit for food stamp recipients was reduced from 60 percent to 30 percent above the poverty line. However, critics of the Reagan initiatives blamed the administration for exacerbating two of the major social problems of American cities in the late 1980s: homelessness and the underclass.

Suggested Reading
Burt, Martha R., and Karen J. Pittman. *Testing the Social Safety Net: The Impact of Changes in Support Programs during the Reagan Administration.* Washington, DC: Urban Institute, 1985.
Levitan, Sar, and Clifford Johnson. *Beyond the Safety Net: Reviving the Promise of Opportunity in America.* Cambridge, MA: Ballinger, 1984.
Palmer, John L., and Isabel V. Sawhill, eds. *The Reagan Record: An Assessment of America's Changing Domestic Priorities.* Cambridge, MA: Ballinger, 1984.

Scatter-Site Housing   Federally subsidized, smaller scale, dispersed residential public-housing projects. Scatter-site housing was mandated by federal district-court decisions (*Gautreaux v. Chicago*

461

Housing Authority, 1969); dispersal requirements contained in the 1974 Housing and Community Development Act; a U.S. Supreme Court decision in *Hills v. Gautreaux,* 425 U.S. 284 (1976); and a subsequent consent decree. These policies sought to improve racial integration by avoiding large housing projects such as the "vertical ghettos" symbolized by the St Louis, Missouri, Pruitt-Igoe project, and required dispersal of public-housing projects away from the central city, toward outlying neighborhoods and suburban communities. In addition, scatter-site provided subsidized housing units leased in buildings that have a racial and class mixture. *See also* HILLS V. GAUTREAUX; HOUSING, PUBLIC; HOUSING SUBSIDY; PRUITT-IGOE; YONKERS-STYLE POLITICS.

Significance   The scatter-site housing program was developed in the 1960s to provide for a mixture of racial and economic groups in a local community. Created as an alternative to large-scale public-housing projects, scatter-site housing also attempted to locate tenants in areas outside of central-city neighborhoods, where increasing job opportunities were becoming available. Many suburban communities resisted scatter-site housing programs when sites in their areas were selected for construction.

Suggested Reading

Warren, Elizabeth C. "The Dispersal of Subsidized Housing in Chicago: An Index for Comparisons." *Urban Affairs Quarterly,* vol. 21, no. 4 (1986), pp. 484–500.
———. Measuring the Dispersal of Subsidized Housing in Three Cities." *Journal of Urban Affairs,* vol. 8, no. 1 (1986), pp. 19–34.

School District   The major organizational structure for providing primary and secondary public education in the United States. Local school districts are defined by the Bureau of Census as either "independent" or "dependent." Approximately 90 percent of all U.S. school districts are independent. Independent school districts have total responsibility for providing local public education, and at least 25 states have fully independent school districts. Several states, including Alaska, Maryland, North Carolina, and Virginia, mandate their local governments to administer the public schools. These are considered dependent school districts. Independent school-district residents elect or appoint local boards of education that make local district policy and select a superintendent of schools as chief administrative officer. Federal and state funding of local programs, with their subsequent imposition of standards, has reduced the discretion of local school boards. School-district scale varies from state to state, but in general, public-school reorganization has decreased drastically the overall number of school districts since World War II. Public schools require proof of residency for attendance. By contrast, private schools do not impose residency restrictions. Hence, compulsory busing caused some parents to select private schools for their children in order to avoid complying with desegregation orders. *See also* BANKRUPTCY, ACADEMIC; BOARD OF EDUCATION; *DE FACTO* SEGREGATION; *DE JURE* SEGREGATION; INDEPENDENT SCHOOL DISTRICT.

Significance   Historically, public education has been left to local decision makers. Some national standardization occurred during the late 1800s in an effort to assimilate the large number of immigrants, but most public education policymaking remained in the hands of local school boards. During the mid-1900s, providing equal educational opportunities among districts became an important national policy issue. The first *Brown v. Board of Education* decision, 347 U.S. 483 (1954), prohibited state-sanctioned segregated school districts. This decision struck down the "separate but equal" provision of *Plessy v. Ferguson*, 163 U.S. 537 (1896). The Court argued that separation alone created a stigma that violated the rights of minorities. With federal aid-to-education statutes passed in the 1960s, Congress took many education decisions out of local hands, and redefined them as civil rights issues. This included mandating provisions for bilingual education imposed by the national government in 1968 (20 U.S.C. 880 et seq.). While this set of policies attempted to eliminate legally sanctioned, or *de jure,* segregation, the national courts used busing as a tool for school-district desegregation.

Suggested Reading

Cronin, Joseph M. *The Control of Urban Schools.* New York: Free Press, 1973.
Pelissero, John P., and David R. Morgan. "State Aid to Public Schools: An Analysis of State Responsiveness to School District Needs." *Social Science Quarterly,* vol. 68, no. 3 (1987), pp. 466–477.
Peterson, Paul E. *School Politics, Chicago Style.* Chicago: University of Chicago Press, 1976.
Zeigler, Harmon, and M. Kent Jennings. *Governing American Schools: Political Interaction in Local Districts.* North Scituate, MA: Duxbury Press, 1974.

Sector Model   The theory of urban growth and land use that focuses on capital outlays in wedge-shaped zones radiating from central locations such as place of work. The sector model was devised in 1939 by Homer Hoyt, a real estate economist, based on the study of a sample of 142 American cities. The terms *zone* and *sector* are used interchangeably. A multipointed star pattern resulted from urban transportation arteries emanating from the central business district (CBD). The overall mosaic was highly influenced by high-rent residential uses, which in turn developed around scenic areas, areas with high ground, and areas adjacent to parkways and waterways, and in the direction of open countryside. High-socioeconomic-status (SES) residences occupy the most valuable space. The lower SES occupy residential areas adjacent to industry. The sector model modified the earlier concentric-zone hypothesis. Hoyt's seven major sectors number two more than Burgess's earlier 1925 mode. The first zone in both is the CBD. Sector two is wholesale and light manufacturing. Sectors three, four, and five are all residential for those paying low, medium, and high rent. The high-rent sector drives all the other areas because it represents the highest bid on land. The sixth zone represents commercial development. The seventh zone represents heavy industry. *See also* CENTRAL BUSINESS DISTRICT; CONCENTRIC ZONE MODEL; MULTINUCLEI MODEL; SHOPPING CENTER; ZONE, URBAN.

Significance   Hoyt's sector theory presented a more complex and better fit to urban geography than the earlier Burgess theory. It was based on long-term patterns of transportation and building development; it allowed an active role for real estate developers' decisions; it was sensitive to the commuting radius by factoring in time as well as linear absolute distance from work; and it was sensitive to agglomeration of similar classes in the same general area. The theory posits that land value is a function of bidding practices of households and locations, accessibility to work and recreation, class formation, and aesthetics. Three major criticisms of the sector model are that (1) it did not account for the dispersion of the modern metropolis; (2) it was not sensitive to post–World War I shopping centers and commercial developments; and (3) it was insensitive to the artificial price structure of housing costs produced by racial segregation, redlining, and real estate steering practices. From these criticisms developed the third urban land-use model, that is, the multinucleated theory.

Suggested Reading

Hoyt, Homer. *The Structure and Growth of Residential Neighborhoods in American Cities.* Washington, DC: U.S. Federal Housing Administration, Government Printing Office, 1939.

Self-insurance   Risk management by an incorporated entity for itself or through a pool designed to cover liability claims. Self-insurance is a major outcome of the liability insurance crisis of the 1980s in which for-profit conventional insurance carriers and their underwriters canceled policies, refused to renew them, or increased costs many times the initial price. A few cities have elected to go "bare," that is to say, not to carry any form of liability insurance because they feel they cannot afford the premiums. Some cities have saved on premiums over those charged out-of-house by pooling costs and creating their own reserve fund. *See also* PRIVATIZATION.

Significance   In the 1980s self-insurance became a major innovation not only among municipalities but for profit-making corporations, not-for-profit groups, and professional corporations. Churches as diverse as the Seventh Day Adventists and Roman Catholic dioceses began to self-insure. More than 10,000 cities were involved in self-insurance by 1989. Having suffered cutbacks in coverage and increases in premiums, previously covered groups looked for ways to take over a traditional private-sector service. As a result of self-insuring and managing their own risk, cities have become more sensitive to recordkeeping and the need for safety checks, and have lowered their exposure to liability suits by abolishing select functions, such as eliminating high-diving boards at public swimming pools. Although such cities as Prescott, Arizona, and Dallas, Texas, have opted for single-city risk-management, pooled coverage is more common because it spreads risk over a larger number of cities. Some authors divide alternatives to acquiring outside commercial insurance between (1) risk pooling though a joint underwriting association (JUA) and (2) a program of individual single-city self-insurance. The insurance industry has responded by claiming that the crisis was brought on by excessive awards in lawsuits filed nationwide.

Suggested Reading
Litan, Robert E., and Clifford M. Winston, eds. *Liability: Perspectives and Policy.* Washington, DC: Brookings Institution, 1988.
Rynard, Thomas W. "The Local Government as Insured or Insurer: Some New Risk Management Alternatives." *Urban Lawyer,* vol. 20, no. 1 (1988), pp. 103–153.

Separation of Powers   The three-way distribution of decision-making authority at the same governmental level among the legislative, executive, and judicial branches. Under separation of powers, the three branches are coequal. The theory is generally adhered to at all levels of general government. There are parallel institutions for the legislature at the national, state, county, township, village, and city levels. The legislatures are variously called Congress, state legislature, county commission, township trustees, village board, and city council.

Executives are variously called president, governor, county executive, township supervisor, village president, and city mayor. The parallel breaks down for the courts. There are only two systems—national and state. National courts of general jurisdiction include the trial level, called the district courts, and two appellate levels—the circuit courts of appeal and the U.S. Supreme Court. Most state courts have these three parallel tiers. Generally there are trial courts for villages, cities, townships, and most counties. The more highly populated states have two appellate levels, with court(s) of appeal and a state supreme court. Whereas the legislature and executive at the national level are partisan, court appointments are often officially nonpartisan. State and substate levels differ markedly in allowing for partisanship, but generally the state level parallels the national pattern, and subcounty elections are more commonly nonpartisan. The assumption is that there is no Republican or Democratic way of collecting refuse. At each level the executive establishes the political agenda by an address, variously called state of the union, state of the state, state of the county, or state of the city. Executives at all levels now generally are responsible for preparing a line-item budget, called an executive budget. *See also* CORPORATION COUNSEL; FEDERALISM.

Significance   The concept of separation of powers originally was sketched out in Book 11 of *Spirit of the Laws* (1748) by Montesquieu. Separation of powers and federalism are the two chief structural devices used in U.S. governments. Each prevents a buildup of power, one by a trifurcation of branches and one by bifurcation of levels. The three-branch theory is not a set of hermetically sealed compartments but rather interacting functional units sharing duties with the familiar checks and balances. At the national level, since the 1880s there also has been a headless fourth branch made up of Independent Regulatory Commissions (IRCs), each of which regulates a segment of the national economy. Separation of powers fragments responsibility so that no one person collects too much authority. This is done by barring a person from simultaneously serving in two branches. In some substate extraconstitutional levels, however, this distinction breaks down. In townships, the supervisor both sits as a voting member of the board of trustees and serves as the chief elected executive. In some cities (and villages), the mayor (president) is a voting member of the council and at the same time the chief elected executive. Where the branches are partisan, separation of powers allows for the possibility of split party control, thereby increasing the chances for deadlock. Each of the three branches represents a separate constituency and is usually elected or appointed by its own procedures, thus encouraging alternate access points for groups. Each branch works on its own priorities—the legislature with its calendars, the executive with its agendas, and the judiciary with its dockets, each at its own pace. The courts alone are passive and decide only those cases that some outside party initiates. The courts are final arbiters for maintaining the boundaries among the three branches through their exercise of judicial review. Corporation counsels are not part of the judiciary but are attached to legislatures or executives. Prosecuting attorneys are also in the executive branch.

Suggested Reading
Goldwin, Robert A., and Art Kaufman, eds. *Separation of Powers: Does It Still Work?* Lanham, MD: American Enterprise Institute, 1986.
Svara, James H. "Conflict, Cooperation, and Separation of Powers in City Government." *Journal of Urban Affairs*, vol. 10, no. 4 (1988), pp. 357–372.

Set-Aside   A form of affirmative action in government contracts reserving a portion of the project cost to be performed by qualified minorities. Set-asides are targeted for "minorities" in some contracts and for "blacks, Hispanics, and women" in others. The program was designed to offer preferential treatment by allocating a portion of competitive bids to groups that had been excluded unjustly. The proportion set aside for minorities ranged nationally from 10 percent of local businesses in Dade County, Florida, to 30 percent in Richmond, Virginia. Detroit's system set aside 14 percent for blacks and 12 percent for other minority- and female-owned enterprises. The national set-aside program expanded the scope of minorities to include blacks, Hispanics, Asians, and Native Americans. The national 10 percent set-aside program was upheld in *Fullilove v. Klutznick,* 448 U.S. 448 (1980). The case affected federal funds designed for businesses on local public works. The program contains an administratively controlled flexible-waiver clause that allows cancellation of the proviso. Minority business enterprises (MBEs) can receive more than 10 percent if they win the bid in sealed competition, or they may receive no work at all. *See also* AFFIRMATIVE-ACTION PROGRAMS; COMPETITIVE BID.

Significance   Set-aside programs established at the national, state, and local levels substantially increased minority business contracts. All the programs monitored qualifications of eligible businesses for truly being minority-run rather than front organizations. Not all minority businesses qualified in terms of capitalization. Local set-asides were severely reduced when the U.S. Supreme Court announced in *City of Richmond, Virginia v. J. C. Croson Co.,* 102 L Ed 2d 854 (1989), that the 30-percent set-aside of construction contracts for minority-owned firms was an impermissible form of reverse discrimination for want of proof of past city discrimination. The new court rule puts the obligation on the state or local level to demonstrate past governmental, rather than societal, discrimination against a minority. As originally enunciated in *Wygant v. Jackson, Michigan Board of Education,* 476 U.S. 267 (1986), favoritism to a minority violates the equal protection of the law clause of the Fourteenth Amendment unless there is a specific finding of a past state-imposed pattern of unfair competition.

Suggested Reading
Note. "The Nonperpetuation of Discrimination in Public Contracting: A Justification for State and Local Minority Business Set-Asides after *Wygant.*" *Harvard Law Review,* vol. 101, no. 8 (1988), pp. 1797–1815.
Weinstein, Stephen L. "New York City's Locally Based Enterprise Set-Aside: Legitimate Exercise of Mayoral Power or Unconstitutional Quota in Disguise?" *Fordham Urban Law Journal,* vol. 12, no. 4 (1983–1984), pp. 703–748.

Shantytown   A squatter settlement on the fringe of an urban area, populated by homeless, underemployed, or unemployed people who may also be recent migrants from rural or foreign areas. Shantytowns have no aesthetic value and few amenities, and they often are located on unappropriated land. They are peopled by the underclass, or what the Marxists call the *lumpenproletariat. See also* HOMELESS; SKID ROW; SLUM; URBAN HOMESTEADING.

Significance   Shantytowns often are situated in major cities of the third world. In French-speaking former colonies they are called "Bidonvilles," and in the subcontinent of India they are "Bustees." During the 1930s in the United States, shantytowns were called Hoovervilles after President Herbert Hoover. Most of the homeless of the George Bush era have not gravitated to shantytowns but live in private or public temporary accommodations or on the street. A slum is a more permanent set of structures than a shantytown and is more centrally located.

Sheriff   The senior police officer of a county, usually elected. The name derives from early England's "shire reeve," who was the county's chief law-enforcement officer. There are approximately 3,000 sheriff's departments in the United States. The largest is in Los Angeles County, which serves 32 cities and a population of more than 3 million. Representing the sheriffs is the National Sheriffs' Association, a professional and lobbying organization headquartered in Washington, D.C. *See also* CRIME; JAIL, LOCAL; LAKEWOOD PLAN; POLICE, PUBLIC.

Significance   A sheriff's duties and authority vary, depending on the level of development and size of the county. County sheriff's officers may serve as county court attendants, process servers, custodians of the county jail, patrol officers, tax collectors, and coroners. A sheriff's jurisdiction usually includes only the unincorporated areas within a county. The office may be called in to support a local police department in certain cases. Some sheriffs have contracts to serve as law-enforcement agents for public authorities such as airports.

Suggested Reading
Newsletter—National Neighborhood Watch Programs, vol. 11. Washington, DC: National Sheriffs' Association, 1972.

Shopping Center   A planned commercial development, privately owned and maintained as a unit, with copious on-site vehicular parking; also known as a plaza or mall. Functionally, shopping centers are to suburbia what main street is to the commercial portion of the central-city business district. Shopping centers are represented by a national trade association, the International Council of Shopping Centers, headquartered in New York City. A major ingredient of shopping centers is a prearranged mix of tenants or a motif, as in the case of discount or outlet malls. There are usually one, two, or three dominant tenants called anchor stores. *See also* CENTRAL BUSINESS DISTRICT; MULTINUCLEI MODEL.

Significance   Shopping centers are a twentieth-century U.S. innovation. Although there is disagreement about which was first, one of the earliest was the Kansas City, Missouri, Country Club Plaza, built in 1925. Upper Darby Center was opened in 1927 in Philadelphia. Highland Park Village was built north of Dallas in 1931. According to the trade association, shopping centers are constructed on four different scales: (1) A neighborhood shopping center is the smallest, usually with a supermarket anchor. A supermarket is defined as a general-line grocery store that carries some soft- and hardware and grosses at least a million dollars in sales annually. Such malls need not be adjacent to an expressway. (2) A community shopping center services several neighborhoods. It usually is connected by an open walkway and is anchored by a discount department store and/or a supermarket. (3) A regional shopping center must have access to an expressway and major surface streets. It has climate-controlled walkways and offers goods and services similar to a small downtown central business district (CBD). (4) The superregional shopping center has covered walkways or is climate-controlled. It is anchored by three or more full-line department stores, has access to at least one expressway, and provides all the amenities associated with a major downtown area. Northland Shopping Mall in suburban Detroit was so important to areawide development that the under-construction mall lent monies to the local township to incorporate as the city of Southfield. The three major distinguishing features of shopping malls are ample on-site circumferential parking, retail and professional offices carefully selected according to a master plan, and centralized, coordinated private management. Because the common area is privately owned, it does not fully serve as a legal equivalent of a conventional public square for the exercise of otherwise protected First Amendment rights of free expression. The U.S. Supreme Court ruled on this issue in *Lloyd v. Tanner,* 407 U.S. 551 (1972), by declaring in a 5–4 vote that the Lloyd Center had not publicly dedicated its walkways so as to entitle protesters to exercise their normally protected right to distribute handbills. Master planners-builders such as Victor Gruen and A. A. Taubman have been major political actors in suburbia and were considered classic absentee landlords by many local politicians. The third and fourth types of centers are blamed for urban sprawl, because they are built to accommodate private automobile traffic at expressway access points, no matter what rural land uses are interspersed between settlements.

Suggested Reading

Bul, A. Alexander, and Nicholas Ordway. "Shopping Center Innovations: The Past 40 Years." *Urban Land,* vol. 20, no. 6 (1987), pp. 22–25.

Gillette, Howard, Jr. "The Evolution of the Planned Shopping Center in Suburb and City." *Journal of the American Planning Association,* vol. 51, no. 4 (1985), pp. 449–460.

Gruen, Victor. *The Heart of Our Cities: The Urban Crisis—Diagnosis and Cure.* New York: Simon & Schuster, 1964. Chap. 14.

Lion, Edgar. *Shopping Centers: Planning, Development, and Administration.* New York: John Wiley, 1976.

Sternlieb, George, and James W. Hughes, ed. *Shopping Centers: USA.* Piscataway, NJ: Rutgers, the State University of New Jersey, 1981.

Sinking Fund   A separate account established by a local government set aside for periodic payments in order to retire a debt or replace operating assets. Most municipal bonds have sinking fund provisions, allowing a municipality to reduce or amortize its financial obligations over a period of time. A sinking fund accumulates money over time through regular contributions along with interest derived from investments allowed under the provisions of the bond. *See also* BOND, MUNICIPAL; DEBT, MUNICIPAL.

Significance   A sinking fund is the most common method of retiring a municipal debt, as a certain amount of money is set aside each year for debt repayment. These accounts are particularly attractive for debt retirement of municipal bonds. Most municipal bonds are issued in a series, whereby different portions of the issue are due at different times, usually on an annual basis. Therefore, a sinking fund becomes a custodial account, allowing a municipality to place money into a separate account to repay the bond debt as each series becomes due. Such practices by a municipality show fiscal responsibility to investors, and the creation of a sinking fund makes their bonds more attractive to potential investors, the bond rating services, and insurers. In some cases, an insurer requires the establishment of a sinking fund, making debt retirement more likely than if a municipality attempted to repay the entire debt at once.

Sister City Program   Primarily a city-to-city linkage focusing on exchange of ideas and personnel in education and culture, manifested by student and adult exchanges as well as contacts in business and social relations, such as dedication of public parks with foreign themes. The program is largely coordinated by the Alexandria, Virginia–based organization Town Affiliation Association of the USA, Inc. More than 700 U.S. cities are affiliated with jurisdictions in more than 80 foreign nations. Begun by the Eisenhower administration in the 1950s, the program originally was designed to be apolitical. *See also* DIVESTMENT.

Significance   The program promotes cooperation on a local level and disperses ideas and technology. The Washington, D.C.–based Council for International Urban Liaison also serves as a facilitator for dispersing innovative urban policy. For those who participate directly, it breaks down ethnocentrism. In conception and its administration from inception, the affiliations were largely educational, such as college-to-college ties or mayor exchanges. Most affiliations have been initiated by American cities. During the escalating war in Vietnam, contacts with these two areas broke off. The apolitical aspect changed with the inception of the Reagan administration's support for the Contras against the government of Nicaragua. Although in a federal system foreign policy is delegated exclusively to the national level, this program gave local American units a way to express dissent with national policy. Nicaragua picked up on this technique and by-passed the Sister City program in setting up even more coordinated programs. Other affiliations also exist, as between Wisconsin and Nicaragua and between Ann Arbor, Michigan, and Seattle, Washington. Both had city-council elections in the 1980s decided in part on the basis of continued aid for Nicaragua. Many American cities have multiple foreign contacts; Los Angeles has 15, while Chicago and New York each have 5. In addition to the Sister City program, there are other avenues for a city to express disagreement with foreign policy, such as conducting a nonbinding referendum, a practice that some cities used to express opposition to the war in Vietnam. Other issues on which cities have developed their own foreign policy include *sanctuary* for refugees, *divestment* of stock holdings for local pension funds in corporations doing business in South Africa, *principled purchasing* of products from contractors who do not produce nuclear weapons, and comprehensive test bans. Starting with Takoma Park, Maryland, more than 900 local governments have declared their cities part of a nuclear-free zone.

Site Plan Review   A comprehensive preconstruction consultation between land developers and one or more public agencies. When site plan review is approved, the community allows building on a specific parcel. It is sometimes known as a design approval. In many cities, only single-family, detached residences built on platted lots are exempt from such review. The review covers all aspects of physical planning from surveys, proof of ownership, soil type identification, layouts of elevations, and contours in the land to parking considerations, scale maps of the immediate vicinity, layout of the facility itself, lighting, traffic circulation maps, and, when called for, approval from agencies protecting floodplains and environmental impact statements of potential air and water pollution. Planning boards and city councils must approve the plans after open hearings. Approval is usually valid for one year, with renewals possible. *See also* BUILDING PERMIT; ENVIRONMENTAL IMPACT STATEMENT; MASTER PLAN; OCCUPANCY PERMIT; PLANNING, FOCAL-POINT.

Significance   This is the first of three stages for public supervision of specific buildings, justified under the police power in order to protect the public's health, safety, and welfare. Whereas master plans are conceptual and forward-looking, site plans refer to the actual space to be occupied by a structure. Because this is a fairly recent concept, most of the built-up portions of American cities have not undergone this public review. Developers are on notice to prepare all documentation at the outset of a project. Developers appeal denials to local trial courts if no other internal administrative remedy is set up by the city.

Skid Row   A type of urban slum, located in a section of the central city near the central business district, that has weekly-rate rooms and flophouses catering to older, single, low-status males. Skid rows are associated with most major metropolitan areas. They serve as havens for otherwise homeless alcoholics and drug addicts. Most skid rows house fewer than 6,000 males, mostly white. The most famous example is New York's Bowery. Detroit's Cass Corridor is typical of skid rows: Its borders are ill defined and have changed over time with urban renewal, fires, relocation drives, historic preservation projects, and expressway construction. *See also* HOMELESS; ZONE, URBAN.

Significance   The notoriety of skid row derives from the area's being home base for society's failures. These people, who are on the skids, have been well studied as classic individual deviants and their neighborhoods as classic social problems. High-incidence crimes committed on skid row include disorderly conduct, vagrancy, fighting, robbery, and burglary. The area typically has poorly maintained low-cost housing, bars, pawn shops, Red Cross blood donation centers, and Salvation Army shelters and soup kitchens. A skid row segregates undesirable, low-status males and increasingly some females from the balance of society and serves as a hiring area for unskilled day laborers needed in nearby business areas. A three-panel longitudinal study of 41 skid rows for the 1950, 1960, and 1970 census reports suggests that the areas are partially disappearing.

Suggested Reading

Bahr, Howard M. *Skid Row: An Instruction to Disaffiliation*. New York: Oxford University Press, 1973.

Lee, Barrett A. "The Disappearance of Skid Row: Some Ecological Evidence." *Urban Affairs Quarterly*, vol. 16, no. 1 (1980), pp. 81–107.

Ward, Jim. "Skid Row as a Geographic Entity." *Professional Geographer*, vol. 27, no. 3 (1975), pp. 286–296.

Wiseman, Jacqueline P. *Stations of the Lost: The Treatment of Skid Row Alcoholics*. Chicago: University of Chicago Press, 1979.

Slum   In federal statute, "an area where dwellings predominate which, by reason of dilapidation, overcrowding, faulty arrangements or design, lack of ventilation, light or sanitation facilities, or any combination of these factors, are detrimental to safety, health, or morals," 42 U.S.C. 1402(3). "Slum" and "blight" both delineate physical decay caused by lack of maintenance and little or no code enforcement. Slums are defined based on the common-law police power concept and not on economic grounds. *See also* BLIGHT; GOLD COAST; HOUSING ACT OF 1949; URBAN RENEWAL.

Significance   Slums are known as the shame of the city. Socially they are areas of disorganization and alienation. Physically they are gray areas of dilapidated buildings. Once a slum has been identified by local public planners and that designation has withstood any court challenges, slum land is subject to renewal. The municipality may acquire and demolish a slum in order to construct and equip low-rent housing under a public housing agency: This stipulation was made in the original Housing Act of 1937, reformulated under Title I of the Housing Act of 1949. Zorbaugh's 1929 case study in Chicago characterized the near North Side slum as tenements housing recent arrivals from overseas plus a jungle of lodging houses containing economic failures and derelicts. *Slum* is preferable to *blight* as a term for designating urban substandard living accommodations because it is based on statutory guidelines.

Suggested Reading

Clinard, Marshall B. *Slums and Community Development: Experiments in Self-help.* New York: Free Press, 1966.
Hunter, David R. *The Slums: Challenge and Response.* New York: Free Press, 1968.
Suttles, Gerald D. *The Social Order of the Slum: Ethnicity and Territory in the Inner City.* Chicago: University of Chicago Press, 1968.
Ward, David. "The Victorian Slum: An Enduring Myth?" *Annals of the Association of American Geographers,* vol. 66, no. 2 (1976), pp. 323–336.

Small Business Administration (SBA)   An independent federal agency founded in 1953 (15 U.S.C. 631 et seq.) to assist modest-scale businesses. The Small Business Administration makes loans, assists businesses in locating government contracts, refinances businesses declared to be part of a disaster area by the Federal Emergency Management Agency (FEMA), functions as a liaison with local banks and investment companies, and sees that minority-owned companies are exposed to the set-aside portion of nationally sponsored contracts. Since 1976 the SBA's regional offices also work with farmers, most of whom have been declared small businesses. Administrative rules governing the SBA are promulgated in Titles 13 and 48 of the *Code of Federal Regulations. See also* AFFIRMATIVE-ACTION PROGRAMS; DISASTER DESIGNATION; FEDERAL EMERGENCY MANAGEMENT AGENCY; GROWTH POLITICS; INCUBATOR; SET-ASIDE.

Significance   The Small Business Administration functions as an analogue to locally sponsored business incubators. Because there is a large turnover in new businesses, government support is greatly needed and wanted by tyro businessmen. In snowbelt cities, where businesses historically have not bid successfully on a proportionate share of federal contracts, the SBA in part is an equalizer in achieving regional parity. Local business boosters know that small businesses tend to be more labor-intensive than large corporations and that future growth is associated with small but innovative concerns. The SBA and business incubators partially compensate for the attention states and cities lavish on large-scale businesses in promoting tax increment financing (TIFs) and long-term tax abatements. However, the SBA is essentially a passive organization waiting for businesses to contact it; it is not part of any broad-based national industrial policy.

Social Indicators   Quantitative measurements of community conditions and personal attitudes over time and by several areal scales. Social indicators are also known as monitoring social change and as social accounting. It is a movement in several of the social sciences systematically to collect and analyze data on well-being. Social indicators variously calibrate conditions at the national, regional, state, city, and neighborhood levels. Subjects covered range from environmental variables such as climate and pollution (both air and water) to subjective personal variables that calibrate internal conditions such as physical and mental health, satisfaction with one's job and family, and stress levels. The movement to collect and use the indicators in physical and social planning represents an interest in creating a bank of information analogous to economic indicators associated with computation of elements in the gross national product (GNP), elements in the leading economic indicators, and such relatively hard data as unemployment rates. Research on social indicators has been sponsored by major research organizations, including the American Academy of Arts and Sciences, The University of Michigan Institute for Social Research (ISR), and the U.S. Bureau of the Census. Many indicators are derived from aggregate data, including vital statistics; others are collected by survey research techniques. The movement has been particularly active in the United States, the United Kingdom, and Canada. *See also* COMMUNITY FACT BOOKS; FORECAST; QUALITY OF LIFE.

Significance   Social indicators were first collected in the 1930s at the city and state levels in an attempt to measure over time and space social pathologies as diverse as child-abuse levels and suicide rates. As with all aggregate data, interpretation of the results is open to the *ecological fallacy* of attributing an overall condition to each individual in the collection area. Critics point to five other major problems: (1) There is no model to suggest what information should be included that would make it analogous to national income accounting, (2) most indicators weigh equally every variable on which information is collected, (3) the indicators lack justification for creating the scales on which they calibrate their information, (4) some of the material represents reliable data whereas some is so subjective that its error range is not even calculated, and (5) in many projects unavailable information for all areas studied precludes uniform analysis. The primary purpose for collecting social indicators has usually been to track trends over time and space so as to assist planners and to develop models to forecast trends. Where survey research is involved, subsamples usually do not allow for special breakouts, thwarting much of the original intent. Properly used, social indicators are intended to assist public decision makers in allocating resources. There has been heavy secondary use of these indicators by others to prepare city-by-city comparisons, a literature usually called "quality of life" (QOL).

Suggested Reading

Bauer, Raymond A., ed. *Social Indicators.* Cambridge, MA: MIT Press, 1966.
Campbell, Angus. *The Sense of Well-Being in America: Recent Patterns and Trends.* New York: McGraw-Hill, 1981.
de Neufville, Judith Innes. *Social Indicators and Public Policy.* Amsterdam: Elsevier Scientific Publications, 1975.
Long, Norton E. "Symposium on Municipal Social and Economic Accounting." *Journal of Urban Affairs,* vol. 8, no. 2 (1986), pp. 1–90.
Murphy, Thomas P. *Urban Indicators: A Guide to Information Sources.* Detroit: Gale Research, 1980.
Pacione, Michael. "The Use of Objective and Subjective Measures of Life Quality in Human Geography." *Progress in Human Geography,* vol. 6, no. 4 (1982), pp. 495–514.
Rossi, Robert J., and Kevin J. Gilmartin. *Handbook of Social Indicators.* New York: Garland STPM Press, 1980. (Glossary.)
Smith, David M. *The Geography of Social Well-Being in the United States: An Introduction to Territorial Social Indicators.* New York: McGraw-Hill, 1973.
U.S. Commission on Civil Rights. *Social Indicators of Equality for Minorities and Women.* Washington, DC: Superintendent of Public Documents, August 1978. CR 1.2:50-1/2.

Solid-Waste Management   The collection and disposal of refuse, usually under the jurisdiction of a local government. Solid waste includes garbage, rubbish, ashes, and industrial refuse, in contrast with *liquid waste* or sewage. Because of increasing costs, many local governments have contracted solid-waste collection to private firms or imposed user fees on refuse disposal, particularly for large items that require special pickup. Industrial waste in particular is commonly collected by private haulers. *See also* CONTRACTING OUT; ENVIRONMENTAL LEGISLATION; PRIVATIZATION; USER FEE.

Significance   Solid-waste management has been a growing concern in many communities, as landfills are reaching their capacity and incineration has created its own set of problems, including air pollution and questions about proper disposal of ashes. The proper management of waste has a substantial effect on the quality of life in any community, from both aesthetic and health standpoints. The federal Solid Waste Disposal Act of 1965 (42 U.S.C. 6901) left most waste-management responsibilities to state and local governments, with technical assistance from the federal level. Subsequent federal legislation attempted to address solid-waste problems by encouraging recycling, with the Resource Recovery Act of 1970 (42 U. S. 3251). Later statutes dealt with hazardous and toxic waste (Resource Conservation and Recovery Act of 1976 [42 U.S.C. 6901]; Toxic Substances Control Act of 1976 [15 U.S.C. 2601]). In earlier times, sanitary landfills generally were adequate. However, land-use controls and increases in per-capita output of solid waste have put a tremendous burden on disposal sites. In addition, many of the dumps are not sanitary, but contain toxic waste that has leached into groundwater supplies. In larger metropolitan areas, the management of solid waste has shifted away from landfills toward incineration. While public concern over the environment has increased, most air, water, and land pollution has occurred within the legal limits established by the Environmental Protection Agency (EPA) or by state and local policy. Further, many violations have gone unpunished, since funding for pollution-control enforcement and monitoring of waste disposal rarely has been adequate at any governmental level. Some municipalities themselves have become major polluters, when their incineration facilities produce toxic-laden effluent and ashes.

Suggested Reading

American Public Works Association, Committee on Refuse Disposal. *Municipal Refuse Disposal*. Chicago: Public Administration Service, 1961.

Council of State Governments. *Waste Management in the States*. Lexington, KY: Council of State Governments, 1982.

Kirschten, Dick. "The New War on Pollution Is over the Land." *National Journal* (April 14, 1979), pp. 603–606.

Kovacs, William L., and John F. Klucsik. "The New Federal Role in Solid Waste Management: The Resource Conservation and Recovery Act of 1976." *Columbia Journal of Environmental Law*, vol. 3 (1977), pp. 205–261.

Lester, James P., and Ann O'M. Bowman, eds. *The Politics of Hazardous Waste Management*. Durham, NC: Duke University Press, 1983.

Nader, Ralph, Ronald Brownstein, and John Richard, eds. *Who's Poisoning America: Corporate Polluters and Their Victims in the Chemical Age*. San Francisco: Sierra Club, 1981.

U.S. General Accounting Office. *Solid Waste Disposal Practices: Open Dumps Not Identified, States Face Funding Problems*. Washington, DC: Government Printing Office, 1981.

Southern Burlington County NAACP v. Township of Mount Laurel, **I and II**   New Jersey supreme court cases decided in 1975 and 1983 that identified impermissible exclusive suburban zoning and then spelled out remedial guidelines. The two Mount Laurel decisions describe the causes of racial and economically segregated housing and propose a statistically based formula for overcoming the condition. Mount Laurel was a rapidly expanding Philadelphia suburb. *Mount Laurel* I invalidated a municipal zoning ordinance that excluded low- and moderate-income families by building "a wall around itself." *Mount Laurel* II asserted that developing communities had an affirmative obligation to accommodate a fair share of the region's needs for modest homes and apartments. *See also* HILLS V. GAUTREAUX; POLICE POWER; SCATTER-SITE HOUSING; ZONING, EXCLUSIONARY.

Significance   *Mount Laurel* I, 336 A.2d 713 (1976), and *Mount Laurel* II, 456 A.2d 390 (1983), were State of New Jersey supreme court decisions that, at the time, were heralded as the most important since the U.S. Supreme Court established the constitutionality of zoning in 1926. Combined, they established judicial standards for land use, bypassing local community standards in favor of a statewide perspective based on regional patterns. The court defined regional needs and fair-share quotas in order to make their initial decision operable. They also defined low and moderate income. Those earning less than one-half of the region median are *low-income* and those earning between one-half and four-fifths of the median are *moderate-income.* Manufactured homes, more commonly known as mobile homes, were given new prominence as a possible solution to affordable housing. To implement the State Development Plan, special court masters were assigned to assist in city master-plan reformulation. Special trial judges were designated to hear the technically oriented litigation. Planners, long described as hired hands protecting parochial upper-class interests, testified that their profession was destroying the broader New Jersey public interest of fair housing for all residents. In 1985 the State of New Jersey set up the Council on Affordable Housing to administer the decisions. Rutgers, the State University of New Jersey, conducted a statewide survey to aid the court and identified six regions. However, the state legislature largely gutted the decisions by allowing developing communities to swap half of their obligations for lower and midrange housing with central cities such as New Brunswick, Jersey City, Newark, and Orange. In addition to these transfers, along with monies to construct or repair housing, cities had to submit modified master plans to the council. As of 1989, about 80 percent of New Jersey communities were in noncompliance. The eroded judicial decisions were being transformed by the governor and legislature into a modest central-city rebuilding project. Implementation defeated the plan for open housing and undermined the two cases. They deteriorated into less than landmark status. State land planning was given a boost over local zoning ordinances, but the fruits of scatter-site housing are yet to be felt.

Suggested Reading

Burchell, Robert W., et al. *Mount Laurel II: Challenge and Delivery of Low-Cost Housing.* New Brunswick, NJ: Center for Urban Policy Research, Rutgers University, 1983.
Erber, Ernest. "The Road to Mount Laurel." *Planning,* vol. 49, no. 10 (1983), pp. 4–9.
Symposium issue. "Mount Laurel II and Development in New Jersey." *Rutgers Law Journal,* vol. 15, no. 3 (1984), pp. 513–788.

Special District   A limited- or single-function local government structurally independent of the general-purpose governments of a state or city. Special districts often are created to receive federal funding for specific programs, to raise money for private development projects, or to administer programs whose scope goes well beyond individual city limits. Examples include public works, water supply, transportation, conservation, economic development, and community colleges. Special districts generally have the power to tax in order to raise revenue. By contrast, local governments also have created public authorities to build specific projects, such as hospitals, bridges, airports, and urban redevelopment projects. Authorities tend to generate their revenues through user fees. *See also* AUTHORITY, PUBLIC; CENSUS OF GOVERNMENTS; DEBT LIMIT, LOCAL; USER FEE; ZONE, URBAN.

Significance   A local government may create a special district to operate a specific project and raise revenue through a separate tax. Most special districts are run by appointed officials, who are less accountable to the electorate than are general government officials. Critics of the proliferation of special districts argue such entities often serve private interests and discourage local government fiscal responsibility. Of all types of local governments, special districts are the most numerous: 29,487 as of 1987. In fact, while most types of local government—county, township, and school district—decreased in number between 1972 and 1987, special district governments increased by 20 percent. States with the most special districts are California, Nevada, and Texas. Of the more than 3,000 counties in the United States, Cook County, Illinois, has the most special districts, with 152.

Suggested Reading
MacManus, Susan. "Special District Governments: A Note on Their Use as Property Tax Relief Mechanisms in the 1970s." *Journal of Politics,* vol. 43, no. 4 (1981), pp. 1207–1214.
———. "Special Districts: A Common Solution to Political Pressures Stemming from City-County Fiscal Inequities." *Journal of Urban Affairs,* vol. 4, no. 2 (1982), pp. 1–10.
Porter, Douglas R., Ben C. Lin, and Richard B. Peiser. *Special Districts: A Useful Technique for Financing Infrastructure.* Washington, DC: Urban Land Institute, 1987.

Spending Limit   A ceiling adopted by executive resolution or legislative action to restrict the amount of public money to be spent per fiscal year for all expenditures. Most state and local governments have statutory limits on debts, and their state constitutions prohibit them from deficit spending. In addition, many local-government officials operating under severe fiscal stress during the mid- to late 1970s voluntarily adopted spending limits through reduced services, layoffs, and other cutbacks. *See also* CAPITAL EXPENDITURE; DEBT LIMIT, LOCAL; REVENUE IMPROVEMENT BOND; USER FEE.

Significance   Calls for spending limits at all levels of government arose during the late 1970s and early 1980s, as taxpayer revolts occurred in several states, and the United States experienced a general economic recession. Many state governments attempted to assert more legislative or executive controls on spending during this time. For example, at least 40 states limit the governor's authority to transfer funds between departments. All state and local governments have stringent restrictions on spending and borrowing for their operating budgets. However, there are fewer restrictions on capital budget expenditures, financed by long-term borrowing approved by the voters. Many states and cities attempted to circumvent the legal and political restrictions of spending and borrowing limits by moving to user fees, revenue bonds, and privatization of some services.

Suggested Reading
Merriman, David. *The Control of Municipal Budgets.* Westport, CT: Quorum Books, 1987.

Stabilization   The condition of a residential neighborhood in which there is a persistence of household by race and class. As used in the human ecology literature, stability exists in home values when sale prices and assessed values reflect long-term and areawide market forces rather than panic selling. Because it is common to have a turnover of residential ownership of about one in each five households each year, stability is measured through homeowner type and rate of turnover. The opposite of a stabilized neighborhood is one undergoing change. Unstable or changing neighborhoods are invaded by another race, ethnic group, or class. Blacks invade white areas or whites gentrify black areas. Hispanics invade Anglo communities, or lower-class families intrude on the middle class. Group homes are said to destabilize neighborhoods, but if they are spaced— as is usually the case—there have been no examples of large-scale panic selling. During the fever pitch of turnover, sellers accept low offers from speculators who in turn sell high to demand-driven minorities. Scatter-site public housing also is said to *destabilize* a neighborhood. Community relations councils, church groups, and public schools have a major role to play in calming owners and checking the spread of panic. *See also* BLOCKBUSTING; BUSING; CHICAGO SCHOOL; FILTERING THEORY, HOUSING; HUMAN ECOLOGY; INTEGRATION, RACIAL; INVASION; SUCCESSION; TIPPING POINT; WHITE FLIGHT; YONKERS-STYLE POLITICS.

Significance   Stabilization is one of the most emotionally charged issues in urban politics. Homes and condominiums are usually the largest investment for most people; hence it is an economic issue. Viable neighborhoods can be maintained by such devices as preventing blockbusting, enforcing fair housing in the entire metropolitan market, preventing real estate agents from steering, and banning redlining in insurance and mortgage markets. Stability becomes an issue in well-maintained sections contiguous to blighted or slum areas. It is also an issue in first-ring suburbs sharing a common boundary with a central city that has substantial unmet minority housing demand. Two of the major issues during peak destabilization are what role the city council/city administration should play and how the mass media should treat the subject in news stories and editorials. Open-housing markets truly deflect destabilization drives because owners are free to buy without the restraints of *de facto* segregation.

Suggested Reading
Downes, Bryan T., and John N. Collins. "Community Stabilization in the Inner Suburbs." *Urban Affairs Quarterly*, vol. 4, no. 1 (1977), pp. 135–159.

State-of-the-City Address   An annual report delivered in some jurisdictions by the mayor, city manager, or city council. The state-of-the-city address is an analogue to the better-known state-of-the-state address by the governor and the state-of-the-union address by the president. It sets forth the problems besetting the city and establishes priorities for the administration in the forthcoming calendar or fiscal year; if the mayor or administrator has been in office before, it often contains a summing up of accomplishments in the form of a stewardship report. The concept behind a stewardship report is an accounting of a position of trust. The address is received by the legislative body in written and/or oral form. *See also* CITY MANAGER.

Significance   Some state-of-the-city addresses are combined with a swearing-in talk. These addresses set the tone for a new administration. They often are not well covered by the press unless they contain substantial new departures in policy, such as promises of major reductions in force (RIFs) or new plans for community growth. By extension, Chief Justice Warren Burger adopted the idea and instituted state-of-the-judiciary addresses, the first of which he delivered at the 1970 midwinter meeting of the American Bar Association (ABA). This was later published in the *American Bar Association Journal*. State-of-the-city addresses delivered after an election are statements of reconciliation with the other factions and parties and a statement of unity for all ethnic and racial groups, as well as a show of unity for all sections of the city. Along with the budget, the state-of-the-city address should be a controlling document indicating a clear agenda. The National Urban League has used this format for preparing an annual state-of-black-America address since 1976.

State Mandate   A state-imposed requirement on substate levels, directing them to perform or refrain from certain functions. Such state-mandated actions may be accompanied by state-generated transfer of funds to cover the cost of the imposition or abstention. Although legislatures conventionally impose these conditions, state mandates occasionally emanate from actions by any branch. The courts, for example, may take superintending control over a local function and require an upgrading of services. From the state perspective, mandates impose uniform standards, which might or might not involve that level with increased expenditures. It locks in local-level decision makers who may not otherwise cooperate. From the local perspective, state mandates are particularly irksome when there are also state-mandated maximum taxing levels. State mandates that have no escape clause for home-rule communities force a reordering of budget priorities from the top. The opposite of a state mandate is a *local option:* In bill-drafting language, it is the difference between requiring that cities *shall* do something and suggesting that cities *may* do something. There are also *federal mandates,* which impose burdens on states and their cities, such as requirements under the 1972 Clean

Water Act to upgrade sewage-treatment facilities so as to limit sewage being dumped into rivers, lakes, and oceans. *See also* CONSTITUTION, STATE; DILLON'S RULE; HOME RULE; INTERGOVERNMENTAL RELATIONS.

Significance   State mandates are the instruments in intergovernmental relations by which the superior level imposes uniform standards and priorities on substate units. They are one tool to enforce state control over municipalities. Because local governments are creatures of the state, the higher level dictates what they can perform or abstain from performing. This is accomplished without the give and take of equals in a political process. Examples include forcing binding arbitration on public safety officials, requiring strict solid-waste management in all general governments, requiring counties to administer and pay in part for worker's compensation and public welfare programs, making local units pay part or all of local court costs, and forcing counties to pay all or part of their residents' costs when they are assigned to group homes. One particularly controversial state mandate requires counties to house state inmates in rough proportion to their contribution of them in the overall state prison population. Local governments react to state mandates by lobbying against new impositions and by initiating litigation to stop mandates that are underfunded or unfunded. In New Hampshire, local units sponsored a constitutional amendment to require the state to pay fully for any newly imposed program. Most new state mandates do not compensate local units for costs incurred. In California, the legislature simply estimates that the impact of the mandate will save funds for the local unit. It may also assert the mandate is a revenue-neutral measure. By law, the state level has the upper hand in this intergovernmental relation, and the local level will always be reactive. Federal mandates have been equally controversial. For example, the Environmental Protection Agency has insisted on states and cities cleaning up sewage operations, while Congress and the federal executive have curtailed the amount of funds to accomplish the project.

Suggested Reading

Advisory Commission on Intergovernmental Relations. *State Mandating of Local Expenditures*. Washington, DC: ACIR, 1978.
Koch, Edward I. "The Mandate Millstone." *Public Interest*, no. 61 (Fall 1980), pp. 42–57.
Lovell, Catherine H., and Charles Tobin. "Mandating—A Key Issue for Cities." *1980 ICMA Year Book*, vol. 47, pp. 73–79.

State-Municipal Affairs Office   An administrative, intergovernmental relations umbrella agency charged with overall local liaison. The purpose of a state-municipal affairs office may range from exercise of some local control to collecting information from local governments. Cities, villages, towns, and counties legally are all products of the state and responsible to that level as well as to the electorate. These offices exist in about half the states. They serve a variety of functions, such as aiding localities in strategic planning, annexation, and locating certified consultants. They serve as clearinghouses for city stewardship reports on local expenditure of state funds and as executive-branch contact for local officials. However, they have not developed into full-fledged control bodies. The dominant pattern has been to decentralize state contact with municipalities. *See also* CONSTITUTION, STATE; DILLON'S RULE; FEDERALISM; INTERGOVERNMENTAL RELATIONS; STATE MANDATE.

Significance   Most state supervision of urban affairs is conducted along functional lines, not from a single state-municipal affairs office. For example, a state treasury department may be charged with investigating finances of cities on the brink of insolvency. State departments of education normally are responsible for monitoring local labor-management relations and school audit reports. Councils of Governments (COGs) and county highway offices intervene between cities and state highway departments. The power of a state-municipal affairs office is severely diminished by direct city-state legislative contact and by direct city–national-level liaison that bypasses state machinery. Cities also are held accountable to courts, as when judges assume superintending control over schools or jails or when they review zoning board of appeals decisions. In brief, the complex web of intergovernmental relations precludes the state-municipal affairs office in the administrative branch from exercising as much control as might appear possible on the face of a state constitution.

Street-Level Bureaucrat   A public employee working under stress who frequently interacts with citizens, exercises discretion in disposing of those contacts, and makes an extensive impact on those citizens' lives. "Street-level bureaucrats" is a neologism coined by Michael Lipsky in 1969 to describe largely but not exclusively urban line administrators. *Line* personnel perform the functions for which the organization was created, in contradistinction to *staff* personnel, who perform either supervisory or support functions. Examples of line personnel include police on the beat, classroom teachers, mental and general hospital duty nurses and physicians, social workers, welfare caseworkers, trial judges, administrative law referees, prosecuting attorneys, public defenders, jailers, and parole officers. These job descriptions are entry-level, and usually require professional or post-secondary education as well as certification. Most of these positions mandate adherence to professional codes as well as staff-level over-sight. *See also* GHETTO; URBAN CRISIS.

Significance   It was Lipsky's thesis that street-level bureaucrats are under siege, working in stressful conditions with overcrowded caseloads/dockets/classes/clientele. They have too few resources, are under physical threat, and live with cross-currents in their job descriptions. Clients criticize them for being insensitive to the unique needs of those they serve. Many of these clients are poor, ethnic, and ill equipped to defend themselves if abused by bureaucrats. There are more than 10 million such bureaucrats in the nation, probably three-fourths working in urban areas. When street-level personnel fail their clients, it brings disrespect on the whole department, school, office, court, hospital, or penal institution. Those bureaucrats who fall back on formal rules fail to personalize the system and often are accused of incompetence, lethargy, and stagnation. They are often burned-out but cannot be moved from their positions by supervisors, nor can they be inspired from below. They sour their clients and bring on a low sense of efficacy in those who cannot get redress from the system. The Lipsky construct suggests that institutional inertia emanates from line administrators who react to stress by oversimplifying the rules, stereotyping the client's needs, and resisting close supervision. They manipulate the information that the organization keeps in its client files, thereby invalidating proper audits. Suggestions for overcoming the problem include reducing student-teacher ratios, precinct size, and caseloads; increasing supervision; improving audits; improving working relationships between unions and management so that the most burned-out can be removed; and decentralizing the units to bring accountability closer to those being served.

Suggested Reading
Brintnall, Michael. "Caseloads, Performance, and Street-Level Bureaucracy." *Urban Affairs Quarterly*, vol. 16, no. 3 (1981), pp. 281–298.
Lipsky, Michael. *Street-Level Bureaucracy: Dilemmas of the Individual in Public Services*. New York: Russell Sage, 1980.
———. "Street-Level Bureaucracy and the Analysis of Urban Reform." *Urban Affairs Quarterly*, vol. 6, no. 4 (1971), pp. 391–409.
Thomas, John Clayton. "The Personal Side of Street-Level Bureaucracy: Discrimination or Neutral Competence?" *Urban Affairs Quarterly*, vol. 22, no. 1 (1986), pp. 84–99.

Subdivision   A tract of land recorded under one owner's name that is subsequently broken down into a series of numbered lots or parcels, and offered for sale or actually sold or leased to others. Some states limit subdivision to land that has or could be developed as un-attached homes. Tracts that fall under plat acts of states for control purposes are bifurcated into minor and major subdivisions, with expe-dited approval available for small-scale breakups. There are various stages in subdivision approval imposed by the state and locality. Since the 1920s, some developers have been forced to construct on-site infra-structure such as roads, sewers, water mains, drainage, and sidewalks. In the 1980s, some major subdivision developers were also forced to plan and construct off-site infrastructure such as roads and areawide drainage facilities under exacting standards imposed on financially hard-pressed local governments. The permissible, government-imposed, on- and off-site standards before the awarding of site plans vary among the states. *See also* ARCHITECTURAL REVIEW BOARD; BUILDING CODES; EXACTION; LEVITTOWN; MANDATORY LAND DEDICATION; MASTER PLAN.

Significance   Most post–World War II housing in U.S. urban areas has been constructed on tracts of land subject to subdivision control ordinances and laws. Because of the federal system, there has been substantial variation in what government standards apply to these projects. Whereas early subdivision developments were sometimes free of responsibility for building improvements or dedicating land in lieu of construction, later developers have been held to rigorous re-view procedures. The high standards protect homeowners and the community from abandoned projects and limit the whole commu-nity's liability for small-area improvement costs such as street paving and sidewalk installation. Planning board review of subdivisions is one of the most important stages in the political life of a community. Failure to lay down proper guidelines and provide for proper code enforcement will produce a multiplier effect of problems in the later stages of the subdivision's history. Undercapacity drains develop sewer backups, improper backfilling yields buckled streets, and wrongly designed access streets later yield high accident rates at inter-sections and long backups during peak traffic.

Suggested Reading

Shultz, Michael M., and Richard Kelly. "Subdivision Improvement Require-ments and Guarantees: A Primer." *Washington University Journal of Ur-ban and Contemporary Law*, vol. 28 (1985), pp. 3–106. (Well documented.)

Weiss, Marc Allan. *The Rise of the Community Builders: The American Real Estate Industry and Urban Land Planning*. New York: Columbia University Press, 1987.

Suburb   A municipal corporation or unincorporated area outside the central city but within the metropolitan area. Suburbs are physi-

cally peripheral to the anchor city. Separately incorporated civil jurisdictions within the central city are called *enclaves*. Affluent governmental units outside the ring of suburbs but still functionally
integrated to central cities by a long commute are called *exurbs*. The
major feature distinguishing a suburb from a central city is racial and
ethnic composition. To a lesser extent, suburbs tend to have residents
of higher social status, a higher rate of home ownership, and more
single-family, unattached households. Suburbs differ in density all the
way from some apartment-dominated, first-ring units to large-lot,
unattached single-unit, outer-ring examples. *See also* BALKANIZATION;
CENSUS OF GOVERNMENTS; CITY CLASSIFICATION; ENCLAVE; EXURBIA;
LEVITTOWN; SUBURBAN TYPOLOGY; URBAN; YONKERS-STYLE POLITICS.

Significance   The United States has become a dominantly suburban
nation. The greatest percentage of people in most metropolitan areas
live in suburbs, not the central city. Amor there are regional
differences between sunbelt and snowbel, subu tend to have more
shopping centers, higher automobile ownership, and fewer sidewalks; they spend more on schools per capita, experience lower crime
rates, and have a higher sense of quality of life than central cities. The
myth of suburban homogeneity is now well debunked: suburbs differ
substantially in life style, electoral turnout, partisan identification,
and economic base. They also differ in form of government, degree
of intermetropolitan governmental cooperation, and rate of taxation. Increasingly suburbs are the sites of new jobs as well as new
homesites.

Suggested Reading
Cervero, Robert. *Suburban Gridlock*. New Brunswick, NJ: Center for Urban
    Policy Research, Rutgers University, 1986.
Danielson, Michael N. *The Politics of Exclusion*. New York: Columbia University
    Press, 1976.
Dolce, Philip C., ed. *Suburbia: The American Dream and Dilemma*. Garden City,
    NY: Doubleday, 1976.
Ebner, Michael H. *Creating Chicago's North Shore: A Suburban History*. Chicago:
    University of Chicago Press, 1988. (Social-political history of eight Lake
    Michigan communities.)
Gober, Patricia, and Michelle Behr. "Central Cities and Suburbs as Distinct
    Place Types: Myth or Fact?" *Economic Geography*, vol. 58, no. 4 (1982),
    pp. 371–385.
Kramer, John, ed. *North American Suburbs: Politics, Diversity, and Change*.
    Berkeley, CA: Glendessary Press, 1972.
Lake, Robert W. *The New Suburbanites: Race and Housing in the Suburbs*. New
    Brunswick, NJ: Center for Urban Policy Research, Rutgers University,
    1981.
Murphy, Thomas P., and John Rehfuss. *Urban Politics in the Suburban Era*.
    Homewood, IL: Dorsey Press, 1976.

Suburban Typology   Use of various characteristics to classify general local governments outside the central city but within the metropolitan area. Suburban typologizing first was developed in the United States in the 1950s when sociologist Leo Schnore noted the diversity of outlying metropolitan cities. Among variables used today to classify suburbs are: (1) *demographic:* absolute population, percentage nonwhite, percentage retired, and mobility rates; (2) *land use:* percentage of land zoned for residences or business and density level; (3) *sociological:* residential life style, ethnicity, occupational breakdown, level of racial integration, and type of residence (detached single-family condos, apartments, and flats); (4) *economic:* tax base relative to budget levels, per-capita wealth, and ratio of daytime to nighttime population; and (5) *political:* reformed versus nonreformed cities, home rule versus state charters, degree of party competition, and diversity of services offered. Thomas Dye established that a community's economic base is more important than its political machinery in predicting policy outcomes. *See also* BEDROOM SUBURB; COMPARATIVE URBAN ANALYSIS; DYE THESIS; EXURBIA; LEVITTOWN; MULTINUCLEI MODEL; PRIVATISM.

Significance   Suburban typology ranges from dormitory, recreation, and industrial examples to slum and business park/shopping center examples. Suburbs differ substantially in the levels and types of services offered, ranging from spartan, privatized jurisdictions all the way to paternalistic, large-budget units. All suburbs are not dominated by white, middle-class residents. This stereotype of the late 1960s and early 1970s spurred critics to argue that it is fallacious to aggregate all social issues. Clearly some political problems are more intractable and serious than others. Classification of suburbs is largely a function of an author's research interests. There are many variables in which suburbs differ. In one study, proximity from the core city may be important. In another, age of incorporation, type of electoral machinery, type of charter, or form of administration may be more relevant.

Suggested Reading
Barth, Ernest A. T., and Stuart D. Johnson. "Community Power and a Typology of Social Issues." *Social Forces,* vol. 38, no. 4 (1959), pp. 29–32.
Berger, Bennett M. *Working Class Suburb: A Study of Auto Workers in Suburbia.* Berkeley: University of California Press, 1971. Chap. 1, "The Myth of Suburbia."
Donaldson, Scott. *The Suburban Myth.* New York: Columbia University Press, 1969.
Kramer, Kathryn Beth, Gordon C. Johanson, Jr., and W. Parker Frisbie. "Suburban Differentiation: On the Contemporary Utility of the Employment-Residence Typology." *Journal of Urban Affairs,* vol. 4, no. 2 (1982), pp. 11–24.

Schnore, Leo F. "The Functions of Metropolitan Suburbs." *American Journal of Sociology,* vol. 61, no. 5 (1956), pp. 453–458.

Zikmund, Joseph. "A Theoretical Structure for the Study of Suburban Politics." *Annals of the Academy of Political and Social Science,* vol. 422 (1975), pp. 45–60.

Suburbanization   Dispersion of metropolitan population from the central city to peripheral communities. Although both jobs and residences are being suburbanized, employment remains more centralized than housing. Suburbanization reflects two demographic trends: (1) *Decentralization,* in which the periphery grows faster than the central city grows; (2) *Deconcentration,* in which central-city density decreases and periphery density increases. *See also* ANNEXATION; DENSITY, URBAN; DISINVESTMENT, URBAN; INFILLING; INTERSTATE HIGHWAY SYSTEM; SUBURBAN TYPOLOGY; WHITE FLIGHT.

Significance   Suburbanization is one of the major demographic trend lines of the twentieth century, especially after World War II. Most explanations attribute the process to push and pull factors. Among the reasons for leaving the central city are excessive densities and high crime rates. On the part of whites, there has been a desire to distance themselves from incoming blacks. Attractions of the suburbs include an exclusionary life style, better public schools, less expensive and larger land parcels, and national tax subsidies for home buying; in addition, the interstate highway system permits faster commuting to jobs. Under the balkanized system of metropolitan government, local tax bases are captured for local service delivery. This allows former central-city dwellers to distance themselves from the inner city's deteriorating tax base.

Suggested Reading

Holly, Brian P., and William E. Denton. "Suburbanization in the Cleveland SMSA, 1950–1970." *Professional Geographer,* vol. 34, no. 2 (1982), pp. 197–207.

Jackson, Kenneth. *Crabgrass Frontier: The Suburbanization of the United States.* New York: Oxford University Press, 1985.

Schwartz, Barry, ed. *The Changing Face of the Suburbs.* Chicago: University of Chicago Press, 1976.

Smith, Joel. "Another Look at Socioeconomic Status Distributions in Urbanized Areas." *Urban Affairs Quarterly,* vol. 5, no. 4 (1970), pp. 423–453.

Succession   A process associated with human ecology theory in which a population or land use is replaced with another group or use within a city neighborhood. Most succession analysis involves unstable neighborhoods where high-status groups are invaded and numerically overcome by low-status groups. It can also involve whites whose areas are invaded by black groups, or assimilated groups who are replaced by ethnic groups who eventually tip the neighborhood into a dominantly ethnic area. Succession also describes an industry invading a residential area or a loft subculture taking over an industrial area. Two of the major issues in succession analysis are the rate of turnover from first to second or later groups and uses, as well as the degree of resistance by *status quo* landowners who either do not want to move or do so only at an economic sacrifice. *See also* FILTERING THEORY, HOUSING; HUMAN ECOLOGY; INVASION; NEIGHBORHOOD; STABILIZATION; TIPPING POINT.

Significance   Succession theory focuses on the cycle of change in small environments within a city. The theory assumes a cycle of activity from equilibrium through transformation and back to some new equilibrium. Most empirical studies on succession are based on residential transformation from white to black communities or from upper- to lower-status ethnic groups. Employed by both sociologists and economic geographers, the operationalization of the concept is suspect because researchers rely upon census tracts that seldom correspond with the changing area. Some of the major findings that emerge from the analysis suggest that age of buildings is not always a major determinant of change. Several successions occur in the same area if a long enough period of time is used. There is an unanswered question whether racially mixed neighborhoods can ever be stable. The roles of gentrification and urban renewal are not well integrated into these studies. Gentrification is displacement by higher-status groups. Urban renewal is largely government-initiated urban land-use change. Most of the succession studies do not account for the roles of antiblockbusting statutes, antiredlining statutes, or real estate agents as initiators of rollover.

Suggested Reading

Aldrich, Howard. "Ecological Succession in Racially Changing Neighborhoods: A Review of the Literature." *Urban Affairs Quarterly*, vol. 10, no. 3 (1975), pp. 327–348.

Andrews, Richard B. *Land Use Succession Theory*, Parts I and II. Theory Discussion Paper Series. Madison, WI: Center for Urban Land Economics Research, 1980 and 1981.

Hudson, James R. "Soho—A Study of Residential Invasion of a Commercial and Industrial Area." *Urban Affairs Quarterly*, vol. 20, no. 1 (1984), pp. 46–63. (Review of the literature and extension of the definition.)

Park, Robert E. "Succession, An Ecological Concept." *American Sociological Review*, vol. 1, no. 2 (1936), pp. 171–179.

Schmidt, Charles G., and Yuk Lee. "Impact of Changing Racial Composition upon Commercial Land Use Succession and Commercial Structure: A Comparative Neighborhood Analysis." *Urban Affairs Quarterly*, vol. 13, no. 3 (1978), pp. 341–353.

White, Michael J. "Racial and Ethnic Succession in Four Cities." *Urban Affairs Quarterly*, vol. 20, no. 2 (1984), pp. 165–183. (Census tract analysis for 1940–1970 for Chicago, Detroit, Cleveland, and St. Louis.)

Sunbelt   The southern region of the United States, extending from Virginia on the Atlantic to central California in the West and on to Hawaii in the Pacific. It is also known as the southern rim. Four terms for the complementary area to the sunbelt are *snowbelt, frostbelt, rustbelt,* and *manufacturing belt.* The term was coined by Kevin Phillips in 1967 and used in his book *The Emerging Republican Majority,* published in 1969. Originally it meant the Southeast, Southwest, and Far West all the way north to Washington State. When operationalized by geographers, it is more restricted and refers to that area with a January mean temperature of 45°F or more, or an area below a latitude drawn from Washington, D.C., to just south of San Francisco. Major sunbelt industries include aerospace, energy exploration, and computer components, all high-growth-employment businesses. The northeast and north-central sections have older central cities that cannot expand through annexation and have high land-abandonment rates, higher unemployment rates, more metal fabrication, and flat or negative population levels. Compared to those areas, the sunbelt has lower energy costs because of better weather and locally available fuel sources, less costly labor (in part because of right-to-work laws), along with relatively higher federal transfer payments. Indicative of the shift in people, jobs, and political power from snowbelt to sunbelt is the shifting population center of the nation, which in 1790 was outside Baltimore but in 1980 was outside St. Louis. The center is moving west and slightly south with each census, signaling interregional economic redistribution. *See also* ANNEXATION; CENTRAL CITY; GROWTH MANAGEMENT.

Significance   In the original Kevin Phillips formulation, sunbelt cities were thought of as antiunion and interested in giving tax incentives to industry to bolster the local economy. Sunbelt meant conservatives, many of whom were retirees in Florida and Arizona, the two states with the highest per-capita retirement incomes. It also meant a young, highly educated, affluent, and mobile work force in high technology and the service sector, all the antitheses of the smokestack industries of the northeast and north-central sections. In the late 1960s, Phillips saw the beginning of a new and Republican-dominated conservative cycle: Barry Goldwater, the 1964 GOP presidential standard-bearer from the sunbelt state of Arizona, was an early manifestation. Richard Nixon, the 1968 and 1972 GOP presidential candidate, who grew up in Whittier, California, also in the sunbelt, was a successful leader in the cycle. Ronald Reagan of California and George Bush of Texas are two other examples. The cycle was a reaction against the established, older, eastern leadership. Nixon's "southern strategy" simply confirmed the wisdom of the power shift. In fact, sunbelt metropolitan areas led the nation in population increase in the 1970s. Of the top 25 Metropolitan Statistical Areas (MSAs) as of 1985, the fastest growing were: Anaheim, California; Phoenix; San Diego; Houston; and Denver. All were lower-density urban areas than those in the North, and all increased in scale through annexation. The sunbelt also had the greatest growth in per-capita wealth: From 1969 to 1975, the Houston MSA recorded the nation's largest increase in total personal income corrected for inflation. As a precise term, *sunbelt* has limited application, because it is so all-encompassing. The major criticism of the term *snowbelt* is that it is an overbroad sectional designation for those areas located in the northeast and north-central United States. The sunbelt region is too varied to be meaningful, bracketing low-income Alabama and Mississippi with wealthy Florida and sparsely settled New Mexico and west Texas.

Suggested Reading

Abbott, Carl. *The New Urban America: Growth and Politics in Sunbelt Cities.* Chapel Hill: University of North Carolina Press, 1981.
Bernard, Richard M., and Bradley Rice, eds. *Sunbelt Cities: Politics and Growth since World War II.* Austin: University of Texas Press, 1983.
Dilger, Robert Jay. *The Sunbelt/Snowbelt Controversy: The War over Federal Funds.* New York: New York University Press, 1982.
Gappert, Gary, ed. *The Future of Winter Cities.* Beverly Hills: Sage Publications, 1987.
Perry, David C., and Alfred J. Watkins, eds. *The Rise of the Sunbelt Cities.* Urban Affairs Annual Reviews, vol. 14. Beverly Hills: Sage Publications, 1977.
Phillips, Kevin P. *Post-Conservative America.* New York: Random House, 1982. Especially Chap. 7, "After the Sun Belt, What New Forces?"
Sale, Kirkpatrick. *Power Shift.* New York: Random House, 1975.
Sawers, Larry, and William K. Tabb, eds. *Sunbelt/Snowbelt: Urban Development and Regional Restructuring.* New York: Oxford University Press, 1984.

Supply-Side Economics   An economic theory that suggests private investment and overall economic growth and prosperity can be stimulated by tax reductions. Supply-side economics supports substantial tax incentives as well as reduced levels of government business regulation. Theoretically, these policy changes would encourage wealthy individuals and corporations to make capital investments that would increase productivity, create jobs, and increase overall governmental revenues because of the resulting economic activity. This theory is considered "supply-side" because it focuses on stimulating a sluggish economy by rewarding private-producer behavior through tax breaks rather than the Keynesian "demand-side" approach, which argued for increased government spending to stimulate demand for goods and services. *See also* PRIVATIZATION.

Significance   Supply-side economics first was advocated by economist Arthur Laffer in the late 1970s. By the time of Ronald Reagan's presidential election in 1980, the supply-side philosophy was embraced by many who supported reductions in governmental spending and regulation. A number of the nation's larger urban centers suffered under the Reagan philosophy, which reduced or eliminated many urban-aid programs initiated under earlier administrations. In addition to reducing taxes to stimulate private investment, the supply-side approach favored reducing welfare assistance because it was thought to encourage labor mobility and individual motivation among the unemployed. Though the supply-side approach reduced governmental expenditures in many categories, the federal deficit grew more under the Reagan administration than in all previous administrations combined. This was due largely to the great increases in "tax expenditures," or costs incurred by the government as reduced revenues generated by the massive tax breaks given to private investors.

Suggested Reading
Bartlett, Bruce R. *Reaganomics: Supply Side Economics in Action*. Westport, CT: Arlington House, 1981.
Bartlett, Bruce R., and Timothy P. Roth, eds. *The Supply-Side Revolution*. Chatham, NJ: Chatham House, 1982.
Gilder, George. *Wealth and Poverty*. New York: Basic Books, 1981.
Lekachman, Robert. *Greed Is Not Enough: Reaganomics*. New York: Pantheon Books, 1982.
Roberts, Paul Craig. *The Supply Side Revolution*. Cambridge: Harvard University Press, 1984.
Stein, Herbert. *Presidential Economics: The Making of Economic Policy from Roosevelt to Reagan and Beyond*, 2nd ed. Lanham, MD: American Enterprise Institute for Public Policy Research, 1988.

T

Taking   A prohibited governmental action that interferes materially with the private use of private property, as cited in the last clause of the Fifth Amendment to the U.S. Constitution: "nor shall private property be taken for public use, without just compensation." In American jurisprudence, a distinction is made among eminent domain, the police power, and a taking. Eminent domain is a government taking of private property for a public purpose with just compensation. The amount of compensation is determined either before or after the fact, depending upon whether the state has a quick-take law. The police power is reserved to the states under the Tenth Amendment. This power permits states or their subdivisions to regulate private property to prevent uses detrimental to the public's health, safety, morals, welfare, well-being, or, occasionally, aesthetics. A taking can be either a temporary or permanent deprivation of property use by a physical invasion or a destruction of the utility of the property as a whole by government action. However, a reduction in the property's value alone does not constitute a taking. If it did, communities could not down-zone parcels. *See also* EMINENT DOMAIN; EXACTION; GROWTH MANAGEMENT; INVERSE CONDEMNATION; MORATORIUM; POLICE POWER; QUICK-TAKE LAW; ZONING, DOWN-.

Significance   The line between a taking on the one hand and permissible police-power regulation and eminent domain on the other is not totally clear. In 1986 the U.S. Supreme Court announced that a taking only occurs where there has been final governmental determination of land use (*MacDonald et al. v. Yolo County et al.*, 477 U.S. 340). The U.S. Supreme Court then wrestled with these issues in a trilogy of celebrated 1987 cases, the merits of which commentators are still debating. The three cases were *Keystone Bituminous Coal v. Benedictis*, 480 U.S. 470; *First English Evangelical Lutheran Church v. Los Angeles County*, 482 U.S. 304; and *Nollan v. California Coastal Commission*,

483 U.S. 825. The most important of the three is *U.S. First English*, which decided that a landowner was eligible to recover damages for the duration of a temporary regulatory taking that precluded any use of the land. The federal executive branch responded to these cases by issuing guidelines for "Governmental Actions and Interference with Constitutionally Protected Property Rights" in the *Federal Register*, vol. 53, no. 53, Executive Order 12630, recorded March 18, 1988. The *Nollan* case invalidated a California Coastal Commission exaction requiring public access to a beach as a precondition to issuing a building permit. However, the court justified the general idea of exactions as a means of managing growth. Takings generate substantial litigation, in part because of the lack of a coherent set of principles in all the previous taking cases.

Suggested Reading
Siemon, Charles L., and Wendy U. Larsen. "The Taking Issue Trilogy: The Beginning of the End?" *Journal of Urban and Contemporary Law*, vol. 33 (1988), pp. 169–200.

Tammany Hall (New York City)   One of the most widely known urban political machines in the United States. The machine became known as Tammany Hall because its members met in the building of that name. As with most urban political machines, Tammany Hall was a highly structured, local political party organization led by a "boss." Urban machines ran candidates for public office and provided jobs and other services to loyal members and to voters who supported the machine's candidates. Tammany Hall began in 1789 as a social and patriotic group, the Society of St. Tammany. While the Tammany Society continued as a social and fraternal group, a separate political arm was created, called the General Committee. By the mid-1800s, the General Committee of Tammany Hall became the controlling faction of the Democratic party in New York City. *See also* BOSS; CORRUPTION, GOVERNMENT; URBAN POLITICAL MACHINE.

Significance   Tammany Hall and urban political machines in general have been widely characterized as purveyors of favoritism, kickbacks, payoffs, and political corruption in general. Machines were often quite powerful. In many states, the local political machine had more political power than the party's state organization. These organizations were the primary targets of the Progressive Movement of the early twentieth century in the United States. The Progressive Era reformers successfully introduced reforms such as at-large city council elections, and open and direct presidential primaries, and they promoted the use of city managers and local civil service employment systems. However, many scholars of urban machines have taken a "functional" approach to studying machines, in which they argue that certain positive social and political functions were performed by machines. In addition to jobs and charitable support, machines provided political and social stability as well as urban service delivery to the working class. Some observers have noted that the increased use of block grants over categorical grants has given local authorities greater discretion over the actual distribution of federal funding. Such increased local discretion has given rise to the possibility of a "new machine" style of politics, in which benefits to political supporters may be distributed through this new vehicle of favoritism.

Suggested Reading

Connable, Alfred, and Edward Silberfarb. *Tigers of Tammany: Nine Men Who Ran New York.* New York: Holt, Rinehart, 1967.
Eisenstein, Louis, and Elliot Rosenberg. *A Stripe of Tammany's Tiger.* New York: Robert Speller, 1966.
Mushkat, Jerome. *Tammany: The Evolution of a Political Machine 1789–1865.* Syracuse, NY: Syracuse University Press, 1971.
Myers, Gustavus. *The History of Tammany Hall,* 2nd ed. New York: Burt Franklin, 1968.
Riordan, William L. *Plunkett of Tammany Hall.* New York: E. P. Dutton, 1963.

Tax, Local Income   A charge imposed by a local government on the wages, profits, interest, and other revenue sources of residents or those who are employed within the city. In many cases, local income tax rates differ between residents and nonresidents. Cities with decreasing property tax bases have begun to use income taxes to offset the losses incurred as businesses and homeowners leave, and as property values decline. *See also* RESIDENT; TAX, PERSONAL PROPERTY; TAX, REAL PROPERTY.

Significance   Once the federal income tax was imposed in 1913, taxes on income became popular with states and cities. About 43 states had income taxes by 1989, as did many cities. In 1939, Philadelphia became the first city to adopt a local income tax. Often, local income taxes have been associated with older, larger, and industrialized cities such as Detroit, Cleveland, Pittsburgh, and Baltimore. However, many other cities have begun to use the local income tax as a source of revenue. Cincinnati, Grand Rapids, Louisville, and Birmingham, Alabama, all have imposed local income taxes on their residents. Most local income taxes have flat rates; exceptions include New York City and Washington, D.C., which employ graduated taxes. Washington, D.C. and Philadelphia have the two highest per-capita taxes.

Suggested Reading

Neenan, William B. *Political Economy of Urban Areas.* Chicago: Markham Publishing, 1972. Chap. 11, "The Municipal Income Tax."
Smith, R. Stafford. *Local Income Taxes: Economic Effects and Equity.* Berkeley: Institute of Governmental Studies, University of California, 1972.

Tax, Motor Fuel   A user charge imposed by both the federal and state governments. The motor fuel tax is generated through the sale of automobile gasoline, with federal revenues going to the Highway Trust Fund to pay for federal highway construction and maintenance. State motor fuel taxes are much more extensively used and pay for the respective state highway systems. Some of the money may be further distributed to county and municipal governments to maintain their road systems under a legislated formula. *See also* INCOME SOURCES, URBAN; TAX, REGRESSIVE; TAX, SALES.

Significance   Because the motor fuel tax is a sales tax on gasoline purchased, it has been criticized by some as a regressive tax that unfairly burdens lower-income individuals. In addition, the motor fuel tax is collected at the gasoline pump, and therefore cannot determine the distribution of highway use in a state or within the federal interstate system. However, it is cheaper and easier to collect the tax in this fashion. In addition, since the pump price does not distinguish between the cost of the gasoline and the taxes assessed on the purchase, the motor fuel tax is essentially hidden from consumers/taxpayers.

Tax, Personal Property   A charge imposed by a taxing authority on items of value other than real property. Personal property can be classified as tangible, such as business machinery and merchandise, or intangible, such as bank accounts and stocks or bonds. Taxes on personal and real property holdings remained an overwhelming proportion of municipal revenues until a decline occurred after World War II, as cities increasingly began to use sales and income taxes. *See also* TAX, LOCAL INCOME; TAX, REAL PROPERTY; TAX, SALES.

Significance   Personal property tax requires that individuals or businesses declare ownership of such items. Assessment and collection of these taxes are often quite difficult, especially for intangible personal property. Taxation of personal property items, particularly against businesses, grew as municipal economies became more complicated and wealth took many forms in addition to property. In an effort to continue some relationship between overall wealth and tax assessments, many states and cities began to impose taxes on these personal property items.

Tax, Progressive   A revenue measure in which the tax rate increases as income increases. By contrast, a regressive tax is one in which the tax rate increases as income decreases. The progressive tax is also called a graduated tax. There is some debate over the progressive or regressive nature of the overall tax system in the United States, especially after the 1986 changes in the federal tax code. *See also* TAX, LOCAL INCOME; TAX, REGRESSIVE.

Significance   In the past, progressive taxes have been supported as a means to redistribute income. However, the progressivity of the federal income tax has been mitigated substantially by a wide variety of loopholes and tax shelters available to those individuals and corporations with very large incomes. Questions of who will pay for government services at all levels likely will remain a controversial issue. Changes in the federal tax code reducing the number of tax brackets to three has further increased the regressive nature of the overall taxation system. While the federal income tax is considered a progressive tax, many state governments have constitutionally prohibited a graduated tax for their state income taxes. Local government taxation also is subject to state constitutional constraints. Critics of the progressive income tax argue that such a tax reduces individual initiative and imposes a penalty on those who work hard. State and local revenues are traditionally subject to the general condition of the economy. When national production decreases, state and local income and sales taxes decline. Such sensitivity to national economic trends provided a strong argument for countercyclical federal aid to states and cities. By 1988, reduced federal aid to cities forced several states to expand local taxing authority and increase revenues by other means. During 1988, Arkansas, Florida, Iowa, and Nevada granted authority to their local governments to impose sales taxes, and other states, such as New Mexico, attempted to increase local revenues by granting authority to establish a lodgers' tax and benefit from an increasing tourism industry in the state.

Suggested Reading

Advisory Commission on Intergovernmental Relations. *Significant Features of Fiscal Federalism*, 1988 ed., Vol. 2. Washington, DC: ACIR, 1988.
MacManus, Susan A. "Tax Structures in American Cities: Levels, Reliance and Rates." *Western Political Quarterly*, vol. 30, no. 2 (1977), pp. 263–287.

Tax, Real Property   An *ad valorem* (that is, according to value) charge imposed by a taxing authority on land ownership. Local governments make the greatest use of the property tax, although most states also levy property taxes. Between 1962 and 1982, property taxes decreased from 27 percent to 15 percent of total state and local government revenue. As of 1985, Alaska and Wyoming had the highest per-capita property tax revenues of any states, and Alabama the lowest. According to the Bureau of the Census, intergovernmental aid comprised the largest share (23.4 percent) of all sources of city government income by 1985–1986. Income from utility and liquor stores, which many cities operate, accounted for about 17.5 percent, user fees and other charges about 21 percent, and property taxes about 16 percent. See also AD VALOREM ; ASSESSMENT; INCOME SOURCES, URBAN; MILLAGE; TAX, PERSONAL PROPERTY.

Significance   Local governments historically have relied on the property tax to generate revenue. However, many larger cities have faced a combination of declining land values and decreasing populations. These factors have greatly reduced the tax base of these cities. Many cities have been forced to increase their millages, reduce or eliminate services, impose user fees, or seek additional funding from the federal or state government. Because state constitutions or legislatures determine State Equalized Value (SEV) formulas and specify types of property that are taxable or exempt, local governments do not have control over several important parts of the taxing process. Local property taxes often appear to be more salient to the average taxpayer than taxes imposed by other levels of government. As such, the property tax tends to force the issue of accountability to the forefront in local politics and creates a more active citizenry at the local level of policymaking.

Suggested Reading

Aaron, Henry J. *Who Pays the Property Tax?* Washington, DC: Brookings Institution, 1975.
Case, Karl E. *Property Taxation: The Need for Reform.* Cambridge, MA: Ballinger, 1978.
Hale, Dennis, "The Evolution of the Property Tax: A Study of the Relations between Public Finance and Political Theory." *Journal of Politics,* vol. 47, no. 2 (1985), pp. 382–404.
Harris, C. Lowell, ed. "Symposium: The Property Tax and Local Finance." *Proceedings of the Academy of Political Science,* vol. 35, no. 1 (1983).
U.S. Bureau of the Census. *Government Finances in 1985–86.* GF-86, no. 5. Washington, DC: Government Printing Office, November 1987.

Tax, Regressive   A government levy in which the tax rate increases as income decreases. A tax is considered regressive, therefore, when the larger proportional burden is placed on individuals with lower incomes. An example of a regressive tax is the sales tax. Because such a tax is uniformly applied without regard to income, individuals with smaller incomes pay a greater proportional share of their income to that tax. State and local governments tend to be the most active users of regressive taxes through the sales tax and property tax, each of which imposes a flat tax regardless of income category. *See also* TAX, PROGRESSIVE; TAX, SALES.

Significance   Debates over tax systems have centered around the question of how governments can generate enough revenue to pay for public services, and the question of who should pay for these services. A regressive tax applies the same percentage to all citizens (or purchasers, for example), but forces those with lower incomes to pay a proportionally larger share of their available funds to that particular tax. This leaves relatively less disposable income for poorer citizens to purchase goods and services. In recent years, many states have attempted to soften the effect of the sales tax by eliminating the tax on necessities such as food, clothing, and prescription drugs. In addition, some have argued that a higher sales tax rate should be placed on luxury items to generate more revenue for the taxing authority and to offset the losses incurred when a sales tax on necessities is no longer imposed. Considerable debate still occurs over the overall progressive or regressive effect of individual taxes and the overall tax system. For example, the Social Security contribution would appear quite regressive, because the tax rate stops increasing beyond a set income level and any kind of property income is exempt. Yet, the benefit formula for Social Security gives low-income earners more dollars of benefit per dollar contributed than high-income earners. Historically, the federal tax system has been more progressive than state and local taxes.

Suggested Reading
Aaron, Henry J. *Who Pays the Property Tax?* Washington, DC: Brookings Institution, 1975.
Cord, Steven. "How To Transform the Property Tax into a Graded Tax." *American Journal of Economics and Sociology*, vol. 34, no. 2 (1975), pp. 127–128.
Hansen, Susan B. "Extraction: The Politics of State Taxation." Chap. 12 in Virginia Gray, et al., eds., *Politics in the American States*, 4th ed. Boston: Little, Brown, 1983.

Tax, Sales   An *ad valorem* tax generally imposed on the purchase of retail items. The taxing power of states first must allow for the imposition of such a tax. The sales tax became popular during the period after the Great Depression, in which states were forced to seek additional revenues to pay for the social services required at the time. This tax remains the largest source of income for states, although more states have recently added income taxes to increase revenues further. At least 45 states have authorized a sales tax. In addition to the state sales tax, some cities (New York City, New Orleans) have levied their own sales taxes in an effort to increase revenues. *See also* AD VALOREM ; TAX, REGRESSIVE.

Significance   The sales tax has remained a popular revenue generator for state governments. This type of tax has been used increasingly by cities, many of which have experienced substantial losses in their property tax base. Cities that rely on tourism also have found the sales tax on hotels and motels a popular generator of additional revenue, because those fees can be charged to nonresidents. The major criticism of the sales tax is that it is equally applied to persons of all income levels, and therefore places a larger proportional burden on lower-income citizens. This regressive nature of the sales tax has been addressed partially in some states, which have exempted some retail commodities that are regarded as necessities, such as food and medicine.

Tax Abatement   A property tax benefit given by a municipality to a business that renovates, expands, or builds a manufacturing plant in a designated district within the city. Tax abatements are not actual tax exemptions, because they are a temporary forgiveness of tax liability. The designated area within which business investments qualify for abatement is usually determined by a formula of economic distress. The tax abatement, or reduction, is usually 50 or 100 percent of the property tax liability on improvements, or for a new facility. Property tax assessments are typically frozen for varying lengths of time, depending on the state. In New York, abatements normally last 10 years; in Michigan up to 12 years; and in Ohio, 20 years. *See also* ECONOMIC DEVELOPMENT; TAX INCENTIVE.

Significance   Tax abatements have become part of the package of incentives that states and municipalities have had to offer to attract business development. Abatements are normally offered for construction of manufacturing facilities; the competition by cities over these increasingly rare high-wage-paying businesses has grown substantially since 1975. With reduced federal support for urban redevelopment, states and cities have been forced to offer the few incentives available at their discretion. Ironically, the original argument for government support of economic development projects—that it would add to the municipal tax base—has been largely undercut by these incentives, at least in the short term. Recent benefit-cost studies evaluating the effect of incentives such as tax abatements have raised serious questions about the economic value to a city that offers such incentives. If used for new construction only, abatements discriminate against on-site local businesses. In addition, critics have argued that abatements and other incentives have little impact on private locational decision making, though some evidence suggests these incentives may influence site selection within, but not between, regions.

Suggested Reading

Blair, John P., and Robert Premus. "Major Factors in Industrial Relocation: A Review." *Economic Development Quarterly*, vol. 1, no. 1 (1987), pp. 72–85.
Warner, Paul D. "Business Climate, Taxes, and Economic Development." *Economic Development Quarterly*, vol. 1, no. 4 (1987), pp. 383–390.
Wolkoff, Michael J. "Chasing a Dream: The Use of Tax Abatements To Spur Urban Economic Development." *Urban Studies*, vol. 22 (1985) pp. 305–315.

Tax Amnesty   A program authorized by states or cities to provide a temporary period for delinquent taxpayers to pay overdue taxes without penalty. By 1988, at least 28 states had created tax amnesty plans. States that offered amnesty programs included Alabama, California, Florida, Maryland, New Jersey, New York, Oklahoma, and West Virginia. In some states, all taxes were covered by the amnesty program, in others only selected taxes. Although the programs vary from state to state, tax amnesty usually requires prompt payment of taxes and interest within a 60- to 90-day period to avoid criminal and civil prosecution. Additional monetary penalties usually applied to overdue payments often are waived. States that collected the most money during their amnesty periods were New York ($401.3 million), New Jersey ($182 million), California ($154 million), and Illinois ($152.4 million). North Dakota received the least overall money, collecting about $150,000. While this has been primarily a state-level program, some cities, such as Chicago, also have offered amnesty programs for the taxes applicable within their jurisdictions. *See also* TAX, LOCAL INCOME; TAX, SALES; TAX DELINQUENCY.

Significance   Tax amnesty programs increasingly became popular during the early 1980s. As unpaid taxes increased at rapid rates in some states, legislatures were forced to consider tax amnesty plans. One aspect of most amnesty programs is increased enforcement after a specified "grace period," in a further effort to encourage delinquent taxpayers to respond promptly. In California and Oklahoma, for example, amnesty offers were limited to individual income and sales taxes; in Texas, to the sales tax alone. Most states have reported success with these plans, as the direct costs of the amnesty programs (mostly publicity and personnel) were small compared to the revenues generated by the responses.

Suggested Reading
Parle, William M., and Mike W. Hirlinger. "Evaluating the Use of Tax Amnesty by State Governments." *Public Administration Review,* vol. 46, no. 3 (1986), pp. 246–255.

Tax Anticipation Note (TAN)   A short-term obligation sold by any public jurisdiction, ranging from a state to an authority, in conventional money markets at a fixed rate of return. The notes are promises to pay, usually in 30 to 120 days, from income to be derived from conventional revenue sources such as property and intangible taxes, transfer payments, fees, and fines. TANs are designed to smooth out irregularities in public revenue receipts. The notes are used to pay for operating expenses and are not to be used for capital budget accounts. *See also* CAPITAL EXPENDITURE; INCOME SOURCES, URBAN; REVENUE SURPLUS.

Significance   Many jurisdictions make use of these notes when they do not have adequate reserves to pay current obligations such as vendors and payroll. The notes often are employed seasonally to carry over the jurisdiction before a tax payment deadline. It is considered desirable for local governments to have at least two months' reserve available as a percentage of the total fiscal year's expenditures. These notes may be a technique for covering up a deficit, however. In that case, the jurisdiction is postponing a decision on raising taxes, cutting services, going into permanent debt, asking other jurisdictions for aid, or some combination thereof. The scale of these notes is calculated as a percentage of total income, and if it is less than 20 percent of expenditures for operations, it is considered a reasonable public policy. Persistent use of these notes is an indication the budget process is not based on enough carryover or enough underlying revenue. Charters may prevent their use or limit the reason for their issuance. They are used to pay off pension underfunding, substantial overtime, back pay in union settlements, and major lawsuits without adequate set-aside provisions.

Suggested Reading
Pickens, Daniel N., and David Unkovic. "TANs Remain a Viable Option Despite Tax Act Restrictions." *American City and County,* vol. 102, no. 6 (1987), p. 74.

Tax Base   The major source of revenue for a government. For municipalities in the United States, the property tax historically has constituted the tax base. Even in the 1980s, U.S. cities continued to rely on the property tax for about 75 percent of their revenues (down from about 86 percent in 1960). However, declining property values and the loss of businesses and residents in many urban centers have created fiscal stress. It has forced these cities to rely on other sources of revenue. These alternative sources have included income taxes, user fees for specific services, intergovernmental fiscal assistance, public lotteries, and local sales taxes. *See also* ECONOMIC BASE ANALYSIS; FISCAL STRESS; TAX, REAL PROPERTY; TAX ABATEMENT; URBAN CRISIS.

Significance   Many of the larger, older, northern cities faced serious fiscal problems beginning in the 1970s. The near-bankruptcy of New York City in 1975 constituted but one of many critical periods for U.S. cities. As the urban tax base declined, citizens needing greater public services (welfare, police and fire protection, health care) replaced many of the middle- and upper-class residents who left for the suburbs. Many cities were left to confront the problem of providing more services with less revenue. During Ronald Reagan's presidency, the federal level cut urban aid and forced cities to reduce services and/or look elsewhere to generate revenue. Many of the investment inducements offered by cities, such as tax abatements, further reduced the municipal tax base.

Tax Base Sharing   The use of the same tax fee by two or more taxing authorities. One taxation authority traditionally collects the tax, then passes a portion of the revenues through to other authorities to share. Sharing can occur *vertically*, as between the federal and state levels, or it can involve local governments, in which case it is said to be *horizontal*. *See also* TAX BASE; TWIN CITIES.

Significance   Traditional tax base sharing generally refers to the historical sharing of property tax revenues (and later, income and sales taxes) by state and local governments. More recently, the term has come to reflect innovations in sharing revenues—and economic development—among municipalities in the same metropolitan area. This more recent type of tax base sharing is associated primarily with the Minnesota Twin Cities—Minneapolis and St. Paul. Under this tax-sharing plan, which began in 1972, a certain percentage of increased tax receipts in industrial and commercial properties goes to the Twin Cities Metropolitan Council. The council then distributes these receipts to all local units in the metropolitan region according to a formula established by the state. The remaining percentage of property tax receipts stays within the local jurisdiction that generated the revenue. In this way, competition for business investment among regional cities is reduced, and all local units share regional economic development.

Suggested Reading
Vogt, Walter. "Tax Base Sharing: Implication from San Diego County." *Journal of the American Planning Association,* vol. 45, no. 2 (1979), pp. 134–142.

Tax Delinquency   The failure to pay a legally imposed tax in a timely fashion. Tax delinquency occurs most frequently in urban areas over the payment of property taxes and is highly correlated with abandonment of urban housing units in declining neighborhoods or business districts. *See also* ABANDONMENT; *IN REM* PROPERTY; MILLAGE; TAX AMNESTY.

Significance   Tax delinquency has become a major problem in large urban centers where the housing markets have suffered great decreases in demand. Cities with high vacancy rates, large populations, and relatively few young couples seeking housing appear to have the greatest problems with defaults on property tax payments. Studies of property tax delinquency have found this problem to exist in all regions of the country. During the early 1970s, for example, Chicago's uncollected property taxes averaged 14.6 percent of the total tax base, while Houston's tax delinquency rate reached 9.4 percent. In general, homeowners or landowners are most likely to default when the return rates on their investments are perceived to be unsatisfactory. Absentee landlords are also more likely to abandon a property and default on the property tax than are owners who occupy the dwellings. High tax-delinquency rates can be seen as a reflection of urban deterioration as well as a factor in the declining revenues of some cities. For cities and states that have imposed income taxes, delinquency also has been identified as a problem of lost revenues. In an effort to encourage compliance quickly and inexpensively, several states and cities have offered tax amnesty plans, in which a grace period is established for delinquent taxpayers to come forward to pay back taxes without penalty.

Tax-Exempt Property   A parcel of real estate or equipment taken off the tax rolls permanently or temporarily by state or local action, thereby shrinking the tax assessment base of the community. Tax-exempt property constitutes a category that state or municipal legislatures feel should not share the burden of paying for services. The decision to exempt parcels must apply to all examples of the same type and cannot violate equal protection standards of the national and state constitutions. The list of privileged land uses excused from paying their fair tax share differs from state to state, but the following is a representative enumeration: public and private streets open to general ingress and egress; public and not-for-profit parks open to the general public; public golf courses; public and nonproprietary schools; public and not-for-profit colleges and universities; preschool cooperatives; churches and church parishes; cultural buildings such as museums, libraries, theaters, and their parking spaces; public buildings owned by municipal, state, or national government; public housing, elderly housing, and housing for those declared to be in poverty; public and nonprofit cemeteries; new business buildings and equipment under abatement; not-for-profit housing for the elderly and retired veterans; riverbeds and publicly owned floodplains; nonprofit and public airstrips; seawalls; energy-conversion land used to harness wind, water, and solar power; technological parks; meeting areas for eleemosynary organizations and social groups such as the YMCA/YWCA and Scout groups; not-for-profit medical clinics and hospitals. *See also* ASSESSMENT; CEMETERY; ELEEMOSYNARY GROUP; HOUSING, PUBLIC; TAX BASE.

Significance   Tax-exempt property is conventionally listed as an exception to the general rule that all property must be subject to property tax. Yet the exceptions, listed in neutral categories without reference to the number of acres or percentage of equipment taken off the rolls, may subtract from one-fourth to more than one-half of all property in a community or all earth-moving machinery in the area. Some states even exempt mobile home parks because they tax the home as such and not the underlying land. Nearly one-third of New York City is tax-exempt, as are some suburbs, such as Dearborn, Michigan, a first-ring suburb of Detroit. Cities that are economically dependent on educational institutions can push this ratio to more than one-half, as in Ann Arbor, Michigan. Assessor associations regularly pass resolutions opposing larger exemption categories, while lobbying groups representing not-for-profit organizations petition the legislature to broaden exemptions. They plead the case that as national tax laws tighten up deductions, the state must loosen the tax base proportionately. In states that do not rely on the real or personal property tax but allow municipalities to use the revenue, exemptions created by state legislature establish goodwill at the expense of cities and counties. As more owners are exempted from property taxes, the argument that an *ad valorem* tax is equitable slips away. The long-term trend is toward increased exemptions and greater reliance on taxing privately owned homes, apartments, and older business establishments. The tax dodge of setting up a family-room ministry is less common today than in the 1970s. Communities may bill tax-exempt institutions for direct services rendered, such as crowd control. Some tax exempts realize they are not paying their own way and contribute monies to the municipality; this is called payment in lieu of taxes, or PILOT.

Suggested Reading
Beebe, Robert L., and Stephen J. Harrison. "A Law in Search of a Policy: A History of New York's Real Property Tax Exemption for Nonprofit Organizations." *Fordham Urban Law Journal*, vol. 9, no. 3 (1981), pp. 533–590.
Larson, Martin, and C. Stanley Lowell. *Praise the Lord for Tax Exemption: How the Churches Grow Rich—While the Cities and You Grow Poor*. Washington, DC: Robert B. Luce, 1969.

Tax Exemption   A government waiver of the obligation for a specified class of taxpayer to pay a certain kind of tax. Many state and local governments allow tax exemptions to consumers on sales taxes for certain retail items such as food and medicine. In the past, the income derived from ownership of state or municipal bonds has been exempt from taxation. One form of exemption is a tax abatement for businesses. Tax abatements differ from exemptions in that exemptions refer to waivers of liability both present and future, while abatements extend only for a specific time period. *See also* BOND, MUNICIPAL; TAX ABATEMENT; TAX BASE; TAX-EXEMPT PROPERTY.

Significance   Tax exemptions can reflect a government's desire to encourage or avoid discouraging certain activities or merely underscore the political influence of special-interest groups. State and local governments have offered a wide variety of tax exemptions, such as abatements or other forgiveness of taxes, for business investment within the state or community. Local governments also have offered exemptions on new housing construction or rehabilitation for specific periods. In many jurisdictions, certain classifications of property are exempt from local property tax. Such exemptions include government-owned properties and those used by religious or charitable organizations.

Suggested Reading
Aronson, J. Richard, and John L. Hilley. *Financing State and Local Government*, 4th ed. Washington, DC: Brookings Institution, 1986.
Meyer, John R., and John M. Quigley. *Local Public Finance and the Fiscal Squeeze: A Case Study*. Cambridge, MA: Ballinger, 1977.

Tax Incentive   A governmental offer to the private sector aimed at inducing firms to select or remain in a particular location based on an overall favorable tax rate. Tax incentives are based on abatement, exemption, increment financing, or low rates. Attempts to cultivate firms to locate in a jurisdiction include land sales at write-down costs, city promises to build infrastructure to accommodate special needs, and zoning redesignation to facilitate expansion. *See also* TAX ABATEMENT; TAX-EXEMPT PROPERTY; TAX INCREMENT FINANCING; WRITE-DOWN.

Significance   Tax incentives and a favorable business climate, including a tax structure that does not inhibit business, are two factors in industrial location decisions. The question of how important these factors are is answered by empirical studies: They are of secondary concern. Costs of space, of which taxes are but one consideration, are often listed highest: Other major location factors include transportation links, proximity to customers, security, opportunity to expand, available labor pool, presence or absence of labor unions and labor unrest, parking, cultural amenities, and proximity to suitable residences and schools. It is not only total tax rate but type of tax structure for which firms look since some types of taxes such as a single-business tax are more onerous on capital-intensive businesses. Firms highly sensitive to total local tax burden may well be more marginal operations.

Suggested Reading

Jones, Bryan D., and Lynn W. Bachelor, with Carter Wilson. *The Sustaining Hand: Community Leadership and Corporate Power.* Lawrence: University Press of Kansas, 1986.

Sternlieb, George. *New Jersey Growth Corridors—Site Selection and Location Satisfaction.* New Brunswick, NJ: Center for Urban Policy Research of Rutgers University, 1987.

Thompson, Wilbur R. "Industrial Location: Causes and Consequences." Chap. 8 in Harvey E. Brazer, ed., *Michigan's Fiscal and Economic Structure.* Ann Arbor: University of Michigan Press, 1982.

Tax Increment Financing (TIF)   A method of financing public improvements by allowing a municipality, a development/redevelopment authority, or a tax increment finance authority to "capture" the increased property tax revenues in a redevelopment area. State enabling legislation is required before local governments can use tax increment financing. Under such legislation, local governments designate a certain area as a TIF district, which will operate under a redevelopment or TIF authority. The increased tax value of property due to a redevelopment project remains within a TIF district and is used to help pay the cost of that project or other projects within the district.

Such financing often is used to pay for infrastructure improvements such as roads or sewers, but can be used for a variety of activities. Tax increment financing is one of several ways in which urban development or redevelopment projects have been financed, primarily since 1975. *See also* DOWNTOWN DEVELOPMENT AUTHORITY; INDUSTRIAL REVENUE BOND; PUBLIC-PRIVATE PARTNERSHIP; TAX ABATEMENT.

Significance   Tax increment financing began in Minnesota and California during the early 1950s. It became most popular during the mid-1970s, as the Carter and then Reagan administrations began reducing direct federal aid to cities and encouraging private investment as a precondition of federal money. By the mid-1980s, over 30 states had passed enabling legislation for the establishment of TIF districts. However, their implementation varies and several states specifically prohibit their use, viewing them as a dedication of general revenue funds to a specific area, and therefore unconstitutional. In some states, TIFs have come under legal challenge from school districts denied those increases in property tax retained in the TIF district. Along with tax abatements, loans, and Industrial Revenue Bonds, tax increment financing is one of several ways in which cities offer inducements to private firms to remain or relocate.

Suggested Reading

Hartz, Debra, and Jack Huddleston. *Tax Increment Financing*. Chicago: Council of Planning Librarians, 1980.

Klemanski, John S. "Using Tax Increment Financing for Urban Redevelopment Projects." *Economic Development Quarterly*, vol. 4, no. 1 (1990), pp. 23–28.

Tax Limit   A rate ceiling or restriction imposed by constitution or statute on governments and other taxing authorities. Many state constitutions mandate limits on a newly created municipality's ability to impose taxes and contract debt. As cities were given home-rule powers during the twentieth century, state legislatures again incorporated into the general law various restrictions on the rate of taxation that could be imposed by a city. During the late 1970s, several proposals (usually referenda) sought to place a ceiling on property tax rates or assessment increases. These proposals typically limited allowable tax rates to 10 or 15 mills of the full value of property. While there have been tax-limit proposals covering personal income tax or prohibitions on specific taxes, the most common has been the property tax limit. Referenda such as Proposition 13 (Jarvis-Gann) in California, Michigan's Headlee Amendment, and Proposition 2½ in Massachusetts are recent examples of property tax limits imposed through a referendum vote. *See also* PROPOSITION 2¹/2; PROPOSITION 13; TAX BASE; TAXPAYERS' REVOLT.

Significance   The 1978 California referendum called Proposition 13 was the first action of a national movement termed the "tax revolt." California property values and assessments had risen dramatically during the 1970s. Many scholars concluded that the popularity of Proposition 13 stemmed in large part from a perception of high taxes imposed by the federal government. In addition, voters saw that the state had a $5 billion budget surplus in 1978. Massachusetts property taxes were limited to 2¹/2 percent of a community's assessed valuation, and any subsequent increases were to be limited to 2¹/2 percent annually. Not surprisingly, the impact of Proposition 13 was felt most directly by local governments and school districts, which rely on property taxes for the bulk of their revenues. Many cities in the affected states were forced to cut services and lay off employees, close schools, rely on increased state aid, and use more revenue bonds rather than general-obligation bonds. However, in 1980, California Proposition 9 (also known as Jarvis II), which would have reduced the state income tax by half, was rejected by the voters. The size and persistence of the taxpayer revolt was thus brought into question. Still, many cities have had to confront three major problems that led to urban fiscal stress during the 1980s: revolt by taxpayers, reduced federal aid, and economic recession without federal antirecession assistance.

Suggested Reading
Danzinger, James, and Peter Ring. "Fiscal Limitations: A Selective Review of Recent Research." *Public Administration Review*, vol. 42, no. 1 (1982), pp. 47–55.
Ladd, Helen F., and T. Nicholas Tideman. *Tax and Expenditure Limitations.* Washington, DC: Urban Institute Press, 1981.
Sharp, Elaine B., and David Elkins. "The Impact of Fiscal Limitation: A Tale of Seven Cities." *Public Administration Review*, vol. 47, no. 5 (1987), pp. 385–392.

Tax Rate   The percentage of the tax base (for example, income or assessed valuation of property) paid to a taxing authority. When the tax rate is applied to the tax base, the overall effect of the rate can be determined. In the case of income taxes, the amount of tax liability is found by multiplying the tax rate by the tax base. Tax rates also help determine the tax structure. For example, the federal income tax rate increases as the base increases; therefore, in theory the tax structure is considered progressive. A proportional-rate structure would find the tax rate remaining constant in comparison to changes in the tax base. A structure in which the tax rate decreases as the base increases is considered a regressive tax, for example, a flat tax such as the sales tax. *See also* TAX, LOCAL INCOME; TAX, PROGRESSIVE; TAX, REGRESSIVE.

Significance   The tax rates for the federal income tax, various state income taxes, and local taxes are under constant scrutiny by concerned taxpayers and decision makers. The question of who pays for public services remains at the heart of politics and public policy at all levels of government. In the case of the local income tax, a two-tiered system of tax rates often is applied—one rate for residents and a lower rate for nonresidents who work in the city that imposes the tax. Although many nonresidents have criticized being taxed at all, cities have justified this nonresident tax by pointing out that nonresidents use many public services (public safety, streets, utilities) while they are within the city limits. Tax rates are manipulated in response to economic forces such as recessions or inflationary periods, to political pressures such as interest group lobbying, and to such budgetary issues as deficits, low revenue projections, and increases in expenditures.

Tax Roll   The list of all taxable properties within the jurisdiction of a taxing authority. All nonexempt properties in a state are assessed each year by local assessors, who then create their tax rolls. The potential for variations in these local assessments is great, so statewide standards through published manuals are established. In addition, State Equalized Value (SEV) ratios may be imposed on the assessments to ensure uniformity. *See also* ASSESSMENT; MAP, CADASTRAL; TAX, REAL PROPERTY; TAX ABATEMENT; TAX-EXEMPT PROPERTY.

Significance   While property tax assessment is essentially reserved to local determination, most important taxation decisions are left to the state legislatures. Therefore, the ultimate tax roll of a local government will be determined largely by decisions made at the state level. For example, a municipality's ability to offer local incentives, such as tax abatements and tax exemptions, is authorized by the state. In cities with many government buildings, religious institutions, and other tax-exempt properties, percentages of properties off the local tax roll can exceed 50 percent. Although not official, abandonment of residential and commercial properties has taken many properties *de facto* off the tax rolls.

Taxation, Double   A duplicate tax on the same transaction or property. Double taxation occurs, for example, when a government taxes a corporation on its profits, then taxes individual stockholders on those corporate dividends. Double taxation also occurs when two or more levels of government use the same tax base. The federal, state, and local governments in some areas all tax an individual's income. In many states, both state and local governments tax real property. This is technically known as "vertical tax overlap." *See also* TAX, LOCAL INCOME, TAX, REAL PROPERTY; TAX BASE SHARING; URBAN FISCAL CRISIS.

Significance   Double taxation is almost inevitable in a federated form of government because different levels of government share some of the same tax sources. Major problems of local government relate to overreliance on the property tax. In older Northeast cities, the property tax base has declined substantially. This not only has reduced the city's revenues, but often means a city must spend more on select services such as police, fire, or social services. This fiscal crisis of cities presents a special problem: Voters have a direct opportunity to turn down millage increases, but they cannot equally object to the more distant and diffuse federal- or state-level income tax rates.

Suggested Reading
Coe, Charles L. "Double Taxation: Identifying the Hidden Tax Burden in America's Cities." *Urban Affairs Quarterly,* vol. 19, no. 2 (1983), pp. 241–254.

Taxpayer Suit   Legal action taken by any taxpayer against a taxing authority, seeking to prohibit alleged illegal expenditures of public funds. Laws of virtually every state give taxpayers legal standing to sue state or local governments, but no such law is present at the federal level. However, federal and state laws have authorized citizens access to courts in cases involving alleged civil violations by individual government employees. *See also* MUNICIPAL TORT LIABILITY.

Significance   In *Frothingham v. Mellon,* 262 U.S. 447 (1923), and its companion case, *Massachusetts v. Mellon,* the U.S. Supreme Court held that a taxpayer may not bring a suit against the federal government to restrict the expenditure of federal monies. These cases determined that a taxpayer who cannot prove harm different from that incurred by the general public has no legal standing to bring suit. The so-called Frothingham rule remained intact until *Flast v. Cohen,* 392 U.S. 83 (1968). In this case, the Court determined that taxpayer suits could be authorized in cases that involve an alleged violation of a constitutional limit on the federal government's power to tax or spend. This case involved the issue of federal aid to parochial schools and raised the constitutional issue of separation of church and state.

Taxpayers' Revolt   A term coined during the late 1970s when voters in several states passed referenda placing limits on property taxes. Because many of these limitations were the result of referenda and voter initiative efforts, some observers thought that a national movement was under way in a taxpayers' revolt against big government. In the period between 1978 and 1980, over 50 fiscal limitations were placed on various state and local governments and their taxing and spending powers. By 1988, 32 states had laws limiting local taxing and expenditure activities. *See also* PROPOSITION 2½; PROPOSITION 13; TAX LIMIT.

Significance   The taxpayers' revolt began in California in June 1978, when citizens passed Proposition 13 (Jarvis-Gann), an amendment to the California constitution. This established a property tax rate of 1 percent for all real property and rolled back assessments to 1975 assessment levels. Proposition 13 also limited property tax increases to 2 percent a year and required that the state legislature have a two-thirds majority in both houses to pass any other tax in the state. Florida, Michigan, and Massachusetts also passed tax limitation referenda. These limitations produced mixed results during the first ten years of their existence. California's skyrocketing land values and housing costs were creating a crisis situation for homeowners, and some homeowners certainly benefited from limits imposed on property tax increases. The resulting loss of revenue in many states, however, has required serious cutbacks in public services and substantial layoffs in public employment. In addition, some critics have argued that Proposition 13 merely shifted the main property-tax burden from older homeowners and businesses to younger families buying homes after 1978. By 1988, the median price of homes in California had doubled relative to 1978 figures. Later buyers of homes thus paid extremely high property taxes. In addition, California needed to find alternative sources of revenue, which resulted in much higher "impact fees" paid by commercial and residential developers for improving infrastructure. However, the impact fee in most cities is the same regardless of the cost of the home or business, and developers have tended to build relatively more expensive houses. This has shifted construction away from moderately priced homes and toward more upscale housing, shopping malls, and hotels.

Suggested Reading

Buchanan, James M. "The Potential for Taxpayer Revolt in American Democracy." *Policy Studies Review Annual,* vol. 3 (1979), pp. 584–590.

Lampman, Robert J. "Taxation and the Taxpayers' Revolt." *Policy Studies Review Annual,* vol. 3 (1979), pp. 591–599.

Slovak, Jeffrey S. "Property Taxes and Community Political Structures." *Urban Affairs Quarterly,* vol. 16, no. 2 (1980), pp. 189–210.

Swartz, Thomas R. "A New Urban Crisis in the Making." *Challenge* (September–October 1987), pp. 34–41.

Think Tank   An unaffiliated, nonprofit, and tax-exempt research organization that conducts public-policy analysis. Think tanks conduct studies commissioned by outsiders and through internally selected topics. The range of research topics is dictated by the tank's mission statement. It may be confined to basic or applied topics. Tanks may focus on public or private alternatives. They may deal with international, national, or state and local concerns. A tank often is well known for its methodological approach, such as econometrics, demographic analysis, or historical studies. Many tanks focus on one public-policy arena such as education, transportation, or housing. A few tanks are generalists and change topics as demand requires. The well-established and well-funded major tanks publish one or more in-house journals. All publish occasional papers and series. These reports are generated by on-staff writers and stringers commissioned by project. The quality of documentation is quite high, because the marketplace is competitive, and the tanks are mindful of academic and governmental review. Think tanks' budgets are funded by contracts from outside sponsors. Foundations, industry, and government agencies also sponsor think tanks. *See also* COST-BENEFIT ANALYSIS.

Significance   Think tanks are a product of the twentieth-century United States. Some are politically centrist, publishing information that is neither consistently pro–national level nor always in favor of austere solutions. Other tanks regularly are biased in favor of nongovernmental solutions to public-policy issues. There are more right-of-center think tanks than other categories, because it is easier for them to find private funding. Products of think tanks include issuing innovative advice, publishing information to a wide readership that otherwise is unobtainable, educating attentive publics through seminars and newsletters, distributing new ideas with great dispatch, and collecting information that government is not reporting in usable form, if at all. Think tanks also regularly publish cost-benefit studies. Common criticisms of tanks include their development of hidden agendas, the uneven quality of their research, their proclivity to be too theoretical for local government decision makers, the often inaccessible nature of their reports, and, most important, the always possible ideological bias. Research topics of think tanks are as diverse as the issues facing government. These stretch from abandoned building reuse through identification of the homeless, to the costs of privatization and the relative merits of organizing public safety, as opposed to separate police and fire departments. Examples of think tanks abound. The American Enterprise Institute (AEI) for Pubic Policy Research of Lanham, Maryland, has sponsored research on referenda, transportation systems, and the diffusion of innovations. The Brookings Institution of Washington, D.C., is one of the oldest think tanks, founded in 1916. It focuses on economic issues and publishes books on such topics as self-insurance and indexing for inflation. The Heritage Foundation of Washington, D.C., champions conservative causes and advocates decentralization of power in the federal system, vouchers for education, and privatization of local services. It was particularly important as a source of ideas and personnel during the Reagan administration. The Urban Institute of Washington, D.C., was founded in 1966 with liberal researchers. It conducts research on domestic priorities, poverty, and homelessness, among other topics. These four think tanks constitute the major Washington, D.C.–based research groups. On the far right of the ideological continuum is the Cato Institute, founded in 1977, which conducts libertarian-based research. This is also a Washington, D.C., organization, with a smaller budget than the big four. The Citizens Research Council of Detroit focuses on only one state. It studies everything from annexation to state mandates to the effect of tax equalization and comparative local taxing capacity. The Committee for Economic Development (CED) of New York City is composed of 200 leading business people and educators. Two of its committees concentrate on government management practices and on education and urban development. It has published studies on the identification of the urban poor and the costs of metropolitan consolidation. The Heartland Institute of Chicago sponsors in-depth studies of special concern to the Midwest. It commissioned a work on the application of tax abatements by localities that are trying to attract and keep industries. The Joint Center for Political Studies of Washington, D.C., conducts research on black-oriented urban issues such as at-large versus ward elections. Its members also study affirmative-action programs and monitor the location and number of elected black officials. The Santa Monica, California–based RAND Corporation, usually associated with defense and international political topics, does sophisticated comparative urban research, using aggregate population statistics on the effect of fiscal stress and population shifts. Resources for the Future, Inc. (RFF), of Washington, D.C., focuses on topics of direct urban concern such as recreation land, water pollution, and waste resource recovery. The most recent think tank in Washington, D.C., is the Progressive Policy Institute, funded by the Democratic party to conduct long-term as well as more conventional analysis. Think tanks such as these examples are not to be confused with university-based urban research centers, which are affiliated with academic institutions. A list of these other centers was published periodically in early issues of the *Urban Affairs Quarterly*.

Suggested Reading
Foundation for Public Affairs. *Public Interest Profiles 1988–1989*. Washington, DC: Congressional Quarterly, 1988.

Three-Tier Reform   An incremental, structural, metropolitan innovation that creates an umbrella regional agency performing line and staff functions, thus constituting a third level of government in addition to the city and county. There are only two examples of three-tier reform in the United States. The Minneapolis–St. Paul Twin Cities Metropolitan Council was established directly by the state legislature in 1967. The electors voted in the Greater Portland, Oregon, Metropolitan Service District (MSD) through a referendum as a merger of two other units in 1978 under state enabling legislation. The Twin Cities Metropolitan Council, not accountable directly to the people, serves a seven-county area. The Twin Cities Metropolitan Council has responsibility for coordinating airports and sports facilities as well as transit, sewer, and regional recreation parks. The Portland MSD is responsible for the area zoo, waste disposal, and the region's convention center. The Portland MSD serves the urbanized portions of a tricounty area and is popularly accountable by direct election. Both are nonpartisan governments. *See also* BALKANIZATION; CONSOLIDATION; COUNCIL OF GOVERNMENTS; METROPOLITAN COUNTY; TWIN CITIES.

Significance   Unlike the voluntary Council of Governments (COG), which is confined to planning functions, the two three-tier reform examples additionally serve as line agencies. Both are deemed successful but limited-scope regional governments. They were difficult to bring about and represent a less complete consolidation of function than Indianapolis and Marion County's Unigov.

Suggested Reading
Harrigan, John J., and William C. Johnson. *Governing the Twin Cities Region: The Metropolitan Council in Comparative Perspective*. Minneapolis: University of Minnesota Press, 1978.

Horan, James F., and G. Thomas Taylor, Jr. *Experiments in Metropolitan Government.* New York: Praeger, 1977. Chap. 8, "Minneapolis–St. Paul: The Twin Cities Region Approach," pp. 173–195.
Walker, David B. "Snow White and the 17 Dwarfs: From Metro Cooperation to Governance." *National Civic Review*, vol. 76, no. 1 (1987), pp. 14–28.

Tiebout Thesis   An economic model proposed by Charles M. Tiebout which posits that local governments in a balkanized metropolis can efficiently allocate public services under certain assumptions. Tiebout's thesis is that cities present residents with different bundles of taxes that pay for various levels and types of services. This assumes citizens are aware of these municipal variations and residents are mobile. Distance from work is not factored in. People with different preferences arrange themselves spatially according to market conditions provided for in the urban area. The thesis was first developed in a 1956 article, and two variations developed in 1961. The general approach has been labeled the *public choice literature* because it looks at prospective residents as making informed economic choices among various policy packages forged by the city councils within a metropolitan area. *See also* BALKANIZATION; CONTRACTING OUT; COPRODUCTION; LAKEWOOD PLAN.

Significance   The Tiebout Thesis is part of the economic allocation approach to studying fragmented metropolitan areas. Rather than decrying balkanization, the thesis suggests it is a mechanism for efficiently matching needs and ability to pay with expenditures, of matching demands with supply. There is now an extensive secondary literature reacting to the Tiebout model, which empirically tests several of the underlying assumptions. They are not met under field conditions. The model suggests services are only consumed by residents of the jurisdiction, overlooking externalities available from, say, a museum for the entire area. Many citizens are not mobile because of noneconomic ties to an area. Because cities do not employ consistent accounting practices and do not report comparatively on their service packages, residents shopping comparatively for a new address do not have the inputs needed to make an informed decision. Additionally, formal balance sheets do not reflect levels of coproduction of services that are contributed by city residents. Insofar as some residents are mobile and have information, the balkanized system is skewed in favor of wealthy residents at the expense of the poor. The thesis brought proper attention to residential location decisions. But it overlooked that firms have different interests in services from consumers. One empirical test found that city expenditures on select services did not correlate with the growth of either poor or affluent families. These studies confirm that the wealthy cluster in cities with a strong tax base and thus have the option, if they wish, to secure services at inordinately high levels.

Suggested Reading

Ostrom, Vincent, Charles M. Tiebout, and Robert Warren. "The Organization of Government in Metropolitan Areas." *The American Political Science Review,* vol. 60, no. 4 (1961), pp. 831–842.

Schneider, Mark, and John R. Logan. "The Effects of Local Government Finance on Community Growth Rates: A Test of the Tiebout Model." *Urban Affairs Quarterly,* vol. 18, no. 1 (1982), pp. 91–105.

Stein, Robert M. "Tiebout's Sorting Hypothesis." *Urban Affairs Quarterly,* vol. 23, no. 1 (1987), pp. 140–160.

Tiebout, Charles M. "Economic Theory of Fiscal Decentralization." In National Bureau of Economic Research, *Public Finances: Needs, Sources, Utilization.* Princeton: Princeton University Press, 1961, pp. 79–96.

———. "A Pure Theory of Local Expenditures." *Journal of Political Economy,* vol. 64 (1956), pp. 416–424.

Tipping Point   The theoretical threshold at which the number or percentage of minority families moving into a neighborhood or school district acts as a catalyst for white flight or discourages whites from moving into the neighborhood. Thus, the tipping point actually is determined by the racial tolerance level of white residents. Once it has reached its tipping point, a racially integrated area begins a process of resegregation, resulting in a neighborhood or housing project entirely populated by minority residents. *See also* BLOCKBUSTING; DISINVESTMENT, URBAN; FAIR HOUSING ACT; RACIAL STEERING; REDLINING; STABILIZATION; WHITE FLIGHT.

Significance   Integration in housing has been a controversial issue for many years in the United States. The notion of a tipping point in the racial mix of a neighborhood has been used primarily by critics of residential desegregation. Opponents argue that integrating neighborhoods will cause massive white flight, leaving the neighborhood segregated again. Tactics by some real estate agents, such as blockbusting and racial steering, have sought to pervert the intention of residential desegregation mandated by such policies as the Fair Housing Title of 1968. Urban economists also have used the term *tipping point* to refer to a threshold of housing abandonment whereby private investment is precluded and a reversal of a neighborhood's deterioration likely will take place only through publicly supported reinvestment. If such abandonment has been reached in a neighborhood, banks and mortgage companies often have "redlined" these areas, so no loans are made for home purchases or rehabilitation, causing the deterioration process to continue or accelerate.

Town   (1) In common usage, a small urban community that is larger than a village but smaller than a city. Some states officially designate towns as a category of municipalities, along with villages and cities. (2) In all six New England states, a basic unit of government that exercises municipal functions and some functions usually carried out by counties in other parts of the nation. Typically, a town serves an urban place and adjacent rural areas. New England towns vary in terms of their professionalization—towns with large populations employ some professional staff, while others rely mainly upon the elected officers. Elected officials are called town officers and *selectmen. See also* BOUNDED CITIES, TYPES OF; CENSUS OF GOVERNMENTS; COUNTERURBANISM; TOWN MEETING; VILLAGE.

Significance   Towns in the twentieth-century United States gave way to cities as the primary residence for most Americans. Town living is defended by Jeffersonian agrarians. Some population losses of towns were stemmed in the 1970s in a decentralization movement away from the major cities and back into small communities. This trend is called counterurbanization. In New England, towns were not laid out geometrically by surveyors but rather focused on a central community and its commuting range, which generally was the adjacent amount of land early settlers could cultivate. The small scale of New England towns reflects the limited transportation technology that defined the immediate commuting area. Many large-scale New England towns have incorporated as cities to bound themselves to their true urban jurisdiction.

Town Meeting   In New England, an open gathering of residents exercising direct democracy over local public business. Town meetings now are used as a general form of local government in Maine, Vermont, New Hampshire, Massachusetts, and Connecticut. They also are used by schools and special districts in these five as well as Rhode Island. In some jurisdictions, this device is used only for adoption of town budgets. *See also* INITIATIVE; REFERENDUM.

Significance   This form of direct political participation is a Yankee tradition that began in Massachusetts in the 1620s. Regular annual meetings have averaged only about 10 percent turnout of the eligible residents in recent years. When major unresolved issues are on the warrant (agenda), turnout is higher. As of 1989, no city with a population of more than 50,000 uses the town meeting to conduct general business. Cities that once did so have gone to an indirect democratic system. Boston, for example, abandoned the town meeting form in the 1820s, when its population exceeded 40,000.

Suggested Reading
Mansbridge, Jane J. *Beyond Adversary Democracy*. Chicago: University of
    Chicago Press, 1980, 1983.

Township   In public surveying, a 6-square-mile unit of land composed of 36 one-mile-square sections. Actual township size varies because of topography. This designation, called a Congressional
Township, was established in 1785 and applies in 19 states established
early in the history of the Republic. In some states, a township serves
as a political subdivision of a county and provides limited general
functions. Political townships can be unorganized, incorporated, or
designated general townships. Charter townships in Michigan provide
a full range of services. The 1982 Census of Governments recognized
them in 21 states, mainly in the north and north-central regions. The
term *township* is sometimes used synonymously with *town*. *See also* CEN-
SUS OF GOVERNMENTS; TWO-TIER LOCAL GOVERNMENT.

Significance   Most townships are rural, but some in metropolitan
areas are highly developed and urban. When cities are incorporated,
the townships may be dissolved if the new city covers the entire township area. In Michigan, villages remain part of the township, thus
creating a two-tier local government. Popularly elected officials include a supervisor, clerk, treasurer, two or more trustees (legislators),
and, in some states, a justice of the peace and constable. Municipal
services provided by townships may include elections administration,
property tax assessing and collection, planning and zoning, cemetery
maintenance, animal control, parks and recreation, water and sewer
service, and primary schools.

Traffic Analysis   The study of moving people and goods, transportation safety, results of traffic sign studies, trip frequency, destinations, purposes, and cost per vehicle mile. In urban areas most traffic
analysis focuses on the automobile and is done in three major data
categories: traffic accidents, traffic law enforcement, and traffic engineering. Occasionally, analysis is done on vehicle movement past a
stationary point to determine the need for road maintenance, while
dynamic studies are used to compare traffic counts over time to forecast trends, one benefit being to aid businesses in site location. Traffic
analysis may examine road use, perhaps to justify infrastructure upgrading or recommend additional parking facilities or one-way
streets. Other studies may look at intermodel breakpoints, such as the
Boston, Chicago, and Cleveland mass-transit links to their metro air-

ports or the Washington, D.C., park-and-ride facilities. *See also* EMER-
GENCY EVACUATION; GRIDLOCK; INFRASTRUCTURE; INTERSTATE HIGHWAY
SYSTEM; MACHINE SPACE; MASTER PLAN; POPULATION, DAYTIME AND NIGHT-
TIME.

Significance   One definition of a metropolitan area is its daily urban
system of commuters (DUS), with its systematic weekday rush-hour
rhythms from 7 to 10 A.M. and 4 to 7 P.M. A hallmark of modern urban
America is congested traffic, high-density expressways, the absence of
a widely used mass-transit system, and, in extreme cases, near gridlock
during peak traffic hours. Much systematic traffic analysis is now
conducted by university safety centers, government councils, and locally sponsored *ad hoc* groups as part of areawide planning. Properly
collected traffic information saves taxpayers and local agencies millions of dollars in reduced traffic accidents, lowered insurance rates,
and reduced vehicle maintenance. Traffic analysis differentiates between limited-access expressways, which presently link about 80 percent of urban America, and surface arteries. Interstate highways are
the key element in this movement, accounting for as much as one-
fourth of all miles traveled. The privately owned and operated automobile is the chief user of the system, accounting for about 70 percent
of all work trips. Large data bases are set up by region and for the
country at large, and master plans contain a section on traffic circulation based on traffic analysis for both present and projected conditions. Police departments often use these analyses to locate evacuation
routes for civil defense emergencies and roads needing special patrols
during peak hours; fire departments use them to identify congested
areas to be blocked off in case of multialarm fires; and schools use
them to place crossing guards.

Suggested Reading
Institute of Transportation Engineers. *Transportation and Traffic Engineering
    Handbook,* 2nd ed. Englewood Cliffs, NJ: Prentice-Hall, 1982.
Pignataro, Louis J. *Traffic Engineering: Theory and Practice.* Englewood Cliffs,
    NJ: Prentice-Hall, 1973.

Transferable Development Right (TDR)   A form of incentive zoning in which the capability to build on property becomes severable
from the underlying land; that capability then can be sold to another
owner. Transferable development rights allow the state or its subdivisions to give owners of restricted land the power to earn the financial
increment that would have attached to the land if it had been developed. It allows the state to maintain open space and protect recreation
or agricultural land. The right to build to a greater than conventional

density elsewhere need not be confined to a contiguous parcel. It can be transferred anywhere the city wishes to designate a contingency density zone. The assumption behind TDRs is that owners deserve the right to land-value increases, while the community has the power to protect the public welfare by shifting the location of construction. *See also* OPEN SPACE; VARIANCE; ZONING, EUCLIDEAN.

Significance   TDRs were an experiment by localities that felt constrained by conventional Euclidean zoning, which confines land-use benefits to the site and not the community at large. They opened up the possibility of greater density levels elsewhere in the community. Their use in New York City was invalidated in 1976 and in New Jersey in 1984. Legal commentators noted that TDRs shifted zoning from a statutory and administrative process to unpredictable negotiations with owners, developers, and city administrators.

Suggested Reading
Marcus, Norman. "A Comparative Look at TDR, Subdivision Exactions, and Zoning as Environmental Preservation Panaceas: The Search for Dr. Jekyll without Mr. Hyde." *Urban Law Annual*, vol. 20 (1980), pp. 3–73.

Transition   (1) The transfer period from one administration to another. It refers to the time from the loser's concession speech to the winner's swearing-in. The period varies from state to state and differs for mayors, supervisors, village presidents, and county executives. The outgoing chief executive takes responsibility for a smooth transfer of power. In large cities, as at the national and state level, this may be done by appointing a transition coordinator and creating a line item in the budget of election years for the possible transfer. The process includes briefings by the outgoing staff for the new chief executive and major appointees. (2) Transition also refers to the changing of the political guard between a heretofore subordinate race or ethnic group and a politically older tradition, as when migrating blacks took over major elective positions from whites-in-flight in Atlanta, Gary, Detroit, Newark, and Washington, D.C., during the 1960s and 1970s. *See also* AD HOC BODY.

Significance   (1) Mayoral and county executive transitions are most likely to be rough when there is a failure by the incoming leader to recognize that the outgoing executive is still in office until the swearing-in, and a failure by the outgoing leader to recognize the need of the new team for information on present policy. Rough transitions also take place when the challenger has campaigned against "city hall," is of the opposite party, and has a defiant attitude toward the former executive's political philosophy. A smooth transition is most likely when the incumbent is retiring; the new officeholder is of the same party, is a protégé, and has a similar ideological outlook; no fiscal crisis exists; and both sides designate transition teams. These weeks or months are prime time for the mayor-designate to select an administrative team, establish priorities, and study options through *ad hoc* commissions. Joint press announcements by the two administrations reassure the public of a smooth flow of power, if not policy continuity. An *interregnum* is the period between rule, when there is no chief executive, such as, for example, the time between the death of a mayor and the swearing-in of a successor. (2) Transition, used as a changing of the guard from English Protestants to Irish Roman Catholics, or whites to blacks, raises the issue of possible turmoil between the old and new order. In a case study of Boston, Atlanta, and Detroit, one author found the transformation of power to be quite smooth. The old order gave way with dignity. It maintained substantial power in the new political climate by acting in a conciliatory and accommodating manner. After all, the new politicians still need access to the old-order private-sector financial elite.

Suggested Reading
Eisinger, Peter K. *The Politics of Displacement: Racial and Ethnic Transition in Three American Cities.* New York: Academic Press, 1980. (Use of definition 2.)

Treasurer   An elected or appointed tax collector at the state or substate level. In most states and in some jurisdictions, the treasurer's office disburses and takes charge of public monies. In larger jurisdictions treasurers collect taxes but deliver funds to be deposited to a *finance department*. Finance officers usually are appointed and have a background as certified public accountants (CPAs) or in public or business administration. When treasurers are also general financial officers, they deal with bonds, pooled funds, certificates of deposit, and commercial paper. Treasurers now work mainly with on-line computer lists of property identified by ownership and assessment. They are often up to three months behind in recording title changes. They prepare periodic statements of balances and disbursements. Many are responsible for investing idle funds awaiting transfer to other units of government, such as schools, for later use as payroll or for capital expenditures. *See also* AUDIT; FISCAL YEAR; MILLAGE.

Significance   Treasurers are a chief source of income for a municipality or state through wise investment of retirement funds and unencumbered balances. They are limited in the types of investment instruments they can select. A few are allowed by statute to invest overseas, but others cannot even invest in securities from the quasi-public Government National Mortgage Association (Ginnie Mae) because they are not direct government obligations. Treasurers cannot spread the millage among taxpayers until the assessor establishes parcel values. On property taxes uncollected over three years or more, the sheriff conducts a tax sale. After a specified date, tax payments are in arrears, with penalties and interest payments charged. With an increasing amount of government self-insurance, many treasurers are taking on increased responsibilities. The two major types of patronage available to treasurers are determining (1) which depository institutions get public funds and (2) which insurance firms carry liability. Usually the treasurer is given council guidance but retains latitude in selecting actual banks and carriers. Treasury records are usually in the public domain, and treasury officials must periodically promulgate a complete list of delinquent taxes in an official newspaper. Most states have a municipal treasurers association that sponsors seminars on changes in legal guidelines. An international Municipal Treasurers Association of the United States and Canada, located in Rancho Palos Verdes, California, offers certification to those members who qualify. Statistically, most treasurers are women, whereas most finance officers are men. Because treasurers and financial officers handle billions of dollars, there is always the temptation for corruption, which is usually uncovered by audits, both pre- and post-, conducted by outside certified public accounting firms or state teams.

Triage Politics   In urban government, sorting out priorities among the many disasters in the central city. It is deciding (1) which businesses and buildings, even with treatment from public funding, will probably still have to be abandoned; (2) which projects will die unless given immediate crisis intervention; (3) which priorities are merely serious, and even if not given infusions of local aid, will be able to limp along for one more fiscal year; and (4) which problems are minor and can be attended to after the preceding two categories, when and if money becomes available. The term and concept first were applied to urban politics in the 1970s. *Triage* is from the French, meaning "to sort out." It is a metaphor borrowed from emergency medicine in the battlefield and hospital, in which a nurse quickly sorts out patients according to the severity of injury from a host of patients who must be attended to simultaneously, permitting some to die without treatment in order to save many others. *See also* ABANDONMENT; BIOLOGICAL FALLACY; CENTRAL CITY; URBAN CRISIS.

Significance Triage is an apt metaphor for those who contend that U.S. central cities do have not just problems but crises. There is no time to plan, only to react to emergencies. It is appropriate for those who talk of sick and dead cities, as opposed to cities that simply are losing population or have a reduced density. The major value of the metaphor is that it focuses attention on the tough choices decision makers face regarding which sectors of the economy to assist, which to leave alone, and which to ameliorate for later full attention. In short, it deals with priorities for limited government resources.

Suggested Reading

Cassidy, R. *Livable Cities: A Grass-Roots Guide to Rebuilding Urban America.* New York: Holt, Rinehart, 1980.

Judd, Dennis R. *The Politics of American Cities: Private Power and Public Policy,* 3rd ed. Glenview, IL: Scott, Foresman, 1988. Pp. 349–350.

Kleniewski, N. "Triage and Urban Planning: A Case Study of Philadelphia." *International Journal of Urban and Regional Research,* vol. 10, no. 4 (1986), pp. 563–579.

Marcuse, Peter, Peter Medoff, and Andrea Pereira. "Triage as Urban Policy." *Social Policy,* vol. 12, no. 3 (1982), pp. 33–37.

Strickland, Donald E., and Dennis R. Judd. "National Urban Policy and Shifting Priorities of Inner-City Revitalization." *Urban Analysis,* vol. 7 (1983), pp. 165–167.

Twin Cities A single metropolitan area composed of two incorporated anchor cities, combined with the suburbs of each. The city with the larger population commonly is designated in capital letters. The most celebrated example is MINNEAPOLIS and St. Paul, Minnesota, separated by the upper Mississippi River. Other examples include FARGO, North Dakota, and Moorhead, Minnesota, on the Red River; Kansas City, Kansas, and KANSAS CITY, Missouri, as well as ST. LOUIS, Missouri, and East St. Louis, Illinois, on the Mississippi; and OMAHA, Nebraska, and Council Bluffs, Iowa, also on the Mississippi. Three major examples of international-border twin cities are DETROIT, Michigan, and Windsor, Ontario, Canada, on the Detroit River; EL PASO, Texas, and Ciudad Juarez, Chihuahua, Mexico, on the Rio Grande River; and NIAGARA FALLS, New York, and Niagara Falls, Ontario, on the Niagara River. The *quad cities* of DAVENPORT, Iowa, along with Moline, East Moline, and ROCK ISLAND, Illinois, are all on the Mississippi River.

Significance Twin cities raise questions of areawide cooperation, planning, forecasting, and perception of problems. Each of these pairs of cities is useful in analyzing how side-by-side jurisdictions approach the same or similar issues. Border towns, although to an extent economically integrated, generally do not have close political working relationships.

Suggested Reading
Freisma, H. Paul. *Metropolitan Political Structure: Intergovernmental Relations and Political Integration in the Quad Cities.* Iowa City: University of Iowa Press, 1971, 1987.

Two-Level Urban Reorganization   Structural urban reform that delegates pan-area functions to a large-scale government while retaining local functions within small-scale governments. The term was coined by John C. Bollens and Henry J. Schmandt in the 1970s, and the model has been widely copied. Two-level reorganization can take three forms: (1) Multifunctional districts or authorities, covering a whole metropolitan area and addressing areawide concerns at the appropriate scale. There are no major examples in operation; most metro authorities have single functions, such as a park authority. Even these modest overall units do not always have the power to tax. (2) The comprehensive urban county with a strong upper level. The first urban county was created in 1957 in Metropolitan Dade County, encompassing Miami, Florida. The form has not been adopted by any other U.S. metropolitan area. (3) The federation plan, based on a newly established, areawide government with overall functions that supplement the retained lower-level villages, cities, and hamlets. No U.S. city has adopted this plan. The 1953 Metropolitan Toronto experiment is the major North American example. *See also* METROPOLITAN COUNTY; PORT OF NEW YORK AND NEW JERSEY AUTHORITY; TWO-TIER LOCAL GOVERNMENT.

Significance   Two-level reorganization is a reaction to the inefficiencies and balkanization of urban America. As part of the reformer's zeal for structural change, it has met with a very low level of success. St. Louis, Pittsburgh, and Boston worked on various plans for two-level government, but the plans failed in votes of the people or in committee. Major structural reform of U.S. cities in the twentieth century is a minor motif; the dominant trend is balkanization and voluntary cooperation through mutual-aid pacts and the Council of Governments movement.

Suggested Reading
Bollens, John C., and Henry J. Schmandt. *The Metropolis: Its People, Politics, and Economic Life*, 4th ed. New York: Harper & Row, 1982. Chap. 11.

Horan, James F., and G. Thomas Taylor. *Experiments in Metropolitan Government.* New York: Praeger, 1977. (Using the model from the first edition of Bollens and Schmandt, 1975.)

League of Women Voters Education Fund. *Supercity/Hometown, U.S.A.: Prospects for Two-Tier Government.* New York: Praeger, 1974. (Note: Here two-tier means two-level. Two-tier can also refer to unintended overlapping governments.)

Safen, Edward. *The Miami Metropolitan Experiment,* rev. ed. Garden City, NY: Anchor Books, 1966.

Two-Tier Local Government   Dually elected general governments that partially overlap, each serving some of the same people. Rather than an intended structural reorganization designed to create economies of scale or service delivery closer to the people, two-tier local government is largely an unintended consequence of state legislative laws. In Michigan, for example, when a city incorporates, it entirely supplants the former township government within its municipal boundaries, whereas when a village incorporates, it does not replace the township; the village becomes a second-tier local government. Townships are governed by boards of trustees, one member of whom serves as elected supervisor. Within the township is the village governed by a village council, one member of whom serves as president, a position similar to a mayor in a city. The township retains residual functions of (1) assessing property, (2) tax collecting for all jurisdictions that use the property tax, (3) voter registration, and (4) the conduct of all elections, except off-year contests that are solely within one school system or village. The balance of services, including public safety, road maintenance, and supply of any utilities, is the responsibility of the incorporated village. In an extreme case, a township might be broken into two cities and the residue of the township broken into three villages, with parcels in the pure township left unattached to any city or village. Such a six-square-mile area accommodates six clerks and six treasurers, not counting the county clerk and county treasurer. Southfield Township in Oakland County, Michigan, has such an arrangement. *See also* BALKANIZATION; COUNCIL OF GOVERNMENTS; TOWNSHIP; TWO-LEVEL URBAN REORGANIZATION.

Significance   Two-tier local government produces such urban anomalies as rump townships with a 1980 census of fewer than 60 people, clustered in noncontiguous units. It is extreme balkanization, illustrating the need for annexation, reincorporation, or consolidation. The two tiers are cost-inefficient, producing a confused electorate and low-visibility government.

U

Ultra Vires   Acting beyond the scope, literally "beyond the powers," authorized by a corporate charter. As applied to incorporated cities and counties, to act *ultra vires* means the jurisdiction's legislature or one of its agents exceeded those powers explicitly granted. A city council or county commission that authorizes its administration to enter a contract beyond its scope under home rule or general statutory provision cannot have its action enforced in a court. *See also* DILLON'S RULE; HOME RULE.

Significance   *Ultra vires* actions are illegal. In a state without home-rule provisions and operating under a strict interpretation of Dillon's Rule, municipalities and counties must have explicit state legislative authority to enter a field, or they will be successfully challenged as acting beyond their narrowly confined power. Many successful challenges to local innovations have been launched in the absence of a broad allocation of power to substate units.

Underclass   The most highly disadvantaged segment of the U.S. urban population. Though the term often refers to minorities, the underclass typically includes those who live in neighborhoods with very high concentrations of long-term unemployment, long-term poverty, or dependency on welfare; it also includes those who have little or no job training or skills. Rather than being based on income levels that define a segment of society, the underclass also is defined by behavioral characteristics. Thus, the underclass includes individuals such as drug dealers and prostitutes, who may have relatively higher incomes, but whose behavior deviates from social norms. Permanently barred from access to society's mainstream, the underclass accounts for a disproportionate share of social pathology—crime, drug addiction, teen pregnancy, and other social ills. *See also* HOMELESS; KERNER COMMISSION; POVERTY PROGRAMS.

Significance   The term *underclass* is a fairly recent addition to the social science vernacular. Indeed, the 1968 Kerner Commission first spoke of a dual society—one white and affluent; the other black and impoverished. However, 20 years later social research has found upward social, political, and economic mobility for some blacks—witness the growing black middle class and the increasing electoral success of black candidates for mayor, city council, and many state-level races. Despite this mobility for some black Americans, a segment of the U.S. population still has few job opportunities and faces permanent dependency on public assistance. Public-policy recommendations differ as how best to deal with the underclass, much as they have for many years over the best approaches to solving poverty and unemployment. Yet, this identification of an underclass suggests a dual society within the black community as well as the Kerner Commission's original dual society of white and black. The term itself has been the center of controversy, since it was coined originally by conservatives investigating social and urban questions. Such an issue would likely have come out of the liberal tradition, and many liberals have fought to keep questions of the underclass pointed toward the problems of society as a whole, rather than blaming individuals. Despite this dispute between conservatives and liberals over the term and its impact, *underclass* and its assumptions have moved research closer to the Marxist notion of an urban "lumpenproletariat," referring to those unemployed and unaware of their class origins. Studies during the late 1980s have indicated that larger, industrialized but declining cities have seen the greatest growth of underclass neighborhoods, due in large part to the inability of the economy to provide jobs, and the behavioral response by individuals who perceive limited or no opportunities. During the 1980s and 1990s, those cities with the greatest numerical increases in underclass populations have been New York City, Chicago, Detroit, and Philadelphia.

Suggested Reading

Auletta, Ken. *The Underclass.* New York: Vintage Books, 1982.
Feiock, Richard C. "The Political Economy of Urban Service Distribution: A Test of the Underclass Hypothesis." *Journal of Urban Affairs,* vol. 8, no. 3 (1986), pp. 31–42.
Glasgow, David G. *The Black Underclass: Poverty, Unemployment, and Entrapment of Ghetto Youth.* San Francisco: Jossey-Bass, 1980.
Lemann, Nicholas. "The Origins of the Underclass." *Atlantic,* vol. 257, no. 6 (1986), pp. 31–68; vol. 258, no. 1 (1986), pp. 54–68.

Nathan, Richard. "Will the Underclass Always Be with Us?" *Society*, vol. 24, no. 3 (1987), pp. 57–62.

Ricketts, E. R., and I. V. Sawhill. "Defining and Measuring the Underclass." *Journal of Policy Analysis and Management*, vol. 7, no. 2 (1988), pp. 218–325.

Wilson, William Julius. *The Truly Disadvantaged: The Inner City, the Underclass, and Public Policy*. Chicago: University of Chicago Press, 1987.

————, ed. "Symposium: The Ghetto Underclass: Social Science Perspectives." *Annals of the American Academy of Political and Social Sciences*, vol. 501 (1989).

Undercount   Failure of the U.S. Bureau of the Census to enumerate accurately all the residents of a civil jurisdiction in the decennial April 1 enumeration of population. The bureau admits to an undercount; the issues are the magnitude of error and the policy implications from resulting misallocation of funds, which are based in part on aggregate population. Causes of the undercount, which vary each decade, include (1) missing illegal aliens, who do not wish to cooperate with any government program for fear of being deported; (2) disproportionately missing members of the lower class, who are reluctant to cooperate with any government program; (3) overlooking the homeless (which is predominantly an urban phenomenon); (4) bypassing migrants, who are very mobile; and (5) missing proportionately more blacks than whites partly because of a difference in socioeconomic status. In more than a score of briefs filed by cities against the Bureau of the Census for the 1980 head count, central cities argued that their jurisdictions had disproportionate numbers in these five categories. *See also* COMMUNITY DEVELOPMENT BLOCK GRANT; POPULATION, DAYTIME AND NIGHTTIME; URBAN MASS TRANSPORTATION ADMINISTRATION.

Significance   The basic public-policy issues stemming from the acknowledged undercount are whether there should be an adjustment, how any such adjustment should be administered, and what the impact would be on transfer payments to localities under various grant programs. In fact, the Census Bureau did not adjust the 1980 figures. There was no adjustment in any grant formula based on the undercount, and all challenges in federal district courts were dismissed. The 1980 error range was estimated to be less than 3 percent. Cities argued that estimated per-capita underfunding spread over the ten years in which the numbers would be used would amount to between $50 and $2,000 per capita per decade, probably nearer the lower end. But, assuming all regions of the nation were adjusted upward at about the same rate, there would be very little reallocation, as the formulas were based on fixed allocations. Every decennial census is likely to raise the issue of undercount and the problem of whether or not to compensate for it. The 1990 Census of Population included a special post–April 1 recount in order better to calibrate the magnitude of undercount.

Suggested Reading
Maurice, Arthur J., and Richard P. Nathan. "The Census Undercount: Effects on Federal Aid to Cities." *Urban Affairs Quarterly,* vol. 17, no. 3 (1982), pp. 251–284.

Underemployment   Any situation in which labor is not used to its fullest potential. Underemployment can take different forms. One, individuals may work in jobs that require less skill than is available from their training and education. Two, individuals may be working fewer hours than they wish or are able. Three, employees may be underutilized because their skill level is lower than needed for a particular job. The Manpower Development and Training Act of 1962 (42 U.S.C. 2571 et seq.) was the first federal statute that accepted into various job-training programs underemployed individuals wishing to upgrade their skill levels. *See also* POVERTY LEVEL; SOCIAL INDICATORS.

Significance   Data on underemployment should be added to the calculus of unemployment and the "discouraged worker" in any effort to understand the state of the economy. Some social scientists have argued that a more accurate measure of the economy to provide "full employment" would include those underemployed as well as the standard unemployment figure. In addition, some economists argue a *two-tiered labor market* exists in the United States, called a "dual labor market," in which a more highly skilled and educated work force enjoys relatively higher wages, better working conditions and benefits, more job security, and better promotional opportunities. The secondary labor market features those less-skilled workers who encounter less job security, greater underemployment, lower wages and worse working conditions, more horizontal movement, seasonal employment, and few or no benefits. Facing a shift in the economy away from manufacturing and toward service employment, many workers take jobs they do not prefer or that do not provide enough hours.

Suggested Reading
Bernick, Michael. *Urban Illusions: New Approaches to Inner City Unemployment.* Westport, CT: Greenwood Press, 1987.

Martin, James E., with Thomas D. Heetderks. *Two-Tier Wage Structures: Their Impact on Unions, Employees and Employers.* Kalamazoo, MI: W. E. Upjohn Institute for Employment Research, 1990.

Unicameral   One-chambered, as applied to a legislature. A two-chambered legislature is *bicameral*; a three-chambered legislature is *tricameral.* South Africa has the world's only tricameral legislature. Forty-nine U.S. states presently use a bicameral legislature. In the 1770s, Georgia, Pennsylvania, and Vermont experimented with unicameralism, but now only Nebraska uses one chamber. Nebraska's unicameral structure initially was proposed by Republican George Norris to the state's constitutional convention in the 1930s. He argued that there was no need to parallel the U.S. Congress, that one chamber would eliminate conference committees, would be more efficient, and would save the salaries of the second chamber. The model bicameral legislature is the United Kingdom Parliament, which is composed of an upper chamber representing peerage, the House of Lords, and a lower chamber representing nontitled citizens, the House of Commons. The U.S. Congress is bicameral because the Connecticut Compromise established an upper chamber, the Senate, to represent all states equally with two senators, and a lower chamber, the House, to represent states by population. Representatives are elected to the House by district or at large. The least populated states must elect congressmen at large, because they are allocated only one seat each. All U.S. county commissions, township boards, school boards, and city councils are unicameral.

Significance   Unicameralism is the norm for local legislatures. However, some cities experimented earlier with bicameralism: In the 1880s, Detroit had a Board of Aldermen and a Board of Councilmen with overlapping responsibility. When the two were melded together, it was appropriately called the Common Council. There is no need for state and local legislatures to copy national bicameralism, because the *federal analogy* is false. The federal analogy states that the U.S. Senate is to a state senate as the U.S. House of Representatives is to a state house. Although states are represented in the upper national chamber, counties are not represented at the state level. All legislative bodies other than the U.S. Senate are under a 1970 Supreme Court decree to base representation on the principle of "one person, one vote as nearly as practical," *Headley v. Junior College District of Kansas City*, 397 U.S. 50. The only basis of representation for all local legislative bodies is population by residence, also known as nighttime population. Local chambers might as well be unitary if all bodies must be based on the same representation. Unicameralism provides no check by a second chamber, but other checks are supplied by mayoral veto, recall, administrative inertia, and judicial review.

Unigov   The consolidated government of Indianapolis and Marion County, Indiana. Unigov was created in 1969 by a vote of the state legislature and did not require voter approval. Consolidation of city and county government responsibilities usually comes in metropolitan areas where local service delivery has experienced serious problems or local politics has had a history of corruption. In the case of Unigov, local leaders were able to convince a newly elected Republican majority in the state legislature to approve the measure. *See also* CONSOLIDATION; COUNCIL OF GOVERNMENTS.

Significance   During the 1960s, three of the largest city-county consolidations occurred: Nashville/Davidson County, Tennessee, in 1962; Jacksonville/Duval County, Florida, in 1967; and the Unigov consolidation of Indianapolis/Marion County, Indiana, in 1969. Unigov is represented by a governing council of 29 members. Unlike other consolidations, Unigov did not eliminate the old administrative units of city and county governments, including the school districts, public authorities, and special districts. Rather, it brought the former city and county administrative agencies under greater control of the mayor. Part of the success in the Unigov consolidation was due to the lack of significant political opposition. Under the Unigov plan, 16 small suburbs were consolidated with the city of Indianapolis. Four of the larger suburbs remained independent.

Suggested Reading
Florestano, Patricia, and Vincent L. Marando. *The States and the Metropolis.* New York: Marcel Dekker, 1981.
Hill, R. Steven, and William P. Maxam. "Unigov: The First Year." *National Civic Review,* vol. 60, no. 6 (1971), pp. 310–314.
Willbern, York. "Unigov: Local Government Reorganization in Indianapolis." Advisory Commission on Intergovernmental Relations, *Report A-41: Substate Regionalism and the Federal System, Volume II, Regional Governance: Promise and Performance—Case Studies.* Washington, DC: Government Printing Office, 1973.

U.S. Conference of Mayors   Established in 1932, this organization of city mayors meets annually to discuss the problems of larger cities in the United States. The U.S. Conference of Mayors also employs a lobbying staff that is permanently housed in Washington, D.C. This group is considered one of the "Big Seven" Public Interest Groups (PIGs) and tends to represent the interests of cities with populations over 50,000. As part of the "urban lobby," the U.S. Conference of Mayors works with other groups to testify before Congress, mobilize public opinion, and assist cities in obtaining federal grants. *See also* LOBBYING BY CITIES; NATIONAL LEAGUE OF CITIES; NATIONAL MUNICIPAL LEAGUE; PUBLIC INTEREST GROUPS.

Significance   The U.S. Conference of Mayors was created during the years of the Great Depression, when large-city mayors attempted to seek direct aid from the federal government. For many years, state legislatures often overlooked the problems of their larger cities. The founding members of the conference sought to circumvent these reluctant state legislatures by dealing directly with the more progressive administration of Franklin D. Roosevelt. Direct federal-city fiscal relations embodied in categorical grants were first institutionalized during the Depression and during the fiscal crises experienced by many U.S. cities at that time. The conference still tends to focus on the political, economic, and social problems of larger cities, whereas the National League of Cities tends to represent the smaller, suburban, and often more conservative cities in the United States.

Urban   A city and surrounding communities with a large number of inhabitants involved in nonagricultural occupations. Urban derives from the Latin *urbs/urbis,* meaning city or town. The antonym of *urban* is *rural.* The two terms often are thought of as points along a continuum. Some commentators add high density and social heterogeneity as components of the definition of urban. Economic geographers who label mining and agriculture as the primary occupation group define urban as those areas associated with higher-order jobs such as manufacturing, also called secondary occupations. This is the industrial urban area. Urban areas focusing on general services are said to concentrate on tertiary occupations. Quaternary services of communications, research, and the professions are associated with the postindustrial city. New York City has the highest density in the United States, with more than 26,000 people per square mile. The U.S. Bureau of the Census defines *urban place* as a geographic area with 2,500 or more people. Researchers who test for urbanism using total population as the sole criterion tend to oversimplify the definition. As used in the Slum Clearance, Urban Renewal, and Farm Housing Statute, 42 U.S.C. 1490 (1986), as amended, *rural* refers to any habitat with population less than 20,000 that is not "associated with an urban area" or "not contained within a metropolitan statistical area." *See also* EKISTICS;

METROPOLITAN STATISTICAL AREA; POSTINDUSTRIAL CITY; CONSOLIDATED
METROPOLITAN STATISTICAL AREA; SUBURB; WIRTH THESIS.

Significance   Urban refers to a physical condition of one or more
cities that may be under- or overbounded. Urban also describes a set
of social conditions where certain occupations and amenities predominate. The two major causes of U.S. urban growth have been market
forces and, to a lesser extent, government decisions allocating capital
improvements. Approximately 70 percent of the U.S. population lives
in 7,000-plus urban places. Urban and surrounding suburban communities constitute a *metropolitan area*. Metropolitan is from the Greek,
meaning "mother or anchor city." The 1980 U.S. Census of Population listed 37 Metropolitan Area cities or urban areas in Level A (from
the New York City Consolidated Metropolitan Statistical Area of almost 18 million residents to the Salt Lake City–Ogden, Utah, Area).
Level B Metropolitan Areas with a population less than a million but
at least 250,000 ranged from Oklahoma City (number 38) through
Columbus, Georgia (number 131). Level C Metropolitan Areas ranged
down to 100,000 and included Sarasota, Florida, through Kokomo,
Indiana (number 256). Level D Metropolitan Areas with populations
less than 100,000 ranged from Sherman-Denison, Texas, through
Grand Forks, North Dakota (number 280), and Enid, Oklahoma
(number 281), with a population of 63,000.

Suggested Reading
Kaufman, Clifford. "Political Urbanism: Urban Spatial Organization." *Urban
    Affairs Quarterly,* vol. 9, no. 4 (1974), pp. 421–436.
Sherbenow, Edgar L., and Victor E. Flango. "An Empirical Test of Size as a
    Measure of Urbanism." *Urban Affairs Quarterly,* vol. 12, no. 1 (1976),
    pp. 3–17.

Urban Coalition   Formalized alliances created in the late 1960s
which tackle severe community problems as a network between heretofore noncooperating segments of citizens. Urban coalitions are of
two related types. The first is a diverse partnership between major
business and professional groups, organized labor, community advocacy groups, civic-oriented religious organizations, youth and women's
associations, along with racial and ethnic associations, and select representatives from government. In many communities, blacks and Hispanics are prominent because they represent the two major urban
minorities in most central cities. The second type is a more restricted
public-private partnership among business, labor, the professions (especially law, banking, and accounting), and local government. This

type is more economically homogeneous and concentrates on economic issues. Examples of issues that the more diverse bridge-building coalitions have focused on include housing rehabilitation, urban homesteading, racial discrimination in hiring, substance abuse, homelessness, minority contract assistance, ministations, and the use of English as a second language. The more homogeneous business-oriented urban coalitions have worked on such issues as central business district (CBD) revitalization, convention hall expansion, and venture capital funding for high-tech entrepreneurs. *See also* AGENDA SETTING; COMMITTEE FOR ECONOMIC DEVELOPMENT; INCUBATOR; KERNER COMMISSION; PUBLIC-PRIVATE PARTNERSHIP; RIOT.

Significance   The immediate catalyst for most of the broad-based local urban coalitions stemmed from the urban riots of 1967. The prototype was New Detroit. Although the National Urban Coalition based in Washington, D.C., has roots in the 1890s, it represents a merger of liaison organizations stemming from the 1960s and an affiliation of about 40 separate city groups. The urban coalition serves as a forum for leaders who would not otherwise ever sit around a common table. Local coalitions are funded by foundations and corporate monies channeled through United Foundation contributions. Public-private partnerships are more often funded out of corporate giving. The greatest success of both types of coalitions has been diffusing racial tension and infusing a sense of urgency in formulating issues for the public agenda that would not otherwise be on the table at all. The National Urban Coalition's primary focus for the 1990s is on upgrading inner-city education, promoting better health, and nurturing the diminishing central-city housing stock. Both types of coalitions advocate regional solutions. Examples of the more diverse coalition type include the Houston Association for the Advancement of Mexican-Americans and the Urban Coalition of the District of Columbia. An example of the public-private partnership coalition is the Metropolitan Affairs Corporation of Detroit and Southeast Michigan.

Suggested Reading

Fosler, R. Scott, and Renee A. Berger. *Public-Private Partnership in American Cities*. Boston: D. C. Heath, 1982. (Seven city case studies sponsored by the Committee for Economic Development [CED], none of which overlaps with affiliates of the National Urban Coalition network.)

Graves, Helen M. *New Detroit Committee/New Detroit, Incorporated, A Case Study of an Urban Coalition, 1967–1972*. Ph.D. dissertation, Wayne State University. 1975.

Harris, Red R., and John V. Lindsay, cochairmen. *The State of the Cities: Report of the Commission on the Cities in the '70s*. Published in cooperation with the National Urban Coalition. New York: Praeger, 1972.

Urban Crisis   A series of interrelated cataclysmic events or turning points that if not adequately addressed cause death or severe displacement for urban dwellers. Some urban issues are so severe that there is neither time nor resources to save lives, buildings, or jobs. Some feel it is best to allow the people to die, the buildings to be abandoned, or the jobs to be transferred to a suburban location, the sunbelt, or overseas. For Marxist analysts the urban crisis is a special manifestation of a more general crisis in capitalism between the classes. Among elements of the urban crisis that have been identified since the urban violence of the 1960s are the following: (1) The AIDS pandemic, measuring casualties in comparison to combat deaths in national wars such as Vietnam. (2) Abandoned property in the form of hospitals, churches, plants, and homes, in short the high level of disinvestment accompanying the shrinking of the inner city. (3) Crime and juvenile delinquency measured by the FBI Uniform Crime statistics and unfavorably compared to strife-torn religious conflicts in Ireland. (4) Deaths and various crimes stemming from drug-related activity, including the crack-heroin crisis, LSD, and so-called designer drugs. (5) Environmental decay of air, water, and toxic waste is a major example of the urban crisis especially linked to cancer rates and respiratory disease. (6) Fiscal stress, defaults, bailouts, and payless paydays are a major type of crisis. (7) The homeless are a major manifestation of the urban crisis, albeit the number of affected people is unknown. (8) The failure to build and maintain the urban infrastructure is a major urban crisis. Catastrophes waiting to happen include possible bridge collapses, burst dams, water line breaks, sewer backups, or uncontrolled fires that spread because of a lack of equipment. (9) For many commentators the major urban crisis consists of the creation of the poverty class, sometimes labeled the underclass. These are the poor in the central cities who do not possess skills needed to survive in the postindustrial society. (10) This failure to develop employment skills is related to the crisis in urban public schools, or blackboard jungles, where basic discipline is out of control and academic standards have slipped to unacceptable levels for literacy and quantitative skills. (11) For most commentators the effect of many of these elements ignited into the 1960s riots, including assassinations of major political leaders. (12) For many other commentators the urban crisis is the racial cauldron in which the rising expectations of blacks for equality met continuing white intransigence. (13) Finally, unemployment, underemployment, the cycle of poverty, generations on welfare rolls, the elimination of the safety net, and the inability of female-headed households to secure work create a permanent crisis of despair, alienation, and disrespect for the law. "Urban crisis" was most discussed in the 1960s and 1970s. A major question in the 1990s is whether the urban crisis is over. For conservative commentators such as Edward Banfield, the answer was to redefine terms and suggest there never was an urban crisis but only a series of major problems that is simply best acknowledged. *See also* BANFIELD THESIS; BIOLOGICAL FALLACY; DIVESTMENT; QUALITY OF LIFE; RIOT; TRIAGE POLITICS; UNDERCLASS; URBAN DEVELOPMENT ACTION GRANT; WHITE FLIGHT; YONKERS-STYLE POLITICS.

Significance   *Urban crisis* is one of the most subjective terms in the political lexicon. Conservatives such as Banfield state that there is no major urban crisis. Other urbanologists, such as George Sternlieb, say there is an urban crisis. It is a matter of values, of ideology, and whether one is looking at Kenilworth, Illinois, where there are no fiscal or demographic crises, or whether one is looking at the South Bronx in New York or Belleville, Illinois, where there are major unresolved and long-lasting dislocations. The social upheavals and riots of the 1960s initiated the term *urban crisis*. Whether contemporary concerns ranging from AIDS to persistent white racism constitute a crisis is a judgment call.

Suggested Reading
Banfield, Edward C. *The Unheavenly City: The Nature and Future of Our Urban Crisis*. Boston: Little, Brown, 1968, 1970.
———. "A Critical View of the Urban Crisis." *Annals of the American Academy of Political and Social Science*, vol. 405 (1973), pp. 7–14.
Castells, Manuel. *City, Class and Power*. Elizabeth Lebas, trans. New York: St. Martin's Press, 1978. Chap. 1.
David, Stephen M., and Paul E. Peterson, eds. *Urban Politics and Public Policy: The City in Crisis*. New York: Praeger, 1973.
Eisenger, Peter K. "The Urban Crisis as a Failure of Community: Some Data." *Urban Affairs Quarterly*, vol. 9, no. 4 (1974), pp. 438–461.
Gottdiener, Mark, ed. *Cities in Stress: A New Look at the Urban Crisis*. Vol. 30, Sage Urban Affairs Annual Reviews. Beverly Hills: Sage Publications, 1986.
———, ed. "Symposium: Whatever Happened to the Urban Crisis?" *Urban Affairs Quarterly*, vol. 20, no. 4 (1985), pp. 421–467.
Healy, Patrick, et al. "The Financial Crisis of Our Cities." Chap. 11 in Louis K. Lowenstein, ed., *Urban Studies: An Introductory Reader*. New York: Free Press, 1971.
Jones, Walter J., and James A. Johnson. "AIDS: The Urban Policymaking Challenge." *Journal of Urban Affairs*, vol: 11, no. 1 (1989), pp. 85–102.
Meyer, Jon K., comp. *Bibliography on the Urban Crisis: The Behavioral, Psychological, and Sociological Aspects of the Urban Crisis*. Chevy Chase, MD: National Institute of Mental Health, 1969.
Sternlieb, George, and James W. Hughes. "New Dimensions of the Urban Crisis." In Hearings before the Subcommittee on Fiscal and Intergovernmental Policy of the Joint Economic Committee. *Is the Urban Crisis Over?* Washington, DC: Government Printing Office, March 2, 1979, pp. 65–84.

Urban Development Action Grant (UDAG)   A federal categorical transfer payment created in 1977, designed to support private development efforts in economically distressed cities and urban counties. UDAGs were part of the federal government's general approach to economic development policymaking, which sought to offer incentives for private investment in urban centers rather than provide direct public-sector expenditures. Authorization for the program was terminated in 1988, after spending $4.5 billion, generating $27 billion in private investment, and creating an estimated 550,000 jobs. With an economic-distress formula built into the granting process, the states receiving the most UDAG money were New York, Pennsylvania, and Michigan. *See also* GRANT-IN-AID; PUBLIC-PRIVATE PARTNERSHIP.

Significance   The Urban Development Action Grant program was the brainchild of Robert Embry, Assistant Secretary of HUD under President Jimmy Carter. In some respects UDAGs constituted a second generation of urban renewal programs, begun after the 1974 demise of urban renewal. Unlike other urban-aid programs, UDAGs were designed to bring declining cities back into economic health by encouraging private investment. Cities were required to prove they had a willing private developer ready to invest $2.50 for each UDAG dollar contributed by the federal government. These so-called "project grants" for the first time allowed nongovernmental bodies to be recipients of federal grants. Criticism of UDAGs eventually came from several sides. Some critics objected to giving federal money to already-wealthy developers and businesses. Others wondered how much federal money should be made available to clinch a commitment from a private developer. Supporters of UDAGs argued these grants leveraged about $5–$6 in private investment for every dollar funded by the UDAG program. In addition, supporters point out that HUD estimated increases in federal taxes and reductions in transfer payments created through UDAG projects totaled $991 million per year, more than double the annual budget of the program itself. In the end, a Congress controlled by the Democratic party eliminated the program with the support of a Reagan administration that wanted market forces to prevail.

Suggested Reading
Honadle, Beth Walter. "Federal Aid and Economic Development in Non-metropolitan Communities: The UDAG Program." *Publius*, vol. 17, no. 4 (1987), pp. 53–64.
Myers, Phyllis. "UDAG and the Urban Environment." *Journal of the American Planning Association*, vol. 48, no. 1 (1982), pp. 99–109.
Rich, Michael J. "Hitting the Target: The Distributional Impacts of the Urban Development Action Grant Program." *Urban Affairs Quarterly*, vol. 17, no. 3 (1982), pp. 285–301.

Stephenson, Max O., Jr. "The Policy and Premises of Urban Development Action Program Implementation: A Comparative Analysis of the Carter and Reagan Presidencies." *Journal of Urban Affairs,* vol. 9, no. 1 (1987), pp. 19–38.
Young, Alma H. "Urban Development Action Grants: The New Orleans Experience." *Public Administration Quarterly,* vol. 8, no. 1 (1984), pp. 112–129.

Urban Homesteading   A self-help, "sweat equity" home ownership program authorized in 1974 to revitalize declining or abandoned urban housing stock, and reduce the inventory of federally owned properties. Properties include those owned by the Department of Housing and Urban Development (HUD), the Department of Veterans Affairs (VA), and the Farmers Home Administration (FmHA). Urban homesteading began as a federal demonstration program involving 23 cities. Under this program, abandoned or vacant properties owned by the federal government would be transferred to state, county, or local governments that create homesteading programs approved by HUD. The local governments then transfer the properties for a small sum to eligible "homesteaders." Homesteaders must bring the home up to local code standards within three years and occupy the property as their principal residence for at least five years. At the end of five years, the homesteader receives full legal title. *See also* ABANDONMENT; COMMUNITY DEVELOPMENT BLOCK GRANT; *IN REM* PROPERTY; URBAN RENEWAL.

Significance   The first local-level homesteading program began in 1973 in Wilmington, Delaware, followed by programs in Philadelphia and Baltimore. Federal action followed within two years as Congress saw the success of these early local efforts. The Housing and Urban Development Department stipulated two conditions for federal funding. One, the areas chosen by a city must be in a declining neighborhood that is not severely blighted and has the potential of regaining its vitality. Two, homesteading was to be one of several components of a more comprehensive program for upgrading and stabilizing neighborhoods. Still a relatively small program, urban homesteading involves about 1 percent of all federal housing stock. By 1988, 157 localities had been approved, with modest funding levels less than $20 million annually during the late 1980s. Major sources of funding for the urban homesteading program include rehabilitation loans available under Section 312, Community Development Block Grant (CDBG) money supporting administrative costs, Section 810 funding to cover property transfers, and private lending institutions.

Suggested Reading
Aryanpour, Azar. *Urban Homesteading: 1975–1986.* Monticello, IL: Vance Bibliographies, February 1987.

Chandler, Mittie Olion. *Urban Homesteading: Programs and Policies.* Westport, CT: Greenwood Press, 1988.
Clark, Anne, and Zelma Rivin. *Homesteading in Urban USA.* New York: Praeger, 1977.
U.S. Department of Housing and Urban Development. *Programs of HUD 1987–88.* Washington, DC: Government Printing Office, August 1988.

Urban Impact Analysis (UIA)   A prediction of the locational and financial effect of all major federal programs on cities. More correctly called urban and community impact analysis, it was based on an order issued by President Jimmy Carter that mandated federal executive agencies to appraise in advance the effect of major new national programs on cities. Based on Executive Order 12074 and Office of Management and Budget Circular A-116 of 1978, UIA became operative in 1980. The obvious analogy to environmental impact statements was intentional but misleading: UIAs were not to be conducted on individual projects but rather on new national programs such as solar energy utilization. The UIAs had no legal standing and were only intended for internal agency use. They were not reviewable by outside groups. The goal of UIAs was to perform spatial analysis of new general government initiatives in terms of their effect on the central-city regions and nonmetropolitan areas. The mandate carried no required methodological format; hence a variety of models and nonquantitative approaches could be used to satisfy the small-area and regional forecasts. Examples of possible topics included income tax policy and regional redistribution effects, defense expenditures, and the spatial ramification of uneven contract allocation, as well as national environmental cleanup policy. *See also* A-95 REVIEW; ENVIRONMENTAL IMPACT STATEMENT; FORECAST; NATIONAL URBAN POLICY.

Significance   Urban impact analysis grew out of President Carter's attempt to formulate a national urban policy. It went into force at the end of his administration and was quashed by Executive Order 12350 of the Reagan administration in the early 1980s. The goal was to initiate national administrative study of major public-policy changes on a spatial basis, using multidisciplinary tools, especially those of geography, economics, and political science. Proponents felt some of the hardships suffered by snowbelt cities may have been brought on by the unintended results of such national programs as the Interstate Highways Program or by Department of Defense military procurement policy. In the few published articles on UIAs, concerns were expressed about methodology, data collection, and explanations for private-sector decisions. The few model studies published on UIAs indicated it was difficult to differentiate between effects that were long- or short-term. In the 1980s, without benefit of the formal machinery of government, academic researchers continued to study the indirect and unintentional effects of national public policy on cities and regions. Like Zero Based Budgeting (ZBB) and Program Planning Budgeting Systems (PPBSs), UIA never realized its innovators' aspirations. There has been no major *postmortem* of the project.

Suggested Reading

Glickman, Norman J., ed. *The Urban Impacts of Federal Policies.* Baltimore, MD: Johns Hopkins University Press, 1980.

Grasso, Patrick G. "Estimating the Urban Impacts of Federal Policies." *Urban Affairs Quarterly,* vol. 16, no. 3 (1981), pp. 377–383.

Urban Land Institute (ULI)   A nonprofit research, educational, and advocacy organization for physical developers. The Urban Land Institute, founded in 1936 and based in Washington, D.C., should not be confused with the Urban Institute, a think tank founded in 1968 and also based in Washington. Both publish reports on urban problems, but the ULI has a narrower developmental focus on the built environment. ULI research covers topics such as industrial parks, real estate, redevelopment, market profiles of individual cities, parking requirements, shopping center development, growth management, and finance and taxation trends. Their major periodical is entitled *Urban Land.* Two other important ULI publications are the monthly *Urban Land Digest,* which relays everything from demographic to historical designation information, and the 20-times-a-year *Project Reference File,* which profiles a major urban development in each issue. Recent examples include Gateway Plaza in Yonkers, New York, and the Barony on Peachtree in Atlanta. *See also* JOINT CENTER FOR HOUSING STUDIES; NATIONAL ASSOCIATION OF HOUSING & REDEVELOPMENT OFFICIALS; PUBLIC INTEREST GROUPS; REAL ESTATE AGENT; THINK TANK.

Significance   The ULI does not qualify as a think tank, because it was incorporated to take a stand favoring a particular position, namely physical development. Nor is the ULI a Public Interest Group (PIG), because it does not purport to represent the public at large in urban controversies. However, it is a highly influential advocacy group with a membership of about 12,000 developers, planners, and academics. The academics represent such diverse specialties as architecture, economics, geography, planning, and political science. ULI publications are used in conventional professional education and for continuing education seminars. ULI research on such topics as parking requirements of developments is adapted into site plan standards by planning departments.

Urban Mass Transportation Administration (UMTA)   A federal agency created by the Urban Mass Transportation Act of 1964 (49 U.S.C. 1601 et seq.), as amended, to coordinate metropolitan public transit in the United States. The administration is charged with (1) assisting in the development of mass-transit facilities, (2) encouraging the planning and implementation of urban mass-transportation systems, where deemed cost effective, (3) providing financial assistance to state and local governments for mass-transit systems, and (4) nurturing private involvement in local mass-transportation systems. One of eight agencies in the Department of Transportation, UMTA has ten regional offices: in Cambridge, Massachusetts; New York City; Philadelphia; Atlanta; Chicago; Fort Worth, Texas; Kansas City, Missouri; Denver; San Francisco; and Seattle. *See also* BAY AREA RAPID TRANSIT; MASS TRANSIT; PARATRANSIT.

Significance   UMTA reviews funding requests for urban mass-transit systems, such as rapid or light-rail transit, or personal rapid transit, such as the "People Mover" systems in Detroit and Morgantown, West Virginia. In fiscal year (FY) 1987, UMTA's budget authority totaled about $1.1 billion. Through 1989, UMTA still carried a specific budgetary line item for the Washington, D.C., metro subway system, which totaled about $150 million for fiscal year 1987. With Ronald Reagan's presidency, a shift away from UMTA funding began. The overall 1980s budgets for UMTA remained relatively high; this reflected the multiyear commitments made during the Jimmy Carter years. Outlays by the mid-1980s averaged slightly over $500 million, compared to FY 1979 outlays of $2.4 billion.

Suggested Reading

National Transportation Policy Study Commission. *National Transportation Policies through the Year 2000: Final Report.* Washington, DC: Government Printing Office, 1979.
Stopher, Peter R., and Arnim H. Meyburg. *Urban Transportation Modeling and Planning.* Lexington, MA: Lexington Books, 1975.

Urban Observatory   A joint nationally and locally funded network of ten major and ten medium-sized U.S. cities that joined with local universities and research institutes to study city problems between the late 1960s and late 1970s. The urban observatory idea was first suggested by Robert C. Wood in a 1962 speech. It was championed by Milwaukee Mayor Henry W. Maier and initially funded by the Department of Housing and Urban Development (HUD) in 1968–1969. The ten large cities were selected first; they included Albuquerque, New Mexico; Atlanta, Georgia; Baltimore, Maryland; Boston, Massachusetts; Cleveland, Ohio; Denver, Colorado; the two Kansas Cities in

Missouri and Kansas; Milwaukee, Wisconsin; Nashville and Davidson County, Tennessee; and San Diego, California. The most active was Milwaukee's program. The large cities selected nine comparable study topics that were to employ the same methodology. They covered such topics as local freeway impacts and the role of vocational education on the local economy. Later HUD funded ten observatories in smaller cities with populations between 30,000 and 125,000. The ten medium-sized cities included Allentown, Pennsylvania; Anchorage, Alaska; Boise City, Idaho; Bridgeport, Connecticut; Charlottesville, Virginia; Durham, North Carolina; Garland, Texas; Hoboken, New Jersey; Lake Charles, Louisiana; and South Bend, Indiana. The most active of these was Allentown's program. Study projects included such topics as animal control, public transportation, citizen involvement with decentralization, and citizen evaluation of community services—items of direct concern to area practitioners. The National League of Cities and U.S. Conference of Mayors coordinated the program. Research projects were selected by the sponsoring university or research staffs in conjunction with the mayor's office and local citizen advisory panels. The network folded for want of continued funding at various times in the 1970s. *See also* CITIZEN ADVISORY BOARD; COMMUNITY FACT BOOKS; COMPARATIVE URBAN ANALYSIS; DETROIT AREA STUDY; OAKLAND PROJECT; PERMANENT COMMUNITY SAMPLE.

Significance   The urban observatory project is widely regarded as a major federal-city and town-gown failure. Milwaukee, twice evaluated as one of the best of the ten units, spent more than $1 million in its six-year existence without producing one well-circulated report. Criticized in two audits for a poor distribution system, the program includes only one urban observatory study that was listed through the Government Printing Office catalog from 1976 through 1988. Individual city studies are available through the National Technical Information Service (NTIS) of the U.S. Department of Commerce. Winnipeg, Manitoba, set up its own system modeled after the early U.S. projects. Research suffered from a lack of clear guidelines, noncomparable methods, and uncertainty about whether to concentrate on short-term projects such as community fact books or long-term projects that had little usefulness to city hall. There has been no major *postmortem* on the project. This form of comparative urban analysis has been discontinued. The next phase in comparative urban studies focused on central coordination through Terry Clark's Permanent Community Sample of a cross-section of cities and through the in-depth field analysis of Aaron Wildavsky's single-city Oakland Community Project and the Detroit Area Study (DAS).

Suggested Reading

Greenleigh Associates, Inc. *Evaluation of the Urban Observatory Program.* Hazel
    S. McCalley, ed. Washington, DC: Department of Housing and Urban
    Development, 1974. Available from National Technical Information
    Service (NTIS) PB80-109556. (Large-city study.)
Irwin, William P. "Symposium on Urban Observatories." *Urban Affairs Quar-
    terly,* vol. 8, no. 1 (1972), pp. 3–34. (An upbeat interim report.)
National League of Cities. *Smaller-City Urban Observatory Program, Final Report.*
    Todd W. Aronson et al. Washington, DC: Department of Housing and
    Urban Development, 1978. Available from National Technical Informa-
    tion Service (NTIS) PB80-109598.
———. *Urban Observatory Research Report.* Washington, DC: Department of
    Housing and Urban Development, 1976. Available from National Tech-
    nical Information Service (NTIS) PB80-109200. (Large-city study.)
———. *Urban Observatory Research Report.* Washington, DC: Department of
    Housing and Urban Development (HUD), 1978. Available from Na-
    tional Technical Information Service (NTIS) PB80-136310. (Small-city
    study.)
Palay, Miriam G., et al. *Summary Report for the U.S. Department of Housing and
    Urban Development on the Milwaukee Urban Observatory: 1969–1974.* Mil-
    waukee: University of Wisconsin-Milwaukee Library, 1974. Mimeo.
    (Obituary notice and disjointed pathology report.)
Wood, Robert C. "Contributions of Political Science to Urban Form." In
    Werner Z. Hirsch, ed., *Urban Life and Form.* New York: Holt, Rinehart,
    1963. (The original idea.)

Urban Political Economy   An analytical framework that attempts
to understand urban problems by investigating the relationship between political and economic institutions of a society. Many or perhaps most contemporary urbanists can be considered urban political
economists, since all recognize the importance of the political (federal
and state relations) and economic (macro- and microeconomic factors)
forces that influence urban life. The differences lie in the various
proposed solutions to those identified problems. Urban political economy therefore can include public-choice theorists on the ideological
right, Marxist or neo-Marxist analysts on the left, and most points in
between the two philosophical camps. *See also* DYE THESIS; MARXIST
URBAN ANALYSIS; PRIVATE SECTOR; PUBLIC SECTOR; URBAN POLITICAL
REGIME.

Significance   The urban political-economy approach recognizes the
relevance of both economics and politics to a local setting. The view
that economics and politics are both important is not a new concept,
nor exclusive to one philosophical perspective. However, a political-
economy approach appears to have reached consensus in urban analysis as it has in no other area of social science inquiry, with the possible
exception of regulatory policymaking. The urban political-economy

perspective has influenced a number of twentieth-century American writers. Many community power studies have focused directly on the relationship between private resources and public policymaking, most notably the studies using the reputational analysis made famous by the Middletown and Regional City studies. The more recent emphasis on urban economic-development issues also has brought the relationship between politics and economics to the forefront. Paul Peterson's seminal 1981 work, *City Limits,* argues that the economic context of cities imposes serious constraints on government officials. His assumption of a unitary model describing all local governments in pursuit of business investment has been challenged by urbanists who subscribe to the perspective that politics always mediates in the process of urban development. This process generates conflict and the need for conflict resolution. Accordingly, economic constraints do not determine the political choices of urban decision makers, but rather are determined by an interaction of a city's political-economic environment and the political orientation of its governing coalition.

Suggested Reading

Elkin, Stephen L. "Twentieth Century Urban Regimes." *Journal of Urban Affairs,* vol. 7, no. 1 (1985), pp. 11–28.

Gottdiener, Mark, and Joe R. Feagin. "The Paradigm Shift in Urban Sociology." *Urban Affairs Quarterly,* vol. 24, no. 2 (1988), pp. 163–187.

Kantor, Paul, with Stephen David. *The Dependent City: The Changing Political Economy of Urban America.* Glenview, IL: Scott, Foresman, 1988.

Lake, Robert W., ed. *Readings in Urban Analysis: Perspectives on Urban Form and Structure.* New Brunswick, NJ: Center for Urban Policy Research, 1983.

Logan, John R., and Harvey L. Molotch. *Urban Fortunes: The Political Economy of Place.* Berkeley: University of California Press, 1987.

Mollenkopf, John H. *The Contested City.* Princeton: Princeton University Press, 1983.

Ostrom, Elinor. *The Delivery of Urban Services.* Beverly Hills: Sage Publications, 1976.

Peterson, Paul E. *City Limits.* Chicago: University of Chicago Press, 1981.

Sackrey, Charles. *The Political Economy of Urban Poverty.* W. W. Norton, 1973.

Schultze, William A. *Urban Politics: A Political Economy Approach.* Englewood Cliffs, NJ: Prentice-Hall, 1985.

Stone, Clarence N. "City Politics and Economic Development: Political Economy Perspectives." *Journal of Politics,* vol. 46, no. 1 (1984), pp. 286–299.

Stone, Clarence N., and Heywood T. Sanders, eds. *The Politics of Urban Development.* Lawrence: University Press of Kansas, 1987.

Tabb, William K. *The Political Economy of the Black Ghetto.* New York: W. W. Norton, 1970.

Tiebout, Charles M. "A Pure Theory of Local Expenditures." *Journal of Political Economy,* vol. 64 (1956), pp. 416–424.

Urban Political Machine   A political party organization of the sort that dominated local politics in many U.S. cities beginning in the early

1800s. Urban political machines were highly structured, yet also highly personalized. The organization was hierarchical, but precinct captains were quite familiar with voters in their precinct. Because machines were party organizations, they sought to elect candidates to official positions in local government. From these positions, favors could be distributed to loyal supporters and voters. Jobs, favorable treatment for local public services, and city contracts with local businesses were all part of the benefits available to supporters. Even though much of the traditional power of urban political machines faded with the social and political reforms of the Progressive Era, some scholars have argued that new machines or vestiges of the old machines still exist. Tammany's William Tweed in New York City, Richard Daley in Chicago, and Thomas Pendergast in Kansas City are among the most notable leaders of urban machines, whose careers ranged from the early 1800s to the mid-1970s. *See also* PATRONAGE, URBAN; REFORM GOVERNMENT; TAMMANY HALL.

Significance   Urban political machines were in part the outgrowth of local politics during the great waves of immigration to the cities. Many reasons have been given to explain the development of machines during this time. Politics became an outlet of power, status, and money for those ethnics who were unable to break into the business world. Machines could mobilize ethnic voters through a combination of political and social support unavailable through other means. It also has been argued that machines provided some stability to cities experiencing social and labor unrest during the tumultuous period of the Industrial Revolution. Because urban machines offered benefits to supporters and voters, numerous examples of corruption surfaced during the late 1800s, and the machines became the primary targets of the social and political reforms of the Progressive Era. However, several twentieth-century scholars have taken a different approach to machines than most of the reformers of the Progressive Movement. Robert Merton has argued that machines performed positive functions in large U.S. cities, and Theodore Lowi has argued that bureaucratic politics has become merely a "new" style of machine politics. Still others have suggested that political machines grew out of the formal powers available to executives in strong-mayor governments, not in weak-mayor systems as has traditionally been believed. As classic examples of exchange between organizations and supporters, urban political machines will remain a primary interest of urbanists, whether they are considered old or new machines, or whether they arise out of strong- or weak-mayor systems.

Suggested Reading
Allswang, John M. *Bosses, Machines and Urban Voters*. Baltimore: Johns Hopkins University Press, 1986.

DiGaetano, Alan. "The Rise and Development of Urban Political Machines: An Alternative to Merton's Functional Analysis." *Urban Affairs Quarterly,* vol. 24, no. 2 (1988), pp. 242–267.

Erie, Steven P. *Rainbow's End: Irish Americans and the Dilemmas of Urban Machine Politics, 1840–1985.* Berkeley: University of California Press, 1988.

Guterbock, Thomas M. *Machine Politics in Transition: Party and Community in Chicago.* Chicago: University of Chicago Press, 1980.

Merton, Robert K. *Social Theory and Social Structure,* rev. ed. Glencoe, IL: Free Press, 1957, pp. 72–84, 192–194.

Rakove, Milton. *Don't Make No Waves, Don't Back No Losers.* Bloomington: Indiana University Press, 1975.

Wolfinger, Raymond E. *The Politics of Progress.* Englewood Cliffs, NJ: Prentice-Hall, 1974. Chap. 4.

Urban Political Regime   A distinctive pattern of urban governance that is shaped by the interaction between the political orientation of a city's governing coalition (liberal, conservative, etc.) and its political-economic environment. In a liberal democracy, different urban political regime types arise, reflecting how the conflict between economics (the private market) and politics (elections and interest-group competition) is resolved. Regime analysis contrasts with Paul Peterson's belief that all cities have a "unitary interest" in economic development. Based on factors of an individual city's economic-growth needs, the political necessities of reelecting city officials, and the force of the city bureaucracy seeking power, Stephen Elkin suggests three distinct types of urban political regimes. They are the pluralist regime, found in many Northeast and Midwest cities of the 1950s and 1960s; the federalist regime, characteristic of many of those same cities after the political movements of the 1960s; and the entrepreneurial regime, found in many of the newer cities of the sunbelt. *See also* AGENDA SETTING; DYE THESIS; ECONOMIC DEVELOPMENT; GROWTH MANAGEMENT; MARXIST URBAN ANALYSIS; POLITICS; URBAN POLITICAL ECONOMY.

Significance   The theory of an urban political regime strikes at the heart of urban political-economy analysis. The notion of regimes attempts to reconcile the relative importance of both economics and politics in urban public policy. Regime analysis directly attacks the economic determinism of both public-choice theorists and adherents of Marxist urban analysis. Elkin and other regime analysts have rejected the view that economic factors essentially control urban policy-making. Rather, the political forces of varying urban electoral coalitions, of urban bureaucracies, and of a city's political approach to economic growth all intrude on the purely economic logic holding that the private market drives all city agendas. Urban political-regime analysis points out the relevance of politics, at least to the extent that political factors mediate the ways in which a city will approach economic growth. Politics also influences how and for whom other urban public policy will be made. Urban regime analysis has placed itself firmly on a continuum between public-choice theory and Marxist urban analysis.

Suggested Reading

Elkin, Stephen L. *City and Regime in the American Republic.* Chicago: University of Chicago Press, 1987.
——. "Twentieth Century Urban Regimes." *Journal of Urban Affairs,* vol. 7, no. 2 (1985), pp. 11–28.
Peterson, Paul E. *City Limits.* Chicago: University of Chicago Press, 1981.
Stone, Clarence N., and T. Sanders Heywood , eds. *The Politics of Urban Development.* Lawrence: University Press of Kansas, 1987.
Swanstrom, Todd. "Semi-sovereign Cities: The Politics of Urban Development." *Polity,* vol. 21, no. 1 (1988), pp. 83–110.

Urban Renewal   A major community-demolition redevelopment program created by the Housing Act of 1949 (42 U.S.C. 1401 et seq.) and its amendments. As a response to the post–World War II housing crisis, urban renewal was intended to eliminate slums and urban blight and replace each dilapidated structure with a new dwelling. The urban-renewal program gave federal funding to local authorities to condemn and clear land, then promote residential or commercial development of the properties. In practice, many more dwellings were razed than were constructed. Although the Housing Act of 1949 meant to increase the availability of affordable housing, most critics claimed the overall effect of urban renewal was to displace many lower income families in favor of private commercial enterprises. In addition, although related authorizing legislation proposed that 135,000 public housing units would be built annually, only about 200,000 total units were built during the six-year period in which the companion legislation was in effect. Urban renewal as a separate grant-in-aid program was eliminated by the Housing and Community Development Act of 1974. *See also* BLIGHT; HOUSING, PUBLIC; HOUSING ACT OF 1949; HOUSING AND COMMUNITY DEVELOPMENT ACT OF 1974; POLETOWN; SLUM; URBAN REVITALIZATION.

Significance   Urban renewal has been a long-standing need for many of the older, industrial cities of the United States. As early as the 1930s, many Northeast central-city buildings were at least 50 years old and deteriorating. Some economic restructuring had occurred in these areas; in many cases surrounding land use had changed dramatically. In addition, cities were so widely blighted that only renewal on a large scale would address the problem. Some public-housing units were built after the Housing Act of 1937, but a particularly large housing shortage occurred after World War II. However, the 1949 Housing Act provided for more development than just public-housing construction. The urban-renewal component of the 1949 Act allowed for the first time up to 30 percent of the cleared land to be used for private commercial purposes. Many critics from both the ideological right and left disliked urban renewal. The right believed it was a wasteful public program better vested in the private housing market. The left argued the program was more correctly an "urban removal" program that did not replace the dwellings it demolished, thereby destroying communities and neighborhoods, forcing poor urban residents to relocate with little or no government assistance.

Suggested Reading

Bellush, Jewell, and Murray Hausknecht, eds. *Urban Renewal: People, Politics and Planning.* Garden City, NY: Doubleday, 1967.

Bennett, Larry. "Beyond Urban Renewal: Chicago's North Loop Redevelopment Project." *Urban Affairs Quarterly,* vol. 22, no. 2 (1986), pp. 242–260.

Mollenkopf, John. *The Contested City.* Princeton, NJ: Princeton University Press, 1983.

Stone, Clarence N. *Economic Growth and Neighborhood Discontent: System Bias in the Urban Renewal Program of Atlanta.* Chapel Hill: University of North Carolina Press, 1976.

U.S. Congress, Legislative Research Service. *The Central City and Urban Renewal Policy.* Washington, DC: Legislative Research Service, 1973.

Wilson, James Q., ed. *Urban Renewal: The Record and the Controversy.* Cambridge, MA: MIT Press, 1966.

Urban Revitalization   Physical redevelopment through reinvestment in and conservation of a city's built environment. In the United Kingdom, urban revitalization is known as *urban regeneration.* A single building is said to be renovated, whereas a neighborhood is revitalized. Funding for the improvements comes from either public investments in infrastructure repair or private monies for housing and office building renovation. Both central business districts (CBDs) and residential neighborhoods have been regenerated through such devices as urban renewal, gentrification, urban homesteading, and strict code enforcement. *See also* DOWNTOWN DEVELOPMENT AUTHORITY; GENTRIFICATION; HISTORIC PRESERVATION; INFRASTRUCTURE; LAND BANKING; URBAN HOMESTEADING; URBAN RENEWAL.

Significance   *Urban revitalization* is the antonym of *disinvestment,* in which money is removed from an area. For major central cities in the snowbelt, disinvestment is the major trend. Urban revitalization is not greatly significant in terms of overall residents, businesses, and capital investment. The back-to-the-city movement is a distinctly minor motif in late-twentieth-century urban America. Revitalization is not necessary in relatively recently developed cities; it is more of a concern as the life cycle of a city lengthens. The scale and very existence of returning people and investments differ among cities and regions. In part this is a function of the quality of initial building stock. Revitalization can be impeded or encouraged by local tax codes, the availability of suburban land, and the demographics of those in search of housing and offices. Empty-nesters are more likely to gravitate to gentrified housing or waterfront apartments. Businesses in need of proximity to CBD services are more likely to settle in retrofitted spaces in the zone of transition.

Suggested Reading

Bryce, Harrington. *Back to the City: An Appraisal of Housing Reinvestment and Population Change in Urban America*. Washington, DC: Urban Institute, 1981.

————. "The Revitalization of Older Urban Housing and Neighborhoods." In Arthur P. Solomon, ed., *The Prospective City*. Cambridge, MA: MIT Press, 1980.

————, ed. *Revitalizing Cities: Policies and Prospects*. Lexington, MA: D. C. Heath, 1979.

Schill, Michael H., and Richard P. Nathan. *Revitalizing America's Cities: Neighborhood Reinvestment and Displacement*. Albany: State University of New York Press, 1983.

Urban Services   Provision of assistance to residents of densely populated areas by government or the private sector or through co-production or public-private partnerships. Urban services are delivered in conventional line functions such as garbage pickup and building inspection, as well as staff functions such as park and recreation planning and transportation design for highways and airports. An extensive literature has emerged on the subject since the 1970s. It generally does not distinguish between capital- and labor-intensive services. Most of the empirical evidence is based on case studies of relatively few services for a short period. Heavily represented in the literature are Chicago, Detroit, and New Haven. One major finding is that most services are distributed unevenly in large cities. One topic studied is whether delivery is systematically biased against the underclass. In fact, there is no evidence of overt class maldistribution. A second topic has been who makes the decisions about service delivery. Is it administrators using professional standards and rational principles, or are politicians responding with political payoffs? The best answer seems to be both. Uneven levels of delivery are caused by the balkanization of metropolitan areas, separating resources from those who need certain services. Issues of service delivery equity, equality, and efficiency also have been studied but are tied up with disagreement over measurement standards and are largely inconclusive. *See also* BALKANIZATION; CITIZEN-INITIATED CONTACTING; COPRODUCTION; OAKLAND PROJECT; QUALITY OF LIFE; STREET-LEVEL BUREAUCRAT; UNDER-CLASS; ZONING, EXCLUSIONARY.

Significance   Most of an urban government's budget provides for services, the two most expensive of which are education and public safety. Who gets what services becomes one of the central questions in metropolitan politics. Theoretical and anecdotal interest in the topic traces back to the 1930s. It was given major impetus by the 1972 Fifth Circuit Court of Appeals case of *Hawkins v. Town of Shaw*, 461 F. 2d 1171, which found intent to discriminate based on race in the delivery of infrastructure services such as paving and lighting. Most subsequent empirical research has been confined to one or a few jurisdictions, not accounting for variation in metropolitan county delivery, private-sector contributions, or coproduction. In the late 1980s, attention shifted to research on the role of citizen-initiated requests for action, a form of political participation referred to as *contact behavior*. Urban services thus are studied both as a form of input and as a type of output. Three elements in any definition of service delivery include (1) the purpose of the service, (2) who decided it should be provided, and (3) the method of its provision. Many services, such as police protection, are universal. But many other services, such as primary school education, are targeted to a limited clientele. Services are not paid for simply by taxes but also by fees, bonds, subsidies, gifts, and transfer payments, and through donated labor or capital. This topic is one of the major research concerns of the social sciences. Researchers are becoming more sensitive to the need for replication studies, operationalization of categories, and analysis of long-term impacts.

Suggested Reading

Baer, William C. "Just What Is an Urban Service, Anyway?" *Journal of Politics*, vol. 47, no. 3 (1985), pp. 881–898. (An alternative definition, pp. 885–886.)

Benton, Edwin, and Platon Rigos. "Patterns of Metropolitan Service Dominance: Central City and Central County Service Roles Compared." *Urban Affairs Quarterly*, vol. 20, no. 3 (1985), pp. 285–302.

Bond, Kenneth W. "Toward Equal Delivery of Municipal Services in the Central Cities." *Fordham Urban Law Journal*, vol. 4, no. 2 (1976), pp. 263–287. (Proposed jurisprudential theory, bypassing the equal protection clause.)

Jones, Bryan D., with Saadia Greenberg and Joseph Drew. *Service Delivery in the City: Citizen Demand and Bureaucratic Rules.* New York: Longman, 1980.

Koehler, David H., and Margaret T. Wrightson. "Inequality in the Delivery of Urban Services: A Reconsideration of the Chicago Parks." *Journal of Politics,* vol. 49, no. 1 (1987), pp. 80–99. (A replication study debunking the role of bureaucrats.)

Lineberry, Robert L. *Equality and Urban Policy: The Distribution of Municipal Services.* Beverly Hills: Sage Publications, 1977.

Mudd, John. *Neighborhood Services: Making Big Cities Work.* New Haven, CT: Yale University Press, 1985.

Rich, R. C., ed. *Analyzing Urban Service Distributions.* Lexington, MA: D. C. Heath, 1982.

———, ed. *The Politics of Urban Public Services.* Lexington, MA: D. C. Heath, 1982.

Urban Sprawl   An area of low-density population that is unplanned and develops as an irregular extension of residences and light industry around an urban fringe, usually outside city boundaries, where it escapes control by governmental planning bodies. Sprawl often consists of ribbon development along major transportation arteries. The term is usually employed in a negative connotation. *See also* BOUNDED CITIES, TYPES OF; DENSITY, URBAN; EXTRATERRITORIAL POWER; GREENBELT; INFILLING; PLANNING, URBAN PHYSICAL.

Significance   Urban sprawl is attractive to home buyers because less populated jurisdictions often enforce building codes more leniently, tax land at lower rates than do central cities, and provide escape from central-city crime. Urban sprawl is unattractive to physical planners because it encroaches on productive agricultural land, usually cropland. Low-density homes are as much as ten times more expensive to serve with infrastructure than are new homes built on infill sites. The costs of water, sewer lines, paved roads, bus routes, and increased police patrols are usually not fully borne by the homeowner or new business but rather are shifted to the entire community. The major purpose of Sir Ebenezer Howard's new-town greenbelts was to provide a physical barrier against sprawl. States that give cities extraterritorial planning power limit sprawl. Councils of Governments (COGs), which delimit future sewer and water hookup areas, also provide a barrier against sprawl.

Suggested Reading

Real Estate Research Corporation. *The Costs of Sprawl: Environmental and Economic Costs of Alternative Residential Development Patterns at the Urban Fringe: Detailed Cost Analysis.* Washington, DC: Superintendent of Documents, 1974.

Sinclair, Robert. "Von Thuenen and Urban Sprawl." *Annals of the Association of American Geographers,* vol. 57, no. 1 (1986), pp. 72–87.

Urban Village   (1) A physical-planning concept delineating a portion of a city that is anchored by a regional shopping center, major industrial plant, or office complex and is composed of a core with a periphery that serves as a transportation nexus within the larger jurisdiction. "Urban village" was coined in the 1920s by New York City planners to characterize an urban scale in which people would conduct most of their daily travel. The spread-out city is a mosaic of villages of relatively self-contained spaces in which people feel comfortable. The multinucleated urban complex has not a dominant central business district (CBD) but a series of activity hubs. (2) *Urban village* is also a term employed in urban sociology to describe a central-city, low-rent ethnic enclave such as the Italian-American community in Boston's West End, which was described by Herbert Gans. *See also* COMMUNITY; COMMUNITY PRESS; MULTINUCLEI MODEL; NEIGHBORHOOD; NEW TOWN; TRAFFIC ANALYSIS; ZONE, URBAN.

Significance   (1) *Urban village* is a twentieth-century term. It was coined in an attempt to break down the impersonal large scale of the city so as to plan on a humane scale. The two major hoped-for results of this scale of planning are a heightened sense of community and decreased traffic volume between sections of the metropolitan area. As employed in the Phoenix, Arizona, master plan, the city is broken down into nine villages. The one empirical study of traffic flow for one of these units—North Mountain Village—suggests the plan is only effective for shopping trips and not for commuting to work. (2) As a descriptive term in sociology used to characterize lower-socioeconomic-status (SES) ethnic neighborhoods, the major empirical study uncovered a high sense of community, strong identity, and satisfaction with the area.

Suggested Reading
Gans, Herbert J. *The Urban Villagers: Group and Class in the Life of Italian-Americans.* New York: Free Press, 1962. (Descriptive use.)
Guest, Avery M., and Barrett A. Lee. "The Social Organization of Local Areas." *Urban Affairs Quarterly,* vol. 19, no. 2 (1983), pp. 217–240. (Uses the distinction between urban village and community of limited liability.)
Picks, John, and Patricia Gober. "Urban Villages and Activity Patterns in Phoenix." *Urban Geography,* vol. 9, no. 1 (1988), pp. 85–97. (Analytic planning term.)

User Fee   A method of funding a public program by applying a specific charge to consumers of that service or good. In the public budget, the user fee often is earmarked for that service or good. The user fee embodies more of a "business" approach to providing public goods or services and has occurred more frequently as tax limits and budgetary constraints have been imposed on state and local governments. A common example of a user fee would be a toll for a bridge or highway. Local governments have applied user fees to an increasing number of services, such as municipal swimming pools, and special assessment fees for sidewalks and other development projects. *See also* INCOME SOURCES, URBAN; PRIVATE SECTOR; PRIVATIZATION; PUBLIC SECTOR; TAX LIMIT.

Significance   User fees have become increasingly popular during the 1970s and 1980s. Fiscal austerity and general complaints about high taxes have forced all levels of government to seek alternative funding mechanisms for the programs they provide. However, user fees have existed for many years, especially at the local level. For example, separate fees commonly have been applied for water and sewerage, and for parks and recreation services, as well as special assessments for street improvements. This method of paying for governmental services "taxes" only those who wish to use a service and avoids general tax increases, which have become highly unpopular. This trend toward alternative funding of public programs also includes the increased privatization of many governmental services and the "contracting out" of other services to private business. Opponents argue that such fees are unfair to the poor and may result in decreased public control over programs and the deterioration of standards for services provided.

Suggested Reading
Mushkin, Selma, and Charles L. Vehorn. "User Fees and Charges." *Governmental Finance*, vol. 6, no. 4 (1977), pp. 42–48.

V

Vacancy Chain   A theoretical process occurring when families move into better housing units, leaving their previous units for families with lower incomes. A vacancy chain is created as a series of housing units become unoccupied when families move into different residences. The concept of vacancy chains is directly related to the filtering theory of housing, which argues that new, and usually more expensive, housing causes a trend in which families of all class strata are able to upgrade their residence. *See also* ABANDONMENT; BLIGHT; FILTERING THEORY, HOUSING; SUCCESSION; URBAN HOMESTEADING.

Significance   The notions of filtering and vacancy chains provide the foundation of housing policy in the United States. Housing policy historically has provided ample opportunities for private real estate agents and developers, while creating minimal governmental intervention into housing construction. Vacancy-chain analysis has become part of the rationale supporting the dominance of the private sector in the provision of housing in the United States and a justification for reduced housing subsidies. The movement of families into different housing units assumes ample housing opportunities for families in all socioeconomic segments of society. Because upgraded housing eventually filters down to lower income families by way of vacancy chains, many economists argue public-housing programs are unnecessary. Problems may arise, however, because housing units of the lowest value and quality at the end of the vacancy chain are likely to be abandoned and create blight and unsafe conditions in these neighborhoods.

Suggested Reading
Marullo, Sam. "Housing Opportunities and Vacancy Chains." *Urban Affairs Quarterly*, vol. 20, no. 3 (1985), pp. 364–388.

White, Harrison C. "Multipliers, Vacancy Chains, and Filtering in Housing." *Journal of the American Institute of Planners,* vol. 37, no. 2 (1971), pp. 88–95.

Vacancy in Office   An elected or appointed position that remains unfilled for some period. State constitutions often define under what conditions an office is considered vacant, whether it is to be filled, and how. State statutes also specify when an office is considered vacant. Generally home-rule charters take precedence in case of conflicts with statutes, unless the enabling statute for the home-rule community stipulates that the statute takes precedence. Vacancies are caused by death, removal by recall, or resignation. Resignation may be voluntary or involuntary; the right to continue in office may be forfeited by failure to attend meetings, conviction of a felony, or failure to maintain residency requirements. Recall removal statutes and ordinances conventionally specify replacement procedure. Whether there is a vacant office is usually a matter subject to judicial review. Filling a vacancy can be by *succession,* as where a vice-president of a village council automatically elevates to the president's position. Provision may exist for the vacancy to remain *unfilled* until the next appropriate election. If the vacancy is to be removed by *interim* or *permanent appointment,* the appointee may be named by the chief executive, president, mayor, supervisor, or county executive at the same level or by a higher geographic level. Or the appointment may be made by the board, commission, or council, in which case it may be by plurality vote, simple majority, or extraordinary vote, conducted by secret ballot, voice vote, or recorded vote. The person who fills the vacancy must possess the qualifications for that office. *See also* CARETAKER GOVERNMENT; CONSTITUTION, STATE; RECALL.

Significance   Substate units of government are characterized by high turnover. How a vacant office is filled, therefore, becomes important because of the frequency with which the procedure is repeated. A majority of some elected bodies are represented by members who originally owed their position to an appointment. State law is not unanimous on whether such officials deserve the designation of incumbent at the next election. Vacancies may be kept open, filled for the balance of the particular legislative term, filled on an interim basis for no more than six months, filled until the next regular election, or filled for the balance of the term of the vacant office. The new appointee does not necessarily inherit all powers of his or her predecessor, especially if the former holder was a chairperson or exercised office by virtue of accumulated seniority. Most disputes on vacancies arise from want of clear guidelines in statute or ordinance and are clarified *ad hoc* through attorney general opinions or litigation.

Variance   A permitted discrepancy in a zoning ordinance requirement that implements a master plan with regard to either land use or the allowable area in which a building can be erected. Nonconforming land use is usually the continuing employment of real property in a manner in which adjacent and similarly situated land cannot be used under a zoning classification. Or it can be a first use of such land. In the former, the Zoning Board of Appeals (ZBA) acknowledges the aberration through a grandfather clause and permits its continuance until the land is sold, for a time certain (such as a decade) or until more than some fraction (such as one-half) of the building needs replacement. The ZBA is much more reluctant to issue a use variance for initial construction, because *ipso facto* the action negates the ordinance's integrity. The other type of variance relates to the permitted area in which there can be construction. Typically a building code or zoning ordinance specifies prohibitions for floodplains, the land over or under easements, or land within certain distances from side lots, streets, or adjacent buildings. Variances often are granted for uninhabited outbuildings in floodplains or for encroachments into open spaces because of hardships caused by terrain or the odd shape of platted lots. Many states stipulate that all platted lots are buildable, thus forcing ZBAs to issue variances or be overturned on appeal. *See also* GROUP HOME; HIGHEST AND BEST USE; PLANNED UNIT DEVELOPMENT; ZONING; ZONING, DOWN-.

Significance   Variances are granted initially by local Zoning Boards of Appeal. They also can be issued because of court action. State legislatures can issue blanket variances for group homes, because state statutes override local ordinances under the principle of the hierarchy of positive laws. It is possible for more than half of a zoning classification to be at variance with the rule when a city council has downzoned or land has been shifted recently in the ordinance from residential to commercial. Zoning ordinances are instituted to protect the general public interest. Hence, variances should not be granted on pleadings of financial hardship from individual owners. A major function of ZBAs or city councils is hearing petitions for relief from zoning ordinance classifications. The question is always whether to approve the request because it is unique or merely a relative hardship.

Suggested Reading
Bair, Frederick H., Jr. *The Zoning Board Manual.* Washington, DC: American Planning Association Planners Press, 1984.

Cohen, Yoram Jerry. "Area Variance Law in New York: A Uniform Approach." *Cardozo Law Review*, vol. 7, no. 1 (1985), pp. 251–279.

Zimmerman, Ruth M. "Impact of Regional Facilities on Local Variance Decisions: *National Merritt v. Weist.*" *Urban Law Annual*, vol. 16 (1979), pp. 405–415.

Village   The legal term for the government of certain small-scale communities. *Town* is a generic term for a small community; however, the government structure of many communities makes them villages. A village may be incorporated or unincorporated. States differ on the population-size requirements for a village, but usually place a limit of 1,000 to 2,500 people. However, the 1990 census records villages with more than 10,000 residents. Villages usually are governed by a part-time mayor and council. In many states, the taxing and borrowing authority of a village is more limited than that of a city. *See also* BALKANIZATION; CENSUS OF GOVERNMENTS; CITY CLASSIFICATION; JEFFERSONIAN AGRARIANISM; OPTIMUM CITY; TOWN; TOWNSHIP.

Significance   Historically, residents of a village demanded only a few basic local services to provide for their relatively small population. As their populations increased, or when the counties or townships could not provide adequate services, villages often incorporated. With even greater populations and a subsequent demand for more services, many villages opted for city status in order to extend the government's taxing and borrowing abilities. Suburban communities sometimes have sought to maintain a quiet environment by continuing their village status. In some states village residents retain affiliation with the township in which they are located, and they pay taxes and vote as township residents in addition to their status as village residents.

Village of Euclid v. Ambler Realty Co., 272 U.S. 365 (1926)   The landmark U.S. Supreme Court case upholding zoning as a proper exercise of the police power. The *Euclid* case was brought by a landowner in a suburb of Cleveland against a comprehensive and complicated 1922 zoning plan, asking that the ordinance be declared null and void in its entirety as violative of due process clauses in the Ohio and U.S. Constitutions. The realty company won at the district level. The village appealed to the U.S. Supreme Court, where, by a 6-3 vote the Court reversed the lower court, ruling there was no confiscatory taking of public property. In an opinion written by Justice Sutherland, the Court found that zoning is a proper exercise of the police power and bears a reasonable relationship to the community's health, safety, and welfare. In upholding land-use restrictions, the Court found there was a reasonable and effective enforcement system. *See also* LAND CLASSIFICATION; POLICE POWER; TAKING; ZONING, EUCLIDEAN.

Significance   In the *Village of Euclid* case, the Court upheld the constitutionality of fixed-classification zoning systems. The very existence of land-use restrictions, and their general scope and exercise, were hereafter sanctioned. In one of the unheralded great Supreme Court quotations of Justice Sutherland, he wrote: "Until recent years, urban life was comparatively simple; but with the great increase and concentration of population, problems have developed, and constantly are developing, which require, and will continue to require, additional restrictions in respect of the use and occupation of private lands in urban communities" (at 386–387).

Suggested Reading
Fluck, T. A. "*Euclid v. Ambler*: A Retrospective." *Journal of the American Planning Association*, vol. 52, no. 3 (1986), pp. 326–327.
Tarrant, John J. *The End of Exurbia*. New York: Stein & Day, 1976. Chap. 3.

Volunteers in Service to America (VISTA)   An independent federal agency that provides volunteer workers in urban or rural community organizations, hospitals, schools, and Indian reservations within the United States. VISTA is headquartered in Washington, D.C., and has nine regional administrative bodies located throughout the country. The VISTA program was established by the 1964 Economic Opportunity Act (42 U.S.C. 2701) and became known as the "domestic Peace Corps." *See also* ECONOMIC OPPORTUNITY ACT OF 1964.

Significance   VISTA became a major part of Lyndon Johnson's War on Poverty program, which gained full thrust after passage of the Economic Opportunity Act. The idea of helping disadvantaged people, both in the United States and abroad, made VISTA and the Peace Corps so popular at their inception that some volunteers initially had to be turned away. Projects pursued by the VISTA campaign included rehabilitating neighborhoods, distributing emergency food and shelter, establishing drug-abuse centers, organizing the poor, creating self-help programs, and providing technical and support service to community organizations. In 1971, VISTA came under the auspices of ACTION, an independent federal agency that also directed other federal voluntary service programs, such as Foster Grandparents and the Retired Senior Volunteer Program. During the 1980s, VISTA and all the other programs administered by ACTION came under severe budgetary constraints, as cuts in social-service programs became a leading initiative under President Ronald Reagan. By 1985, the entire ACTION budget totaled just $129 million.

Suggested Reading
Reeves, T. Zane. *The Politics of the Peace Corps and VISTA.* Tuscaloosa: University of Alabama Press, 1988.

Vote Dilution Cases   A series of judicial decisions that have litigated the meaning of a portion of the Voting Rights Act of 1965, as amended in 1982, which provides that states and their political subdivisions must eliminate "voting procedures and methods of election which inhibit or dilute equal access to the electoral process." The vote dilution cases are based on 42 U.S.C. 1973b(a)(F)(i). Initially the Supreme Court interpreted locally imposed rules for elections in multimember districts to be a violation of statute if their purpose canceled out the voting power of racial and/or ethnic minorities, *White v. Regester,* 412 U.S. 755 (1973). The high court later decided *City of Mobile v. Bolden,* 446 U.S. 55 (1980), which upheld at-large election procedures against claims that the rules diluted a minority's voting power. It put the burden of proof on the challengers. Congress reacted to this case with the 1982 amendments, effectively nullifying the *Mobile* holding. It replaced that decision's intent test with a result-type test borrowed from the earlier *White* ruling. Vote dilution refers to watering down the impact of racial and ethnic bloc voting. The case of first impression on the 1982 Voting Rights Amendments addressing vote dilution was *Thornburg v. Gingles,* 478 U.S. 30 (1986). In this North Carolina case dealing with multimember state legislative districts, the high bench declared that a series of factors and circumstances must be investigated in order to determine whether there was racially polarized voting (at 79). *See also* AT-LARGE ELECTION; ELECTIONS, TYPES OF; VOTING RIGHTS ACT OF 1965.

Significance   The vote dilution cases are a challenge to at-large and multimember district elections based on the assumption that groups as well as individuals can be discriminated against by electoral machinery. As with most cases based on a statute, legislative history became important. With these amendments, it was a series of seven major and two additional factors listed in a Senate committee report used by the Court to determine discrimination against racial or ethnic groups (Senate Report No. 97-417, 97th Congress, 2nd Session). Based on the line of cases, the actual outcome of racially polarized bloc voting becomes a factor that courts can consider in judging the validity of electoral machinery. The issue undoubtedly will spawn a long line of cases before judicial tests for dilution are fully explicated.

Suggested Reading
Davidson, Chandler, ed. *Minority Vote Dilution.* Washington, DC: Howard University Press, 1984.
Hunter, Robert N., Jr. "Racial Gerrymandering and the Voting Rights Act in North Carolina." *Campbell Law Review,* vol. 9, no. 2 (1987), pp. 255–291.
Jacobs, Paul W. II, and Timothy G. O'Rourke. "Racial Polarization in Vote Dilution Cases under Section 2 of the Voting Rights Act: The Impact of *Thornburg v. Gingles." The Journal of Law and Politics,* vol. 3, no. 2 (1986), pp. 295–353.
MacManus, Susan A. "Constituency Size and Minority Representation." *State and Local Government Review,* vol. 19, no. 1 (1987), pp. 3–7.
Miller, Andrew P., and Mark A. Packman. "Amended Section 2 of the Voting Rights Act: What Is the Intent of the Results Test?" *Emory Law Review,* vol. 36, no. 1 (1987), pp. 1–74.

Voter Fatigue   The failure of a citizen, once at the polls, to complete filling out a ballot. Voter fatigue, also known as roll-off, typically manifests itself when voters ignore some local offices and propositions. The *official canvass of votes* and *certified election results* include the degree of roll-off in on years between presidential totals and those for local office. In off years, voter fatigue is tabulated by subtracting the vote for governor or congressional races from the total vote cast for local contests. Combined low turnout and voter fatigue can pull participation rates to less than 5 percent of the eligible electorate for some local contests. *See also* BALLOT, SHORT; OFF YEAR; PLUNKING.

Significance   Voter fatigue indicates urban politics is not necessarily closest to the people. If it were, turnout and voter response to local contests would be as high as national and statewide contests, if not higher. Empirical evidence suggests voter fatigue is higher on voting machines than with paper ballots. Ballot form also affects voter fatigue. The Massachusetts or office block form, which requires multiple selections, produces greater fatigue than the Indiana or party column, single-choice system. Voter fatigue is to be differentiated from *ticket splitting,* in which voters divide between both major parties in the same contest. Voter fatigue is also to be differentiated from *turnout,* which is measured by the number of voters who exercise their prerogative to go to the polls relative to those who register.

Suggested Reading
DeVires, Walter, and V. Lance Tarrance. *The Ticket Splitter: A New Force in American Politics.* Grand Rapids, MI: William B. Erdman Publishing, 1972.

Walker, Jack L. "Ballot Forms and Voter Fatigue: An Analysis of the Office Block and Party Column Ballots." *Midwest Journal of Political Science,* vol. 10, no. 4 (1966), pp. 448–463.

Voting Rights Act of 1965   A national statute passed under the Lyndon Johnson administration (42 U.S.C. 1971 et seq.) and designed to cure problems of voting discrimination. The 1965 Voting Rights Act was preceded by related legislation in 1957, 1960, and 1964. The 1965 act was amended in 1970 and 1975, and extended with amendments in 1982 to the year 2007. The 1982 amendment provided that localities with less than 50 percent minority turnout in 1964 be required to receive preclearance from the national attorney general's office or the national courts before changing voting laws. Preclearance places the burden for proving nondiscrimination on the locality, not the minority. Provisions of the original act include assignment of federal registrars, poll watchers, the elimination of literacy tests, and simplification of residency requirements. The 1965 act was found constitutional in *South Carolina v. Katzenbach,* 383 U.S. 301 (1965). *See also* AT-LARGE ELECTION; ELECTIONS, TYPES OF; QUALIFICATIONS FOR OFFICE; VOTE DILUTION CASES.

Significance   The Voting Rights Act of 1965 initially applied to seven southern states. Ten states were added later. In addition to affecting the number of eligible black voters, the statute opened the way for more registration of Spanish-speaking voters. The act removed some state and local electoral supervision and in certain cases made it a national responsibility. It resulted in increased voter turnout for minorities and the white majority. Voter registration drives successfully franchised many previously inactive citizens. Blacks and whites now vote in approximate proportion to their population totals. The major policy shift in the 1982 amendments acknowledged that voting is not only an individual right, but that groups may be discriminated against and their collective votes diluted if legislative bodies are elected at large or in multimember districts. Substantial litigation followed the 1982 law, seeking to clarify what constitutes a permissible electoral unit.

Suggested Reading
Boyd,Thomas M., and Stephen J. Markman. "The 1982 Amendments to the Voting Rights Act: A Legislative History." *Washington and Lee Law Review,* vol. 40, no. 4 (1983), pp. 1347–1428.
MacManus, Susan A. "Constituency Size and Minority Representation." *State and Local Government Review,* vol. 19, no. 1 (1987), pp. 3–7.

W

War on Poverty   A massive effort begun by the federal government in the mid-1960s to alleviate poverty, with an emphasis on programs of economic opportunity and political participation for the impoverished. John F. Kennedy often is credited with planting the policy seeds for the War on Poverty after he discovered the grim poverty of Appalachian coal miners during his campaign for the presidency in 1960, followed by his reading of Michael Harrington's *The Other America* (1963). On January 8, 1964, President Lyndon B. Johnson declared a war on poverty before a joint session of Congress, proclaiming an end to all poverty as a national goal. The chief legislative vehicle of the War on Poverty was the 1964 Economic Opportunity Act (42 U.S.C. 2701), which provided for job training and education programs, Project Head Start, Community Action Programs, Economic Development Corporations, the Volunteers in Service to America (VISTA) program, and legal services for the poor. *See also* COMMUNITY ACTION PROGRAM; ECONOMIC OPPORTUNITY ACT OF 1964; MAXIMUM FEASIBLE PARTICIPATION; POVERTY PROGRAMS; UNDERCLASS; VOLUNTEERS IN SERVICE TO AMERICA.

Significance   Though the War on Poverty programs came under substantial criticism during the 1970s and 1980s, considerable public support formed behind these initiatives during their first few years of operation. Administration of the War on Poverty programs was given to the Office of Economic Opportunity (OEO), which was placed within the executive office of the president. President Johnson appointed R. Sargent Shriver, Jr., to head the office as his "personal chief of staff in the war against poverty." During this time the Council of Economic Advisers (CEA) identified six major groups of the estimated 35 million poor to be most susceptible to poverty: (1) families headed by persons 65 years or older, (2) nonwhite families, (3) families headed by women, (4) families with no wage earners, (5) families headed by unemployed persons, and (6) farm families. Many criticisms were leveled at the administration and funding of the programs, among them that patronage had taken over the programs, that maximum feasible participation was a failure, and that many local program officials were overpaid. As a consequence, the OEO director was given authority to override state or local attempts to subvert the intent of the programs. In addition, the OEO removed a provision in the act that required Job Corps participants to sign an affidavit stating they did not espouse a violent overthrow of the government. In fiscal year 1966, $1.75 billion was authorized for the War on Poverty. However, funding and enthusiasm for these programs dropped as the war in Vietnam escalated and Richard Nixon took office in 1969. By the early 1970s, President Nixon began impounding OEO funds, and in 1973, he disbanded the Office of Economic Opportunity entirely. Congress and the courts salvaged some of the programs and transformed the former OEO into the Community Service Agency.

Suggested Reading

Greenstone, J. David, and Paul E. Peterson. *Race and Authority in Urban Politics: Community Participation and the War on Poverty.* New York: Russell Sage, 1973.

Harrington, Michael. *The Other America: Poverty in the United States.* Baltimore: Penguin Books, 1963.

Kaplan, Marshall, and Peggy Cuciti, eds. *The Great Society Revisited.* Durham, NC: Duke University Press, 1986.

Levitan, Sar. *The Great Society's Poor Law.* Baltimore: Johns Hopkins University Press, 1969.

Piven, Frances Fox, and Richard Cloward. *Regulating the Poor.* New York: Pantheon Books, 1971.

Ward   A division of a city intermediate between a precinct and a legislative, judicial, or citywide level. Wards, where they exist, are two tiers below the county party organization. In most states, counties are the most important local-level party organization. Wards also are used as the units in which the municipal assembly is elected if the vote is not conducted at large, and in some jurisdictions wards are used for the administration of municipal works. *See also* PRECINCT; URBAN POLITICAL MACHINE.

Significance   In contemporary city politics, ward leaders are employed by the political party organization to coordinate a set of precincts, organize election day activity, and canvass to get out the vote. In the era of city party machines, wards were used also to organize patronage, keep a tab on public opinion, and recruit leaders. Such wards were headed by *ward healers,* a term with negative connotations.

In the boss era, Chicago's First Ward, one of fifty, was particularly infamous for voting turnouts in excess of the number of registered voters. Wards are still important levels of party activity in Boston, New York City, and Philadelphia.

Suggested Reading

Fremon, David K. *Chicago Politics Ward by Ward.* Bloomington: Indiana University Press, 1988.

Rakove, Milton L. *Don't Make No Waves, Don't Back No Losers: An Insider's Analysis of the Daley Machine.* Bloomington: Indiana University Press, 1975. Chap. 4, "The Ward Organizations."

Sorauf, Frank J., and Paul Allen Beck. *Party Politics in America,* 6th ed. Glenview, IL: Scott, Foresman, 1988. Chap. 3, "The State and Local Party Organizations."

Washington, District of Columbia   A unique, 10-square-mile area of over 600,000 residents, originally carved out of Virginia and Maryland, that serves as the seat of the national government. Washington, D.C's official government is established by Article I, Section 8, Clause 17 of the U.S. Constitution and subordinated to the control of Congress. In short, Washington, D.C., is not part of any state but was set up expressly by the founders to be a district set apart so it could not embarrass the national level. Although there is a minor House standing committee on the District of Columbia, Congress authorized home rule in 1973, permitting residents to elect their own mayor and city council. Congress reserves the right to reject city ordinances and budgets and does so on a regular basis. Because Washington, D.C., is not part of a state, it has no vote in the Senate or House, although it does have a delegate to Congress. Residents of the District do have a voice in electing the president under the Twenty-third Amendment, ratified in 1961. Its three electoral votes are equal to that of "the least populous state," which is Alaska. This electoral vote has remained constant in all seven presidential elections in which District voters have participated. Reapportionment of legislative bodies in the United States has two exceptions, namely the electoral votes of the U.S. Senate and Washington, D.C., both of which are frozen by constitutional mandate. To correct the lack of congressional representation, there have been repeated attempts to enfranchise District voters since 1800, when the capital was moved there from Philadelphia. In 1978, Congress proposed a formal constitutional amendment to correct this. Three-fourths of the states failed to ratify by 1985, and the proposal failed. *See also* HOME RULE; NATIONAL CAPITAL PLANNING COMMISSION.

Significance   Washington, D.C., is an atypical central city in many respects. It has one of the highest percentages of the labor force in public administration (more than one-third of the work force) and one of the highest percentages of black populations (three-fourths). It is one of the most consistent Democratic areas in the nation, having voted Democratic in every presidential election from 1964 through 1988. Congress has experimented with a series of distinct government structures over 200 years. The current statute is the District of Columbia Self-government and Governmental Reorganization Act, creating a strong mayor and a 13-member city council. Congress retains near-complete jurisdiction over the areas of District courts and city planning. Recent presidents have assigned a liaison officer within the Executive Office of the President to deal with the sensitive issues of town and crown. For example, in the Nixon White House, Egil "Bud" Krogh, Jr., a white, was in charge of District-presidential matters, including the often-present anti–Vietnam War demonstrations. The two elected mayors from 1973 through 1990, Walter Washington and Marion S. Barry, were both black. Successful opposition to enfranchising the District of Columbia came from conservatives who did not wish to see two types of units at the lower level in the federal system (namely states, and one quasi-state or district), as well as from partisan Republicans who were aware Democrats were bound to win the two Senate seats and one House seat. Because of the large financial impact that national government operations make on local public facilities, the national level has issued an annual "federal payment" in lieu of taxes since 1925. This is known as PILOT, or payment in lieu of taxes. It has been necessary because, under the doctrine of intergovernmental tax immunity, approximately 50 percent of total District property is tax-exempt. District borrowing is also atypical. Washington, D.C., alone is permitted to borrow directly from the federal treasury. Congress routinely interferes with District governance, including mandating the location of a fire station and the classic of symbolic politics, the renaming of the city's streets.

Suggested Reading

Green, Constance Winsor. *The Secret City: A History of Race Relations in the Nation's Capital.* Princeton: Princeton University Press, 1967.

Hatch, Orrin G. "Should the Capitol Vote in Congress? A Critical Analysis of the Proposed D.C. Representation Amendment." *Fordham Urban Law Journal,* vol. 7 (1979), pp. 479–539.

Smith, Sam. *Captive Capitol: Colonial Life in Modern Washington.* Bloomington: Indiana University Press, 1974.

Welfare, Public   Financial or in-kind assistance provided by governments to eligible recipients. Eligibility is determined through a needs or "means test." The means test is more accurately a lack-of-means test, because one qualifies for these assistance programs only if annual income is less than an established standard. There are four basic public-assistance programs that use income as the exclusive test for eligibility: Aid to Families with Dependent Children (AFDC); Supplemental Security Income (SSI); Food Stamps; and General Assistance (GA). Each of these programs provides to qualifying recipients direct cash payments or food stamp equivalents. Public welfare is to be distinguished from the wide variety of private charities that have operated for many years in the United States and have been encouraged specifically by the Reagan and Bush administrations. *See also* AID TO FAMILIES WITH DEPENDENT CHILDREN; ELEEMOSYNARY GROUP; POVERTY PROGRAMS; WORKFARE.

Significance   Many other social welfare programs in existence can also be considered public welfare support programs, but require partial payment or are a form of insurance. Public criticism of welfare has focused on means test programs because they give money directly to low-income individuals. Other governmental programs with greater expenditures, such as Social Security, receive more public support, often because they are entitlements and are viewed as going to the more "deserving." Critics of these means test programs argue that such assistance promotes laziness and fraud. However, program supporters argue that appropriate amounts of money are spent on these programs, and that they provide needed assistance for those unable to work or find employment.

Suggested Reading
Albert, Vicky N. *Welfare Dependence and Welfare Policy: A Statistical Study.* Westport, CT: Greenwood Press, 1988.
Berkowitz, Edward D., and Kim McQuaid. *Creating the Welfare State: The Political Economy of Twentieth Century Reform.* New York: Praeger, 1980.
Freeman, Roger A. *The Wayward Welfare State.* Stanford, CA: Hoover Institution, Stanford University, 1981.
Schwartz, John E. *America's Hidden Success: A Reassessment of Public Policy from Kennedy to Reagan,* rev. ed. New York: W. W. Norton, 1988.

White Flight   A large-scale movement of Caucasians, usually from a central city to outlying suburban or rural areas. White flight occurred in many northern, industrialized U.S. cities after World War II when minority populations began replacing white residents. Major migrations of whites out of urban centers took place in cities that experienced riots in the 1960s—such as Detroit, Los Angeles, and Newark—and after busing plans for public school desegregation were implemented during the 1970s. *See also* BLOCKBUSTING; CLOSING, SCHOOL; RESTRICTIVE COVENANT; ZONING, EXCLUSIONARY.

Significance White flight typically occurred in the older, declining, industrialized cities of the Northeast and Midwest between 1950 and 1970. After World War II, large numbers of minorities began moving to northern urban centers, primarily from the rural South. At the same time, blockbusting tactics by real estate salesmen created fear among white homeowners who previously had lived in segregated neighborhoods. As exclusionary zoning and restrictive covenants became illegal, some housing markets began opening up for minority homeowners. Between 1950 and 1970, the northern industrialized cities lost between one-third and one-half of their English-speaking populations. These same cities experienced no net influx of whites compared to the rest of the nation. Younger cities tended to experience above-average increases in their white populations, while older cities were losing their white residents. By 1983, 23 percent of the total U.S. white population lived in central cities, 43 percent lived in suburban communities, and 34 percent lived in nonmetropolitan areas. According to the Census Bureau's 1983 Current Population Survey (CPS), whites were more likely to move between counties, while blacks tended to move within the same county.

Suggested Reading
Molotch, Harvey Luskin. *Managed Integration: Dilemmas of Doing Good in the City.* Berkeley: University of California Press, 1972. Chap. 8, "Property Turnover: Measuring White Flight."
Wurdock, Clarence J. "Neighborhood Racial Transition: A Study of the Role of White Flight." *Urban Affairs Quarterly,* vol. 17, no. 1 (September 1981), pp. 75–89.

Wired City The postindustrial community equipped with electronic devices that allow residents to spend substantially more time at home. Among major examples of the wired city are (1) fax (facsimile) machines, which allow transfer of information over telephone lines; (2) cable television, allowing multiple channel access; (3) video machines, which facilitate home or office use of film; (4) computer modems, which allow remote access to data bases and hence less need for access to conventional libraries; (5) inter-university communications such as BITNET that allow owners to send and receive mail; (6) debit cards, which work through electronic banks; (7) telecourses transmitted over narrowcast channels; (8) teleshopping; and (9) the CD-ROM technology (Compact Disc—Read Only Memory), which microminiaturizes information storage for fast retrieval. The wired city allows for interaction heretofore limited to face-to-face transactions. *See also* CABLE FRANCHISE; COUNTERURBANISM; POSTINDUSTRIAL CITY.

Significance   The wired city is a product of twentieth-century technology. There is less need for central business districts (CBDs) or multinucleated centers in a wired city. Because of the proximity of major computer companies located in the same city, there are already suburbs such as Southfield, Michigan, where telephone consumption per 1,000 people exceeds 1,000 phones. Home and office can be situated remote from other terminals without need for daily physical contact. Life styles will develop that do not require physical proximity to the great museums, libraries, orchestra halls, and banking institutions in order to utilize them. Four of the most important elements of this new wired city will be increased home-communication capability, home-based learning, home entertainment, and less need to transact business face to face.

Suggested Reading
Frendreis, John P. "The Information Revolution and Urban Life." *Journal of Urban Affairs*, vol. 11, no. 4 (1989), pp. 327–338, 355–359.
Wilson, Josh L., Jr. "Electronic Village™: Information Technology Creates New Space." *Computer/Law Journal*, vol. 6, no. 2 (1985), pp. 365–386. (Describes the electronic village proposed for Placer County, California.)

Wirth Thesis   Urbanism represents a large number of socially heterogeneous residents living in dense settlements characterized by social pathologies. The Wirth Thesis is named after University of Chicago sociologist Louis Wirth (1897–1952), who wrote an influential article in 1938 defining the city and explaining the consequences of urbanism. It was instrumental in guiding a generation of urbanologists in their choice of research topics. Individually, Wirth argued, urban residents are overstimulated by a plethora of sights and sounds. They retreat from this jungle of impressions and become aloof or alienated from their surroundings. Socially, urbanism produces the highest possible specialization of labor, which differentially rewards workers and produces diverse life styles. Cities produce mutual exploitation, nervous tensions, isolation, anomie, a sense of anonymity, and superficial social contacts. Segmental relationships develop in which firm ties to primary groups fail to develop. Weakened secondary ties to the union, occupation, or profession substitute for a true sense of community. Interest groups and the mass media take their place as sources of information. High density causes high levels of deviance, for both innovation and conventional types of deprivation. *See also* CHICAGO SCHOOL; JEFFERSONIAN AGRARIANISM; URBAN VILLAGE.

Significance   Wirth's thesis of the pathologies that are *ipso facto* associated with big cities was accepted by a large number of urbanologists from the 1930s into the 1960s. Implicit in Wirth's argument is that cities are abnormal, and eventually city density levels must decline or pathological behavior will increase. Later writers claimed alcoholism was directly related to density levels, not questioning whether these related to persons per room or persons per unit acre of land. Others found larger cities overrepresented on relief rolls because of city size *per se*. It was claimed that mental disorders inherently occur in larger cities more than smaller cities because of the city's density and forced isolation. The thesis is now rejected and was never supported by well-grounded empirical studies. Most urbanites do not even perceive the city in its entirety but live their lives within a much smaller portion of the city or suburb. In studying a city, density levels are less important a factor than income levels because pathologies are less likely to occur in a gold coast than in an economic ghetto. The thesis, however, lives on in its continued Jeffersonian agrarian bias against the city and the assumption that it is best to look at the city in terms of its many segments, such as the central business district (CBD), the ghetto, or the Zone of Transition.

Suggested Reading

Berry, Brian J. L. *Comparative Urbanization: Divergent Paths in the Twentieth Century.* New York: St. Martin's Press, 1973, 1981, pp. 14–15, 30–36.

Peterson, Elmer T., ed. *Cities Are Abnormal.* Norman: University of Oklahoma Press, 1946.

Wirth, Louis. "Urbanism as a Way of Life." In Albert J. Reiss, Jr., ed., *Louis Wirth on Cities and Social Life: Selected Papers.* Chicago: University of Chicago Press, 1964. Chap. 4, pp. 60–83.

Workfare   A set of mandatory employment or job training requirements for recipients of Aid to Families with Dependent Children (AFDC). Workfare is meant to take the poor off the welfare rolls and require some employment for aid recipients. Earlier federal work requirements for AFDC mothers began in 1967 under the Work Incentive Program (WIN), but a 1975 study found only about 16 percent of those registered in WIN received job training or located permanent employment. California's Greater Avenues to Independence (GAIN) and Massachusetts' Employment and Training (ET) programs were the earliest state-level efforts in what is now called workfare. Federal workfare programs sponsored at the federal level by Senator Patrick Moynihan (D-NY) usually involve joint federal and state funding. In 1988, federal appropriations for workfare amounted to $3.5 billion. *See also* AID TO FAMILIES WITH DEPENDENT CHILDREN; POVERTY PROGRAMS.

Significance   Workfare was hailed as the first major welfare reform passed by Congress since the late 1960s. This represents an attempt to accommodate the conservative criticism of welfare as encouraging laziness and dependency. It is also an attempt to address some of the functional problems of the poor by providing jobs and day-care facilities for working mothers. The federal government has established guidelines for states to participate in the workfare program, including enrollment goals for welfare recipients in education, training, work-experience, or job-search programs. By 1990, each state was to have enrolled at least 7 percent of its welfare mothers who have children older than three and increase that enrollment to 20 percent by 1995. A welfare recipient is eligible for subsidized day care and medicaid insurance for one year after leaving public support. In its early stages, workfare has come under criticism. Often workfare participants cannot join labor unions, receive pay, have health insurance entitlements or worker's compensation, or receive sick time or job security. In a time of public-sector layoffs and cutbacks, workfare participants often replace unionized employees who have been laid off. Early evaluations of some programs have suggested that individuals have not been permanently removed from welfare rolls any more quickly than before implementation of workfare.

Suggested Reading
Englander, Valerie, and Fred Englander. "Workfare in New Jersey: A Five-Year Assessment." *Policy Studies Review*, vol. 5, no. 1 (1985), pp. 33–41.
Kirk, David L. "The California Work/Welfare Scheme." *Public Interest*, no. 83 (1986), pp. 34–48.
Morris, Michael, and John B. Williamson. "Workfare: The Poverty/Dependence Trade-off." *Social Policy*, vol. 18, no. 1 (1987), pp. 13–16.
Reischauer, Robert D. "Six Welfare Questions Still Searching for Answers." *Brookings Review*, vol. 5, no. 3 (1984), pp. 9–16.

Write-down   The difference between the value of land to the public sector and the reduced cost of that land when it is offered to a private developer. Write-down costs have become part of the package of incentives given to private developers and businesses to encourage business investment in a given area. The term literally means that the price of the land is "written down" to a lower amount so as to reduce taxes and assessments and building costs to make certain land more attractive for development. Such write-downs have been an integral part of federal housing policy at least since the 1949 Housing Act. *See also* HOUSING ACT OF 1949; INFILLING.

Significance While write-downs have been a long-standing practice, they became increasingly common during the 1980s. Cities have been forced to create a package of incentives to make business investment in their city more desirable. During the 1940s and 1950s, most of the write-down subsidies were jointly paid through federal and local funding. Title I of the 1949 Housing act provided for $500 million in write-down subsidies to be available through the Housing and Home Finance Agency (HHFA). The emphasis during these years was primarily on residential development. In addition, such subsidies were generally offered only on land that had declined in value and held little interest for private developments. More recently, local governments have offered write-down subsidies for commercial, retail, or industrial developments in an effort to redevelop central-city areas.

Y

Yankee City   A camouflaged urban case study of Newburyport, Massachusetts (population 17,000), between 1930 and 1935 and less intensely to 1959. The classic Yankee City team study, headed by W. Lloyd Warner, was based on social anthropology and social psychology theories and published in the 1940s and 1950s. It focused on the dynamics of the New England community's social stratification, ethnic composition, and economic base activities. The team studied such institutions as the factory, church, school, and local government. Using reputational analysis, the team identified a sixfold local social class system or socioeconomic system (SES), ranging from an upper-upper class of old family (2 percent) to a lower-lower class (25 percent). In a less well known follow-up urban case study of a camouflaged community dubbed Jonesville (Morris, Illinois), Warner's team did not find the upper-upper class and settled for a fivefold typology. *See also* CAMOUFLAGED CASE STUDY; CASE STUDY; MIDDLETOWN.

Significance   The Yankee City studies were among the pioneering empirical in-depth field studies inspired by anthropologically derived structural-functional analysis. As with the Middletown studies, which were headed by the Lynds, Warner's group tried unsuccessfully to mask the community's true identity. There are four traditions from this study that persist in contemporary urban social science analysis. First, the city is studied in depth, with information collected on a host of variables. Second, the city is studied over time to capture the dynamics of events, rather than using a snapshot approach. Third, a team is employed in order to collect diverse information. Fourth, the information is generalized so as to be useful in building overall theory. To some extent, the community must be a microcosm of the nation, typical of all communities. Specific theories derived from Yankee City have been refined further since the 1940s, yet the reputational analysis field technique continued to be employed into the 1970s by com-

munity power studies. The Jonesville follow-up study has been criticized as based on a biased, blue-ribbon community panel. Neither
Yankee City nor Jonesville was ever demonstrated to be typical, and
the modest population of each is not necessarily indicative of class and
ethnicity in the larger nearby primary cities of Boston or Chicago. The
Yankee City books were devoid of specific-policy case studies.

Suggested Reading
Stein, Maurice R. *The Eclipse of Community: An Interpretation of American Studies.*
    New York: Harper & Row, 1960. Chap. 3, "Lloyd Warner and Bureau-
    cratization in Yankee City."
Warner, W. Lloyd, ed. *Yankee City,* 1 vol., abridged ed. New Haven, CT: Yale
    University Press, 1963.
Warner, W. Lloyd, et al. *Democracy in Jonesville: A Study in Quality and Inequality.*
    New York: Harper, 1949.

Yonkers-Style Politics   A dominantly white New York City metropolitan suburb that was found guilty of perpetuating 40 years of
housing segregation but long refused to abide by an earlier agreed-
upon, binding court decree to accept low- and moderate-cost housing
for blacks and Hispanics. In 1988 Yonkers became a national symbol
of northern white defiance by refusing to end *de facto* racial housing
segregation. After receiving a 1984 bailout from the State of New
York, Yonkers went into state financial receivership by the Emergency
Financial Control Board when it was slapped with crippling, escalating
contempt-of-court fines by a federal judge of the Southern District of
New York. The judge presided over the protracted case for eight
years. He found there was racial intent to confine public housing to
one city area, thereby segregating public school attendance lines. In
the highly emotional theater of politics that followed the increasing
schedule of fines, two of the four opposition councilmembers refused
to budge until they actually saw the list of personnel who were to be
laid off unless they changed their votes to favor compliance. *See also DE
FACTO* SEGREGATION; *HILLS V. GAUTREAUX* ; SCATTER-SITE HOUSING.

Significance   Yonkers-style politics typifies emotional defiance of
federal court orders to integrate housing and hence public school
boundaries. As the fourth largest city in New York State, Yonkers had
carefully confined previous low- and moderate-income public housing so as to segregate blacks and Hispanics. After the 600-plus-page
judicial opinion chronicled this plan, a majority of four of the Yonkers
council reversed an earlier consent decree, bringing on crippling
fines, threatened layoffs, and ultimately bankruptcy. Opponents of
the recalcitrant council noted they wasted taxpayers' monies in a futile

effort. Professional planners acting as consultants acquiesced in the city's efforts at evasion by designing the *de facto* segregation effort, contrary to their professional code of ethics. Two of the seven city council members never did agree to the federal judge's plan, thus placing a higher premium on local constituent opinion than the supremacy of the national constitution.

Z

Zero Coupon Bond (ZCB)   A debt instrument that pays no interest until due date and is sold at a large discount relative to maturity value. Zero Coupon Bonds were first introduced by the private sector in 1981, coming to maturity in 1989. They sold at a deep enough discount that a compound rate of 14 percent interest yielded $1,000 at maturity. Municipalities soon entered the market with ZCBs that carried a lower yield than the private ZCBs but were more desirable, because owners were not taxed annually for the interest that was accruing but not being received. A second type of ZCB is called a *compound interest bond,* or municipal multiplier. This type of bond increases by some agreed-upon interest rate relative to its maturity every six months. For example, a bond at face value of $5,000 will increase every six months by 1.04 times the number of six-month intervals to surrender date. *See also* SINKING FUND.

Significance   Zero Coupon Bonds were introduced at the height of the high-interest cycle in the early 1980s because they attracted investors. The whole investment stays within the instrument for its entire life, and there is no reinvestment risk for buyers who might worry that they cannot capture that level again. The advantage to the municipality is no worry about coupon repayment schedules but only a single balloon payment. The investor's advantage in holding municipal ZCBs is exemption from federal income tax. The disadvantage is that a municipality may not set up a sinking fund to prepare for the payoff, and an investor might have to wait for the conclusion of municipal bankruptcy proceedings before being paid. If interest rates go down, cities want the right to redeem the bonds early, whereas investors do not want an early-call provision attached, because they want to lock in the rates for the life of the instrument.

Suggested Reading
Feldstein, Sylvan G., and Frank J. Fabozzi. "Zero Coupon Bonds." In Sylvan
G. Feldstein, Frank J. Fabozzi, and Irving M. Pollack, eds., *The Munici-
pal Bond Handbook,* Vol. II. Homewood, IL: Dow Jones–Irwin, 1983.
Chap. 24.

Zone, Urban   A formal or informal district characterized either by
common governmental, commercial, physical, or social features.
Some urban zones are recorded on published maps with demarcated
boundaries. Others are imprecise, informal designations. Land-use
zones are stipulated in ordinances and relate to building use and site
restrictions. Newspaper zones are area designations for parochial
news coverage and distribution. Sociological zones are distinguished
by types of buildings and the different categories of people who use
them, such as the central business district (CBD), upper-class residential zones (gold coast), and ethnic group enclaves (barrios and Chinatowns). Governmental zones include postal zip-code zones, police and
fire precincts, voting precincts, wards, and census tracts. *See also* UR-
BAN VILLAGE; ZONE OF TRANSITION; ZONED EDITION; ZONING, EUCLIDEAN.

Significance   Urban zones are an indication that the built environment is too complex to be grasped as a totality. Cities are understood
primarily by small-scale parts. Metropolitan areas are divided into
zones to accommodate better management and better understanding
of the urban areas' problems. The zones of a city are as varied as the
people using them. City retail sales territories are seldom the same for
any two products or companies. Geographers talk of zones of transition. Human ecologists talk of concentric zones. Only rarely do such
zones correspond with neighborhoods, communities, census tracts, or
subdivisions.

Suggested Reading
Weiss, Michael J. *The Clustering of America.* New York: Harper & Row,
1988.

Zone of Transition   An indefinite area of urban land peripheral to
the central business district (CBD) with lowered population density
and land values, exhibiting mixed commercial and noncommercial
land uses that change over time. The term *zone of transition* was coined
by E. W. Burgess in 1925 to describe the second zone in his concentric
theory. The zone is a buffer to the residential portions of the city that
exhibit less intensive land uses than those associated with the city core.

It is characterized by a succession of building uses. Most of the property is physically deteriorating. Part of the zone may be under active assimilation into the CBD, whereas other parts may be relatively static. Administratively the zone is an area of lowered public maintenance in comparison to the CBD. It is often located in a separate police and fire precinct because of different types or levels of crime and fire activity. Financially, it is an area where land values are changing, both deteriorating and improving, and tax collections are in arrears. Variances exist without formal approval. In a reversal of the CBD pattern, nighttime population exceeds daytime population. *See also* BLIGHT; CONCENTRIC ZONE MODEL; GENTRIFICATION; INVASION; MACHINE SPACE; SKID ROW; SLUM; URBAN RENEWAL.

Significance   The zone of transition describes a discontinuous and heterogeneous land-use belt near the central business district whose boundaries are unstable. The zone's human space has both itinerant housing and vital pockets of ethnic communities (Puerto Ricans and Chinese, e.g.) along with pockets of the underclass (skid row). More commonly the space is devoted to machines—parking lots, repair facilities, transportation terminals, electrical transforming equipment, and expressway interchanges. It is a characteristic North American urban space that represents a set of interrelated planning issues that differ from location to location and do not yield to a simple or uniform public policy.

Suggested Reading

Griffin, Donald W., and Richard E. Preston. "A Restatement of the 'Transition Zone' Concept." *Annals of the Association of American Geographers*, vol. 56, no. 2 (1966), pp. 339–350. (Review of the literature.)

Preston, Richard E. "A Detailed Comparison of Land Use in Three Transition Zones." *Annals of the Association of American Geographers*, vol. 58, no. 3 (1968), pp. 461–484.

Zoned Edition   A term used by journalists and marketing specialists to refer to any of two or more issues of a newspaper printed on the same day for different geographic areas. Within the same daily publication, zoned editions have different advertising and/or news accounts designed for different distribution. The concept is based on the assumption that not all readers have similar disposable income or interest in the same local news. This allows major metropolitan dailies, such as the *New York Times, Chicago Tribune,* and *Los Angeles Times,* to expand local coverage in order to compete better against the suburban weeklies and biweeklies. Suburban newspapers, such as the Lowell

(Massachusetts) *Sun* and the Michigan *Observer & Eccentric* chain, also break down their audience into subgroups, better to serve local interest in community announcements. *See also* COMMUNITY PRESS.

Significance   Zoned editions pinpoint audiences and permit mass-media newspapers, through automation, to package a more nearly "neighborhood" product. Newspapers accomplish this either by separate and well-defined local sections or different blends of page makeup. There are more than 1,800 suburban newspapers in the United States, with a total readership in excess of 23 million. These suburban papers often cater to a more affluent readership than the median readership profile of the big-city dailies. Yet these news sources often are overlooked by scholars because they are not *newspapers of record*; that is to say, publishers do not prepare a compilation of articles in bound index form available in libraries. Major dailies may not be eligible for promulgation of legal notices because they may not be acknowledged as papers of local general circulation. Because the last city edition of a daily newspaper is usually employed in preparing the index, many citations to page and column by scholars who use an earlier-deadline edition of newspapers are erroneous.

Zoning   The process by which general-purpose substate governments regulate land usage and occupancy. Zoning is accomplished by passage of an ordinance that establishes districts (zones) to promote the health, safety, morals, welfare, well-being, and occasionally aesthetics of the community. Inherently, a zoned district of real property has uniform requirements. Between zones land-use requirements differ. Zoning ordinances consist of definitions, specifications of district requirements, and one or more maps. Specifications, or performance standards, include such factors as lot size, setbacks, maximum buildable heights, and required number of parking spaces relative to floor space. Land that does not conform to a zoning ordinance is either issued a variance or is said to be out of compliance and subject to fine, stoppage of construction, or other government action. *See also* INVERSE CONDEMNATION; PLANNING, URBAN PHYSICAL; RESTRICTIVE COVENANT; *VILLAGE OF EUCLID V. AMBLER*; ZONING, EUCLIDEAN.

Significance   Zoning establishes laws of permitted and prohibited usages under the police power. It applies to specific lots, plats, and parcels. On the other hand, a master plan is an overall statement and is usually established by resolution of a city council or by planning commission promulgation. Zoning is a set of present restrictions. Physical planning forecasts where a community wants to be. Zoning prohibits and is current policy, whereas planning promotes and is prospective. Zoning refutes the maxim that a man's home is his castle and that he can do what he wishes therein. Under zoning an owner is governed by the maxim that one must use private property in a manner that does not injure others. The law of zoning is one of the major topics of local government jurisprudence. It is undergoing substantial review at all levels each year. Frequently, courts impose their zoning decisions on a city where there is a finding of overreaching or arbitrary action. To comport with court standards, zoning ordinances must not be arbitrary, must relate use to the topographic character of the land as well as the circulation pattern, and must fit into reasonable categories. The New Jersey courts have been especially active superintending land-use policy, substituting their ideas for local general-purpose governments. In 1927, the first impression case on zoning's constitutionality was decided by the U.S. Supreme Court in *Village of Euclid v. Ambler Realty Co.*, 272 U.S. 364 (1926). Since then a complex body of law has developed. Clearly, state statutes override substate zoning on group homes for the developmentally disabled. The Texas case of *Cleburne v. Cleburne Living Center*, 473 U.S. 432 (1985), established the rule nationally. In addition, local zoning ordinances are preempted by the Department of Interior Historic Designations for buildings declared part of the national heritage. The purpose of zoning includes restrictions on all property to prevent misuse, promotion of public policy, and protection of property values. The first village sanctioned to zone property, the village of Euclid, Ohio, was a bastion for wealthy residents. Not all cities have adopted zoning ordinances; two of the most notable are in Texas, namely Houston and Wichita Falls.

Suggested Reading

Babcock, Richard F. "Houston, Unzoned, Unfettered, and Mostly Unrepentant." *Planning*, vol. 48, no. 2 (1982), pp. 21–23.

Babcock, Richard F., and Charles L. Siemon. *The Zoning Game Revisited.* Boston: Oelgeschlager, Gunn & Hain, 1985. (Eleven case studies.)

Hartman, Robert J. "Beyond Invalidation: The Judicial Power to Zone." *Urban Law Annual*, vol. 9 (1975), pp. 159–177.

Makielski, S. J., Jr. *The Politics of Zoning: The New York Experience.* New York: Columbia University Press, 1966.

Rathkopf, Charles A., and Arden H. Rathkopf. *The Law of Zoning and Planning*, 5 vols., 4th ed. New York: Boardman Clark, 1977.

Zoning News. Chicago: American Planning Association. (A monthly publication.)

Zoning, Aesthetic   Regulating structures, individual buildings, and open spaces to achieve a pleasant visual quality. Aesthetics refers to that which is beautiful, leaves a positive visual impression, provides a pleasant ambience, and is in good taste. The term encompasses overall design as well as effective use of construction materials. Well-established standards of aesthetics include balance, spaciousness, and the preservation for the public of views of lakes, rivers, and open spaces. The courts have upheld cities in imposing setbacks, street beautification, height requirements, and general skyline appearance in order to promote light and circulating air for all parcels of property. The opposite of an aesthetic area is a blighted area. *See also* ARCHITECTURAL REVIEW BOARD; POLICE POWER; QUALITY OF LIFE; ZONING.

Significance   Aesthetic standards are a controversial issue in cities that use setbacks and height limits on skyscrapers, thereby reducing functional capacity. The question is whether a community has the right to curb land utilization by those in pursuit of extracting maximum rent. The U.S. Supreme Court supported the municipality's power to plan for continuity and beautification standards in *Brennan v. Parker,* 348 U.S. 26 (1954). Justice Douglas found for the community's right to demand spaciousness and well-balanced design. Aesthetic controls at the local level translate into design review and architectural review boards that look at a building's facade and its setting in the context of the adjacent urban profile. The American Institute of Architects (AIA) presents "onion awards" in some communities to developers that have built offensive projects. Architecture should be applied art. In an attempt to avoid low-quality work, communities impose review design and force compliance with generally accepted principles of art so as to preserve the integrity of the community. In a capitalist system with loose public controls, and in the absence of long-standing master plans, no U.S. city will uniformly be a community work of art in the style of Florence, Italy.

Suggested Reading
Redding, Martin J., Project Officer. *Aesthetics in Environmental Planning.* Washington Environmental Research Center, Office of Research and Development, U.S. Environmental Protection Agency. Washington, DC: Superintendent of Documents, November 1973. EP 1.23/3.600/5-73-009.
Whittick, Arnold. "Aesthetics." In Arnold Whittick, ed.-in-chief, *Encyclopedia of Urban Planning.* New York: McGraw-Hill, 1974, pp. 11 ff.

Zoning, Down-   Reclassification of land use to a more restrictive category. Examples of downzoning include changes from industrial to commercial use, from commercial to residential use, from residential to agricultural use, or from small-lot to large-lot requirements. Downzoning, through more stringent limitations on the number of allowable stories on buildings, was employed in the 1980s in San Francisco's and Seattle's central business districts (CBDs). Densely developed condominium property was zoned into an R-A single-family residential classification in Beverly Hills, Michigan. The obverse is *up-zoning*, that is, allowing denser development than previously. *See also* GROWTH MANAGEMENT; HIGHEST AND BEST USE; INVERSE CONDEMNATION; TAKING.

Significance   The major issue attached to downzoning is whether the state should pay affected property owners for the diminution of their property value. The oft-litigated question is whether land, once zoned, can be rezoned. The judicial answers are consistently affirmative. Downzoning is not inverse condemnation or a taking. Cities and villages must have a viable public-policy option of changing their master plan. A California supreme court case, *HFH, Ltd. v. Superior Court*, 542 P. 2d 273 (1975), summarizes common law in several states and finds that social needs interpreted by zoning decisions are free from the financial impact such decisions have, so long as owners do not hold a valid building permit under the old system. One of the techniques for managing growth is through downzoning substantial unbuilt parcels.

Suggested Reading
Northrup, Melinda. "Limiting Availability of Inverse Condemnation as a Landowner's Remedy for Downzoning." *Urban Law Annual*, vol. 13 (1977), pp. 263–275.

Zoning, Euclidean   A system of fixed land-use designations designed to manage growth and protect property values. It is named after the village of Euclid, Ohio, which was the first jurisdiction to receive U.S. Supreme Court sanction to regulate parcels by designating permitted land uses in *Village of Euclid v. Ambler Realty Co.*, 272 U.S. 365 (1926). General-purpose substate governments have authority under the police power to divide public and private land comprehensively into several districts or zones, within which there is to be uniform land use and among which there is to be variable use. The assumption is that the benefits of such restrictions extend to each site. They do not necessarily benefit the larger regional community. *See also* HIGHEST AND BEST USE; PLANNED UNIT DEVELOPMENT; *SOUTHERN BURLINGTON COUNTY NAACP V. MOUNT LAUREL.*

Significance   Euclidean zoning assumes that distinct areas within a community should develop either under an exclusive pattern or for a higher use than that which is permitted. Such categories cover public property, business, light and heavy industry, single-family residences, and more densely developed apartment complexes. Each district has a special use, the highest category being low-density, single-family unattached residences.

Suggested Reading
Siegan, Bernard H. *Land Use without Zoning.* Lexington, MA: Lexington Books, 1972. (The case for no zoning as exemplified by Houston.)

Zoning, Exclusionary   Land-use restrictions employed typically by high-status suburbs to bar entry by low- and moderate-income residences and all industry. Exclusionary zoning is also known as snob zoning. It originated with suburbs that wished to maintain the high character of their community by outlawing mobile homes, now more properly known as manufactured homes. Exclusionary zoning is a redundancy, because the purpose of all zoning is to restrict permitted functions. The R-1 land category is the most controversial, for this is the designation for the highest type of single-family dwelling. In the extreme, one city, Weston, Connecticut, was zoned entirely for detached residences. This situation was litigated in *Cadoux v. Planning & Zoning Commission,* 294 A. 2d 582 (1972). A city also may successfully exclude a single use, as in the case of San Francisco's ban on cemeteries. Seven other zoning devices are employed to achieve exclusionary zoning: (1) requiring single-family lots while concurrently outlawing apartments; (2) limiting the number of bedrooms so as to discourage families with children; (3) preventing mobile/manufactured homes; (4) mandating large lots; (5) requiring minimum building size, expressed in cubic feet; (6) regulating minimum frontage on a street; and (7) enforcing long setbacks. These practices shift the burden of more modest housing to other communities. The practice is a negative externality from the region's perspective and a positive internal control from the single city's vantage. Exclusionary rules taken individually are valid exercises of the local police power. *See also* CEMETERY; EXTERNALITY; *HILLS V. GAUTREAUX*; *SOUTHERN BURLINGTON COUNTY NAACP V. MOUNT LAUREL*; SUBURBANIZATION.

Significance   Exclusionary zoning produces racial and ethnic segregation as well as economic separation, because blacks, Hispanics, and many other Americans as groups have comparatively low socioeconomic status. Snob zoning has resulted in public housing ghettos. The U.S. Supreme Court addressed that problem in the Chicago scatter-site public housing case of *Hills v. Gautreaux.* Snob zoning produced by private housing segregation in wealthy suburbs has been addressed in many state courts, especially in the New Jersey supreme court cases of *Southern Burlington County NAACP v. Mount Laurel I* and *II*. When jobs leave the central city and the people cannot follow because of inadequate amounts of housing, low- and moderate-income workers must *reverse commute*, that is, travel from the central city to their employment in suburbs. Wealthy suburbs have ample tax base on which to collect revenue to fund the better-quality suburban public schools. Large-lot requirements produce a spread city or urban sprawl. This increases the costs of providing infrastructure. Snob zoning is employed as part of an antigrowth strategy to prevent newcomers from moving in.

Suggested Reading
Davidoff, Paul, and Mary E. Brooks. "Zoning Out the Poor." In Philip C. Dolce, ed., *Suburbia: The American Dream and Dilemma*. Garden City, NY: Doubleday, 1976, pp. 135–166.

Zoning, Flexible   Creation of open-ended land-use designations to be determined by negotiations between developers and a city administration in conjunction with the Zoning Board of Appeal (ZBA). The opposite of flexible zoning is fixed Euclidean zoning. Flexible zoning also is called Planned Unit Development (PUD), mixed-use zoning, performance-based zoning, floating zoning, and concomitant agreement zoning (CAZ). Rather than assuming an exclusive land use, flexible zoning stresses neighborhood compatibility, transit tie-ins, environmentally sensitive development, and the opportunities that arise in the market as economic factors change. The idea began in the 1950s. This relatively new form of zoning puts a premium on negotiation under the spirit of the law rather than literal legal compliance. Often, flexible zoning is granted for a project that meets a certain number of points on a scorecard. *See also* PLANNED URBAN DEVELOPMENT; ZONING, EUCLIDEAN.

Significance   To be eligible for flexible zoning, projects usually must be of a certain size, such as 20 acres or more. One form is called mixed-use zoning. It is most appropriate for convention sites, large offices with attached residential developments, or phased-growth industrial parks combined with light manufacturing. Modest-sized areas such as Buckingham Township, Pennsylvania, and Duxbury, Massachusetts, have experimented with mixed-use zoning. So too have major jurisdictions such as Washington, D.C., and St. Louis County, Missouri. A major advantage of this form of land planning is that it avoids the need to rezone parcels. Another advantage is that it accommodates new technology.

Suggested Reading

Brown, Jennifer G. "Concomitant Agreement Zoning: An Economic Analysis." *Land Use and Environmental Law Review,* vol. 17 (1986), pp. 183–210.
Frank, Michael J. "Performance Zoning." *Planning,* vol. 48, no. 11 (1982), pp. 21–24.
Meshenberg, Michael J. *The Administration of Flexible Zoning Techniques.* Report No. 318, Planning Advisory Service. Chicago: American Planning Association, 1975.
Porter, Douglas R. "Flexible Zoning: How It Works." *Urban Land* (April 1988), pp. 6–11.

Zoning, Inclusionary　　The concept and practice of creating a land-use plan that requires developers to build a certain number or percentage of low- or moderate-income dwellings in an area. Inclusionary zoning enables low-income families to live in previously exclusive high-income neighborhoods. Such zoning ordinances attempt to create a mixture of both classes and races in neighborhoods, thus addressing the problem of *de facto* segregation. *See also* DE FACTO SEGREGATION; *SOUTHERN BURLINGTON COUNTY NAACP V. TOWNSHIP OF MOUNT LAUREL* ; ZONING, EXCLUSIONARY.

Significance　　Inclusionary zoning regulations attempt to provide inducements for private developers to build low- or moderate-income residences. Legally sanctioned segregation and segregated living patterns have created many racially divided cities. In some, such as New York City, inclusionary zoning allows developers to build taller, more profitable, luxury apartments than traditional height regulations would allow; the *quid pro quo* would be the construction or renovation of low-income housing situated near the high-income building. In addition, cities such as Seattle have made housing linkage arrangements with developers to increase height restrictions on high-rise offices in exchange for developments in and around the buildings considered to be of public value. Such public-purpose developments include day-care centers, public courtyards, and atriums. The developer of Seattle's Washington Mutual building was allowed to add 13 stories over the city's height limit in exchange for a $2.5 million donation to preserve and build 196 units of downtown residential housing.

Suggested Reading

Hagman, Donald. "Taking Care of One's Own through Inclusionary Zoning: Bootstrapping Low- and Moderate-Income Housing." *Urban Law and Policy,* vol. 5 (1982), pp. 169–187.
Hill, Henry A. "Government Manipulation of Land Values To Build Affordable Housing: The Issue of Compensating Benefits." *Land Use and Environmental Law Review,* vol. 16 (1985), pp. 147–171.

Mallach, Alan. *Inclusionary Housing Programs*. New Brunswick, NJ: Center for Urban Policy Research, 1984.
Merriam, Dwight, et al., eds. *Inclusionary Zoning Moves Downtown*. Chicago: American Planners Press, 1985.

Zoning, Spot   The illegal creation of an arbitrary and unreasonable small-scale area of land use within a large-scale designated land plan. Spot zoning can invalidate the entire zoning ordinance when properly brought to judicial notice. It is to be distinguished from a *variance*, which is issued to a nonconforming land use by a zoning body or in blanket form to all out-of-sync parcels at the time of the ordinance's passage. A variance is created to preserve the zoning ordinance from judicial scrutiny so that the nonconforming use cannot be said to be a taking or an inverse condemnation. *See also* ULTRA VIRES ; ZONING.

Significance   Spot zoning is against the law *per se*. It is an inexact term subject to court interpretation of what constitutes small scale and what is reasonable justification. Plaintiffs in a spot-zoning case challenging a municipal land classification as unreasonable argue the jurisdiction acted *ultra vires*, that is to say, beyond the scope of its legitimate authority. The policy judgment of the local legislature is thus subject to judicial second-guessing.

Zoning Classification   Designations within a land-use ordinance for categories of permitted or prohibited activity and occupancy. Zoning classification designations are as diverse as cities in the United States. Under conventional Euclidean zoning, the classes are relatively few. They contain such designations as:

AP	Agricultural-Preservation
B	Business
C	Commercial
FP	Floodplain
I	Industrial
IP	Industrial Park
O	Office
P	Parking
PP	Public Park
R	Residential

Under flexible zoning, classifications cannot be fixed on a map, as they are a function of negotiation between developer and city administration.

Significance   Zoning classification is relatively simple for small suburban communities. A suburb of 12,000 might get by with 5 uses where industry is excluded. Larger suburbs of 100,000 may have only 15 classes, although residential uses may be broken down into 5 residential subcategories relative to density and height requirements. New York City has ten classes of residential use alone. It is conventional for zoning classifications not to take into account adjacent jurisdictional land uses. Total reclassification review takes place anywhere from every 25 to 50 years. Such projects are conducted by both in-house staff and consultants. Especially important in the 1990s are the innovations caused by the creation of new industrial and research parks. It is common for variances to account for 1–10 percent of the total acreage under classification.

Suggested Reading

Meshenberg, Michael J. *The Language of Zoning: A Glossary of Words and Phrases.* Report No. 322, Planning Advisory Service. Chicago: American Society of Planning Officials, 1976.

INDEX

A-95 Review, 3–4, 96, 192, 280
AAA. *See* American Arbitration Association
Abandonment, 4–5
Abrogation, 5–6
abu-Lughod, Janet, 117
ACIR. *See* Advisory Commission on Intergovernmental Relations
ACORN. *See* Association of Community Organizations for Reform Now
ACTION. *See* American Council To Improve Our Neighborhoods
ACWU. *See* Amalgamated Clothing Workers Union
ACYF. *See* Administration for Children, Youth, and Families
Ad hoc body, 6–7
Ad valorem, 7, 25–27, 498
Administration for Children, Youth, and Families (ACYF), 238
Adult entertainment, zoning, 106
Adult foster-care home, 231–232
Adult-only community, 7–8
Advisory Commission on Intergovernmental Relations (ACIR), 8–9, 85, 282
AEC. *See* Atomic Energy Commission
AEI. *See* American Enterprise Institiue for Public Policy Research
AFDC. *See* Aid to Families with Dependent Children
AFDC-UP. *See* Aid to Families with Dependent Children–Unemployed Parent
Affirmative-action programs, 9–11
AFL-CIO. *See* American Federation of Labor–Congress of Industrial Organizations
Afro-American press. *See* Black press
AFSCME. *See* American Federation of State, County and Municipal Employees

Agenda setting, 11–13
AHA. *See* American Hospital Association
AIA. *See* American Institute of Architects
AICPA. *See* American Institute of Certified Public Accountants
Aid to Families with Dependent Children (AFDC), 13–14, 246, 409, 568, 571
Aid to Families with Dependent Children–Unemployed Parent (AFDC-UP), 13
Aid to Impacted Areas program, 282
AIP. *See* American Institute of Planners
Air Pollution Clean Air Act, 185
Air Quality Act, 185
Air rights, 14, 72
Airports, 9, 405
Alabama, 12, 19, 21, 195, 442, 494
    taxation, 499, 502
    See also various cities
Alameda County (CA), 40
Alaska, 18, 34, 54, 158, 272, 462, 499.
    See also Anchorage
Albuquerque, 543
Alcohol, Drug Abuse, and Mental Health Administration, 245
Alderman, 14–15
Alinsky, Saul, 12, 359, 373
Allegheny County Industrial Development Authority, 298
Allegheny Pittsburgh Coal Company v. County Commission of Webster County, West Virginia, 27
Allentown (PA), 544
Almonaster-Michoud Industrial Corridor, 375
Alternative school, 15–16
Amalgamated Clothing Workers Union (ACWU), 250
Amenities, 16

American Arbitration Association
  (AAA), 23, 328, 436
American Council To Improve Our
  Neighborhoods (ACTION), 17
American Enterprise Institute (AEI) for
  Public Policy Research, 515
American Federation of
  Labor–Congress of Industrial
  Organizations (AFL-CIO), 17
American Federation of State, County
  and Municipal Employees
  (AFSCME), 17–18
American Hospital Association (AHA),
  98
American Institute of Architects (AIA),
  63, 582
American Institute of Certified Public
  Accountants (AICPA), 456
American Institute of Planners (AIP),
  387, 393
American Institute of Real Estate
  Appraisers, 22
American Insurance Association
  National Building Code, 61
American Municipal Association. See
  National League of Cities
American Planning Association, 103
American Society of Appraisers (ASA),
  22
American Society of Public
  Administration (ASPA), 103
American Society of Real Estate
  Counselors, 22
American Statistical Index (ASI), 162
America's Housing Needs: 1970 to 1980,
  289–290
Amsterdam News Weekly (newspaper), 45
Anaheim (CA), 492
Anchorage, 129, 369, 544
Anchorage Borough, 129
Annexation, 18–19, 58, 160, 195
Antiquities Act, 242
Antirecession fiscal assistance, 20
Anton, Thomas J., 161
Apartheid, 20–21
Apartments, condominium conversion,
  126, 250
Appraisal, 21–22
  vs. assessment, 26
Arbitration, 22–24
Architectural review board, 24–25
Archives, clearinghouse, 96
Argins v. City of Tiburon, 286
Arizona, 8, 134, 441, 492. *See also*
  various cities, towns
Arkansas, 38, 498
  school districts, 36–37, 272
  See also various cities, towns

Arlington County (VA), 350
Army Corps of Engineers, 25, 274, 378,
  389
ASA. *See* American Society of
  Appraisers
Ashtabula (OH), 418
ASI. *See* American Statistical Index
ASPA. *See* American Society of Public
  Administration
Assessment, 25–27
  appeals, 48–49
  vs. appraisal, 21–22
*Associated Home Builders of Greater East
  Bay, Inc., v. City of Walnut Creek,* 316
Association of Community Organizations
  for Reform Now (ACORN), 12,
  27–28, 373
Association of University Related
  Research Parks, 379
At-large election, 28–29
Atlanta (GA), 16, 76, 284, 543
  case study of, 66, 69, 450
  politics, 93, 365, 395
Atomic Energy Commission (AEC), 361
Audit, 29
Auditor, 30
Authority
  ad hoc, 7
  public, 30–31
Avery v. Midland County, Texas, 440
Ayer Directory of Publications, 97

Bachrach, Peter, 396
Baker v. Carr, 439–440
Balanced ticket, 32–33
Balkanization, 33–34, 296, 489
Ballot, short, 34–35, 445
Baltimore, 29, 157 (table), 326, 329, 350,
  496, 543
  housing, 229, 540
Banfield, Edward C., 35, 189, 538
Banfield thesis, 35–36
Bankruptcy, 208–209
  academic, 36–37
  municipal, 37–38
Bankruptcy Reform Act, 37
Baratz, Morton, 396
Barrio, 39
Barron v. Baltimore, 286
Barry, Marion S., 567
BART. *See* Bay Area Rapid Transit
Baton Rouge, 129
Battlement Mesa (CO), 362
Bay Area Rapid Transit (BART), 39–40,
  274
BBBs. *See* Better Business Bureaus
Beame, Abe, 341
Bedroom communities, 404

Bedroom suburb, 40
Bell, Daniel, 406–407
Bellaire (TX), 181
Beltway, 41
Benign neglect, 41–42
Berkeley (CA), 43, 369
Better Business Bureaus (BBBs), 228
Beverly Hills (CA), 181
Beverly Hills (MI), 583
Bilandic, Michael A., 12
Bilingual Education Act, 188–189
Biological fallacy, 42
Birmingham (AL), 496
Black, Hugo, 440
Black American (newspaper), 45
Black Executive Exchange, 354
Black Panthers, 43
Black power, 43–44
Black press, 44–45
Black United Fund (BUF), 114–115, 178
Blackmun, Harry, 353
Blacks, 39, 42, 138, 179, 354
    education, 103–104
    housing, 47–48, 198, 207, 251
Bledsoe, Timothy, 69
Blight, 46–47. See also Slum
Bliss, Ray C., 47
Bliss thesis, 47
Block grant. See Community
    Development Block Grant
Blockbusting, 47–48
Blue Cross, 79
Board of Aldermen, 15
Board of Assessment appeal, 48–49
Board of Education, 49–50
Board of Estimate of the City of New York v.
    Morris, 440
Board of Regents, University of California,
    Davis v. Bakke, 10
BOCA. See Building Officials and Code
    Administrators International, Inc.;
    Building Officials Conference of
    America Basic Building Code
BOCA Basic Building Code, 62
Boise City (ID), 544
Bollens, John C., 526
Bond, municipal, 50–51, 53, 208, 471,
    577
Bond and rating services, 51–52
Bond election, 52–53
Bond types, 269–270
    industrial revenue, 272–273
    moral-obligation, 337
    revenue improvement, 455–456
Book of the States, 441
Borough, 53–54
Borrowing limit, 54–55
Boss, 55–56

Boston, 72, 84, 106, 197, 329, 339, 379,
    442, 519, 526, 543
    housing, 126, 251, 448
    politics, 93, 326, 566
    transportation, 284, 520
Boston Massacre, 457
Boulder (CO), 233, 418
Boulder City (NV), 361
Boundary, 56–57
Bounded cities, types of, 57–58
Bourne, L. S., 174
Bowen, Bruce, 161
Bowery, 473
Bradley, Tom, 325
Branti v. Finkel, 382
Brennan, William, 217
Brennan v. Parker, 582
Brenner, Clifford, 15
Bridgeport (CT), 544
Bristol (PA), 306
Broadacre City, 16, 58–59, 371, 393
Brookings Institution, 515
Brooklyn (OH), 71
Brown v. Board of Education of Topeka,
    Kansas, 59–60, 63, 147, 159, 257,
    279, 346, 463
Brownstown Township (MI), 460
Bryan v. Koch, Mayor of the City of New
    York, 98
Buckingham Township (PA), 585
Bucklin preferential voting plan, 418
Budget types, 60–61
Budgets, control, 54–55
BUF. See Black United Fund
Buffalo (NY), 20, 428
Building codes, 61–62, 102, 367
    manufactured homes, 316–317
Building Officials and Code
    Administrators International, Inc.
    (BOCA), 62, 63, 367
Building Officials Conference of
    America (BOCA) Basic Building
    permit, 62–63
Buildings, 80
    abandonment, 4–5
    regulations, 24, 278
Bullet voting, 394
Bureau of Construction Code, 61
Bureau of Labor Statistics, 132
Bureau of Outdoor Recreation, 378
Bureau of the Budget, 3
Bureau of the Census, 72–74, 249, 332,
    530
Burger, Warren, 52
Burgess, Ernest W., 76, 83, 125, 126, 578
Burnham, Daniel H., 89, 90
Bush, George, 47, 275, 355, 468, 492,
    568

Business, 94, 421, 431
  incubators, 270–271
Busing, 59, 63–64, 104, 147
Byrne, Jane, 12

CAAs. *See* Community Action Agencies
Cable franchise, 65–66
CADD. *See* Computer-Aided Design and
  Drafting, 300
Cadoux v. Planning & Zoning Commission,
  584
California, 39, 65, 77, 277, 316, 448, 479,
  483, 492, 571
  exaction policy, 19, 268
  schools, 272, 428
  special purpose units, 72–73
  taxation, 419–420, 502, 509, 510, 513
  See also various cities, counties, towns
Calvert County (MD), 197
Cambridge (MA), 418, 446, 543
Camouflaged case studies, 66, 334
Camp Dearborn (MI), 196
Canada, 42, 174, 298
CAP. *See* Community Action Program
Cape Cod (MA), 233
Capital expenditure, 67–68
Caplow, Theodore, 66
Caretaker government, 68
Carlisle (MA), 197
Carmichael, Stokley, 44
Carter, Jimmy, aid to cities, 20, 267,
  355, 509, 539, 541
Case study, 66, 68–70, 152
Cass corridor, 473
Categorical grant, 70–71
Cato Institute, 515
Catt, Carrie Chapman, 304
CATV. *See* Community Antennae
  Television
CBD. *See* Central business district
CDBG. *See* Community Development
  Block Grant
CEA. *See* Council of Economic Advisors
CED. *See* Committee for Economic
  Development
Cemetery, 71–72
Census of Governments, 33–34, 72–73
Census of Housing, 73, 74, 249
Census of Population, 73–75
Census of Retail Trade, 76
Census tract, 75
Central Atlanta Progress, 76
Central business district (CBD), 14,
  75–77, 404, 464
  zone of transition, 578–579
Central city, 77–78
Central county, 77
Centralized purchasing, 78

CEQ. *See* Council on Environmental
  Quality
Certificate of need (CON), 79–80
Certificate of occupancy (CO), 80
CES. *See* Consumer Expenditure Survey
CETA. *See* Comprehensive Employment
  and Training Act
CHA. *See* Chicago Housing Authority
Chamber of Commerce, 81
CHAP. *See* Comprehensive Homeless
  Assistance Plan
Charity, 177
Charlotte (NC), school segregation,
  63–64
Charlottesville (VA), 544
Charter, 81–82
Chicago, 12, 14, 16, 19, 77, 84, 114, 116,
  128, 136, 150, 157 (table), 180, 223,
  236, 274, 339, 357, 373, 472, 505,
  529, 543, 551
  housing, 4, 198, 240, 246, 252, 254,
    261, 474
  mass transit, 322, 520
  newspapers, 44–45
  political organization, 15, 382, 566
  politics, 55, 93, 547
Chicago Housing Authority (CHA), 240,
  424
Chicago Police Riot, 457
Chicago School of Urban Sociology,
  83–84
Chicanos, 39. *See also* Hispanics
Children, housing, 7, 8
Chinatown, 84–85
Chrysler Corporation, 356, 429
Churches, self-insurance, 465
Cicero (IL), 452
CIJE. *See* Current Index to Journals in
  Education
Cincinnati, 181, 418, 496
Circuit breaker, 85
Circulation plan, 85–86
Cities, 4, 16, 42, 76, 88–89, 143, 148, 219
  annexation, 18–19
  bonds, 51–52
  borrowing limits, 54–55
  boundaries, 56–57
  bounded, 57–58
  central, 77–78
  charters, 81–82
  classification, 90–91
  concentric zone model, 125–126, 300
  decentralization, 149–150
  federal assistance, 20, 164
  planning, 89–90
  postindustrial, 406–407
  reapportionment, 439–440
  services, 295–296

The Citizen (newspaper), 116
Citizen advisory board, 86–87
Citizen advisory committees, 324
Citizen-initiated contacting, 87–88
Citizens Research Council, 515
Citizens to Preserve Overton Park v. Volpe, 284
City Beautiful, 89–90
City classification, 90–91
City council, 91–92, 327, 446
  at-large elections, 28–29
  organization of, 14–15
City Limits, 411
City manager, 92–93, 141
City of Canton, OH v. Harris, 343
City of Lafayette v. Louisian Power & Light Co., 343
City of Mobile v. Bolden, 561
City of Pleasant Grove v. United States, 19
City of Richmond v. J. A. Croson Co., 10, 467–468
City political profile, 93–94
Ciudad Juarez, 525
Civic association, 94–95, 436
Civil Rights Act, 147, 188, 347, 429, 443
  Title VIII, 7, 198–199, 252, 438
Civil Rights Commission, 438
Civil rights movement, 43, 127, 346, 354
  housing, 251–252
  organization of, 347–348
Civil Service, 445
Civil Service Reform Act, 281
Civil Works Program, 25
Civilian Conservation Corps, 68
Clark, Kenneth B., 279
Clark, Mamie, 279
Clark, Mark, 43
Clark, Terry, 69, 122, 123, 544
Clean Air Act, 185
Clean Air Act Amendments, 185
Clean Water Act, 185
Clearinghouse, 95–97, 312
Clearwater (FL), 196
Cleaver, Eldrige, 43
Cleburne v. Cleburne Living Center, 231–232, 581
Clerk, 97–98
Cleveland, 79, 181, 326, 418, 446, 496, 520, 559
  municipal bankruptcy, 38, 209
Closings
  hospital, 98–99
  plant, 99–101
  school, 101–102
CMSA. *See* Consolidated Metropolitan Statistical Area
CO. *See* Certificate of occupancy
Coalition on Temporary Shelter (COTS), 248

Code enforcement, 102
Codes
  clean up, 6
  housing, 255
Codes of ethics, 102–103
COG. *See* Council of governments
COLA. *See* Cost-of-living adjustment
Coleman, James S., 103
Coleman Report, 103–105
Coleman Young v. American Mini Theatres II, 106
Collective bargaining, 105–107
Colorado, 73, 268, 328. *See also* various cities, towns
Columbia (MD), 323, 362
Columbia (SC), 123
Columbia University, 175
Columbus (GA), 129
Columbus Board of Education v. Penick, 64
Combat zone, 106–107
Commercial strip development, 107–108
Commission plan, 108–109
Commissions, *ad hoc*, 6
Committee, *ad hoc*, 6
Committee for Economic Development (CED), 109, 515
Common Cause, 95
Communities, 109–111
  adult-only, 7–8
  ethnic, 84
  planning, 58–59
Community Action Agency (CAA), 324
Community Action Program (CAP), 111–112, 173, 324, 564
Community Antennae Television (CATV), 65
Community control, 112–113
Community Development Block Grant (CDBG), 113–114, 156, 158, 159, 248, 255, 259, 271, 332, 349, 540
Community Disaster Loans, 163
Community Dispute Services, 328
Community Fact Books, 114–115
Community Mental Health Centers Act, 154, 232
Community of limited liability, 115
Community power, case studies of, 66, 69. *See also* Pluralism; Reputational analysis
Community Power Structure, 450
Community press, 116
Community Reinvestment Act, 116–117, 244
Community Service Agency, 565
Commuting, zone of, 146
Comparative urban analysis, 117–118
  demographic, 118–119
  economic, 119–120

Comparative urban analysis, *(cont.)*
  geographic, 120–121
  historic, 121–122
  political, 122–123
  sociological, 123–124
Competency Based Education Action
    Act (Arkansas), 36–37
Competitive bid, 124
Comprehensive Employment and
    Training Act (CETA), 124–125,
    246, 288
Comprehensive Health Planning Act, 79
Comprehensive Homeless Assistance
    Plan (CHAP), 247
Comptroller, 30
Comptroller general, 29, 30
Comptroller of the Currency, 117, 243
Computer-Aided Design and Drafting
    (CADD), 300
CON. *See* Certificate of need
Concentric zone model, 125–126, 300
Conciliation, 22–23
Condemnation, inverse, 286
Condominium conversion, 126
Condominiums, 249–250
Congress of Racial Equality (CORE), 127
Connecticut, 54, 519. *See also* various
    cities, counties, towns
Conservancy, land, 300–301
Conservator (newspaper), 44–45
Consolidated Metropolitan Statistical
    Area (CMSA), 127–128, 332, 333
Consolidation, 128–130
Constitutional Convention, 204
Constitutions
  definitions in, 152–153
  state, 130–131
Consuetude, 5
Consultant, local government, 131–132
Consumer Expenditure Survey (CES), 249
Consumer Price Index (CPI), 79,
    132–133, 336
Contra Costa County (CA), 40
Contracting out, 133–134
Contractors, minority-owned, 10
Contracts, public, 422–423
Control Data Corporation, 311
Controller, 134–135
Conurbation, 135–136, 174
Cook County (IL), 479
Cook County Forest Preserve (IL), 305
Cooperatives, 250–251
Copper Canyon, 136
Coproduction, 136–137
CORE. *See* Congress of Racial Equality
Corporation counsel, 137–138
Corporations
  government, 31
  self-insurance, 465

Corruption, government, 138–140
Cost-benefit analysis, 140–141
Cost-of-living adjustment (COLA), 133
COTS. *See* Coalition on Temporary
    Shelter
Council Bluffs (IA), 525
Council for International Urban Liaison,
    471
Council-manager government, 141–142
Council of Economic Advisors (CEA), 564
Council of governments (COG), 34,
    142–143, 333
  A-95 review, 3, 96, 192
  role, 86, 263, 275, 300, 312, 345, 350,
    389
Council of State Governments (CSG), 8,
    352, 425
Council on Environmental Quality, 183,
    184, 186
Counselors of Real Estate (CRE), 22
Counterurbanism, 143–144
Counties, charters, 81–82
County administrator, 144
Courts
  housing, 260–261
  juvenile, 291
  municipal, 342
CPI. *See* Consumer Price Index
CPS. *See* Current Population Survey
CRE. *See* Counselors of Real Estate
Crime, 144–145
CSG. *See* Council of State Governments
Culver City (CA), 181
Current Index to Journals in Education
    (CIJE), 175
Current Population Report, 249
Current Population Survey (CPS), 249,
    569

Dade County (FL), 467
Dahl, Robert A., 69, 122, 371, 450
  on pluralism, 394–395
Daily urban commute (DUC), 404
Daily urban system (DUS), 146, 521
Daley, Richard J., 55, 325, 547
Dallas, 77, 141, 157 (table), 181, 195,
    365, 465, 469
Danville (IL), 28
DAS. *See* Detroit Area Study
Data bases, 96, 162, 174–175, 308,
    311–312
Davenport (IA), 525
Davidson (TN), 129
Davidson County (TN), 129, 533, 544
Dayton (OH), 64, 92, 284
Dayton Board of Education v. Brinkman, 64
Dayton County (OH), 369
DDA. *See* Downtown Development
    Authority

De facto segregation, 147, 576
De jure segregation, 147–148
Dearborn (MI), 129, 196, 506
Dearborn Towers, 196
Debt, municipal, 51–52, 148–149,
     470–471
Debt limit, local, 149
Decentralization, 149–150, 489
Deconcentration, 489
Dedication, 150–151
Defender (newspaper), 45
Definition
     operational, 151–152
     sources of, 152–154
Deinstitutionalization, 154–155
Delaware, 328, 392. *See also* Wilmington
Democratic party, 32, 78
Demography, 118
Demonstration Cities and Metropolitan
     Development Act, 155–156
Density, urban, 156–158
Denver, 76, 129, 492, 543
     annexation, 19, 161
     political organization, 326, 365
Denver County, 129
Department of Agriculture, 177–178,
     377
Department of Commerce, 72, 73, 100
Department of Defense, 25, 247, 356
Department of Education, 247
Department of Health and Human
     Services (HHS), 90, 238, 247
Department of Health, Education and
     Welfare (HEW), 79
Department of Housing and Urban
     Development (HUD), 156, 158–159,
     193, 227, 246, 247, 255, 257, 269,
     356, 378, 424, 543
     local program review, 259–260
     programs, 203, 250, 264, 447, 540
     regulations, 8, 198, 316
Department of Justice, 252
     bounded cities, 58
Department of Labor, 100, 247
Department of the Interior, 241, 377,
     378
Department of Transportation (DOT),
     227, 283
Department of Veterans Affairs (VA),
     224, 247, 262
     manufactured homes, 316–317
Depressed area, 159
Depressed Areas Act, 159
Depression, 534
     capital projects, 67–68
     housing, 202, 203, 204
Derogation, 5
Desegregation, 159–160. *See also* Busing;
     Segregation

Desuetude, 5
Detachment, 160–161
Detroit, 72, 77, 145, 146, 150, 157
     (table), 176, 181, 197, 207, 269, 322,
     345, 375, 525, 405, 441, 470, 473,
     496, 529, 551, 568
     ethnic groups, 84, 116
     government organization, 117, 142, 532
     health services, 79, 98
     housing, 248, 251
     mortgage subsidies, 5, 260
     newspapers, 45, 290
     Poletown in, 397–398, 437, 447
     political organization, 32, 93, 365, 369
     riots, 292, 457
     zoning, 106, 443
Detroit Area Study (DAS), 123, 161–162
Development, exaction fees, 190–191
Development, 375
DIALOG, 162, 312
El Diario (newspaper), 188
Dillon, John F., 162
Dillon's Rule, 36, 162–163, 341, 528
Directories, 97
Disaster area, 159
Disaster designation, 163–164
Disaster Relief Act, 164
Disasters, 12, 201–202
Discrimination, 10, 160, 429, 552
     affirmative action and, 10–11
     housing, 198, 251–252
Disincorporation, 160
Disinvestment, urban, 164–165,
     550–551
Displacement, 165–166
Divestment, 166–167, 443, 472
Domhoff, G. William, 69
DOT. *See* Department of Transportation
Douglas, William O., 199, 582
Downsizing, 157
Downtown. *See* Central business district
Downtown Development Authority
     (DDA), 167, 426
Doxiadis, Constantinos A., 153, 174, 176
Drake, St. Clair, 83
DUC. *See* Daily urban commute
Ducks Unlimited, 301
Duluth (MN), 100
Duncan, Otis Dudley, 371
Durham (NC), 544
DUS. *See* Daily urban system
Dusch v. Davis, 440
Duval County (FL), 129, 533
Duxbury (MA), 585
Dye, Thomas R., 167, 488
Dye thesis, 167–169

Earmarked fund, 170
Easement, 170–171

East Baton Rouge Parish, 129
East Coast Ministry of Self-defense, 43
East Los Angeles, 39
East Moline (IL), 525
East Saginaw (MI), 129
East St. Louis, 525
Ebony (magazine), 45
Economic base analysis, 171
Economic development, 172
Economic Development Administration
    for Community and Business
    Development, 100
Economic Development Corporations,
    564
Economic Opportunity Act, 173, 227,
    238, 288, 564
Economic Recovery Tax Act, 241, 242
Economics, supply-side, 492–493
Economy, 118
    trends in, 132–133
    urban political, 545–546
Ecorse (MI), 442
Ecumenopolis, 174
Edison, Thomas A., 379
Education, 227
    alternative, 15–16
    bilingual, 188–189
    minorities, 103–104, 238–239
    public, 462–463
    See also School board; School district;
    Schools
Educational Resources Information
    Center (ERIC), 96, 162, 173–174,
    312
EHAP. *See* Experimental Housing
    Allowance Program
EIS. *See* Environmental Impact
    Statement
Eisenhower, Dwight D., 283
Ekistics, 175–176
El Paso, 93, 525
Elazar, Daniel, 117, 122
Eldersveld, Samuel J., 161
Elections
    at-large, 28
    balanced tickets, 32–33
    bond, 52–53
    nonpartisan, 364–365
    proportional representation, 418
    recall, 440–441
    reform, 445–446
    short ballots, 34
    types of, 176–177
Eleemosynary group, 177–178
Elkin, Stephen, 548
Elmtown, 66
Elmwood Place (OH), 180
Elrod v. Burns, 382

Embry, Robert, 539
Emergency Employment Act of 1971,
    178–179
Emergency evacuation, 179–180
Emergency Relief Act, 361
The Emerging Republican Majority, 491
Eminent domain, 180
Employees
    public, 105, 423–424
    transfer of, 281
Employment
    federal act, 178–179
    public service, 125
    training for, 124–125
Employment and Securities Commission,
    100
Employment and Training (ET)
    program, 571
Enclave, 180–181
Endorsement, municipal political,
    181–182
Enforcement, date, 182
Enfranchisement, 214
English as a Second Language (ESL),
    188
Enterprise zone, 159, 182–183
Environmental Impact Statement (EIS),
    183–184, 185, 267, 389
Environmental legislation, 185–186
Environmental Protection Agency (EPA),
    185, 477, 483
EPA. *See* Environmental Protection
    Agency
Equal Credit Opportunity Act, 443
Equality of Educational Opportunity, 103
ERIC. *See* Educational Resources
    Information Center
ESL. *See* English as a Second Language
ET. *See* Employment and Training
    program
Ethnic group, 32, 84, 95, 186–187
Ethnic media, 187–188
Ethos theory, 189–190
ETJ. *See* Extraterritoral jurisdiction
Euclid (OH), 299–300, 581
*Evaluation, Review, and Coordination of
    Federal and Federally Assisted Programs
    and Projects*, 3
Evanston (IL), 236, 379
Ex officio, 190
Exaction, 190–192, 268
Executive Order 11063, 252
Executive Order 11365, 292
Executive Order 12350, 541
Executive Order 12372, 3–4, 96, 192
Executive Orders, 10
Exhaustion of administrative remedies,
    193

Experimental Housing Allowance
    Program (EHAP), 193–194
Expressways, 283–284
Externality, 194–195
Extraterritorial jurisdiction (ETJ),
    195–196
Extraterritorial power, 195–196
Exurbia, 196–197

FACE. *See* Federally Assisted Code
    Enforcement
Factories. *See* Plants
Facts on File, 162
FAH. *See* Federation of American
    Hospitals
Fair Housing Amendments Act, 7, 8
Fair Housing Title, 198, 252
Fair Labor Standards Act, 217, 352, 353
Fairfax County (VA), 233, 350
Fairfield County (CT), 196
Falls Township (PA), 306
Family, 7, 8, 13, 199–200
Fannie Mae. *See* Federal National
    Mortgage Association
Fargo (ND), 525
Farmer, James, 127
Farmers Home Administration (FmHA),
    540
Fayette County (KY), 129
FBI. *See* Federal Bureau of Investigation
FCB. *See* Fiscal Control Board
FCC. *See* Federal Communications
    Commission
Federal Aid Highway Act, 283
Federal aid to impacted areas, 200–201
Federal Bureau of Investigation (FBI),
    43, 96, 144
Federal Communications Commission
    (FCC), 65, 431
Federal Deposit Insurance Corporation
    (FDIC), 243
Federal Emergency Management
    Agency (FEMA), 163, 164, 179,
    201–202, 246, 247, 458, 474
    planning, 388, 389
Federal Highway Administration, 283
Federal Home Loan Bank Board, 117
Federal Home Loan Mortgage
    Corporation (FHLMC), 202,
    203–204, 262
Federal Housing Administration (FHA),
    158, 202–203, 224, 455
    loans, 251, 262, 443
    manufactured homes, 316–317
Federal Impacted Areas Aid Act,
    200–201
Federal Insurance Administration, 201
Federal Magnet School Grants, 315

Federal Mediation and Conciliation
    Service, 328
Federal National Mortgage Association,
    (FNMA), 203–204, 262, 436
Federal National Mortgage Charter Act,
    203
Federal Regional Councils, 3
Federal Reserve Board, 117, 208, 243
Federal Security Agency, 200
Federal Tax Reform Act, municipal
    bonds, 50, 53
Federal Water Pollution Control Act,
    185
Federalism, 204–206
    fiscal, 209–210
Federally Assisted Code Enforcement
    (FACE), 206, 260
Federation of American Hospitals
    (FAH), 98
Fees
    exaction, 190–191, 268
    user, 555
FEMA. *See* Federal Emergency
    Management Agency
FHA. *See* Federal Housing
    Administration
FHLMC. *See* Federal Home Loan
    Mortgage Corporation
Filtering theory, housing, 206–208
*First English Evangelical Lutheran Church
    of Glendale v. County of Los Angeles,*
    233, 338
Fiscal Control Board (FCB), 341
Fiscal crisis, 208–209
Fiscal federalism, 209–210
Fiscal year (FY), 210
Flast v. Cohen, 512
Flint (MI), 119
Floods, 201
Florida, 8, 272, 277, 323, 328
    impact analysis, 267, 268
    taxation, 498, 502, 513
    See also various cities, counties, towns
Flower Mound (TX), 362
Fluoridation politics, 210–211
FmHA. *See* Farmers Home
    Administration
FNMA. *See* Federal National Mortgage
    Association
FOIA. *See* Freedom of Information Act
Food Stamps, 568
Ford, Gerald, 188
Fordson (MI), 129
Forecast, 212–213
Foreign trade zone (FTZ), 213–214
Forest Park (IL), 362
Fort Halifax Packing Co. v. Coyne, 100
Fort Lauderdale, 427

Fort Worth, 145, 328, 543
Foster Grandparents, 560
Fragmentation. *See* Balkanization
Franchise
    elective, 214–215
    government, 215–216
Freddie Mae. *See* Federal Home Loan
    Mortgage Corporation
Freedom of Information Act (FOIA),
    216
Freedom rides, 127
Freeways, 284
Frothingham v. Mellon, 512
FTZ. *See* Foreign trade zone
Fullilove v. Klutznick, 467
Funds, earmarked, 170
FY. *See* Fiscal year

GA. *See* General Assistance
GAIN. *See* Greater Avenues to
    Independence
Galbraith, John Kenneth, 275
Gale Directory of Publications, 97
Gallaher, Art, Jr., 66
Galveston, 108
GAO. *See* General Accounting Office
*Garcia v. San Antonio Metropolitan Transit
    Authority*, 217, 352, 353
Garden city, 217–218, 361
Garland (TX), 544
Gautreaux v. Chicago Housing Authority,
    461–462
Geddes, Patrick, 153, 174
General Accounting Office (GAO), 29, 30
General Assistance (GA), 409
General Electric, 391
General Motors, 397, 437, 447
General Revenue Sharing (GRS),
    218–219
Gentrification, 207, 219–221, 242–243,
    490
Georgia, 18, 36. *See also* various cities,
    counties, towns
GFOA. *See* Government Finance Officers
    Association
GGL. *See* Good Government League
Ghetto, 221–222
Gift to government, 222
Gini coefficient, 408
Ginnie Mae. *See* Government National
    Mortgage Association
GNMA. *See* Government National
    Mortgage Association
Goal setting, 222–223
Gold coast, 223–224
Golden v. Ramapo, 233
Goldwater, Barry, 492
Good-government educational and
    reform groups (goo-goos), 17, 95

Good Government League (GGL), 33
Gordon v. Lance, 52
Gottmann, Jean, 120, 128, 153, 174, 329
Government
    caretaker, 68
    contracting out, 133–134
    county, 144
    decentralization, 149–150
    franchise, 215–216
    local, 54–55, 72–73, 122, 519
    merging, 128–129
    organization of, 204–205, 465–466,
        526, 532–533
    reform, 445–446
    regional planning, 3–4
    state, 130–131
    two-tier local, 527
Government Finance Officers Associ-
    ation (GFOA), 135, 308, 425, 456
Government National Mortgage
    Association (GNMA), 158, 203, 224,
    262, 524
Grace, J. Peter, 225
Grace Commission, 225
Granger case, 431
Grand Rapids (MI), 496
Grant-in-aid, 159, 163, 167, 225–226,
    315
    categorical, 70–71
    federal, 9, 209–210
    See also Community Development
        Block Grant; General Revenue
        Sharing
Grantsmanship, 226–227
Great Compromise, 204
Great Society, 173, 227–228, 355
Greater Avenues to Independence
    (GAIN), 571
Greater Portland, Oregon, Metropolitan
    Service District (MSD), 516
Green River Ordinance, 228–229
Greenbelt, 229–230, 361, 553
Greenbelt (MD), 229, 361
Greenbelt Act, 229
Greendale (WI), 229, 361
Greenhills (OH), 229, 361
Gridlock, 230–231
Griggs v. Duke Power, 309
Group home, 231–232
Growth management, 233–234
Growth Management Act, 323
Growth politics, 234–235
GRS. *See* General Revenue Sharing
Gun control, local, 236

Habitat Company, 240
*Hadley v. Junior College District of Metro-
    politan Kansas City, Missouri*, 440

Hague, Frank, 55
Haider, Donald, 396
Halfway house, 237–238
Hampton, Fred, 43
Hampton (VA), 129
Hamtramck (MI), 116, 181, 336, 437
Handicapped, housing for, 247
Hare, Thomas, 417
Hare plan, 417
Harrington, Michael, 564
Harris, Chauncy, multinuclei model,
    125, 339–340
Harris, Fred, 293
Harris, Patricia, 158
Hartford (CT), 145
Harvard University, housing studies,
    289–290
Harwood Heights (IL), 180
Hawaii, 34, 233, 328. *See also* various
    cities, counties
Hawkins v. Town of Shaw, 552
Hawley, Amos, 371
HCDA. *See* Housing and Community
    Development Act
Head Start, Project, 173, 238–239, 390,
    564
Headlee Amendment, 509
*Headley v. Junior College District of Kansas
    City*, 532
Health and Hospital Planning Council,
    79
Health facilities, 79
Heart of Atlanta Motel v. U.S., 147, 429
Heartland Institute, 515
Heller, Walter, 219
Hempstead (NY), 306
Heritage Foundation, 515
HEW. *See* Department of Health,
    Education, and Welfare
HFH, Ltd. v. Superior Court, 583
HHFA. *See* Housing and Home Finance
    Agency
Highest and best use, 239–240
Highland Park (TX), 181
Highway commissions, 86
Highway Trust Fund, 497
Highways, 356
Hill-Burton Act, 79, 99
Hillman, Sidney, 250
Hills, Carla, 158
Hills v. Gautreaux, 240–241, 424, 462,
    584
Hispanics, 39, 187
Historic area, 241
Historic preservation, 242–243
Historic Preservation (magazine), 242
Historic preservation review boards, 24
Historic Sites Act, 242

*Historical Statistics of the United States,
    Colonial Times to 1980*, 74
Hoboken (NJ), 544
Hollinghead, August B., 66
Holt Civic Club v. Tuscaloosa, 195
Home loan programs, 158
Home Mortgage Disclosure Act,
    243–244, 443
Home rule, 244–245, 446
Homeless, 245–247
Homeless Assistance Act, 246,
    247–248
Homeless Housing Act, 246
Homeless Reintegration Project, 247
Honolulu, 129
Hoover, Herbert, 468
Hoover, J. Edgar, 43
Hoovervilles, 468
Hospital Survey and Construction Act,
    79, 99
Hospitals, 79, 98
Household, 248–249
Housing, 5, 73, 110, 206, 227, 438
    abandonment, 4–5
    age-segregated, 7, 8
    building codes, 61–62
    condominium, 126, 249–250
    cooperative, 250–251
    family, 199–200
    filtering theory, 206–207
    financing, 202–203, 262–263
    mobile homes, 251, 376–377
    open, 198, 251–252
    ownership vs. rental, 253
    prefabricated or temporary, 253–254
    programs, 193–194, 257–260, 356
    public, 158, 240, 254–255, 421–422
    rehabilitation of, 255–256
    scatter-site, 461–462
    Section 8, 193, 256, 264
    segregated, 256–257
    studies of, 289–290
Housing Act of 1937, 254, 256,
    257–258, 264, 474, 550
Housing Act of 1949, 258–259, 260,
    262, 447, 475, 549
Housing Act of 1965, 206
Housing and Community Development
    Act (HCDA), 113, 156, 172, 255,
    259–260, 462
Housing and Home Finance Agency
    (HHFA), 158, 262, 573
Housing and Urban Development Act,
    260, 362
Housing court, 260–261
Housing finance agencies, 262–263
Housing starts, 263
Housing subsidy, 263–264

Houston, 19, 77, 84, 181, 195, 365
population, 157 (table), 492
Houston Association for the
Advancement of Mexican-
Americans, 536
Howard, Ebenezer, 59, 218, 229, 361,
553
Hoyt, Homer, sector model, 125,
463–464
HUD. See Department of Housing and
Urban Development
Human ecology, 264–266
Hunter, Floyd, 66, 69, 395, 450–451
Hurd v. Hodge, 455
Hutton, Bobby, 43
Hyperpluralism, 396

ICBO. See International Conference of
Building Officials Uniform Building
Code
ICMA. See International City
Management Association
ICMA Municipal Year Book, 96, 344
Idaho, 294
IFGs. See Individual and family grants
IGR. See Intergovernmental relations,
282
IIMC. See International Institute of
Municipal Clerks
Illinois, 28, 409, 502. See also various
cities, counties, towns
Immigration Act of 1921, 354
Immigration and Naturalization Service
(INS), 454
Impact analysis, 267, 541–542
Impact fee, 268
In rem property, 268–269
Income sources, urban, 269–270
Incorporation, 82, 160, 460
Incubator, 270–271
Independent Regulatory Commissions
(IRCs), 466
Independent school district, 271–272
Indianapolis, 106, 129, 533
Individual and family grants (IFGs), 163
Industrial districts, 374. See also Parks,
industrial
Industrial revenue bond (IRB), 272–273
Infilling, 273–274
Infrastructure, 67, 274–275
Initiative, 276–277
Innovation groups, 277–278
INS. See Immigration and Naturalization
Service
Inspection, building and food, 278–279
Insurance, self-, 464–465
Integration, racial, 159–160, 279–280,
518

Interest groups, agenda setting, 12. See
also Public Interest Groups
Intergovernmental Cooperation Act,
280–281
Intergovernmental Personnel Act (IPA),
281–282
Intergovernmental relations (IGR), 282,
345
Intergovernmental tax immunity,
282–283
International City Management
Association (ICMA), 19, 29, 88, 96,
103, 141–142, 308, 348, 352, 425
International Conference of Building
Officials (ICBO) Uniform Building
Code, 61
International Council of Shopping
Centers, 469
International Institute of Municipal
Clerks (IIMC), 97–98
International Red Cross, 177
International Studies of Value in Politics
Project, 117
Interstate Commerce Commission, 432
Interstate Highway System, 41, 283–284
Inter-University Consoritum for Political
and Social Research, 96, 162
Invasion, 285–286
Inverse condemnation, 286
Iowa, 498. See also various cities
IPA. See Intergovernmental Personnel Act
IRB. See Industrial revenue bond
IRCs. See Independent Regulatory
Commissions
Irvine Ranch (CA), 362
Islip (NY), 186

Jackson, George, 43
Jacksonville (FL), 129, 533
Jail, local, 287
James v. Valtierra, 444
Jamestown (NY), 369
Janowitz, Morris, 83, 115
Jarvis, Howard A., 419
Jaycees. See Junior Chamber of
Commerce
Jefferson, Thomas, 288
Jeffersonian agrarianism, 288, 519
Jennings, M. Kent, 66, 69
Jersey City, 37, 55
Jet (magazine), 45
JOA. See Joint Operating Agreement
Job Corps, 173, 288–289, 565
Job Training Partnership Act, 124
Johnson, Lyndon, social programs, 10,
156, 158, 173, 198, 227, 292, 355,
458, 560

Johnson, Tom L., 446
Joint Center for Housing Studies of
    Massachusetts Institute of
    Technology and Harvard
    University, 289–290
Joint Center for Political Studies, 515
Joint Operating Agreement (JOA), 290
Jonathan (MN), 362
Jones, James G., 237
Jones, Samuel "Golden Rule," 446
Jones v. Mayer, 252, 257
Jonesville, 575
Journal of Housing, 349
Judges, agenda setting, 12
Junior Chamber of Commerce (Jaycees),
    81, 429
Juvenile court, 291
Juvenile Court of Cook County, 291

Kansas, 18, 214, 272. *See also* various
    cities, counties, towns
Kansas City (KS), 525, 543
Kansas City (MO), 55, 336, 469, 525,
    543, 547
Katz, Daniel, 161
Katzenbach v. McClung, 147, 429
Kemp, Jack, 158, 183
Kennedy, John F., 47
    programs, 10, 154, 158, 252, 564
Kennedy, Robert, 236
Kentucky, 36, 94
Kerner, Otto, 292
Kerner Commission, 48, 292–293, 399,
    402, 457, 529
Kestnbaum Commission on
    Intergovernmental Relations, 282
Key, V. O., 93
Keystone Bituminous Coal v. Benedictis, 494
King, Martin Luther, Jr., 44, 198, 252
King County (WA), 369
Kiwanis, 94
KKK. *See* Ku Klux Klan
Koch, Ed, 341
Krogh, Egil "Bud," Jr., 567
Ku Klux Klan (KKK), 293–294
Kucinich, Dennis J., 38, 209

Labor unions, 250
Lake Charles (LA), 544
LaGuardia, Fiorello, 33
Lakewood (CA), 295
Lakewood Plan, 295–296, 344
Land
    mandatory dedication, 316
    ownership, 150–151
    raw, 296–297
    vacant urban, 297
    valuing, 572–573

Land banking, 297–299
Land classification, 299–300
Land conservancy, 300–301
Land use, 494–495
    concentric zone model, 125–126
    control, 301–302
    nonconforming, 364
Landfills, 186
Landlocked property, 302–303
Landrieu, Moon, 158
Las Colinas (TX), 362
Lau v. Nichols, 188
*Laurel Hill Cemetery v. City and County of
    San Francisco*, 71
Law, 5, 48, 153
    quick-take, 436–437
    See also Legislation
Law enforcement, local, 287
Law Enforcement Assistance Admin-
    istration (LEAA), 303–304, 458
Lawyers, corporation, 137–138
LEAA. *See* Law Enforcement Assistance
    Administration
League of Women Voters, 95, 304–305
Lease-back, 305
Le Corbusier, population density, 157
Legal Defense and Educational Fund
    (LDF). *See* NAACP
Legal Defense and Educational Fund, Inc.
Legislation
    environmental, 185–186
    passage of, 5–6
    See also various acts
L'Enfant, Pierre Charles, 16
Letchworth (England), 218
Levittowns, 305–306
Levittown v. Nyquist, 428
Lewis, John L., 373
Lexington (KY), 129
Libraries, 96, 188
Licensing, adult entertainment, 106
LILCO. *See* Long Island Lighting
    Company
Lindsay, John, 293
Line personnel, 484
Lineberry, Robert, 396
Lipsky, Michael, 484–485
Little Rock, 161
Lobbying
    by cities, 306–308
    for civil rights, 347
LOCAL EXCHANGE, 308, 312, 352
Local Government Information
    Network. *See* LOGIN
Local merit system, 308–309
Locally Unwanted Land Use (LULU),
    71, 232, 246, 309–310
    invasion by, 285–286

Lockheed Corporation, 356, 429
Lockup, 310–312
Loftin, Colin, 161
LOGIN, 311–312
Long Beach (CA), 307, 339
Long Island (NY), 196
Long Island Lighting Company
    (LILCO), 179
Lorenz Curve, 408
Los Alamos (NM), 361
Los Angeles, 77, 93, 116, 142, 157
    (table), 181, 188, 128, 231, 280, 307,
    339, 441, 472, 568
  housing, 246, 448
  riots, 292, 457
  transportation, 284, 322
Los Angeles County, 39, 468
Lottery, 312–313
Loudoun County (VA), 350
Louis, Arthur, 434
Louisiana, 34. See also various cities, towns
Louisville (KY), 496
Lowell (MA), 186
Lower class, Banfield thesis on, 35, 36
Lowi, Theodore, 396, 547
LULU. See Locally Unwanted Land Use
Lynd, Helen M., 66, 334, 395, 450
Lynd, Robert S., 66, 334, 395, 450

MAC. See Municipal Assistance
    Corporation
McCulloch v. Maryland, 26, 282
MacDonald et al. v. Yolo County et al., 494
Machine politics, 326, 546–547
Machine space, 314–315
McKenzie, Roderick, 264
McKinney, Stewart B., Homeless
    Assistance Act. See Homeless
    Assistance Act
MacKinnon, R. D., 174
Macomb County (MI), 345
Madison (WI), 16
Magazines, black, 45
Magnet school, 315
Mahoney City (PA), 65
Maier, Henry W., 543
Maine, 100, 133, 272, 519
Maine v. Thiboutot, 343
Mainstreaming. See Deinstitutionalization
MALDEF. See Mexican-American Legal
    Defense and Educational Fund
Mandatory land dedication, 316
Manpower Development and Training
    Act (MDTA), 124, 125, 531
Manufactured home, 316–317
Map, 317–318
  cadastral, 318
  types of, 318–320

Marion County (IN), 129, 533
Marshall, Thurgood, 346
Martin v. Wilks, 10
Marx, Karl, 320
Marxist urban analysis, 320–321, 537
Maryland, 462, 502. See also various
    cities, counties, towns
Mass media, agenda setting, 12
Mass transit, 322, 520, 543
Massachusetts, 180, 191, 267, 434, 519
  poverty programs, 409, 571
  property tax, 418–419, 509, 510, 513
Massachusetts Institute of Technology
    (MIT), 289
Massachusetts v. Mellon, 512
Master plan, 322–324
Maui County (HI), 369
Maximum feasible participation, 324–325
Mayor, 327
  strong, 325–326
  weak, 326
Mayor-council government, 327
MBS. See Mortgage-backed securities
MDTA. See Manpower Development and
    Training Act
Media, ethnic, 187–188. See also Mass
    media
Mediation, 23, 327–328
Medicaid, 246
Medicare, 246, 409
Megalopolis, 120, 128, 174, 175,
    329–330
Melting pot, 330
Memphis (TN), 284
Mencken, H. L., 434
Menlo Park (NJ), 378–379
Mennonite Board of Missions v. Adams, 417
Mental health, 154
Mergers, 160
Merit system, local, 308–309
Merton, Robert, 547
Metropolitan area, 135, 146, 331
  balkanization, 33–34
  regional planning, 3–4
Metropolitan Council on Housing, 449
Metropolitan county, 331–332
Metropolitan Dade County, 526
Metropolitan Statistical Area (MSA),
    128, 152, 331, 332–333, 492
Metropolitanization, 333–334
Mexican-American Legal Defense and
    Educational Fund (MALDEF), 39
Miami, 93, 145, 290, 427, 458, 526
Michigan, 26, 38, 46, 85, 191, 272, 294,
    313, 316, 375, 414, 527
  city mergers, 19, 129
  jurisdiction, 460, 520
  State Historic Commission, 241

taxation, 501, 509, 513
See also various cities, counties, towns
Michigan Chronicle (newspaper), 45
Middletown, 66, 152, 334, 450
Middletown (PA), 306
Migration
  rates of, 119
  urban, 335–337
Milford Township (MI), 196
Millage, 336–337
Miller, Samuel F., 454
Miller, Warren E. 161
Milliken v. Bradley, 59, 64, 104, 240
Mills, C. Wright, 395, 450
Milwaukee, 114, 284, 298, 544
Minimum wages, 217, 352–353
Minneapolis, 284, 504, 512
Minneapolis–St. Paul Twin Cities
  Metropolitan Council, 516
Minnesota, 328, 509. *See also* various
  cities, counties, towns
Minorities, 9, 21, 39
  balanced tickets, 32–33
  housing, 251–252
  set-asides, 467–468
Mississippi, 19, 272, 434, 494
Mississippi River, 12
Missouri, 245, 409. *See also* various cities,
  counties, towns
MIT. *See* Massachusetts Institute of
  Technology
MJA. *See* Multijurisdictional agency
Mobile, 12
Mobile home parks, 376–377. *See also*
  Manufactured home
Mobility, 119
Mobro, 186
Model Cities, 113, 155, 158, 227. *See also*
  Demonstration Cities and
  Metropolitan Development Act
Model Cities Act, 156
Moline (IL), 525
*Monell v. Department of Social Services,
  New York City*, 343
Montesquieu, 466
Montgomery County (MD), 350
Montgomery County (OH), 369
Moody's Investor's Service, 53
Moore v. City of East Cleveland, 199
Moorhead (MN), 525
Moral-obligation bond, 337
Moratorium, 337–338
Morgantown (WV), 543
Morocco, 180
Morrill Land-Grant College Act, 209–210
Mortgage-backed securities (MBS), 224
Mortgage subsidy programs, 4–5,
  203–204, 260

Morton Grove (IL), 236
Mount Laurel (NJ), 478
Moynihan, Daniel Patrick, 41, 572
MSA. *See* Metropolitan Statistical Area
Mueller, John E., 211
Muhammad Speaks (newspaper), 45
*Mullane v. Central Hanover Bank and Trust
  Co.*, 417
Multijurisdictional agency (MJA),
  338–339
Multinuclei model, 125, 339–340, 554
Mumford, Lewis, 90
Muncie (IN), 66, 334, 450
Municipal Assistance Corporation
  (MAC), 340–341
Municipal corporations, 162, 341–342
Municipal court, 342
Municipal tort liability, 342–343
Municipal Treasurers Association of the
  United States and Canada, 524
Municipal Union–Financial Leaders
  organization, 341
Municipal Year Book, 19, 29, 344, 348
Munn v. Illinois, 431
Muscogee County (GA), 129
Mutual-aid pact, 344–345

NAACP. *See* National Association for the
  Advancement of Colored People
NAACP Legal Defense and Education
  Fund, Inc. (LDF), 346–347
NACo. *See* National Association of
  Counties
NACo-ICMA County Year Book, 96
NAHRO. *See* National Association of
  Housing & Redevelopment Officials
NAHRO Monitor (journal), 349
NAIOP. *See* National Association of
  Industrial and Office Parks
NAR. *See* National Association of Realtors
Nashville, 114, 129, 533, 544
Nassau County (NY), 369
National Advisory Commission on Civil
  Disorders, 292
National Association for the Advance-
  ment of Colored People (NAACP),
  44, 347–348
National Association of Clerks and
  Treasurers, 96
National Association of Counties (NACo),
  8, 96, 348, 352, 425
National Association of Home Builders,
  253–254
National Association of Housing &
  Redevelopment Officials (NAHRO),
  348–349, 425
National Association of Impacted
  Districts, 200

National Association of Industrial and
Office Parks (NAIOP), 375
National Association of Realtors (NAR),
22, 439
National Audubon Society, 301
National Capital Planning Commission
(NCPC), 349–350
National Conference of Black Lawyers,
138
National Conference of Commissioners
on Uniform Laws, 126
National Conference of State Legislators
(NCSL), 425
National Council for Good Cities, 17
National Environmental Policy Act, 183,
185–186
National Governor's Association (NGA),
425
National Governor's Conference, 352
National Historic Preservation Act, 242
National Homeless Union, 246
National Housing Act, 202, 203
National industrial policy, 350–351
National Industrial Recovery Act, 258
National Institute of Dental Research,
211
National Institute of Municipal Lawyers,
138
National Institutes of Health (NIH), 211
National League of Cities (NLC), 307,
308, 351–352, 425, 534, 544
National League of Cities v. Usery, 217,
352–353
National Legislative Conference, 352
National Manufactured Home Construc-
tion and Safety Standards, 316
National Mobile Home Construction and
Safety Act, 376
National Municipal League, 353–354,
418
National Newspaper Publishers
Association (NNPA), 45
National Opinion Research Center
(NORC), 384–385
National Park Service, 241
National Park Service Act, 242
National Petroleum Council, 86
National Register of Historic Places, 241,
242
National Rifle Association (NRA), 236
National Science Foundation, 384
National Seashore Recreation Area, 378
National Sheriff's Association, 468
National Trust for Historic Preservation,
242
National Urban Coalition (NUC), 17, 536
National Urban League, 354
National urban policy, 355–356

Nation's Cities Weekly, 352
Nature Conservancy, 300
NBO. See Neighborhood-based
organizations
NCPC. See National Capital Planning
Commission
NCSL. See National Conference of State
Legislators
NDO. See Neighborhood development
organization
Nebraska, 38, 532
Negro press. See Black press
Neighborhood, 260, 357–358, 397, 436,
455, 518
copper canyon, 136
gold coast, 223–224
stabilized, 480–481
See also Barrio; Ghetto
Neighborhood-based organizations
(NBOs), 359
Neighborhood development
organization (NDO), 359
Neighborhood justice center (NJC), 261,
358–359
Neighborhood movement, 359–360
Neighborhood Opportunity Fund, 255
Neighborhood unit, 357
Neighborhood watch, 360–361
Neighborhood Youth Corps, 173
Nevada, 8, 106, 479, 498. See also various
cities, towns
New Communities Act, 362
New Deal, 258, 355
New Federalism, 210
New Hampshire, 180, 313, 483, 519
New Haven (CT), 69, 76, 122, 366, 450,
551
politics, 93, 394–395
New Jersey, 31, 34, 54, 158, 185, 306,
313, 448, 502, 522
schools, 36, 272, 428
zoning, 159, 478–479
See also various cities, counties, towns
New Jersey Tenant's Organization, 449
New Left, 150, 359
New Mexico, 94, 492, 498. See also
Albuquerque
New Orleans, 32, 106, 284, 326, 375,
501
A New Partnership to Conserve American
Cities, 355
New town, 361–363
New York Black Enterprise (magazine), 45
New York (state), 31, 250, 306, 313
nuclear power, 179, 180
municipal assistance corporation,
340–341
schools, 272, 428

taxation, 501, 502
See also various cities, counties, towns
New York Adirondack Park Agency, 389
New York City, 77, 79, 102, 114, 119,
  123, 128, 142, 146, 196, 269, 284,
  300, 302, 414, 457, 472, 529, 543
  balanced tickets, 32, 33
  balkanization, 33, 34
  development rights, 14, 522
  health services, 98–99
  housing, 126, 246, 250–251, 254, 448,
  449, 473
  Landmark Preservation Act, 242
  minorities, 84, 188
  municipal assistance corporations,
  340–341
  newspapers, 44, 45
  planning, 16, 554
  political organization, 53–54, 150,
  369, 418, 566
  politics, 55, 93, 95, 140
  population density, 157 (table), 534
  schools, 428, 446
  taxation, 496, 501, 504, 506
  zoning, 106, 299, 586, 588
New York City bailout, 356, 363–364
New York ex. rel. Bryant v. Zimmerman, 293
New York v. United States, 421
Newark, 20, 37, 43, 292, 369, 434, 568
Newburyport (MA), 66, 574
Newspaper Preservation Act, 290
Newspapers, 181
  black, 44–45
  community, 116
  Hispanic, 188
  joint operation of, 290
  official, 368–369
  zoned edition, 579–580
Newton, Huey, 43
NGA. See National Governor's
  Association
Niagara Falls (NY), 525
Niagara Falls (Ontario), 525
Nicaragua, Sister City program, 471
NIH. See National Institutes of Health
NIMBY. See Not in My Backyard
Nixon, Richard, 47, 112, 113, 179, 228,
  458, 492
  benign neglect, 41, 42
  federal programs, 193, 210, 219, 355,
  565
NJC. See Neighborhood justice center
NLC. See National League of Cities
NNPA. See National Newspapers
  Association
Noise Control Act, 185
Nollan v. California Coastal Commission,
  191, 268, 494

Nonconforming use, 364
Nonpartisan election, 364–365
NORC. See National Opinion Research
  Center
Norfolk County (VA), 129
Norridge (IL), 180
Norris (TN), 361
North Carolina, 94, 268, 355
  elections, 28, 561
  schools, 63, 462
North Dakota, 441, 502
North Las Vegas, 161
North Lawndale (Chicago), 4
Northwestern/Evanston Research Park
  (IL), 379
Norwood (OH), 180
Not in My Backyard (NIMBY), 238, 309
Notes, as income sources, 269–270
NRA. See National Rifle Association
NRC. See Nuclear Regulatory
  Commission
NUC. See National Urban Coalition
Nuclear power plants, evacuation plans,
  179–180
Nuclear Regulatory Commission (NRC),
  179
Nursing homes, 79

Oak Park (IL), gun control, 236
Oak Ridge (TN), 361
Oakland (CA), 39, 84, 106, 307, 366, 373
Oakland County (MI), 38, 196, 197, 284
Oakland Project, 366–367
Obrogation, 5
Occupancy permit, 367–368
OEO. See Office of Economic Opportunity
Off year, 368
Office of Community Planning and
  Development, 447
Office of Economic Opportunity (OEO),
  112, 173, 324, 565–565
Office of Management and Budget
  (OMB), 153
  review procedures, 3, 96, 280
Office of Personnel Management, 281
Official newspaper, 368–369
Ohio, 38, 501. See also various cities,
  counties, towns
Oklahoma, 185, 502. See also various
  cities
Olmsted, Frederick Law, 16, 90, 378
Omaha, 525
OMB. See Office of Management and
  Budget
Ombudsman, 369–370
Omnibus Crime Control and Safe
  Streets Act, 303
Open space, 297, 305, 370–371

Optimum city, 371–372
Orange County (CA), 233
Ordinance, 182, 372
    abrogation of, 5, 6
    announcement of, 368–369
    building design, 24
    Green River, 228–229
    zoning, 232
Oregon, 185, 233, 441. See also Portland
Organic community, 361
Ostrom, Vincent, 136
The Other America, 564
Outpatient facilities, 79
Outside influence, 372–373
Overtime, 217
Oxnard (CA), 123

PAC. See Political Action Committee
PAIS. See Public Affairs Information
    Service
Palo Alto (CA), 379
Panel studies, 152
Paratransit, 374
Parent-Teacher Association (PTA), 95
Park, Robert Ezra, 83, 264, 379
Park, 90
    industrial, 374–376
    mobile home, 376–377
    recreation, 377–378
    research, 378–379
Park Thesis, 379–380
Parkway School, 15
Participation, 380–382
Patronage, urban, 382–383
Payments in lieu of taxes (PILOT), 222,
    282, 507, 567
PCD. See Planned Commercial District
PCS. See Permanent Community Sample
Peets, Elbert, 90
Pendergast, Thomas, 55, 547
Pendleton Act, 281
Penn Central, 356
Pennell v. San Jose, 448
Pennsylvania, 54, 65, 306. See also various
    cities, counties, towns
Pension fund politics, 383–384
Performance, 416
Permanent Community Sample (PCS), 69,
    122, 123, 384–386, 544
Permits, building, 62–63
Petaluma v. Construction Industry Association,
    233
Peterson, Paul, 411, 548
PHA. See Public Housing Authority
Philadelphia, 15, 84, 93, 117, 142, 185,
    329, 339, 412, 469, 496, 566
    demographics, 157 (table), 529
    housing, 220, 540
    Market Square East, 76

Phillips, Kevin, 153, 491–492
Phoenix, 77, 141, 157 (table), 365, 414,
    492, 554
PID. See Planned Industrial Development
Pierce, Samuel, 158
PIGs. See Public Interest Groups
PILOT. See Payments in lieu of taxes
Pittsburgh, 100, 298, 496, 526
    Golden Triangle, 76
    SMSA, 33–34, 143
Plainville, 66
Planned Commercial District (PCD),
    386
Planned Industrial Development (PID),
    386
Planned Unit Development (PUD),
    386–387, 585
Planned Unit Residential Development,
    386
Planning
    advocacy, 387–388
    city, 89–90
    community, 58–59
    contingency, 388–389
    focal-point, 389–390
    master, 322–324
    metropolitan and regional, 3–4
    social, 390–391
    strategic, 391–392
    urban, 16, 392–394, 554
Plants, closing, 99–101
Plessy v. Ferguson, 147, 463
Plunk, 394
Pluralism, 394–397. See also Community
    power
PMSA. See Primary Metropolitan
    Statistical Area
PNYA. See Port of New York and New
    Jersey Authority
Poletown, 397–398, 437, 447
Poletown Neighborhood Council v. City of
    Detroit, 397
Police
    private, 398–399
    public, 399–400
Police power, 400–401
Police review board, 401–402
Polish Century Club, 95
Political Action Committee (PAC), 81
Political machines, 92–93
Political parties, 32, 55–56
Political profiles, city, 93–94
Politics, 402–404
    fluoridation, 210–211
    growth, 234–235
    machine, 326, 546–548
    pension fund, 383–384
    triage, 524–525
    Yonkers-style, 575–576

Pollock v. Farmers' Loan & Trust Company,
  283
Pollution, 185–186
Population, 118, 120, 143, 157, 371
  census of, 73–75
  daytime and nighttime, 404–405
Port of New York and New Jersey
    Authority (PNYA), 31, 405–406
Portland (OR), 108, 145
Postindustrial city, 406–407
Poverty level, 407–408
Poverty programs, 408–409, 461
Powell, Lewis, 199
The Power Elite, 450
PPBS. *See* Program Planning Budgeting
  System
PR. See Proportional representation
Precinct, 410
Prescott (AZ), self-insurance, 465
Preservation News, 242
Primary Metropolitan Statistical Area
  (PMSA), 127
Prince George's County (MD), 350
Prince William County (VA), 350
Princess Anne County (VA), 129
Princeton (NJ), 16, 233
Principled purchasing, 472
Prisons, 287
Private sector, 410–411
Private street, 412
Privatism, 412–413
Privatization, 413–415, 429–430
Productivity, 415–416
Progation, 5
Program Planning Budgeting System
  (PPBS), 60, 140
Progressive Era, 78
  reform, 91, 92, 353, 444, 445–446,
    495–496, 547
Progressive Policy Institute, 517
Project Head Start. *See* Head Start,
  Project
Project Reference File, 542
Promulgate, 416–417
Property, 14, 180, 268
  appraisal, 21–22
  development rights, 521–522
  easements, 170–171
  rights to, 494–495
  taxes on, 27, 418–420, 497, 509–513
  tax-exempt, 505–507
  titles to, 446–447
  See also Real property
Proportional representation (PR),
  417–418, 446
Proposition 2½, 418–419, 509
Proposition 9, 510
Proposition 13, 419–420, 509, 510, 513
Proprietary function, 420–421

Pruitt-Igoe Project, 421–422, 462
PTA. *See* Parent-Teacher Association
Public Affairs Information Service
  (PAIS), 162
Public contract, 422–423
Public employee strike, 423–424
Public Housing Administration, 158
Public Housing Authority (PHA),
  424–425
Public Interest Groups (PIGs), 348, 352,
  425, 534
Public policy
  agenda setting, 11–12
  public employee unions, 17–18
Public/private partnership, 426–427, 436
Public safety, 427
Public-school financing cases, 427–428
Public sector, 105, 429–430
  private market, 194–195
Public Technology, Inc., 352
Public utility, 430–432
Public Works Administration, 31, 258
Public Works Employment Act, 20
PUD. *See* Planned Unit Development
Puerto Rico, 188
Purchasing, centralized, 78
PURD. *See* Planned Unit Residential
  Development

QOL. *See* Quality of life
Quad cities, 525
Qualifications for office, 433–434
Quality of life, 434–435, 476
Quasi-public, 435–436
Quick-take law, 436–437

Race, 41–42, 118
Race riots, 457
Racial steering, 438
Racism, 21, 292–293, 387
Radburn (NJ), 361, 436
Radio, 188
RAND Corporation, 515, 123
Rapid-transit systems. *See* Bay Area
    Rapid Transit; Mass transit
RC2s. *See* Regional Clearinghouse Review
    Committees
RDAs. *See* Redevelopment authorities
RD&E. *See* Research, development, and
    engineering
Reading, John, 43
Reagan, Ronald, 47, 134, 140, 236, 421,
    471, 492, 515, 568
  A-95 Review, 3–4, 281
  economy, 172, 183, 213, 492–493
  federal aid, 20, 164, 192, 201, 259, 275,
    281–282, 355, 461, 504, 509, 539
  government services, 124, 225, 426,
    541, 543, 561
  homeless, 246, 247

Real estate, highest and best use, 239.
  See also Real property
Real estate agent, 439
Real property, 222, 253
  covenants, 454–455
  dedication of, 150–151
  taxes on, 498–499
Realtor, 439
Reapportionment, city, 439–440
Recall, 440–441
Receivership, 441–442
Reconstruction Finance Corporation
  (RFC), 31
Recycling, 185
Red Cross, 164
Redevelopment authorities (RDAs), 426
Redfield, Robert, 83
Redlining, 442–444
Referendum, 444–445
Reform government, 445–446
Refuse Act, 185
Regime analysis, 548
Regional City, 66, 450
Regional Clearinghouse Review
  Committees (RC2s), 96
Registrar of deeds, 446–447
Rehabilitation, of housing, 255–256
Rehnquist, William, 195, 353
Rehnquist Court, 10
Relocation, 447–448
Rent, 253, federal subsidies, 4, 5, 256.
  See also Housing, Section 8
Rent control, 448
Rent strike, 449
"Rent-a-cops," 398
Renton v. Playtime Theatres, 106
Replication, 151–152
Representation, proportional, 417–418
Republican party, 47
Reputational analysis, 449–452. *See also*
  Community power
Research, development, and engineering
  (RD&E), 277, 378
Resettlement Administration, 229
Residency requirement, 452–453
Resident, 453–454
Resident alien, 453–454
Residential community, 40
Resource Conservation and Recovery
  Act, 185
Resource Recovery Act, 185, 477
Resources for the Future (RFF),
  515–516
Resources in Education (RIE), 175
Reston (VA), 16, 323, 362
Restrictive covenant, 454–455
Retired Senior Volunteer Program, 560
Retirement communities, 7

Revenue, lottery, 312–313. *See also* Tax
Revenue improvement bond (RIB),
  269–270, 455–456
Revenue surplus, 456–457
Reynolds v. Simms, 440
RFC. *See* Reconstruction Finance
  Corporation
RFF. *See* Resources for the Future
Rhode Island, 185
RIB. *See* Revenue improvement bond
Richland (WA), 361
Richmond (VA), 284, 467
*Ridgemont Development Co. v. City of East
  Detroit*, 316
RIE. *See* Resources in Education
Riot, 292, 457–459, 536
Road classification, 459
Robinson v. Cahill, 428
Rochester (NY), 373, 414, 428
Rock Island (IL), 525
Roe v. Wade, 403, 436
Rogation, 5
Romney, George, 158
Roosevelt, Franklin D., 10, 204, 258,
  355, 361, 534
Roper Center, 96
Rosenstone, Steven J., 161
Rotary, 94
Roth, Stephen, 64
Royal Oak Township (MI), 38, 460
Rule of contiguity, 459–460
Rural, 534
Rural/Metro system, 134

Sacramento, 65
Safe Streets Act, 458
Safety net, 461
Saginaw, 129
St. Bernard (OH), 180
St. Louis, 93, 207, 269, 434, 443, 525,
  526
  balkanization, 33, 34
  public housing, 4, 254, 421–422, 462
St. Louis County, 295, 435, 585
St. Paul, 504, 525
*Salyer Land Co. v. Tulare Lake Basin Water
  Storage District*, 440
San Antonio, 93, 77, 119, 122, 141
  elections, 32–33, 365
*San Antonio Independent School District v.
  Rodriguez*, 428
San Bruno Mountains conservancy, 389
San Diego, 16, 77, 119, 141, 186, 544
  population, 157 (table), 492
San Fernando (CA), 181
San Francisco, 12, 14, 43, 71, 76, 84,
  142, 186, 234, 290, 307, 448
  politics, 93, 140

transportation, 39, 274, 284, 543
zoning, 583, 584
San Francisco County, 40
San Jose (CA), 448
San Marino (CA), 180
Sanctuary, 472
Santa Monica (CA), 233
Saugus (MA), 186
SBA. *See* Small Business Administration
Scatter-site housing, 461–462
Schmandt, Henry J., 526
Schnore, Leo, 488
School board, 150
   bankruptcy, 36–37
   See also Board of education;
      Education; School district; Schools
School district, 59, 446, 462–463
   accountability, 36–37
   busing, 63–64
   independent, 271–272
   See also Education; School board;
      Schools
Schools
   closing of, 101–102
   financing, 222, 427–428
   magnet, 315
   See also Education; School board;
      School district
Scott, Geoffrey, 42
SCSA. *See* Consolidated Metropolitan
   Statistical Area
Seabrook power plant (NH), 180
Seale, Bobby, 43
Seattle, 126, 142, 207, 290, 369, 434,
   543
   elections, 365, 441
   zoning, 106, 583
Section 8 Housing. *See* Housing, Section 8
Sector model, 125, 207, 463–464
Segregation, 20–21, 59, 63, 84
   de facto, 104, 147, 576
   de jure, 147–148
   housing, 7, 8, 48, 256–257
   hyper, 280
Self-insurance, 464–465
SEMLOL. *See* Southeast Michigan
   League of Libraries
Seniors in Community Service, 354
Separation of powers, 465–467
Serrano v. Priest, 428
Service clubs, 94
Services, 134, 410, 534
   metropolitization of, 333–334
   mutual-aid pacts, 344–345
   provision of, 426, 517–518
   urban, 551–552
SES. *See* Socioeconomic status
Set-aside, 467–468

700 Club, 178
Sewerage treatment facilities, 113
Sex ratios, 118
Shantytown, 468
Shapiro v. Thompson, 452
Sharkansky, Ira, 396
Shelly v. Kramer, 455
Shelters, homeless, 248
Sheriff, 468–469
Shopping centers, 41, 469–470
Shriver, Sargent, Jr., 564
Silicon Valley, 379
Sinking fund, 470–471
SIPP. *See* Survey of Income and
   Program Participation
Sister City program, 471–472
Site plan review, 472
Skid row, 472–473
Slaughterhouse cases, 454
Slums, 224, 258, 472–474
Small Business Administration (SBA),
   163, 271, 474–475
SMSA. *See* Standard Metropolitan
   Statistical Area
SNCC. *See* Student Nonviolent
   Coordinating Committee
Social engineering, 390
Social indicators, 475–476
Social programs, federal involvement, 4
Social Security, 409
Social Security Act, 13, 154, 246
Society of Real Estate Appraisers (SRA),
   22
Society of St. Tammany, 495
Socioeconomic status (SES), 464
Sociology, Chicago School of, 83
Solid Waste Disposal Act, 185, 477
Solid waste managment, 476–477
South Africa, 20
   divestment, 166, 472
South Bend (IN), 544
South Carolina, 36. *See also* various
   cities
South Carolina v. Baker, 50, 282–283
South Norfolk (VA), 129
Southeast Michigan Council of
   Governments, 142
Southeast Michigan League of Libraries
   (SEMLOL), 333
Southern Building Code Congress
   Standard Building Code, 61
*Southern Burlington County NAACP v.
   Township of Mt. Laurel*, 157,
   478–479, 585
Southfield (MI), 470, 570
Spanish language, 188
SPAs. *See* State planning agencies
Special district, 386, 479–480

Special purpose units, 72–73
Special Use District (SUD), 386
Spectovsky, Auguste C., 196
Spending limit, 480
Spirit of the Laws, 466
Springfield (IL), 28
Springfield (MA), 123
SRA. *See* Society of Real Estate
    Appraisers
SSI. *See* Supplemental Security Income
Stabilization, 480–481
Standard and Poor's, 53
Standard Consolidated Statistical Area
    (SCSA). *See* Consolidated
    Metropolitan Statistical Area
    (CMSA)
Standard Metropolitan Statistical Area
    (SMSA), 33, 76, 143, 333. *See also*
    Metropolitan Statistical Area (MSA)
Stanford Research Park (CA), 379
State and Local Programs and Support
    Directorate, 201
State government
    constitution, 130–131
    regional planning, 3–4
State mandate, 482–483
State-municipal affairs office, 483–484
State of Black America, 354
State-of-the-city address, 481–482
State of Utah v. Hutchinson, 163
State planning agencies (SPAs), 303
Statutes, 5, 153, 182
Steagall, Henry B., 258
Sternleib, George, 538
Stockholm, 295
Stokes, Donald E., 161
Street-level bureaucrat, 484–485
Strikes, public employees, 423–424
Strip development, commercial, 107–108
Student Nonviolent Coordinating
    Committee (SNCC), 44
Subdivision, 485–486
Suburb, 404, 486–487
Suburban typology, 488–489
Suburbanization, 489
Succession, 489–491
SUD. *See* Special Use District
Suffolk County (NY), 179
Suffrage, 214
Sumpter (SC), 445
Sun Cities, 8
Sunbelt, 77, 78, 491–492
    population density, 157–158
Supervisors Inter-County Committee,
    152
Supplemental Security Income (SSI), 13,
    409, 568
Supply-side economics, 492–493

Supportive Housing Demonstration
    Program, 247
Survey of Income and Program
    Participation (SIPP), 249
Sutherland, George, 560
*Swann v. Charlotte-Mecklenburg Board of
    Education,* 69, 63–64, 104
Syracuse, 428

Tahoe Regional Planning Agency, 389
Taking, 494–495
Takoma Park (MD), 472
Tammany Hall, 495–496, 547
Tampa, 119, 145
TAN. *See* Tax anticipation note
TARP. *See* Tunnel and Reservoir Project
Tax, 85, 191, 242, 250, 268, 269, 370,
    497, 498
    ad valorem, 7, 25–27
    foreign trade zones, 213–214
    intergovernmental immunity, 282–283
    local income, 496–497
    millage, 336–337
    property, 418–419
    real property, 498–499
    regressive, 499–500
    sales, 500–501
Tax abatement, 501–502
Tax amnesty, 502–503
Tax anticipation note (TAN), 53, 270,
    456, 503
Tax base, 504
Tax base sharing, 504–505
Tax delinquency, 505
Tax-exempt property, 505–507
Tax exemption, 421, 507
Tax incentive, 165, 508
Tax increment financing (TIF), 508–509
Tax limit, 509–510
Tax rate, 510–511
Tax role, 511
Taxation, double, 511–512
Taxpayer suit, 512–513
Taxpayers' revolts, 419–420, 513–514
TDRs. *See* Transferable development
    rights
Technology, 12
Telemundo, 188
Television, 188
Tennessee, 94, 272. *See also* various
    cities, counties, towns
Tennessee Valley Authority (TVA), 25,
    31, 361–362
Terms of office, 445
Texas, 18, 39, 77, 277, 479, 492, 503, 581
    exaction policy, 191, 268
    school boards, 36, 37
    See also various cities, counties, towns

Texas Municipal Annexation Statute, 195
Think tank, 514–516
Thornburg v. Gingles, 28, 561
Three-tier reform, 516–517
Ticket-splitting, 562
Tiebout, Charles M., 517
Tiebout Thesis, 517–518
TIF. *See* Tax increment financing
Tipping point, 517
Title VIII. *See* Fair Housing Title
Toledo, 79, 418, 446
Toll roads, 284
Tonnies, Ferdinand, 115
Topeka, 161
Toronto, 339, 526
Town, 519
Town Affiliation Association of the USA,
    Inc., 471
Town and Country Planning Act, 229
Town meeting, 519–520
Township, 520
Toxic Substances Control Act, 477
Toxic Waste Superfund Act, 185
Trade groups, 153
Traditional Housing Demonstration
    Program, 247
Traffic, circulation plan, 85–86. *See also*
    Expressways; Mass transit; Traffic
    analysis
Traffic analysis, 520–521
Training and Education Directorate, 201
Transferable development rights,
    521–522
Transition, 522–523
Transportation, 146, 374
Treasurer, 523–524
*A Treatise on the Election of Representatives,
    Parliamentary and Municipal,* 417
Triage politics, 524–525
Triangle Park (NC), 119, 379
Tricameral, 532
Tullytown (PA), 306
Tulsa, 108, 434
Tunnel and Reservoir Project (TARP),
    274
Turnpikes, 284
Tuskegee (AL), 21
TVA. *See* Tennessee Valley Authority
Tweed, William Marcy, 55, 547
Tweed Ring, 55
Twin Cities, 525–526
Two-level urban reorganization, 526
Two-tier local government, 527
Two-tiered labor market, 531

UCA. *See* Uniform Condominium Act
UCCC. *See* Uniform Consumer Credit
    Code

UCR. *See* Uniform Crime Reports
UDAG. *See* Urban Development Action
    Grants
UIA. *See* Urban impact analysis, 541
ULI. *See* Urban Land Institute
Ullman, Edward, multinuclei model, 125,
    339–340
Ultra vires, 528
UMTA. *See* Urban Mass Transportation
    Administration
Underclass, 528–530
Undercount, 530–531
Underemployment, 531–532
Unemployment, 179
Unemployment compensation, 409
UNESCO. *See* United Nations
    Educational, Scientific, and Cultural
    Organization
Unicameral, 532–533
Uniform Condominium Act (UCA), 126
Uniform Consumer Credit Code
    (UCCC), 228
Uniform Crime Reports (UCR), 96, 144
Uniform Relocation Act, 166
Uniform Relocation Assistance and Real
    Property Acquisition Policies Act, 447
Unigov, 533
Unincorporated areas, 160
Unions, 32
    public employee, 17–18
United Housing Federation, 251
United Kingdom
    greenbelt, 218, 229, 230
    new towns, 362
United Nations Educational, Scientific,
    and Cultural Organization
    (UNESCO), 242
United Organization of Taxpayers, 419
U.S. Conference of Mayors, 352, 425,
    533–534, 544
U.S. Constitution, 74, 205
U.S. Fire Administration, 201
*U.S. First English Evangelical Lutheran
    Church v. Los Angeles County,* 494, 495
U.S. Fish and Wildlife Service, 389
U.S. Foreign Disaster Assistance
    Program, 388
U.S. Housing Authority, 257
U.S. Office of Human Development
    Services, 231
U.S. Postal Service, 31
U.S. Public Health Services, 245
U.S. Senate, 205
U.S. Superintendent of Documents, 188
U.S. Supreme Court cases
    condemnation, 286
    desegregation, 59–60, 63, 147, 159,
        257, 279, 346, 463

U.S. Supreme Court cases, *(cont.)*
  developer impact, 268
  discrimination, 10, 21, 455, 467–468
  election, 28
  extraterritorial power, 195
  family, 199
  freeways, 284
  housing, 231, 240, 252, 448, 461–462
  Ku Klux Klan, 293
  land, 494–495
  merit systems, 309
  municipal annexation, 58
  patronage, 382
  public/private issues, 429, 436
  public utilities, 431
  reapportionment, 439–440
  referenda, 444
  representation, 532
  residency, 452, 454
  role, 205
  schools, 428
  taxes, 26, 282–283, 421, 512
  voting, 28, 561
  wages, 217, 352–353
  zoning, 299–300, 302, 559–560,
    581–583
U.S. Treasury, 341
United Way, 114, 178
Universities, as clearinghouses, 97
University of California at Berkeley, 366
University of Chicago, 384, 385
  Department of Sociology, 83, 114, 264
University of Delaware Disaster
    Research Center, 388
Univisa Satellite Communications, 188
Univision, 188
Urban, 534–535
Urban Affairs Abstracts, 308, 352
Urban Affairs Council, 355
Urban Affairs Quarterly, 516
Urban agglomerations, 135
Urban areas, 297, 335
  income sources, 269–270
  See also Cities; Metropolitan area
Urban coalition, 293, 535–536
Urban Coalition of the District of
    Columbia, 536
Urban crisis, 35, 537–538
Urban Development Action Grants
    (UDAG), 159, 167, 172, 426,
    539–540
Urban enterprise zones, 159
Urban Growth and New Community
    Development Act, 355, 362
Urban homesteading, 540–541
Urban impact analysis (UIA), 541–542
Urban Institute, 515
Urban Land, 542

Urban Land Digest, 542
Urban Land Institute (ULI), 386, 542
Urban League News, 354
Urban League Review, 354
Urban Mass Transportation Act, 322, 543
Urban Mass Transportation
    Administration (UMTA), 543
Urban Observatory, 543–545
Urban place, 534
Urban planning, 16, 58, 158
Urban political economy, 545–546
Urban political machine, 546–548
Urban political regime, 548–549
Urban renewal, 27, 113, 158, 165,
    258–259, 437, 490, 549–550
Urban revitalization, 550–551
Urban services, 551–553
Urban sprawl, 553–554
Urban studies, 83
Urban village, 554
USCM. *See* U.S. Conference of Mayors
User fee, 555
Utah, 18, 272
Utilities, public, 430–432

VA. *See* Department of Veterans Affairs
Vacancy chain, 556–557
Vacancy in office, 557–558
Variance, 558–559
Vatican, 180
Vermont, 233, 519
Veterans, housing for, 247
Veterans Administration. *See*
Department of Veterans Affairs
Vice, 106
Vietnam, Sister City program, 471, 472
Village, 559
Village of Belle Terre v. Boras, 199
Village of Braetenahl, 181
Village of Euclid v. Ambler Realty Company,
    559–560, 581, 583
Virginia, 16, 18, 159, 462. *See also*
various cities, counties, towns
Virginia Beach (VA), 129
VISTA. *See* Volunteers in Service to
America
Volunteers in Service to America
    (VISTA), 560–561, 564
Vote dilution cases, 561–562
Voter fatigue, 562
Voting, 214, 394, 417
Voting Rights Act of 1965, 19, 28, 58,
    347, 440, 561, 563
Voting Rights Amendments, 561

Wages, 217, 352–353
Wagner, Robert F., 258

Wagner-Steagall Housing Act, 258
Waite, Morrison R., 431
Walker Commission Report, 457
War on Poverty, 173, 227, 560, 564–565
Ward, 565–566
Ward's Cove Packing Co. v. Antonio, 10–11
Warner, Sam Bass, 117, 412, 413
Warner, William Lloyd, 66, 574
Warren (MI), 452
Washington, Walter, 567
Washington (state), 64, 106. *See also*
    various cities, counties, towns
Washington, DC, 197, 214, 313, 329,
    362, 443, 448, 496, 521, 566–567,
    585
  planning, 16, 323, 349–350
Washington v. Seattle School District No. 1,
    64
Waste management, solid, 476–477
Water and sewerage programs, 113, 158
Water Quality Act, 185
Water Quality and Improvement Act, 185
Watts riots, 292
Wayland (MA), 197
Wayne County (MI), 38
Weaver, Robert, 158
Webb, Del E., corporations, 8
Webster v. Reproductive Health Services, 429
Welch, Susan, 69
Welfare, 452
  public, 567–568
Welwyn (UK), 218
West Berlin, 181
West Bloomfield Township (MI), 460
West Virginia, 26, 52, 126, 502. *See also*
    Morgantown
West University Place (TX), 181
Westbury v. Sanders, 440
Weston (CT), 584
Weston (MA), 197
White flight, 568–569
*White v. Massachusetts Council of Construc-
    tion Employers*, 454
White v. Regester, 561
Who Governs?, 394, 450
Whyte, William Foote, 83
Wichita (KS), 369
Wildavsky, Aaron, 366
Williams, Oliver, 122
Willingsboro (NJ), 306
Wilmington (DE), 540
Wilson, James Q., 189
WIN. *See* Work Incentive Program
Windsor (Ontario), 525
Wired City, 569–570
Wirt, Douglas, 396
Wirth, Louis, 83, 88, 570
Wirth Thesis, 570–571

Wisconsin, 85. *See also* Madison
Withers, Carl, 66
Women, 9, 214, 409
Wood, Robert C., 543
Worcester (MA), 418
Work Incentive Program (WIN), 571
Workfare, 571–572
World Trade Center, 405
World's Columbian Exposition, 89
Wright, Frank Lloyd, 16, 157
  Broadacre City, 58–59, 371, 393
Write-down, 572–573
WSKQ, 188
*Wygant v. Jackson, Michigan Board of
    Education*, 468
Wyoming, 214, 499

Yankee City, 66, 574–575
Yates, Douglas, 396
Yonkers (NY), 340, 387
Yonkers-style politics, 575–576
Youngstown (OH), 100
Youngtown (AZ), 8
Yuba City (CA), 434–435

ZBA. *See* Zoning Board of Appeal
ZBB. *See* Zero-Based Budgeting
ZCB. *See* Zero coupon bond
Zephyrhills (FL), 8
Zero-Based Budgeting (ZBB), 60, 140
Zero coupon bond (ZCB), 577–578
Zone, urban, 578
Zone of transition, 578–579
Zoned edition, 579–580
Zoning, 580–581
  aesthetic, 581–582
  cases, 559–560
  down-, 582–583
  Euclidean, 522, 583–584
  exclusionary, 584–585
  exclusive, 478–479
  family, 199
  flexible, 585–586
  inclusionary, 586–587
  land, 299–300, 301–302
  nonconforming use, 364
  open space, 370
  ordinances, 232, 234
  planned unit development, 386–387
  restrictive, 106, 257
  spot, 587
  variances, 558
Zoning Board of Appeal (ZBA), 558, 585
Zoning classification, 587–588
Zoot-Suit Race Riots, 457
Zorbough, Harvey, 83, 223, 474
Zunz, Oliver, 117